AN ISLAND
NAMED
DAUFUSKIE

Other Publications by Billie Burn

Mary Dunn Cemetery, Daufuskie Island, South Carolina
Stirrin' the Pots on Daufuskie

Left: Daufuskie Island—Right: Hilton Head Island

(Aerial photograph, U.S. Department of Interior, 1985. Geological survey, EROS Center, Sioux Falls, South Dakota, 57198)

AN ISLAND

NAMED

DAUFUSKIE

Billie Burn

Published In Association With
Billie Burn Books
By

THE REPRINT COMPANY, PUBLISHERS
SPARTANBURG, SOUTH CAROLINA
1991

An original publication, 1991, in association with
Billie Burn Books
Daufuskie Island, South Carolina 29915

The Reprint Company, Publishers
Spartanburg, South Carolina 29304

ISBN 0-87152-454-6
Library of Congress Catalog Card Number 91-31046
Manufactured in the United States of America

The paper used in this publication meets the requirements of American
National Standard for Information Sciences—Permanence of Paper for
Printed Library Materials, ANSI Z39.48-1984.

Library of Congress Cataloging-in-Publication Data

Burn, Billie.
    An island named Daufuskie / Billie Burn.
        p.   cm.
    Includes bibliographical references and index.
    ISBN 0-87152-454-6 (alk. paper)
    1. Daufuskie Island (S.C.)—History. I. Title.
F277.B3B86 1991
975.7'99—dc20   91-31046
                                                       CIP

For those past and present who have found in this Island a haven. May these treasures of history, legend, and lore be deemed worthy of preserving and may this book find a special place in each home of those who truly love Daufuskie.

I shall pass through this world
    but once
If therefore, there be any kindness
    I can show
or any good thing I can do
    let me do it now
let me not deter it or neglect it
for I shall not pass this way again

    —Grellet, *Kindness*

The treasure of antiquity laid up in
old historic rolls, I opened.

    —Beaumond

Contents

Preface

HISTORY? I hated it with a passion and only through the good graces of my teachers was a passing grade made. Write a history about the people of Daufuskie Island? Never! No way!

But when God instilled in my heart to do just that, a complete turn about was made. Not only did He make me like this living history, but He filled me with joy while pursuing it. It was like being served a favorite desert—the more you eat, the more you want—I just could not get enough! Notes were taken, hundreds of letters were written, questions asked, phone calls and visits were made. The fervor grew! The search was on!

(Had I known that I would have to beat my body to do the work involved—the research and enormous time consumed in such a project—I would have had second thoughts agreeing to such an awesome task. But love and joy prevailed—and led!)

It all began in 1963 when I became postmaster[1] and was hired to drive the school bus to transport the black children to Mary Fields Elementary. The two jobs sorta went together—like hand in glove.

In almost every home there was a child who attended school. Each morning, it was through the children that mail was given to me as they boarded the bus. In the afternoon, it was through the children that the incoming mail was given to them to take to their parents. Those who had no children would be standing by the side of the road with their mail. For nine (school) months out of the year the Island had free mail-delivery service.

The school bus became a life-line for everyone as there were so few cars back in those days. Anyone walking along the road was picked up whether they were going or coming—from Cooper River to Benjie's point. Packages and messages were carried from one end of the Island to the other—from okra to live chickens—it all went on the school bus. Whatever it was—it was always "a package." Never were the contents revealed; only the name of the person the "package" was for was ever mentioned.

There was not a family that my life did not touch in some way. Not only were they provided with postal services but they needed birth

certificates, death certificates, hunting licenses, assistance with income taxes and catalog orders—whatever they needed—inquiries were made as to where or how it could be done. There was very little that could not be accomplished through the mail. I was the Registrar (recording births and deaths). I also operated the sheriff's ship-to-shore-radio, which was the only contact with the Island as there were no phones.

After becoming active in the PTA, I also became the first white member. The bus was used to take everyone to PTA parties, to Halloween parties, and to church. Each funeral was attended and I also helped with injuries and visited the sick. Appointed secretary to the Daufuskie Island Community Improvement Club, I served from its inception in 1985 until February 1988. As president of the Daufuskie Cooperative during 1985, I was also chairman of Daufuskie Day activities, 22 June, same year.

Love for the Island blossomed from my very first visit, but it was through the close association with the people that I was drawn to them. We all became one big family—what affected one affected us all. My husband Lance aptly put it when he made this remark, "We are not white; we are not black; we are Daufuskians."

Occasionally, there was a death on the Island, but it was this winter back in the mid-1960s when five people died (supposedly) of the flu or pneumonia that really got me to thinking. (Since there was no doctor and no way to get one here, exact cause of death was not determined.) Having lost those five precious people in so short a time, it suddenly dawned on me that the Island was slowly dying—that only the very young or the very old lived here. It was then that God gave me this thought:

"There is no history written about these people. They are all dying and something has to be done to preserve their way of life."

Although the message was a quiet revelation, to me it seemed like a strong command!

Death has no voice, so I decided I'd better get busy and begin asking questions of the older people who yet lived. Having some small note pads, I clamped one to the dashboard, and each time someone caught a ride on the bus I would question them about the Island or themselves. Their information was then scribbled on the little pad. Arriving back home, I'd take that little piece of paper and place it in an old-

dimestore-ledger-book. When anyone came to the Post Office, questions were asked and answers jotted down on a small scrap of paper, then it was tucked safely away in the ledger-book. This procedure continued until my retirement in 1984, which completed twenty-one years as Postmaster.

After retirement, all of those precious treasures were taken out of the old-dimestore-ledger-book and typed into readable form. Visits to libraries, historical societies, and court houses and personal interviews have yielded much information, but it is impossible for one person to give a complete history of Daufuskie. To the reader who might think some references or explanations are too lengthy—please bear in mind that some Daufuskians will never have the opportunity to darken any door in quest for reference materials—it is to these Islanders that the in-depth information is directed.

The primary motive for the writing of this book was to obey God's command and leave my legacy: a permanent record of the history, stories, and accounts that I have collected—mainly from Daufuskie people. However, pertinent information has come to my attention through people whom I have yet to meet.

This book was humbly written as a labor of love, and although deeply grateful, I'm not totally satisfied with what I have managed to find. Time and research have been limited by unavoidable happenings, but it's a beginning . . . a start . . . a foundation upon which I trust others might build.

Billie Burn

1. There are only PostMASTERS in the Postal Service. Dr. Robert E.H. Peeples quoted Hilton Head Postmaster, "Miss Milley," as saying, "There are no "Mistresses" in the Postal Department; they don't pay us enough for that."

Acknowledgments

There is a lot of merit in this wisdom given by a dear, black lady, Sarah Hudson Grant: "Sometimes, friends will get you where money can't buy."

Without Lucille (Cilie) Sutton, much of this book could not have been written. As an officer in the Daufuskie Historical Society (of two members), she is secretary—better known as "Most Faithful Scribe." Cilie, with the support of her husband, Bill (who made scads of copies), and daughter, Susan (who tagged along and loved it all as much as her mother), furnished much of the foundation information.

Cilie made numerous phone calls, visited homes, and obtained valuable material and photographs. Sometimes she ventured where "angels feared to tread." She camped on the front steps of the Georgia Historical Society and made inroads in the floor covering of the Savannah Library. Every time a lead was presented, like a watch dog, Cilie hit the trail. Thank you, Cilie and family.

To Mrs. William (Jo) Scouten I owe so much for the Daufuskie-Scouten history and pictures. Thanks, also, to Jo's daughter, Dana Myers, for sending me a copy of an *entire* book for my research. And to Jo's sister-in-law, Edith Scouten—thank you.

My thanks and gratitude to Dr. Rebecca Kirk Starr, who earned her doctorate degree from Oxford, June 1990. She played a vital and important role in giving permission to use her material concerning the early history of the island. Dr. Starr is now employed as a professor in England's educational system.

Thanks and appreciation to Mr. Albert Stoddard III, who answered the innumerable questions with which I kept bombarding him. For the documents, history, and pictures of the Mongin/Stoddard families and for giving me permission to quote from his father's "Gullah Tales"— Mr. Stoddard, I'm so thankful that your thread of kindness and patience endured and held beyond the breaking point. And to Jack Stoddard who possessed the only picture of Oakley Hall, the mansion at Bloody Point, and for your stereoscopic pictures you cut in half to share with me—thanks.

To Alex S. Hopkins, Jr., although we have never met, thanks. I

could have never gotten through this without your shared knowledge concerning all of the early plantation owners, especially the Hopkins and Martinangele families. Flying back and forth so much and so fast, our letters are in sufficient numbers to fill a book.

Words are inadequate to express my appreciation for those at the Beaufort Public Library: Julia Zachowski, Dennis J. Adams, and former library members Betty Ragsdale and Emma Bishop. You acted above and beyond the call of duty with books, copies, and information—all sent through the mail.

To Robert Marchman III, thanks for family information and for steering me to the Martinangele ring. And thanks to Mrs. E.H. Anderson who was so kind as to send pictures of the ring now in her possession.

Much gratitude to Mrs. Mary Booth, librarian, Livermore, Maine, and to her assistant, Penny Pelletier.

To Dennis Cox, thank you for the book, uniform buttons, and your knowledge of the Civil War concerning Daufuskie which you so generously shared.

For the aerial photograph of Daufuskie, my special thanks to the U.S. Department of Agriculture—Agricultural Stabilization and Conservation Service (ASCS), Aerial Photography Field Office, Salt Lake City, Utah. For other Daufuskie photographs, thanks to Betsy Caldwell, Joy Fripp Canady, Robert L. Chaplin, Joann Dierks, Charles and Catharine Ellis II, Jimmy and Lawrence Hopkins, Davis Humphrey, Josephine Johnson, W. J. "Skippy" Keith, Glen McCaskey, Gilbert J. Maggioni, Roger Pinckney, Freddie and Robert Sisson, Eleanor K. Strain, Ida White Tatum, and Sen. James M. Waddell.

Thanks to Christina Roth Bates for her lovely art work. And to Cheryl Dickey Smith, thank you for the portrait of Theodosia Burr.

Dr. Curtis Hitchcock, you were very generous to give permission to quote from your "Dear Sister" book—thanks.

To you who have been so kind and shared so much, thank you: Rick Acres, George Anderson, Ragnor E. Anderson, Carol and Jim Alberto, Nancy Amons; Harley Badders, Sophia Barnes, Tom Bass, Provost (Bud) Bates, Jim and Tootie Black, Prof. J. Herman Blake, Leon Bond, Stephen Bond, Harriette Boyd, Colin Brooker; Catherine Campbell, Joe Cavanah, Robert L. Chaplin, Niels and Sarah Christensen, Audrey Harley Clanton, Douglas Cooper, Sister Sharon

Culhane, Dr. Wayne Lee Cummings; Robert H. Dunlap; Charles Ellis III; Bill Fleetwood, Rusty Fleetwood, Claude Fripp, Bessie Futch; Edward Gay, Theresa A. Gould, the Rev. Ervin and Ardell Greene, Romana Grunden; Charlie Haigh, the Rev. C. L. Hanshew, Paul K. and Evelyn Helmly, Jr., Bessie Hookstra, John Horry; International Paper Realty Corporation of South Carolina; Charles and Amy Lebey, George Lenhart, Dr. Larry and Lisa Lepionka; Frances McAlister, Annie McDonald, Thomas McTeer, Margaret Mellinger, Frank M. Moore, Prof. John C. Morse; Carol Noonan; Mable Parker, Dr. Robert E.H. Peeples, Bill Phillips; Margaret Chaplin Rawstrom, S. Henry Rodgers, Loring Rosemond, Don Rutledge; Walter Schaaf, Claude and Priscilla Sharpe, Beth Swindell Shirley; Mike Taylor, Larry Thompson, Laura Fripp Timmons, Mike Trinkley; Captain Marion T. Wright.

To those institutions that were prompt and cooperative in responding to the many requests, thank you: the libraries in Beaufort, Boston, Columbia, Livermore (Maine), Philadelphia, Savannah; the Archives in Columbia and Washington, D.C.; the Historical Societies in Bluffton, Hilton Head, St. Paul (Minnesota), Savannah; the South Carolina Wildlife and Marine Resources Department, Charleston; the Department of Entomology, Clemson University; U.S. Engineers Department and the Probate and Superior Court Judge's Record Rooms, Savannah; and Beaufort County Clerk and Register of Mesne Conveyance Offices.

My gratitude to present and former Daufuskie black people who never once hesitated to share history concerning themselves or the island: Betty Bright Brown, William (Hamp) Bryan, Sarah (Edna) Bryan, Cleveland Bryan, Agnes Graves, Sarah Hudson Grant, Johnny Hamilton, Hezekiah Hudson, Isabelle Hudson, Ella Mae Jenkins, Lawrence Jenkins, Frances E. Jones, Gracie Miller, Agnes Simmons, Janie Simmons, Lillie Simmons, Sier (Si) Simmons, Willis Simmons, Albertha (Bertha) Stafford, Thomas Stafford, Susie Smith, Flossie Washington, Ethel Mae Wiley, Geneva Wiley, Louise Wilson.

To present and former white Daufuskie people, thank you for your loyalty and support: Nell Palmer Duckett, James Goodwin, Josephine Johnson, Juanita Goodwin Kennerly, Hazel Marchant, Annie White Morgan, Gage Scouten, Leonard "Sonny" Smith, Jerry Smith, Ida White Tatum, Charlie Ward, George Ward, Fred White, George

White, Gillian Ward White, Hinson White, Geraldine Ward Wheelihan, and Stewart Wheelihan, Gene and Joann Yarbrough.

My indebtedness and thanks to Judge Francis A. (Frank) Burn, Sr., who gave the "fact truth" and had an overflowing knowledge of 'Fuskie history. And thanks to Frank's sister, Leonella Burn Padgett, for filling in the gaps.

Much sincere love and gratitude goes to my family: to my husband, Alfred Lance Burn, who was reasonably patient and tolerated our "divorce" while I was "wedded" to the typewriter; to daughter June and her husband Bob Crumley; to our son Robert L. (Bob) Burn and his wife Emily; to son Gene and his wife Gail; to my grandchildren, Alan and his Jackie, Eric, Marc and his Debbie, Blain, Jennifer; and to my great grandchildren, Ashley, Heather, Erica, Lance, Christian, and baby Kylee.

Hopefully, everyone has been remembered, but if someone's name is missing, your forgiveness is being asked. Whether your contribution has been large or small, please know—all of you—that I love you very much and may God continue to richly bless you is my prayer.

If this acknowledgement seems long, let me give flowers now, for "I shall not pass this way but once."

Billie Burn

In Memory

To those who have gone home to be with the Lord—you are truly loved and missed: to my beloved husband, Alfred Lance Burn, and his father, Arthur Ashley "Papy" Burn, Stephen Bond, Mary Booth, Rose Brisbane, William (Hamp) Bryan, Sarah (Edna) Bryan, Viola Bryan, Emil Cetchovich, Jr., Johnny Hamilton, Sarah Hudson Grant, S. Henry Rodgers, Sier (Si) Simmons, George White, Hinson White.

Introduction

DAUFUSKIE lies between Hilton Head and Tybee Islands on the east Atlantic coast. It is the first inhabited Carolina Sea Island and the most southern tip of South Carolina territory.

> Daufuskie Island is a Pleistocene remnant, estimated to be between 80,000 and 120,000 years old. Located well on the 100-year flood level and a significant portion is above the 500-year flood level. It has been inhabited almost continuously for nearly 4,000 years."[1]

Without a bridge, an Island, two and one half miles wide by five miles long, Daufuskie is bordered on the

North,   by Cooper River, a name, no doubt derived from Anthony Ashley Cooper, one of the eight Lords proprietors of South Carolina:[2]

East,   by two bodies of water: Calibogue Sound, an Indian name meaning "Sweet Water,"[3] and by the Atlantic Ocean (lest you forget or never knew), derived its name from ". . . Mount Atlas in Libya, on which the heavens were fabled to rest. Hence applied to the sea near the western shore of Africa, and afterwards extended to the whole ocean lying between Europe and Africa on the east and America on the west;"[4]

South,   by Mongin Creek, named for the David Mongin family;

West,   by New River, believed to be the name of a Catawba Indian chief. ". . . New River whose real name he refused to divulge preferring to be called "New River" for a battle in which he won early distinction by killing the chief [King Haigler] of the Shawnee tribe. In the American Revolution, New River, recently made chief of the Catawbas, and already an old man, served with 40 other Catawba warriors. . . ."[5]

On the west, between Piney Islands and Daufuskie, is a cut that joins Cooper River to New River. Because of its shape, this stretch of

xxi

water was called *Ram's Horn Creek*. Due to the sharp turns, large steamers maneuvered with great difficulty.

The James P. Chaplin heirs owned Piney Islands Plantation but in 1923 sold (to the Corps of Engineers, Savannah, Georgia) an easement on the east side to make a cut that would help shorten the inland water route to some degree. However, in 1926, before this cut was made, the Chaplins had sold Piney Islands Plantation to Charles J. Butler.[6] So, when the cut was finally completed, it was named for the Butler family, hence its proper title—*Butler Cut*. It has continued to be addressed as Ram's Horn Creek or Butler Cut—dependent upon the knowledge of the person doing the talking.

The name *Daufuskie* has been spelled and pronounced so many different ways through the years: Dawfuskie, Daufushey, Dafuskee, Danfusky, Dafatchkee, Defawshee, Daufusky, Daufuskey, Dawfuski, Daufuskee, D'awfuskie, Dawfusky, Dawffus Tee, Deefuski, Dafuskey, DIAwfuskee, Dawfuskee, D'Awfoskee, D'Awfoskie, Defuska, Daufuski, Daffuskey, Defawshee, Delfuska, Dogfuskie, Danfuskeel, Daufeskie, Dawfatckee, Dawiusket, Dafouskie, Dawfoske, Dawfuskey, Danfushie, Dewfoskey, Dawaskee, Defoskie, Daw Fuskie and 'Fuskie. But the last and certainly by the least, our three-year-old daughter June, who had trouble pronouncing certain words. When asked where she lived, June replied, "On 'Fuckie Island." Her answer brought much laughter and the question was repeated.

Natural, beautiful, serene, quiet, content, and tranquil—all of these attributes belong to Daufuskie. To those who have lived here, these qualities loom large in comparison to its comparatively small size. An Island so tiny, remote, and seemingly insignificant, that through the years it has barely been mentioned in times of war, storm, or other major happenings. Its history so well hidden through the eons of time that one has to spend much effort in digging up any information concerning it.

It was not until recently, when property (especially beach property) had been nearly depleted on other islands in Beaufort County, that all eyes have been focused on Daufuskie. Rarely had most people even heard of this Island, but suddenly, it has become the "in place" to be. Developers are now on the scene with bulldozers and earth movers; the trees are being cut and burned, the roads turned into sand dunes. Strangers and new vehicles are crowding the roads, tourists are

coming by the hundreds—and this is just the beginning!

Soon, those who once walked alone on the seven mile beach will no longer be allowed to even *go* there. Gathering clams, oysters, conch, arrow heads, and shells will be a thing of the past.

And yet, developers have provided jobs for which the island is grateful. The island was dying, and development has brought life! The island is entering a new phase of its history. What the result will be, only time can tell.

From moccasin, plantation, slavery, war, and plough, Daufuskie has been many things to many people: to the Indian, it was a secluded place to live, fish, hunt, and yes, to war; to the Indian trader, it meant greed and wealth; to the plantation owner, it meant wealth, mansions, slaves, and prestige; to the plantation children, it meant security with expensive tastes, the finest education in schools here and abroad—with little sense of responsibility and servants on every hand; to the Revolutionary War Tories, it was a gathering place, a hide-away; to the slave, it meant hard work, sacrifice, and restriction; to the freed-man (after the Civil War), it meant freedom to own a piece of land, freedom to build a little hut, freedom to plant a vine—a fig tree—and never fear that someone could take it from him; to the pioneer white people (who came after the plantation owners had been stripped of their wealth and left), the Island became a sanctuary, literally the land of milk and honey.

Although the living was tough, there was a natural pasture for animals as they were contained within the boundary of the Island. There was plenty of land to farm, a constant supply of game and seafood, plenty of space to raise a family, with an environment of peace and contentment—where they were the boss with a daily work-load judged by their own pace and need.

To all of those (black and white) who have loved Daufuskie, there has been a sense of belonging—so clothed with a depth of security and satisfaction, with such a feeling of oneness and warmth between the people and the place, it was as though they wore the Island like a cloak.

Years have passed, times have changed—gone are most of the older generation, scarcely a few remain. Population in 1984 B.D. (Before Developers), had dwindled to sixty people, only eighteen of whom were white. The Island was slowly dying.

Being at one with the Island through so many years, having mi-

nutely touched its heart, pulse, and soul, having unlocked and un-earthed a small segment of its history, I invite you to join me now in presenting *An Island Named Daufuskie.*

Notes

1. An excerpt from Senator Strom Thurmond's letter, 1 July 1982, addressed to the Daufuskie Island Community Improvement Club, in regard to Daufuskie being considered one of the barrier islands.

2. Edward McCrady, *The History of South Carolina Under the Proprietary Government, 1670-1719* (1897, reissue, New York: Russell and Russell, 1969), p. 62.

3. From the files of Dr. Robert. E.H. Peeples, president, Hilton Head Historical Society, Hilton Head, South Carolina.

4. Oxford English Dictionary, s.v. "Atlantic."

5. Ron Chepesiuk and Louise Pettus (Winthrop College Faculty), "Catawba Woman Preserves 550 Acres for Posterity," Hilton Head, S.C., *Island Packet,* 18 November 1983.

6. Files of David Humphrey, Savannah, Georgia; Beaufort County Courthouse, Deed Book 39, pp. 459-50.

1

TRADITIONS CLARIFIED

There are several traditions and stumbling blocks that need to be untangled and unraveled in order to better understand certain history about Daufuskie.

The main one to be addressed is the word *Daufuskie*. Some say that it is Gullah and means "The First Key"; others think it Indian and means "Island of Blood." Both of these meanings are incorrect and far from the truth, and this will be proved in the following explanations.

Daufuskie: An Indian Name

Daufuskie is an Indian name. Indians inhabited this island long before there were white people, plantations, and slaves. In 1962, potsherds that the Burn family found were dated back to 350 B.C. by Dr. A. J. Waring, a Savannah, Georgia, Indian artifacts specialist; a former school teacher, Jim Alberto, found an arrow head that South Carolina Archaeologist Jim Michie dated back to 9,000 years; the Smith family found arrowheads and potsherds that archaeologist Stanley South proved interesting:

> The [your] collection contains artifacts from the Early Archaic Period, primary a spear point type called Morrow Mountain, that dates from around 7 to 8,000 years ago and are known as Savannah River Points.... From around 500 B.C. to the time of Spanish contact, Indians were making pottery on the Island and you have some of these types in your collection.... Eighteenth and nineteenth century artifacts reveal the presence of Europeans on the Island.[1]

In 1666 Robert Sanford, newly appointed Clerk and Register for the Lords Proprietors of the new (Carolina) county, had been in conversation with the Indians and took aboard his vessel an Indian

(the Cassique's nephew) to be his guide and protector (from other Indians) as they sailed the rivers and creeks. Two days were spent exploring the islands that joined Calibogue Sound. On these islands, he found ". . . good firm soil as he had ever seen and better timbered with live oak, cedar and bay trees. . . ."[2]

Sanford did not mention seeing one white person or slave. As he had already stated, all of the islands were *covered* with a forest of excellent trees. He saw only that these islands would provide habitation for thousands where English settlements could be established.

As early as 1706, Indian trader Samuel Hilden acquired land on Daufuskie.[3]

One of the earliest known warrants recorded thus far was for 500 acres of land on "Dawffus Tee Island" issued to Thomas Cowte in 1707.[4]

In 1716, according to McCrady's chart of the estimated population of South Carolina under the Royal Government, there were 6,400 white people listed but not one slave.[5]

Ramsay states that between 1696-1730 no great amount of emigrants had even settled in South Carolina.[6] Johnson reiterates that prior to 1730 slaves were scarce in South Carolina, but that after that year the number increased.[7]

What has been proven is—that this island was named *Daufuskie* and inhabited by Indians long before white man and slaves were ever thought of.

But to make it a little more interesting, I got this rather brilliant idea: if I wanted to know the meaning of the Indian word *Daufuskie*—ask a real-live Indian!

Letters had been written to the University of Oklahoma concerning my own Indian background and this was what I had in mind to do. Before I could write the letter (and knowing that I was interested in anything at all about the Island), The Reverend Clarence L. Hanshew approached me one Sunday morning and related the following story: He had attended a Baptist Convention in Tennessee and while there, he met a very interesting Indian preacher, The Reverend Bill Barnett, from Seminole, Oklahoma. Right away, he had taken a liking to this "man of the cloth" and, as they were parting, invited him down to Ridgeland and he (Mr. Hanshew) would take him to Daufuskie to preach at the First Union Baptist Church. When Mr. Barnett heard

the name *Daufuskie*, it caught his attention and he quickly replied, "That is a Creek Indian word and means *Land With a Point.*"

"Then," The Reverend Mr. Hanshew said, "he went on to explain to me just how this meaning came about, but just so that I don't get it all mixed up, I'll give you the Indian preacher's name and address and you can get his phone number and talk to him personally and let him explain it all to you."

To say that I was elated would be putting it mildly! Right away, I wrote to the preacher but not satisfied with that (and feeling that I couldn't wait), I called him at The Indian Nations Baptist Church where he is pastor. At first, no one answered (this was on Saturday). Then I waited about an hour and when I called again, who should answer the phone but the preacher himself! I was beside myself with anticipation—I introduced myself and explained my motive for calling. He asked me, "Haven't you received my letter?" I told him that I had not. "Well," he said, "I mailed you a letter right after the Tennessee Convention in February [this was in June]. Reverend Hanshew had informed me about your writing a book about this island and that you would be interested in knowing the Indian meaning of the word Daufuskie."

The Reverend Mr. Barnett went on to explain to me just how this name was derived. But, in order to have something concrete (and something that I could actually show in black and white and not just relate), I asked him to please write and include something about himself. After three more weeks of waiting, and chewing my fingernails, his letter (dated 20 August 1986) finally arrived! Following is his long awaited explanation:

> Now as to the word: *Daufuskie*: In the Muscogee language (called Creeks in English, given to us) the word would have to mean "Sharp Feather." It is actually a combined word of two distinct two words. "Daufa" means "Feather"—"Fuskie" means *sharp* or *pointed.* So, rather than saying "Dau*fa*fuskie," it becomes easier to say "Daufuskie" in a spoken conversation.

I called to question him how a "feather" could apply to land that had a point. He explained that the Indian language was not a progressive one—that once a word was established for an object or thing, it never changed. "For instance," he said, "the first airplane that we saw, we called it a *flying boat.* To this day, it remains the same—it is still called a *flying boat* and not an airplane."

3

"The most logical explanation concerning your island being called Daufuskie that I can give you," Mr. Barnett stated, "is that the first Indians who saw it noticed that it had a point—*reminding* them of a feather which had been trimmed to a point. The name stuck and forever after was known to them as *Daufuskie* or *Land With a Point.*"

How grateful, after nearly 300 years—revealed at last—we now have the true meaning of the word *Daufuskie* from a full-blooded Indian who does not speak with forked tongue.[8]

A MAP OF SOUTH CAROLINA AND PARTS OF GEORGIA—1780
William Faden

This map shows more clearly why the Indians called this Island Daufuskie, "Land with a Point."

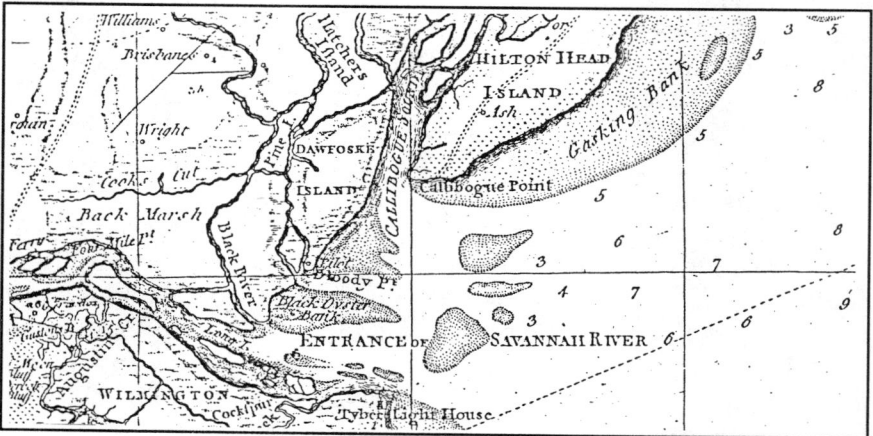

Mongin and Phillip Martinangele Names

The names of Mongin and Phillip Martinangele have been misspelled through the years but the following should clarify any doubt: the residents of the island were faced with a problem. To get to the north end of the island to embark to Hilton Head, or to the south end for those going to Savannah, permission had to be granted to cross property lines. They realized what a time-saver it would be to have a public road on which they could travel freely from one end of the island to the other.

The residents and interested parties of St. Luke's Parish got to-

4

gether and formed a petition for the first public road on Daufuskie. On 2 October 1805 this petition was presented to the House of Representatives, State of South Carolina.[9]

On this petition are the personal signatures of John D. Mongin and Phillip Martinangele. Therefore, there will be no further question as to the proper spelling of these names.

MAP OF BEAUFORT DISTRICT, S.C.
By C. Vignole and H. Ravenel, 1820
Mills' *Atlas*—1825

This map shows the road that was approved (1805) and established from the north end to the south end of Daufuskie.

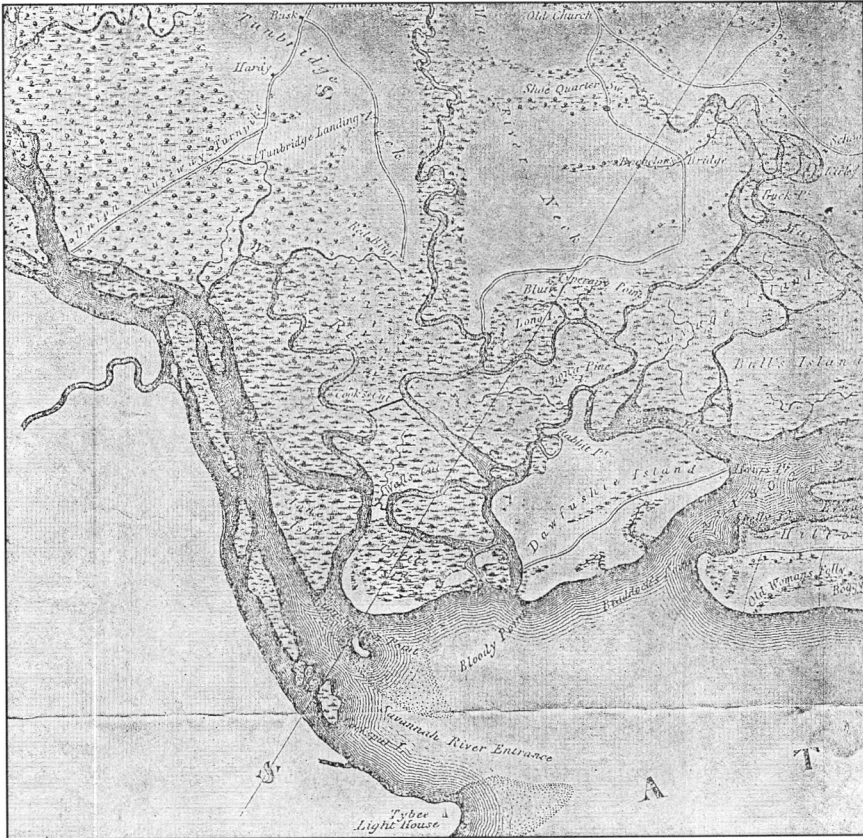

The petition was acted upon and put into law. Regrettably, a plat for such a road has not surfaced as yet. But, just for the record, in the *Acts Relating to Roads, Bridges, and Ferries* appears the following:

> XIII. And be it further enacted by the authority aforesaid, That the commissioners of the roads of the parish of Saint Luke's, be directed, and are hereby authorized, to lay out a road on the Island of Daufuskie, for the benefit of the inhabitants thereof.[10]

David Mongin Not Granted Daufuskie [11]

That Captain David Mongin (No. 1), British privateer, was given Daufuskie as a *King's Grant*, has not proven to be accurate.

In 1730 Governor Robert Johnson of Carolina had been ordered by the British crown to lay out townships and populate them as defense against Indian attacks. From Neufchatel, Switzerland, came John Peter (Jean Pierre) Purry to see just what Carolina had to offer. After much observation (and checking the soil and climate), he was completely satisfied with the excellence and freedom of the provincial government, and, with a contract from the British government that he would be given land and 400 pounds sterling for each one hundred effective men brought into the area, Mr. Purry returned to his native land. From his favorable report, 170 Switzers followed him back to Carolina. Sometime later, 200 additional men came to join the settlement.[12]

The governor, pleased with these new settlers, allotted forty thousand acres of land for the use of the Swiss, et al., on the northeast side of the Savannah River. Each person was granted a certain portion of land and the town became known as Purrysburg (*Pure-es-burg*), so named for its promoter, John Peter Purry.[13]

It was to the town of Purrysburg that George the *Second*, King of Great Britain, 12 August *1737*, granted to David (No.1) and brother, Francis Mongin, 650 acres of land. [15]

David Mongin (No. 1) had died in *1770*. It was his son, David [John] Mongin I (No. 2), to whom George the *Third*, King of Great Britain, 28 July 1775, granted one thousand acres of land at St. Peter's Parish.[16]

(Thus far, there have been no records found to substantiate a claim that any part of Daufuskie was ever granted to a David Mongin by any King of England.)

In 1783, when John David Mongin's (half) uncle, William Edwards

6

N
E
W
S

722×75

| No. 21 Frances Mongin | No. 22 David Mongin |
| No. 79 Anthone Ingeron | No. 20 Peter Chas. Mason |

S. E. 17-D

| No. 23 Barbara Traur | No. 24 Andrew Winkler |
| No. 21 Dofo Bourquin | No. 22 Jos. Robart |

| No. 77 Donnie Morrat | No. 78 |
| No. 75 Jacob Metzger | No. 76 |

South St.

| No. 19 Dr. Bra- bant | No. 20 David |
| No. 17 Bourquin | No. 12 |

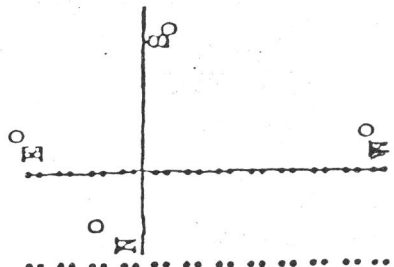

Taken from the Original Plat of Purysburg

This 26 day of May, 1776—187 John Linden, S.C. for David Mongin. [No. 2].[14]

Mongin, married Margaret Martinangele Pendarvis, the couple moved to Daufuskie and resided on her one-hundred-acre-plantation.

In 1762 Margaret's mother, Mary Foster Martinangele, had purchased 500 acres of land on Daufuskie. But it wasn't until 1785 (after the death of son Phillip) that Mary had a survey and plat made, dividing the land into one-hundred-acre-tracts for her five remaining children: Simeon, Abraham, Isaac, Mary M. Hopkins, and Margaret.[17] (It is believed that Mary Hopkins sold her one-hundred-acre-tract to sister, Margaret, thus increasing Margaret's plantation to two hundred acres.)

Sometime after Margaret's death in 1808, her heirs sold her two hundred acres of land to Christian Eigleberger and the plantation became known as Eigleberger.[18]

In 1790, John David Mongin (No. 3) married Sarah Watts. Sarah was heiress to her father Robert Watts' 400 acres of land known as Bloody Point. In 1816, at Sarah's death, John David became the heir of his wife's property—his first Daufuskie plantation.

On 13 March 1818, from the sale of Richard Russell Ash's Daufuskie property, in Charleston, South Carolina, John David Mongin (No. 3), purchased three plantations: Melrose (Salt Pond), Oak Ridge, and Maryfield, a total "on the whole about eight hundred acres" for $60,672.[19]

Christian Eigleberger had died and Eigleberger Plantation was publicly auctioned off at the Beaufort Court of Equity, 7 March 1831. John David Mongin (No. 3), the highest bidder, purchased the plantation (with house) for $2,200.00.[20] He then owned five plantations—a total of approximately 2561 acres.

Just when David John Mongin (No. 4) bought Haig's Point is unknown, but the following verifies the fact that he did:

> ... William Pope, who died on the 10th day of March, 1862, came into possession of Haig's Point Plantation in 1850 by purchase from Rev. Herman M. Blodgett, in the convenance of which all the heirs of *David John Mungin* [No. 4], who, at his death in 1823, owned the property, joined, as the property had not been distributed.[21]

David John Mongin (No. 4) also owned Freeport Plantation. Verification of this is found in the marriage contract of his widow, Sarah I. Mongin, 6 January 1825, Marriage Settlements, Book 9, pp. 149-53, South Carolina Archives:

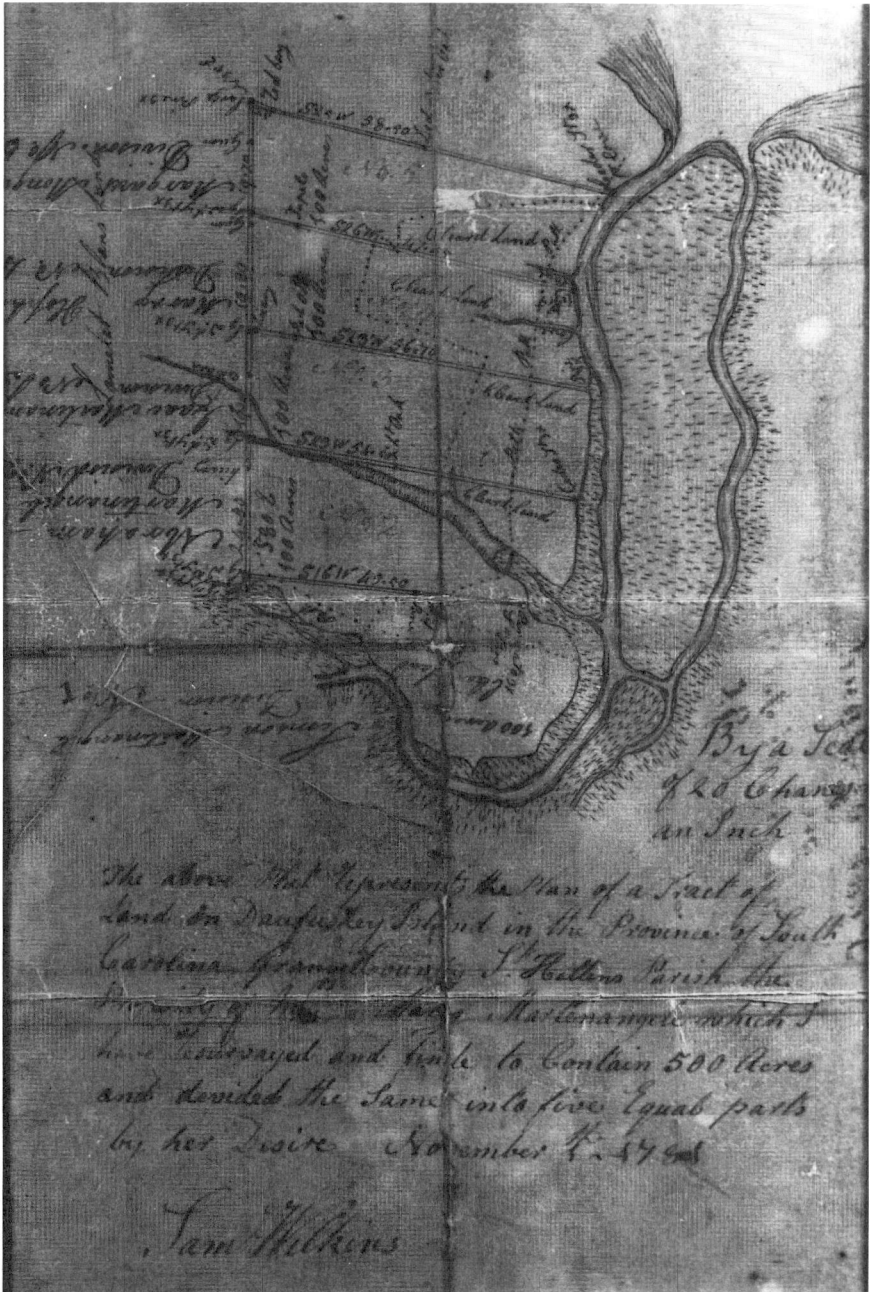

Plat, 5 November 1785, showing the division of the 500 acres Mary Foster Martinangele shared with her children.

According to the settlement between Sarah [Irwin Mongin] of Daufuskie, her intended husband, Himan M. Blodgett, of Daufuskie, and George W. Coe of Savannah and Samuel B. Webb of Daufuskie, Trustees, Sarah Mongin had inherited from her husband's [David John (No. 4)] estate two plantations on Daufuskie called Freeport (600a. more or less) and Haig's Point (358a. more or less). Also see Michie, p. 27.)

(Following this marriage settlement, Freeport and Haig's Point Plantations were combined and known only thereafter as Haig's Point, consisting of 958 acres more or less.

In 1801, Chatham County, Georgia, records show that John Andrew Mongin, son of David Mongin (No. 1) by his second wife, Elizabeth Edwards, purchased Piney (Pine) Island Plantation of 240 (some state 350) acres, from the estate of Rebecca Davies Stebbins.[22] However, John Andrew did not keep this plantation; he sold it to Jesse Mount whose wife was Love Martinangele, daughter of Isaac Martinangele. Jesse in turn sold Piney Island Plantation 23 April 1849 to James P. Chaplin, Sr., Love's nephew. [23]

Just when Cooper River Plantation was purchased is yet unknown, but, at John David Mongin's (No. 3) death in 1833, his Daufuskie holdings also included Cooper River, 540 acres, plus 300 acres of salt marsh.[24]

It can only be assumed (no record) that John David Mongin (No. 3) purchased the 274 acre plantation known as the Estate of Webb and later as Benjie's Point. But we do know that it was in Mongin-Stoddard possession before and after the Civil War.

At some point in time, the Mongin family were in possession of eleven of the twelve Daufuskie plantations. Only the 300 acre Mary Dunn tract was never theirs.

Summary of Mongin Plantations on Daufuskie

Piney Island	240	1801	John Andrew Mongin, son of David (No. 1).
Bloody Point	400a.	1816	John David Mongin (No. 3)
Melrose	770a.	1818	Ditto
Oak Ridge	596a.	1818	"
Maryfield	530a.	1818 circa	"

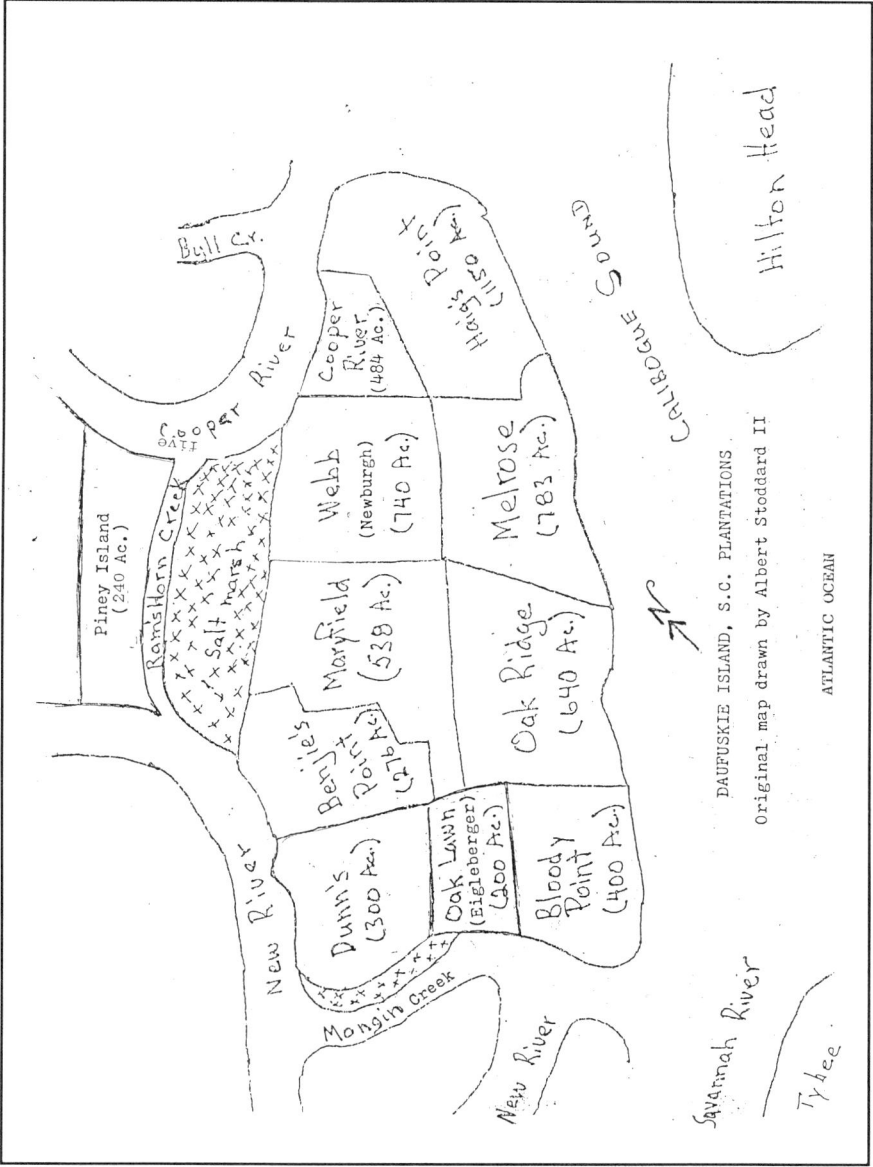

Bull Cr.

Cooper River

Piney Island
(240 Ac.)

Ramshorn Creek

Salt marsh

New River

Benjie's Point
(276 Ac.)

Dunn's
(300 Ac.)

Oak Lawn
(Eigleberger)
(200 Ac.)

Mongin Creek

New River

Savannah River

Tybee

Maryfield
(538 Ac.)

Webb
(Newburgh)
(740 Ac.)

Cooper
River
(484 Ac.)

Haig's Point
(1,050 Ac.)

Bloody
Point
(400 Ac.)

Oak Ridge
(640 Ac.)

Melrose
(783 Ac.)

CALIBOGUE SOUND

Hilton Head

DAUFUSKIE ISLAND, S.C. PLANTATIONS

Original map drawn by Albert Stoddard II

ATLANTIC OCEAN

Haig's Point	358a.	1820 circa	David John Mongin (No. 4)
Freeport	600a.	1820 circa	Ditto
Cooper River	484a.	1828 circa	John David Mongin (No. 3)
Benjie's Point	276a.	1830 circa	Ditto
Newburg (Webb)	740a.	1830	"
Eigleberger	200a.	1831	"

The acreage in these plantations varies from family and legal records, therefore should be addressed as "more or less."

As mentioned previously, sometime after 1825 Haig's Point and Freeport were combined and known only as Haig's Point.

How Bloody Point Got Its Name

Although this subject is not in controversy, very few know how "the point" (from which the Indians derived the name *Daufuskie*) got bloody. There were three skirmishes, two of which the white men won. They lost the last one to the Indians. For information leading up to these events,we need to go back prior to the Yemassee (Indian) War of 1715. So let the drama begin.

When the first white men set foot on Carolina soil, they displayed their guns, hoes, axes, knives, and other farm tools. Ever alert, the Indians watched patiently as the white men shot deer with little effort, dug holes, and planted seed in half the time it took them with their crude shell tools. With amazement, they watched the white men cut down trees with their axes; and what the white men could do with a knife was unbelievable. The Indians had to have some of all the tools the white men had in order to make their work a great deal easier. With envy, they saw the colorful clothing and sturdy shoes the white men wore. It was because of this supply and demand situation that the Indian trader appeared in their midst.

Indian traders were well educated white merchants, recognizing the need for a trading post (or store) whereby goods could be supplied to the Indians. The Indians could obtain items through trade (barter) or purchase.

The Indian trader also realized the wealth that could be obtained

in trading with the Indians. In fact, the first fortunes made in this new country were made by these traders.

Indian traders recorded as being on Daufuskie were Samuel Hilden (1706), Nicholas Day (1707), James Cockran (1711), and John Wright (1712).[25]

When the Indian trader first opened his door, he probably had all kinds of tools, guns, ammunition, rum, clothing, hats, shoes, cloth, thread, ribbons, beads, and trinkets.

For trade or sale, the Indian might have had corn, beans, squash, rice, potatoes, pumpkins, seafoods, deer meat and skins, furs of all kinds, and perhaps handmade baskets.

The trouble began when the Indian had no cash, nothing to trade, and the trader let the Indian have things on credit. Especially rum bills were allowed to run so high that when the trader demanded payment and the Indian couldn't pay, the Indian was slapped about, sometimes killed, or made to raid other tribes bringing back young Indian males to give as payment of their debt. The trader would in turn sell these Indians as slaves, put them aboard ships, and send them to the West Indies. The abuses were numerous.

The trader would swap a few pieces of fancy colorful ribbon for acres of Indian land. For some cheap trinket, the Indian would have to give maybe twenty bushels of corn. Because of this greed and the fact that the trader could outsmart him on every hand, animosity and hatred were beginning to build within the Indian for the trader. This terrible abuse, resentment, and mistrust was the *first factor* in the cause of the Indian uprising of 1715.

The *second factor* that brought on this war was caused by the Spanish wanting to prevent the establishment of the town of Beaufort.

Landing on the Sea Islands of Carolina in 1521, the Spanish later made claim of all that territory between Charles Town and St. Augustine. When a group of Scots, led by Henry Erskine (Lord Cardross), founded Stuart Town (on Port Royal Island) in 1684, Spanish resentment grew—this was their land and they wanted no permanent colony settled thereon. Lord Cardross had warned Governor Morton of Spanish hostility and threatened invasion, but his concern fell on deaf ears. Suddenly, without warning, in the summer of 1686 the Spanish appeared with three galleys, and with the force of Indians (and others), the Spaniards pilfered, whipped, killed, took

others captive, and completely destroyed Stuart Town.[26]

The same thing was happening again: Beaufort Town had been established in 1711, but the Spanish (continuing to claim the land upon which the town was built), as before, set the Indians against the English in order to get their help to destroy not only Beaufort, but to completely annihilate all Englishmen from Carolina territory.

On the day before the war began, the traders had noticed their gloomy faces and were aware of unrest among the Indians. Something was wrong, but they could not quite put their finger on the problem. Because they lived among the Indians, Governor Charles Craven dispatched Captain Thomas Nairne, agent for Indian affairs, Indian trader John Cockran, and other traders to meet with the Indians to find the nature of their discontent. The men went immediately to the chief warriors at Pocotaligo and offered to right any wrong that had been done. The chiefs met the traders with a false pretense of friendliness. The Indians claimed they had no complaints against anyone—they were only preparing to go on an early hunt the next morning.

(Had the English been observant, they would have been aware that the Indians had sent their wives and children to St. Augustine that very same day.)

After eating an evening meal that the Indians had provided, Captain Nairne and Mr. Cockran went home and slept with a sense of complete harmony—their fears were unfounded and all was well between them and the Indians.

(Little did they know that ten thousand Indians were encamped round about them.)

At day break the next morning, Good Friday, 15 April 1715, all were alarmed by Indian war cries—the bloody battle had begun. At Pocotaligo, the Indians massacred ninety people in a matter of a few hours, including Captain Nairne. They had taken John Cockran captive, later killing him. Traders were their main target, but they plundered neighboring plantations, murdering all of those who had not escaped. It was called the Yemassee War because they spearheaded the attack, but it was the Creeks, Appalachians, Congarees, the Catawbas, the Cherokees, and others who fought with them. Every Indian tribe from Florida to Cape Fear had joined in the conspiracy.

Governor Craven proclaimed martial law and sought aid from

North Carolina, Virginia, and as far away as New England. Fighting groups were formed that pursued the Indians. The war had turned in their favor; the English chased the Indians completely from Carolina soil.[27]

The Yemassees retreated to the Spaniards at St. Augustine. But they did not forget being driven from their land and had ill-will toward all Carolinians. At every opportunity, an Indian war party would sneak up from Florida and make quick raids on unguarded plantations along the coast. They would pilfer and steal, then take their loot and head back toward St. Augustine, usually stopping off at Daufuskie.

Roving English scout boats plied Carolina waters to protect plantations and the entrance to Port Royal Sound.

Captain John Palmer's scout boat lay at anchor in Daufuskie Creek, a branch of the Inland Passage which flowed past the southern end of Daufuskie Island. The crew of perhaps 15 scouts waited, enveloped in swarms of insects and summer heat, some thinking, some trying to sleep, some talking quietly. Suddenly, about 150 yards to the northwest, Captain William Stone's scout boat appeared from upstream and landed on Daufuskie Island. Captain Stone and several men disembarked and hid themselves in the nearby woods. Yemassees were coming! Captain Palmer's crew primed the swivel-guns and secured their oars.

The date was about the last week of August 1715. For three months the Yemassee Indians had been raiding the South Carolina frontier from their Spanish Florida Sanctuary. Three days ago the scouts had been at Port Royal Fort when information arrived that several canoes full of Yemassees were looting abandoned plantations. The scouts had quickly rowed to Daufuskie Island where the Indians would have to pass in their return to Florida.

A few minutes after Captain Stone and his scouts disappeared among the trees and their boat had moved on, a war party in eight canoes paddled around the Island's southwest point and came into view. Captain Palmer and his crew weighed anchor and began hurriedly rowing toward the plunder-laden canoes. The Yemassees spied the scout boat bearing down on them and decided to flee to the safety of the Island's woods. As they approached the Island the pursuing scout boat drew within swivel-gun range, forcing them to abandon their canoes and swim, every man for himself. They reached the shore and were running to the cover of the woods when the trees unexpectedly erupted with blasts and smoke from the muskets of Captain Stone's scouts. When

"Daufuskie Fight" was ended the Yemassee casualties were about 30 dead and two captured. One scout had been killed.[28]

Thus ended the *first skirmish* when the beach sand on "the point" was red with the blood of those slain. (A map reference is made concerning a "Daufuskie fight—1715."[29])

The *second skirmish* began when the Indians had pilfered and stolen from plantations on Hilton Head. They had jumped in their canoes and taken off through Skulk (Scull) Creek. The settlers were angry and followed them in hot pursuit. Friendly Indians had informed the settlers that the raiding party would be found having a feast on the southern tip of Daufuskie. The settlers rowed to the northern end of Daufuskie, anchored their boats and began wading the length of the Island, hoping to catch the Indians by surprise.

When the Indians had reached Daufuskie, for protection from the rough waters, they had secured their canoes along the shore of the creek on the west side of "the point."

They had taken their loot, had built a fire, and were having a feast on the oceanside, which was a good distance from their canoes.

As the settlers neared the southern end of Daufuskie, they saw the smoke from their fire, heard the loud noise of the raiding party, and saw the canoes pulled up along the shore of the creek. Quietly coming between the Indians and their canoes (making retreat impossible), they bore down on the Indians with guns blazing. They killed twenty eight—all of the Indians but two, who jumped in the water and escaped.[30]

(This is the second time the beach was crimson with Indian blood.)

There is a little interesting anecdote to this story: Tradition has it that the two escaping Indians swam to Tybee Island, found their way back to Hilton Head and murdered the Indians who had informed the settlers of their whereabouts, went back to St. Augustine, and were never heard of again.

The *third skirmish* happened in 1728. Since 1715 "the point" had been referred to as *Bloody Point*, but this last incident that caused blood to flow for the third time cemented the name forever:

> ... In December 1717, one of the two scout boat crews stationed at Beaufort was ordered to build and garrison a new fort, subsequently named Passage Fort, at Bloody Point on Daufuskie Island. It occupied the same site as the earlier (1701) lookout. In 1728, after a fresh

outbreak of waterborne raids against South Carolina, a Yemassee war party surprised the garrison at Passage Fort, killing everyone except the commander, Captain Barnabas Gilbert [whom they held captive and carried back to St. Augustine with them]. . . .[31]

Thus ended the third time that the beach was crimson, but this time it was the whitemen's blood. It took them thirteen years, but the Yemassee Indians finally had their revenge! Apparently they were satisfied, as there have not surfaced any more records of Bloody Point raids by them.

Notes

1. An excerpt from a letter addressed to Sonny and Mrs. Ruby (Shorty) Smith, dated 20 June 1984, from Stanley South, Archaeologist, and Santa Elena Crew: Bill Hunt, John Goldsborough, Russ Skowronek, Chuck Mastran, Bob Strickland, and Linda South. This team is from the Institute of Archeology and Anthropology, University of South Carolina, 29208.

2. Edward McCrady, *The History of South Carolina Under the Proprietary Government, 1670-1719,* (1897, reissued, New York: Russell & Russell, 1969), pp. 82-90; Guion Griffis Johnson, Ph. D., *A History of the Sea Islands* (Chapel Hill: University of North Carolina Press, 1930; reprint, New York: Negro University Press, 1969) p. 4.

3. Memorial Books, v. 1, pp. 447-48, and v. 3, pp. 165-67: Proprietary Grants, Records of the Secretary of the Province, 1711-1715, pp. 231-32, South Carolina Archives; Rebecca K. Starr, "A Place Called Daufuskie: Island Bridge to Georgia, 1520-1830," (M. A. Thesis, University of South Carolina, 1984), p. 7.

4. A. S. Salley, Jr., and R. Nicholas Olsberg, *Warrants for Land in South Carolina, 1672-1711* (Columbia: University of South Carolina Press, 1973), p. 639; Starr, pp. 7, 8.

5. Edward McCrady, *The History of South Carolina Under the Royal Government, 1719-1776,* (1899, reissued New York: Russell & Russell, 1969), p. 807.

6. David Ramsay, M.D., *History of South Carolina, From Its First Settlement in 1670 to the Year 1808* , 3 vols., (pub. and sold by W. J. Duffie, Newberry, S. C. (Charleston: Walker, Evans & Co., 1858; reprint, Spartanburg: The Reprint Company, 1959, 1968), 1:5.

7. Johnson, p. 31.

8. Reverend Bill Barnett is three-quarters Creek and one-quarter Seminole Indian. His Indian name is *Tok'se* which means "Spoiler." He is pastor of The Indian Nations Baptist Church, Seminole, Oklahoma, and is a teacher at the Centennial Bacone College, Muskogee, Oklahoma.

9. "Petition of Inhabitants of Dawfuskie Island and St. Luke's for a Public Road," 28 November 1805, General Assembly Petitions, S. C. Archives; Starr, p. 66. (See Appendix I.)

10. Thomas Cooper & David J. McCord, eds., *The Statutes at Large of South Carolina*, 10 vols., (Columbia: A. S. Johnson, 1841), 9:419.

11. See Mongin Family Pedigree Chart, Appendix II.

12. David Ramsay, M.D., *Ramsay's History of South Carolina From Its First*

Settlement in 1670 to the Year 1808, 3 vols., (Charleston: Walker, Evans & Son, 1858), 1:58-61.

13. Ibid.; Purrysburg was situated on the Savannah River, due west of Hardeeville, S.C. Only the cemetery remains. To visit: leave Savannah on Hwy 17 to Hardeeville, turn left at traffic light (Main St./Hwy 46). Cross the railroad track and keep straight. Following this road will lead directly to the cemetery/river. (Directions, courtesy: Dr. Robert E. H. Peeples.)

14. This map comes from the personal Mongin-Martinangele files of Charles Ellis III, Robert L. Marchman III of Atlanta, Georgia, and Ben Anderson, Jr., Greensboro, North Carolina.

15. S. C. Royal Grants, vol. 45, p. 162, Archives, Columbia.

16. S. C. Pre-Rev. Land Grants, vol. 37, p. 368, Archives, Columbia; Personal files, Charles Ellis III and Robert Marchman III, Atlanta, Ga.

17. The original cloth plat made by Sam Wilkins, 5 November 1785, in the possession of Lance and Billie Burn, was a gift to them from Laura Fripp Timmons, who inherited it from her grandmother, Margaret Chaplin Fripp.

18. "Record of the Martinangele Family Connected With the Mongins of South Carolina, Copied 1899," unpublished typescript in the possession of Charles Ellis III, Robert L. Marchman III—both of Atlanta, Ga., and E. H. Anderson, Greensboro, N. C., 24-B.

19. Thomas Hunt, Commissioner of the Honorable Court of Equity, Charleston, S. C., 13 March 1818; from the personal files of Albert Henry Stoddard III, Savannah, Ga.

20. Beaufort County Courthouse, Deed Book 16, p. 601.

21. See Records of the Lighthouse Service, United States Coast Guard, Record Group 26, National Archives, Washington, D. C.

22. Chatham County, Georgia, Records of Mesne Conveyance, Deed Book V, p. 390; Starr, p. 65, n. 4.

23. Chaplin family records from the files of David Humphrey.

24. Declaration of John Stoddard, trustee for the estate of John David Mongin [No. 3], 20 September 1865, Restorations Applications (unregistered), Bureau of Refugees, Freedmen, at South Carolina Archives; Starr, p. 65, n. 6.

25. Starr, p. 7.

26. Edward McCrady, *The History of S. C. Under the Proprietory Government,* pp. 215-17.

27. Ramsay, pp. 89-92; McCrady, pp. 531-46; Chapman J. Milling, *Red Carolinians* (Chapel Hill: University of South Carolina Press, 1940), pp. 135-48.

28. Larry E. Ivers, "Scouting the Inland Passage, 1685-1737, "*South Carolina Historical Magazine* 73 (July 1972): 117-19, 128.

29. John Barnwell, "Map of Southeastern America," ca. 1722. British Public Record Office, copy at South Carolina Archives.

30. Nell S. Graydon, *Tales of Beaufort,* rev. ed., (Beaufort: Beaufort Book Shop, Inc., 1964), pp. 140-41.

31. Larry E. Ivers, *Colonial Forts of South Carolina, 1760-1775* (Columbia: University of South Carolina Press, 1970), pp. 11, 65-66; Ivers, "Scouting," p. 126; Starr, p. 16.

2

INHABITANTS ON DAUFUSKIE

Native Americans were the first on Daufuskie soil. Artifacts found are proof that the Indians were here at least nine thousand years ago, but some go further to state that they might have lived here as far back as fifteen thousand years. Future research might prove this to be true.

The Spanish came to Carolina in 1521. They were on this island but it is not known just when.

The French followed in 1525. They settled on the coast and gave Port Royal its name. No record has been found of them having lived on Daufuskie that early; however, John David Mongin (No. 3), Frenchman, came in ca. 1790.

In 1670 the English settled in Carolina. The Proprietors named their colony *Carolina* that year, but it was not until 1693 that they first designated it as *South* Carolina—according to *Names in South Carolina*.[1] We know the English were on the island as they were well represented by Indian agents and traders who lived among the natives. In fact, the traders were probably the *first white people* to actually live on Daufuskie.

The Italian influence came in 1762 when the Mary Foster Martinangele family arrived on the island.

First Inhabitants: Indians

This segment is not intended to give a complete history of the Indians in South Carolina, but only to acquaint the reader with those tribes that lived in this state and along the Savannah River that might have lived on or visited Daufuskie.

From north to south, from east to west, American Indians roamed

19

this land thousands of years before the white man knew of its exis-tance. Our continent derived its name *America* from Italian explorer, Amerigo Vespucci, who was really searching for India when he sailed here in 1497. These early Europeans who landed on our shores called the copper-colored natives who greeted them *Indians*, whether or not this was India.[2]

James Adair, Esq., Indian trader, who lived for forty years in Indian country, knew not only the Indian language but Hebrew and Latin as well. From his observation, he declared that Indians were descended from the Jews.[3] (Could they be one of the ten lost northern tribes of Israel?)

Indians were here—then gone—before the white man really knew their thoughts, their ideas, or where they really came from. From this continent's first discovery ca. 1497, until 1838-1839 when the military escorted the remaining tribes to middle and western America, it had taken less than four hundred years for the white man to corral the Indians to reservations.

Bushels of arrowheads, a peace pipe, conch shell tools, stone axes, and other artifacts have been found on this island. While working on Webb Tract, Jim Michie, South Carolina archeologist, unearthed human bones and other relics, suggesting that a Yemassee Indian village was located at Rabbit Point, which is located on a small creek that flows off Cooper River on the northwest perimeter of the island.[4]

There were approximately thirty tribes of Indians in South Caro-lina. Just how many of these set foot on this island, no one knows. However, we do know from records that the *Creeks* were here because they gave Daufuskie its name; we know the *Yemassee* were here because of the three massacres on Bloody Point and we have the Michie report; from Bierer, we also know that a "*Palachocola*: Wonoya of *Daufuskey*" was here.[5] Rebecca Starr went further to say, ". . . Wonoya is evidently an *Appalachicola* Indian procuring for the [Indian] slave trade."[6]

It can be assumed that those Indian tribes living around the area now known as Savannah and those living along the Georgia coast, could have been on this island at some point in time—the Guale, Savannah, Cusabo, Apalachee, and the Westo. Other tribes that were farther west but who were associated with the foregoing tribes should

also be mentioned—the Chickasaw and the Yuchi (whom Bierer states were part of the Westo tribe).[7]

Many of the Indian tribes in the southeast area are herewith listed according to language:

Algonquion linguistic family: Saluda and Shawnee.

Iroquoian linguistic family: Cherokee and the Chiaha. (The Cherokee, being the largest of all the nations, were the most advanced in knowledge and the first to have their own written alphabet.)

Muskhogean linguistic family: Chiaha, Chickasaw, Coosa, Creeks, Cusabo, Guale, Natchez, Westo, Yemassee, and the Yuchi.

Siouan linguistic family: Catawba, Congaree, Eno, Issa, Iswa, Keyauwee, Pedee, Santee, Sewee, Shakori, Sissipahaw, Sugeree, Waccamaw, Wateree, Waxhaw, Winyah, and the Ysa.[8]

Following the Yemassee War of 1715, many of the smaller tribes joined the larger ones: the Cherokee in Tennessee, the Creeks of the Chattahoochee, the Seminole in southern Florida, and the Yemassee at St. Augustine.

After the Revolution in 1783, the United States of America was formed, causing the Indians to eventually sell or relinquish their land. As a devastating blow, *The Indian Removal Act* was signed by President Andrew Jackson on 28 May 1830. Those tribes surviving in the southeast—the Cherokees, Seminoles, Choctaws, Chickasaws, Creeks, and others—were forced to barren reservations in Oklahoma, Arkansas, New Mexico, and Arizona.

Using legal action, the Cherokees resisted for awhile, but sometime between 1838-1839, with military assistance, sixteen thousand of them were forced from their territory. Through the lack of food, bad weather, and disregard for pregnant women and small children, thousands died enroute to Oklahoma. Because they lost their land and their nation, this forced migration was called "The Trail of Tears."[9]

Although the Catawba Indians sided with South Carolina whites in their aid to North Carolina to fight the Tuscarora Wars (1711-1713), and, although they joined the Yemassee in their war of 1715 against the English, the Catawbas were faithful in remaining loyal to the colonists after peace was declared. The Catawbas retained their iden-

tity longer than any other tribe and they are the only ones to remain in South Carolina. In 1842 an eight-hundred-acre reservation was set aside for them near present-day Rock Hill and they continue to remain there.[10]

According to President Tom Claus, Chief of the Indian Nation,

> Of the one thousand treaties made by the white man—less than one hundred were ever kept. . . .
>
> Indians did not understand fences around land that they thought all should share. . . .
>
> When the Indian killed an animal, the meat fed *all* the tribe—not just the warrior (and family) who killed it. . . .
>
> The Indians shared their meager supply of food with the white man and showed him how to plant corn, potatoes and pumpkin in order to survive.[11]

The Indians made a lasting impression on this continent. Throughout the United States, whatever was named by the Indians has remained the same. Found in South Carolina are names of cities, places, and rivers, such as Oatie, Calibogue, Edisto, Coosawatchie, Pocotaligo, Okeetee, Cheraw, Awensdaw, Peedee, Stono, Ashepoo, Coosa, Santee, Combahee, Congees, Wando, Etiwaw, and many others.

An article that appeared in a local newspaper is so apropos concerning the thoughts of the Indians that it bears quoting in its entirety.

The following is taken from a letter written to President Franklin Pierce in 1855. It was sent to him by Chief Sealth [of] the Duwanish Tribe in the state of Washington:

> The great chief in Washington sends word that he wishes to buy our land. How can you buy or sell the sky—the warmth of the land? The idea is strange to us. We do not own the freshness of the air or the sparkle of the water. How can you buy them from us? Every part of this earth is sacred to my people. Every shiny pine needle, every sandy shore, every mist in the dark woods, every clearing and humming insect is holy in the memory and experience of my people.
>
> We know that the white man does not understand our ways. One portion of the land is the same to him as the next, for he is a stranger who comes in the night and takes from the land whatever he needs. The earth is not his brother but his enemy, and his children's birth right is forgotten.

There is no quiet place in the white man's cities. No place to hear the leaves of spring or the rustle of insect wings. But perhaps because I am savage and do not understand, the clatter seems to insult the ears. And what is there to life if a man cannot hear the lovely cry of the whippoorwill or the arguments of the frogs around the pond at night.

The whites, too shall pass—perhaps sooner than other tribes. Continue to contaminate your bed, and you will one night suffocate in your own waste. When the buffalo are all slaughtered, the wild horses all tamed, the secret corners of the forest heavy with the scent of many men, and the views of the ripe hills blotted by talking wires. Where is the thicket? Gone. Where is the eagle? Gone. And what is it to say goodbye to the swift pony and the hunt, the end of living and the beginning of survival."[12]

Buffaloes were slain for their tongues; giraffes, for their tails to make fly swats; elephants, for their tusks to make ornaments and souvenirs; ostriches, for their plumes to adorn ladies' hats; furry animals, for their pelts to make coats, rugs, and bedspreads; and alligators, for their hides to make shoes and handbags—the list goes on.

Before life does become "survival" as Chief Sealth predicted, let us learn from our mistakes. Like the Indians, let us consider them sacred and not pollute our air and contaminate our waters, for it is upon these things that our very life depends.

The Spanish on Daufuskie

We know the Spanish were on this island but just *when* remains an enigma. However, we do have evidence of their influence. The small horse known as "marsh tackey" was either brought here by the Spanish or by the Indians who traded with them. For the knowledge of making tabby, we have them to thank. And, the word "dollar" was adopted from the Spanish "dollar" or piece-of-eight.

A very interesting little story surfaced when Mrs. Marguerite Wright Rawstrom was called concerning her family history. During the course of the conversation, she mentioned that when a child, her brother had found some Spanish artifacts.

A letter was written to Mrs. Rawstrom's brother, Captain Marion T. Wright of Tampa, Florida, asking him about the Spanish relics that he had found on Daufuskie. He sent this explanation:

The information that you requested happened 72 years ago, in 1914. My sister, Bessie Ella Wright, and I were digging around the roots of a very old oak tree, when, we suddenly saw something shiny [Toledo steel]. We continued digging and uncovered—what my grandfather, James Peto Chaplin, Jr., said was—a piece of Spanish armor (a breast piece), also—part of a chain-link arm piece. We, my sister and I, were very proud of our findings. Not so! Grandfather Chaplin ordered us to rebury the armor *at once!*[13]

Captain Wright explained that his grandfather wasn't pleased when things like that were dug up—let the dead remain buried.

With sadness Marion and Bessie returned their treasure by the old oak tree, where they so joyously had uncovered it.

Notes

1. Claude Henry Neuffer, *Names in South Carolina*, 30 vols. (Columbia: Department of English, University of South Carolina, 1967), v. 17; 49.
2. Virginia C. Holmgren, *Hilton Head: A Sea Island Chronicle* (South Carolina: Hilton Head Island Publishing Company, 1959), pp. 2, 3.
3. Edward McCrady, *The History of South Carolina Under the Royal Government 1719-1776*, p. 297, n. 2.
4. James L. Michie, *An Archeological Reconnaissance Survey of the Haig Point, Webb, and Oak Ridge Tracts, Daufuskie Island, South Carolina* (Columbia: University of South Carolina Institute of Archaeology and Anthropology, 1983), p. 82.
5. Bert W. Bierer, *Indians and Artifacts in the Southeast* (1977; reprint, South Carolina: The State Printing Company, 1982), p. 477.
6. Rebecca Starr, p. 10.
7. Bert W. Bierer, p. 395.
8. Ibid, pp. 388-398 passim.
9. Bierer, p. 359; Milling, pp. 332-365.
10. Bierer, pp. 388-390.
11. NBC, "Feed the Children," 4 January 1987, Larry Jones.
12. "Indians Question Buying of Land," *Beaufort Gazette*, n.d.
13. Captain Marion T. Wright's personal letter, 22 June 1986.

3

THE MONGINS
AND THE MARTINANGELES

This country was forged from the Indians, founded and populated by those seeking religious freedom. Daufuskie was no different and became a haven for those French and Italians who had, in time past, fled their countries because of their faith. The Mongin and Martinangeles were mainly responsible for the plantations that flourished on this island.

David Mongin (No. 1)

Record of the Mongin family copied from the family Bible of David Mongin, Sr., who emigrated from France to London after the revocation of the Edict of Nantes 1685. David Mongin did not leave France until 1725 when the persecution of the Huguenots became intolerable, and when his aged father entreated him to leave his country and take his young brother Francis Mongin with him.

A faithful servant of the family informed them that a number of Roman Catholics were then on the way to the Chateau to pilfer, burn and murder. After the Edict of Nantes was revoked, the Huguenots had no protection and those who refused to embrace the Roman Catholic religion were compelled to flee the country or be slaughtered or burned at the stake. Collecting what valuables he and his brother could carry and all available money in the house, together with old pieces of silver they made their way by night to the sea shore. They hired a fishing boat and landed on the coast of England in 1725, from thence he proceeded with his brother and resided several years in London. David Mongin received intelligence in London that his aged father was tortured severely to make him renounce his religion, that he died from [these] tortures.[1]

His father, a watchmaker,[2] had taught this artistic craft to his son;

so, there is a possibility that David might have operated a watch shop while in London.

David married Persille Dair on 4 September 1726. On 19 September 1728, twin girls, Elizabeth and Margaret, were born. Only Elizabeth survived as she is mentioned as Elizabeth *Harvey* in David's Will.[3] Two children, born 1730 and 1735, did not live; however, David John, born in 1739, and Jane Mary, born in 1741, lived to maturity. Persille died in 1747. She and the three deceased children are supposed to be buried in Westminster Abbey, but research has proven there are no Mongins listed in Abbey records.[4]

David had owned property in Charleston when a fire destroyed three hundred buildings between Tradd and Church Streets according to the following: ". . . In 1742, David Mongin's name was among property owners who had suffered losses in a Charles Town fire, with a claim for 115 pounds sterling."[5]

Tradition states that Captain David Mongin was a British privateer operating against Spanish pirates. On 12 August 1737, King George II of England *did* grant David and his brother, Francis, 650 acres of land at Purrysburg in South Carolina, but whether it was for services rendered on the high seas is not certain. It's difficult to believe that brother Francis would have been included in a grant that only David had earned for *his* services.

Perhaps both David and Francis were privateers. It is also possible that the brothers had heard about the governor's plea for settlers and applied for this grant themselves.

David, with his three children and Francis, left London for Liverpool where they sailed for America. They landed in New Jersey on 10 November 1747.

Shortly after his arrival, David proceeded to Princeton where he made the acquaintance of the Reverend Jonathan Edwards, who later became the president of Princeton College and David's father-in-law.

After visiting for a few weeks, David, Francis, and the children, made their way to Carolina to claim their land at Purrysburg.

The Mongin and Edwards Families
Connected Through Marriage

The Edwards family was not only prominent in New England but throughout the country as well. One of the latter grandsons remarked,

"It is very pleasant to know that we came of gentle birth, and are not mushrooms popped up in the night."

The Reverend Jonathan Edwards' father was The Reverend Timothy Edwards, pastor of the Church of Windsor, Connecticut. His mother was Esther Stoddard, daughter of the famous Solomon Stoddard (Fourth Generation) of Northampton, Massachusetts.

All of the Edwards men were pastors, beginning with Jonathan's great grandfather, The Reverend Richard Edwards, of London, England, whose wife Anne _____, was a young lady of the court of Queen Elizabeth. (Anne had made a ruff for the neck of the Queen, which was highly appreciated.) The Reverend Richard Edwards had died, so his wife Anne, with their son William, came to America and settled in Hartford, Connecticut. William became a minister and begat The Reverend Richard Edwards II, who begat The Reverend Timothy Edwards, who begat The Reverend Jonathan Edwards.

The Reverend Jonathan Edwards married Sarah Pierrepont of New Haven, Connecticut. They had eleven children but only two of their girls—Elizabeth and an older sister Sarah—will be mentioned in this segment.[6]

When David Mongin (No. 1) became acquainted with the Edwards family in 1747, Elizabeth was only fifteen years old. David and Elizabeth had been very seriously attracted to each other and on 23 December 1749, they were married in Princeton, New Jersey. Elizabeth was now seventeen. Immediately following the ceremony, David, with his young wife, two children from his former marriage, and his brother Francis, departed for their Walnut Grove Plantation on South May River.

In 1750 Elizabeth gave birth to their first child, William Edwards Mongin (who would later marry Margaret Martinangele). After having three other children by 1758, Elizabeth Edwards Mongin died in 1759. Family records state that she was buried on Daufuskie but so far, there are no *legal* records found to prove that she or David were ever on Daufuskie.

David married for the third time in 1765 to a Mary Ann, who is mentioned in his will. Whether David's wife was formerly Mrs. Burgoyne, a relict of General Burgoyne of the British Army, Charleston,[7] as one record states, or a Miss Bekin, the daughter of old General Bekin of South Carolina, from another record,[8] is unknown. There

were no children from this marriage.

David lived in Charleston and attended church regularly. He even went so far as to have his private pew identified with his initials, D.M. When he became an old gentleman, every Sunday he would walk up the aisle with his gold-headed cane, wearing his royal purple velvet suit with its fancy gold buttons.[9]

One family record states that when David died in 1770, he was buried in the French Huguenot Churchyard. Another record states that his burial was at St. Michael's Episcopal Church. Research has been made at both churches in Charleston. He is not listed at either of them; records for the years prior to 1865 were burned during the Civil War and are unavailable.

Sarah Edwards and The Reverend Aaron Burr Wed

In 1752, Elizabeth Edwards' older sister Sarah was married to The Reverend Aaron Burr, a German divine and the first president of Princeton College, New Jersey.

Sarah gave birth to a daughter (1753) and then to a son, Aaron Burr, Jr., in 1755. Sarah Edwards Burr died in 1757. The historian records that she had no sickness that he could call by name; the physician said, "A messenger was sent to suddenly call her out of the world." A woman of great piety, she was converted when she was seven or eight years old and attached herself to the Presbyterian Church at the age of fifteen.[10]

Aaron Burr, Jr., was educated at Yale College. He was on General George Washington's staff during the Revolutionary War. He was vice-president of the United States (and only lost the presidency by one vote). He attempted separating the South and North and was subsequently tried for treason 19 February 1807; but proofs were not sufficient and he was acquitted. He was the challenger in a duel with Alexander Hamilton in which Hamilton was killed. Following the code of honor, he had been forced to challenge Hamilton, who had insulted Burr. Hamilton was Burr's schoolmate and had once been a close friend.

Aaron Burr, Jr., married a Mrs. Converse. Their only child was a daughter, Theodosia Burr (21 June 1783-January 1813). Just a few years after marriage, his wife died.

In 1802, Aaron Burr, Jr., and daughter Theodosia visited Captain

William Edwards Mongin (his first cousin and grandson of The Reverend Jonathan Edwards) at their Walnut Grove Plantation on South May River. During their stay, they were visited by the Governor of South Carolina, Joseph Alston, who was served a large dinner party given in honor of Colonel Aaron Burr.

Governor Alston became so enamored with the lovely Theodosia, that soon after Colonel Burr's return to New York, the governor offered his hand in marriage to Miss Burr, who accepted it.

When Governor Alston went to New York, he took the pastor of

Theodosia Burr

Daughter of Aaron Burr and wife of Governor Joseph Alston of South Carolina. A photograph of her may be seen in *Tales of the Coast*, page 27. (Portrait compliments of artist, Mrs. Cheryl Dickey Smith, 5 January 1987.)

29

his own church with him to perform the ceremony. Governor Joseph Alston and Theodosia Burr were married in New York City, in 1803, by The Reverend P. S. Van Pelt, D.D.[11]

A son, Aaron Burr Alston, was the only child from this union. Governor Alston died and left Theodosia a very young widow. Her father, Aaron Burr, Jr., asked Theodosia to leave her home in South Carolina and to meet him in New Orleans, Louisiana, with her son. Colonel Burr was detained in New York on business and advised his daughter to take a sailing ship and come to New York via the Gulf of Mexico.

Theodosia and her son embarked as requested, but they never reached her father in New York. The ship in which they sailed was never heard of again. Colonel Burr became a lonely desolate man. He sailed for Europe where he lived for several years and then returned to his native New York.

Before his death in a New York hospital, a sailor confessed that he was on a piratical ship when Theodosia Burr Alston and her son were captured. The captain and the crew on the ill-fated ship were killed but Mrs. Alston and her son were made to walk the plank and perished in the sea.[12] The sailor could never forget ". . . the beautiful face of the only lady aboard as it sank into the deep."[13]

David John Mongin (No. 2)

Born in London, England (1739), David John Mongin was the son of Persille Dair and David Mongin (No. 1). After his mother's death, it was at the age of eight (in 1747) that David John left England with his father and sisters Elizabeth and Jane Mary, and came to America. He visited the Edwards family with his father in New Jersey, then came south to claim their land at Purrysburg.

Two years later (1749) he returned to Princeton, New Jersey, to attend the wedding of his father and Elizabeth Edwards. The family brought the new bride (and stepmother) back to their Walnut Grove Plantation on South May River.

David John Mongin married Sarah Grimkie at Walnut Grove in 1762. He was taught the watchmaking trade by his father and might have earned his livelihood from this craft and inherited his father's watch shop. The following ad appeared in a local newspaper:

The subscriber intending to *carry on* the WATCHMAKING BUSI-NESS in all its branches in Purysburgh, all gentlemen and ladies who may be pleased to favour him with their work may depend on having it done in the nicest manner, and with the quickest dispatch by their humble servant, DAVID MONGIN.[14]

In 1766 David John Mongin (No. 2) received Spanish Wells Plantation on Hilton Head as a gift from a friend.[15]

In 1775 David John was given a King's Grant for one thousand acres of land, St. Peter's Parish.[16]

David John and Sarah Grimkie had five children.*

During the Revolution, David John (No. 2) and his son John David (No. 3) were members of the Whig gang on Hilton Head, known as the "Bloody Legion." Members of this group went to Daufuskie on Christmas, 1781, and murdered Tory Captain Phillip Martinangele in his bed.

Their son Daniel William's daughter married in Charleston, according to the *Charleston City Gazette* 4 June 1818:

... married on Thursday evening, 28th ult. at the residence of D. W. Mongin, Esq. in South Carolina, by the Rev. Mr. Swea, Mr. George A. Turkneth, of Augusta, (Ga.) to Miss Mary C. Mongin, daughter of Daniel W. Mongin, Esq. of the former place.[17]

David John (No. 2) died in Charleston (1815) and is assumed buried in the same churchyard as his father—wherever that might be.

John David Mongin (No. 3)

Born in 1763 at Walnut Grove, John David was the eldest of the five children of David John and Sarah Grimkie Mongin.

Having grown up on his father's plantation, he took a vital interest in its management and he visited his father's watchmaking shop quite often at Purrysburg. If he were taught the watchmaking trade he did not pursue it, but rather chose to be one of the most successful planters and landowners of South Carolina and Georgia.

In 1783 David's (half) uncle, William Edwards Mongin, married Margaret Martinangele Pendarvis. The couple moved to Daufuskie and lived on her two-hundred-acre plantation on Mongin Creek.

---

*See Appendix IV for the David John I (No. 2) Family Genealogy Record.

John David Mongin's "Capital Dwelling House"
24 Habersham Street, Savannah, Georgia

Robert Watts, the shipbuilder at Bloody Point, had left his daughter, Sarah (Sally) Watts, a ward of William Edwards Mongin.

Having vivacious Sarah Watts living in the Mongin home gave John David numerous excuses to call on his Uncle William and Aunt Margaret on Daufuskie. It was only natural that John David and Sarah fall in love. They had a lavish wedding at Walnut Grove Plantation in 1790 and their only child, David John Mongin II, was born there in 1791. However, in his will, John David mentions an adopted daughter, Mary Ann Taylor Mongin, who shares as an heir.[18]

Sarah Watts Mongin had inherited her father's Bloody Point property. She and John David paid short visits to Oakley Hall (the Bloody Point mansion) but did not live there permanently. An overseer was in control of the plantation as John David could not be confined to a monotonous situation on such an isolated place for any length of time because of his other lands and businesses in Georgia and South Carolina.

John David's trips to Daufuskie were only to see first hand the condition and management of his slaves and plantations. (Read the section: "David Mongin Not Granted Daufuskie.")

His plantations on the island only accounted for a portion of John David's interests: In 1778 he was a partner in Whittendel & Mongin, a business operated on a Savannah wharf by John T. Whittendel and John David Mongin "... who have in their power to supply plantations with all kinds of groceries as well as many other supplies...."[19] In 1790 he owned a store on Bolton's Wharf which was convenient to handle all the cotton and produce from his Daufuskie plantations.[20] In 1797 he built a "capital dwelling house" in Savannah. (The house has been restored and may be seen at 24 Habersham Street.) John David owned Litchfield, a 1040-acre rice plantation on the Great Ogheechee River; a 1000-acre plantation in Jefferson County, Georgia; and in Bryan County, Georgia, 500 acres of land known as the Eastern Half of the Belfast and [Hume] Tract.[21]

In South Carolina in Beaufort County, known as "New River Neck," John David (who by now was known as "Money Mongin") owned Good Hope Tract, 1107 acres; Ficklin Tract, 2194 acres; and a 500-acre tract known as Point Place.[22]

According to Walter C. Hartridge, "Prosperity led him to seek a more pretentious home," and in 1805 John David sold his "capital dwelling house" in Savannah. He could have built a mansion there and moved to his Litchfield Plantation on the Great Ogheechee River.

His son, David John (No. 4), married Sarah Irwin in 1812, taking his bride to Daufuskie where they lived at Bloody Point.

In 1816 John David's wife, Sarah Watts, died and left him heir of the Bloody Point property. While there is no record of proof, it is believed that after he purchased Melrose in 1818 John David built the Melrose mansion as early as 1823 to be near his grandchildren. There's a possibility that he might have had some of his grandchildren living in the house with him, since Mrs. Virginia Susan (Chaplin) Wright stated the following:

> There was a very rich man called *Money Mongin*. . . . He had a large plantation on Daufuskie and lots of slaves. . . . He had a teacher to teach his children in his home. His home was called Melrose. . . ."[23]

At that time (circa 1823), John David had no children at home. His son and only child, David John, was living with his wife, Sarah Irwin, at the Bloody Point mansion with their two children, William Henry (7) and Mary Lavinia (4). If there were children at Melrose it would have to be these. As son David John had a drinking problem, it could be that John David took his grandchildren to live with him at Melrose.

It is known that John David was living on Daufuskie in 1823 as he is a "witness" to Love Martinangele's will.[24]

John David (No. 3) married for the third time in 1823 to Ann Harrison. There were no children from this marriage. He died in 1833. Requested in his will was that he be "buried in the family burial place on May River." His body was later moved to Bonaventure Cemetery, Savannah, Georgia, and placed in the Mongin-Stoddard vault with his first wife, Sarah Watts.*

•

A little story concerning John David Mongin (No. 3) surfaced through Mrs. William (Jo) Scouten:

> From Haig's Point, old Mr. Mongin had a ferry (barge) ready at each river crossing and a roadway built across each hammock to the mainland. When he wanted to go to the city, he would take his horse and

*See Appendix V for John David (No. 3) Family Genealogy Record.

buggy and ride on to the ferry. Slaves would pole him across a body of water. When they came to a hammock, John David would ride off the barge and across the hammock until he reached the next body of water. He repeated this procedure until he got to the mainland, which was on the road to Savannah. He would ride off the ferry, go to the city, tend to his business, then return the same way.

David John II (No. 4)

The only child born to John David and Sarah Watts Mongin was David John II. His birthplace was Walnut Grove on South May River in 1791.

Having a father who was wealthy beyond measure, David John was given everything that a young boy could possibly need or want. He was educated at Princeton.

Of all of his father's plantations, his apparent favorite place was on Daufuskie; in 1812, David John married Sarah Irwin and the couple made Oakley Hall, the mansion at Bloody Point, their permanent residence.

Just when is unknown, but David John bought Haig's Point and Freeport Plantations and had an overseer to manage them.

Of David and Sarah's six children, only two lived to maturity: William Henry, who was born in 1816, and Mary Lavinia, the survivor of twin girls born in 1819.

David John, not controlling his alcoholic problem, died at the age of thirty-two in 1823 at the Bloody Point mansion.

His body is interred in the Mongin-Stoddard vault at Bonaventure Cemetery, Savannah.

(For further detailed information concerning David John Mongin (No. 4),* see Bloody Point Plantation section.)

Mary Lavinia Mongin (No. 5)

Mary Lavinia was born to David John II and Sarah Irwin in 1819 on Daufuskie. Her twin sister, Sarah, died in 1822 and was buried on the island with her two brothers, Edmund and David John, and her sister,

---

*Appendix VI, p. 1, for David John Mongin (No. 4) Family Genealogy Record. See p. 2 for information concerning Mongin-Stoddard vault at Bonaventure Cemetery.

Jane J. (The bodies of all four children were later moved to the Bonaventure Cemetery in Savannah.)

Mary Lavinia lived with her parents at Bloody Point. It is thought that she and her brother, William Henry, might have stayed at length with their grandfather, John David Mongin (No. 3), who could have been living at Melrose.

In 1823 Mary Lavinia's father died and in 1825 her mother married The Reverend Herman M. Blodgett. As a marriage settlement, her mother was given Haig's Point and Freeport Plantations and it is assumed that the family moved to a smaller mansion which faced Cooper River on the Haig's Point property. An avenue of oaks led to this house.

Where she was educated is unknown, but when her mother and grandfather both died in 1833, Mary Lavinia could have been sent to school in France. Her grandfather had stated in his will, "I desire and direct that my grandchildren be well educated and supported from my estate . . . and I desire my Executors to be liberal . . . in this regard."[25] Who knows? Perhaps she was living with distant relatives in France, from where her great grandfather, David Mongin (No. 1), had fled in 1725. However, it was while in Paris that she met John Stoddard.

John Stoddard Not Tutor to Mongin Children

Contrary to popular belief, John Stoddard did not come to Daufuskie as a tutor for the Mongin children. He was the lineal descendant of Anthony Stoddard, who came to the "Plantations of America" from England in 1630 with his wife Mary and settled in Boston.

John was born 11 March 1809 in Northampton, Massachusetts, to Solomon Stoddard (Fifth Generation) and Mary Tappan. John's brother Charles was a partner in the importing business of Edwards & Stoddard. At the age of sixteen, John was taken into the firm and taught the many aspects of the importing trade. At the age of twenty, he had demonstrated his business acumen to the extent that he had gained the confidence and respect of his employers who admitted him into the firm. John was sent to France to conduct the branch houses at Paris and Lyons, where, after seven years, he became wealthy in his own right.

Brought up in the pure doctrine of his illustrious kinsman, The Reverend Jonathan Edwards, at the age of eighteen John was a

consistent member of the Church of Christ and lived what he believed. "The lures and gayeties of the French capital were resisted with the stern denial of his Puritan predecessors, never during his Paris life being induced to enter opera or theatre."[26]

It was while in Paris that John met Mary Lavinia Mongin. A beautiful courtship led them to be married in Paris at the American Consulate, 7 January 1836, by The Reverend Baird.[27]

They lived abroad until after their first child, Mary Helen, was born in London, 4 January 1837.* With the vast inheritance given Mary Lavinia by her grandfather, John David Mongin (No. 3), John Stoddard thought it in the best interest of his wife for them to leave France and come to South Carolina to handle her estate—which they did that same year (1837).

It had been stated that "her income, already of opulent dimensions, was, by her husband's judicious management, enhanced to the extent of two and a half times at her demise in 1865."

(Continued in Melrose Plantation section.)

The Martinangeles[28]

Prince Filippo de Martinangelo is speaking:

My father was Lord Protector of Italy. Our family consisted of my father, my mother, two sisters, and an elder brother. My brother was by right entitled to the titles, honor, wealth and estate of the family, as for me, I was reserved for the church.

After awhile, there was a young Englishman who visiting Rome on account of his health. We became acquainted and proved in sequel to be the most inseparable of friends. This young gentleman was exceedingly pious, while I, on the other hand, was a rigid Romanist. So one day while we were conversing, he begged of me to read my Bible. After awhile I consented, and behold, my eyes were opened and I became a protestant.

This could not be long kept a secret from my family as I was compelled (being one of the young nobles) to attend every morning at the Vatican and carry to our Confessor his stated salary. When this was handed me, instead of taking it to this Worthy Father, I retained it. It passed on for some time. Finally, my mother requested my presence in

---

*See Stoddard Family Group Record, Appendix VII.

the library. I tremblingly entered. She at once questioned me as regarding my strange proceedings and said that it was by accident that our Confessor had been questioned and that the money appropriated for his benefits, he had never received and she wished to be informed by me, as to what use I had employed it. She hoped that it had not been squandered at the gaming-table, neither in riotous living, for if this were the case, she devoutly hoped I would make a confession immediately to my saintly Father and promise her never to have this occur again, and at the same time, every cent that was coming to the venerated friend should be paid.

I felt as if the breath were leaving my body, but I determined to tell the truth, dare all things and leave the rest 'in the hands of that Good Being Who orders all things for the best.' I fell on my knees before my mother and confessed everything and concluded with these words: that I was unchangeable and was at heart a confirmed Protestant. Who very sadly turned away from me and then walked to the window. There rolled the Tiber in its beautiful grandeur and above towered our castle. At last, my mother turned away sorrowfully. She gazed into my eyes and said, 'Philip de Marteangel, do you know the end of this decision? do you know that we shall be compelled to give you up to the all-powerful Inquisition and that you will be condemned by your own testimony?'

What avails it to say more? I was to be given to the Inquisition and by parents who loved their children to adoration and in this, they thought they were doing a good service. But fortunately, I possessed the love of my youngest sister, Margaret, for she passionately loved me, her youngest brother.

There was on the east wing of our castle a postern gate that was scarcely ever used at all, or if known was little used. To this secluded spot my darling sister caused a swift horse to be taken. It was midnight when she came to my room and awakened me out of my sleep.

"Arise, my brother, you must be away [before] it is light."

I hurriedly followed her to the spot. She then bade me an eternal farewell and placed in my hands a purse of gold and her watch.

"Go," said my sister, pressing me to her heart, "and may God speed you."

I immediately threw myself on my horse and just arrived at the last gate as it was closing. I attempted to pass, but was prevented by a soldier, for he told me that one of the young nobles had been given up to the Inquisition and he was commanded to close the gate.

I offered him the purse of gold. He would not take it. I then offered him the purse of gold and my watch. To this, the soldier very readily

agreed as his love for the precious metal overcame all things. He allowed me to pass through and I immediately hurried on to Paris and to the residence of my aunt who was my godmother. I rode so hard that when I entered, I was unable to stand and had to be swathed in linen bandages for several days. I immediately confessed everything to this lady. She did all in her power to induce me to return to the Catholic faith and even volunteered to regain for me the love of my parents if I would only consent. But all that would not do— the die had been cast. I had crossed the Rubicon, and this alone was enough. Still my trouble was not over. The Inquisition was still out against me, but my lady aunt had me secreted in a distant wing of the chateau and waited on me herself. Her apartment connected with mine by a secret door in a wall. My aunt said to me that she could never bring herself to give me up for my limbs to be torn to pieces by the infernal rack.

She then provided me with money and I crossed over to Dover and then sailed for America where I have since married and have become the father of a number of children. I settled first in Charleston, South Carolina, but then afterwards removed to Dawfuskie Island, Beaufort District, South Carolina.[29]

What the greedy soldier did not see that dark night was the de Martinangelo red cornelian ring that Prince Filippo was wearing. Engraved in the brownish-red stone is the family coat of arms—a sunflower turning to the sun with this inscription: "*Tibi Soli* (*Soli Tibi*), Latin, which means "To Thee Alone." Mrs. E. H. (Bertha) Anderson, who is in possession of the ring, gives another spiritual meaning: "As the Flower Turns to the Sun, So We Turn to God."[30]

According to Anderson Genealogy, "Parents of Filippo de Martinangelo were a Tuscan nobleman and wife, living in Rome." Filippo was probably born around 1720.

When Prince Filippo de Martinangelo settled in America (circa 1740), he anglicized his name, and became known as Phillip Martinangele. He married Mary Foster in 1743. Traditional accounts state that he lived on Daufuskie but no records have surfaced to substantiate this.

As a Granville (Beaufort) County planter, Phillip bought on 13 October 1754, from Christopher Dawson of Prince William Parish, two hundred acres on Skull Creek, Hilton Head Island, South Carolina, adjoining two hundred acres he had bought earlier from Sarah Blakeway.[31]

The Phillip Martinangele Ring

Stone is Solid Brownish Red. *Tibi Soli*—Latin
which means "To Thee Alone." (Compliments of
Mrs. E. H. [Bertha] Anderson.)

In 1756 Phillip Martinangele (and David Mongin) were enrolled in
the Euthaws Company of the county militia on the South Side of Port
Royal River. And in 1757, Phillip served on the Beaufort petit jury.[32]

On May 1759: "...Philep Martonangels...for the sum of fifty pound
Sterling being the Revnd. Mr. Jones Legacy For the Encouragement of
a School Master & Educating of poor Children in This parish...."[33]

And on 10 October 1759, Phillip was granted Lot 91 in Beaufort.[34]
Phillip died prior to 6 October 1761, when an inventory of his estate
was presented. He is probably buried on Port Royal where he lived.
On 7 April 1762, "Mary Martinangele, widow of Phillip Martin-
angele, planter of Port Royal, bought from Lancelot Bland of Prince
William's Parish Plantation of five hundred acres on Daufuskie
Island, Granville [Beaufort] County."[35]
Phillip and Mary Foster had eight children, all of whom were born
on Port Royal Island. Birth records of five of them may be found in St.

Helena's Parish Register; however, all eight of the children are listed in the Anderson Genealogy.

Little is known concerning some of the children, but any history at all is noteworthy, because the Martinangeles were one of the first permanent families on Daufuskie and until today their descendants continue to own 4.6 acres of land known as the Mary (Martinangele) Dunn Cemetery.

Francis Martinangele

Born 2 February 1744, Francis was baptized 28 May 1744 by The Reverend Lewis Jones, St. Helena Church.

South Carolina rigidly adhered to the English common law, particularly regarding the inheritance of property, estates, and wills. There were no exceptions to the laws of primogeniture, whereby the eldest son was the heir-at-law, inheriting all real property. Therefore, it may be assumed that at his father's death in 1761, Francis, being the oldest son and heir-at-law, would have inherited all of the family property holdings (or realty).

There is no record of a wife, but that does not mean that Francis did not marry. If he received his father's estate, this would have put him in a financial position to marry early. Listed on the 1790 Census are two Martinangeles, Joseph and Lewie (or Lewis) who might have been sons of Francis. Assuming they were of age in 1790, Francis would be the most logical of the Martinangele males to have been their father. No other records of them exist.

"He assumes responsibility for his father's loan by the Vestry of 6 of the Rev. Lewis Jones Legacy, paying the interest in 1772."[36] Francis, listed as a private in the Granville County, South Carolina, Royal Militia, was serving duty on Daufuskie in 1781.[37] No death record was found.

Mary Martinangele

Mary was born 16 December 1745. On 5 May 1767 she married John Hopkins, a British seaman and a pilot of the Savannah Bar. Their second son, Francis (and the only one to survive of three children), was born near Bluffton, 10 November 1770.[38]

John Hopkins was fiercely loyal in defending the British cause. It was on 24 July 1775 that he was overheard to have muttered "Dam-

nation to America" in drinking a toast, thus offending the Sons of Liberty. They determined to make an example of him by ordering him to either recant and drink "Damnation to all Tories and Success to American Liberty," or be hanged immediately.

About nine o'clock that same evening, while John was having supper with his family in their home on Lot #12 in Yamacraw, a group of rowdy Liberty Boys, without a word, opened the door, dragged him out of the house, and carried him to the outskirts of the city to be tarred and feathered.

The majority decided that it should be done in a more public place so they took him to the middle of the square in the center of town. There, they stripped off his jacket and shirt, reluctantly leaving on him the remainder of his clothing. They proceeded to tar and feather John, put him in an open cart, then paraded him up and down the streets of Savannah for three hours in that condition.

Abused and cursed, he was carried to the Liberty tree to be hanged but they changed their minds. Between midnight and 1:00, they left him at the Vendue house ordering him to beg "all America pardon."[39]

Shortly thereafter, being on the Georgia Confiscation List, he lost everything and left Savannah for East Florida. He, Mary, and son Francis left Florida for the Bahamas, where they settled. John Hopkins supposedly died in 1788 while on a voyage to Charlotte Amelia.

Following the death of John, Mary and son returned to Daufuskie. Probably in need of finances, Mary sold her one-hundred-acre inheritance to sister Margaret, and moved to the area of Bluffton.

In the first United States Census, 1790, Mary Hopkins is listed as head of a household with three males. We will never know for certain who these males were, or even whether they were Martinangele kin, but we do know that her son Francis, at age twenty, is also listed as head of a separate household. In 1794, Francis married Rebecca Saye and had several children. They are depicted as living with Francis' mother on a large plantation on May River until the awful storm of 1804, which destroyed much property along the coast. That same year, his friend, Thomas Spalding, persuaded Francis to move with his family (including his mother) to Sapelo Island, McIntosh County, Georgia.[41]

Francis's mother Mary died in 1812. Family lore states that "her son took her body back to the old home to be placed in the tomb of her

father."[42] It is uncertain just where Mary is buried as her father, Phillip Martinangele, Sr., is buried at Port Royal and the tombstone of Mary Foster Martinangele, her mother, may be found in the Mary Dunn Cemetery on Daufuskie.

Francis Hopkins served in the Georgia Legislature 1808-1814, and in the Georgia Senate 1815-1816. He was a Justice of the Inferior Court of McIntosh County from 1811 until his death in 1821. He served as Major in the Georgia Militia during the War of 1812, and was elevated to the rank of Major General during the Indian Wars. Six of his sons served in the legislatures of Georgia and Florida.

Duel of Col. John Livingston Hopkins

General Francis Hopkins's son John Livingston, when very young, enlisted in the United States Navy. He served as a midshipman on the frigate *Constitution* and saw service on the African coast in the war with the Barbary States. After returning home, where the ship was stationed at Hoboken, New Jersey, John L. Hopkins became involved in a bad situation with a Lieutenant Keith.

An amusing caricature of Keith had been circulated about, which annoyed the Lieutenant. Being clever with a pencil, John Livingston was accused by Keith in an insulting way of being the artist. Hopkins was innocent of the charge, but because he felt outraged, he resigned his commission and sent Keith a challenge, which was accepted. A duel was arranged and Hopkins slew Keith.

After the duel, John Livingston Hopkins returned home to Sapelo, studied law, and was admitted to the bar. In 1817 he was elected as a representative to the Georgia Legislature from McIntosh County. Because of his title, Hopkins is now referred to as "Colonel."

Col. John Livingston Hopkins Kills McQueen McIntosh

The Hopkins and the McIntosh clan were really old friends. They were all high strung and easily irritated. Because of political slander, petty arguments, accusations, and, using vile language during times of anger, they had many close encounters using pistols and swords.

Hopkins was also ridiculed because of the loss of his left eye. (Would you believe a marsh-bird swooped down and plucked it out when he was a young boy?)[43]

On one occasion, bearing the brunt of a fight for McQueen, Col. Hopkins had received three dangerous stabs, two in the head and one in the breast that had confined him to bed for over two months.

It seemed that everytime a Hopkins and a McIntosh met, some sort of disagreement was sure to follow. When John L. Hopkins and Capt. William R. McIntosh were dining at the Darien Hotel, they got into an argument and Hopkins threw a glass of wine in McIntosh's face, then McIntosh threw a bottle of wine at Hopkins' head—"a waste of good wine on both sides."

The finale came when Col. John L. Hopkins and McQueen McIntosh had a brawl on the streets of Darien, Georgia. McQueen was killed, having been shot through the body, and Col. Hopkins walked away with a shattered arm.

During a course of events, Col. Hopkins was jailed, indicted for murder, then sentenced to a term of years in the penitentiary. He was allowed to visit his plantation High Point on Sapelo before serving his sentence. Secret action was taken to have Hopkins rowed out of Sapelo Sound to the ocean where he boarded a sailing ship. For the sum of $5000, the captain carried him to England where he lived in safety for three years.[44]

Col. John L. Hopkins returned to America and was pardoned by Gov. John Clarke. Hopkins later moved to Monroe County, Tennessee, where he resumed his practice of law and taught at the local Academy. In September of 1828, while on muster with the County Militia, he became involved in an altercation with a man to whom he had loaned money. Hopkins was struck on the head with the butt of a rifle, and died three days later. His only son, John Livingston Hopkins, Jr., was born just six days before his father's death and lived to become one of Georgia's noted lawyers and jurists, dying in Atlanta in 1912.[45]

Phillip Martinangele, Jr.

Born 20 November 1747, Phillip came to Daufuskie with his mother, Mary, circa 1762. In 1776 he was elected to the St. Helena Safety Committee. He married circa 1777 to a young lady by the name of Elizabeth. (She was not Mary Green as has been portrayed, but her surname remains a mystery.) After Phillip's death in 1781, she remarried to William Williams, December 1783. We know her name was

Elizabeth, for at her death in 1786, the following legal notice appeared in the Savannah newspaper by Benjamin Lloyd, Esquire, Register of Probate of Chatham County, Georgia:

> Whereas William Williams, of the county and state aforesaid, planter, hath this day made humble suit to me to grant him letters of administration on the estate of Phillip Martinangel, unadministered by his widow, *Elizabeth*, now deceased, and late the wife of said Williams. . . .[46]

Phillip and Elizabeth's first child was Phillip III, baptized by The Rev. John Joachim Zubly at Middlesex[47] (near Purrysburg), South Carolina, in 1778.[48]

It is thought their second child may have been Thomas Martinangele, whose marriage announcement appeared in the Savannah newspaper 8 July 1800: "Thursday evening by Rev. Mr. Cloud, Mr. Thomas Martinangel to the agreeable Miss Susan Hover, both late of South Carolina."

No daughters have been positively identified, but Martinangele lore states that Margaret Martinangele (who married John Chapman) could have been their third child. Margaret, then three weeks old, was supposedly lying in bed by her father's side when he was slain December 1781. Family legend gives this account of Phillip's death:

> Lee Craft's party landed on Dawfuski Island. There they visited the Martinangel plantation. [Phillip] de Martinangel had been very ill and they had left his little daughter [Margaret], about three weeks old, on the bed with him. The breakfast table was set waiting the assembling of the family, when lo, the stillness of the scene was interrupted by the visit of Lee Craft's party. They entered and all [the family] fled like frightened birds. The [raiding party] stole the silver from the table. Then they entered the room of the invalid and murdered him in his bed and left yelling like so many bloodhounds let loose. When quietness returned to the family, the husband and father was no more and the little baby was [nearly] strangled in her father's blood.[49]

(Contrary to prior records, it was not Abraham who was murdered. He appears in the 1790 Census. See notes on the Revolutionary War concerning Phillip.)

Because Phillip died on Daufuskie, logic would say that he is buried here, but no one really knows.

Until the Revolution, his home and activities were centered around Savannah. Possibly it was for safety reasons only that Phillip might

have brought his family to be with his mother, Mary, during the War, especially since his wife Elizabeth had an infant baby at the time of his death. No record has been found connecting Phillip to any land on the island. However, whether he owned, leased, or perhaps had permission from his mother to use her plantation, one record has surfaced of his having a herd of cattle on Daufuskie. A notice appeared in a Savannah newspaper after his widow Elizabeth married William Williams. (The copy is almost too faint to read.):

> Received of William Williams & Elizabeth Williams his wife the sum of Ninety four___less shillings by purchase of seventy head cattle ___ ___calves & sold at Venue on the Defusky Island S. Carolina now late the property of Philip Martinangell desceased . . . (Date of sale at Venue, February 1784, by Edward Davies.)[50]

In 1983 the Hilton Head Historical Society had an impressive ceremony dedicating a memorial marker in honor of Phillip Martinangele, Jr. (For further details of this occasion, see the Mary Dunn Cemetery segment.)

Thomas Martinangele

The thoughts of several are that Phillip and Mary Foster Martinangele did not have a son named Thomas. However, he does appear in the Anderson Genealogy as having been born "about 1749." There is nothing more to substantiate this and no records have surfaced concerning him. A possibility is that he might have died as an infant.

Isaac Martinangele

Isaac was born in 1752 on Port Royal Island. He served as a private with his brothers in the Royal Militia on Daufuskie in 1781. He married Elizabeth Ladson-Godfrey (widow of Anthony Godfrey), 20 March 1782. (In 1780, while he and Elizabeth were living on Daufuskie, Anthony Godfrey died from a rattlesnake bite.)

Brought into Isaac's marriage was Elizabeth's daughter, Elizabeth Ladson Godfrey, Jr., who was the first person baptized in the Savannah Baptist Church, Chippewa Square, Savannah, Georgia, by the Reverend Henry Holcombe in 1800. Elizabeth, Jr., married William E. Jones.[51] They had a son, Æneas Jones, who is listed on his mother's tomb, Mary Dunn Cemetery.

Isaac and Elizabeth had six children, all born on Daufuskie. (They will be discussed here, but a Family Group Record may be found in Appendix IX.)

Phillip IV was born, 1783, remained a bachelor, killed by lightening in 1852, buried on Daufuskie.

Mary, born 1785, married Francis Dunn. Both buried on Daufuskie. No children.

Love, born 1788, married first to a Mr. _____ Mead. At his death, she married a Mr. _____ Forsythe. Following his death, she married Jessie Mount. They had one daughter, Amanda Mount. Jesse and Love sold her inheritance of land (one-fifth of 200 acres) from her Uncle Simeon, to her sister, Mary Dunn, and brother, Phillip IV, 1826.[52] Jesse purchased Piney Islands Plantation from John Andrew Mongin. (See Mongin segment.) Jesse later sold the plantation to Love's nephew, James Peto Chaplin, sister Harriet's son. No record of Love's death or burial.

Jesse is buried in the Baptist Churchyard, Beaufort, South Carolina.[53]

Isaac, Jr., born 1790. No record of marriage or death.

Mary Ann, born 1791, was married first to James Peto of Godalming, Surry, England. They had one daughter, Mary Elizabeth, and one son, James Peto, Jr. After James Peto, Sr.'s, death, Mary Ann married Paul Grimball and had four sons, Francis Dunn, William Peto (William Paul), B. Jenkins, and Paul L. Mary Ann Grimball sold her inheritance of land from her Uncle Simeon (one-fifth of 200 acres) to her sister, Mary Dunn, 1830.[54]

Harriet Louise was born 1797. According to David Humphrey family records, she was a tiny woman, only 4 feet tall. She married William Fripp Chaplin in 1811. He had fifteen children from a previous marriage. He and Harriet had ten, six of whom are listed on her horizonal marble slab. (See Mary Dunn Cemetery section.) Harriet had four other children:

Francis and John Joseph—no birth or death dates.

William Fripp Chaplin, Jr., married his first cousin, Elizabeth Mary (Mary Elizabeth) Peto, Harriet's sister, Mary Ann's daughter.

James Peto Chaplin born 1818, married Mary Caroline Rhodes. Both are buried on Daufuskie.

Abraham Martinangele

Abraham was born 20 July 1754 on Port Royal Island. By his first wife (name unknown) he had one child, Elizabeth. By his second wife (name unknown) he had two children, Ellen and Margaret. Census of Daufuskie Island on the eve of the Revolution lists Abraham as a Loyalist and a farmer.[55] However, he is not listed in 1781 as serving in the Royal Militia with his brothers.[56]

Abraham was not murdered December 1781 in his bed on Daufuskie by the Bloody Legion—it was his brother Phillip, Jr. Abraham wasn't on Daufuskie in 1781. The following facts quoted from the files of Alex S. Hopkins, Jr., prove that Abraham was alive and well at that time:

> The first adult record of Abraham is when he is shown with one other adult male on a list of Loyalist refugees sailing from Savannah to East Florida at the evacuation of Savannah. (BPRO, C. O. 5/560, #2351.) In all probability the other male was Simeon, the two younger boys being sent away by their family to escape the fate of their brother, Phillip, Jr. and their brother-in-law, Richard Pendarvis. It would be logical that they would go to East Florida where their sister Mary, and her husband, John Hopkins, had gone earlier.
>
> Abraham Martinangele appears on the Census of Refugees in East Florida with one other adult male in 1782/3. John Hopkins appears on the same list.
>
> Abraham is next recorded on a list of refugees to the Bahamas who settled there during the years 1783 and 1784, in A. Talbot Bethell's book, *The Early Settlers of the Bahamas and Colonists of North America.*
>
> A petition to address the inequities being suffered by the "new" inhabitants of the Islands was presented in 1788 to the British Government. The petition from the Island of Abaco dated January 1788 was signed by Abraham Martinangele.
>
> We know that Abraham returned to this country after January 1788. . . .

Because the names of his wives were not known, it is believed that Abraham might have married while in the Bahamas and perhaps all of his children were born there.

In 1785 Abraham was given one hundred acres of land from his mother, Mary Foster Martinangele;[57] and he is back in South Carolina

and listed in the 1790 Census as having four males, four females, and two slaves.

A deed confirms that Abraham sold his one hundred acres of land to his brother Simeon.[58] There is no record of Abraham returning to Daufuskie after the Revolution. His daughter, Elizabeth, married George Stoney of Bluffton, South Carolina.[59] There is no record, but it is perhaps there that Abraham died and is buried.

Simeon Martinangele

The only source available states that Simeon was born after 1751. Extensive research by Alex S. Hopkins, Jr., has traced Simeon as having been born around 1757.

In 1775 Simeon was an apprentice to shipwright Charlie Watts (Robert Watts' cousin) who was building ships at Bloody Point. Simeon lacked fifteen more months of completing his apprenticeship when Charlie Watts was forced by the Rebel Committee to give up the indenture and flee Daufuskie. (See Bloody Point segment, n. 49.)

In February 1781 Simeon is listed as a private in Col. Nicholas Lechmere's Regiment of Loyalist troops.

In order to keep them safe from abuses of the Liberty Boys, it is believed that in 1782/83, Simeon and his brother Abraham were sent to East Florida to be with their older sister Mary and her husband, John Hopkins. Abraham went to the Bahamas with Mary, John, and their son Francis.

Coming to light recently was a document found in the Governor's Papers of Gov. John Martin of Georgia at the University of Georgia. It is a letter from Patrick Tonyn, British Governor of East Florida, written to Gov. Martin concerning Simeon Martinangele. It reads in its entirety:

> Sir, I had the honor of writing to your Excellency by Colonel Cooper, who set out from here on the 15th instant, and I hope all the gentlemen have got safe to Savannah.
>
> The Bearer has requested a flag of truce to settle his private affairs, and I have complied with his desire, and have given to Mr. Simeon Martinangel in the sloop Sally and Nancy proper powers for that purpose, who will wait on you with my respects, and I beg you will grant him your countenance and protection.

I have the honour to be with great respect, Sir,

> Your Excellency's
> most obedient and
> most humble servant
>
> /s/Pat. Tonyn

His Excellency   St. Augustine 20th Nov.
Governor Martin 1782.[60]

In 1785 Simeon married Love Tucker. Mrs. Elizabeth (Bettye) Derst was given the Prayer Book of her great-grandmother, Mary Green Lebey, Savannah, Georgia. In this Prayer Book, the Tucker family is recorded:

> . . . Love was born, Love Tucker 11 March 1739. Her father was George Tucker [possibly from Bermuda] who died 10 June 1773. Love was married three times; 1st Robert Henning, 12 April 1765; 2nd Charles Rowland, 9 July 1769. He died 26 January 1782; 3rd Simeon Martinagele 14 February 1785. She died 30 November 1823, apparently making her home with Mary Green Lebey and Christian [David] Lebey.[61]

On 5 November 1785 Simeon was given one hundred acres of land from his mother, Mary Foster Martinangele. Simeon is listed as head of household in the 1800 Census.

There is no record, but Simeon had died prior to the 1810 Census as Love is listed as head of household. But Milner Tucker, who was presumably her brother, is listed on Daufuskie in 1805, and could be the male over forty-five who was living with Love in the 1810 Census. Perhaps in his old age, and after Simeon's death, Milner came to live with Love and is buried on Daufuskie, maybe next to Simeon.

Margaret Martinangele

Margaret was born circa 1758 on Port Royal Island, South Carolina. She and Richard Pendarvis ("Tory Dick") were married in 1781. He was murdered while they were on their honeymoon, living at Stephenville Plantation on South May River. (Read details in the Revolutionary War segment.) After Richard's death, Margaret probably came back to Daufuskie to live with her mother at Eigleberger. On 25 May 1783, she and William Edwards Mongin were married. (He was the son of David Mongin and David's second wife, Elizabeth Edwards

50

Mongin.) William and Margaret divided their time living at the Mongin mansion, Walnut Grove, on South May River, and with her mother Mary at Eigleberger. Margaret and William had nine children, viz.:

Mary Mongin, 14 September 1784, died 20 September 1784, born and buried on Daufuskie.

Elizabeth Edwards Mongin, 25 December 1785, Daufuskie. She married Robert H. Pettigrew (of Charleston) 21 December 1815 at the Mongin Walnut Grove mansion on South May River. She had no children but Elizabeth (Eliza) Edwards Mongin was a "mother" to Margaret Cornelia Sanford Mongin after the death of her mother, Adeline C. Lewis. Robert H. Pettigrew died 30 November 1840. Elizabeth Edwards Mongin Pettigrew died in Savannah 9 February 1847, buried on Daufuskie.

Margaret Mongin, 4 March 1788, Walnut Grove, died 12 October 1792, buried on Daufuskie

William Henry Mongin, 3 March 1790, Walnut Grove, died 12 October 1792, buried on Daufuskie.

Sarah Watts Mongin, 14 August 1792, Walnut Grove, died 1 September 1794, buried on Daufuskie.

William Edwards Mongin, Jr., 12 August 1794, Walnut Grove, died 16 September 1799, buried on Daufuskie.

Richard Thomas Pendarvis Mongin, 7 August 1797, Daufuskie. (He was named after Margaret's first husband.) Richard married Adeline Cornelia Lewis, 17 August 1820, New Haven, Connecticut. Adeline was his second cousin and great granddaughter of Reverend Jonathan Edwards of Princeton, N. J. She died 2 September 1822—only daughter was Margaret Cornelia (above). Richard died 2 September 1837 in Savannah, buried on Daufuskie.

Simeon Mongin (named after her brother), 22 September 1799, died 21 October 1800, born and buried on Daufuskie.

Ralph David Mongin, 5 January 1802, Daufuskie, married Elizabeth Catherine Maner, 15 December 1824, South May River. They lived at Oak Island Plantation, South Carolina. He died 31 October 1850, Savannah, buried on Daufuskie.

In 1785, from her mother, Mary Foster Martinangele, Margaret was given one hundred acres of land, on which stood the Eigleberger

mansion. Margaret at some point in time and in some way, acquired her sister Mary's one hundred acres, thus increasing Eigleberger to two hundred acres.

William Edwards Mongin's mother, Elizabeth Edwards Mongin, had died in 1759 when William was nine years of age, therefore, she could not have come to Daufuskie and lived with him and Margaret as has been stated. It was probably *her* mother, Mary Foster Martinangele, who lived with them until her death in 1790.

Margaret Martinangele-Pendarvis-Mongin died Saturday morning, 6 February 1808, buried on Daufuskie.[62]

The Green Family
and Their Association With the Martinangeles

Old records state that William Green married Mary Rutledge, daughter of Gov. Rutledge of Charleston, South Carolina; that William and Mary had two children, Mary and William, Jr.; that Mary Green was supposed to have married Phillip Martinangele, Jr.; and that William, Jr.'s, granddaughter, Love Green, married Simeon Martinangele, Phillip's brother. None of the preceding is accurate.

Research has been made into the Rutledge genealogy. There were two Governors Rutledge of South Carolina, John (1776-1778 and again 1778-1779), who was also the first governor of South Carolina, and Edward (1798-1800). There is no reference to a daughter of either Rutledge marrying a Phillip Martinangele, Jr.[63]

Being also related to the Green family, Alex S. Hopkins, Jr., in his research, has proven that the William Green, planter, who lived on Daufuskie prior to 1781 and associated with the Martinangele family, was the son of Josiah Green and Catherine Beale Green of Hilton Head. This is also confirmed through the Prayer Book of Mary Green Lebey (William's daughter).[64] William had two sisters, Catherine and Elizabeth, but no *Love*.

Josiah Green died and Catherine Beale Green married the second time to Daniel Williams. Her third husband was Joseph Steel, boat builder. Catherine and Joseph are found living on Daufuskie. They had two sons—John Steel, born 8 May 1770, and Joseph Steel, born (on Daufuskie) 21 September 1772.[65] Naturally, John and Joseph were half brothers of William Green. Joseph followed his father's trade and was also a ship carpenter, possibly on Daufuskie.

Records show that circa 1789, William Green (born 24 June 1755—died 13 Sept. 1812) married Mary Roberts (born 8 May 1754—died 24 March 1812) of Robertsville, South Carolina. When Savannah was evacuated during the Revolution, William, Mary, and son Josiah (along with Abraham Martinangele), left for East Florida and then on to the Bahamas, where their daughter, Mary Green, was born at New Providence (1792).[66] They had another daughter, Catherine, and another son, William.

William, Mary, and family returned to Savannah, Georgia, (1793). Their daughter, Mary Green, married Christian David Lebey, with whom Love Tucker Martinangele lived out her final years. Daughter Catherine Green married Charles Flinn of Daufuskie.

(As you have already read in the Phillip, Jr., and Simeon Martinangele segments, Phillip married Elizabeth _____ [last name unknown], and Simeon married Love Tucker.)

Early Martinangele family accounts indicated that Love Tucker Martinangele was somehow related to Mary Foster Martinangele prior to Love's marriage to Simeon, although no connection has been found. The inclusion in the Prayer Book of Mary Green Lebey of records relating to Love and the Tucker family indicate a relationship between the Tuckers and the Greens. This is further borne out by the will of Love Martinangele which refers to the son of Mary Green Lebey as her "grand Nephew." When coupled with the very close association between William Green and the Martinangele family in many documents and during the Revolution, some kinship between these three families is indicated, but no record has been found.

•

Last minute facts have brought to light more information concerning the Martinangeles that will help to assist those interested in this family's history.

On 27 September 1735, directed by James St. John, Esq., "his majesty's surveyor gen'l, Philip Martainang," was granted Lot Number 121 in the Town of "Purrisburgh."[67]

With this information, it is evident that Phillip Martinangele, Sr., was in South Carolina a few years earlier than other records have indicated. It also shows that Phillip, Sr., and David Mongin, Sr. (having both given grants to Purrysburgh land), perhaps knew each other prior to coming to America.

53

The second piece of information concerns Simeon Martinangele. From research in the Bahama Island, New Providence Archives, comes the will of Simeon, dated 3 April 1787, which states:

> First, I give and bequeath to my well beloved wife, Love Martin-angele, all my estate real and personal moveables and unmoveables for her to make use of as she shall think proper and Secondly, I desire all my debts may be paid by my Executors or by my Executrix, and I do nereby appoint my well beloved wife, Love Martinangele, my whole Executrix, to do as she shall think proper with my estate and I do acknowledge and constitute this to be my last will and testament.

The will is witnessed by William Green and Robert Tucker (Love Tucker Martinangele's relative).

This proves that apparently Simeon too evacuated Savannah along with his brother Abraham, Francis Hopkins, and others during the closing days of the Revolution.

The third piece of information also concerns Simeon Martinangele. He did not remain in the Bahamas but returned to South Carolina. Surveyed for Simeon on 1 February 1800, a 357-acre March Island that now joins the north and west shores of Mongin Creek on the south side of Daufuskie. This island lies west of Bloody Point and borders the north shore of what is now known as New River that flows to Bloody Point.[68]

The fourth bit of information concerns Simeon's wife, Love Tucker and the will of her father, sent to Alex S. Hopkins, Jr., from Mrs. A.C.H. Hallett, Bermuda.

> The Will of George Tucker, father of Love and Milner and others, is filed in the Books of Wills here, probate taking place here 1773, June 28. (Book 9, p. 68, and Book 12b, p. 392.)
> Here is a summary of that Will:
> George Tucker, mariner, of Sandys Parish
> Wife: Elizabeth
> Sons: Milner, Richard, John
> Daughters: Rachel, Martha, LOVE
> 2 Deceased sons, not named
> Grandsons: Stephen and Henry Tucker
> House and 7 acres of land in Sandys, known as "Flemish Wreck"
> Executors: sons Richard and Milner
> Date of Will: 1772, May 19

George Tucker was buried 1773, June 11 (ref: Register of Rev. J. Moore, Rector of Sandys Parish).

Notes

1. "Record of the Mongin Family," p. 5.
2. Walter C. Hartridge, *John David Mongin's 'Capital Dwelling House' on Warren Square,* guide book published by the author in Savannah, n.d.
3. Will of David Mongin, Index to Inventories, Records of Wills and Miscellaneous Records of Charleston County, 1687-1785, p. 1001, Charleston Main Library.
4. Jarrold and Sons Limited, *Westminster Abbey, Official Guide* (Norwich, Great Britain: Jarrold and Sons, Ltd., Revised Edition: 1988). Mrs. William (Jo) Scouten, Jr. visited London 20 April 1989, and was kind to mail the guide book to verify the fact that not one Mongin was listed there.
5. Gerhard Spieler, "Romantic Tales Tend to Linger and Become Part of Tradition," *Beaufort Gazette,* 30 November 1982.
6. "Record of the Edwards Family of New England, Connected With the Mongin Family of South Carolina by Marriage," p. 1. Copied from the life of Rev. Jonathan Edwards, the greatest divine [who] has ever lived in the United States of America, unpublished typescript in possession of Mrs. Charles Ellis, Jr., Savannah, Georgia, Mr. Robert L. Marchman III, Atlanta, Georgia, and Mr. Ben Anderson, Jr., Greensboro, North Carolina.
7. "Record of the Mongin Family," p. 6.
8. "Record of the Edwards Family of New England," p. 14. (See Appendix III for David Mongin (No. 1) Family Genealogy Record.)
9. "Mongin-Gregory-Anderson Genealogy," unpublished typescript in possession of Ben Anderson, Jr., Greensboro, N.C., Robert Marchman III, Atlanta, Georgia, p. 14.
10. "Record of the Edwards Family of New England Connected With the Mongin Family of South Carolina by Marriage," pp. 2, 3.
11. Ibid., pp. 3, 4.
12. Ibid., p. 4.
13. Merchants & Miners Transportation Company, *Tales of the Coast and a Brief History of the Merchants & Miners Transportation Co.* (Baltimore, Maryland: 1852, Seventh-Fifth Anniversary Copyright, 1927), p. 46. For an entirely different story see: Edith Tunis Sale, *Old Time Belles and Cavaliers,* (Philadelphia & London: J. B. Lippincott of the Washington Square Press, 1912), pp. 247-58.
14. *Georgia Gazette,* 9 May 1765, p. 4, c. 2, Savannah Historical Society.
15. Dr. Robert E. H. Peeples.
16. S. C. Pre-Rev. Land Grants v. 37, p. 368, Archives, Columbia.
17. Gerhard Spieler, "Romantic tales . . .," *Beaufort Gazette,* 30 November 1982.
18. John David Mongin's Will, Probate Judge's Office, Savannah, Ga., File #15, document nos., 308-311.
19. *Columbian Museum & Savannah Advertiser,* 27 November 1778, p. 2, c. 1.
20. Starr, p. 65.
21. Probate Judge's Office, Savannah, Ga., Index to Estates A—Z, 1742 through 1955, #15, Martinangele, Philip, [Mongin, J. D.], MF Adm., 1786, MI 169—175.
22. National Archives, Records of Freedman Bureau, Restoration Applications

(Unregistered L-2). (These three plantations are mentioned in a letter written 20 September 1865 to Maj. Genl. Rufus Saxton from Albert Henry Stoddard I, Attorney, in regard to the estate of his deceased mother, Mary Lavinia Mongin Stoddard (No. 5), who had inherited these plantations from her grandfather, John David Mongin (No. 3).

23. David Humphrey, Savannah, personal files.

24. "Will of Love Martinangele," Probate Judge's office, Savannah Courthouse, File #15, document #1578.

25. John David Mongin's Will, Document No. 310.

26. Obituary of John Stoddard, *New York Observer*, 7 July 1879; Charles Stoddard and Elijah W. Stoddard, *Anthony Stoddard, of Boston, Mass., and His Descendants: A Genealogy* (New York: J. M. Bradstreet & Son, 1865), p. 83.

27. Ibid.

28. For a Family Record Group, see Appendix VIII.

29. "Martinangele-Mongin family notes of Miss A. Haviland Gregory, written 10 August 1865," unpublished typescript in the possession of Robert Marchman III, Atlanta and Ben Anderson, Jr., Greensboro, North Carolina, pp. 2-5.

30. Ibid., p. 9; Mrs. Edward Haviland (Bertha) Anderson, Peoria, Illinois, personal letter, 1 July 1983.

31. Christopher Dawson to Phillip Martinangele, Charleston Deeds, Book N N, p. 524; Sarah Blakeway, widow of William Blakeway, to Phillip Martinangele, Charleston Deeds, Book N N, pp. 543, 550.

32. Robert M. Weir, "Muster Rolls of the South Carolina Granville and Colleton County Regiments of Militia, 1756" South Carolina Hisstorical and Genealogical Magazine, v. 70, p. 230; Mary Bonduraut Warren, *South Carolina Jury Lists, 1718-1783* (Danielsville, Ga.: by the author, 1977), p. 83; Starr, pp. 28, 29.

33. A. S. Salley, Jr., ed., *Minutes of the Vestry of St. Helena's Parish, South Carolina, 1726-1812* (Columbia: The State Printing Company, 1919), pp. 104, 110.

34. *SCHGM*, v. p, p. 154; Anderson.

35. Charleston Deeds E-3, p. 20.

36. St. Helena Vestry Records, p. 181.

37. Starr, p. 76.

38. Georgia Historical Society, Savannah, Manuscripts Collection, John Livingston Hopkins' Papers, Collection #395, Item 15; Alex S. Hopkins, Jr., Atlanta, a descendant of Mary Martinangele Hopkins, has spent several years researching the Martinangele, Hopkins, and Green families. Much gratitude goes to him for having so graciously shared the information that he found, which in some cases expounded on or changed some of the early family lore.

39,. Hopkins' personal file; Catherine S. Crary, *The Price of Liberty, Tory Writings from the Revolutionary Era* (New York: McGraw-Hill Book Company, 1973), pp. 62-3, Georgia Department of Archives and History; Ronald G Killion and Charles T. Waller, *Georgia and the Revolution,* (Atlanta: Cherokee Publishing Company, 1975), p. 171.

40. Hopkins' file.

41. Thomas Gamble, *Savannah Duels and Duellists, 1733-1977* (Savannah: Review Publishing & Printing Co., 1923), pp. 137-38.

42. Mrs. W. Cabell (Frances Fullerton) Hopkins, personal letter addressed to Mr. & Mrs. Henry Netherton (Vista Volunteers), Daufuskie Island, 1968.

43. Hopkins.

44. Gamble, pp. 138-48.

45. Hopkins.

46. *Georgia Gazette,* 17 August 1786, p. 3, c. 2.

47. Virginia Bowe Strickland, "A Liberty of Conscience and Commerce for All," *Ancestoring VII,* ed., Carrie M. Adamson (Augusta: McGowen Printing Co., 1983), p. 25.

48. Georgia Historical Society, Savannah, "The Diary of the Reverend John Joachim Zubly," Entry of 5 April 1778. From a transcription made by Mrs. Lilla Mills Hawes, Savannah.

49. Marchman III, Anderson, p. 13.

50. Chatham County Deeds 1797-1798, v. 1S, p. 67; Hopkins.

51. Marchman, Anderson, p. 27.

52. Beaufort Court House, Deed Book 3, p. 153.

53. Mrs. Leonard (Sophie) M. Barnes' personal files, Savannah, Georgia.

54. Beaufort County Court House, Deed Book 3, p. 153.

55. Rebecca Starr, p. 76.

56. Ibid., p. 81.

57. Original plat in possession of Lance & Billie Burn.

58. Beaufort County Courthouse, Deed Book 3, p. 154.

59. Alex S. Hopkins, Jr., files; Mongin-Martinangele family records, p. 25.

60. Hopkins' file.

61. For granting permission to use quotes from Mary Green Lebey's Prayer Book, much gratitude goes to Mrs. E. J. (Elizabeth Courtenay Morgan) Derst, Savannah, Georgia; A personal letter from Mrs. Derst to Alex S. Hopkins, Jr., Atlanta, Georgia, 28 February 1989.

62. Mongin-Martinangele Family Records, p. 16.

63. South Carolina Historical Society, *South Carolina Genealogies* (Spartanburg: The Reprint Company, 1983) v. 4, pp. 133-35, 141-42.

64. Mrs. E. J. Derst, Savannah, Georgia.

65. Ibid.

66. Charles A. Lebey files, Savannah, Georgia.

67. S.C. Colonial Plats, vol. 18, p. 43, Archives, Columbia, S.C. All of this new information is shared through the courtesy of Alex S. Hopkins, Jr.

68. S.C. State Plat, vol. 36, p. 267, Archives, Columbia. Shared through the courtesy of Alex S. Hopkins, Jr.

4

PLANTATION LIFE

Plantations on Daufuskie ranged in size from two hundred to
eleven hundred acres of land. Each planter had the number of
slaves it took to operate his particular plantation successfully. One
man had two hundred acres with eleven slaves. If the land was all
farmed, there would be the need for more slaves. If there was a good
bit of pasture land for cattle, hogs, sheep, and other livestock, the need
for slaves would be less—so it all depended upon what the planter
needed as to the number of slaves he possessed.

Plantations were self-contained. Almost everything they needed
was raised, produced or made—very little was bought. Probably the
main item that was purchased was a coarse, off-white material called
"negro cloth" from which all the clothing the slaves wore was made.
Sugar, called "short-sweetening," if available, was purchased for use
at the "big house." Slaves were allowed "long-sweetening" which was
a syrup made from boiling down the juices of sugar cane or sorghum
that they grew. They raised bees for honey and used the wax for
making candles.

Cow hides were tanned into leather to make shoes for the slaves,
harness for the horses, and other farm items. Meats were cured by
packing in barrels with salt, or were smoked, dried, or pickled in
vinegar.[1]

Lard for frying, baking, and general cooking was rendered from the
fat of hogs. Tallow used for grease, and for making candles and soap,
was made from the fat of the cow. Fiber from cotton and wool from
sheep were used for making pillows and mattresses, or for handweav-
ing into fine cloth for beautiful counterpanes and other items for the
home and personal use. Down and feathers plucked from geese and

chickens were also used in making pillows and feather beds.

(Slaves had mattresses and pillows stuffed with corn shucks and dried Spanish moss.) Wooden bed frames were laced with rope to hold the mattress.

Huge brick fireplaces were built for cooking. Metal hooks were embedded in the brick work for hanging heavy pots over the fire. An oven for baking loaves of bread was also built into the fireplace. Used for baking cornbread were iron pots that had long legs (called "spiders") that would sit comfortably over red hot coals on the hearth. Their heavy iron lids were indented to hold additional hot coals so the bread could also cook from the top and get golden brown.

Herbs of all kinds were grown for flavoring foods and for medicinal purposes. Wild plants and roots were also collected to make teas and poultices for the sick: "pine tops, holly bush, John worts, life-everlasting," sassafras leaves and roots, mullen, castor bean leaves, and many others. Special rooms or buildings were used to dry and store the herbs and plants.

Preserving foods was a never ending task. Like clothes hanging on a line, green beans were strung on twine and hung in the sun. When dry, they were called "leather breeches." Okra, pumpkin (peeled and cut in strips), and slices of apples and pears were placed on sheets and dried in the sun. Peas were dried in the hull, put into bags, sprinkled with a little lime to discourage beetles, then hung from the rafters in the barn or some other place to keep them dry. Sweet potatoes were dug and banked for winter use. Irish potatoes were put into the storehouse. Fruits and vegetables were grown the year round.

Two kinds of soap were made—soft and hard. It was cooked in an old heavy iron wash pot because a pot made of thinner metal would be dissolved by the lye. Soft soap was used for scrubbing floors, washing dishes, and putting in the pot to boil the clothes. Soap was made by boiling together water, old lard or fat and pieces of scrap meat left over from hog-killing time, and homemade lye. To make soap soft, it was cooked a shorter time. When cooked to the proper consistency, the soap was poured into a vat made from a section of a tree at least two feet in diameter. This was laid down horizontally and a cavity hewn out the width and length of it to hold the soap. To make the soap hard, it was cooked longer, then left in the old iron wash pot until it was firm. The soap was then cut into squares, stored on boards

in a dry place, and left to harden. This was the soap that was used on the clothes when scrubbing them by hand or on a scrub board, then putting them in the iron wash pot to boil and whiten. The clothes were stirred occasionally with a broom stick. After they boiled awhile, they were removed, rinsed in cold water two or three times, then hung on the line to dry. When making face soap, after the mixture was properly cooked, a perfume was added, then the soap was cooled and cut into small pieces (or rolled into small balls) and left to harden.

Lye was made by making a V-shaped wooden trough (hopper) tall enough to hold oak ashes (no other ashes would do). Another V-shaped wooden trough was placed at the opening at the bottom to catch the lye. Ashes from the fireplace were cooled then poured into the hopper until it was full. Boards were placed over the top to keep out the rain. When it was time to make lye, water was poured in the top of the ashes and let trickle down to the trough below. Water was continually poured into the top of the hopper until the needed volume of lye was reached.[2]

Cows were milked before dawn. The milk was strained then set aside in pans to cool. Some was used for drinking and cooking; some was allowed to clabber and churned for butter and buttermilk; and some was reserved for making curds. Milk from goats was used to drink and make hard cheeses.

Plantation life was hard and mean, working from 'till to can't. Slaves performed all the menial tasks: some farmed, others made the candles, smoked the meat, washed the clothes; some were nannies, cooked and did all the kitchen chores, spun the fiber into thread, and wove the cloth. Others operated the blacksmith shop, cut the wood and sawed the lumber, sewed the clothes, slaughtered the animals for food, milked the cows, churned the butter, made the cheese. Still others gathered oysters, caught the fish, shrimp, and crabs, made the shoes, burned the oyster shells to make the lime, mixed and poured the tabby—work was never ending.

Work also played no favorites. The planter ("Massa") was the head of the operation. He usually had two or more plantations and busied himself between them. He took care of the finances, bought and sold the slaves, and used his complete authority in seeing that the plantation operated as smoothly as possible.

The wife ("Missus") supervised the entire operation of the house-

hold. She planned the menus, instructed the slaves in the mixing of herbs for medicine. She cared for the sick whether they were family or slave. She saw that garments and shoes were made for all the slaves. She usually was the one to guide and teach her children concerning their education, to read the Bible to them, and to see that they went to church on Sunday. Slaves were not allowed to attend church. Being a very sensitive and compassionate person, the wife was probably responsible for praise houses being built for the slaves so that they could meet, pray, and sing their spiritual songs. Even though they were not free physically, they did have the freedom within to meditate spiritually. They possessed nothing but faith—the Lord was all they had. No one could enslave their feelings concerning a power higher and mightier than they. (Their prayers and faith in God ultimately led to their freedom.)

Because the planter could not be present at all times, he had an "overseer" who was usually white and lived with his family on the premises and knew more about the personal operation of the plantation than the owner. He kept abreast of all that was going on and informed the planter when any need or problem arose.

Next to the "overseer"was the "driver," a slave himself who had been given a certain amount of authority.[3] He designated the work load for each slave, taught them how to gather oyster shells and burn them to make lime, and showed them how to hoe the beds to plant the seeds. He carried a whip or a club to make sure his wishes were carried out. He sounded the conch horn for the day's work to begin. He was responsible for doling out (or withholding) rations of corn or potatoes. (The slaves were allowed no meat except at Christmas time.) One of the most important requirements of the "driver" was to teach the new slaves how to speak and understand commands. This was not easy, for the new slaves had a language of their own and had to be taught a different one in a matter of a few days. Sentences were never used for not only were they too long, but the "driver" himself could not speak in sentences. He used only short, terse phrases or just one word to make it easier for the slave to understand. The result was a broken English called Gullah or Geechee, which had a link historically and structurally with West Indian Creole English.

The most disliked among the slaves were the "drivers." This is reflected in some of their songs after the Civil War.[4]

The planters on Daufuskie had elegant homes in Savannah or other places, spending most of their winters there, leaving the plantation in the charge of their "overseer." However, they returned for the summer and gave elaborate parties for their many visiting friends and relatives who had to arrive by boat.

Slaves

On Daufuskie, Indians could have been the first slaves. Allowed to buy so much rum on credit and unable to pay, the Indians were forced to raid other tribes and to capture and sell young warriors to the traders to clear the debt. Traders would ship these Indians as slaves to the Caribbean or the West Indies.[5] Going through rigorous training to perform the duties of a slave, many of the Indians died under the pressure of forced, brutal labor. It was the African, with his determination to live, who stood up under the pressure and the heat and proved the most valuable.[6]

Spain and Portugal were the first to import slaves—followed by the Dutch, French and British. With their mighty sea power, the British controlled the slave trade.

The majority of the slaves came from Africa, but some came from as far away as New Guinea and Borneo.

When merchants and planters in Barbados and on other West Indies Islands were unable to expand their plantations, they looked to the new country to purchase land. When they came, they brought their slaves with them. This was the beginning of black slavery in South Carolina.

In all the states prior to the American Revolution, it was legal to own slaves. Shortly after the war ended (1783), all of the northern states abolished slavery.

Even though the northern states had abolished chattel slavery, they imposed slavery of a different nature. They enslaved their people by having them work in sewing or "sweat factories," paying their employees "dirt wages," and requiring them to be on call twenty-four hours a day.[7] (These "sweat factories" continue today, especially for foreigners who cannot find other employment.)

On the eve of the Civil War, the slave states were Alabama, Arkansas, Delaware, Florida, Georgia, Kentucky, Louisiana, Maryland, Mississippi, Missouri, North Carolina, South Carolina, Tennessee, Texas, and Virginia.[8]

Prices of slaves varied and were judged by age, sex, worth, and origin.[9] No doubt many slaves were mistreated by their masters, but many others were loved and cared for. There was such a strong bond between President Andrew Jackson and his personal slave, Alfred Jackson, that they were buried near each other at the Hermitage, the President's mansion, Nashville, Tennessee.

After they were freed, many slaves had no place to go or were reluctant to leave. Some were allowed to continue living in the old slave quarters while others bought land and built small cabins of their own.

On Daufuskie, according to family records, Mary Dunn's slaves did not leave and stood by her until the very end. A few old slaves remained at John Stoddard's Melrose Plantation.[10]

Gullah

Gullah is a language derived from broken English mingled with the native tongue of the African or other dialect. It was the "driver" who had the responsibility of teaching the slave orders and commands. He taught what he knew in a language that the slave could understand quickly—short and to the point.[11]

Albert H. Stoddard II (1872-1954) was the only surviving child of his parents, Albert H. and Elizabeth Hamilton-Stoddard. Melrose was their permanent home. Young Albert's only playmates were the black children who lived on the plantation. He learned to speak their Gullah (or Geechee) as fluently as they. In later years, he wrote many island stories laced with Gullah. (Mr. Stoddard's son, Albert H. Stoddard III, kindly gave permission to quote from his father's writings. Rabbit Point [Webb Tract] is a familiar name on Daufuskie, and the reason this particular story was chosen to share.)

Whey Da Million Dey

Moses' wife was very fond of watermelons and one very rainy summer which ruined practically all the melons, she heard that a man on the other side of the island had some. She walked over to his place, bought a melon and brought it back on her head [approximately a six-mile trip].

When she got home she was tired and hot so she hid the melon behind the door and lay down and went to sleep.

While she slept, Moses came in, spied the melon and proceeded to eat

it. When she woke up and found the melon gone there was a battle royal.

The row assumed such proportions that it was brought to "The Big House" for settlement.

"Uh walk da hot road clean tuh Rabbit Pint fuh git da million, en den uh had tuh pay uh whole ten en uh fibe cent fuh um, en tote um clean home. Mose ain tun e han fuh da million. Den come behime me en eat muh million while uh duh sleep, Uh could kill Mose. E ought to be shoot. Wuh you duh gwine do wid Mose?"

Moses was sentenced to get her another melon at once, if possible. Otherwise his next pay was to be docked "two ten and a five cents." The extra dime to pay her for her walk.

I never understood what this was to accomplish, as I believe she got all his wages anyway. However, it seemed to satisfy justice.[12]

Daufuskie Gullah Tales

Mrs. Sarah Grant told this tale:

This mother was leaving to work in the field and she told her two daughters not to speak to a soul while she was gone, especially to strangers. In order to keep them busy, she left them some mending to do.

After the mother left the house, the two girls were sitting out on the porch sewing away when a strange man came up to the edge of the porch and asked, "What's your name?" The girls said not a word, remembering what their mother had told them.

One girl's thread was giving out so she said to her sister, "Gimme de tret."

"Tawt ma tel yu no fuh tauk," was the reply.

"Ent fuh tauk, Tituh, gimme de tret," the sister answered.

"Tengk Gawd, me no fuh tauk," the other girl replied, pretty pleased with herself.

•

Another story by Mrs. Sarah Grant:

This man said that he would marry this woman's daughter if she would tell him three ridiculous things about life.

So, she told him this story: "One time uh ooman binnuh struk e dautuh. E tel um se, 'Wen you don scrub de kitchin flo, mek de sunhot een fuh de flo dry mo soon.'

"De gal don scrub de flo. Den e git de wheel barruh en e tuk um out tuh de yaad. E full um wid sunhot en a tote um eentuh de kitchin fuh dry de flo."

"Well," the man said, "That was one ridiculous situation, tell me another one."

The woman said, "One time uh nyung man ent waan fuh pit an e pans

regluh fashun. So e tuk e pans en e tan um op puntop de flo al by demsef. Den e run en jump slap eenth dem."

"Well," the man said, "that was two, tell me another one."

The woman told the third tale: She said, "Uh man tel e son se, 'Go feed de cow. Gi um some moss outuh de tree.' So de nyung man go out en git one rope. E tie um roun de middle ub de cow en pu de cow. E pu dat cow slap op eentuh de tree we de moss da grow."

The man said, "That's it, you win, that's the three wildest tales I ever heard." So he married the daughter.

•

A story told by Mrs. Estell (Stella) Hamilton:

The scene was in the chicken house where some turkeys also stayed. A thief was coming each night and taking some of the chickens out of the house. Late this one night a chicken asked a turkey, "See ary uh man tief dem chikin?"

"No," the turkey said, "uh sleep wid me hed onniit me wing en uh yent see uh ting."

About that time a noise was heard at the door and a figure could be seen entering the hen house.

"Bot," the turkey said, 'uh tingk huh com de SOB now," as she quickly tucked her head back under her wing.

The moral of the story: Tief ent bad, gittn ketched iz uh waasa sumpin.

•

The school children were leaving on the boat this day as they were taking a field-trip to the mainland. I gave this black girl a pack of chewing gum and when I did, my friend, Mrs. Viola Bryan, said to the child, "Ebbry ting fuh eat ent fuh tauk." The little girl said, "Yassum," and went on her way.

"Viola, what did you say?" I asked.

"Ebby ting fuh eat ent fuh tauk," she replied.

"What in the world does that mean?" was my next question.

"Well," she said, "ef dat chile go tel dem todduh chillun se, 'Mis Billie gimme gum,' den de all binnuh obbuh hyuh waan yu gi um gum too."

•

Johnny Hamilton was in the Post Office 7 June 1982. I asked him if he had gone to church Sunday.

"Yassum" was his reply.

"Did you meet Mr. Alex Haley who wrote the book *Roots* ?

"Yassum," was his answer, "e so easy en quite, luk lak e kidn bruk uh aig."

"What do you mean by that?" was my question. I understood what he

meant, I just wanted him to repeat it.

"Wel, lak de ol fok se, 'uh quite caaf dringk de mos milk'— Misa Haley, e so easy en quite, luk lak he kidn bruk uh aig."

•

David Brown had bought a chain saw in Savannah and it wouldn't work, so he asked Charlie Richards if he would take it back to Savannah when he went and have it fixed for him. Charlie told him, yes, just to bring it over to Lance Burn's dock and he would take care of it for him. When David brought the saw, Charlie thought it might still be under warranty and asked David, "Does this saw have a guarantee?"

"Gantee? No suh, uh duh pay kesh fuh dis saw."

•

This black girl was warning about a tornado that might be coming to this area and it came out like this: "Gret Gawd, dat topedo kid com tru dis ilant, sen yuh eentuh maternty en yuh ent nubbuh know wuh happun to yuh."

•

This white man was talking to his black friend when a beautiful red bird flew down on the ground before them.

"What a beautiful Cardinal," the white man exclaimed.

"Caadnyl, Caadnyl, ent no Caadnyl, taint nuttin beta ol red bud," replied the colored gentleman.

•

The battery was low and the father was having trouble starting the car. He sent his daughter to Ben Smith (living in a trailer on Mongin Creek) to bring some jumper cables to help get the car started. When the girl reached the Smiths', this is what she said to Ben's wife:"Mis. Shorty, tell Mr. Ben if he aint too tired, Daddy sed ta please cum over and give him a jump-off."

•

The husband had been sick for sometime. The wife was bemoaning the fact that their love-life was not what it should be. This is how she summed up the situation: "Me ol man n me ain ka-neck-up n de bed fa moos tu ears now."[13]

Tabby

A lot of slave quarters were constructed of wood. Through the years they either were torn down or deteriorated. Many quarters, however, were made from a very durable cement material known as "tabby." On Daufuskie, Haig's Point was the only plantation with

tabby slave quarters, remnants of which remain evident today. Gable roofs were covered with wood shingles. Most of the "floors" were dirt.

The word "tabby" was derived from possibly two sources: either from the Spanish word "tapia," meaning "mud wall," or it could have come from the mottled or "tabby cat" appearance of the structure before a final protective coating of plaster or stucco was applied. The mottled coloring was caused by partially burned and blackened shells from the lime burning process.

This construction material had also been referred to as "tappy" because the process called for pouring the mixture into wooden forms then tapping it down with a heavy object to fill it in firmly to eliminate air bubbles or loose spots which would weaken the structure.[14]

The Process in Making Lime

In making tabby, lime is one of the most important ingredients and is made by burning *old* oyster shells (never fresh or live ones) washed free of salt. Salt causes decay.

Begin by digging a pit about four feet square and three feet deep. On opposite sides, dig two trenches two feet wide for cross ventilation to make sure the fire burns freely. Fill the pit with heart pine with smaller pieces on top to ignite and burn quickly.

Dry pine logs need to be cut about eight feet long. Larger logs are used at the base. As the stack gets higher, for stability smaller logs are used. The first two logs are to be placed across the pit perpendicular to the trenches. The next two will go perpendicular to the first ones in pig-pen fashion, making sure they are all level. On the ground, over the pit and between the third and fourth logs, lay four shorter logs to form a "bed." Chink any open space between these logs with smaller logs and pieces of heart pine to prevent the shells from falling through into the pit area. Next, completely cover the bed of logs with several bushels of oyster shells, making sure they stay within the bed area or they won't burn. This completes the first tier.

Keep repeating the first tier structure (using smaller logs) until you have as much lime as you think you will need. Usually three tiers are sufficient.

After the tiers are completed, cover the shells on top with a thick layer of dry scrap wood and stand up short logs all around the outside. This will help prevent the oyster shells from popping all over the place

and burning someone. The best time to ignite the fire is just before dark so it can burn all night.

After the pile has burned, a little water can be thrown on the pile to help cool it down. The ashes will be on the bottom and the lime on the top. Use the lime immediately or store in a dry place.[15]

History of Georgia and South Carolina Tabby

It was Thomas Spalding, Sapelo, Georgia, who as early as 1805 revived the use of tabby and perfected its construction. Spalding, in a letter to his friend, relates that when General Oglethorpe settled Frederica on St. Simons Island—the fort, barracks, quarters for his officers and men—all of the buildings were made of tabby. Spalding further states that General Oglethorpe was a very wise, observing man and probably had seen buildings made of this material in Spain or along the Mediterranean coast. Being friendly with the Spanish in the adjacent Province of Florida gave him an excellent opportunity to have them instruct his men in the making of this material.

"Tabby and not Tappy," he said, "is a mixture of shells, lime, sand and water in equal proportions by measure and not by weight."

Thomas Spalding's manner of building with tabby:

Two planks as long as convenient to handle, 2 inches thick and about 12 inches wide, are made to unite and to go the round of your building. These planks are kept apart by spreaker pins with a double head as thus: The first head keeps the outer plank in its place, the last with the pin run through the point, keeps the inner plank firm while the workmen are filling in the material and setting it down, either with a spade or a light rammer, which, if shells, bring these into a flat position. Then, the planks at the ends are let into each other thus:

with an iron wire ⊙═══════ with an eye

to draw it out at each round of Tabby. The corners of the building are thus: the same kind of iron wire binding the sides together.

All that is necessary when you construct doors or windows, is to drop a short board

across the wall between the outer and inner planks and steady it with
two poles, to be drawn out at each round and replaced at the next, and
so continue until you have reached the height you intend your doors and
windows. When you then drop your Lintall into the Tabby Box so as to
secure the next round of Tabby your wall then becomes an intire
whole.[16]

Spalding's further instructions were that the holes for the pins that
held the box in place be drilled one inch above the lower edge of the
twelve-inch inch planks [approximately two feet from each end of the
box]. This box was easily disassembled and moved up to make the next
course. Spalding liked old, whole shells washed free of mildew or salt,
and he preferred pit sand because it was free of salt—salt caused decay
in the tabby. He also liked a mixture of fine and course sand but was

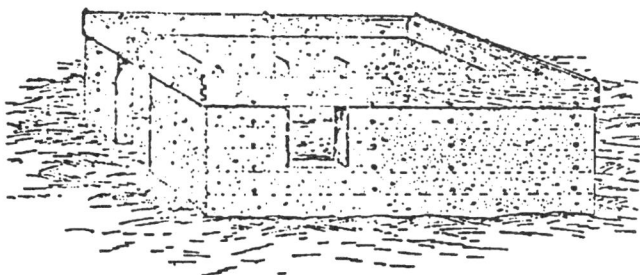

not too concerned about that. He mixed his tabby one day and let it
set until the following day. The mixture was very soft—the better to
amalgamate. His tabby mix was equal parts by *measure*, not by weight:
ten bushels of lime, ten bushels of sand, ten bushels of shells, and ten
bushels of water; this made sixteen cubic feet of wall. He had made his
walls fourteen inches thick—two feet thick below ground and ten
inches thick for the second floor—beyond which he would not erect
tabby.[17] (The thickness of any tabby wall was determined by the
builder, based upon the type of building being constructed.)

The roof (flat) of Spalding's house was of tar and sand upon
"sheathing paper three fold resting on 2 layers of boards. The house
is of the Ionic order. This house was built by six men, two boys, and two
mules (one white man superintending) in two years." Every year, a
fresh coat of two barrels of tar was applied to the roof.[18]

Specimens of Spalding's method of construction are found in the tabby ruins on "St. Helena and *Daufuskie* islands."[19]

Although certain builders later used eighteen-inch-high tabby boxes instead of twelve-inch ones, the construction was still by the Spalding method.

Christmas on a Lowcountry Plantation

Christmas is such a beautiful time of the year. No record has surfaced describing exactly how this holiday was spent on a Daufuskie plantation. But there is the next best thing—a record of a Christmas spent on a plantation in Beaufort, written by Dr. James Stuart who was a trustee of Beaufort College (1799-1810).[20] Since most of the plantations had similarities in their operation, it can only be assumed that some of the things that Dr. Stuart talks about happened somewhat in the same manner on Daufuskie.

Dr. Stuart's account seems centered around the time he was in his early teens, possibly in the 1760s. The only date available is that his father Francis came to America from Inverness, Scotland, in 1746, settled in Charleston, South Carolina, and married a Miss Barnwell. Their only son was James.

Dr. James Stuart begins his story by relating that he, as a boy, spent only two months in the country—December and May. The other ten months were spent in Beaufort going to school.

He tells about his father's death when he was only six years old, how his Uncle Henry Barnwell took over the operation of his father's plantation and came weekly to make sure that everything was in order. Apparently, James and his mother lived in the grandfather's old mansion with his grandmother and his two maiden aunts, Sarah and Emily Barnwell (his mother's two sisters). He also mentions "we boys" so it can be assumed that some of his three uncles had sons (his cousins), who were spending a portion of their holiday with James.

He goes on to say that although the Negroes were immune, summer months were death to the white man because of malaria and fever. It was only after the vegetation was killed by frost that the planter could live on his plantation—from November to May.

Negroes were required to have passes to leave the plantation. As a blessing during the Christmas season, slaves were given three-day passes (plus Sunday) to leave the plantation and go anywhere they

wanted to, usually to another plantation to visit relatives, who might be husband or wife. They were free to take things that they raised (or made) to sell or trade at the local store for something they wanted. James remembers their coachman, Sam, walking ten miles with a bushel or two of corn on his head to trade it off at the little Jewish store in Beaufort.

Christmas was a boon for the slaves in another way—they received probably the only meat that they would get until the following year. Several head of beef cattle were killed and shared according to the size of the family. James and his cousins were allowed to take turns killing an animal by walking right up to the cow and putting a bullet in the forehead. It was fun for them to see the cattle hung up, skinned, and quartered. The boys got the bladder to "treat it in hot ashes and strip the outside until we could insert a joint of cane & blow it up, tie it to a stick & use it as the mountebanks used to."

Christmas was a time for other gifts as well and came in the form of an extra barrel of molasses distributed, winter clothes and shoes provided, and wool caps given to the men with head-kerchiefs for the women. Prizes were sometimes given for exceptional services rendered. James states that Christmas presents were not often given to them. However, their chimneys were large enough for "Santa Claus to come down foot foremost easily & the fireplace wide with its brass fire dogs and wood fires."

It was a cheerful time for all on the plantation and gave the slave something pleasant to look forward to through all the rest of the year.

James and his company were up by two or three o'clock in the morning. The slaves never slept on the night before Christmas but held prayers in the largest home of the settlement, Daddy January's. Jack, the foreman, and August Baker, the house servant, could read. James's mother had given them each a Testament and a Prayer Book. After singing and shouting all night, at daylight the next morning (Christmas Day), the meeting broke up and the singers strode over to sing on the piazza of the plantation. At such an early hour, the ladies of the household were still in bed asleep. What a wonderful feeling to be waked up by the voices of men and women—all singing their beautiful hymns in perfect harmony, with the depth and feeling of the holiday season. After thirty minutes, the singing stopped. Then each slave woman would "bring out from her pocket or in her hand from

under her wrap, two or three eggs, as morning Christmas gifts" to James and his cousins. A large basket was brought forth which was filled with eggs for egg nog that night. The negroes would all go home, then James and the other boys would get ready for their special treat: *Firecrackers*!

James's grandmother and his two aunts had given each of the boys a quarter the day before. The Fourth of July and Christmas were the only times they saw any money, all of which was spent on fireworks. "The beautiful packs of firecrackers were brought out with their red rice paper and Chinese inscriptions." Pieces of burning wood were brought from the kitchen, then the excitement of lighting the fire-crackers began.

James was never allowed to play with any of the black children except a young houseboy, who was kept clean by a mother who was also a house servant. But on this occasion, some of the other black children were allowed to share in the firecracker fun. Happiness at Christmas was felt and shared by all. James recalls that he had three uncles on whose plantations he had constantly visited as a boy and never, never had he seen one slave whipped on any of them or on his own. Of course it was done, but he never saw it happen—not once.

The noise of the firecrackers had made the dogs sneak off in a corner, the chickens run wildly about, the geese honk, and the turkeys gobble—all of which added to the merriment of the occasion.

It was now time for breakfast. Hog-killing time having just passed, on the table were sausage, spareribs, pigs feet, and Daddy Moses' buckwheat pancakes with plenty of dark, thick, sweet molasses. Nobody, but nobody, ever made buckwheat pancakes like Daddy Moses. The boys ate their fill which only whetted their appetites for all the good food they would be having for dinner around 3 P.M.

The whole plantation was in a stir. Everyone had on his or her best Sunday clothes. There was singing, gossiping, and the voices of the settlement children ringing out happily. More than once a passing boat, loaded with negroes going to visit friends, would start up a boatsong with a full chorus that was timed to match the pulling of the oars.

No hunting was done on Christmas. They would spend time putting the finishing touches on their bonfire. There was a pile of materials that James and his cousins had spent several weeks putting together

with their own hands. On days they were not being worked on the plantation, a team of horses, a wagon, and boardsled had been used by the boys to haul cornstalks, old discarded fence rails, tree branches, and pieces of fat-lightwood, making a pile ten feet high or more. They topped this off with branches of green wild myrtle, cedar, and other evergreen shrubs, then left it to light later that night.

Dinner time had arrived. Wafting from the kitchen were odors of spices and all the good food that added to the spirit of Christmas. They all went to their rooms to bathe and dress for the occasion. The table was laden with "calf-head soup, turkey, ham, oysters, turnips, tanyah, and sweet potatoes." The choice for dessert was plum pudding or mincemeat pie. Wine was not served for some of the family were teetotallers.

James and the boys ate so much that "we felt like anacondas with an antelope inside." They had to go outside and lay down in the grass, "too full for utterance."

As the sun was getting low, James and the boys might meander down to the pen to see the cows come in. Dick, the grandmother's houseboy, was allowed to go with them. Dick was a little older than the other boys and was full of fun. He would jump on the back of one of the yearlings which would kick and bellow from fright, then throw Dick over its head. He would get up with a big grin on his face. He was like that. James had known Dick all of his life and never saw him angry. His mother, who was a privileged character in James's grandmother's household, was called for in times of sickness, even to go half way across Georgia if necessary. She had the sweetest of voices and a terrible temper at times. Dick had to hurry home, as it was his job to hand the bread-waiter at tea.

There was no supper table. Tea on a large waiter was brought into the parlor by a house-servant. A smaller waiter filled with wafers, toast, and teacakes was brought in by a houseboy.

As soon as everyone had finished eating, it was time to light the bonfire. As it burned, a crowd ran around it like a bunch of wild Indians. The greenery on the stack crackled and popped and the cloud of smoke pouring up from it was very aromatic. There was something special about a bonfire besides its warmth, and it always burned too quickly for the time it took to build it.

When only the dying embers were left, it was time to go back to the

house and make the egg nog—a lot of eggs but only a little nog. James remembers the beating of the egg yolks and sugar in a bowl until they were light in color. The whites of the eggs were beaten in a platter until they were firm, then tossed in with the yolk mixture. Old Madeira wine was added to give it flavor.

James doesn't say so, but it is certain that after that night-cap was finished off, all went up to bed and slept soundly with "sugar plums dancing in their heads."

(This is such a beautiful account of a young man's Christmas, but wouldn't it be extra special if there was also a record of a young lady's Christmas at that point in time!)

Slavery on Daufuskie

Thinking perhaps that slavery tales had been handed down from generation to generation, all of the older people on the island were asked about this, but only three responded.

Mrs. Lillie Mongin Simmons, whose grandfather Bradley Mongin was a slave to the David Mongin family, stated that all she was told about slavery times was that when a mother had a small baby and had to go to the field and work, she would put the baby in a box and place it under a tree just at the edge of the branches so that she could easily see it; this also protected the baby from the sun.

Mr. Johnny Hamilton said that all he heard about old slavery times was that when the Massa was leaving, he would give the slave so many tasks to do while he was away. If the work was not finished by the time the Massa returned, the slave would either be whipped or sold.

Mrs. Rose Bryan Brisbane stated that in slavery time a pen on the outside of Beaufort, South Carolina, was where the slaves were herded together and sold, either separately or as a family. Her mother and family were sold in Beaufort to Mary Dunn and brought to Daufuskie. Her mother was used solely as a breeder (fifteen children) to produce more slaves for her Missus. Mrs. Rose always wanted to go to Beaufort and see just where her mother and family were put on the "slave block" and sold, but she never had the opportunity. She died when she was in her mid-nineties (1968).

Since there seemed so few tales of slavery times passed down, it is hoped that the slaves on the island did not have many horror stories to relate and were treated kinder than most.

Daufuskie Slave Count

The number of slaves one had was not determined by the acreage of the plantation, because needs were different.

The majority of the slave schedules seen thus far have included slaves from all of the plantations a person owned in the entire County, but the following are only those from the 18 June 1860 St. Luke's Parish Slave Census that represent plantations on Daufuskie:

Planter	Slaves	Slave Houses
James Peto Chaplin, Sr.	20	4
John Stoddard	51	13
Isabella Mongin	38	8
Mary Dunn	17	—

The above list needs clarification: James P. Chaplin, Sr., owned Piney Islands Plantation that contained 250 acres which was located on New River and Rams Horn Creek.

John Stoddard and his wife, Mary Lavinia Mongin Stoddard, owned Melrose, Oak Ridge, Maryfield, and Eigleberger plantations which totaled approximately 2000 acres. On the 1840 Slave Census, John had 200 but had sold most of his slaves as early as 1858 in order to build his brick cotton warehouses on the river front in Savannah.

Isabella Mongin was the widow of William Henry Mongin (brother of Mary Lavinia Mongin Stoddard). She was owner/planter at Bloody Point which consisted of 400 acres. Her husband had 142 slaves on the 1840 Census record, but at that time he also owned Cooper River Tract of 484 acres.

Mary Dunn owned the 300-acre plantation named after her. She was the daughter of Isaac Martinangele and the widow of Francis Dunn.

Eigleberger Slave Count

On the 1850 Slave Schedule, Christian Eigleberger owned 50 slaves.[21] His plantation consisted of 200 acres on Mongin Creek—the former land of Margaret Martinangele Mongin (Mrs. William Edwards Mongin).

An interesting thing about Eigleberger—after the mansion burned, the barn and a 12-hole outhouse survived until the early 1920s. (The Burn and Harley families lived in the barn at different times. This information came from Lance Burn and Audrey Harley Clanton.)

Notes

1. See Appendix X.

2. See Appendix XI.

3. Guion Griffis Johnson, *A Social History of the Sea Islands* (New York: Negro Universities Press, 1930), pp. 78, 79. (For those interested in plantation life, please read this book.)

4. Donald Daise, *Reminiscences of Sea Island Heritage* (Orangeburg: Sandlapper Publishing Company, 1986), p. 108.,

5. Starr, "Daufuskie," pp. 8-12. The Indian traders who actually operated trading posts or camps on Daufuskie were Samuel Hilden (1706) and John Wright (1712).

6. Harry A. Ploski and James Williams, eds., *The Negro Almanac A Reference Work on the Afro-American* (New York: Bellwether Publishing Company, 1983), p. 1367.

7. His name cannot be mentioned, but one man on the island stated that one of his grandmothers who lived in New York had worked 18 hours a day for five center an hour.

8. Charles Scribner's Sons, *Dictionary of American History,* rev. ed., 7 vols. (New York: Charles Scribner's Sons, 1940), 6: 309.

9. See Appendix XII for names of slaves and prices.

10. Chlotilde Rowell Martin, *A Soldier's Diary,* Beaufort Gazette, _____ 1931. ("... Down to the 'Quarters' only 6 or 8 of the old helpless darkies are left.")

11. Johnson, p. 78.

12. Albert H. Stoddard, ed., *Gullah Tales* (Savannah: A. H. Stoddard, 1940), p. 215. (His tapes and records may be purchased from the Library of Congress, Washington, D. C. 20540.)

13. See Appendix XIII for Daufuskie Gullah words and phrases.

14. E. Merton Coulter, *Georgia's Disputed Ruins* (Chapel Hill: University of North Carolina Press, 1937), p. 86.

15. Curtis Childs, "Lime Kiln Procedure," unpublished typescript (Frederica Town, Georgia: A. & A. Tabby Company, 30 August 1980), p. 1; Interview with Mrs. Gillian Ward White, 10 November 1984.

16. Coulter, pp. 71-74.

17. Ibid., pp. 74-76.

18. Ibid., p. 76.

19. Ibid., p. 78

20. Dr. James Stuart, "Christmas on the Plantation," a gift to the Beaufort Township Library from Mrs. Ruth Rhett Holmes, unpublished typescript, n. d. May be found in the Beaufort County Library, Beaufort, South Carolina, under reference: "VF Beaufort County—Stuart Family."

21. Slave Schedules, Archives, Columbia, South Carolina.

5

PLANTATIONS ON DAUFUSKIE

There were eleven plantations on the eve of the Civil War: Benjie's Point, Bloody Point, Cooper River, Eigleberger, Haig's Point (which included Freeport), Mary Dunn, Maryfield, Melrose, Oak Ridge, Piney Islands, and Webb Tract. Titles to Daufuskie land changed hands often and most of it was under absentee ownership until these plantations were well established. (Discussion of plantations will be in order of interest.)

Foreseeing huge profits to be made in Indian trade, the earliest provincial government land grants on Daufuskie were made to Indian traders. The first of these traders to recognize its value and invest in this land were Samuel Hilden (1706), Nicholas Day (1707), and James Cockran (1711). "In less than a decade over half the island was in the hands of traders."[1]

Cockran/Ash/Livingston/Fraser Land and Plantations

The Ash/Livingston/Fraser families possessed up to three-fourths of the land on Daufuskie. Land acquisition by this family began with James Cockran I, a Granville and Colleton Counties planter, physician, and Indian trader. In 1709 he was appointed a Commissioner of the Indian trade, working to control some of the abuses practiced by unscrupulous traders. Cockran was one of several traders who saw profits by investing in Daufuskie land. He was granted 1000 acres in two separate transactions of 500 acres each in 1711.[2] On 16 February 1714, he purchased 1200 acres from Landgrave Robert Daniel.[3]

His wife is unknown but James had three children: James Cockran II, Mary Cockran, and Elizabeth Cockran. James II was a bachelor; Mary Cockran married Richard Ash and had a son, Richard Cockran

Ash; Elizabeth, who married Charleston merchant Samuel Peronneau, had a son, Samuel Peronneau, Jr.

James Cockran I died intestate in about 1724, and son James II inherited his father's property.[4] When James II died 17 March 1739, he left the land to be equally divided to the children of his two sisters, Mary Ash and Elizabeth Peronneau. On 8 November 1758, partition of the land was made.[5]

Elizabeth's son, Samuel Peronneau, Jr., is seen in July 1761 conveying his 1220 [sic] acres of land to his first cousin, Richard Cockran Ash, son of his Aunt Mary Cockran Ash. Adding this to his five hundred acres inherited from his Uncle James and acquiring an additional five hundred acres, Richard Cockran Ash increased his property to twenty-two hundred acres.[6]

According to a plat dated 3 March 1795, James Cockran and Robert Daniel had land grants amounting to 2995 1/2 acres. James' grandson, Richard Cockran Ash, and wife Ann had four sons: John, Joseph, Richard, and Algernon Sidney Ash. When Richard Cockran Ash died in 1767, his land remained undivided until after nineteen-year-old Algernon Sidney's death in 1784. It is evident that said plat had been submitted by surveyor John Talbird, for Richard Cockran's son, John Ash, who inherited one third of his father's land which consisted of 1983 3/4 acres. (Plat was recorded in Book 6, pp. 22-23, 10 March 1798, Beaufort.)[7]

John Ash came from England, lived in South Carolina, married, and had several children, one of whom was Cato Ash, whose wife was Sarah. Sarah and Cato Ash had three children: Theodora, Richard Russell, and Mary Ash. Theodora was thought perhaps to have been an invalid and Richard Russell remained a bachelor.[8] In 1771 Mary Ash married Dr. James Fraser, a native of Liverpool, England. Through her brother, Richard Ruseell Ash, Dr. Fraser purchased 350 acres of land on Daufuskie, built a house and barn, farmed, and raised cattle (Dr. James Fraser died on Daufuskie in 1803 at the age of fifty-eight.)[9]

Cato Ash died about 1757 and his widow, Sarah, remarried to Henry Livingston, Jr. They had two sons, William West and John Cattel Livingston, who were half brothers to Richard Russell Ash and Mary Ash Fraser. At the death of Henry Livingston, Jr., Sarah married for the third time to Charles Odingsell.[10]

John Cattel Livingston lived on the island with his slave Mag and had five children by her: Mary Ann, Paul, Rose, Lydia, and Salina. At his death, he left a deed of emancipation, money, and land to Mag and the children, with the residue of his estate going to his four nephews, George, William, John, and Alexander Fraser, children of his half-sister, Mary Ash Fraser.[11]

On a deed dated 6 December 1785 John Ash and wife Catharine are selling to William West Livingston and John Cattel Livingston a "third part or share of those several plantations or tracts of land containing in the whole two thousand one hundred acres more or less" entitled to John through the will of his father, Richard Cockran Ash, which, as shown on said plat mentioned before, is land that would later become Freeport and Cooper River Plantations.[12]

Richard Cockran Ash's widow, Ann, married John Berwick,[13] a commissioner of the Confiscation Act. When Dr. James Fraser purchased 350 acres from his brother-in-law, Richard Russell Ash, he never bothered to have the title legally transferred to his name. The land, therefore, remained under the name of Richard Russell. Because John Berwick was also a very powerful Whig, the Ash property was retained after the Revolution.

Whatever the reason (possibly because of the war and economic conditions), the Frasers had fallen on very difficult times financially, and had gotten heavily in debt to Francis Hopkins, grandson of John and Mary Martinangele Hopkins.

Having named his first son John Livingston Hopkins, Francis unquestionably was a devoted friend of these families. In John Cattel Livingston's will, he left money and property to his children by "my wench, Mag," and the residue of his property to his four Fraser nephews "to be divided as they come of age." Evidently all the children were minors, as John Cattel instructed that his 1803 plantation crop be placed in trust "to my friends Charles Odingsell(s) of the State of Georgia and Francis Hopkins of the State of S. Carolina." Executors of his will were Francis Hopkins and Paul Hamilton for South Carolina and Charles Odingsell and John Bolton for Georgia.[14]

(It is unknown, but there might have been a house built for Francis Hopkins on a section of the Livingston land—perhaps he occupied the two-story house near Cooper River landing? Or, did he live in the one-and-a-half-story house built on Livingston property on the west road

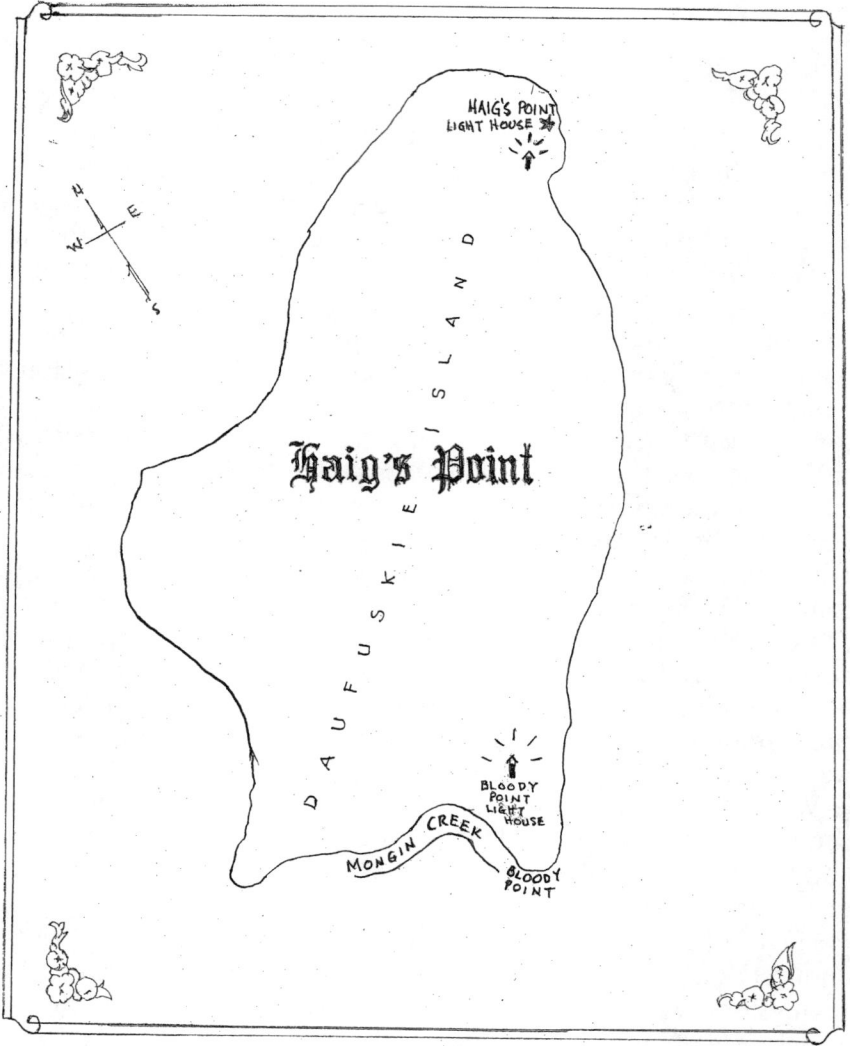

(Courtesy of artist Stephen Pennington Bond II, 1985.)

that led to the Haig's Point property line?)

Several documents found in Georgia indicate that both George and John Fraser were heavily in debt and that Francis Hopkins loaned them money. They didn't pay, so after deeding over to Francis 738 acres of land near Savannah, they still owed him $7,500.00 for which Francis took slaves. George's deed in 1810 states: "George Fraser of the Island of Daufuskie in the State of S. C. . . ."[15]

It might have been because of bad debts that a sheriff's sale of Livingston property was held sometime around 1810, and could have been when John David Mongin (No. 3) purchased Cooper River and Freeport Plantations for his young son, David John Mongin (No. 4).

Richard Russell Ash died in 1806. A plat of that same year shows that the Ash/Fraser lands were in his possession. Since there is no record of Richard Russell having married, either his sister Mary Ash Fraser, or her four sons, are the apparent heirs to his property. She is seen having the authority to have the 2630 acres of land surveyed by Hezekiah Roberts. Thus, Mary Ash Fraser is responsible for the birth and names of four plantations, viz.: (1) Newburgh, 740 acres; (2) Melrose (Salt Pond), 770 acres; (3) Maryfield, 530 acres; and (4) Oak Ridge, 590 acres.[16]

Through distress sales, deaths, or for other reasons, three of the four plantations—Melrose, Maryfield, and Oak Ridge—were placed in the Court of Equity, Charleston, 1818, and sold to John David Mongin (No. 3), the highest bidder, for the sum of $63,000. There is no record to substantiate this, but it is assumed that Samuel B. Webb might have purchased Newburgh about this same time, as the plantation since then has been referred to as the Webb Tract.

The sale of these plantations thus ended the Ash/Livingston/Fraser dynasty, removing the land from their hands and putting it into the possession of John David Mongin, with the exception of Newburgh, which went to Webb.

Haig's Point Plantation

George Haig I, a Scots merchant of Charleston, was also an agent and trader among the Catawba Indians. As other traders, he saw profits to be made in purchasing land on Daufuskie. It is not known if he was a trader on Daufuskie.

...On April 6, 1733, Hugh Evans, a Charleston tailor was granted 800 acres on Daufuskie. He sold it on the 11th and 12th of January 1733 to Indian traders George Haig I and Frederick Myers. Likewise, Elizabeth Varner, widow of another Charleston tailor, was granted 500 acres on Daufuskie on 8 August 1735. She sold out to George Haig and Frederick Myers three days later on 11 August 1735. . . .[17]

The earliest record of Haig's Point is a 500-acre tract certified by Archibald Neile in 1735, delineating the land as being on the northern tip of Daufuskie.[18] Neile sold the land to George Haig I. In 1748 George Haig I was abducted by "a party of Warriors chiefly consisting of Seneka Indians and barbarously murdered by them."[19]

George Haig II, born about 1743, was just a lad when he inherited the estate of his father. He was sent to England to attend the University of Edinburgh (1762-1763) to study medicine. Although he did not receive a degree, he called himself "Dr." George Haig for the remainder of his life. He was back in South Carolina by 1768 trying to sell Haig's Point by private sale or public auction (*Georgia Gazette*, 2 March 1768). He did not find a buyer.

David John Mongin (No. 4) Owns Haig's Point and Freeport

Dr. George Haig II died in 1790 and Haig's Point went to his son, George Haig III, who died in 1860 and was probably the one who sold it to John David Mongin (No. 3) or his son, David John II (No. 4), sometime between 1810-1820. No record.

Freeport Plantation was part of the Cockran/Ash/Livingston/Fraser lands. Consisting of 600 acres, the property joined Haig's Point on the south. When he purchased it is unknown, but David John Mongin (No. 4) is seen in possession of it before his death in 1823. Verification is found in the marriage settlement of David John's widow, Sarah Irwin Mongin, and her intended husband, Reverend Herman M. Blodgett, 6 January 1825.[20] After this settlement, the two plantations were combined and known only as Haig's Point: Freeport Plantation was no more. The only reminder of the name is Freeport Creek which empties into Calibogue Sound and lies just north of the Melrose/Haig's Point border.

Blodgetts at Haig's Point

It is the belief that Herman and Sarah Blodgett lived in a house that faced Calibogue and stood just west of the present Haig's Point lighthouse. (Herman's second wife, Catharine, said of this dwelling: "I am not very much prepared for dinner parties as our cottage has but one parlor or sitting area."[21]

Sarah took her two children, William Henry and Mary Lavinia Mongin, into her second marriage. (Blodgett was very unpopular with the Mongin family because of his drinking.) Sarah and Herman had three children that we know of, but no birth dates for any of them have been found: Benjamin died 1827, Joseph died 1831, and Sarah M. died 1840. All three are buried in the Mongin vault at Bonaventure Cemetery, Savannah, Georgia. It is not certain, but there could have been two other children, William and Emily (mentioned in Catharine Blodgett's letters, 1838-1840), who might have lived to maturity.

Sarah I. Mongin-Blodgett Dies

In 1833 Sarah Irwin-Mongin-Blodgett died and was buried in an Egyptian-type vault that stood just inside the fence at the eastern gate entrance at Haig's Point. The vault faced south by the Haig's Point-Melrose boundary road and directly in front of the only church built on the island just for white people. Circa 1880 the ten-capacity vault was literally moved intact to Bonaventure Cemetery, and there Sarah lies by her first husband, David John Mongin (No. 4) and her three Blodgett children. (See Appendix VI, p. 2.)

Blodgett Buys Haig's Point—Remarries

After Sarah's death, Herman M. Blodgett bought from the Mongin heirs the Haig's Point Plantation (which now included Freeport as well—a total today of approximately eleven hundred acres). On 21 October 1837, Reverend Herman M. Blodgett married again:

> At Lancaster, Pa., on the 3d ult., by the Rev. Richard W. Dickinson of New York, the Rev. H. M. Blodgett, of S. C., to Miss Catharine O. Hall, of Lancaster, Pa.[22]

Rev. Herman M. Blodgett Builds Mansion

It was the Rev. Herman M. Blodgett who in 1838 was having the huge tabby mansion built (where the lighthouse now stands). His wife Catharine wrote in her letter:

... The *new house* progresses very slowly. I am fearful it will not be planned and arranged as conveniently as I desire. I cannot bring it before my mind exactly how it will do when finished. ...[23]

An avenue of live oaks guided the way to the mansion.

Only a few of the present tabby slave quarters were built about the same time as the house, but all were patterned after the Thomas Spalding method of tabby construction.[24]

"Squire" William Pope, Jr., Purchases Haig's Point

Squire Pope, Jr. (1788-1862), was a very prosperous man on Hilton Head and owned several plantations among which were included Cotton Hope, Coggins Point, Point Comfort, Leamington, and Pineland. There is also a fine "William Pope" dwelling, 419 E. St. Julian Street, Savannah, Georgia, that either he or his father built circa 1810.

Squire Pope was considered one of the more romantic males on Hilton Head and was said to be "gorgeous to look at." Ladies were said to swoon over him. He married Ann Scott in 1806. They had several children, and after her death he married Sarah Lavinia Pope in 1816.

In 1850 he bought Haig's Point from the Reverend Herman M. Blodgett. With all of his other plantations he might not have spent much time at the mansion that Blodgett had built. However, Squire Pope's son-in-law, the Reverend Alsop Park Vail Woodward, was planting Haig's Point for him when the Reverend died at the mansion, November 1858. (From the files of Mrs. M. B. Strain.)

Haig's Point Confiscated—Squire Pope's Son Dies

When northern soldiers invaded the island in 1861, they took possession of Haig's Point. Squire Pope's Hilton Head plantations were also confiscated, his mansions burned. One of the northern soldiers remarked, "What a shame" as they were burning the Pope papers and records, some dating back to 1712.

Squire Pope's son William J. Pope, who was attending Princeton,

Slave Tabby Ruins—Haig's Point Plantation, 1930
(Photograph courtesy Mrs. W.W. [Jo] Scouten.)

William "Squire" Pope

(Photograph courtesy Mrs. M.B.[Eleanor K.] Strain.)

William Pope
Town House,
419 E. St. Julian
Street, Savannah,
Georgia.

Town House of
WILLIAM POPE,
Planter

HILTON HEAD ISL.

BUILT ABOUT 1810

died (the son's wife had preceded him) and left orphaned his two little girls, Anna S. Pope and Hepsibah J. Pope. They were very close to their grandfather. At the time, Squire's Pope's second wife was living, but both of them were up in years and not able to care for the little girls. The maternal grandmother came, took the children back with her to Beaufort, and raised them.

Demise of Squire Pope

For sometime Squire Pope had been in very bad health. The death of his son, the loss of his granddaughters, confiscation of his plantations, the burning of his mansions—all added to his affliction and caused an earlier demise on 10 March 1862 at Sandersville, Georgia, a refuge from his beloved Hilton Head. He reposes at Hilton Head Cemetery.[25]

Haig's Point Mansion Torn Down

The battle of Port Royal had ended 7 November 1861. All of the islands had been confiscated. The next move for the northern army was to take Ft. Pulaski and stop the supply route by water to Savannah.

The only way to secure Ft. Pulaski was to bombard it with gunfire. Gun placements would have to be established directly across the Savannah River at Venus Point on Jones Island. The island was so boggy that in order to support the heavy guns, sufficient timbers would have to be laid to make a road the length of it.

Spying the mansion at Haig's Point, they realized that tearing down this huge building would supply a good many heavy timbers needed to get a road established. This is what they did. They tore down the Blodgett mansion, probably salvaging the nails and using them also. After razing the building, they burned what was left. Other houses were treated in the same manner.[26]

Popes Redeem Haig's Point

In 1866, J. J. Pope paid the taxes and reclaimed Haig's Point for the heirs of [Squire] William Pope (NARG 26/State file, S.C. #9).[27]

Popes Sell Land to United States Government

Shipping had increased to the extent that in order to safely channel ocean-going vessels into Savannah River and Calibogue Sound, it was

necessary for the government to purchase land on Daufuskie to build two lighthouses, one of which would be located at Haig's Point. A three-acre tract was needed for the lighthouse-keeper's dwelling; south of this a two-acre tract was needed for the range light.

After negotiating with the Pope heirs, on 20 May 1872 the United States Government paid $745.00 for the five acres of land. Between the two parcels the government would have certain privileges:

> . . . a right of way sufficiently wide for the convenient passage of vehicles, wagons, carts, etc., over and across the land lying between the two pieces or parcels of land and entrance to the highway and . . . keep said way free from all obstructions and in good safe passable condition . . . and cut down any shrubbery bushes or trees that may obstruct the view of the light houses to be erected upon said pieces of land from each other or from Calibogue Sound. . . .[28]

Popes Lose—Regain—Haig's Point

Ida Leila Erwin and Julia Adelaide Erwin were sisters. Ida Leila married James F. Woodward, a grandson of Squire Pope. Julia Adelaide married Evan Park Howell. At a distress sale (auction) held by Henry D. Elliott, Sheriff of Beaufort County, on 5 January 1886, Evan Park Howell was the highest bidder ($500.00) and was given title to the Haig's Point property.[29]

Through a generous and kind heart, for the amount of $1.00 on 22 March 1895, Evan Park Howell returned the Haig's Point property to the hands of the Squire Pope heirs.[30]

William Wiser Scouten Buys Haig's Point

Born in Hiawatha, Kansas, 2 November 1871, William Wiser Scouten was in the Spanish American War (1898) earning the rank of lieutenant. He was on assignment in Beaufort when he met Myra Dana Gage. Myra was the daughter of Sarah Marshall Ely Gage, born 28 September 1834, Lambertville, N.J. Educated in Philadelphia, Pennsylvania, Sarah went to St. Helena Island, Beaufort County, South Carolina, in January 1865 at the request of Alfred Love, founder of the first "Peace Society" in America. She married George Gage, Lambertville, New Jersey, 20 May 1868. George and Sarah made their home in Beaufort. He was a surveyor, had a saw mill, and was Captain of the Port of Beaufort.[31]

In order to perform his duties, W. W. Scouten commuted between Beaufort and the Charleston Navy Yard. Hearing about Daufuskie, he visited the island to observe available land for sale and was very impressed with the Haig's Point property.

At that time there were no decent roads on the mainland, thus, few trucks for transport of goods. However, there were steamers making regular schedules all up and down the coast which provided much faster service. The rivers were the highways for shipping freight to all

WILLIAM W. SCOUTEN HOUSE

(Photograph courtesy Mrs. William [Jo] Scouten, Jr.)

of the South Carolina islands. William was interested in truck farming and selling produce to the Savannah market.

From the Squire Pope heirs, 27 December 1899, W. W. Scouten purchased Haig's Point "containing 1100 acres (more or less)" for the sum of $2500.00.[32]

W. W. Scouten married Myra Dana Gage 6 November 1902. They came to Haig's Point, bringing her brother Albert ("Bert") Gage with them. The Scoutens chose to build a house facing Cooper River near the tabby slave ruins, on the same spot where supposedly on some old maps a former dwelling had stood. The Scouten house was built with

a porch on three sides with the roof on the front porch side so high that the windows of the second story bedroom and storage room were under the front porch roof. That was his own idea, so that the windows of the upstairs rooms stayed open all summer, because all the porches were screened.

William and Myra's two children were boys: George Gage (1903) and William Wiser, Jr. (1907).

W. W. Scouten, Sr., became the magistrate of Daufuskie. Myra was the first teacher at the little wooden Daufuskie School built for white children, circa 1913.

When World War I began, W. W. Scouten was called back into service (1915), stationed at the Charleston Navy Yard, and assigned to Admiral Beatty's staff. He carried Myra and the boys with him, returning to the Island in 1918.

The Scoutens rendered many services to the people on Daufuskie. He hired several men and women from Cooper River and Benjie's Point as farm hands. They would bring babies to the field in baskets and leave them under a tree with an older one watching. The babies had "basket names" like Gold Wire, Sweet Boy, Missy, Blossom, Handful, Lemon, Pinkie, Two Time, Donkey, and others. These names followed them through their adult lives.

Mr. Scouten was a surveyor, operated a commissary, and assisted the blacks in legal matters. As a teacher, Mrs. Scouten was also concerned about the nutritional welfare of the children. For recreation she played the piano and had a large, glass-enclosed, hothouse where she grew many beautiful flowers. They operated a very successful truck farm until the mid-1930s when he became ill. W. W. Scouten, Sr., died 11 July 1940 at the Veterans Hospital in Columbia. Myra Gage Scouten was born 10 August 1871, died 6 May 1955. Both are buried in the Spanish American War section of Arlington National Cemetery, Washington, D.C.[33]

Scouten Sons—Gage and Bill

Gage and Bill Scouten attended Daufuskie and Charleston schools. Becoming bored while in Charleston in 1917, Gage joined the Navy at the age of fourteen and was assigned to his father's office as a (bicycle) messenger boy. He was discharged from the Sixth Naval District, Charleston, in 1921.

Gage went to Vermont where he enrolled in Randolph High School, graduating in 1930. In 1942 he graduated as an Ensign from the United States Maritime Service, New London, Connecticut.

Employed by the U. S. Engineering Corps, Gage worked as Chief Warrant Officer on several Savannah dredges, two of which were the *Kingman* and the *Calebra*. The *Calebra*, known as a Hopper-Dredge, was built in such a way as to hold the mud it dredged. When the vessel was loaded, it went well off shore, the valves were opened, and the mud dumped at sea. When the dredge that he was working on went to New Jersey, Gage went with it. There he met and married Edith Evelyn Coburn, 1943. They had two sons, George Gage, Jr., and William Wiser III.

Joining the Army in 1943, Gage served with the engineering section during World War II. He was an officer on the seagoing dredge *Hains*, which had a war record like that of a fighting vessel. Besides clearing Apra Harbor at Guam and Manila, the *Hains* was credited with shooting down two Japanese bombers off Tacloban, Leyte, as well as withstanding 113 air raids in forty-four days. Warrant Officer Scouten was third mate and later second mate on the dredge, and was her gunnery officer when she shot down the Japanese planes. As the youngest veteran of World War I, he wore Victory ribbons for both wars. In addition, he wore the Maritime ribbon for 1942, American theater ribbon with one star, the Asiatic-Pacific theater ribbon with three stars, and the Philippine Liberation ribbon with two stars. He was discharged 19 May 1942 from the Separation Center, Fort Dix, New Jersey.

Gage operated an auto and aircraft shop, living out his life (1973) in Plainsfield, New Jersey. Edith continues to live there and shared this family history.

Bill Scouten lost his leg when a child. (See story in White School section.) He was a lock and gunsmith, having a thriving shop in Savannah when his father became ill in 1935. Bill gave up the shop and returned to the island to give aid and support to his parents.

In 1936 Josephine (Jo) Cofer was working in a business office in Atlanta; she looked forward to a much needed vacation from a very demanding boss. She wanted to get as far away as possible from the bustle and noise of the city, to the tiniest place she could find. Daufuskie Island, South Carolina, appeared as the smallest spot on

the map. That was it! That was where she would go! Jo contacted Postmaster Gus Ohman to find out if there was a place she could spend her vacation. Gus asked around and found the Marchants willing to give Jo "bed and board."

Jo came to Savannah by train and caught the steamer *Clivedon* to Daufuskie. When she got off the boat, some of the Marchant men were there to meet her in one of their wagons, taking her to Melrose where the family farmed and lived in the old boat-house.

The Post Office was a meeting place for islanders and where Bill Scouten met Jo. The "new girl on the block" was the center of attention. Late one afternoon Bill drove to Melrose and picked up Jo in his 1928 Model A Ford. As it was beginning to get dark, Bill stopped, got out, and hung a lantern on the back of the car. Jo asked him why on earth was he hanging a lantern on the back of the car and not on the front. Well, Bill told her, he could see where he was going without lights in front, but the lantern was placed on the back to prevent other cars from ramming him in the rear.

The romance between Jo and Bill did not end when she left the island; Bill continued to visit her in Atlanta. They were married 30 May 1937, moving to the Haig's Point lighthouse.

For a living they fished one tide down and the next up, raised chickens, sold eggs to Savannah restaurants and fish to Frank C. Mathews. Jo learned how to cast for shrimp, as Bill (using a crutch) could not keep his balance well in throwing a net. Out in all kinds of weather, exposed too much to the elements, Jo became ill.

Leaving the Island in 1939, they moved to Brunswick, Georgia. They had three children: Charlie, Judith, and Dana. Bill operated a lock and gunsmith shop until his death, 6 November 1965.

Jo joined the Peace Corps and was sent to Monrovia, Liberia, where she worked as a secretary. She loved the place and the people, but because of ill health she had to return to the States. The children married and gone, Jo sold her property in Brunswick and moved to Penney Farms, Florida, in 1987.

Stiles M. Harper Buys Haig's Point

Because of taxes and living in other states, Gage and Bill Scouten on 9 November 1957 sold Haig's Point to Stiles M. Harper of Estill, South Carolina, for the sum of $44,000.[34]

Harper Sells Haig's Point to George H. Bostwick

Keeping the property for almost four years, on 22 August 1961 Stiles Harper sold to G. H. Bostwick the Haig's Point property for $134,187.[35] (Harper retained a fifteen-acre tract near Mullet Hole and Beacon Creek, later selling it to International Paper for $750,000.[36]

On 24 February 1965 Bostwick also bought the lighthouse and the five acres of ground that had been sold by the Pope family to the government in 1872. The lighthouse was in deplorable condition, and in 1967 Mr. Bostwick repaired it, preventing further deterioration, but he did not restore it to its authentic condition. (See Haig's Point Lighthouse section.)

Manning Woods of Bluffton was the manager for all of Mr. Bostwick's plantations, which included Tomotley and Hogg. In Beaufort County alone he owned 25,000 acres of land.

In 1967 Mr. Woods contacted Lance Burn to tear down the old Scouten house. Prince Rivers, a colored man, had worked for no one but the Scoutens all of his life. As they were leaving the island, the Scoutens gave Prince permission to live in their house to look after the place. He was still living there when Mr. Bostwick bought Haig's Point. Prince dropped dead in the yard, and after his funeral Mr. Woods got in touch with Lance Burn to dismantle the house.

Bostwick Heirs Sell Haig's Point

From the Bostwick heirs the deal was closed 9 May 1980, when Charles Cauthen and a group of investors bought Haig's Point, Webb, and Oak Ridge Plantations—2300 acres at $1250.00 per acre.[37] Their plans were to develop low-key, allowing horse-drawn carriages and electric golf carts as the only modes of transportation. Their vision was never completed.

International Paper Buys Haig's Point

Charles Cauthen and investors sold out to International Paper Realty Corporation of South Carolina on 23 October 1984 for $8,453,328.18, buying Haig's Point, with an option to purchase Webb Tract and Oak Ridge by 8 August 1989[38] (which they did not do). IP has the reputation of being one of the most outstanding environmentally-conscious companies known.

The first thing IP did was to build a dock and change the name to "Haig Point," forever losing its identity as a plantation. The next thing they did was really commendable: they hired archaeologist Larry Lepionka and historical architect Colin Brooker, and team, to date the existing tabby slave ruins, and to locate the foundation of a large mansion that was at Haig's Point on the eve of the Civil War.

On 9 August 1985, under the existing lighthouse building, the mansion foundation was discovered—a seventy-five-foot by seventy-five-foot, two-and-a-half or three-story building made completely of tabby, dating from 1790-1820. Everyone was elated. It was the largest building so far discovered on any of the Sea Islands.[39] (As stated previously, built by Reverend Herman M. Blodgett, the mansion was under construction 16 January 1838.)

Golf Course and Other Amenities
for Haig Point Club Members

Buying into Haig Point is the qualification to become a member of the Haig Point Club. The first of its kind, a twenty-hole golf course designed by Rees Jones was built for the Club's membership.

Electric carts and several lovely, horse-drawn carriages are available for every need and whim. Many buildings have been completed, including a welcome center, a country store, large private homes, apartments, a carriage house, horse stables, and more. Named streets have been laid out and covered with clam shells brought on barges from Louisiana. Haig Point has its own security guards.

Chief Tom Carucci heads the private fire department, consisting of two red fire engines, four staff firefighters, and twenty volunteers. For a mascot, Chief Carucci has Haiggie, a beautiful female Dalmatian mix that he chose from the Hilton Head Island Humane Association Animal Shelter.

Strachan Mansion Moves to Haig Point

In 1986 the seventy-seven-year-old (1910) Strachan mansion on St. Simons Island, Georgia, was to be given to anyone for the amount of $1.00, with the provision that it be moved. In 1986 International Paper accepted the challenge, paid the $1.00, and, to have the mansion moved to Daufuskie, paid $100,000 to Bill Phillips who had the huge

mansion put on two barges, towed 100 miles along the Intercoastal Waterway, then placed near the dock at Haig Point. This feat became really big news; its progress was viewed on TV daily. The voyage of the house began 27 March 1986 and ended 29 April 1986.

The house is restored with an elegance vastly beyond that of its original condition. It is furnished beautifully, and on 28 March 1987 was opened for use as an inn for food and lodging.

Boats Built for Haig Point

For transporting club members, prospective owners, and guests, IP had two large boats custom built, the *Haig Point I* and the *Haig Point II*. These boats were designed by naval architect Timothy Graul of Sturgeon Bay, Wisconsin, but were constructed by the Breaux Brothers of Louisiana.

To transport building materials and other freight, a Haig Point towboat and barge are berthed at their private wharf on Hutchinson Island, Savannah, Georgia.

Something new is constantly being built or added for the comfort and pleasure of the clientele.

Growth at Haig Point is astronomical and has to be seen to really appreciate its beauty and grandeur. It will take several years for their plans to be implemented.

Security gates prevent outsiders from entering the premises and private gasoline powered vehicles are prohibited.

Melrose Plantation

Regressing for just a moment and reviewing the John Stoddard segment, after several years managing the Paris and Lyon (France) offices of Edwards & Stoddard importing firm, John Stoddard has accumulated much wealth; he has met and married Mary Lavinia Mongin, 7 January 1836.

Mary Lavinia's grandfather, John David Mongin (No. 3), has died in 1833, leaving her and her brother, William Henry Mongin, heirs of his vast estate. Their mother, Sarah Irwin-Mongin-Blodgett, has also died in 1833, leaving them two more plantations on Daufuskie: Haig's Point and Freeport.

John Stoddard decides that it is in their best interest to leave France and come to South Carolina to manage his wife's inheritance. Mary is

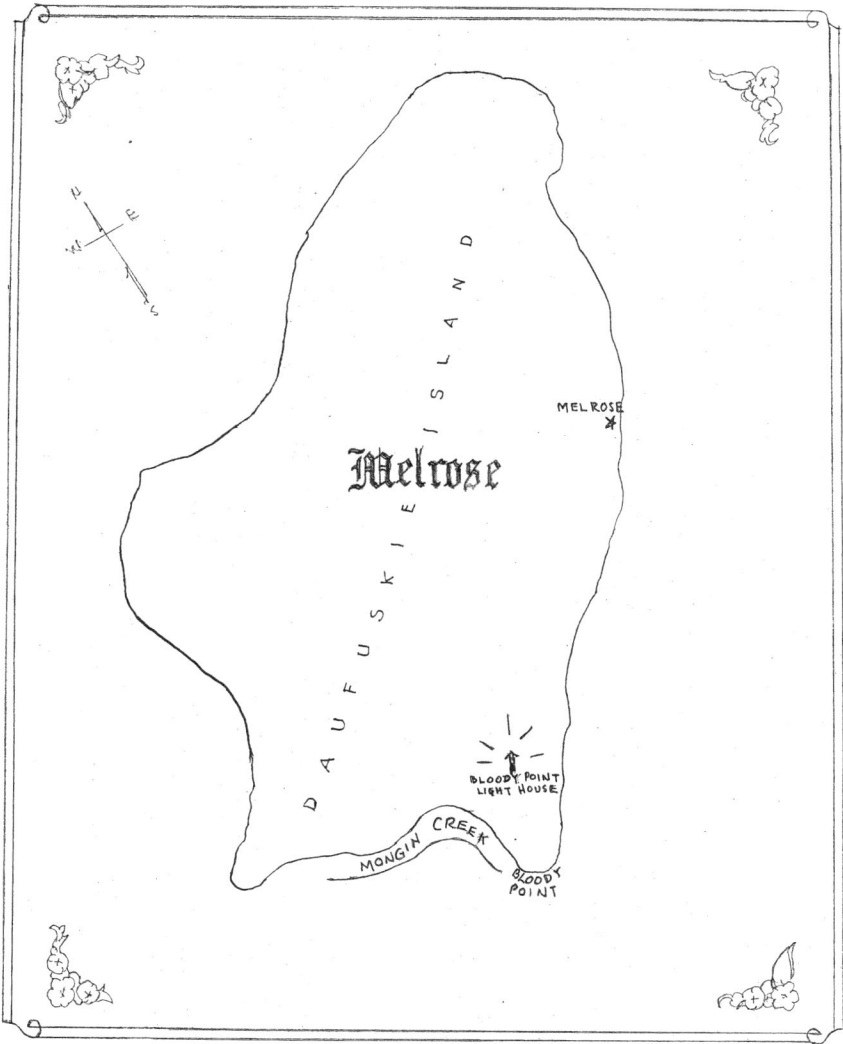

(Courtesy of artist Stephen Pennington Bond II, 1985.)

Melrose Plantation about 1890, Daufuskie
(Courtesy Mr. Charles Ellis, Jr.)

expecting their first child. They leave France and for some unknown reason they are in London where their little daughter, Mary Helen (Helen Mary), is born 4 January 1837.

(Just when Melrose mansion was built and who built it is another mystery. It is assumed that it was built by John David Mongin (No. 3) shortly after he acquired the property in 1818; he was living there in 1822 with his two grandchildren, William Henry and Mary Lavinia Mongin.)

1837: Stoddards Living in Melrose Mansion

It is now known that John, Mary Lavinia, and their daughter, Mary Helen, had arrived on Daufuskie and were living in the Melrose house sometime during 1837. Mrs. Catharine Blodgett writes in a letter to her sister, 16 January 1838, during which time whooping cough was apparently rampant:

Mary Lavinia Mongin Stoddard	John Stoddard
1819-1865	1809-1879

(Photographs courtesy Mr. Albert H. Stoddard III. Mrs. Stoddard's picture is from an original portrait in possession of Mr. Stoddard, Savannah, Ga.)

...Mrs. Stoddard's little babe is teething and has coughed very hard. When they had it in town, it appeared as if it would have a hard struggle. But the physician ordered its return to the country—and it is not nearly well—altho' it has cut several teeth during that period. . . .[40]

John Stoddard has bought a beautiful spacious home in Savannah, 17 W. McDonough Street, which can still be seen today. They are spending some time in the city, but John returns to Daufuskie to supervise the plantations: Melrose, Cooper River, Maryfield, Oak Ridge, Bloody Point, and Eigleberger. Haig's Point and Freeport have been sold to Reverend Herman M. Blodgett, who combines the two plantations which are known hereafter only as Haig's Point.

Melrose Mansion

Built of lumber, the house consisted of two stories built over a brick basement. Used as flooring in the basement, large four-inch-thick pieces of slate were cut and fitted to cover the whole ground area. The basement had a wine cellar, plenty of storage space, and a large fireplace where slaves cooked the food, carrying it upstairs to the dining room.

The first floor was the living area, built with a wide hall down the center separating two large rooms on either side. Between the rooms were very deep spacious closets which were very rare in those days. The four rooms consisted of the parlor, library, music, and dining area. The door to each of these rooms opened into the wide hall.

A stairway on the left side of the hall led to the second floor, which was built identical to the first and contained the four bedrooms with the same closet arrangement between them. Except for air vents, a windowless attic topped the whole structure.

A wide porch graced all four sides of the house with a set of steps at the front and rear. Attached to the back porch on either end were separate buildings of wood built over a brick basement (like the house). These could have been used for house-servant and nanny quarters.

There were four chimneys, two each built on the north and south sides of the house, which gave a fireplace for the four rooms both up and down stairs. The fireplaces and mantles were constructed of black and white marble brought from Italy. The inside walls were plastered

View from the front yard of the Melrose mansion— a steam ship is seen off shore.

The Melrose dock.

Flower gardens in the back yard of the Melrose manstion.

on wood lathe. Bits of horsehair were imbedded in the plaster mixture to give added strength and to prevent cracking. The floors and trim were oak.

The house was furnished with massive and elegant furniture brought from England. The china and porcelain were from France.

The Flower Gardens

Pete Henderson owned a feed and seed store in Savannah. His brother, an English gardener, was hired by John Stoddard to landscape the flower gardens at Melrose. No one knew the given name of the brother, but because Pete was so well known, he was always referred to as "Pete Henderson's brother."

Surrounding the mansion, the gardens were magnificent with walkways lined with hedges. Beds were bordered and filled with many different types of flowers. There were acres of roses of every kind and color. The whole panorama was breathtakingly beautiful with a heavenly fragrance perfuming the air.

Gazebo or Summer House

Pete Henderson's brother built a gazebo in the midst of the north garden. It was an octagon-shaped wooden structure, ten feet wide, with stained glass over hinged windows. The roof contained eight sections to correspond with the walls. A weathercock perched precariously atop a cupola. A closed-in seating space was built along all the inside walls.

The English were inventors of "rustic furniture." One idea was to take short pieces of wood, attach them side by side with nails onto the solid wood along the outside edge of a table top, or around a box and on top of the lid. The various patterns and designs proved very interesting.

After completing the little gazebo, Pete Henderson's brother chose to cover the outside and inside walls, including the seating area, with these tiny pieces of wood. He wanted wood with the bark on to present a pleasing effect. In order to do this, the wood had to be gotten in the winter so that the bark would adhere and not slip off.

He chose the tulip poplar which was prevalent throughout the island. Cutting one-inch diameter branches, he sawed or split them down the center, then cut them into eight, ten, twelve inches, or

Melrose Gazebo

(Courtesy Mr. Albert H. Stoddard III.)

Melrose Gazebo—
Inside Walls.
(Courtesy Mrs. W.W.
[Jo] Scouten.)

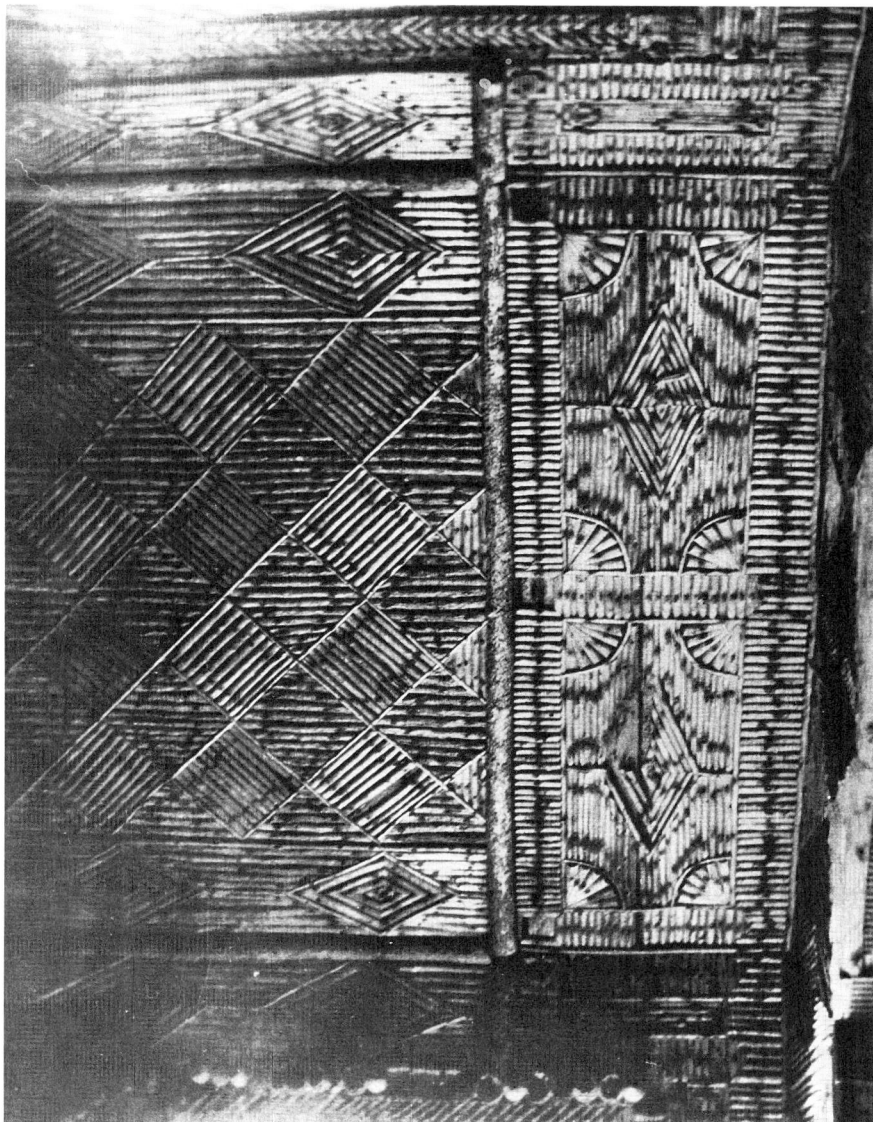

Melrose Gazebo—Inside Walls. (Courtesy Mrs. W.W. [Jo] Scouten.)

whatever length he needed. He made intricate designs in all shapes and sizes, using six thousand little pieces of wood.

When the walls were completed inside, he decided to cover the ceiling with hundreds of pinecone rosettes, which resembled zinnias. Brushing the entire masterpiece with varnish brought out the color and detail of the bark.

Visitors who came admired the house, but the lovely flower gardens and the gazebo—these they never forgot.

Peter Henderson's Brother
Builds Plantation Office for Blodgett

Probably because he admired the gazebo so much, The Reverend Herman M. Blodgett, who was living at Haig's Point, had the brother build a two-room plantation office in the back yard of the mansion. In the south room, which was the office itself, the little pieces of wood made into triangles, squares, etc., covered the walls from the wainscot up. The adjoining northern room had only plain wooden walls and was used for storing supplies.

(This little building withstood the Civil War and was still standing in 1935 when I first came to the island to live. I had the privilege of walking around in it and staring with amazement at the intricate work involved in piecing together the patterns that were used on the walls. I could only imagine the time-consuming work in just gathering, preparing, and cutting all of those little pieces of wood, then nailing them on the wall—one by one. Truly this was a labor of love.)

Farmer's Dwelling

Six hundred feet behind the mansion stood a twenty-by-sixty-foot wooden building. Partitioned down the center, with a door on either end, it was large enough for two families, probably the farmer and driver.

Artesian Wells

Between the mansion and the farmer's building was an artesian well. (A ditch was dug to the beach to take care of the overflow.) A brick meat house was built not far from the well. There were two patches of bamboo fishing canes—one near the meat house and the

other near the farmer's dwelling. Some of the canes grew to a height of twenty feet.

Orchard

Beyond the farmer's building on the west was a twenty-acre pear and pecan orchard. Dotted about the yard were fig, orange, lemon, cherry, and peach trees. The winters were mild enough that citrus fruit was grown without fear of freezing.

The Barn

Just south of the farmer's dwelling was a huge barn that could stable eighteen to twenty cows or horses at a time. The old farm bell that called the slaves to and from work or for dinner was attached to a large live oak that stood in front of the barn near the door. The barn was still standing in 1945.

Slave Quarters

Joining the orchard on the south side, running north and south, were quarters for twenty-two families, representing at least forty-four slaves. The quarters consisted of two rows facing each other—the first row contained seven cabins, the second row, fifteen.[41]

These quarters were built of wood, leaving no trace of them. They could have deteriorated or been torn down and given to freed slaves to build their own cabins.

Oak-Lined Road

As was the custom of the larger plantations, carefully planted live oak trees graced each side of the road leading up to the Melrose mansion. It has been said that when some of the planters gave a special party in the evening, slaves, holding torches, would stand at intervals along the avenue of oaks to light the way for those attending the gala affair.

Other Stoddard Children

Albert Henry I was born in February 1838, Isabelle in March 1840, John Irwin in July 1842, and Henry Mongin Stoddard in July 1844. The family was living permanently in Savannah. Melrose was strictly a summer or week-end home.

Just where the children were educated is not known, but Mary Helen at sixteen was a singer. In a letter dated Saturday, 3 May 1856:

... It seems that Miss [Mary Helen] Stoddard and Miss [Lucy] Sorrel are rival singers, and it is "diamond cut diamond" with them just now. . . .[42]

John Stoddard Invests in More Land and Buildings

Purchased from the Reverend Herman M. Blodgett for $1140.00 in 1845, John Stoddard added to the north of Melrose a twenty-acre tract of land Blodgett called Beachfield, situated in the southeast corner of the former Freeport Plantation. Beachfield bordered Melrose on the south, Freeport Creek on the west, and Calibogue Sound on the east.[43]

In 1854-1855, as an investment, John Stoddard built massive structures at Nos. 19, 21, 23, and 25 West Perry Street in Savannah.

An astute business man and knowledgeable about the economy of Europe, John Stoddard was also aware of the storm clouds brewing between the North and the South. Being a northern man, he could no doubt judge the outcome should there be a civil war. In order to avoid complete disaster, John Stoddard, as early as circa 1857, wisely sold Mary Lavinia's slaves which she had inherited from her grandfather, John David Mongin (No. 3). With this money, John built warehouses at 12 through 45 W. Bay, known as Stoddard's Upper Range, and at 208 through 230 W. Bay, known as the Lower Range. The two upper floors on the Bay Street level were built on top of the River Street warehouses owned by the Mongins.[44]

Daufuskie Island Abandoned

Having sold most of the slaves, John Stoddard retained a few to supply a labor force at Melrose. He continued to carry cotton and farm products to his warehouses in Savannah until Union warships were headed to South Carolina waters.

Leaving his slaves on the plantation, he also left Pete Henderson's brother in charge at the Melrose mansion. John Stoddard, along with every other planter, left Daufuskie before the invasion, forsaking everything they possessed, including fields white with cotton, waiting to be picked.

Northern Troops on Daufuskie

After the Battle of Port Royal 7 November 1861, all of the South Carolina sea islands were confiscated and were in Union hands as abandoned lands and for non-payment of taxes. (It didn't matter that they did not inform the planters how much their taxes really were.)

Gen. Egbert L. Viele was stationed a short time at the Melrose house, later moving down on the south end at the Mary Dunn Plantation to watch more closely the shelling of Ft. Pulaski.

Northern Officer Impressed with Melrose

Lieut. Charles Fred Monroe, of the Eighth Maine Regiment, Company C, of the Federal Army, was one of the 1,600 Union soldiers stationed about on Daufuskie. Lieut. Monroe was camped at the Dunn plantation on Mongin Creek. He kept a diary during his two year stay in this area and liked what he saw at Melrose:

> ...March 2, 1862: The Sergt., Maj., and myself started on a tramp and walked down the island a mile and turned to the shore and followed the beach down for two miles to a plantation called the Stoddard Place, and a finer never was, large elegant and tasteful mansion with an abundance of outbuildings; then farther back the 'Quarters'. Such a garden never was, I do believe.
>
> Stoddard kept an English gardener, whose residence ... a prince might envy. Such walks, hedges, arbors, vines, graveled walks, shade trees, flowers of every hue, and of all descriptions, I never imagined. Birds of all kinds, singing their sweetest songs; grounds all laid out on a very expensive scale, winding gravel walks going in all directions, divided off neatly trimmed hawthorn hedges; orange, lemon, fig, plum, cherry and peach trees in profusion. I noticed the castor-oil tree, mighty live oaks, gum trees, tulip and other trees, with mansion and all the outbuildings completely overgrown with grape vines and hanging rose vines, ivy, etc.
>
> The mansion furnished with marble fireplaces and mantles, black and white; some $10,000.00 of furniture was removed [by northern troops] to Port Royal except two massive bedsteads. There is a large hot house, in which are 200 different kinds of plants, withering and dying for the want of water.
>
> Amid the blossoming stocks stands the crown-lily of the island: a summer house of octagonal form about ten feet across, surmounted by

a cupola and a weather cock. This house is built of pieces of wood, in the natural state with bark on. The sticks are split and nailed on in such as way as to form the most pleasing figures, checks, squares, diamonds, arches, parallels and circles. Stained glass over the swinging glass windows and an arched roof. There are eight pillars around the outside, made octagonal in form, all done with those pieces of wood, then varnished and the different colors brought out with a pleasing effect. It is said that there are 6,000 pieces of wood in this little house.

A guard of a corporal and four men are stationed to protect and show visitors about. Down to the 'Quarters' only 6 or 8 of the old helpless darkies are left. . . .*

The diary continues from 3 July 1862 to 3 March 1863, with Lieut. Monroe being sent to Beaufort. He talks about Port Royal, Seabrook, St. Helena, and then about sailing to Fernandine and Jacksonville.

On 1 April 1863 he arrives at Hilton Head then back to Beaufort again. On 11 April 1863, he boards the steamer *Fulton* bound for Virginia. His last entry was simply: "April 17, 1864: Gloster, Yorktown."[45]

Who Was This Lieut. Monroe?
Where in Maine Was He From?

Curiosity was aroused concerning this enemy soldier who had left such valuable information. He was so knowledgeable concerning flowers, trees, wood, soil, and architecture. Where was he actually from? What happened to him? Did he survive the war? Did he return home? Marry, and live happily ever after?

Letters were written to Maine to locate the Eighth Maine Regiment. Lieut. Charles Fred Monroe was finally traced to Livermore. With much excitement a letter was sent to the librarian of that city, asking for any information concerning this man.

What a delight when a favorable response was received from Mrs. Mary Booth, volunteer librarian at Livermore, Maine. Yes, Charles Fred Monroe was listed in the Civil War records. Mrs. Booth stated that she could not find Daufuskie on her map—where was it?

---

*Something needs to be clarified here concerning Lieut. Monroe's Diary: The reason that Monroe thought the Melrose mansion belonged to the gardener was that John Stoddard had left the gardener in charge of the house and slaves. So Monroe, not seeing anyone else, assumed that the house *belonged* to the gardener.

Above: Ira Thompson Monroe.
Right: Charles F. Monroe.
Below: Livermore, Maine, Library.
Librarians Penny Pelletier, Mary
Booth, Marion Irish.

111

Mrs. Booth's letter was answered with information about Daufuskie and where it was located, explaining that being so small it rarely appeared on most maps of this area. A copy of "The Soldier's Diary" was also mailed to her.

Mrs. Booth was kind to send the following information with this remark: "You know more about Charles F. Monroe than I do."

> Lieut. Charles F. Monroe was Provost Marshall of the city of Beaufort, S.C., while the Union troops occupied that locality. He was wounded May 18th and killed June 3, 1864.

Mrs. Booth further stated that Charles' brother, Ira Monroe, had written a book, *The History of Livermore*. As she was thumbing through the book, she found this notation that Ira had found in Charles' diary: "Edwin T. Quimby lies buried under a beech tree on Danfusky, Hilton Head." Quimby was also a soldier from Livermore, Maine, and a friend of Charles Monroe.

Ira Monroe had found the diary among his brother Charles' possessions. In 1931 (when Ira was 79 years old), he and his wife, Ida, paid a visit to Beaufort to see where his brother had served during the war. Chlotilde Rowell Martin wrote in her article:

> Ira brought with him a door knob that Charles had taken from an old plantation home belonging to a Dr. Pope on Ladies Island.
>
> The house no longer standing, the knob was presented to R. F. Ford, superintendent of the large estate of Dr. A. W. Elting, prominent New York surgeon who then owned the Pope plantation.

Mrs. Mary Booth also sent pictures of Charles and his brother Ira Monroe, through the courtesy of volunteer librarian Penny Pelletier, who was very good with a camera. A debt of gratitude goes to these two women for the unfolding of this remarkable story.

Mrs. Booth had found an old Civil War book and promised that she would go through it and send any information she found concerning Gen. Egbert L. Viele, commander of all the troops on Daufuskie. Mrs. Booth had a terminal disease, and before she could keep her promise, her husband, Mr. Arthur Booth, wrote that she had died in December 1986.

Mary, although never meeting, through correspondence you became a dear friend. If there is a library in Heaven—you've got to be its HEAD LIBRARIAN. Thank you and God bless.

Melrose—School for Freedmen

As soon as the islands fell into Union hands, the Freedmen's Bureau immediately sent women who not only could teach school but who also were Christians and taught Sabbath school as well.

The exact date is unknown, but two young white teachers, Ellen (Esther) W. Douglas and Frances Littlefield, were sent to Daufuskie through the American Missionary Association, probably as early as 1862. The ladies lived in the Melrose mansion, but whether they held school in the mansion itself or in one of the out buildings, no one knows. There were as many as 86 black children (no whites) enrolled. Classes were taught for three hours each week day. There was also a night session for adults or older children who had to work during the day.[46]

Hilton Head Teachers Visit Melrose

There were two other white teachers, Eliza Ann Summers and her home town friend, Julie Benedict, who were sent by boat to Hilton Head, also under the auspices of the American Missionary Association. They lived in the Lawton Plantation mansion.

On 11 April 1867, Eliza Ann, Julie, and party decided to visit Ellen and Frances, the teachers on Daufuskie. This is how Eliza Ann described the trip that day in her letter.

> ... I commenced to tell you about Mr. Judkins & Miss Hill's coming out. She staid over night so as to be here the next day, Saturday, to go to Daw Fuskie Island to call on some teachers there. It is nearly opposite from our plantation. We are seven miles from them, and the nearest white people to them. It is quite a large island and they are the only white people on the whole island. The next morning we got up early and cooked for ourselves and oarsmen. Mr. Elmore furnished boat and took five more men to row while he steered, making nine of us in all. We took the ladies [Ellen and Frances] quite by surprise. But if I only could describe the place. Its useless to try, for in all my life I never saw such a beautiful place. I felt like just sitting down and crying. So did we all, and were almost wild. It is a very large nice house but for that I do not care. It was the grounds and flowers. I thought I had seen beautiful places & flowers before but I have never seen anything that would be a thousandth part compared with this. Such beautiful roses and a great variety of japonicas. I should think there was as many as 50 varieties of roses without stretching it one bit. Some beautiful lemon colored roses,

called the cloth of gold, as large as the top of a large teasaucer. And another kind the buds of which are as large as a good sized hen's egg. You can imagine the size of the blossom. I could not begin to describe the different sizes, shades, and colors of these roses besides the many other flowers that I never heard of or seen before, and such beautiful summer houses and arbors made of barks and avenues and walks & drives. I told Julie I felt like crying because my mother could not see the place & flowers, and she said that was just the way she felt. We all ran around the garden and yard, or rather it was all in one, each with a colored man at our heels to climb for flowers. I tore my brown dress in twenty places or more, and got six large bouquets of beautiful roses and other flowers. Julie & I got together almost a bushel of roses. We landed in front of the house, and the men had to carry us from the boat to the shore. They took us up in their arms as they would a child. The teachers were very glad to see us and wanted us to come again as soon as we could. We did not get home until nearly dark. . . .[47]

Teachers Leave Melrose

According to Ellen W. Douglas' letter of 2 May 1867, she had sent in her last Monthly Teachers Report and left the island for good. She also states in her letter that one of her former Bible class members had written to her that they were keeping up the Sabbath and evening schools and praying every day for some way to open by which "we may return."[48]

Albert Henry Stoddard Joins Army/Mary Lavinia Dies

John and Mary Lavinia's oldest son, Albert Henry Stoddard, 3 November 1863, received his Commission as First Lieut. and Aide de Camp in the Provisional Army in the service of the Confederate States.[49]

Without a doubt, the War in general and her son's being in service were in part the cause of Mary Lavinia Mongin-Stoddard's death on 22 February 1865. She is buried at Bonaventure Cemetery in Savannah, Georgia.

Melrose Restored to John Stoddard

On 13 January 1866 John Stoddard, Trustee, is granted restoration of Melrose by the Bureau of Refugees, Freedmen and Abandoned Lands, with the provision that he promise that . . .

he will secure to the Refugees and Freedmen now resident on [Melrose] the crops of the present season harvested or unharvested; also, that the said Refugees Freedmen shall be allowed to remain at their present houses or other homes on the island, so long as the Refugees and Freedmen . . . shall enter into contracts by leases or for wages in terms satisfactory to the Supervising Board.[50]

Lease Agreement with Freedmen[51]

On 28 December 1865, from the Board of Supervisors, constituted by order of Maj. Gen. Howard, Charleston, S.C., Mr. John Stoddard, Trustee, let use with no rent for one year, 5 acres of land for twenty-two former slave families . . . 2-1/2 acres in the cornfield and 2-1/2 acres in the cotton field was allotted to each family. The property was to return to the owner after one year. The former slaves who had made their "X" on the document were Peter, Edmond, Jack, Tom, Cinder, Price, John, Tom Abram, Samson, Dennis, Bob, Beck, Horace, August, Phebe, Luch, Bess, Maria, Tena Eley, Phillie, Funo, and Virginia.

The War had changed things. After regaining control of his plantations, John Stoddard now had to pay wages to former slaves for their labor, if he wanted to continue to plant.

John Stoddard's Death 1879

John Stoddard, being a consistent member of the Church of Christ at the early age of 18, was a good, honest, and pious man. In any decision it was principle that concerned him, not policy. In a group of men who were discussing martyrs, the question was asked, "Who in all the town, if persecution were revived, would burn at the stake rather than give in?"

One man spoke up. "I know one—John Stoddard. . . ."

On 13 July 1840, John became a member of the Georgia Historical Society and for one year, beginning 12 February 1867, he became its president.

In 1844 he was elected elder of the Independent Presbyterian Church of Savannah, which office he filled until his death. During his forty-two years of Savannah life, John occupied many offices of trust. In accepting the office his request was that he receive no pay. Until his demise he held the offices of President of the Board of Education of

Chatham County, President of the Georgia Infirmary, Chairman of the Commissioners of Pilotage and Conservators of the Savannah River, and Treasurer of the Industrial Home. He was active with, and gave generously to, his favorite charities.

Acting as trustee over the estate of his wife Mary Lavinia, John Stoddard enhanced her property to two and one half times its original value. At her death in 1865 John shared their entire estate with her children, receiving nothing for himself although his own personal fortune had been "swept away with the War."

He was strong and unwavering in his faith in Christ, and death had no sting for him. He had said to a friend just weeks prior to his death:

> ...when you hear of my departure, you are not to think of me as lying under the oaks at Bonaventure Cemetery, for I shall not be there—I shall be yonder working for Christ; I have tried to work for Him here all these years and I feel that He will have work for me there.

And thus, leaving to his sorrowing children the priceless inheritance of an unstained name, he went—

> Beyond the smiling and the weeping
> Beyond the waking and the sleeping
> Beyond the sowing and the reaping
> —to the Master.[52]

Melrose Given to Albert Stoddard I

After Mary Lavinia's death in 1865, Albert Henry Stoddard I was given Melrose in the distribution of his mother's property. In 1865 he married Elizabeth, daughter of a Dr. Hamilton of Charleston. They made Melrose their permanent home.

Albert and Elizabeth had two children, but only Albert Henry Stoddard II, born September 1872, survived.

Elizabeth Hamilton Stoddard died 1 April 1873 leaving her husband with a seven-month-old child to raise alone.

Albert Henry Stoddard I kept his little son on Daufuskie, tutoring him personally, as there was no school available.

In November 1880 Albert Henry Stoddard I married for the second time to Leila Pegram, bringing her to live at Melrose. Leila Pegram Stoddard embraced Albert Henry Stoddard's son as her own; new friends she met were never told the difference.

116

Stoddards and Doyle Visit

John Michael Doyle had received an order from J. C. LaCosta to erect the rear metal beacon tower for the Bloody Point Light Range. During his stay on Daufuskie, Mr. Doyle kept a diary of his activities. Becoming acquainted with Albert and Leila Stoddard, he made notations of each visit.

John Michael Doyle appreciated their friendship as it was rather lonely at times:

SUNDAY, NOV. 9, 1882

. . . The day was nice & warm so I took a long walk along the beach gathering some shells & on my way back to the quarters came through the grounds of Mr. [Albert Henry] Stoddard [I] & gathered a bunch of fine roses.

SATURDAY, DEC. 2, 1882

Mr. LaCoste went to Savannah this morning having a passenger, Mr. and Mrs. [Albert and Leila] StoddardI & their little son.

TUESDAY, DEC. 12, 1882

We had a call this afternoon at the work from Mr. and Mrs. Albert Stoddard, Mrs. Hains [Haig's Pt. Lighthouse] & Capt. Anderson of the schooner *Pharos*. The ladies are both lovely ladies and it was quite a treat to see their bright faces among us when it is remembered that they are the only white ladies we get to see on the Island. . .

MONDAY, JAN 1, 1883

. . . The men discharged the flat of her load of shells & I was putting in the time as best I could when we had the pleasure of a visit from Mr. & Mrs. Stoddard, the lady was very gracious to me & I had her to chat all to myself for a little while, too. She very kindly invited me to visit them at Melrose & asked me in surprise, why I had not called on them before & I told her that I had only been waiting for an invitation. Well, said she had given a general invitation to all us gentlemen on this work to call, which was meant for me as well as Mr. LaCoste and Mr. Gowers. Well I promised to visit Melrose soon & mean to keep my promise. Auntie [Pender Hamilton, his cook] said it was a good omen that I should have such a pleasant caller on the first day of the year & I was disposed to regard the matter in that light myself.

WEDNESDAY, JAN. 3, 1883

. . . Mr. & Mrs. Stoddard made a flying call in the afternoon.

TUESDAY, JAN. 9, 1883

No work again today on account of the rain which fell almost without ceasing throughout the day. We spent the day in the usual manner, reading, talking, smoking & occasionally playing a game of cards, & by the way we were surprised at the latter amusement during a lull in the storm in the afternoon by a call from Mr. & Mrs. Stoddard. They only staid a few minutes but the old house seemed brighter the balance of the day. . . .

SUNDAY, FEB. 4, 1883

For a wonder this has been a lovely bright day, the first nice Sunday we have had for over a month. After dinner, I hitched up the mule & Mr. Gowers & I went riding, we visited first the front beacon & then the rear & after that took a turn around through the woods & when we returned found Mr. LaCoste had got back & just as I got unhitched Mr. Stoddard drove up with the lady [Mrs. Stoddard] in the buggy, with one of the little English pups in her lap and her old nurse with another.

Those pups are certainly to be envied. They did not stay long but what a pleasure to see her & converse with her for a few minutes. . . .

THURSDAY, FEB. 8, 1883

. . . When I got to the quarters this evening, there was a beautiful present of flowers there, brought during the day by Mrs. [Leila] Stoddard, & not a mere bouquet either but about a half a bushel of the most lovely Japonicas of all colors & shades of color & a lot of fragrant Johnquils.

SUNDAY, FEB. 11, 1883

I determined this morning to make my long promised visit to Melrose & had a very pleasant visit there. The place is a beautiful one inside and out. The house is filled with rich & rare objects from all parts of the globe. Among which there is a bulls head fastened to the wall of the hall upon which are a pair of horns brought by Mr. Stoddard from Rome. Then there are curiosities from everywhere, every nation and every clime. But it was in the garden I spent most of my time among the flowers, of which there are are millions & the oranges on the trees look lovely. I was very cordially treated by Mr. & Mrs. Stoddard & my visit was to me at least a very pleasant one. . . .[53]

Mrs. Leila Pegram Stoddard Dies

Two daughters were born to Leila and Albert Henry Stoddard I: Isabelle was born 23 May 1884, died 24 May 1884, and Ethel Spencer was born May 1885 (no record of her death).

Leila Pegram Stoddard died January 1886; interment was in Elizabeth City, New Jersey.

Albert Henry Stoddard I and II at Melrose

Following the death of wife Leila, Albert Henry is back at Melrose with his son Albert Henry II. The father continues to personally tutor the fourteen-year-old boy who is now referred to as "Bertie."

Being a lonely child, Bertie has had to play with the only companions available—black children of former slaves his father has now hired to farm the plantation. Young Albert learns to speak Gullah as fluently as they. (See Gullah in the Plantation Life segment.)

Bertie naturally liked the company of other young people, so he frequently attended parties in Savannah and Bluffton. He often went "under his own oars" to Savannah—there on the flood and back on the ebb—using the tide to cut down his rowing time, the complete trip taking about nine hours. If he wasn't going to a party he was having one at Melrose. Members of the Cotillion Club (formally known as the German Club) came from Savannah on large steamers and enjoyed several outings a year at Melrose.

Mrs. Sarah Grant said that at low tide steamers going to Beaufort would not travel through New River but would go directly to Melrose and discharge their passengers. Men in small batteaus would row out to meet them and bring them to shore.

Storm of 1893

In the storm of 1893 the house stood, but the lovely flower gardens that had been a conversation piece since 1838 were completely destroyed. They were replanted, but not as extensively as they had been previously.

Bertie Stoddard was home alone at the time of the storm and found refuge in the attic. He figured that if the house were to move, he could feel it best at that position and could get out quickly if the need arose. The house groaned and quaked, but held fast.

119

Albert Stoddard II Attends College, Weds

So completely educated by his father, with no formal grammar or high school education, Bertie Stoddard was accepted at the University of Virginia. There he met and in 1909 married Evelyn Byrd Pollard from King William County. The young couple settled permanently at Melrose.

Farming Continues at Melrose

Albert Henry I and his son Bertie continued to farm Melrose. Mrs. Sarah Grant said that the people on the island would work for them in the orchard. The young men would climb the trees and throw down fruit—the firm fruit only. The girls and women would then pick up and pack the pears in wooden barrels, at a rate of ten cents a barrel. The ripe fruit was given to the people to take home. They also thrashed the pecans and sacked them for market. The barrels and sacks were hauled in wagons and loaded on steamers at Benjie's Point, then shipped to Savannah.

The blacks worked ten hours a day hoeing cotton and corn, or gathering other crops and picking cotton in the fall. They cut hay with a scythe until they got a grass mower that was ridden and pulled by two mules. With a reap-hook they cut tender marsh to feed the cattle and

Melrose after the Storm of 1893

120

horses. To summon field workers for an emergency at the house Mr. Stoddard would shoot a 12-gauge shotgun twice, after he rang the bell that was up in the huge oak in front of the old red barn.

Sam Jefferson was a gardener and farmer at Melrose. Sam's wife Annie was the cook and prepared meals in an open fireplace in the brick basement. The Jefferson children were James, Abraham, Frankie, Alec, Lizzie Bell, Annie, Lucy, and Ella. Years later when the Jeffersons died, Mrs. Agnes (Genia) Brown-Washington became the cook; she stayed with the Stoddards until they moved to Savannah in 1918.

Mrs. Sarah Grant said that Mr. Stoddard would not have a stove in the house and he continued to have meals prepared in the fireplace until the house burned.[54]

Teacher Lives at Melrose

In 1911 Sarah Constable, Evelyn's cousin, came to live with them at Melrose and taught the white children on the island. She was living with the Stoddards when the house burned. Sarah left the island and did not return as there was no place for her to stay. (Read more about her in the White Daufuskie School segment.)

Bertie and Evelyn Have a Son—Melrose Burns

In 1912 Evelyn goes to Savannah where their first son, Dan Hamilton, is born. She returns to Melrose as soon as possible.

The baby is just a few months old when the mansion burns to the ground. The following are excerpts from the *Savannah Press* on Wednesday, 7 August 1912:

It was Melrose, the beautiful home of Mr. & Mrs. A. H. Stoddard, Jr., which burned early Monday morning at Daufuskie. . . . Melrose was a total loss and it is practically impossible to estimate the value of the house and contents, but it will reach easily $25,000.

. . . for the past two generations it has been famous for the house parties held there. The house faced the Atlantic Ocean and was surrounded by spacious and beautiful gardens.

Mr. Albert Stoddard [I], the son of Mr. John Stoddard, occupied the house and he lived there with Mr. & Mrs. A. H. Stoddard, Jr., who with their baby were at home at the time of the fire.

The blaze was discovered in the attic by Mr. Stoddard Monday

morning about 10 o'clock. It is thought rats started the fire. It was impossible to save anything, and in a very short time the entire place had burned.

It is hard to estimate the loss of the contents. A magnificent library, the foundations of which were made by Mr. John Stoddard, who brought over from Europe many books in the original French and Italian, besides hundreds of more modern books, were burned. The family plate, the old music and instruments in the music room and the billiard and pool tables in the billiard room were all destroyed, as well as the contents of the living apartments.

Bertie Stoddard Builds Cottage

With no place to live, Evelyn left the island to visit her parents in Virginia. While she was away, Bertie tore down the old long, thirty-by-sixty-foot farmer's building, and with other lumber built a cottage on the same spot.[55]

It was a rather spacious story-and-a-half structure, built on six-foot brick pillars which gave a lot of open space under the house. In fact, it was so high off the ground that boats were stored underneath; thus, the Stoddards dubbed it "The Boat House." It was also the house with which most of us, who came to the island long after the mansion had burned, were familiar.

On the main floor of this cottage was a large living room with a monstrous fireplace, one bedroom, a dining room, and a kitchen. A large porch was across the front, a sun porch off the south side of the living room, and a small porch off the kitchen. Upstairs was just one large bedroom.

Post Office at Melrose—Stoddards Have Another Son

After the house was finished, Evelyn returned to the island. The family lived comfortably in the new dwelling.

Steamers on the Savannah-Beaufort line would drop off sacks of mail at the public landing. Everyone would go through them looking for their own letters and packages. This handling of the mail distressed Evelyn because she too would have mail in the bags. She applied for and received a commission as the first Daufuskie Postmaster sometime in 1912. The tack room in the old barn became the first Post Office.

122

Stoddard's "Boat-House" at Melrose

Robbie Butler, a young black man who had a fine horse and who lived across the road from Gus Ohman's store at Benjie's Point, would ride all the way to Melrose (about six miles) and bring back anyone's mail for twenty-five cents per family.

Evelyn's expecting their second child might have had something to do with it, but she was not postmaster for very long. She gave birth to Spotswood Douglas in Savannah in 1913. The Stoddards continued to farm successfully and grow cotton at Melrose until 1917.

James (Jim) W. White: Sharecropper at Melrose

In 1918 the elder Stoddard child, Dan, was six years old and was required to attend school. The family would be leaving Melrose for good except for summer vacations and special weekends. Much time would be needed to make the move to Savannah. Bertie Stoddard, therefore, decided to rent the land out that year to Seacoast Farm Company. This company also had contracts to farm three other plantations. Melrose was farmed by Jim White and family; Haig's Point was farmed by Mr. Burns and his family. (The Scoutens had gone to Charleston. It was during World War I and Mr. W. W. Scouten had been called back into service.) Cooper River was farmed by Plummey Simmons and Tom Joiner; and Webb Tract was farmed by William (Geechee) Brown and Chance Sanders.

There were several little houses dotted about Melrose and the Jim White family lived in one of them. George White remembers two families of black people who lived up there about that time—the Dennis family and the Whaleys. He also remembers the Cannon house at Freeport being moved to Melrose. In fact, he and his brother Hinson stayed in that house for a short while when they helped with the farming.

The Seacoast Farm Company furnished all the seeds, two-hundred-pound sacks of fertilizer, and eighteen head of mules (most of which were mares).

Since Jim White and his two sons, Hinson, nineteen, and George, fifteen, would be doing the farming at Melrose, they were given four mules. Fourteen mules were distributed to the other three plantations. The mules were worked all week, then brought from the other three plantations and kept at Melrose over the weekend.

One mule each was allotted to Jim White and his two sons. The fourth mule was used when they needed a double team for the double wagon to haul heavy loads of cotton or potatoes out of the field. Each man with a mule was allowed to buy $15.00 a month from the commissary that Bertie had in the old brick meat house. (At one time the brick meat house had been used as a wine cellar.)

The Whites took a chance with the boll weevil and planted twenty acres of Sea Island cotton, twenty acres of Irish potatoes, twenty acres of corn, and, of course, a lot of other garden vegetables. Money was scarce, so cotton was always planted as a cash crop.

There were only five pieces of machinery needed for the farm work: a big cultivator that had a seat on it to ride, pulled by two mules; a harrow that had no seat but which had to be pulled by two mules, one of them being saddled so a rider could direct it over the field; a turn plough; a stock plough; and a scythe with a three-foot blade.

When it was time for harvest, representatives from the company would come and buy while the produce was growing right in the field. Then, the farmers and their families would get in there and pick the cotton, dig the potatoes, and break the corn.

As it was picked, cotton was packed in bags. Irish potatoes were hauled in sacks and then packed in 200-pound wooden barrels with the open top covered with a piece of burlap held on with wire hooks. Pears were always packed in barrels that had wooden heads to keep the fruit from being bruised.

The produce was hauled in large two-horse wagons. They worked all day and most of the night hauling to Benjie's Point dock to put everything aboard the steamer *Attaquin*. Sometimes they were put aboard the *Louise*, but the *Attaquin* operated the Savannah-Beaufort Line and came more frequently than other steamers.

George White said that they worked so hard distributing those two-hundred-pound sacks of fertilizer and hauling those two-hundred-pound sacks of cotton down those long rows, even though he was a young boy at the time his bones and body ached at night from handling such heavy loads. He said even the little kids and his pregnant mother would go to the field and pick cotton. He didn't know how his mother did it, but she did.

George said he loved Melrose and liked to live there better than any place on Daufuskie. He left the island in 1936 and settled in New

Jersey. Every time he came back to the island he never failed to visit Melrose before he left.

Stoddards Leave Melrose—Albert Henry Stoddard III Born

At the close of the 1918 farming season, the Stoddards left the island for good. Their last child, Albert Henry Stoddard III, was born in 1920. They settled at 101 W. Gordon Street on famous Gordon Row. Mrs. Stoddard operated an antique shop at 230 E. Bay Street, which was on the corner of Bay and Lincoln. Bertie Stoddard, like George White, also loved Melrose. . . . For years, every chance he got, Bertie caught steamers—*Louise, Attaquin,* or the *Clivedon*—to visit the old place once more. For the first time since 1837 there was not one Stoddard living on Daufuskie.

Boll Weevils Kill Cotton

It was in 1916 that the first boll weevils were discovered in South Carolina. That year the first specimen was caught on Daufuskie. Each year the population of the weevil increased until by 1920 King Cotton had been wiped out completely. Only small patches for home use could be harvested.

Hoskiss Family Moves to Melrose

The Stoddard "Boat House" did not remain vacant for long. Joe Hoskiss, his wife Liza, and his brother Ed moved there the winter of 1918. They not only farmed, but, according to Sarah Grant, they also had a grist mill, and Rose Brisbane said they had a small dairy.

A little story goes that Joe Hoskiss became the magistrate and held court at Melrose. On one particular occasion court was in session and a black man just kept yapping and interrupting the proceedings. After reprimanding the man several times to shut him up, Joe pulled out his pistol and shot him in the foot. After the man was carried from the room, court continued very quietly and in order.

Other Families at Melrose

After several years of farming, the Hoskiss family left Melrose and moved to Benjie's Point. Through the years white families on Daufuskie who lived at Melrose one or more times were Charlie and Pearlie Lee

126

Palmer, Jim and Annie White, Jim and Lula Goodwin, and Hinson and Agnes White. Everyone who ever lived at Melrose loved the place and always wanted to go back.

Marchants: Sharecroppers at Melrose

In 1934 a family from Tifton, Georgia, moved into the "Boat House" and were sharecroppers for H. D. Pollard, Evelyn Stoddard's brother, who was in charge of Melrose at the time. The Marchants were a large family of true farmers: Isaac and Lessie Marchant, parents; their older son Lemmie and his wife Hazel; a daughter Ruby Gibbs and her son Gordie Lee "Buddy" Gibbs; and the younger children of Isaac and Lessie—Gladys, James, Henry, Doris, and Ruth. Katie, an older married daughter, and her children would visit the family occasionally.

Mr. Pollard furnished mules, seeds, fertilizer, and food for the family until the crops came in. The steamer *Clivedon* was running the Savannah-Beaufort Line at the time and brought everything they needed to the landing at Benjie's Point on New River. Farming for the Marchants proved not to be very profitable, so they left the island in 1937. The "Boat House" remained vacant until possibly sometime in 1942.

Coast Guard at Melrose During World War II

During World War II it was necessary for the shore along the east coast to be guarded and protected, therefore, the United States Coast Guard had a station in the "Boat House" at Melrose. Coast Guardsmen were living in the house, riding horses to patrol the beach, and using trained dogs. Telephone wires were strung in the trees along the six-mile stretch of beach. There were phones placed at intervals along the line in order to contact the person stationed in the house.

Leon (Lee) Bond, who later married Lance Burn's niece, Beatrice (Beezie) Ellis, was stationed at Melrose. Lee was kind to share pictures of some of the men, the house, barn and animals, and Lee also told some interesting stories concerning his stay on the island.

I do not know when the Coast Guard came to or left Melrose but I came in June 1943 and left July 1944. The "Mounted Beach Patrol"

MEN, DOGS AND HORSES PUT BARBS ON ATLANTIC BEACHES---Scenes as C. G. Mounted Beach Patrolmen go through phases of training at Hilton Head. In picture No.1 is the famous gray horse battery of Fort Myer, Va., whose battery drill thrilled crowds at the major horse shows of the country. In No.2 squadron maneuvers on the beach constitute a riding test. In Nos.3&4, dogs and men exhibit thorough military discipline, the upper photo showing dog class on march to the beach. A moment later, at the order "halt", both human and canine Coast Guardsmen come to attention in perfect unison. No.5 shows a section of the Canine Park Housing Project at Hilton Head. No.6 on guard where America meets the ocean. No.7-Commander Ceballos, Commanding Officer, Mounted Beach Patrol of the Sixth Naval District. No.8-Coast Guard dogs do not shrink from a fired pistol. In the hands of a stranger it means three things...attack, attack and attack. No.9-shows men, horses and dogs wading into swamps behind beaches in the black of night. The dog is on the warpath, while the mounted man stands in reserve, ready to communicate for reinforcements if the other two stir up something too hot to handle. No.10-The "stranger" fired a pistol and then advanced before these attackers. The results all along the line as he ran the gamut in his distinctly undesirable assignment, are illustrated by the center dog who hit the leash so hard he was somersaulted and is shown several feet in the air. (Pictures shown are official U.S. Coast Guard photographs).

All of the Daufuskie Coast Guardsmen were trained on Hilton Head, South Carolina.

128

Coast Guardsmen left to right: Leon (Lee) Bond, Lester Hobbs, Lawrence (Buck) Lane, Zeno Graham, Robert Owens. A funeral is being held for SPARKY, one of the horses. Buck Lane is reading from the Bible and Lester Hobbs and Zeno Graham are ready to fire a rifle salute to the loved and faithful animal.

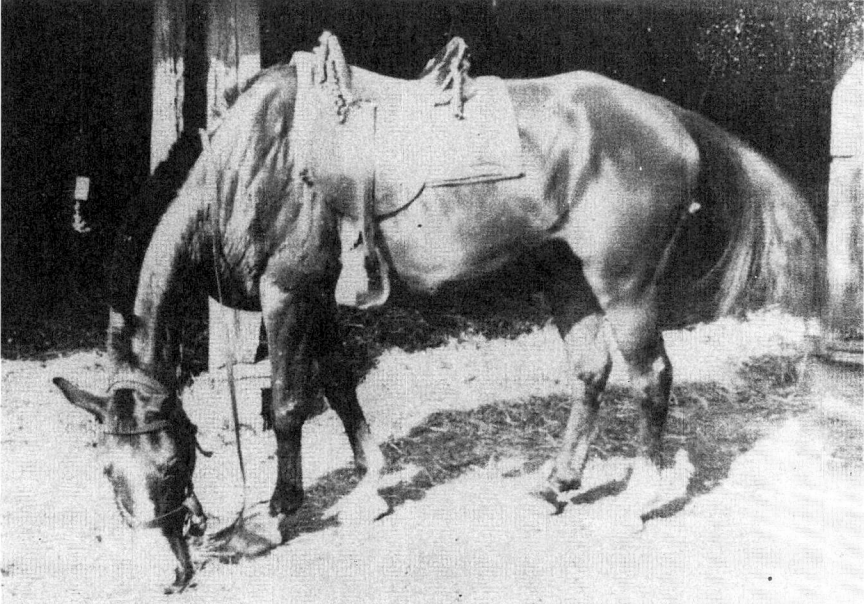

BUTCH—the horse designated to Lee Bond in front of the Melrose barn. (Pictures courtesy Lee Bond, 1943.)

Steamer *Clivedon*
The bow loaded with hay for the Coast Guard horses at Melrose.
(Photograph courtesy of Lee Bond, 1943.)

received basic training at Hilton Head where I was also stationed before coming to Daufuskie.

The Melrose house and barn were in real good shape when I was there. In the front yard was a well that supplied the best drinking water I ever tasted. Underneath the house was a generator that furnished us with lights and a walk-in freezer that preserved our meat and vegetables.

We had 10 days on duty and 4 days off duty. Our main job was to patrol the seaward side of Daufuskie (by horseback) from the Haig's Point Lighthouse on the north end, to Bloody Point on the south end. We had wires strung along the trees for telephone connections. We carried weapons—38 pistols on our hips and shotguns in scabbards on the saddle. We also used trained dogs.

We patrolled Daufuskie every night no matter how rough the weather. Here is a list of the men who were there when I was:

Joe Morrison	Chief in Charge	Savannah, GA
Zeno Graham	Cook	Augusta, GA
Lester Hobbs	Patrol	Thompson, GA
Lawrence (Buck) Lane	Patrol	Augusta, GA
Robert Owens	"	Up North?
Tip Dooley	"	_____, Arkansas
Leon Bond	"	Houston, TX
Arthur Graves	"	Bluffton, SC
Henry Sapp	"	Beaufort, SC
"Woody" Woods	"	Beaufort, SC

There were several things that happened while I was there. In the winter of 1943, three Germans slipped from a submarine and went across Daufuskie, stole a rowboat from the inner-side of the Island and somehow got caught on the mainland.

We would use binoculars and scan the ocean for subs. This one morning, I was on patrol with a buddy as it was just beginning to break day. We spotted a sub, so we called Melrose and I think Chief Morrison in turn called Hilton Head, and between us and them we got a fixed-point on it. The sub disappeared but about thirty minutes later, two planes from Hunter Field (Savannah, Ga.) came and dropped four bombs in the area. Later, on the in-coming tide, we found several life jackets, some oil slicks, some bread and pieces of clothing It wasn't much, but no one claimed any sinkings and we heard no more about it. I believed the sub was sunk, myself.

The steamer *Clivedon* brought down our supplies and hay for the horses from Savannah. When I first got to Melrose, we were hauling our groceries and feed in a two-wheeled cart borrowed from one of the colored families on the Island. Later, we got a four-wheeled wagon.

I would like to say at this point, the most precious memories (but I did not realize it then) was how sweet and kind the colored people were on Daufuskie. Some of us went to their church on Sunday morning and they had a special place for us and treated us real good.

On the lighter side: Lester Hobbs and me would meet this cart driven by two black girls who would bring moonshine down to the landing at Benjie's Point. Their paw was scared to bring it down and he'd get them to do it for him.

We'd load that whiskey in the boat—have on our uniforms and if we passed the Coast Guard boat in the river, we'd just wave at them and putt, putt on to Savannah. They wouldn't stop and board us (which they

131

did to every boat they passed) for they could see our uniforms and would think everything was all right.

We'd take that liquor in at East Broad Street and sell it to a store up on Bay. This would give us some money to spend so we would live it up in a hotel for two or three days, then come back to the Island until we got ready to take up another load.

I remember this night I went to visit a girl on the Island. When I got ready to leave her house, I was so drunk that every time I tried to get on my horse, I'd fall off. I kept doing this a few times until she finally tied me to the saddle.

I charged off down the road and when I got right about in front of the church, some kind of animal let off this God-awful scream! It scared me and the horse so bad, he took off and didn't slow down until we reached Melrose. This "thing" followed us all the way there.

I pulled back on the reins and made a screeching halt. Forgetting I was tied to the saddle, I liked to have fallen out on my head trying to dismount. With 14 thumbs, I finally freed myself, jumped off the horse and ran in the house to tell Chief Morrison what had happened. I was almost out of breath but I told him about this terrible wild animal and that something had to be done about it. After smelling my breath and seeing my condition, he laughed and said, "Boy, go on to bed."

I remember Mr. Gus Ohman would come to Melrose and play poker with all the crew. I must say he was an excellent player as he would take most of the boys' money home with him. He was a heavy drinker, too.

Mr. Arthur A. (Papy) Burn (my future wife's grandfather) made wine and would hide it in gallon jugs by the fence posts around his yard. Us boys would dig it up, drink about half, then put the jug back like we found it. I often wonder what he thought when he would dig up his jugs and find so much of the contents missing. Later, after knowning Papy, he probably scratched his head, laughed, then kept on hiding gallons of wine by the fence posts.

Melrose "Boat House" Torn Down

After World War II ended, the Coast Guard left and the house stayed vacant until 1954 when the Brabham family moved in. They farmed only on a small scale and raised a few cattle. After they moved away in the late 1950s the barn deteriorated and the house started going down until 1969, when Clifford Boyd (Lance Burn's nephew) was given permission by Albert H. Stoddard III to tear it down.

Clifford used the lumber to build a camp site near where the house stood. A careless forest fire in the early 1980s completely destroyed the camp.

With the tearing down of the Melrose "Boat House," an era of Daufuskie history had suddenly ended. Since the mansion had been built sometime before 1837, there had been a dwelling at Melrose. The "Boat House" was the last vestige of a building belonging to a Stoddard.

In closing it might be added that Melrose was the "darling" of all the plantations. Love of the place and the people was expressed through all of the Stoddards and others who were fortunate to live there. This love permeated Melrose and was felt by visitor and friend alike.

Melrose Sold

In October of 1971 the Stoddard brothers, Dan and Albert Henry III, sold Melrose's 700 acres for $950 an acre to Bluffton Timber and Land Company, owned by a group of investors that included Charles Fraser of Sea Pines, Joseph H. Harrison, Jr., of Bluffton, and his brother Robert, of Savannah.[56] With that transaction completed, no more did they own one piece of lumber nor one grain of sand—the Stoddard reign on Daufuskie had come to an abrupt end.

Melrose Resold

In October 1984 for $6.5 million the Bluffton Timber and Land Company sold Melrose to The Melrose Company, a group of fifty investors represented by three Hilton Head partners: Steve Kiser, Jim Coleman, and Robert Kolb.[57]

There are great plans for the development of Melrose: a Jack Nicklaus Golf Course has been built; a beautiful fifty-two-room Melrose Inn is gracing the place, and one hundred beach cottages are in the process of being built. Tennis courts, horse stables, a country store, sportsman's lodge, and other buildings have been added at a rapid pace, with more to come.

There are numerous lakes. Lovely flowers, shrubs, and trees flourish throughout the whole scheme of things. The beauty and awe of the place is too much to describe; it must be seen.

From their dock at Palmetto Bay Marina on Hilton Head, large and small boats are used for transporting members and/or workers daily to Daufuskie. A towboat and barge are available for bringing building materials, freight, vehicles, or whatever the need might be.

All of the amenities at Melrose are built for their Club members only, with security gates to prevent uninvited guests from entering the premises.

Bloody Point Plantation

Bloody Point, having deep water on the inlet side, gave protection for boat travelers who might have need of a safer haven during a storm, or to wait on an in-coming (flood) tide. It became a necessary part of many lives and situations through the years.

In 1701 a lookout post was established on Bloody Point to guard against Spanish and Indian raiding parties. Similar lookouts were again established for the same purpose in 1717 and 1728.

The earliest ownership record of Bloody Point's five hundred acres was Samuel Hilden, Indian Trader, operating on Daufuskie circa 1708. Samuel Hilden sold the property to Indian Trader, John Wright, and Indian Agent, Joseph Wright, circa 1714.[58]

Soldier-scouts manned lookouts at Bloody Point in the 1740s and 1750s. In the later 1740s, John Joyner, a Port Royal harbor pilot, occupied a pilot house on Bloody Point. In 1770 John Dobrins had opened a house of entertainment there.[59]

Permanent ownership of Bloody Point could have been established by Robert Watts as early as 1751, when the plantation was advertised for sale after the death of John Wright.[60] Robert operated the first shipyard on Daufuskie and in 1768 launched the *Georgia Packet*, a one-hundred-ton brigantine.[61] In 1770 he had under construction the *Cowles*, a two-hundred-sixty-ton vessel,[62] and in 1772 he launched the *Friendship,* a two-hundred-sixty-ton, galley-built, ocean-going vessel.[63]

Charles Watts, a first cousin of Robert Watts, had come to Savannah in 1763 and joined in partnership with Robert in his shipbuilding trade. In 1771 Charles had leased a house and moved to Bloody Point:

> . . . in the view of carrying on his shipbuilding to greater advantage and there he lived, prospering, until the troubles arrived at a height in 1775, and constantly refusing to sign or join the Rebel association. He was compelled to leave the province and return to his former residence

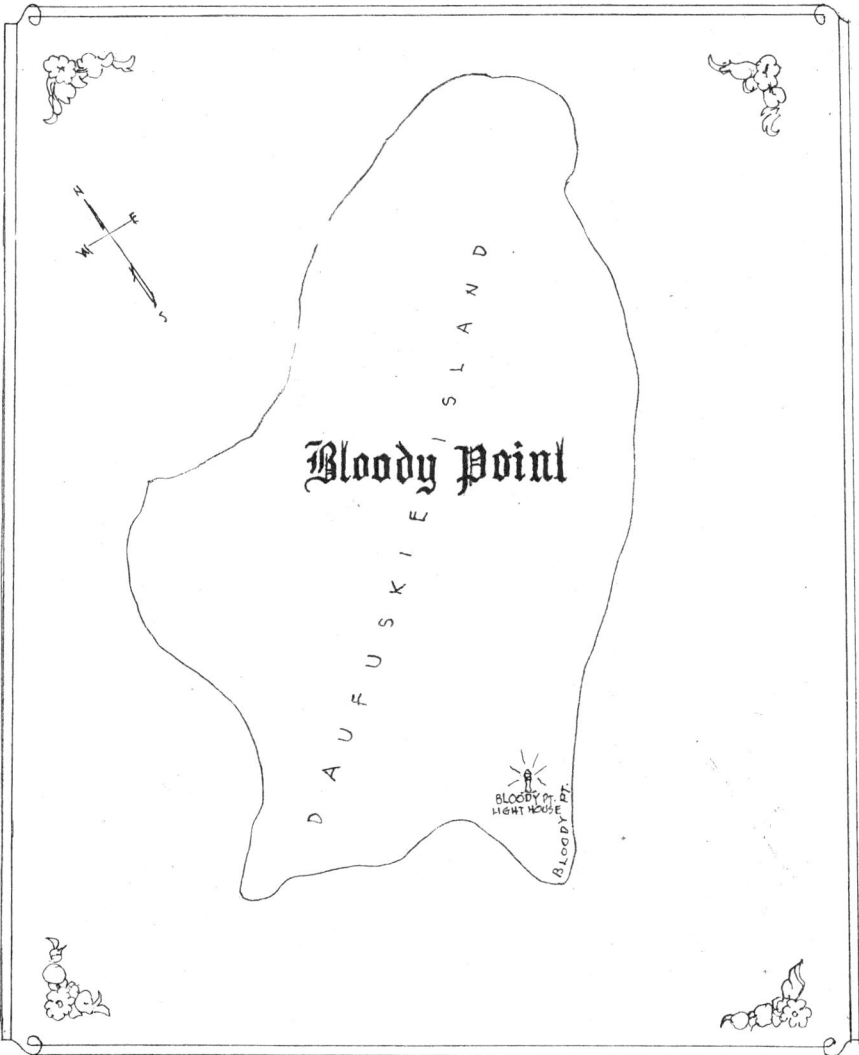

Bloody Point

DAUFUSKIE ISLAND

BLOODY PT. LIGHTHOUSE
BLOODY PT.

(Courtesy of artist Stephen Pennington Bond II—1935.)

Oakley Hall—circa 1874
(Photograph courtesy John [Jack] Stoddard, Noank, Ct.)

136

and property in Georgia. [Watts was tarred and feathered on Daufuskie because he would not join the "Association.]

The date he began is unknown, but in order to learn the shipbuilding trade Simeon Martinangele in 1775 had apprenticed himself out to Charles Watts at Bloody Point. Simeon . . .

had 15 months to serve on his apprenticeship when Watts was forced by the Rebel Committee to give up the indenture and flee Daufuskie.[64]

Robert Watts' wife's name was Jane. Records show that they had two daughters: Jane, who married Richard Hall in 1790 at Bloody Point and Sarah (Sally), who later became the ward of William Edwards Mongin, who lived with his wife Margaret (Martinangele) at her plantation that would later be called Eigleberger.[65]

Oakley Hall Mansion

The mansion at Bloody Point was called Oakley Hall.[66] There is no record as to when or by whom the house was built. Knowing that Robert Watts built his ships of live oak, it would only seem natural that he would also build a house of the same type of lumber, calling it a rather ingenious name to suggest the wood of his trade.

Standing more than a quarter of a mile from the Atlantic Ocean on the south, and near Mongin Creek on the west, the mansion was a wooden, two-story house built over a brick, ground-floor basement.

Completely covering the dirt on the basement floor were huge pieces of four-inch-thick gray slate. In the basement, or ground floor, there were two or more large brick fireplaces where slaves did the cooking. The food to be served was taken through a stairway that led to a "closet" in the upstairs dining room. Also in the basement was a wine cellar and plenty of space for crocks of lard, barrels of different kinds of meat, flour, meal, sugar, and potatoes.

On the first floor were two rooms (twenty-four by twenty-four feet) rooms on either side of a fifteen-foot hall that had a lovely stairway on the left leading up to the second floor. The second floor was built identical to the first, except at the end of the hall, facing the front of the house, was a bathroom complete with tub (with feet), basin, and commode, all made of copper with brass fittings. The water closet hung high on the wall and was flushed by pulling a long chain. Water

used in the bathroom was stored in a four-by-four-by-three-foot lead-lined box that was built into the attic. Slaves kept the tank filled with water. (This bathroom could have been added by the Stoddard family when Oakley Hall came into their possession sometime after 1860.)

The walls were made of plaster on wood lathe. Horsehair was added to the plaster mix to give durability and to prevent cracking. On the first floor were the living room, library, music and dining rooms; on the second floor were the four bedrooms.

In the living room, on the right of the front hall, beautiful cornice work bordered the walls near the ten-foot ceilings and encircled the carbide light chandelier that hung from the center of the room. The chandelier consisted of six small lights. Picture moldings were several feet down from the ceilings on all the walls.

Midway on the inside walls between the rooms, upstairs and down, were lovely black and white marble fireplaces that opened on either side providing heat to each room. Giving entrance into the first floor rooms were seven-foot black cathedral doors.

Wide porches graced the front and back of the house. A windowless attic topped the whole structure. Due to Robert Watts' using all the live oaks on Bloody Point in his shipbuilding trade, there was no oak-lined avenue leading up to the Oakley Hall mansion.

An artesian well on the west side of the house provided an abundant supply of water.

Approximately one hundred fifty feet behind the mansion on the west—or inlet side—was a log cabin that was probably used as "nanny" quarters. Beyond this cabin was a hot house and gardener's cottage and even farther back was the barn.[67]

Toward the northeast and several hundred feet from the mansion, running north and south, was one row of eight slave huts built of wood.[68] They either were torn down or deteriorated after the Civil War.

Sarah Watts, Ward of William Edwards Mongin

Margaret Martinangele Mongin owned two hundred acres of land that later became known as Eigleberger, which was adjacent to Bloody Point. She and William Edwards Mongin had married in 1783 and moved to her Daufuskie plantation mansion. The Mongins were apparently very close friends of Robert Watts, for when he died his

daughter Sarah (Sally) became heir to Bloody Point and a ward of William Edwards Mongin.

John David Mongin (No. 3) and Sarah Watts Marry

William's nephew John David Mongin, living at Walnut Grove on South May River, met Sarah Watts on visits to see his Uncle William and Margaret. He and Sarah fell in love. Their courtship led to a lavish wedding at the Walnut Grove mansion.

Following their marriage in 1790, John David and Sarah moved to Oakley Hall, but not for long. With other plantations and businesses, he entrusted Bloody Point Plantation to an overseer and moved to his house on Warren Square in Savannah. Their only child, David John (No. 4), was born in 1791.

Sarah Dies—John David Inherits Bloody Point

Sarah Watts Mongin died in 1816 leaving John David as heir to her Bloody Point estate. Sarah was buried on Daufuskie, but her body was later moved to Bonaventure Cemetery, Savannah, Georgia.

David John Mongin (No. 4) Marries, Lives at Bloody Point

David John II was only seventeen when his mother died. Daufuskie was a very special place to him, although he frequently visited Walnut Grove with his father. From all indications, being an only child, he was pampered and spoiled, with servants and wealth at his command. He completed his education at Princeton.

Wanting to be married in the same house as his father and mother— on South May River at the Mongin Walnut Grove Plantation mansion—David John II and Sarah Irwin had an elaborate wedding around 1881-1812, then promptly moved to Oakley Hall at Bloody Point.

They had six children born on Daufuskie, but only two lived to maturity—William Henry, born in 1816, and Mary Lavinia, the survivor of twin girls, born in 1819.[69]

With his father John David in full command of all business affairs, and with an overseer successfully operating the plantation, David John II had little or no responsibilities and soon became a victim of alcohol. When one is weak in character with no apparent ambition, the lap of luxury can become a curse and a weapon that destroys.

Jeremiah Evarts Visits David John II: 1822

Jeremiah Evarts (1781-1831) was born in Vermont. He was a teacher, lawyer, philanthropist, and a very religious man throughout his life. He was one of the founders of the American Board of Commissioners for Foreign Missions. He investigated the condition of Indian tribes east of the Mississippi, and strongly opposed the removal of the Cherokees to western reservations. He also visited plantations in the south to see how the slaves were being treated.

It was on one of his trips in 1822 that he, along with a Mr. Eddy (probably a friend living in Savannah who knew the people on this island), visited the plantations on Daufuskie and was a guest of David John Mongin II at Bloody Point.

Mr. Evarts' diary concerning the island is of such interest that it is quoted here in its entirety.

> Tuesday, April 2: At half past one, left Savannah for a visit of a day or two on Dawfuskie, with Mr. Eddy and the family of his host, Mr. Mongin, jun. With five oars we reached the island, 13 miles, against wind and tide, in 4 hours. Thought I feared the passage would be unpleasant, it was not. Saw three alligators, of different sizes. At Mr. Mongin's were a large family of visitors, entertained in the true style of southern hospitality.
>
> Wednesday, April 3: Rode on horseback to the east end of the island, by the road, and back on the beach: 13 miles in the whole: a pleasant excursion, in company with Mr. Eddy. Weather fine.
>
> Thursday, April 4: Took the same ride as yesterday. . . . Attended a meeting of negroes with Mr. E. in the evening.
>
> Friday, April 5: Took a ride of about 4 miles on horseback. At 10 minutes before 4 set out for Savannah in a boat with four negroes. Reached the wharf 5 minutes after 7.
>
> I have resided now three days on a sea-island plantation, where I was treated with all the hospitality, which the owner was master of. The house was large, the rooms airy, the furniture costly, the provisions of the table profusely abundant. I had a horse to ride, and spent my time principally alone and with Mr. Eddy. The master of the house was incapable of society from drinking brandy, and consequent stupidity and ignorance. He had been educated at Princeton College, and is probably somewhat under 40. Every evening he is so far overcome with strong drink, as to be silly, every morning, full of pain, languor, and destitute appetite. The state of the slaves, as physical, intellectual, and

moral beings, is abject beyond my powers of description; yet the state of the master is more to be pitied, as it exposes him to a more aggravated condemnation.

At Mr. Mongin's table there were always a number of visitors and generally some retainers. Food is provided in most abundant quantities, and in great variety. I observed not fewer than 10 or 12 hot dishes for breakfast and supper, besides many cold ones. These dishes were generally excellent in their kinds. The bill of fare was as follows:

Beef steaks broiled, and others fried, three times a day; cold ham and sliced corned beef also at every meal. Often stewed and roasted oysters, boiled and fried fresh fish, crabs, shrimps.

Coffee and tea, both morning and evening, waffles, buck wheat cakes, hominy, toast, and wheat bread at breakfast; the same thing at tea, omitting hominy and buckwheat cakes, and adding corn meal and wheat flour cakes.

How all these things could be cooked would puzzle a northern man to tell. I was once in the kitchen, and could not see half utensils enough to cook a common article with ease. Yet the cooking was always well done, and with great regularity as to time. Slaves have few conveniences for any kind of labor. They are obliged to do everything by the hardest.

It was not a pleasant thought, that while such unlimited profusion reigned on the table of the master, a large portion of his slaves rarely tasted flesh. At Christmas, indeed, all are feasted, but generally the fare of plantation slaves is coarse and scanty.

The furniture of this mansion was expensive, but was little attended to. The general aspect of things indicated slackness, and listlessness. There seemed to be no enjoyment in the place. Nothing like cheerfulness was seen.

Mrs. M. recently professed religion, and appeared seriously engaged in it. She seemed a prey to affliction, and took little interest in what was going forward.

Condition of Blacks

... In my repeated rides I have seen many negroes. Those on the plantations near Savannah appear to be in a very abject condition. The young appear cheerful—the aged very miserable. Their poor bodies appear to be worn out, by hard service and scanty fare, while their minds are in perpetual infancy, not having advanced toward enlarged thought, or made the least progress as immortal beings.

Mr. Eddy says, that the negroes on the islands are generally through their tasks by 2 o'clock; that they have as much land as they can till for their own use, and that they might be in very comfortable circumstances

if they were industrious. Everything which they can carry to market, is sold for liquor.

In one of my excursions, I counted 25 slaves at work in one field. The females have the same tasks assigned them as the males. The clothing of almost all the negroes out of town is very wretched, always coarse and dirty, and generally old and tattered.

I have just returned from an excursion of three days on an island, on which are several cotton plantations. The situation of the slaves is more abject and degraded than I had ever supposed. I refer not to cruelty (of which instances are not lacking), but to that incomparable ignorance, which must exist, of course, where there is a total want of instruction of every kind; where there is no thought or reflection; and where every germ of enterprize is crushed by harsh and contemptuous treatment. Yet I am fully convinced, that there are no difficulties but moral ones, in the way of a thorough renovation of this whole southern country; and these God can remove, by the mild and gracious operations of his Providence, whenever he sees best. Let every possible mean be used by his children, and the work will proceed. But every scheme of meliorating the condition of the slaveholding country without the aid of the Gospel must be chimerical. The first step in the process is to get a competent number of religious teachers, who will cheerfully and heartily devote themselves to the work; and this number is much greater than has ever been estimated. One minister of the Gospel to 1000 people is by no means enough; unless the deficiency be made up by intelligent catechists. It is greatly to be desired, that as many pious young men, natives of the southern states, as God shall endue with the requisite qualifications, may be employed as spiritual teachers of their countrymen. They have many advantages over northern young men; as they are able to bear the climate, and there are fewer projudices against their efforts. But, in the present state of things, how are these young men to be prepared for the work? How are the rising generation to become religious? The means of a religion are not enjoyed; the youth are tempted in a thousand ways to a life of idleness and sensuality; and even the pious have little energy, and little perserverance. To those who come from the north, the whole employment seems like an exile; and they hasten back, with all possible speed, to the land of their fathers.

In the meantime, the instruction of the blacks is a slow process, and requires uncommon disinterestedness and patience and self-denial. Still it implies no impossibility. If all Christians would engage in the work of renovating every part of our own country, they would find that God would interpose in their behalf, and by new methods would carry forward the plans of infinite benevolence.[70]

David John (No. 4) Dies; Widow Remarries

In 1823 David John succumbed to alcohol at the age of thirty-two. Buried on Daufuskie, his body was later interred at Bonaventure Cemetery, Savannah.

Sarah Irwin Mongin, David John's widow, married the Reverend Herman M. Blodgett in 1825. It could be that Blodgett was a pastor at the white church on Melrose property. For a marriage settlement, Sarah was given Haig's Point and Freeport Plantations, as they had belonged to her husband David John.

Death of Sarah Blodgett and John David Mongin (No. 3)

Sarah and the Reverend Blodgett moved to the small Haig's Point mansion which put John David Mongin (No. 3) back in full possession of Bloody Point. The plantation was managed by overseers until John David's death in 1833. Sarah Irwin-Mongin-Blodgett also died in 1833, leaving her children, William Henry and Mary Lavinia Mongin, as sole heirs of their mother's and grandfather's vast estate. From Sarah's heirs, the Reverend Herman M. Blodgett bought Haig's Point and Freeport plantations.

William Henry Marries, Moves to Bloody Point

William became heir to several plantations, among which was Bloody Point. In 1836 William Henry Mongin married Isabella Rae Habersham in Savannah. They moved to Oakley Hall and became planters of this plantation. Proof of their living here is found in a letter that Catharine Blodgett (Herman's second wife) had written to her sister, 16 January 1838:

> . . . We reached Bloody Point (Mr. [Wm. Henry] Mongin's) in somewhat more than two hours, dined and left the children there to pass some days with their friends. . . . [71]

William and Isabella divided their time between Bloody Point and his other inherited plantations in Chatham and McIntosh Counties, Georgia.

William Henry Dies; Isabella Is Bloody Point Planter

They had no children. In 1851 William Henry Mongin died and in his will his wife Isabella was to live at Bloody Point as long as she

chose, and then it was to go to his nephew, Mary Lavinia Stoddard's youngest son, Henry Mongin Stoddard, who also was to share equally with her other children in William Henry's remaining plantations.[72]

Recorded in the census of 1860, Isabella Mongin is listed as a "planter," but vacated Bloody Point before the Civil War.

Bloody Point Confiscated by Northern Troops

Confiscated as abandoned lands and for non-payment of taxes, Bloody Point remained in the possession of the Union Army until John Stoddard redeemed it along with his plantations in 1866.

Henry Mongin Stoddard Claims Bloody Point

With no slaves to work the land, apparently Isabella Habersham Mongin gave up all interest in Bloody Point. On 1 April 1867, Henry Mongin Stoddard was pardoned by Andrew Johnson, President of the United States.[73] This pardon gave Henry the right to claim his Bloody Point inheritance from his deceased uncle, William Henry Mongin. Henry Mongin moved to Oakley Hall, using it as a summer or country home. In a local newspaper ran the following item of interest:

> The steamship *Cleopatra* brought out for H. M. Stoddard, Esq., a steam yacht called the *Spitfire* of Bloody Point, built by Herreshoff Meft., Company of Bristol, R. I. She has made a satisfactory trial trip from Bristol to N. Y. The *Spitfire* is intended for the owner's private use between Savannah and his place on Daufuskie Island.[74]

Whether Henry actually planted Bloody Point is unknown, but he was a party person and kept Oakley Hall jumping with gaiety from private parties to groups that came from Savannah. The following account relates one of such outings:[75]

> This is a sketch of Savannah, a charming old Southern city in the decade between 1880 and 1890. The writer has selected that decade particularly, for two reasons, first, because it shows what a quick reaction Savannah made socially and economically in the fifteen years following the close of the "War Between the States" and secondly, because she has had access to a diary, also old notes, and theatre programs of that period which give her the opportunity to draw a true picture of Society in Savannah at that time.
>
> Daufuskie Island at that time was owned by the Stoddard brothers, Messrs. Harry and Albert Stoddard. "Melrose," the home of Mr. Albert

Stoddard, was at the north end of the island, and Bloody Point at the southern end was owned by Mr. Harry [Henry Mongin] Stoddard. Between the two was Mr. John I Stoddard's place "Oak Ridge" [Eigleberger].

. . . The island, like all of our coastal golden isles, is beautifully wooded, and the beach cannot be surpassed.

Every spring Mr. Harry Stoddard would offer his place, Bloody Point, to the officers of the "German Club" for a picnic, and that affair was the winding up of the social season. The Club chartered a large river boat which left the wharf at the foot of Abecorn Street about 9:30 A. M. The Daufuskie Picnic was regarded as such an elegant affair that everyone wore his or her best. As in the case of the Germans, each girl was asked weeks ahead of time by her partner for the day, who called for her, looked after her all day and escorted her home after the return trip to Savannah.

The regular chaperones of the Club were always there, as well as many other persons who were invited. There were always between two and three hundred persons attending. The tide and moon played an important part in the selection of the date as the boat had to make a landing on the back river according to a high tide on arriving in the morning, and in departing at night.

That annual Picnic was a gay party, for the music never seemed to stop. It was furnished by an orchestra[76] and a brass band. A piano, for the orchestra, was carried to the boat at Savannah and a wagon was at the Daufuskie wharf ready to haul it to the house. The dancing was in the house and the piano was placed in the parlor.

The house was a large two-story one with two rooms on either side of a long hall and the dressing rooms were upstairs. Dancing continued all day except at luncheon time. First the orchestra in the house would play, and when that stopped, the brass band which was just below the house under the trees, would begin, and so on and off all day.

The luncheon was served at the rear of the house under the trees, and was placed on long tables covered with white table cloths. The matrons vied with each other in the quality and quantity of the food, which really could not have been excelled. The Club furnished champagne.

About half-past six the band played a march which was the signal for everyone to go down to the beach, which was only two or three hundred yards from the house, and there the Master of Ceremonies arranged a long double line for the Virginia Reel. Old and young took part in this dance and it made a merry ending before boarding the boat for the homeward trip.

145

On the way back groups of young people sang college songs or the songs of the day, or many of the songs from Gilbert and Sullivan operas much in vogue at that time, until the boat docked at the wharf in Savannah.

The above description seems hardly adequate for such an affair, which was known of throughout the Southern Coastal States, even Ward McAllister of New York (whose family were originally from Savannah), in his book "Society as I have Found It," referred to the Daufuskie Picnic in the following words,"A Savannah Picnic, which is an institution peculiar to the place.[77]

Martha G. Waring's Version of Bloody Point Soiree

Martha gives a more personal insight of one of the parties held at Bloody Point:

The soirees, before mentioned, were the most formal dances of the winter season, and to the last one was awarded the honour of being the Moonlight Picnic at Daufuskie Island, the home of the Stoddard family. Picture to yourselves the beaux and belles of the [18] seventies boarding a steamboat from a wharf at the river front in mid-afternoon; the men in just the proper outfit for that hour; the ladies in gala costumes of muslin or piqué. One of these belles thus describes a Daufuskie picnic of her young lady-hood: "We had a good band on board and danced on the way down the river. The girls wore lovely big hats trimmed with flowers, and the neat stylish dresses are white pique elaborately trimmed with patterns in black or write braid. When we landed at Daufuskie we usually went to Mr. Harry's house or sometime to Mr. Albert's as Mr. John's was too far away. We danced on the beach, square dances, of course, until time for supper, which was eaten there, and it was always a wonderful spread of good things. After supper we danced or strolled on the beach until time to get on the boat and go home. Some funny things happened, sometimes. One very dignified old gentleman had his wig blown off. The wind rolled it on the smooth beach sand like a child's hoop while he gave chase—very bald, furiously angry, and as red as a turkey cock. There were then, she said shyly, no beach costumes and no slacks or shorts, not even in manners.[78]

Flower Gardens and Avenues at Oakley Hall

It was Henry Mongin Stoddard who had his father's English gardener to landscape the yards at Bloody Point mansion. In the front of the house was a round mound tiered and filled with all kinds of

Pictures of Walks, Gardens, and Avenues—Bloody Point Mansion, "Oakley Hall"

Camellia tree—southeast garden.

From front piazza.

One of three walks in front of house.

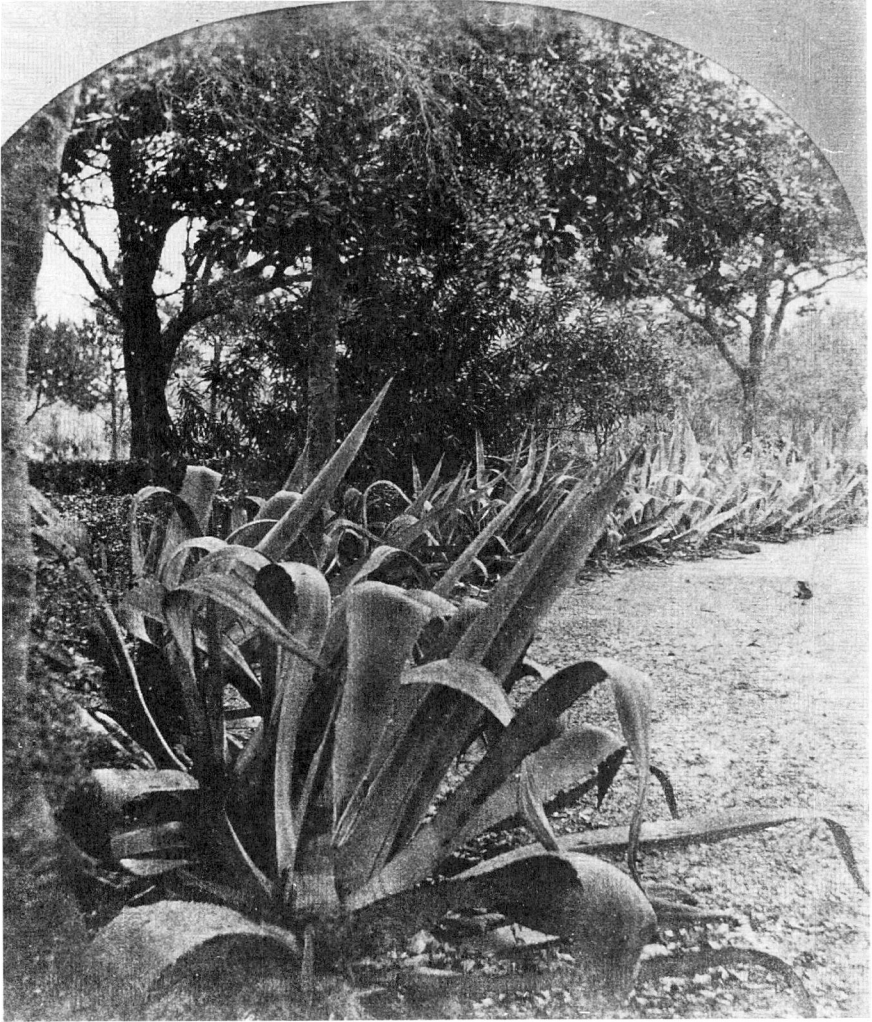

Century plants north side of front sweep.

From stable to dwelling.

Taken from back door.

Left: Rifle gallery. Right: From back door to stable—the part nearest the dwelling.

Serpentine walk.

Avenue from back door to river landing.

Left: From back door to old boat-house via labyrinth view of river. Right: Avenue from outhouse to dwelling.

flowers. Radiating out from this were three avenues: an avenue of cedars trimmed and trained to form an arch, ran a quarter of a mile east to the Atlantic Ocean; two other avenues ran south and west, bordered with hedges, forming flower beds filled with bulbs and other flowers. A summer house trimmed with cypress knees stood on the west near Mongin Creek. Ward McAllister stated that there were five acres of roses.[79] Along the north side of the front sweep of the house ran a row of fifty or more century plants. A profusion of japonicas, azaleas, shrubs, and fruit trees graced the yards. There was also a rifle gallery, an avenue to the stables and barn, a serpentine walk, and an avenue from the back door to the old boat house on Mongin Creek. The gardens were just too beautiful to put into words.

Henry M. Stoddard Sells Land to Government

For a light house to be built on the south end of Daufuskie, on 14 April 1882, Henry Mongin Stoddard sold to the United States government for $425.00, two pieces of Bloody Point land consisting of 1.72 acres on the beach for the Front Beacon Range, including a 4,350 foot right-of-way to a five-acre tract inland for the Rear Beacon Range.[80] (See the Bloody Point Lighthouse segment for further detail.)

Henry Mongin Stoddard Sells Land to John Michael Doyle

In the extreme southwest corner of Bloody Point, for the sum of $200.00 on 11 February 1891, Henry Mongin Stoddard sold ten acres of land to John Michael Doyle, who was responsible for the erection of the Bloody Point Rear Range Light tower.

This ten acres of land changed hands several times, from Doyle to Margaret E. Fripp (1893); from Fripp to Martha S. Sisson (1908); from Sisson to Mrs. H. R. Padgett (1910); from Padgett to Icim Donald Goodwin (1915); from Goodwin to Thomas Lee Harley (1915). The last sale of the land was in 1927 from Harley to Arthur A. Burn, who named it "The Little Place."[81] It is now in the possession of two of his children, Francis A. Burn, Sr., and Leonella Burn Padgett.

The Storm of 1893

During the storm of 1893, like Melrose, the house stood firm, but the water that inundated the island swept away most of the gardens at

Bloody Point. They were replaced to some extent but were never like they were previously.

Edward Stoddard in Control of Bloody Point

It was Edward Stoddard, the son of Henry Mongin Stoddard, who the people on the island remember most. It was to him they paid twenty-five cents for each task (one fourth acre) of ground rented in order to grow the food they needed. Mrs. Sarah Grant said that one had to really hustle about in the spring to rent land, as there was not enough for everyone. Edward rented it out on a "first come, first serve" basis. What happened with the black people was that the majority of them only owned one-to-five-acre plots, which was not enough to grow the produce needed for themselves and their animals, and have a surplus to sell at the Savannah market.

Oakley Hall Rented to Jim and Annie White

Not only did Edward Stoddard rent out the land, he also rented out Oakley Hall to various white families who wanted to farm. The Whites had come from Bluffton to the island in 1901, bringing with them four children: Frank, Inez, Alease, and Hinson. Born on the island were George, Clarence, Allen and Alene (twins), and Fred, who was born in 1911 at Bloody Point.

When the family first arrived on Daufuskie, they lived in a "salt box" type house at Rabbit Point.

During the Whites' stay at Oakley Hall, they used the brick basement for their kitchen and did all of the cooking in one of its huge fireplaces.

They were living here when Dr. William E. Diller of New York decided to build a cottage on his Oak Ridge property. While building the doctor's house, the carpenters boarded with the Whites at Bloody Point. In 1914 Jim and Annie White bought land, built a house, and moved their family to Maryfield.[82]

Lanes Move to Bloody Point

Shortly after the Whites left, George and Hattie Avant-Lane settled in at Bloody Point in 1915, farming and raising a lot of cattle. They brought with them eight children: Braddie, Leonard, Janie and

Eugene (twins), Corrine and Irene (twins), Myrtle and Lola. With the aid of a black midwife, Mrs. Lane gave birth to a son, James W. Lane in June 1917.

Wesley Avant, Mrs. Lane's brother, was a preacher and held services in the little white Daufuskie School.

While the Lanes lived on the island, two black women, Phyllis Hudson and "Mom" Pender Hamilton, cooked and helped them with the housework. Two boats, the *Attaquin* and the *Louise*, supplied their transportation to and from the island.

In January 1919 Hattie Avant-Lane, carrying her tenth child, died with influenza and was buried just west of Margaret and Ashley Burn in Mary Dunn Cemetery.

After Mrs. Lane's death, the family remained only one year, leaving for Savannah in 1920.[83]

Goodwins: The Last Family to Live at Oakley Hall

In 1925 Capt. Marion E. Boyd of Savannah moved Jim and Lula Goodwin to Daufuskie. The Goodwins had a bunch of children: Ethel, Oscar, Ned, B. S., Juanita, Barney, and twins Lucy and James. Capt. Boyd stated that after they finished unloading all of the furniture, everyone was very tired and hungry as a bear. Rummaging through all of her packing boxes, Mrs. Goodwin managed to find a loaf of bread and a can of condensed milk. She spread the milk on the bread and shared with all. Capt. Boyd said it was delicious—the best thing he had ever tasted.

Through the years the Goodwins rented Melrose, lived at Jack Rowe Island a couple of times, moved into the house with the Arthur A. Burn family at the Bloody Point Lighthouse, then rented Oakley Hall mansion sometime in the early 1930s. They continued to farm Bloody Point until circa 1938 when they bought land and moved in their own house at Benjie's Point.[84]

Oakley Hall Torn Down

Before the Goodwins moved out, Oakley Hall was beginning to need major repairs and water was lapping up under the front porch. For $90.00 Edward S. Stoddard sold the mansion to Emil Cetchovich, Sr., who tore it down sometime between 1937 and 1939. Oakley Hall was no more. To give an idea of its age, Mr. Cetchovich stated that the

structure of the house was put together with oak pegs—not one nail was used.

In order to have more land to farm, the black people continued to rent tasks of Bloody Point land until 1940.

Stoddards Sell Bloody Point to Morton Deutsch

On 14 January 1957 Edward S. and Ethel B. Stoddard (children of Henry Mongin Stoddard) sold Bloody Point to Morton Deutsch for the sum of $10,500.00. Morton in turn sold it for the same price to Surfside Development Company, the title later reverting to Morton.[85]

Morton was quite a character. Leaving the Savannah wharf, heading for Daufuskie in the 1950s, I met him while we were riding on the boat *Bessie M. Lewis*. Morton looked to be about 5'11" tall, 175 pounds, a rather nice looking man with a beaked nose. To complete his attire he wore a fedora and a topcoat. It amused me that he had a small compass to direct his way should he get lost on Bloody Point. As open and cleared as that land was, I chuckled to think that anyone could get lost there.

Bloody Point had somewhat eroded through the years and Morton wrote to the Beaufort Tax Office and instructed them not to bill him for the 519 acres that he originally purchased, but to reduce the acreage for the erosion, so that his taxes would not be so high. Then, when he considered selling Bloody Point, he requested them to put the acreage back to the original amount so that he could get more money for it.

If Morton was getting mail that he did not want, he would call the postmaster in Savannah and give him a bad time, informing him in no uncertain terms not to let the mail carrier bring that trash to his door. And, he insisted that "mail be delivered at residences, at a fixed time, day after day, and not before the sun is high in the heavens."

For sometime this lumber company had been after Morton to sell them timber rights on his Bloody Point property. Morton refused. But on one particular occasion the same lumber company had come to Daufuskie to cut other timber. Their workers had been misguided and erroneously had cut down ten trees on Bloody Point. Morton was furious. He had his lawyer sue them. The court awarded Morton $1,000.00 per tree.

A Beaufort surveyor was hired to survey Oak Ridge. That is sepa-

rated from Bloody Point by the beach road, which Morton owned. When Morton heard about this, he contacted the surveyor and asked him if he walked down his road. They surveyor informed Morton that he had to walk the road in order to complete the survey. Morton said, "Well, you'd better get you a lawyer for I'm going to sue you."

Morton owned several rent houses in Savannah. He would let them run down and the city would request that he either repair them or board them up. He was forever in the news.

In 1983 a letter was written to Morton, asking him if he would please

Bloody Point's "Oakley Hall" in disrepair, 1930s. Torn down by Emil Cetchovich I, circa 1942.

send copies of some of his Bloody Point history. The letters that were received from him were rambling, and he wrote absolutely nothing of the history that had been requested. After exchanging several letters, I just gave up hope that he would ever share what he knew.

Hidden behind his acid tongue and pen was a Morton Deutsch who had a benevolent heart. He donated Pine and Page Islands to the Scottish Rite Hospital for Crippled Children in Atlanta. (Not being in

the real estate business, the hospital sold the islands and used the money to enlarge their facilities.)

Morton donated large contributions for construction of wings to several hospitals, including Emory in Atlanta and a hospital in Israel. He also donated land to the United States Government for (Savannah) Hunter Field Army Base on White Bluff Road.

In 1977 Morton signed an agreement with Hebrew Union College, promising them his Bloody Point land in exchange for the college endowing a chair in the name of Morton and his deceased parents; making repairs to the gravestone of his grandfather in Jerusalem; providing for his nursing and medical care in his later years; and publishing a book that he had written.

Morton contacted Alfred Gottschalk, president of Hebrew Union College, in September 1985, and informed him that he was ready to execute a deed conveying Bloody Point to them. But when Gottschalk arrived on 6 September 1985 and presented Morton with a deed to execute—he refused. It seems that the stipulations that Morton had made had not been carried out.

Because of ill health, on 10 September 1985, Morton was appointed a guardian, Louis R. Alexander of Savannah.

He remained a bachelor, but one admirable thing that Morton did was to take care of his mother until her death. He objected to anyone's presence in his home. With all of his wealth, he chose to live secluded and almost in poverty in a white clapboard house, 14 E. 40th Street, until he could no longer remain alone.

Morton had a chronic ailment. Being partially paralyzed kept him in a wheel chair and a part time resident of Azalealand Nursing Home. He was in and out of the hospital at intervals before his death, 1 January 1987, at the age of ninety-three. Morton Deutsch had to be admired, for in spite of his affliction he continued to be very witty, and until the ultimate end he had a mind like a steel trap.

After his death, the Hebrew Union College wanted to claim Morton Deutsch's property, which included Bloody Point (519 acres) and Oaklawn (Eigleberger—200 acres), but he had never signed a deed. After much controversy, and the finding of a relative, S. Richard Morrison—a first cousin once removed—a settlement out of court called for the properties to be sold.[86]

On 28 July 1988, heirs of Morton Deutsch sold to Bloody Point Limited Partnership, c/o The Melrose Company, Inc., Bloody Point and Oaklawn Plantations (741.02 acres) for the sum of $6,865,400.[87]

Martinangele Plantations

Through the years, the 500-acre Martinangele tract was at times divided and known as Eigleberger, Twins Point, and Mary Dunn Plantations.

From Lancelot Bland in 1762, Mary Foster Martinangele purchased 500 acres of land on Daufuskie; the property was situated in the extreme southwest corner of the island, bordering on New River and Mongin Creek, then extending to the public road that separated it from Bloody Point.

Mary brought with her her eight children:

Francis, 18; Mary, 17; Phillip, Jr., 15; Thomas (?), 13; Isaac, 10; Abraham, 8; Simeon, 5; and Margaret, 3. It is believed that Mary F. Martinangele built a mansion on Mongin Creek nearest Bloody Point.

A census on the eve of the Revolution lists Mary as being a "widow." All of her sons except Thomas are listed as "farmers."

Phillip Martinangele, Jr., was murdered in 1781 during the Revolution.

Although there is no record, Francis was presumably dead, for on 5 November 1785 Mary Foster Martinangele had her land surveyed by Sam Wilkins, giving one hundred acres each to her five remaining children: Margaret Mongin, Mary Hopkins, Isaac, Abraham, and Simeon.[88]

Eigleberger Plantation

Margaret Martinangele Mongin was given the one hundred acres that possibly contained the family mansion. Her sister, Mary Hopkins, apparently sold Margaret her one hundred acres, which increased Margaret's tract to 200 acres. Margaret married William Edwards Mongin in 1783 and gave birth to nine children. After her death in 1801, her heirs sold her property to Christian Eigleberger, after whom the plantation was named, thus taking it out of Martinangele ownership. At Eigleberger's death, George Sterly (Stearly), administrator of the estate, had William Joyner, Commissioner of the Beaufort Court of Equity, offer the property for Public Auction. On 7 March

Eigleberger, Home of John I Stoddard, 1869-1888

(Stereoscopic photograph, compliments John [Jack] Stoddard, 21 March 1982.)

Eigleberger Gazebo on Mongin Creek
Decorated with cypress knees from Bloody Point's summer house.
(Stereoscopic photograph, compliments John [Jack] Stoddard, 21 March 1982.)

1831, William E. Mongin's half-nephew, John David Mongin (No. 3), being the highest bidder, purchased Eigleberger for the sum of $2,000.[89]

When John David died (1833), it became the property of his granddaughter, Mary Lavinia Mongin Stoddard, who died in 1865. In the distribution of her mother's property, 23 November 1868, Eigleberger was given to Isabelle Stoddard Green,[90] who on 9 March 1869 exchanged it to her brother, John Irwin Stoddard, for his Estate of Webb tract (later Benjie's Point).[91]

John I. Stoddard Calls Plantation Oak Ridge

A strange thing happened when Eigleberger became the property of John I. Stoddard. For some unknown reason he called it Oak Ridge, after the plantation by the same name that was situated between Bloody Point on the south and Melrose on the north. All of the older black people on the island today refer to Eigleberger as Oak Ridge, because they worked at an oyster shucking house there, circa 1880-1940.

Samuel K. and Mary E. Rich Buy Eigleberger

In 1888, for the sum of $6,000.00, John I. Stoddard sold Eigleberger to Samuel K. and Mary E. Rich.[92]

Snellings Purchase Eigleberger

In 1890 Samuel K. and Mary E. Rich sold Eigleberger to Alonzo F. and Annie E. Snelling.[93]

Richard Fuller Fripp, Sr., Buys Eigleberger

In 1893, for the sum of $3,000.00, Alonzo F. and Annie E. Snelling sold Eigleberger to Richard Fuller Fripp, Sr.,[94] thus putting the plantation back in Martinangele hands, since Fuller's wife Margaret E. Chaplin was the great-granddaughter of Isaac Martinangele. Fuller changed the name of the one-hundred-acre tract to Oaklawn. The Eigleberger mansion burned during Fuller Fripp's ownership.

At the death of Richard Fuller Fripp, Sr. (1922), his daughter Margaret M. Fripp inherited Oaklawn.

In 1923, Margaret deeded one hundred acres of Oaklawn to her

brother Richard Fuller Fripp, Jr., and fifty acres each to her niece and nephew, Laura and Claude Francis Fripp, children of her deceased brother, John Francis Fripp.[95]

At the death of Richard Fuller Fripp, Jr., in 1928, Laura and her brother Claude became heirs of Oaklawn. Laura married William (Bill) Timmons.

Morton Deutsch Buys Oaklawn

In 1947 Laura F. Timmons and Claude Fripp sold Oaklawn (Eigleberger) to Morton Deutsch for $3,000.00,[96] removing the plantation from Martinangele ownership forever.

Morton Deutsch's Heir Sells to Melrose Company

Morton Deutsch died 1 January 1987. His heir sold Oaklawn to Bloody Point Limited Partnership, c/o The Melrose Company, Inc., on 28 July 1988.[97]

Twins Point Plantation

Simeon Martinangele was given one hundred acres bordering New River on the west and Mongin Creek on the south. His tract included a small island on the south from which he derived the name of Twins Point. Abraham sold his adjacent one hundred acres to Simeon which gave Twins Point two hundred acres.

Simeon had married Love Tucker Rowland in 1785. From Charles A. Lebey family records, after Simeon's death (no record), Love leased Twins Point to Christian David Lebey, 3 January 1818. Simeon's Will was found (see end of Martinangele segment), leaving Love sole heir to her husband's estate. At her death (1823), the 200-acre tract was equally distributed to the children of Simeon's brother, Isaac.

Mary Dunn Plantation

There is no record of Isaac Martinangele having given his one hundred acres of land a name. Isaac died in 1796. His wife Elizabeth died in 1847. Isaac's land was divided between their children: Phillip IV, Mary Dunn, Love Mount, Isaac, Jr., Mary Ann Grimball, and Harriet Chaplin.

There is no mention as to what happened to Isaac, Jr., but we know

that son Phillip IV who was killed by lightning in 1852 was a bachelor. Through a partnership, Phillip and Mary Dunn had invested in buying out their sister Love's shares, with the understanding that if either should die, the property would automatically belong to the survivor. Thus, Mary Dunn was the beneficiary of all of her brother Phillip's property.

Mary Martinangele, who had married Francis Dunn in 1807, not only bought out her sister's shares of their father's estate, but she also bought out shares the sisters had received from their Uncle Simeon's Twins Point—thus giving Mary Martinangele Dunn full possession of a three-hundred-acre plantation named after her. Mary M. Dunn was a planter until the Civil War, when her land was confiscated by the Union Army. The plantation was redeemed by Mary sometime during or after 1867.

On 17 November 1874, for the sum of $1,200.00, Mary M. Dunn sold her 300-acre plantation, "except the burial ground which contains four acres more or less" to her brother-in-law William Fripp Chaplin, Sr., who had been the husband of her sister, Harriet, now deceased.

Prospect Hill Subdivision

William Fripp Chaplin, Sr., had the 296 acres of the Mary Dunn Plantation surveyed by F. S. Williams (1874), subdivided into thirty-one lots, and renamed it Prospect Hill, thus ending the Mary Dunn Plantation.[99]

The majority of the lots were sold to black people, most of whom were Mary Dunn's former slaves. Aaron Miller (black man) purchased thirteen acres that contained the Mary Dunn mansion, tearing it down sometime in the 1920s-30s. Miller heirs sold the property to Mary Fee Barbee in the 1960s and it remains in her possession.

Richard Fuller Fripp, Sr., purchased (as Trustee for his wife Margaret E. Chaplin Fripp) Lots 22-24, 27-31, consisting of eighty acres, becoming known as the Fuller Fripp Place.[100] Through a course of events, a home and fifty-four acres belonged to Fuller's son, John, with John's daughter, Laura, falling heir to Fuller's home and thirty acres. In 1927 Edward Gary and Gillian White Ward bought from Juanita Goodwin Fripp, John's widow, the house and 53.1 acres of land. In 1947, Laura Fripp Timmons sold the Fuller Fripp house and 30 acres (more or less) to Lance and Billie Burn.

Piney Islands Plantation

Consisting of 240 acres, Piney Islands Plantation was on the western side of Daufuskie and in the possession of the Martinangele family for many decades.

Records show that in 1801 John Andrew Mongin, son of David Mongin (No. 1) by his second wife Elizabeth Edwards, purchased Piney Islands from the estate of Rebecca Davies Stebbins and her son Edward Thomas Lloyd Davies.[101]

John Andrew Mongin probably farmed the plantation, selling it to Jesse Mount, third husband of Love Martinangele, Isaac Martinangele's daughter.

On 23 April 1849 Jesse sold Piney Islands to James Peto Chaplin I, son of Love's sister, Harriet Martinangele Chaplin.[102] J. P. Chaplin I, owning several slaves, operated a very successful cotton plantation. Chaplin grandchildren relate stories handed down by their grandparents of hearing the slaves singing in perfect harmony, their voices resounding across the still waters in the early evening.

Ram's Horn Creek Widened

James P. Chaplin I died in 1865. His widow, Mary Rhodes Chaplin, and daughters Harriet L. Fripp and Margaret E. Fripp (who had married brothers) sell their interest in Piney Islands Plantation to James Peto Chaplin II, 20 February 1890.[103]

From injuries received when his horse fell on him, James P. Chaplin II died in Savannah, 1919. On 30 October 1923, his widow, Tallulah C. Chaplin, and children James P. Chaplin III, Robert Lee, William F., Mary F. Robertson, Georgia C. Padgett, and Virginia C. Wright, sold "right and easement" to the Corps of Engineers, Savannah, Georgia, to enter, cut away, and remove a strip of land on the northern shore of Ram's Horn Creek "needed to straighten the creek for a cut-off" into Cooper River for the Intracoastal Water Route.[104]

Captain Butler was in charge of the *Creighton* dredge and crew that did the blasting and dredging, and when the cut-off was completed, they named it after him, calling it Butler's Cut.[105] However, the name did not stick but reverted to its original name of Ram's Horn Creek.

Chaplins Sell Piney Islands Plantation

In 1926, Tallulah C. Chaplin, James P. Chaplin III, William F. Chaplin, et al., sold their remaining interest on Daufuskie to Charles J. Butler.[106]

Morton Deutsch purchased Pine and Page Islands and in 1981 donated them to the Scottish Rite Crippled Children's Hospital in Atlanta.[107] In 1984 that institution sold both islands to United Coal Company and James Wedgeworth.[108]

Cooper River Place

This land was part of the Ash/Livingston/Fraser property, consisting of 483.84 acres, plus 300 acres of salt marsh. No one knows just when it was purchased, but Cooper River Place was listed as one of his plantations after John David Mongin (No. 3) died in 1833.[109]

John David's grandson, William Henry Mongin, inherited the plantation and after his death it was given to Henry (Harry) Mongin Stoddard, son of Mary Lavinia Mongin Stoddard, William Henry Mongin's sister.

Shown on an 1850 map is a two-story mansion (on the approximate spot as the present Sam Stevens/Wick Scurry building), but who built it and lived there during slavery-time is unknown.[110]

Confiscated during the War, the plantation was redeemed circa 1867 by John Stoddard, Henry Mongin's father.

Cooper River Place was later divided into small tracts and sold to former slaves and others. Cato McIntyre bought Parcel No. 4 that contained the mansion,[111] which completely burned down in the 1940s.[112]

Maryfield Plantation

Maryfield was purchased by John David Mongin (No. 3) from the sale of Richard Russell Ashe's property, 1818.[113]

At John David's death in 1833 it became the property of his granddaughter, Mary Lavinia Mongin Stoddard.

Confiscated during the Civil War, Maryfield was redeemed by Mary's husband, John Stoddard, then given to their son, John I. Stoddard.

Consisting of 530 acres, Maryfield Plantation was surveyed and laid

off in forty-two lots which were sold to former slaves and their families.[114]

Newburgh or Webb Tract

It has already been stated that Richard Russell Ash owned this land, but at his demise his sister, Mary Ash Fraser, wife of Dr. James Fraser, had the land surveyed and named this 740-acre plantation, Newburgh.[115]

The 1806 plat shows a large house at Rabbit Point, but just who built it is unknown.

When the Richard R. Ash property sold in the Court of Equity, Charleston, 1818, it is believed (no proof) that Samuel B. Webb purchased Newburgh the same time that John David Mongin (No. 3) purchased the other three plantations—Melrose, Maryfield, and Oak Ridge.

Someone was living there and planting watermelons on Webb Tract for in Albert Stoddard's "Gullah Tales," this Melrose female slave walked to Rabbit Point (Webb Tract) just a buy a melon.[116]

Abraham Martinangele's daughter, Mary Elizabeth, married George Stoney, brother of James and John, sons of Capt. Jack Stoney.[117]

George and Elizabeth Stoney lived at Daufuskie and are shown here on the 1800 census. The Stoneys had three daughters, one of whom, Mary Elizabeth, became the second wife of Samuel B. Webb circa 1820.[118]

Samuel and Mary Elizabeth Stoney lived in a mansion on Daufuskie within a mile of the beach. Jeremiah Evarts confirmed this when he visited the island in 1822, thus recording in this diary:

> Took the same [horseback] ride as yesterday [along the beach], except that we [he and a Mr. Eddy] turned off to *Mr. Webb's* about three-quarters of a mile to the left. . . .[119]

According to family records, Samuel and Elizabeth had five children. The youngest, George S. Webb, as stated in the 1860 census, was born on Daufuskie in 1832.[120]

Samuel B. Webb died in 1836 and "Mrs. S. Webb" is shown as head of household on Daufuskie in the 1840 census.

On 5 December 1844 there is a record of a marriage contract

between Samuel's daughter, Elizabeth Lydia Webb and William M. Wilson:

> Elizabeth L. Webb is one of the heirs at law of her father, the late Samuel B. Webb, deceased, and whereas the said Samuel B. Webb left at his death a considerable estate both real and personal which is yet undivided consisting of a plantation or tract of land situate and being on Daufuskie Island and a number of slaves and other property both real and personal, and where as Elizabeth L. Webb is entitled to and will shortly be lawfully seized & possessed of an undivided portion of said plantation of Samuel B. Webb, whatever and wherever it may be. . . .[121]

By 1845 Mrs. Samuel B. Webb left the island and moved to Savannah as she appears there in the 1850 and 1860 census.

During the War, the Webb Tract was claimed by Union soldiers. It remained confiscated for unpaid taxes by the United States Direct Tax Commission for the District of South Carolina and was sold at a Public Auction 31 December 1875 to W. D. Brown, the highest bidder, for $260.00.[121]

On 8 February 1910, for the sum of $1,000.00, W. D. Brown (grantor) conveyed to Lawrence B. Ackerman (grantee), a timber deed to Webb Tract containing 700 acres more or less:

> . . . all the pinetrees [twelve-inches or more in diameter two-feet from the ground] of every sort and description, standing, lying and growing, or that may grow during the term herein after stated. . . . When said grantee logs said premises. . . full right of ingress and egress and the right to have and use permanent rights of way 30 feet wide upon, across and through the lands of the said grantor, to be selected and located by the said grantee . . . for railroads, tramways, wagon roads, and all branch railroads and tramways, and the right to obtain and use material for same for said lands. And all other privileges necessary or desirable to said grantee for the carrying on or continuance of the sawmill, railroad, tramway, wagon road or logging operations . . . including mill locations, skidder camps and other improvements and the privilege of running said railroads and tramways, including branches at any time. . . . It is agreed that the time limit for the removal of the timber and trees above conveyed shall be *five years* from the date of this conveyance. And it is further agreed that all said railroads and other improvements may be removed from said lands within *one year* from the time said grantee ceases to use the same. . . ."[123]

Hilton-Dodge Lumber Train on Daufuskie 1910-1915

For several years after the Civil War, coastal island residents were in a terrible condition. Plantation owners were financially ruined, and even though they were free, former slaves had no money, no place to live, and practically nothing to eat. On St. Simons Island some of the former planters gave to their free slaves small plots of land on which to build modest cabins and to plant gardens.

Once a month the Government sent supplies by ship and unloaded them on the beaches, but it wasn't enough nor often enough. Norman W. Dodge and Titus B. Meigs, both from New York, started a lumber mill known as Dodge, Meigs & Company, and purchased the James Hamilton Cooper plantation on Frederica River. They employed hundreds of men which fed many families, bringing hope, life, and activity once again to the community.[124]

Mr. Meigs' share of the lumber mill changed ownership and it was not until 27 October 1888, when a petition was filed in the Office of Clerk, Superior Court, McIntosh County, that "Hilton" was added to the company name.

> The petition of Joseph Hilton, Norman W. Dodge [et al], ... desire ... to be incorporated for twenty years under the corporate name of the "Hilton & Dodge Lumber Company;" that their principle place of doing business shall be the city of Darien, Georgia.[125]

The company consisted of four mills. Their supply of timber was gotten from "up country" and logs were floated on rafts down the Satilla and Altamaha Rivers into a large basin near the mills.

After the Webb Tract timber deed was signed 8 February 1910, it was the Hilton & Dodge Lumber Company that was to do all the cutting and shipping of the logs.

A coal burning train, ten to fifteen flatcars, timber carts, miles of iron tracks, wooden crossties, and other necessary tools and equipment were brought to Daufuskie on large wooden barges, pulled by towboats.

Making Jimmy Lee's Landing on Mongin Creek the point of embarkation, railroad tracks were laid in a northerly direction, which took them across Oaklawn, then crossing "tram road" (beach road) half way between the school house road and Papy Burn's Landing road, east of Joseph and Peggy Michael (now Frances Jones), east of

the lake in front of the Union Baptist Church and the home of Emily Manuel, east of the Webb Cemetery (near the present Hargray Telephone tower), the track ended at Freeport, which belonged to W.W. Scouten at the time.[126]

There were three "arms or branches" that were laid west of the main tract: the first one ran across lands of Sipio Robinson (near the Beach Road), ending on lands of Morris and Pender Hamilton (in the vicinity of where Willis and Janie Simmons now live) and used as a switch yard; the second one ran west about where the Hargray Telephone tower now stands on Cooper River Road, and the third one was just south of the Cooper River Landing road—these last two branches ran westward deep into Webb Tract toward Cooper River. Near the third arm or branch, there was what was called a "rig tree."

According to Hamp Bryan, a rig tree was a pine tree with its top cut out and pulleys and rigging attached to it. After the oxen had snaked a log to a sufficient distance out of the woods, cables were attached to it and pulled by the "steam boiler" (tractor) up toward the rig tree where the stick was hoisted and put on a flatcar.

For the residence, where the train tract crossed the island roads, a "trestle" was made by filling the area between the tracks with dirt, so that wagon wheels could roll over the rails without any difficulty.

Perhaps as many as thirty-five to fifty oxen (some with horns and some butt headed) were barged over and kept in a pasture that was fenced in from about where the Hargray Telephone tower is now and ran north to the road that goes down to Cooper River Landing. The animals were grazed, fed, and watered every night after work. Oxen were used because they were cheaper and required only one feeding a day; their hides were tougher and their necks did not chafe and turn to sores under their collars like a horse or mule, and they were very obedient. Only one rope was used to guide them. They obeyed with three commands: Gee—which meant turn to the right; Haw—meaning turn to the left; and Hack and See—which meant get moving. Sometimes it would take as many as eight to ten animals just to "snake" one huge log (stick) out of the deep woods or bog. Two or more oxen were harnessed to one timber cart. A timber cart was simply a single axle made of oak, connected to two, five-to-eight-inch iron rimmed wooden wheels, which ranged from six to twelve feet in diameter. A long tongue was attached that separated the animals and

171

Hilton-Dodge Lumber Train on Daufuskie, 1910–1915
(Drawing courtesy of Daufuskie artist Christina Roth Bates.)

"acted as a lever, hoisting the stick under the axle and swinging it off the ground." A chain was used to secure the stick to the tongue.[127]

When the flatcars were loaded, the train would take them down to Jimmy Lee's Landing, stopping near the water's edge. A canthook was then used to turn each stick and flip it into the water on hightide. The logs were then rafted together with wire cable. When a sufficient number of rafts were made, they were joined together, tied behind a diesel-engined tugboat, and carried to Savannah or perhaps Darien. Sometimes the rafts behind the tow boat would measure as much as two or three hundred feet and were lighted to let other boats know that they were pulling a tow.

William (Hamp) Bryan said that he worked different shifts on the dredge in Savannah and that he would pass log-barges day and night being towed; the river was busy with the logging business.

A sawmill for the lumber company was down on Oaklawn near Mongin Creek. There was also a store near the mill where the workers could buy goods and the natives could sell fish and other things.[128]

Some of the men on the island found work with the lumber business either cutting or logging while others had the job of feeding and watering the oxen. The pay was just a few dollars per day for up to twelve hours of work. They labored from "day clean" to "just jew" (first dew), according to William (Hamp) Bryan.

Mr. Meeks, a white man, was overseer on the train. He and his family lived in Toby and Kate Holmes' house at Cooper River. Mr. Lewis (black) was the "skidder man." There was a black man by the name of John Pearl who did most of the work on the train. John and his wife, Annie Pearl, lived on the island. A Casey Jones (a white man) was the engineer for a while.

There were others, but the only island men who were remembered that worked with the lumber company were Ben Miller, Joe Riley, Alfred Mike, Frank Jenkins, Bobby Jenkins, Gabe Washington, and George Simmons.[129]

Young men would catch the train and ride to the end of the line, walk through the Melrose gate, pick up their family's mail from Postmaster Evelyn P. Stoddard, then ride the train back home.[130]

The only death reported during the timber cutting was when two brothers were sawing down a huge pine—one was killed when the tree fell on him.[131]

Timber Cart Used in Hauling Logs (Sticks) to Train
(Drawing courtesy of Daufuskie artist Christina Roth Bates. A photograph may be found in *Live Oaking*, page 116.)

The older people remembered the chugging of the train and the sound of its shrill whistle as it made its way through the woods. The train stayed awhile, left for a period, then returned. It was a good time, a busy time. They all missed it when the train was finally removed from the island in 1915. Some of the tracks remain and numerous railroad spikes have been found. The only remnants left of the timber carts are two iron wheel rims, five or six feet in diameter, in the yard of the Hargray Telephone Company on New River.

Artesian Wells

Before leaving Hilton & Dodge Lumber Company, it may be added that they might have been responsible for drilling the three or four artesian wells that were on Daufuskie. On St. Simons they had drilled these wells to supply water for the train and for families to have good drinking water and inside plumbing.[132]

Webb Tract Owner Murdered

In 1923 W. D. (Old Man) Brown was said to be the best known white man living on Hilton Head. He and his wife, Lulie, ran their general store, which also housed the post office. Lulie had been the postmaster since 1907.

They had two married daughters, Helen Campbell and Fannie Holmes, who lived on the mainland. Brown helped the black people in any way that he could—aided two congregations in getting land for their churches—even selling them some of his property at a reasonable price.

The Browns took in a good bit of money each day and if W. D. had not had a chance to take it to the bank on the mainland, he stored the cash upstairs in a box under his bed. It never occurred to them that they would be robbed, as everyone on Hilton Head was just one big family; they had no reason not to trust their neighbors, black or white.

Quickly spotted on July third were two black men. They were strangers to the island, but perhaps they were visitors or kin to some other black family, so there was no more thought given to them.

Being the Fourth of July, there was not much going on in the way of celebration on Hilton Head, so the Browns' two daughters remained on the mainland where there were lots of people, parties, and fireworks.

Just after midnight a fire broke out on Hilton Head and everyone knew it was in the direction of W. D. Brown's store. Before the men could scramble to get dressed, jump on their horses (or mules), and get to the fire, the store burned to the ground. There had been no time to haul out any of the furnishings and too late to save the Browns.

It took a long time for the embers to cool down enough to search for the bodies, but when they were found, both skulls had been bashed in with an axe or club.

Then everyone remembered the strangers. They started beating the brushes and marsh grass looking for them. Spying the dangling rope where a row boat was once tied, the crowd knew the killers had escaped to the mainland. The police were notified and a search rounded up the two suspects.

At the trial, one of the black men told how they hid in the church loft and watched the store burn. The other man was wearing Mr. Brown's watch with his initials on the cover. The two men were found guilty and were executed, thus closing the case.[133]

Brown Heirs Sell Webb Tract

On 18 July 1960 the Brown heirs, Fannie B. Holmes of New Hanover County, North Carolina, and Helen B. Campbell, of Beaufort, sold Webb Tract (753 acres) to Inland Corporation, Savannah, Georgia, for the sum of $22,590.[134]

G. H. Bostwick Buys Webb Tract

George H. Bostwick buys Webb from Inland Corporation, 28 July 1961, for $41,415.[135]

Bostwick Sells Out

On 6 May 1980, George H. Bostwick and his wife Dolly von Stade Bostwick sell as a package deal Haig's Point and Webb Tract, to partners William H. Grimball, Joseph W. Cabaniss, William H. Vaughan, Edward P. Guerard, Jr., and Neil C. Robinson, Jr., in a certain Trust Agreement for the sum of $10.00 and other valuable consideration.

Charles L. Cauthen acted as witness in the deal and became a representative to the partners.[136]

On 16 October 1984, Robinson, Craver & Wall Professional Asso-

ciation, Trustee, holds title to Webb Tract (and other plantations) as successor to Grimball, Cabaniss, Vaughan & Guerard.[137]

Robinson, Craver & Wall Professional Association, Trustee, on 19 October 1984, sell Webb (and other properties) to Plantation Land Company, in consideration of $10.00 and other valuable consideration.[138]

Plantation Land Company sold Haig's Point to International Paper Realty Corporation of South Carolina, 13 October 1984, with an option to purchase Webb Tract by 8 August 1989.[139] (IP did not honor this option.)

Oak Ridge Plantation

This plantation was formed when Mary Ash Fraser had the land of her brother, Richard Russell Ash, surveyed in 1806. It was sold from the Charleston Court of Equity in 1818 to John David Mongin (No. 3). If there was a mansion at Oak Ridge, no one ever knew about it. John David planted the land until his death in 1833, when it became the property of his granddaughter, Mary Lavinia Mongin Stoddard. it then became a marriage settlement for Mary Lavinia's daughter, "made and entered into between Helen M. Stoddard (Mrs. Helen M. Hardee), John Stoddard [her father] and John L. Hardee [her husband], 4 February 1861."[140]

On 31 October 1889, John L. Hardee, trustee for Helen M. Stoddard Hardee, sold to William E. Diller, a doctor from New York city, Oak Ridge Plantation consisting of 596 acres. According to the family, Oak Ridge was exchanged for one dollar plus some property that Dr. Diller owned in New York.[141]

William E. Diller, on 5 November 1914, conveyed to his wife, Elizabeth A. Diller, Oak Ridge Plantation.[142]

According to George White, Dr. W. E. Diller in 1913 built a modest house on what was now called Diller Woods. George was very knowledgeable concerning this, as the men who built the house for Dr. Diller boarded with his parents, Jim and Annie White, who were living in the Bloody Point mansion at the time.

The doctor only used the house for summer vacations and special occasions. Working for Dr. Diller were Joseph and Margaret (Peggy) Michael; she did the cooking and cleaning while her husband did all the maintenance and outside work. They also watched over the place

when the doctor was away and prepared the house and yards each time upon his return.

•

Francis (Frank) A. Burn relates an interesting story concerning Dr. Diller. The Burn family was living in the Bloody Point Lighthouse. About the middle of the last week of December 1928, Frank and his sister Leonella (Nell) decided they would take a walk to Gus Ohman's store, a good two-mile journey. With his 410 ga. shotgun in hand, Frank had thoughts of killing some game on the way. He was not disappointed. They had not gone far when a squirrel ran across the road and up a tree. By aiming carefully, with one shot, Frank brought the squirrel to the ground.

Carrying the squirrel by the tail, Frank and Nell were continuing their tramp to the store when Dr. Diller and his grandson approached them. The Dillers were dressed in their fancy hunting clothes and carrying automatic shotguns, but had not seen anything to shoot. Noticing the squirrel that Frank was carrying, Dr. Diller asked if he might buy it. Frank agreed on the price of twenty-five cents that was offered, and handed the squirrel to Dr. Diller.

Before parting company, Frank and Nell received a special invitation from Dr. Diller to visit their home on New Year's Day.

When Frank and Nell arrived at Dr. Diller's in the early afternoon of 1 January 1929, to their amazement tacked by one foot on the outside wall of the house was the squirrel they had sold him several days previously, along with a few birds and a rabbit. The puzzled look on Frank's face brought an explanation from Dr. Diller: they didn't eat wild game right after it was killed; they hung it up for several days to let it "age"—until the hair or feathers could be plucked with ease—at which time the meat would be tender and the wild taste would be gone.

Seeing that wild game hanging on the side of Dr. Diller's house impressed Frank so much that he never forgot it. And, after Dr. Diller took the squirrel and handed the twenty-five cents to Frank, he and Nell went on to Mr. Ohman's store, spent the whole quarter on two-cent Johnny cakes, taking some back home to share with an older sister, Bessie Cook, and her son Curtis.

•

178

Elizabeth A. Diller on 20 February 1929 sold to J. A. Coleman and H. R. Williams, co-partners under the trade name of Coleman & Williams, Hardeeville, South Carolina, "all of the Pine timber of every kind and description above the size of 10" Ten inches, Twelve inches from the ground," on the 596 acres (with the exception of twenty-nine acres that surrounded the house) for the sum of $2,500.00.[143]

Elizabeth A. Diller willed to her daughter, Mary Elizabeth Diller McConnell, Oak Ridge Plantation, 6 June 1938.[144]

On 27 April 1945 Mary Elizabeth Diller McConnell sold to Lafayette McLaws Oak Ridge Plantation for $9,500.[145]

Charles Cauthen et al., under the name of Plantation Land Company, Inc., bought from Lafayette McLaws, Oak Ridge Plantation in 1980.

On 23 October 1984 Plantation Land Company, Inc., sold Haig Point to International Paper Realty Corporation with an option to purchase Oak Ridge by 8 August 1989.[146] (The option was not honored by IP.)

Benjie's Point Plantation

This 276 acre plantation was known as the "Estate of Webb." When he came in possession of it is not known, but in the distribution of John Stoddard's plantations after the Civil War, it was given to his son John I. Stoddard. John I. in turn exchanged it for the Eigleberger Plantation of his sister, Isabelle S. Green. (See Eigleberger section.)

Isabelle no doubt named the Plantation Benjie's Point after Benjamin Green whom she married 11 November 1860. Benjamin Green, born circa 1826, was the son of Charles Green, a very wealthy Savannah cotton merchant.[147]

On the west side of Savannah's Madison Square, 24 Macon Street, Charles Green had built a magnificent mansion that was completed in 1861. During the Union Army's occupation of Savannah, 1864-65, General Sherman used the "Green House" as his headquarters. It might have been from this same house, 22 December 1864, that Major General William Tecumseh Sherman sent this message to President Lincoln:

> I beg to present you as a Christmas Gift, the city of Savannah with 150 heavy guns and plenty of ammunition and also about 25,000 bales of cotton.[148]

Confiscated during the War, it can only be assumed that Benjie's Point was redeemed by John Stoddard circa 1867. Benjamin Green died in 1865 and on 6 February 1872 Isabelle married Major William D. Waples. The plantation, at that point in her possession, had been subdivided and she was selling lots in her Waples name.[149] No one has a plat of the subdivision but all of the lots were sold.

It was at Benjie's Point that the County purchased land circa 1920s and built the only public dock on the island.

Benjie's Point has always been a busy place with steamers loading or unloading passengers, freight, and mail. About the only entertainment the islanders had, and something they looked forward to, was to be at the dock upon the arrival of a steamer to see who was coming to or leaving the island. And if a stranger or a new piece of furniture came, the news spread over the island like "wildfire."

For the natives, there are only two places on the island—Cooper River and Benjie's Point. They are either going "up" to Cooper River, or "down" to "Banges Pint."

Notes

1. Starr, "A Place Called Daufuskie," pp. 6-8.

2. Records of the Secretary of the Province, vol. 1711-1715, p. 231, South Carolina Archives; Larry Lepionka, "Cooper River Landing, An Archaeological Survey of a Thirty Acre Tract on Daufuskie Island, Beaufort County, South Carolina," unpublished typescript, 1989, p. 8; Rebecca Starr, "Haig Point: A Land Use History," unpublished typescript, 1986, p. 31. (Rebecca's early chain of title to land in "Haig Point" typescript, cannot be improved upon.)

3. Memorials of James Cockran, 12 May 1733, Memorial vol. I, pp. 165-67; Lepionka, p. 8.

4. Memorials, vol. 3, p. 167; vol. 9, pp. 298, 301, South Carolina Archives; Starr, "Haig Point," p. 29.

5. Memorials, vol. 7, p. 223; Lepionka, p. 9; Starr, "Haig Point," p. 31.

6. Ibid., p. 6; Memorials, vol. 9, p. 298; Will of Richard Cockran Ash, Charleston Wills Book RR, pp. 441-43, South Carolina Archives.

7. Office of Register Mesne Conveyance, Charleston County, Charleston, South Carolina, Book W-6, pp. 21-24, Charleston Main Library.

8. *South Carolina Historical and Genealogical Magazine* (hereafter cited as *SCHGM*), "The Excommunication of Joseph Ash," vol. 22, pp. 53-55; Hopkins.

9. *The* (Charleston) *Times,* 10 September 1803; Starr, "A Place Called Daufuskie," pp. 50-52.

10. *SCHGM* 22 (April, 1921): 54.

11. Will of John Cattel Livingston, Chatham County, Georgia Probate, folio 114-115, microfilm # L1 573-578.

12. Charleston County Deed Book W-6, pp. 21-24.

13. *South Carolina Gazette,* 3 January 1774; Mrs. William Lawson Peel, ed., *Historical Collections of the Joseph Habersham Chapter, Daughters American Revolution* (Baltimore: Genealogical Publishing Company, 1968), 2: 588; Hopkins.

14. Will of John Cattel Livingston.

15. Chatham County Deed Book 2C & 2D 1809-1812. Deed Book 2C, p. 495 has the Fraser/Hopkins Deed to 738 acres. Book 2C, p. 503, has the two deeds for slaves from George and John Fraser. The number of slaves is not given—they are named—but it appeared that there were about fourteen slaves in one deed and twelve to fifteen in the other. They were hard to read and impossible to copy, so the number is estimated. Apparently both Frasers' bad debts to Hopkins, due in January 1811 (against which they had put up slaves as collateral), were by these deeds, settling the debt by the slaves; *Republican and Savannah Evening Ledger,* 2 February 1810; Hopkins.

16. Plat of 1806 in the possession of Albert H. Stoddard.

17. Ibid., p. 22; Charleston County, Records of Mesne Conveyance, Deed Book N, p. 83; S. C. Memorials, v. 7, p. 501; Charleston Wills, Inventories, and Miscellaneous Records (WPA transcripts), v. 62B, p. 812, South Carolina Archives.

18. Colonial Plats, vol. 3 p. 336, South Carolina Archives.

19. Milling, pp. 90-91. ("Barbarously murdered by the Indians" might have meant that George Haig was scalped and his body pierced with lightwood splinters resembling a porcupine, set afire, and let slowly burn, sometimes taking two days to die.)

20. Marriage Settlements, Book 9, pp. 149-53, South Carolina Archives (Columbia).

21. Catharine Blodgett's personal letter to her sister, Mrs. R. W. Dickinson, 16 January 1838; letter in the possession of Dr. Robert E. H. Peeples, President, Hilton Head Historical Society. (John David Mongin [No. 3] and his son David John [No. 4] might have lived in this house at one time.)

22. Brent Holcomb, *Marriage and Death Notices from the Charleston Observer, 1817-1845* (Greenville: A Press, Inc., 1980), p. 131. (Information courtesy The Historical Society of Pennsylvania, Philadelphia, Pennsylvania.)

23. Catharine Blodgett, p. 1.

24. Coulter, p. 78.

25. Mrs. M. B. (Eleanor K.) Strain, telephone conversation 7 June 1987. Mrs. Strain is a member of the Pope family and has been very kind in sharing much information.

26. *The War of the Rebellion: A Compilation of the Official Records of the Union and Confederate Armies,* Prepared under the direction of the Secretary of War by Bvt. Lieut. Col. Robert N. Scott, Third U. S. Artillery, and Published Pursuant to Act of Congress Approved 16 June 1880, 4 ser., 70 vol. (Washington: Government Printing Office, 1882), ser. 1, 6: 144.

27. Michie, p. 27.

28. Beaufort County Courthouse, Deed Book 6, pp. 341-44.

29. Beaufort County Courthouse, Deed Book 14, p. 638.

30. Ibid., Deed Book 19, p. 578; Mrs. M. B. (Eleanor Knorr) Strain's personal files.

31. Mrs. W. W. (Jo) Scouten's personal files.

32. Beaufort County Courthouse, Deed Book 24, p. 320.

33. Jo Scouten's personal files.

34. Beaufort County Courthouse, Deed Book 87, p. 375.

35. Ibid., Deed Book 108, p. 77.

36. Charles Cauthen, telephone conversation, 23 August 1988.

37. Ibid., Beaufort County Deed Book 300, p. 1328.

38. Ibid., Deed Book 406, p. 64.

39. *Island Packet* , 16 August 1985; Ibid., 25 September 1985.

40. Catharine Blodgett, pp. 1-2.

41. Cleveland Rockwell Map of 1860, United States Survey.

42. Robert Manson Myers, *Children of Pride* (Connecticut: New Haven & London, Yale University Press, 1973), p. 215.

43. Beaufort County Courthouse, Deed Book 19, p. 289.

44. Albert H. Stoddard III personal files.

45. Chlotilde Rowell Martin, "A Soldier's Diary," Beaufort South Carolina, 1931. This typewritten article was shared by Mrs. W. W. (Jo) Scouten, Sr. The article does not state, but it can only be assumed that Ms Martin was perhaps a reporter for the *Beaufort Gazette.*

46. American Missionary Association Archives, Fisk University, Microfilm Document Nos. H 6656, H6572, copies at South Carolina Library, Columbia.

47. Josephine W. Martin, ed., *Dear Sister, Letters Written on Hilton Head Island 1867* (Beaufort: Beaufort Book Co., Inc., 1977), pp. 63-4. Permission graciously and thankfully granted by Dr. Curtis S. Hitchcock to quote from book.

48. American Missionary Association, Document No. H 6598.

49. Albert H. Stoddard III has original Commission.

50. War Department, Bureau Refugees, Freedmen and Abandoned Lands, Charleston, South Carolina. Albert H. Stoddard III shared a copy from his personal files.

51. Albert Henry Stoddard III has copy of lease agreement in his personal files.

52. Obituary of John Stoddard, *New York Observer,* 7 July 1879; Robert Manson Myers, p. 1694.

53. "Diary of John Michael Doyle," unpublished typescript in the possession of Paul K. and Evelyn Helmly, Jr., Savannah, Georgia, pp. 63, 65, 68, 74-6, 79, 85, 87-8. Evelyn typed from Mr. Doyle's handwritten Diary and sent a copy, 21 May 1982; Mr. Walter Schaaf, Savannah, also shared a copy.

54. Mrs. Sarah Hudson-Grant was a black lady who worked in the orchard at Melrose. She was well acquainted with the Stoddards and knew much about the mansion and the activities there. She was also an oyster shucker, a midwife, and a spiritual pillar of the First Union African Baptist Church. Sarah was very knowledgeable as to what was going on all over the island, and was sometimes called the "Mayor" of Daufuskie.

55. George White information. George was born on Daufuskie in 1903. He had entertained the Stoddard children and visited the mansion often before it burned. Now living in New Jersey, George has been contacted many times by letter and phone for the past several years.

56. *Beaufort Gazette,* 23 October 1971.

57. *Island Packet,* 7 February 1986.

58. Samuel Hilden: S.C. Memorials, v. 1, pp. 447-48; John Wright: Colonial plats, v. 1, p. 156; Joseph Wright: S. C. Memorials, v. 9, p. 298; Starr, "Daufuskie," p. 75.

59. William DeBrahm, "Map of South Carolina and Georgia," London: T. Jeffreys, 20 October 1757; *Georgia Gazette* , 24 August 1768; 4 April 1770; Starr, p. 30.

60. *South Carolina Gazette,* 19-26 April 1751.

61. Charleston County, S.C., Records of Mesne Conveyance, Deed Book M-5, p. 1; K-5, p. 438, S. C. Archives; *Georgia Gazette,* 24 August 1768; Starr, p. 45.

62. Rusty Fleetwood, *Tidecraft* (Savannah: Coastal Heritage Society, 1982), p. 66;

Quoting from Rusty's 28 March 1983 letter, "This info came from a letter to Wm. Cowles from Henry Laurens (may be seen in *The Papers of Henry Laurens,* USC Press, 1967 and an article in the *South Carolina Gazette* of August 8, 1771). Watts is also mentioned as early in my notes as 1765 (SCG, 9/8/65, when he was reported to have launched a ship near Beaufort. A year later he is mentioned again by the *Gazette,* building a ship with two more under contract (SCG, 10/20/66). . . ."

63. George C. Rogers, Jr., et al., eds., *The Papers of Henry Laurens,* 9 vols. (Columbia: University of South Carolina Press, 1968-1981), 7: 508; 8: 250; Starr, p. 45.

64. Peter Wilson Coldham, F. A. S. G., *American Loyalist Claims,* 13 vols. (Washington, D.C.: National Genealogical Society, 1980), 1: pp. 517-18, Ga. Dept. of Archives and History; Hopkins.

65. *Georgia Gazette,* 19 August 1790; Hopkins.

66. Personal files, John (Jack) Stoddard, Noank, Connecticut. Thanks to Jack: he sent the only picture available of the Bloody Point mansion.

67. Oakley Hall was the last of the mansions to survive on Daufuskie. So many of us were privileged to have seen this once lovely home. For those who helped to recreate the house and its surroundings, appreciation goes to Francis A. Burn, George White, and Mrs. Juanita Goodwin-Kennerly.

68. Cleveland Rockwell Map of 1860. Sea Coast of South Carolina from the mouth of the Savannah River to May River. United states Coast Survey.

69. Mongin/Martinangele family records.

70. "Jeremiah Evarts' Diary: 1822," Manuscript #240, typescript, pp. 15-18, 20-22, Georgia Historical Society, Savannah. (Please note that although Mr. and Mrs. David John Mongin [No. 4] have a three-year-old daughter and a six-year-old son, they are not even mentioned by Mr. Evarts. Surely he would have seen them had they been there. This leads me to believe that either John David Mongin [No. 3] has already built Melrose and has his grandchildren living with him there, or, he and the children could be living at the small mansion at Haig's Point which David John [No. 4] owns.)

71. Catharine Blodgett's letter, p. 1; letter in the files of Dr. Robert E. H. Peeples, Hilton Head.

72. William Henry Mongin's will, Probate Judge's Office, Savannah, Deed Book K, pp. 432-34, 4 November 1851.

73. Mr. Bill Fleetwood, 216 E. Bay Street, Savannah, Georgia, has the pardon hanging on his living room wall. Years ago, Mr. Fleetwood had bought a former Stoddard building and found stored in the attic was the pardon and numerous other historical Stoddard plantation records, Civil War newspapers, plats, cotton receipts, and much more.

74. *Savannah Morning News,* 6 October 1875.

75. Eugenia Marion Johnston's pamphlet, "Social Life and Interesting Events in Savannah Between 1880-1890," February 1935, pp. 64-66, Savannah Public Library.

76. Ibid. Orchestra consisted of three instruments: piano, violin, and cello, with "Natty Solomans" at the piano—a player of waltzes, par excellence—so popular was he that "his and no other orchestra furnished music for any party in that decade."

77. Ward McAllister, *Society as I Have Found It* (New York: Cassell Publishing Company, 1890), pp. 102-03.

78. Martha Gallandet Waring's pamphlet, "The Striving [18] Seventies in Savannah," October 1935, pp. 45-46, Savannah Public Library.

79. McAllister, p. 103.

80. Records of the Lighthouse Service, United States Coast Guard, Record Group 26, National Archives, Washington, D.C.; #8, South Carolina Archives.

81. Beaufort County Courthouse, Deed Book A, p. 13; Deed Book, B, n.p.n.; Deed Book B, p. 111; Deed Book B, p. 113; Deed Book, B, p. 205; Deed Book B, p. 352.

82. Interviews and phone calls, George and Fred White, 1987-1988.

83. George White told me about the Lanes and showed me where Mrs. Lane was buried; interviews with Mrs. Myrtle Lane Marsh and Mrs. Corrine Lane Rice of Charleston, S. C. Tuesday, 14 June 1988. The women had returned to the island after sixty-eight years to see where their mother was buried. Corrine's twin sister, Mrs. Irene Lane Craven, was too sick to come—she died 30 June 1988.

84. Interview and many phone calls, Mrs. Juanita Goodwin Kennerly, Savannah, Georgia, 1988-1989.

85. Beaufort Courthouse, Deed Book 69, p. 460; Obituary of Morton Deutsch, *Savannah Morning News*, 2 January 1987; Gerhard Spieler, "Morton Deutsch Added Color to Daufuskie Island History," *Beaufort Gazette,* 8 March 1988.

86. Deutsch Obituary; Spieler; *Island Packet,* 12 June 1988.

87. Beaufort County Coiurthouse, Deed Book 506, Document Nos. 1969-70, Exhibit "A," pp. 1-2. It is understood that Mr. Morrison retained ten acres of Oaklawn for himself.

88. Original cloth plat in possession of Lance and Billie Burn.

89. Beaufort County Courthouse, Deed Book 16, pp. 601-02.

90. Ibid., Deed Book 3, pp. 71-72.

91. Ibid., Deed Book 3, pp. 442-43.

92. Ibid., Deed Book 16, pp. 240-41.

93. Ibid.

94. Ibid., Deed Book 19, 326-27.

95. Ibid., Deed Book 42, 215.

96. Ibid., Deed Book 65, p. 318.

97. Ibid., Deed Book 506, Document Nos. 1969-70, Exhibit "A," pp. 1-2.

98. Ibid., Deed Book 9, pp. 11-12.

99. The original plat of Prospect Hill could not be found in Beaufort County. There is a possibility of it being in Savannah records since William Fripp Chaplin, Sr., was a resident of that city. However, Mr. Arthur Christensen, surveyor, Beaufort, S.C., through recorded deeds and tax records, reconstructed a plat now available at the courthouse in Beaufort.

100. Ibid., Deed Book 11, p. 453; Deed Book 19, p. 28; Deed Book 19, p. 31; Deed Book 19, p. 326; Deed Book 9, p. 366. It might be added that this land of eighty acres was four-fifths of Simeon Martinangele's original one hundred acres known as Twins Point.

101. Chatham County, Georgia, Records of Mesne Conveyance, Deed Book V, p. 390; Starr, p. 64.

102. Chatham County Courthouse, Deed Book 17, p. 222; Chaplin family records from the files of David Humphrey.

103. Ibid.

104. Ibid., Deed Book 39, p. 459.

105. Interviews and phone calls from Fred White and Francis A. Burn, Sr., at intervals during 1988.

106. Beaufort County Courthouse, Deed Book 44, p. 591; Humphrey.

107. Morton Deutsch's Obituary, following his death in Savannah, 1 January 1987; *Beaufort Gazette,* 8 March 1988.

108. Telephone conversation 24 January 1989, James Wedgeworth, Charter I Realty & Marketing Company, Hilton Head, S. C.

109. Declaration of John Stoddard, trustee for the estate of John David Mongin [No. 3], 20 September 1865, Restorations Applications (unregistered), Bureau of Refugees, Freedmen, and Abandoned Lands, National Archives, microfilm copy at S. C. Archives; Starr, p. 65, n. 6.

110. Survey made 17 November 1850 for John Stoddard, a tract of land containing 840 acres (300 of which is marsh), surveyor, J.S. Jones, plat dated 29 March 1851.

111. Plat of lands, H.M. Stoddard, surveyed and subdivided into fifty-two parcels by O.P. Law, 15 February 1884.

112. Interview with Mrs. Agnes Mitchell Simmons, 26 January 1989. Mrs. Simmons came to the island from Bluffton in 1911 at the age of nine. She was in the mansion many times.

113. Court of Equity, Charleston, 1818.

114. Subdivision plat of Maryfield, for John I. Stoddard, by surveyor, O. P. Law, 9 January 1879, Beaufort County Courthouse, Deed Book 12, p. 260.

115. Mary Ash Fraser 1806 Plat; Stoddard files.

116. Stoddard, "Gullah Tales," p. 15.

117. Hopkins.

118. Ibid.

119. Evarts, p. 16.

120. Hopkins.

121. Georgia Archives, Chatham County Deeds, v. 3C-3D, p. 29; Hopkins.

122. Beaufort County Courthouse, Deed Book 12, p. 28.

123. Ibid., Deed Book 28, pp. 388-89.

124. St. Simons Public Library, *Old Mill Days 1874-1908* (St. Simons: Glover Printing Company, 1976), p. 6.

125. Ibid., p. 27.

126. Gage Scouten's personal letter, 18 July 1967.

127. Virginia Steele Wood, *Live Oaking, Southern Timber for Tall Ships* (Boston: Northeastern University Press, 1981), pp. 111-16. (Highly recommended reading for anyone interested in logging or live oak shipbuilding.)

128. Mrs. Geneva Bryan Wiley, interview, 3 June 1989.

129. Johnny Hamilton, interview, 20 July 1978.

130. William (Hamp) Bryan, interview 8 September 1983.

131. Wiley.

132. *Old Mill Days,* p. 23. (For further information concerning Hilton-Dodge Lumber Company, read *High Water on the Bar,* written at Savannah, Georgia in the summer of 1951 by Thomas Hilton, Beaufort County Library.)

133. Holmgren, pp. 121-22.

134. Beaufort County Courthouse, Deed Book 102, p. 245.

135. Ibid., Deed Book 107, p. 224.

136. Ibid., Deed Book 300, pp. 1330-33.

137. Ibid., Deed Book 405, p. 992.

138. Ibid., 485, pp. 1500-36.

139. Ibid., 406, p. 64; Charles Cauthen, telephone conversation, 30 January 1989.

140. Ibid., Deed Book 16, p. 497.

141. Ibid., Deed Book 16, pp. 497-99.

142. Ibid., Deed Book 32, pp. 371-72.

143. Ibid., Deed Book 45, p. 215.

144. Ibid., Office of the Judge of Probate, 11 July 1940, Will Book 6, pp. 418-19.

145. Beaufort County Courthouse, Deed Book 62, p. 468.

146. Charles Cauthen, 30 January 1989.

147. Hopkins.

148. Betty Rauers, Terry Victor, and Franklin Traub, eds., *Sojourn in Savannah* (Savannah: Printcraft Press, 1968), pp. 47-48.

149. Beaufort County Courthouse, Deed Book 19, pp. 30-31.

6

LIGHTHOUSES

To assure safety, especially for sailing vessels, it was necessary to have lights placed at entrances to harbors and sounds along the coast to prevent ships from going aground on sand bars or meeting disaster on shoals. Merchants and stores depended upon imports and exports to sustain their economy. Proper markers, range and beacon lights provided easy access to waterways not only for shipping, but were also useful and necessary during times of war.

As early as 1673, to direct passage of ships into ports of entry, lights were merely simple braziers, lit at sundown with "fier balls of pitch and ocum," and extinguished at dawn. The original light in South Carolina seemed to be one of these.

Lighthouses prior to the Revolution were private affairs. During George Washington's administration as president, on 7 August 1789, a lighthouse service was born when an act of Congress accepted title to the structures and agreed to maintain them.

The first true lighthouse in South Carolina was built on Morris Island at the mouth of Charleston Harbor. Its construction initially began 30 May 1767. There were several lighthouses built between that date and the years just prior to the Civil War, which began on 12 April 1861. By the last of April every light that could aid a federal ship was extinguished. The Morris Island lighthouse was destroyed the latter part of 1861 and was not rebuilt until 1872.[1]

Because of extensive shipping and passenger service to Savannah and Port Royal, it was necessary to keep the waters safe. The earliest record shows that appropriation was made 3 August 1854 for two separate beacons to serve as a range for Calibogue Sound, one of which was a ship known as *Calibogue Lightvessel*, anchored at

Braddock's Point, just off the southern tip of Hilton Head, South Carolina.[2]

Changing currents repeatedly causing shifting sand to form shoals, this lightship had served its usefulness and plans were made to replace it and the second range light.

Haig's Point Lighthouse

The appropriation asked for the range beacons on this island [Daufuskie], to mark the entrance to Calibogue Sound, and to facilitate the passage from Port Royal Harbor to Savannah River, was made by Act of Congress approved 3 March 1871. The plans and specifications have been made for the structures, and it only remains to secure a proper site before commencing work.

. . . The sites were selected on the northeastern end of Daufuskie Island; in the aggregate, they amount to five acres.[3]

For the price of $745, on 20 May 1872, Sarah Lavinia Pope (widow of William "Squire" Pope), their daughter Eliza C. Pope Woodward, and their two granddaughters, Anna S. Pope and Heph J. Pope (children of their deceased son William J. Pope), sold to the United States Government two tracts of Haig's Point Plantation land consisting of a triangular three acres on the extreme northeast corner, bordering Cooper River and Calibogue Sound, and 750 yards southward, bordering Calibogue Sound, a triangular two-acre tract, with permission to cut trees and bushes that might obstruct the light and for convenient passage of carts or wagons on a right of way between the two parcels.[4]

On the three-acre, most northern tract, would be built a small forty-nine-foot light tower (above its base) on the keeper's dwelling; on the southern two-acre tract would stand an open-frame, fifteen-foot structure.

On 26 December 1872 James H. Reed of Washington, D.C., was given the contract to build the keeper's dwelling and range beacons, to furnish all labor, and to furnish and deliver all materials to Daufuskie, for the sum of $7,681.[5]

Standing on the same spot where the rear or northern range light and keeper's dwelling was to be built were the the charred remains of a large tabby mansion built in 1838 by the Reverend Herman M. Blodgett. Before the work began, in order for the rear range to have

Haig's Point Lighthouse—North Range

(Photographer, Major Jared A. Smith, 11 June 1885; courtesy Senator James M. Waddell, Jr., 20 September 1966.)

Haig's Point South Range Light

(Photographer, Major Jared A. Smith, 11 June 1885; courtesy Senator James M. Waddell, Jr., 20 September 1966.)

a focal plane of sixty-five feet above meantide, the walls, which also included some of the fireplaces in the mansion, had to be filled in and all completely covered with dirt to make a "hill" on which the dwelling would sit.

The two-story house with its light tower was built of virgin timber, without a single knothole. Including the halls, there were four rooms on each floor. Both range lights were painted white with lead-color trim; the lanterns were painted red. The job was supposed to have been finished by 15 May 1873, but due to sickness and bad weather, the work was delayed. The job was completed and the lights exhibited for the first time 1 October 1873.[6]

Both lights were of the fifth order, both white and fixed. Lens of the rear or northern beacon was dioptric of the fifth order of Fresnel and illuminated an arc of 270 [degrees] of the horizon. The light had a focal plane of sixty-five feet above meantide.

The southern or front light was fifteen feet high, built as a separate entity from the foundation frame so that it could rest on the foundation but would be free to be adjusted in any direction to correspond with any change in the build-up of shifting sands in the water. It had a focal plane of twenty-two feet above meantide. This light had a steamer lens, illuminating an arc of 90 [degrees]. Both lights marked the channel into Calibogue Sound from Tybee Roads, Georgia.[7]

> Sailing Directions: Vessels coming up from Tybee Roads will bring the beacons in range when Tybee main light bears SW by W; the course is then N 1/2 W, keeping the beacons in range until Braddock's Point is passed, then haul up N by E in mid-channel.
>
> Shoals lie in close proximity to the range line near the South End, and a strong current sets directly across it. Eight and a half (8-1/2) feet can be carried through the channel where it crosses the shoal at low tide.[8]

Built for the lighthouse were a boat-landing and boathouse (1875); a fence completely surrounding the place to keep off cattle (1879); a nine-by-eleven foot fireproof (brick) oil house, with shelves that would receive 450 five-gallon oil cans (1892); and a bathtub (1914). An outside privy was in use continuously.

A four-thousand-gallon-capacity brick cistern was built to store rainwater that was collected through metal gutters attached along the eaves of the roof. In 1895 this cistern was replaced with a six-thousand-gallon one that was filled with water via the use of a well.[9]

Haig's Point Lighthouse: Daufuskie Island, South Carolina, 1920s
(Courtesy Mrs. Jo Scouten.)

Lighthouse Keepers

The first lighthouse keeper, Patrick Comer, born in Ireland, was appointed 29 August 1873, at a salary of $560 per annum. His wife, Bridget Comer, was the assistant keeper and was paid $400 per annum. On 16 October 1885, when Comer received a pay increase to $720, Bridget's position was abolished. Patrick Comer died 5 March 1891, which forced Bridget to leave the island.[10]

The second keeper was Richard Stonebridge, appointed 5 March 1891. He served until he retired, 1 July 1923.

The third keeper was Charles L. Sisson, appointed July 1923; he served until the lights were discontinued, July 1924.[11]

It might be added that keepers and their assistants were sometimes shifted about to different light stations as temporary replacements for those who might be on vacation, sick, or when a death had occurred.

U. S. Government Sells Lighthouse

The need for lighthouses had passed. With advanced technology of automatic lights not requiring the attention of a keeper, it was easier and cheaper to place markers, buoys, or lights on pilings out in the water where they could be easily changed in position, repaired, or replaced through the use of a boat, rather than to pay high prices for land and/or lighthouses and their upkeep.

Since the Haig's Point lighthouse could no longer be profitably used in the work of the lighthouse service, buildings and land were placed on public sale by sealed proposals on 6 September 1924.

On 2 December 1925 all was sold to an assistant United States Engineer, M. V. Haas of Savannah, Georgia, who was the highest bidder at the sum of $1,499.99.[12]

Chain of Title—1926 to 1965

Haas did not keep the lighthouse property for long. On 26 August 1926 it was sold to Davis Freedman, Jr., of Savannah "for the sum of $10.00 and other good and valuable considerations."[13]

The next transaction is not exactly clear, but it appears that James R. Sheldon, Jr., brought an action in Beaufort County against Davis Freeman, Jr., which resulted in the property being sold at Public Auction on 16 January 1930 to Livingston McLaws of Savannah, for the sum of $1,500.00.[14]

Haig's Point Lighthouse in Disrepair, 1960

(Photographs may be found, *Savannah Morning News*, 14 July 1963. Courtesy Glen McCaskey and Tom Bass, 24 July 1985, International Paper.)

Haig's Point Lighthouse, 1960's

(Photographs may be found, *Savannah Morning News*, 14 July 1963. Courtesy Glen McCaskey and Tom Bass, 24 July 1985, International Paper.)

Tower of Haig's Point Light in Disrepair, 1960's

(Photographs may be found, *Savannah Morning News*, 14 July 1963. Courtesy: Glen McCaskey and Tom Bass, 24 July 1985, International Paper.)

Haig's Point Dwelling in Disrepair, 1960's

(Photographs may be found, *Savannah Morning News*, 14 July 1963. Courtesy Glen McCaskey and Tom Bass, 24 July 1985, International Paper.)

The Haig's Point lighthouse was turned into a hunting lodge. Members gave "wild" house parties quite frequently until one inebriated man climbed to the top of the tower. When he leaned against the wooden fence that surrounded the light, the structure gave way, plunging him to the roof below and to his death. That was also the end of the hunting lodge.

The lighthouse remained vacant for several years and was in terrible need of repairs when newlyweds Bill and Josephine (Jo) Scouten were approached to live in the house, rent free, if they would fix the hole in the roof and do other things that were needed to make the house liveable. They made all the necessary repairs and occupied the house from 1937-1939. For a livelihood they fished, raised chickens, and sold eggs to restaurants in Savannah.

After Bill and Jo left the island, the house stood empty and became forbidding as the years went by. The wind and rain took their toll. Although the original shingles were made of wood, they had been replaced (1914) with asbestos ones over just the back half of the roof, which then was beginning to leak, decaying some of the timbers and causing a gaping hole over the kitchen. Shutters flapping in the breeze caused the hinges to give way. Windows were broken, doors sagged on rusty hinges. All of the glass was broken and the whole light tower was fast falling apart. Hunters and fishermen sought refuge in the lighthouse during inclement weather. It was heartbreaking to see this one-time noble structure in such disrepair. Why it never burned down was a mystery.

James R. Sheldon of Dade County, Florida, bought the property from the Livingston McLaws heirs for $1.00 each on two separate deeds, dated 28 December 1964[15] and 22 January 1965.[16] For some reason Sheldon did not pay full value for the property, as there are no Documentary Stamps affixed to either of the deeds—perhaps he was a relative or something.

Bostwick Buys Lighthouse Property

George H. Bostwick had purchased Haig's Point plantation from Styles Harper in 1961. On 24 February 1965, for the sum of $6,500, Bostwick bought the lighthouse and property from James R. Sheldon of Dade County, Florida, formerly of Fairfield County, Connecticut.[17]

Under the supervision of Manning Woods, manager of Bostwick

plantations, the lighthouse (or rear range) was *preserved* but not restored to its original status. The front range structure had long since weathered away or had been torn down.

Notice of the lighthouse restoration appeared in a Beaufort County newspaper:

"Once a desolate ruin that gazed from the tip of Daufuskie Island through shattered windows, the structure [Haig's Point lighthouse] now (1967) boasts fresh white paint, a new roof, refinished floors, modern electrical wiring, screened windows, and other refinements. The glasses in the lamp house have been replaced and the tower is capped with red roof paint."[18]

When Bostwick purchased the lighthouse property, it was the first time since 1872 that Haig's Point plantation was brought back to its original acreage. Once again it was all in one piece, having one owner.

International Paper Buys Haig's Point

When International Paper Realty Corporation purchased Haig's Point 23 October 1984, their first concern was to search for Indian and other artifacts on the property that might have historical significance.

Tabby Mansion Found

Then came the most exciting part of all: to find the ruins of the old mansion that was supposed to have been on the same spot as the lighthouse.

Archaeologist Larry Lepionka and crew, along with English architect and tabby expert Colin Brooker, were contacted for the research work. Finally, they were led to look under the dwelling where they found that parts of the lighthouse foundation walls were actually sections of the original tabby walls of the mansion. Digging through the dirt and rubble that had been used to fill the whole structure of the house, on 9 August 1985 directly below the lighthouse kitchen was found a fireplace of the original mansion. (Glass has been placed over this section so that it can be seen by all of those who wish to visit the lighthouse.) When excavation was completed, the remaining walls of a mansion, 75.5 by 75.5 feet, estimated to have been built sometime between 1790 and 1820, had been found.[19] Everyone was elated.

Discovered were sections of tabby walls that suggested a mansion with two main floors over an elevated basement. The first main floor

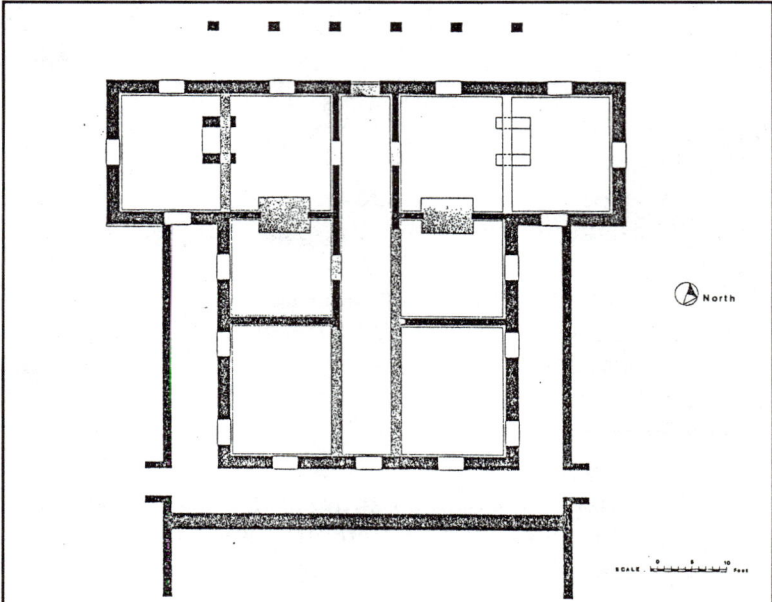

Main Tabby Mansion Excavation

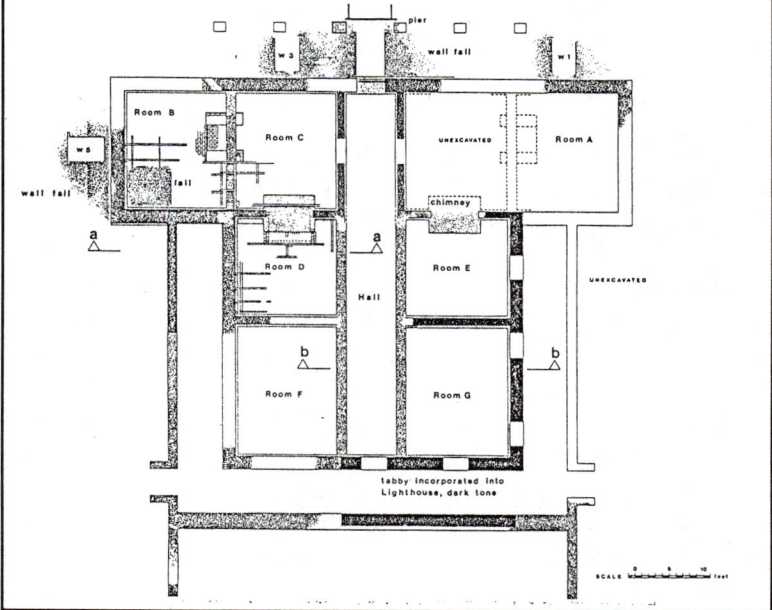

Restored Main Tabby Mansion, Haig Point Plantation
(Courtesy International Paper Realty Corporation of South Carolina.)

200

Haig Point Lighthouse

Seen surrounding the house are "strips" of tabby which shows the outline of the 1838 Blodgett Tabby Mansion. (Photograph courtesy International Paper Realty Corporation of South Carolina.)

consisted of eight rooms—four rooms on either side of a central hall. In order to "catch the breeze," there was a porch that extended along three sides of the house in a "U"-shaped fashion.[20] There may well have been a second main floor built identical to the first, as an elderly Pope cousin wrote in 1862:

> ... My mother spoke so often of visiting Grandpa and Grandma on one of the islands, as a little girl. She mentioned a beautiful colonial home of 25 or 30 rooms. . . .[21]

Very little evidence was found of lumber or nails, for prior to burning the remains, Union soldiers had removed the massive timbers from the mansion (and from other mansions on the island) as they were needed to make a road across the marsh (on Jones Island) heavy and substantial enough to support the guns that were necessary to bombard and capture Ft. Pulaski before taking Savannah.[22]

After all the material was photographed and recorded, the mansion walls were once again filled with dirt. A concrete footing was poured on the surface of the ground to outline the exact floor plan of the tabby structure.

•

There was no record of any large tabby buildings erected between the colonial period and the nineteenth century. However, as early as 1805 Thomas Spalding had revived the art and use of tabby construction. In a letter written to N. C. Whiting, Esq., New Haven, Connecticut, 19 July 1844, from his home at Sapelo Island, Georgia, Spalding wrote:

> ... I have made my walls 14 inches thick; below the lower floor 1 feet; for the *second story* 10 inches—*beyond that I would not erect Tabby buildings*. My house at Sapelo is one story, 4 feet from the ground, and sixteen (16) feet in the the ceiling, 20 feet in wall. It is 90 feet by 65 feet in depth besides *the wings*.[23]

Coulter wrote in his book:

> ... The tabby ruins on St. Helena and *Daufuskie i*slands are plainly seen to follow Spalding's method of construction. . . .[24]

•

Lighthouse Restored

After the excitement of finding the old tabby mansion remains, attention was given to the restoration of the lighthouse itself.

Bill Phillips, well known architect and engineer, was contracted for work on the building. He was fortunate to obtain the authentic plans for the range light and dwelling. Some of the structural timbers had to be replaced, but under the watchful eye and supervision of Bill, every phase and minute details were meticulously carried out from top to bottom, with the aid of Tom Bass et al. The house was brought back to its original grandeur and exquisitely furnished.

Haig Point Light Shines Again

The light had first become operative 1 October 1873. After its restoration had been completed, permission had been granted for the light to shine once more.

Earlier in the afternoon on Saturday, 18 October 1986, arriving by boat at Haig's Point were several hundred people, including members of the Savannah Symphony. As the orchestra played, with the additional audience of a full moon, the historic light tower was illumined by strains of "Stars and Stripes Forever," while a beautiful, colorful display of fireworks burst overhead from a barge anchored off shore.[25]

> The new [permanent] light has a nominal range of 6.9 miles, although at its height of 70 feet it is expected to be visible up to 9.6 miles across water. The Haig Point light has a 12-second cycle, blinking on for a duration of two seconds followed by an off frame of 10 seconds.[26]

Bloody Point Range Beacons

There became a need for lights to be placed on Daufuskie to insure passage for ships leaving the Atlantic Ocean and entering Savannah River to reach the port of Savannah.

Agreement had been made that the land needed on which to place two range lights belonged to Henry Mongin Stoddard who owned Bloody Point Plantation. Mr. Stoddard had been contacted and negotiations had been discussed concerning the necessary land that was required on which to place the lights, and the cost involved.

On 12 August 1881, Mr. Peter C. Hains, Major of Light House Engineers, sent a letter to the Office of Light House Engineers, Sixth

District, Charleston, South Carolina, stating that he had heard from Mr. H. M. Stoddard:

> I propose that the Board purchase from him five (5) acres as the site for the rear beacon at his price, $25.00 per acre, and three hundred (300) feet front on the beach for the front light at his price, $2.00 per foot, beach front: that will make $425.00 for both sights. I enclose tracings which will show the tracts selected. . . .[27]

On 14 April 1882 the United States Government, for the sum of $425.00, purchased from Mr. H. M. Stoddard 1.72 acres of land for the front beacon and 5 acres of land for the rear range light, "with the right to cut down any trees that may obstruct the view between the light houses to be erected upon the said pieces of land."[28]

On 22 October 1881 Cooper Manufacturing Company of Mt. Vernon, Ohio, received a letter from the Light House Board in session at Charleston, S.C., that their company had been awarded the contract of building eleven new iron lighthouses (towers) for the coast and Savannah River harbor.[29]

Mr. Julius E. Rettig, a member of the Light House Board, not only designed and drew the plans for the towers and lighthouses, but he also acted as inspector of the completed work.

It was the Cooper Company's chief machinist, John Michael Doyle, who was given the job of seeing that each foundation plate, column, rail casting, tension rod, strut, slat, and everything needed was meticulously measured, formed, or made, so that each piece of the tower would fit perfectly.

When the Cooper Manufacturing Company had completed the actual iron work on the towers, Mr. James C. LaCoste of Sullivans Island near Charleston, South Carolina, had been given a contract in September, 1882, to see that the tower and lighthouse were erected on Daufuskie.[29]

John Michael Doyle would supervise the erection of the rear metal light range tower and brick oil house, while Mr. LaCoste would build on the 1.72 acre beach site the lighthouse that would incorporate the front light.

Diary of John Michael Doyle

Doyle, having worked with the Lighthouse Department for sometime, was familiar with all aspects of the construction and erection of

their metal towers and oil houses. He and a Mr. Nevil Whitesides had just completed the tower at Parris Island, which was identical to the one to be built at the Bloody Point site and described as follows:

An interesting specimen of these skeleton iron structures was erected in 1881 at Parris Island, Port Royal Sound, South Carolina, and exhibits the rear light of the Paris Island ranges. Altogether it is the most economical structure of its kind in the history of light-house construction. The plan was born of necessity, it being found that the appropriation made by Congress was not sufficient to put up the kind of structure which it was usual to place in such a position. The light exhibited is simply a locomotive head-light in form of a powerful parabolic reflector. It is claimed, however, that it is possible to use on it a lenticular apparatus. The tower is composed of columns, sockets, struts, and tension-rods, framed in the form of a triangular pyramid. It rests on six circular iron disks, anchored to a concrete foundation. The top sections of the side facing the channel, for which the tower is the guide, are provided with horizontal slats to increase the visibility of the beacon by day. The light, which runs up and down in rails in the plane of the structure, is housed by day and at night is hoisted to its place at the apex of the triangle by machinery worked in the oil-house. The large foundation-plates are about 40 feet 4 inches apart. The focal plane of the light is 120 feet above the sea level, but the top of the structure is 132 feet from the ground. The cost of the iron work set up is $9,400.00, and that of the structure complete and lighted about $12,000.00.[30]

Prior to his arriving on Daufuskie, Mr. Doyle had kept a most interesting Diary. The first entry began on 7 March 1861 at Mt. Vernon, Ohio. Doyle had been as far as Savannah (1865) when he was with the Union Army, but had not been back to the South since that time.

Riding the Columbus & Mt. Vernon R.R. train that morning, he tells about his journey southward. On his way down to Atlanta he meets a real life Georgian, John W. Klins, who, with tears in his eyes, drew a very vivid picture of how it was after the War. His wife (whom he had lost by death just a short time before) would say to him when they lay down at night, "I am hungry." Those were dark days for the South after the War, when a man might ride for days and weeks and not find a bushel of corn, a cow or steer, a fowl, a hog, not a dollar in good money, not a fence or bridge, railroad torn up, houses burnt down, everything of any value swept away, women and children

starving and the men powerless to help them. They had to mortgage their lands and pay $1.90 per bushel for seed corn in the spring of '66, and the drought burnt this up so they got no crop. With hope, they kept on working hard and through the years everyone was finally prospering.

After leaving Atlanta, they passed through Augusta and on to Charleston where Doyle took a turn around the city, going through the markets where he saw turkey buzzards, Charleston's scavengers. On Friday, 11 March 1881, he visited the Citadel, a very large castle which was the military school of the State before the War. It was now deserted, the windows broken, the great gates off the hinges, and everything had an appearance of decay.

On 12 March 1881 Doyle rode the Charleston-Savannah R.R. to Yemassee and from there the Augusta and Port Royal R.R. to Port Royal, where he took a Light House boat to Parris Island. Growing on the island were sweet and common potatoes, figs, and oranges—but their principle crop was cotton. The population was eight hundred, with only two white families. Doyle boarded with the Snows. Mr. Snow was a white man, tall and military looking, while Mrs. Snow was "about as black a piece of furniture as I have ever met." Mr. Snow was a cook aboard the *Pawnee*, an old U.S. gunboat which was anchored in the river about a mile off the shore from Parris Island. Mr. Snow came home every Saturday, while Mrs. Snow lived in style on some land that she owned.

After supper on 2 April 1881, Doyle goes to the cabin of a colored family to attend what they call a "shout." The house was about ten by twenty, and divided into two rooms. By nine o'clock, packed into one of these rooms were about thirty men, women, and children. Some of them commenced singing, stamping, and clapping their hands, and then a number of them formed a ring and began a sort of shuffling, sea-sawing dance around the room, keeping time with the hands, feet, and head. The exercise seemed to be hard, for some of them were sweating like a steer, and imagine the flavor. It beat anything Doyle had ever experienced. He left at 11 P.M., but the "shout" was still going strong after daylight.

He was working on the Parris Island light tower on the morning of 5 April 1881 when he made the acquaintance of Mr. [Robert] Sisson, the lighthouse keeper from Hilton Head. After a short conversation,

he learned that Sisson was an old comrade in arms, being a former member of the 157th New York Regiment, which was brigaded with Doyle in the Army of the Potomac. Sisson had been in government employ in that section most all the time since the War, and at one time was clerk of the carpetbag senate at Columbia.

After the job was completed at Parris Island, Doyle took the train back to Charleston to the Custom House to report the work completed. He spent the night at the Mansion House. In the early morning he walked about the city admiring the old mansions with their verandas and the steepled and domed buildings and churches; he visited Sulllivans Island and walked around Ft. Moultrie; from the beach he saw "Castle Pinckney" and the 160-feet-high Morris Island lighthouse and Point Pleasant. On the morning of Friday, 6 May 1881, he sailed aboard the steamer *S.S. Calvert* to Baltimore. In the harbor he counted thirty-eight tugboats and thousands of ships of all sizes, styles, and nationalities whose masts were so numerous they looked like a forest in mid-winter. The steamer then took him to Boston harbor where he went ashore and boarded a train for Washington, D.C., and then home to Mt. Vernon on Wednesday, 11 May 1881.

On Monday, 4 July 1881, Doyle mentions that President James Abram Garfield had been mortally wounded by a gunman. Doyle remained at home that winter and spring, working at the Cooper Manufacturing Company. On the morning of Friday, 3 June 1882, he mentions that Charles J. Guiteau, the assassin of President Garfield, was hanged in the jail of the District of Columbia where he had been confined since the murder. Guiteau had borne up tolerably well till the fatal moment arrived when he broke down and showed himself to be the cowardly wretch which his act proved him to be. His brother, John W. Guiteau, was one of the spectators who witnessed the execution.

Doyle, with a friend, had taken a train trip to Newark, N.J., on Wednesday, 30 August 1882. They had an elegant dinner at the hotel near the depot, and occupying a seat near them was John Sherman, brother of General William Tecumseh Sherman. They got a good view of him and saw the resemblance—even a certain poise of the head peculiar to the old general.

By October 1882 all the material for the Bloody Point Rear Range tower had been completed, packed, and shipped. Doyle left Mt.

207

Vernon, Ohio, by train the morning of 1 November 1882 for Daufuskie. Arriving in Savannah on 13 November, he got his mail, bought a few purchases, then walked about the city. He mentions the changes since that winter of 1865. The Savannah streets were now full of business wagons. The large buildings that were then closed and silent, or full of soldiers, were now full of cotton or merchandise. The docks, which then were the refuge and shelter of the newly-made-free citizens, were now lined with shipping and all was noise and bustle. Even the grand old oaks, with their banners of moss, which lined many of the streets, now looked like old acquaintances.

Mr. LaCoste had a boat waiting, so Doyle was taken to Daufuskie, leaving Savannah about noon on the 13th of November. Passing old Fort Jackson and Fort Pulaski while sailing down the Savannah River, they arrived on Daufuskie at 10 P.M.

On the morning of Wednesday, 15 November 1882, the first ground was broken for the lighthouse work. The digging of the foundation was completed Monday, 7 December 1882, and on that same day the first concrete was poured. Doyle used a mixture that was composed of one barrel of Rosendale cement, three barrels of sharp sand, and six barrels of shells. There were 6,000 bricks to build the oil house.

While Doyle was on the island, he lived in a small house on Mongin Creek near the government wharf that had been built just for lighthouse use. "Auntie" Pender Hamilton cooked for him and did his washing, ironing, and cleaning. Doyle visited the Stoddards at Melrose and the Comers at the Haig's Point lighthouse. He also mentions that he met the Comers' young and lovely daughter, "Miss Maggie."

That winter, activity at the range tower went very slowly because of rain and extremely stormy weather which delayed materials and supplies arriving by "flats." Three months after the work began, the ninety-one-foot iron range tower and brick oil house were completed, and the final inspection was made on 22 February 1883 by Mr. Gowers, the officer in charge of the Sixth Light-House District. After packing up his things, that same afternoon Doyle boarded the *Crouch* with Mr. LaCoste and made sail for Savannah.

Leaving Savannah on 23 February, Doyle boarded a train that took him to Charleston. By boat he visited Sullivans Island on Sunday, 25 February 1883. Mr. LaCoste's son Jim met him with his pony and

phaeton and rode Doyle to the LaCoste house where he was warmly received by Mrs. LaCoste and her two daughters. Flora, one of the daughters, rode with little Jim and Doyle on the beach and visited Fort Moultrie where they explored the whole grounds. After a pleasant day, ending with a delicious dinner, little Jim brought his pony and carriage, taking Doyle to catch the evening boat back to Charleston.

Heading for home to Mt. Vernon, Ohio, Doyle left Charleston by train at 1 A.M. on 1 March 1883. He arrived in Augusta at 7:30 A.M.:

> . . . and had some of the stuff that is usually palmed off on travellers for breakfast & continued my trip to Atlanta which place I reached at noon. After dinner I took a stroll through the city to see if I could recall any of the old points that were once so familiar to me but no. All was changed.[31]

This was the last entry in John Michael Doyle's Diary. I can't thank enough Mrs. Paul (Evelyn) Helmly, Jr., and Mr. Walter Schaff for sharing it.

However, this was not the end of Mr. Doyle!

John Michael Doyle First Bloody Point Lightkeeper

It is evident that after Doyle (born in Wexford, Ireland) left the island, he applied for the government position on Daufuskie. On 4 April 1883 he was appointed the Bloody Point Lighthouse Keeper at a yearly salary of $620.00.[32]

There is no record as to when Mr. LaCoste completed the lighthouse dwelling at the beach or front range sight, but it can be assured that the lights were operative prior to Doyle taking oath that April.

Painted white with lead trim, the lighthouse was a two-story dwelling with porches all the way across the front and back. The first floor consisted of two rooms separated by a closet and front hall, with a stairway leading to the upper floor. After reaching the top of the stairway on the second floor, there was a narrow hallway that led to a small dormer-window room that housed the light. Two doors led to bedrooms on either side of the hall. Each room had a path—not a bath.

The light that shone from the roof of the lighthouse dwelling had a brass stand and wind-up clockwork to turn the light.[33] When synchronized with the rear beacon range, these lights guided ships into the Savannah River Channel.

In 1886 a kitchen twelve by twenty feet was built off the southwest corner of the lighthouse and was accessible from the rear porch. Also that year a boat-house was built.

By 1887 the encroachment of the sea had caused the boat-house to be moved thirty feet inland.

In 1888 the boat-house was moved inland another twenty-five feet and a storage house twelve by fifteen feet was built near the dwelling.

Doyle remained as Keeper for seven years, his salary increasing to $660.00 before he resigned on 15 August 1890.[34] Family lore states that he left the island, moved to Savannah, and became a fireman.

Robert Augustus Sisson Replaces Doyle

On 15 August 1890 Canadian born Robert A. Sisson became the second Bloody Point Lighthouse Keeper.[35]

During the cyclone that occurred on the 27 and 28 of August 1893, the kitchen, storehouse, and boathouse were rolled from their places where the tide had carried them, but were later reerected in their previous positions. The Sisson family lost furniture, food, and personal items. To claim reimbursement, Keeper Sisson on 17 October 1893 sent the following to the Light-House Inspector, Sixth District, Charleston, S.C.:

List of losses, with their value.

PROVISIONS

1 barrel best four $5.12
1/2 dozen cans roast beef 1.15
15 pounds coffee 3.75
1/2 pound tea 40
40 pounds white bacon 6.00
50 pounds lard 5.00
1/2 dozen cans corn beef 75
25 extra C sugar 1.43
3 pounds Royal Baking Powder 1.50
2 demijohns 95
1 bottle essence lemon 35
1/2 bushel salt 25
Spices (assorted) 35
3 pounds starch 15

12 cans roast beef 2.25
1 pound cocoa 60
4 quarts rice 40
l pound pepper 25
l pound D tobacco 60
3 scrubbing brushes 45

KITCHEN FURNITURE

1 safe 5.00
Dining table 4.00
1 kitchen table 2.00
2 chairs 3.00
2 tubs 1.00
Crockery, dinner, and tea set 10.00

HORSE FEED

1 sack oats, 141 pounds 2.25
1 sack corn 1.80
500 pounds fodder 3.75

SHOES

1 pair 1.50
1 pair 1.75
2 pairs 4.00
1 pair 2.00
Total $74.68

With regard to necessity of keeping a horse my reasons are that I am obliged to have one to haul my provisions from steamer landing, 3 miles from station; haul my wood from rear light, from where I at times purchase it, several miles off, and many other reasons—among them to get to steamer landing, 6 miles off. My horse is also used to haul oil and other supplies to the rear light, for which I receive no pay. On each and every inspection the horse is used to transport the inspector of the district to and from the rear light, for which no pay is asked, nor is it expected. I also use the horse to get to rear light in bad weather and when grass is wet. In fact, it would be impossible to live here without a horse, on account of the high prices asked for teaming, and the nearest horse that a person could hire is miles off and could not be got when wanted. The distance from here to the post-office (Savannah, Ga.) is 17

miles, and there is no provision store on the island where a white man would deal, their goods being of the most inferior kind, for which they charge 50 to 100 percent more than in Savannah or Beaufort. only the Marsh Island or swamp negroes buy in these stores.

Yours respectfully,

> R. A. Sisson, Keeper
> Bloody Point Lights,
> 17 October 1893

Sir: We also lost 46 head of fine chickens, valued at $13.80, and other things for which we don't expect any remuneration.

Respectfully,

> R. A. Sisson, Keeper

Lieut. Commander M.R.S. Mackenzie, U.S.N.
Inspector, Office of Light-House, Sixth District, Charleston, S.C.

Relief in the sum of $88.48 respectfully recommended.

> M.R.S. Mackenzie
> 26 October 1893[36]

Because of constant erosion, again in 1897 the boathouse had to be set back another 250 feet. By 1898, because of the encroachment of the sea, it was proposed "that the dwelling be taken down and moved about three-fourths of a mile to the site of the rear beacon." At the same time, a metal light tower from Venus Point range, South Carolina, would be moved to the extreme western boundary of the site of the front beacon. By December 1899 the dwelling had been moved and the Venus Point range tower had been put in place. "The new sight was thoroughly drained and a ditch dug about 7000 feet long to connect with a natural outlet [Mongin Creek]."[37]

The front range site had eroded beyond the 1.72 acres first purchased, and on 15 July 1911 land had to be leased by the year from the Stoddards to keep moving the light tower westward. The tower was moved back on three different occasions.[38]

Son Relieves Robert A. Sisson as Keeper

On 1 May 1908 Charles Leslie Sisson, son of R. A. Sisson, was appointed Keeper. But on 10 August 1910, Charles L. was sent to Fernandina, Florida, and R. A. Sisson returned as keeper to the Bloody Point Light.[39]

Gustaf Ohman Lighthouse Keeper

Gustaf (Gus) Ohman had come from Sweden on a sailing schooner that anchored at Charleston Harbor. As soon as he came ashore he had no intention of returning home, so he hid in a place where he could see the masts of the ship. The day he saw the masts moving away from the mooring, Gus came from his hiding place and found work along the waterfront.[40] He later married Edith Loper, but they had no children. He worked in many ports before settling down in Savannah and getting a job as a laborer at the Venus Point Light Station. On 16 August 1899, for $300.00 per year, Gus was appointed Assistant under Lighthouse Keeper Charles Leslie Sisson at the Venus Point Light. In 1910 he was sent as Assistant Keeper to R. A. Sisson. Shortly afterwards, earning the title of Keeper, Gus replaced R. A. Sisson at the Bloody Point Range Light.

John A. Robertson, Jr., Assistant Keeper

John A. Robertson, Jr., became Gus' assistant. John (Johnny) had a son, William Robertson, who boarded with the James Peto Chaplin, Jr., family on New River. William had a boat and carried passengers and mail to Savannah. The Chaplin girls would occasionally visit Johnny at the lighthouse and with Johnny's help they were allowed to raise or lower the rear range light. William later married Mary Chaplin, one of J. P. Chaplin's daughters.[41]

Arthur Ashley Burn, Jr., Assistant Keeper

Johnny Robertson resigned his position and in June 1913 Arthur A. Burn, Jr., became the Assistant Keeper under Gus Ohman.

A. A. Burn had assumed other duties in his fourteen-year career with the Weather Bureau at the Charleston Custom House, but being a messenger was one of the most important. After the weather reports along the coast had been sent by telegraph to the Weather Bureau Office, the data was transmitted by symbols to maps. Because their activity would be affected by the weather, Arthur would take mimeograph copies of these maps and distribute them by hand to merchants and boat captains along the waterfront.

Having lived on or near Charleston waters practically all of his life, rowing his bateau and salvaging wood along the waterway, and his

father having been a ferry captain and bridge tender at the Ashley River crossing, and having had relatives as lighthouse keepers at the Cape Romain and Ripley Lights, Arthur made application on 9 May 1913 when a vacancy became available at the Bloody Point Light, and received his appointment 21 May 1913, at a salary of $540.00 per annum.[42] When Arthur came to Daufuskie in 1913, he brought his family with him—his wife Catherine Elizabeth Nolte Burn and five children: Bessie (12), Louise (9), Ashley (7), Theodora (4), and Lance (21 months).

Arthur did not stay permanently at this station but was sent temporarily to Oyster Bed Lights (Savannah River). His next assignment was Assistant Keeper to Tybee Knoll Cut Light Station, which was just north of Ft. Pulaski on Cockspur Island. He moved his family and furnishings to this new light station in February, 1916, at a salary of $576.00 per annum. In November, 1918, Arthur was appointed Keeper, with a salary increase to $780.00 per annum. By 20 July 1920 his salary increased to $900.00 and on 9 September 1921 it went to $960.00. Now, however, he was required to furnish his own place to live and buy his own boat.[43]

On 31 July 1923 Arthur Ashley Burn, Sr., resigned his position with the Lighthouse Service and went to work for the U.S. Corps of Engineers, Savannah, Georgia, advancing to leverman on the dredge *Gilmer.*

Bloody Point Lights Extinguished and Property Sold

Gus Ohman remained at the Bloody Point Lighthouse until the lights were discontinued circa 1922. The Government having no further need for the lighthouse or land, they were placed on Public Auction 9 January 1922 and sold to Francis M. Keenan, the highest bidder, for $525.15.[44] This price included the lighthouse dwelling and other buildings, five acres of land, plus the road leading to the front range light. The 1.72 acres for the front range had long since been claimed by the sea.

Gus Ohman Buys Bloody Point Lighthouse Property

On 10 October 1924 Francis M. Keenan sold to Gustaf Ohman the lighthouse buildings and property for $450.00.[45] Gus had bought some land at Benjie's Point and built a store and a house to which he moved.

For the next two years he rented the lighthouse to different families on the island.

Gus Ohman Sells to A. A. Burn, Jr.

The happiest day in the life of Arthur A. Burn, Jr., was when Gus Ohman sold him the Bloody Point lighthouse and property for $700.00 in November 1926. But it was not until the final payment was made that he received his deed, dated 24 February 1930.[46] It was the first place that Arthur had ever actually owned and he was so proud of it. He was not interested in the beach road that was now in his possession, so on 22 June 1935 he swapped the two acres that the road entailed to Edward and John Stoddard for two acres of Bloody Point land joining Arthur's on the south side, thus increasing the lighthouse property where the dwelling stood to seven acres.[47]

Arthur A. Burn, Jr., Lived a Good Life at the Lighthouse.

Affectionately becoming known as "Papy (Pa-pi) Burn, he lived King of his domain. He loved this island so much that he stated he would not give a teaspoon of Daufuskie for the whole state of South Carolina—that Daufuskie was the nearest place to heaven as one could get on this earth.

James F. Byrnes, who was governor of South Carolina and later a U.S. Secretary of State, was a classmate of Arthur A. Burn. Papy said there was only one grade between them—*Medium* ; Jimmy was *High* and Papy was *Low*. Every time Jimmy Byrnes came to Beaufort or Hilton Head, he never failed to visit Daufuskie to see his good friend, Arthur Burn.

After his first wife died, in 1915 Arthur married Margaret Catherine Keenan, whose father Francis M. Keenan had made the first purchase of the property from the Lighthouse Department. Arthur and Margaret had two children, Francis Arthur Burn, born 1916, and Leonella Lillian Margaret Burn, born 1918.

Papy Burn had studied some law in his earlier years. He had also studied to be a preacher, taught a Baptist Sunday School, and was a substitute teacher (both he and his wife Margaret) at the little white Daufuskie school. He was a taxidermist until his hands became affected by the arsenic that was used in the preparation of the animal and bird skins.

Papy's oldest son, Ashley, had joined the U. S. Coast and Geodetic Survey and was serving aboard the ship *Bache.* Just before his twentieth birthday in 1926, Ashley drowned off the north end of Old Tampa Bay, Florida. Ashley is buried at Mary Field Cemetery here on the island. At the time, Papy cursed the Government, everything, and everybody. The case of the accidental drowning was settled in the House of Representatives, and Papy was to receive a cash settlement.[48] He loved Ashley so much and never really got over this terrible tragedy. They were great pals and went everywhere together. Ashley would accompany Papy and help row the boat to tend the Savannah River lights, sometimes taking them all night to make the rounds. Papy could not understand how his son, who was such a good swimmer since a young child, could drown. The only logical answer was that when the small work-boat sank, Ashley was trying to save his buddy, J. B. Ryland, who could not swim—both perishing together.

Margaret C. Keenan Burn, Papy's second wife, died in 1927. She, too, is buried at Mary Field Cemetery.

Papy quit the dredge and farmed his land. An old brown mule that he used to plow was toothless and a leftover from the Army—some even kidded him and said that it had belonged to Sherman when he came through here in 1861. At any rate, being without teeth, the old mule could not eat grass so they had to feed him on cooked cornbread and cornmush, which was a lot of trouble. When the old mule finally died, the hole that was dug to bury him was too small and too shallow, so his head and legs had to be cut off to plant him deep enough.

Early in the morning Papy and his son Lance would take out old *Missy* on the high ebb, sail to the jetty's at the Savannah River entrance, catch a load of fish, string them on palmetto strips, and sell them at Ft. Screven near Tybee. They would wait for the first of the flood and sail back home in the afternoon. It was on one of these trips that while fishing Lance had caught a brown pelican that swooped down on the shrimp Lance had thrown out on the end of his hand-line; the fishhook snared the pelican. Lance pulled him in, removed the hook from his beak, and put him on a box that was built in on the boat to bring him home for a pet. From nowhere, a summer squall hit them and before the sails could be reefed, the boat turned upside down. Papy and Lance hung on to the bottom of the boat, but Papy, with his heavy boots filled with water, kept slipping away, and Lance had a

time bringing him back; they pulled off Papy's boots and let them go, so he could hang on until the blow was over. When the wind subsided, they righted the boat and bailed it out, but the poor pelican had drowned. Papy blamed Lance for the storm because he had caught the pelican and Papy didn't think he should have—to catch a wild thing like that was a bad omen. Anyway, they sailed safely home, but Lance never, during his lifetime, ever caught another pelican.

It was on another of these fishing trips to Tybee in 1933 where Papy met this little widow woman who had come down from Augusta to enjoy the beach. He was captivated by her and she thought he was a bronzed, Greek God. Thus, Papy Burn married again, taking for his third wife Laura (Dyer) Greiner, whom right away he nicknamed "Susie."

In 1934, seven years after Ashley's death, the Government sent Papy a settlement check and he began receiving a monthly pension. Using some of the money to buy white lead, zinc, turpentine, color, and linseed oil, he used the lighthouse formula to mix his own paint and painted the inside and outside walls of the lighthouse. He converted the porch off the east side of the kitchen into a sunroom. With the many windows, they enjoyed the summer breezes, protection from the winter winds, and it was nice to have a place to store many of their favorite flowers from the cold. A bathroom was added on the south side of the kitchen.

Papy also bought a shrimp boat and named it *Ashley*. His son Francis would help him shrimp and do repairs on the engine. Sometimes his son Lance would go along and give them a hand. They caught tons of shrimp and sold them for six to eight cents per pound to L. P. Maggioni at Jenkins Island dock, Hilton Head, and to Frank C. Mathews Seafood in Savannah. The small shrimp that no one really wanted only brought two cents per pound.

Papy loved his wild birds and flowers. Across the banisters at the corner of the porch he would put a wide board on which he would place left over grits, rice, or bread scraps. After he finished, he called the birds by making a loud fluttering noise with his tongue, and here the birds would come. At any time the birds found the board empty, they would hop on the nearby window sill and peck on the window panes until he came out and fed them.

Papy had all kinds of zinnias, petunia boxes on the porches,

217

morning glories running on trellises, and all sorts of pot plants, but his favorite flowers came from bulbs. Huge trumpet lilies lined the driveway. All around his house, using a diamond pattern, he planted thousands of white and yellow narcissus, and beautiful yellow King Alfred daffodils. An eighteen-inch row of one kind would be followed by a wide row of another kind and color. Sometimes he used snow-drops as border plants. In early spring the yard would be a conglomerate of color and the fragrance of the flowers filled the air. It was truly a beautiful sight to see and to smell. He even dug a hothouse, using windows around the top so that he could save his flowers through the winter.

Papy and Susie built a chicken house from lumber that he salvaged out of the river. Many pleasant hours were spent in watching little biddies with their funny antics. At the end of the day, with a great sense of satisfaction, they gathered the large brown eggs that their Rhode Island red hens had laid.

During World War II Papy and Susie moved to Savannah where Papy worked in the shipyard, returning to the island after the war ended. His happy years with Susie ended when she died in 1947.

Papy married divorcee Addie (Tyrrell) Jervey (his first sweetheart and his fourth—and last—wife) in 1948. He was seventy and she was sixty-eight. He and Addie had some good times together and they had some bad times. They went fishing a lot and on one occasion they were using hand-lines with a one-pound lead sinker and pieces of cut mullet, with which to catch a thirty-five pound bass. Papy swung the line around over his head in order to throw it out into the deep, but instead he let it go too soon because he was caught off balance by a wave, and he hit Addie with the full force of the swing. When that heavy lead hit her, it knocked her out and blood started pouring from her forehead. Thinking he had killed her, Papy hurried to her side and took off her old straw hat, then checked her pulse. She was still breathing. He reached over the side of the boat with his hat and filled it with water which he poured on her face until she finally came to. He rowed the boat to the shore, got Addie to the car, and sympathetically said, "Baby, I'll drive you home." Knowing what a terrible driver he was, through her tears Addie cried, "No, you won't! You're not about to finish killing me today." So, *she* drove them home. The next day, even with the big lump and a gash on her head, they had a good laugh

over the whole thing and were grateful that she was still among the living.

It's hard to believe that Papy took Frank Beard (his son-in-law) fishing in the same way that he took Addie, and hit Frank in the same way that he had hit Addie, but with a slight difference. Papy had left some of the entrails on the piece of cut mullet, and when it slammed up by the side of Frank's head, he reached up and felt the entrails and yelled, "Mr. Arthur, you've knocked out my brains!" The only thing that Frank had was a gash and a big lump on his head.

Papy and Addie started making wine in the oilhouse in 1953. He made it all legal by obtaining a license and calling his operation the "Silver Dew Winery." From that time forth, the building has been known as "the winery" and unless they are aware of its history, no one knows that it was once an oilhouse.

The wine was made in five gallon glass jugs, with corks and plastic tubing that ran down to a water-filled jar that caught the bubbles as the fruit fermented. It was a very clean operation. In fact, the inspector stated that it was the first wine that he had ever seen that wasn't infested with roach bugs and mice.

Papy and Addie would go to the beach and pick buckets of blackberries. He made other kinds of wine using bananas, plums, elderberries, scuppernongs, bunch grapes, and oranges. He would make wine out of anything he could find, but he never drank any and he never sold any; he only tasted it and gave it away to his friends. He made wine legally that one year, but he continued to make at least ten gallons at a time just for the sheer pleasure he got out of it.

During his wine making days, he had repainted the kitchen so I went by to see how it looked. As I entered the room, the transformation was really refreshing. The walls were a soothing, cool, sea-green color. As my eyes circled the kitchen, I noticed two, five-gallon glass jugs of freshly squeezed scuppernongs perched on the end of the wooden extension that he had added to the sink, then my gaze lifted upward, and there on that freshly painted snow-white ceiling were bits of grape pulp and seeds where one of the jugs had exploded. Shocked, I looked at Papy and said, "Papy, you didn't!"

He laughingly replied, "That's nothing—you should see the winery. It looks like someone took a dose of salts and did cartwheels."

Papy had the wit, and with that twinkle in his eyes, in his later years, had even the look of Will Rogers.

In the early 1960s, Papy was the first person to divide some of his property into small lots, selling all seven of them. Papy was the magistrate for many years. He was getting in ill health, so in order to be near a doctor, on 25 June 1966 he sold his beloved Daufuskie Lighthouse (completely furnished) and his remaining property (3.8 acres) to Simon P. Kehoe III and his sister Mary Kehoe Cummings, for the sum of $6,000.00.[49] Knowing his love for the island, Papy's family and friends deeply regretted his leaving.

Papy and Addie moved to Sullivans Island near Charleston, but he was never happy and cursed the day he left Daufuskie. He had several pin-strokes, was in and out of the Veterans Hospital and nursing homes in and around Charleston, dying on 20 January 1968. His body was brought back home to Daufuskie where he is buried not far from his son Ashley, in Mary Dunn Cemetery.

Kehoe & Cummings at the Bloody Point Lighthouse

While the Kehoe/Cummings owned the lighthouse, because they all worked, their visits to the island were limited to weekends, holidays, and summer vacations. The only change they made to the house was to tear off the old bathroom at the back of the kitchen and add a new one at the end of the sunroom, thus cutting off any exit to the south side of the house. Their visits grew less and less. Not having a new coat of paint since 1934, and needing repairs, the house was beginning to look pretty run down and uncared for. On 7 March 1979, Mary Kehoe Cummings conveyed her interest in the place to her brother, Simon P. Kehoe III.[50]

James (Jim) Batey Makes Lighthouse Bloom Again

On 18 August 1981, for $82,500.00, Drayton Shipyard, Inc., Jim Batey's company on Hilton Head, purchased the Bloody Point lighthouse property from Simon P. Kehoe III.[51]

Moving to Daufuskie, Jim and his wife Sandra accomplished two things: first, in 1981, their children were three of the four white children who integrated the black Mary Fields Elementary School for the first time; and second, Jim gave the lighthouse a thorough face lifting and almost complete renovation.

220

Some of the foundation timbers had decayed, so new ones were added; window panes were replaced and reglazed; the closet, staircase, and front hall downstairs were removed and the first floor was made into one large room; a new stairway led to the upper floor; wood that encased the two fireplaces was removed, exposing the naked brick; a bathroom was added upstairs in the little dormer window room that had housed the light; the banisters on the porches were revived; the steps to the east porch that were completely gone were replaced, with banisters added; and the steps to the west side porch were renewed; insulation was incorporated in all the outside walls, and the house was painted a Cape Cod red with ivory trim. The inside walls were stripped of their paint,and with the floors, the wood was refinished and left in its natural state. The lumber throughout the house did not contain one knot hole. Lovely, etched half-glass doors were added to the west entrance and to the sunroom. For cooling, ceiling fans were used throughout the house and on both porches. The dwelling was beautiful both inside and out, with the exception of the inside of the kitchen and no shutters.

(During the time the Bateys lived in the house, a friendly ghost— whom they named "Arthur," and who was believed to be the spirit of Papy Burn—would mysteriously turn out the light; or, a chair would rock, and noises were made like someone walking up the stairs. The children even saw his misty form sitting in a rocking chair on the west porch.)

An added attraction that Jim was ready to have built was a barn, to replace the one that had been on the premises in years past. The plans for the barn had been carried out to the letter, with an apartment upstairs for Sal Strozzi, who was an old friend and who had become a member of the family—the children adored him. All of the timbers had been cut to size and everything was ready to be pegged together, with not one nail to be used, when Jim got in trouble with the IRS. The barn was never assembled.

Seizing the Bloody Point Lighthouse and property, the Beaufort County Court of Common Pleas, on 19 November 1982, placed a judgment against Drayton Shipyard, Inc., and a Foreclosure and Sale was advertised for Public Auction of said property, in order to claim the money that Jim Batey owed in back income taxes.[52]

James P. Black, Highest Bidder

On the steps of the Beaufort County Courthouse, 4 April 1983, James P. Black was the highest bidder for $54,500.00.[53]

This price satisfied the court, and Jim Black was the proud owner of the Bloody Point Lighthouse property, an investment that had cost Jim Batey over twice that amount.

Jim Batey took counter action that delayed the case for awhile, but the end result was that he had to relinquish his claim to the property, and the family left the island.

When Jim Black and his wife Tootie moved to the lighthouse, they began to finish what Jim Batey had started. Heating was accomplished by fireplaces and wood-burning stoves, but they replaced these with three air-conditioning units. The six windows in the sunroom were reduced to three in order to balance with the main house. A door was cut in the living room to give access to the sunroom without having to approach it via the outside porch. All of the inside wood in the walls and ceiling of the kitchen was removed, new electrical wiring and insulation installed, then each board was sanded and replaced. The ceiling was painted. The old built-in kitchen cupboard was dismantled, stripped, and re-assembled. The grocery pantry where Papy Burn had stored hundred-pound sacks of sugar, rice, and grits was cut down to size to match the kitchen cupboard on the opposite side of the same wall. Beautiful, custom-built kitchen cabinets were installed. A master bedroom was provided on the first floor by adding a petition to the one large room. A wooden lattice skirt was attached along the high foundation pillars under the house, hiding the cistern that once furnished water. A house was built over the deep well pump. A white board fence graces a large portion of the yard. The last thing that gave added beauty to the place was a good-sized lagoon (or pond) on the east side of the house.

When all the improvements had been completed, it was advertised as the Daufuskie Lighthouse Inn, available by the week or weekend.[54] Because of the lack of renters, the idea was abandoned.

Jim and Tootie tried to live permanently at the lighthouse, but— due to Jim's work and their son Perry's being in school, both of them having to be in Savannah on time—it came to be one big hassle with the bad winter weather and summer squalls. They gave it up, and placed the house on the market.

222

Beach Road Associates Purchase Lighthouse

For the sum of $284,000.00, 26 October 1988, the Beach Road Associates purchased the lighthouse and its 2.85 acres of land.[55] They landscaped the yards with azaleas, boxwood, and other plants, and added a skeet-shoot tower. Shutters for the windows remain lacking. The only outward activity seen about the place has been cook-outs in the yard. Their plans for the property have not been disclosed as yet. It can only be assumed that the house is now being used as a Welcome Center or Sales Office.

NOTES

1. *Charleston Evening Post, Tricentennial Edition*, 31 March 1970, Charleston Main Library.
2. Records of the United States Coast Guard, Record Group No. 26, Lighthouse Site File, South Carolina No. 9, National Archives (GSA), Washington, D., 20408.
3. Ibid.
4. Beaufort County Courthouse, Deed Book 6, pp. 341-4; Strain.
5. Record Group No. 26.
6. Ibid.
7. Ibid.
8. By order of the Lighthouse Board: Joseph Henry, Chairman; *Savannah Morning News* , 22 September 1873, Savannah Public Library; Strain.
9. Record Group No. 26.
10. Ibid.
11. Ibid.
12. Beaufort County Courthouse, Deed Book 43, p. 256.
13. Ibid., Deed Book 43, p. 436.
14. Ibid., Deed Book 48, p. 38.
15. Ibid., Deed Book 128, p. 116.
16. Ibid., Deed Book 128, p. 117.
17. Ibid., Deed Book 128, p. 118.
18. *Beaufort Gazette* , 7 December 1967.
19. *Island Packet*, 24 July 1985, 16 August 1985, 25 September 1985, 29 November 1985; *Beaufort Gazette*, 13 August 1985, 25 September 1985.
20. Mike Trinkley, Ph. D., ed., *Archaeological Investigations at Haig Point, Webb, and Oak Ridge, Daufuskie Island, Beaufort County, South Carolina* (Columbia: Chicora Foundation Research Series 15, 1989), pp. 91-93.
21. Strain.
22. *War of the Rebellion* , 4 series, 70 vols. (Washington: Government Printing Office, 1882), series I, 6:143-44.
23. Coulter, pp. 72-76.
24. Ibid., p.78.
25.. *Island Packet*, 20 October 1986.
26. Ibid.

27. Records of the United States Coast Guard, Record Group 26, in the custody of the Judicial and Fiscal Branch of the National Archives, Washington, D. C>

28. Beaufort County Courthouse, Deed Book, vol. 13, p. 24. See Appendix XIV.

29. Doyle Diary, p. 56.

30. Arnold Burgess Johnson, *The Modern Light-House Service* (Washington: Government Printing Office, 1889), pp. 29-30.

31. Doyle Diary, pp. 3095, passim.

32. Coast Guard Record Group 26; F. Robert Sisson, Jr., personal letter, 14 March 1981.

33. Robert Sisson, personal letter, 18 July 1981.

34. Coast Guard Group 26; Sisson, Jr.

35. Ibid.

36. U. S., Congress, House, *Personal Losses Sustained by Certain Light-House Employees,* Ex Doc. No. 9, 53d Cong., 2d sess., 1893, pp. 3-4.

37. C. G. Group 26.

38. Ibid.

39. Ibid.; Robert Sisson.

40. Samuel Henry Rodgers, interview, 14 June 1983.

41. George White, telephone interview, 14 June 1983; A. A. Burn's personal file; Mrs. Fred (Marguerite) Rawstrom files.

42. A. A. Burn's personal file.

43. Ibid.

44. C. G. Group 26.

45. Beaufort Courthouse, Deed Book 42, p. 537.

46. Ibid., Deed Book 47, p. 569.

47. Ibid., Deed Book 48, pp. 297-98; Deed Book 52, p. 149.

48. U. S. Congress, House, *Arthur A. Burn, Sr., and J. Ryland* Report No. 780 to Accompany H. R. 7631, 73d Cong., 2d sess., 1934, p p. 1-5.

49. Beaufort County Courthouse, Deed Book 138, p. 217.

50. Ibid., Deed Book 2788, p., 389.

51. Ibid., Deed Book 330, pp. 1773-75.

52. Ibid., Deed Book 367, p. 595.

53. Ibid.

54. *Savannah Morning News,* Thursday, 9 June 1988, sec. C.

55. Beaufort County Courthouse, Deed Book 514, pp. 716-20; Steve Kaiser telephone interview, 21 November 1988. Steve would not reveal the prices involved..

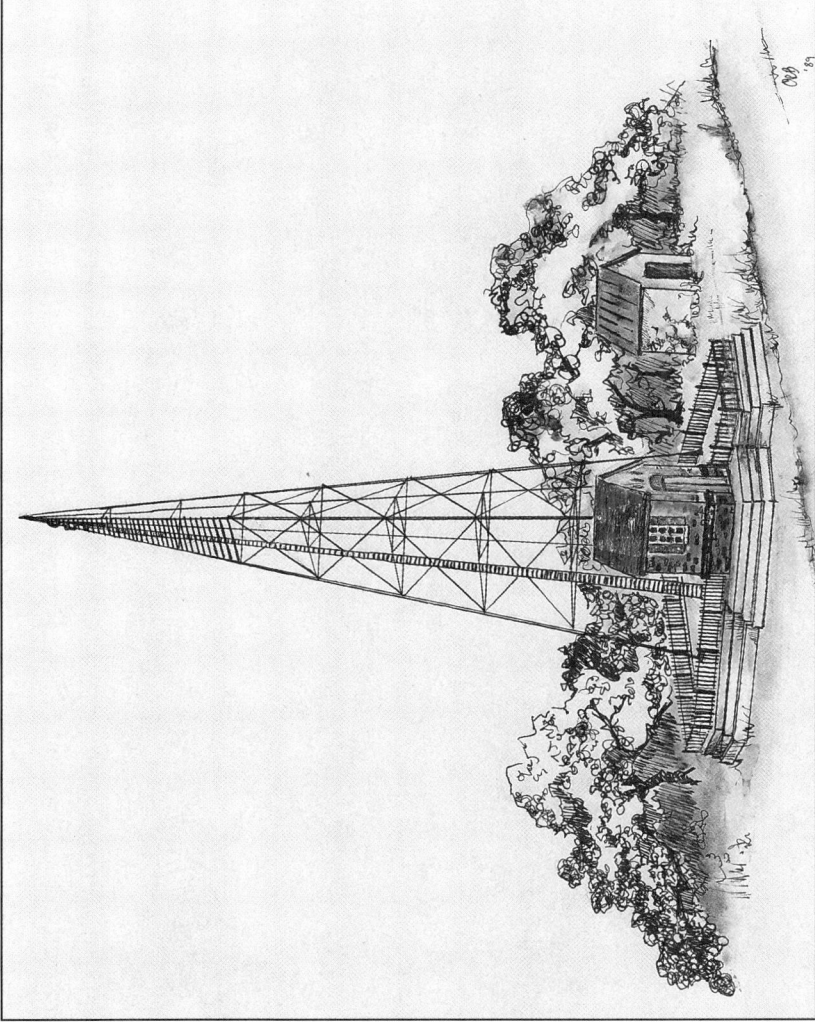

Rear Beacon for Bloody Point Range 1883
(Courtesy artist, Christina Roth Bates.)

This metal tower (circa 1899-1922) was the Front Range Light after the Bloody Point Lighthouse was removed to the Rear Range Site. Remains of this tower continues to be seen on low tide off the front beach. (Courtesy National Archives, Washington, D.C.)

Center Front: Col. Robert Augustus Sisson, Bloody Point Lighthouse Keeper (circa 1890s). His staff, left to right: Maj. Salvador Lupo, Maj. William Dufloque, Maj. G. Yulee Park, Capt. Adj. John L. Wall. (Photograph and names of men courtesy Gilbert Joseph Maggioni.)

Kate C. Sisson, Robert and Martha Sisson's daughter, circa 1900, standing by Eastern entrance steps, Bloody Point Lighthouse. (Photograph courtesy Fred Sisson.)

227

Bloody Point Lighthouse (circa 1900) after it was moved from the beach site in 1899. The white tower shown on the right is the back range light built by John Michael Doyle in 1883. (Photograph courtesy Gilbert Joseph Maggioni.)

Bloody Point keeper, Robert A. Sisson and his wife Martha, Western entrance to lighthouse. (Photograph courtesy Gilbert J. Maggioni.)

Photograph taken on west side of Bloody Point Lighthouse, circa 1900-1912. In wagon seated left to right: Gustaf Ohman, Bloody Point Lighthouse Keeper, Mr. Loper, Mrs. Loper (Mrs. Ohman's parents), Edith Loper Ohman, Gus's wife. "Captain" is the name of the horse. (Courtesy Mrs. Ralph (Ida) Tatum.)

Arthur Ashley Burn, Jr., circa 1920-1923. Bloody Point Assistant Lighthouse Keeper.

Bloody Point Lighthouse in Disrepair, March 1976
(Photograph courtesy R.H. Dunlap, S.C. Wildlife and Marine Resources Department.)

Bloody Point Lighthouse, 23 December 1989. Photograph made during Daufuskie's first white Christmas in history. (Courtesy Robert L. Burn.)

1953 "Silver Dew Winery." Photograph made during snow 23 December 1989. (Courtesy Robert L. Burn.)

7

WARS—THEIR IMPACT
ON DAUFUSKIE

Being a barrier island, Daufuskie has always been one of the first places to feel the impact of a hurricane. There has been no difference in wars that have touched its shores. During several conflicts the island has continued to be one of the first to be invaded and/or occupied by friend or foe.

The Yemassee War

The Indian War of 1715 has already been discussed in the segment *How Bloody Point Got Its Name.*

The Revolutionary War 1775-1783

"Daufuskie came to be called *Little Bermuda* since, like the real Bermuda, it served as a loyalist (Tory) refuge."[1] On Hilton Head was a group of patriots (Whigs). Because of their guerilla tactics the two parties turned the Revolution into a civil war. As an injustice was committed on one side, retaliation quickly followed by the other.

Phillip Martinangele II of Daufuskie was a captain in the Granville County, South Carolina, Royal Militia. Serving under Colonel Nicholas Lechemere and Major Andrew DeVeaux with Phillip were his brothers, Privates Francis, Issac, and Simeon Martinangele.[2] Other members included Lt. William Green, George Lewis, William Petty, Joseph Hill, John Albritton, George Calton, Joseph Page, Thomas Scott, Alexander Hutchison, Joseph Downer, James Scott, Jesse Patterson, Benjamin Jefferson, Alexander Stewart, Joseph Palmentor, Mark Fortune, Richard Fortune, Abraham McGowan, Edward Calton, and John Blucke.

Sometime in 1781, at their own expense, the Royal Militia built a fort on Daufuskie that only lasted six months when they all deserted and left for Savannah.[3]

The first account of the Tory-Whig skirmishes concerned Richard Thomas ("Tory Dick") Pendarvis:

> ... In early January of 1781, Pendarvis and 'a party of militia' perhaps including the Martinangele brothers, went to Bear Island, South Carolina, to apprehend one Dougherty, a 'rebel' officer on parole, for 'not complying with militia regulations.' They found him with six or seven others, were fired upon and returned the fire. Doughtery was killed, the rest escaped.[4]

According to the Whig viewpoint from records that later surfaced, this incident inspired Dougherty's nephew, John Leaycraft of Hilton Head, to form a partisan group called the Bloody Legion, with the purpose in mind of avenging his uncle's death. Members of this gang were John Erving, Lewis Bona, Daniel Savage, Christian Rankin, James Devant, John Bull, James Eving, James Allan, Charles Floyd, Isaac Davids, Nathaniel Gambal, William Chiswell, Thomas Roberts, (David) John Mongin, Sr. (No. 2), John (David) Mongin, Jr. (No. 3), David Ross, Patrick M'Mullin, Isaac Bolder, Meredith Rich, John Fenden, and William Scott.

On 19 April 1781 "Tory Dick" Pendarvis was killed. Family records relate this interesting story:

> Margaret de Martinangel, the youngest daughter of Philip de Martin-angel, was married first to Rear Admiral Richard Penda[r]vis, H.M.N. They were spending their honeymoon at a beautiful residence called "Stephenville," situated on the banks of the South May River. The Admiral had reluctantly left his young bride and returned to the cares of everyday life in the city of Charleston, but of course he felt very anxious to return again and be with the choice of his heart. He returned after an absence of three weeks to enjoy the company of his young wife.
>
> He had scarcely gained the pathway leading from the river to the house when his housegirl, Nancy, said, "Oh, Mistress, Master is coming!"
>
> At the same moment, before his lady could come, one of the waiting boys, Tom, called out, "Master, the rebel scouting party is coming down the road."
>
> His lady called out, exclaiming, "Oh, Mr. Penda[r]vis, run and hide yourself or you will be shot."

He faced her, saying, "Why, for shame, Margaret," kissing her gaily, "I will immediately go out to them and deliver myself up as a prisoner of war and in a very short time I will be exchanged."

He left her, but went out to meet his death, for as he was approaching, Lee Craft [John Leaycraft], who was leader of the party, raised his rifle and fired at one hundred paces. The Admiral fell. His lady rushed out and clasped his bleeding body in her arms and prayed—yes, called down the maledictions of heaven on the murderer and his name. She prayed that he might die like a dog in a ditch and might have neither son nor nephew to bear his name.

. . . Would you know the end of this man? When he died, he was buried on Hilton Head, South Carolina, and had his grave planted around with the American cactus—to keep the women, as he vulgarly termed them, from shaking their petticoats over his head.

And singular to admit, the prayer was granted, he left neither son nor nephew to bear his name.[5]

The death of Martinangele's brother-in-law Pendarvis demanded counteraction. In December of 1781 Captain Phillip Martinangele and five of his men rowed to Hilton Head where they ambushed Charles Davant.

Holmgren gives a full account of this incident. Word had been received by the Whigs on Hilton Head that the Tories on Daufuskie were planning an attack. This message was quickly passed from one plantation to the next. Well-armed men rode their horses to the rendezvous on the southwest corner of the island. The party anxiously glanced at the faint shoreline of Daufuskie expecting any moment to hear the sound of muffled oars. In vain they waited all through the cold winter night, but saw or heard nothing.

Weary and chilled to the bone, at early dawn the men rode back toward their homes. Charles Davant and John Andrews rode side by side ahead of the others. Shortly after making a turn in the road, they were approaching two mighty oaks with their long branches heavily draped in Spanish moss. Charles Davant leaned forward in his saddle to see more clearly if that was something moving in the shadow, when a shot rang out. John Andrews wheeled his horse around and headed back to inform the other men, but Charles Davant slumped in his saddle with a bullet in his chest. His horse bolted from fear and galloped wildly for home. Clinging desperately to the saddle horn, Davant got a brief glance of his assassin—Martinangele. Through the

234

pain, he managed to keep that name on his lips until his horse halted at the doorway to his home.

Awakened by the shot at Two Oaks, Charles' son was waiting on the piazza. The lad rushed to catch the blood-stained body of his father as it slipped from the saddle. "Martinangele, get Martinangele," were the last words that Charles Davant ever uttered.[6]

From an account in a Charleston newspaper, retaliation quickly followed:

> We are informed from Savannah, that about Christmas last, a gang of banditti came to a house on Daufusky Island, where Capt. [Phillip] Martinangel of the Royal Militia was lying sick, and whilst two of them held his wife, another, named Israel Andrews, shot him dead; they afterwards plundered Mrs. Martinangel and her children of almost everything they had. These wretches came from Hilton Head; they stile themselves the Bloody Legion, and are commanded by John Leaycraft. . . .[7]

After the war ended, all animosity and hatred ceased. With the exception of Abraham, all of the surviving Martinangele brothers quietly returned to the family plantation on Daufuskie. When Savannah was evacuated by the British, Abraham, together with the John Hopkins and William Green families, left for East Florida and then on to the Bahamas. However, Abraham was back in South Carolina by 1790, and was listed as "Head of the Family" in the census taken that year.

And even though Margaret Martinangele Pendarvis held John Leaycraft (leader of the Bloody Legion) responsible for her husband's and brother's murders, in 1783 she married Captain William Edwards Mongin. Captain Mongin was not only a Whig (patriot), but was also a half-brother to David John Mongin (No. 2) and half-uncle to his son John David Mongin (No. 3), who were both members of the Bloody Legion. Margaret and William moved to Daufuskie and made their home at her estate on Mongin Creek.

Major Events During and Following the Revolution

There were four eventful things that happened during and after the Revolution pertaining to South Carolina and to the nation as well: The Declaration of Independence was formed; South Carolina became known as the Palmetto State; the Colonial Flag with its thirteen stars

235

representing the thirteen colonies was made; and the Pledge of Allegiance was adopted.

The Declaration of Independence

Having failed every effort at their reconciliation with the English government, the American colonies declared their independence. Written by Thomas Jefferson, the Declaration of Independence was adopted by the Second Continental Congress, 4 July 1776, declaring the thirteen American colonies free and independent of Great Britain. The document was signed by fifty-six revolutionaries, including four South Carolinians: Edward Rutledge, age twenty-six; Thomas Heyward, Jr., age twenty-nine; Thomas Lynch, Jr., twenty-six; and Arthur Middleton, thirty-four.[8]

How South Carolina Became Known as the Palmetto State

On the same day that the committee reported to Congress to draft the Declaration of Independence, the British made their first attempt in Charlestown harbor to crush the revolt in the south.

Having been cut from Dewees Island, Palmetto tree logs were transported to Sullivan's Island in order to construct a hastily built fort which was named Fort Sullivan and was commanded by General William Moultrie.

(Moultrie's executive officer was Francis "Marsh Rat" Marion.[9])

Long Island, now known as the Isle of Palms, lay just north of Sullivan's Island.

Moultrie's 435 men came from two units: the Second South Carolina Infantry and the Fourth South Carolina Regiment. The north end of Sullivan's Island was made secure by 780 men under the command of Colonel William Thompson of Orangeburg. "Thompson and his rangers, dragoons, and 50 'Raccoon Riflemen' (from their coonskin caps) awaited the British from behind two small sand batteries."[10]

The British had 50 ships and 3,000 soldiers under the command of Sir Henry Clinton and Lord Charles Cornwallis. Their strategy was to land soldiers on Long Island, cross Beach Inlet (which separated the two islands) while the ships bombarded Fort Sullivan. What the British were not aware of was that Beach Inlet was not only deep, but also it had always been a treacherous span of water.

After the 11 British ships, carrying 270 guns, anchored off the

island, the bombardment of Fort Sullivan began. The fort's spongy palmetto tree logs held and although the British aim was good, their shots did very little damage.

Things went badly for the British; they suffered a terrible defeat: The flagship *Bristol* was severely damaged and all men on board were wounded; both the *Bristol* and the *Experiment* captains were killed. On the shoals where Fort Sumter now stands three British ships went aground, which prevented them from attacking the fort on its vulnerable side. The British lost one hundred men and one ship, with extensive damage to the remaining ships. The Americans reported only twelve men killed.

Having witnessed their first victory of the Revolution, the people of Charlestown were elated, and for the next three years Charlestown was spared further military involvement in the war.[11]

Following this victory, because of its logs helping win the battle, the palmetto tree was given honor by being affixed to the state flag and South Carolina became known as the Palmetto State. Fort Sullivan was renamed Fort Moultrie in honor of General William Moultrie and Colonel William Thompson had a bridge named after him over Beach Inlet—Thompson Bridge.[12]

Stars and Stripes Sewn by Betsy Ross

This legendary flag maker was born Elizabeth Griscom in Philadelphia, Pennsylvania, 1 January 1752, to Samuel and Rebecca James Griscom. While growing up she was taught by her mother how to do needlework, at which she became extremely skillful. Elizabeth was married 4 November 1773 to John Ross. John, who had been an apprentice to an upholsterer, began his own upholstery business with his wife, now referred to as Betsy Ross. In January, 1776, John was on militia duty and was fatally injured by an explosion of gunpowder on Philadelphia's waterfront.[13]

Mrs. Ross continued to sew and supplemented her income by making flags for the State of Pennsylvania. Legend has it that in June 1776 (some say 1777) Betsy Ross was visited in her upholstery shop by George Washington, Robert Morris, and George Ross (uncle of her late husband), all of whom were members of a secret committee of the Continental Congress authorized to design a flag for the nation-to-be [The United States of America].

237

Her idea that she make a five-pointed star rather than a six-pointed one (as their model revealed) was accepted, after she demonstrated how quickly a five-pointed star could be made with only one snip of the scissors (by folding the cloth a certain way). They entrusted her good judgment in making the flag, using a circle of thirteen white stars on a blue background (representing a new constellation) incorporated with thirteen red and white stripes.

According to some versions of this story, Betsy was given a contract to manufacture flags for the government, and she continued to do so until here death, 30 January 1836.[14]

Meaning of the Flag and Colors

General George Washington expressed his theory on the evolution and symbolism of the Stars and Stripes as follows:

"We take the star from Heaven, the red from our mother country [Great Britain], separating it by white stripes, thus showing that we have separated from her, and the white stripes shall go down to posterity representing liberty."[15]

Stars have long been used to denote dominion and sovereignty; the blue signifies vigilance, perseverance, and justice; the red is for hardiness and valor; and the white means purity and innocence.[16]

In regard to rules and customs of heraldry, there is a distinct rank among the colors: blue is one of the honor colors and outranks white and red. Therefore, it is technically incorrect to speak of the American flag as being "red, white, and blue;" it would be correctly described as "blue, white, and red."[17]

Pledge to the Flag

In 1892 President Benjamin Harrison called for patriotic exercises in school as part of the celebration of Columbus Day, the Four Hundredth Anniversary of the discovery of America. The Pledge of Allegiance, taken from a children's magazine the *Youth's Companion*, was recited by public school children as they saluted the flag that same year.[18]

There were only two men working with *Youth's Companion*— Francis Bellamy and James Uphan, both of whom were concerned about the pledge's publication. The pledge was left anonymous until

after the death of the two men, when each family claimed authorship. The United States Flag Association, through an investigating committee, proved without a doubt that Francis Bellamy was the author. As first published, it read:

> I pledge allegiance to my flag and to the republic for which it stands: one nation, indivisible, with liberty and justice for all.[19]

In 1923 "my flag" was removed and replaced with "the flag of the United States of America."[20]

In 1942 Congress made the pledge a part of the code for use with the flag.[21]

It was not until 14 June 1954 that President Eisenhower signed a bill which added the phrase "under God." The pledge now reads:

> I pledge allegiance to the flag of the United States of America and to the republic for which it stands: one nation under God, indivisible, with liberty and justice for all.[22]

The War of 1812-1815

If this war reached Daufuskie it was probably the same as Holmgren states that happened on Hilton Head:

> . . . On August 22, 1813, the British landed in force on Hilton Head shores and repeated their plundering of Revolutionary War days. The island was defenseless, with no fortifications, and its homes too widely scattered to unite against sudden attack. Once again homes were burned and looted. . . .[23]

The Star-Spangled Banner

Out of this 1812 War came our national anthem. The song was inspired by the British attack on Fort McHenry, Baltimore, Maryland. On the night of the attack, Francis Scott Key, a young Baltimore lawyer who had gone with a group of friends to the British admiral to seek his help in the release of a prominent physician whom they had captured. Key and his friends were detained aboard a ship in the harbor and spent the night of 13-14 September 1814 watching the British bombard the fort. With all of the shooting, Key felt sure that the British had been successful in the attack, but when the dawn disclosed the American flag still flying, Key's emotions were so

239

overwhelming that he wrote the words of the "Star-Spangled Banner" on the back of an old envelope. He adopted the words to the music (at that time) of a popular drinking song, "To Anacreon in Heaven." The next day the original version was printed in the form of a handbill, but a week later it appeared in a Baltimore newspaper. The song soon became the national anthem, but Congress did not recognize it officially as such until 1931. The "star-spangled banner" that flew over Fort McHenry that night may be seen at the Smithsonian Institution, Washington, D.C.[24]

The War of the Rebellion or the Civil War: 1861-1865

Daufuskie played an interesting and very unique roll in this War Between the States. By the time the Battle of Port Royal was over, 7 November 1861, all of the islands along the coast had been invaded by Union Forces. Each island was a sight to behold as there were fields of snow-white cotton bolls ready to be picked.

Leaving the slaves in charge, every white planter had fled Daufuskie and their property was confiscated by the enemy as "abandoned lands." Without notification, taxes were levied against the plantations, but were unpaid since there were no funds with which to pay them—Confederate money was worthless.[25]

For several weeks now, following the Battle of Port Royal, Brigadier General Thomas West Sherman had been aboard the flagship *Wabash* anchored off Hilton Head. He was working out the strategy for the ground and naval forces to cut off all supplies and aid by water, in order to take Ft. Pulaski and Savannah. The troops were beginning to get restless and wanted to get moving.

By January, 1862, Brigadier-General Egbert L. Viele was stationed on Daufuskie with several regiments of troops. Others came by the first of February. These men consisted of a detachment of the Third Rhode Island Artillery, a detachment of Volunteer Engineers, a battalion of the Eighth Maine Regiment Volunteers, parts of the Sixth & Seventh Regiment Connecticut Volunteers, Twenty-eighth Massachusetts, several companies of the Forty-sixth, Forth-seventh, and Forty-eight New York Volunteers, and seven companies of the Third New Hampshire.[26] (The total number of troops stationed on Daufuskie was 1600.)[27]

Some of the men were embarked to the island on the steamers *Winfield Scott* and *Mayflower*, while others came in smaller boats and lighters. Most of the troops disembarked at Haig's Point while the boats were sent to the Engineer's Wharf built in New River (on property now belonging to Lance and Billie Burn). Several companies were stationed at Cooper River Landing and others sent to exposed places on the island, while the majority of the troops marched down the seven-mile length of the island to the Dunn Plantation on Mongin Creek. Officers occupied the big white mansion, while the men were quartered in out buildings and sheds or bivouacked near the woods behind the house. The Dunn mansion was on a very high hill and from this vantage point, and from the Mongin mansion at Bloody Point, bombardment of Ft. Pulaski could be seen and heard.[28]

Soon after arriving on Daufuskie pickets were established and sentries posted. Mail was given out and one soldier stated that he had gotten a letter from a loving sister and a small packet of tea. After reading his letter by the dim light of a short piece of candle which he carried in his pocket, he lay down on his bed of earth and pillow of boughs to dream of home. The morning after they got settled, detachments were sent out to secure the cattle, pigs, and poultry abandoned by the owners who had fled, and to collect whatever else was edible, as most of their supplies were on the steamer *Winfield Scott* which had wrecked on "Long Pine Island" the afternoon before.[29]

The soldiers noticed the beauty of Daufuskie and were amazed at the huge live oaks covered with long streamers of Spanish moss. They revelled in the beauty of the gardens of the Stoddard mansion at Melrose and the Mongin house on Bloody Point:

> . . . Both gave evidence of large wealth and cultivated tastes, in the character of the houses and beauty of their surroundings, and as we wandered through the shaded avenues, and among the shrubs and flowers, in gardens where roses and japonicas grew in tropical luxuriance, where the air was full of sweet odors, and the eye confused with the multitude and variety of brilliant colors, and remembered that these abodes of happiness and beauty had been abandoned to pillage and destruction, and that wherever our armies penetrated, homes would be broken up, and in the place of comfort would come suffering, and in the place of beauty, desolation, we cursed the madness of those who had brought such miseries on the land.[30]

Guns Mounted on Islands in Savannah River

General Thomas West Sherman had given his plans for securing Savannah and Fort Pulaski. Their intentions were to "cork up Savannah like a bottle." All cuts and creeks coming into Savannah would have to be patrolled and made secure. in order to cut off communication and prevent re-enforcements and supplies reaching Fort Pulaski, batteries would have to be placed on Tybee, Jones, Long, and Bird Islands of the Savannah River.

Stopping passage of enemy boats to Savannah, the Confederates had sunk in Wall's Cut (between Wrights and New Rivers) a 90 foot schooner that was 25 feet wide and anchored with rows of piles driven across on either side. By 14 January 1862 this obstruction had been removed by the Forty-eighth Regiment New York Volunteers and a company of the Volunteer Engineers, in order that their gunboats might enter the Savannah River and cover them in the placement of their batteries. Three companies of the Seventh Connecticut Volunteers were left to guard and protect this Cut.[31]

Between 1-4 February 1862, in order to build a wharf at Mud River (Fields Cut), to build a 1000 foot corduroy road across Jones Island, and in order for gun placements to be constructed on islands in Savannah River, nine-feet long poles, five to six inches in diameter, were cut from ten thousand trees on Daufuskie. Hundreds of bags were filled with sand, and several of the larger plantation houses were torn down for boards and heavy timbers that would provide a platform on top of the logs to roll the guns. After these logs were cut, on 5-6 February 1862 men of the Forty-eighth New York, of the Seventh Connecticut Volunteers, and a portion of the engineer forces were all engaged in transporting these logs on their shoulders for a mile and sometimes a mile and a half to get them to the Engineers Wharf on New River, place them aboard small boats, and row them the four miles to Mud River where they built a wharf of some of the sand bags, logs, and timbers. A swath of reeds and grass was cut across Jones Island to prevent the enemy from burning the island over. When the wharf was completed, a wheelbarrow track of planks laid end to end was constructed across Jones Island to Venus Point. On the night of 10 February 1862, guns and ammunition were brought to the wharf at Mud River and transported across the marsh to Venus Point.[32] A

detailed description of what the men had to go through for seven gruesome weeks to get the guns distributed on the islands in Savannah River (against wind, rain, and cold—including a flurry of snow on 7 March) needs to be addressed.

The effort it took for placing the guns on Jones Island alone was explained by Brigadier-General Gillmore, chief engineer Expeditionary Corps, in his journal 11 February 1862:

> The work was done in the following manner: The pieces, mounted on their carriages and limbered up, were moved forward on shifting runways of planks about 15 feet long, 1 foot wide, and 3 inches thick, laid end to end. Lieutenant Wilson, with a party of 35 men, took charge of the two pieces in advance, one 8-inch siege howitzer and a 30-pounder Parrott, and Major Beard and Lieutenant Porter, with a somewhat larger force, of the four pieces in the rear, two 20 and two 30 pounder Parrotts. Each party had one pair of planks in excess of the number required for the guns and limbers to rest upon when closed together. This extra pair of planks being placed in front, in prolongation of those already under the carriages, the pieces were then drawn forward with drag-ropes one after the other the length of a plank, thus freeing the two planks in the rear, which in their turn were carried to the front. This labor is of the most fatiguing kind. In most places the men sank to their knees in the mud, in some places much deeper. This mud being of the most slippery and slimy kind and perfectly free from grit and sand, the planks soon became entirely smeared over with it. Many delays and much exhausting labor were occasioned by the gun-carriages slipping off the planks. When this occurred the wheels would suddenly sink to the hubs, and powerful levers had to be devised to raise them up again. I authorized the men to encase their feet in sand bags to keep the mud out of their shoes. Many did this, tying the strings just below the knees. The magazines and platforms were ready for service at daybreak.[33]

On 12 February a fresh crew of men had to return to Jones Island and throw up a dike around the battery to keep the spring tide out. That day the tide had come within eight inches of the surface at Venus Point.

For gun placements on Tybee Island, which was mostly a mud marsh, the work was extra laborious and dangerous:

> No one except an eye-witness can form any but a faint conception of the Herculean labor by which mortars of 8-1/2 tons' weight and columbiads but a trifle lighter were moved in the dead of night over a narrow

causeway, bordered by swamps on either side, and liable at any moment to be overturned and buried in the mud beyond reach. The stratum of mud is about 12 feet deep, and on several occasions the heaviest pieces, particularly the mortars, became detached from the sling-carts, and were with great difficulty, by the use of planks and skids, kept from sinking to the bottom. Two hundred and fifty men were barely sufficient to move a single piece on slingcarts. The men were not allowed to speak above a whisper, and were guided by the notes of a whistle.[34]

All of the activity had to be done at night, then just before dawn their work was carefully concealed by straw and grass to prevent the

Noiseless Hauling of the Guns

Sometimes it took as many as 250 men for one gun. (The original sketch may be found in "Perry's Saints," p. 165.)

rebels from discovering just what was taking place. As a consequence of the heavy lifting and the amount of energy used, sometimes without the proper amount of food, many of the best Union soldiers were "ruptured or otherwise injured, and crept out of the service, maimed and ruined for life. Whiskey and quinine were powerless to stay the effects of such labor and exposure."[35]

When the work was completed, the armament comprised thirty-six pieces, distributed in eleven batteries at various distances from Ft. Pulaski. The shortest distance a shell would have to travel to hit the fort was 1,650 yards, while the longest distance was 3,400 yards.[36]

Those troops that participated in supplying all of the fatiguing labor

244

for the batteries were of the Forty-sixth New York Volunteers, the Seventh Connecticut Volunteers, two companies of the New York Volunteer Engineers, two companies of the Third Rhode Island Artillery, and a small detachment from Company A, Corps of Engineers.[37]

Brigadier-General T. W. Sherman Relieved of Command

When General Sherman's strategy to reduce Fort Pulaski and Savannah simultaneously became known, letters of opposition flew back and forth from Washington. The Navy refused to partake in this battle of Savannah. With the main obstructions in the river, the risk was too great; this was the duty of the ground forces. On 14 February 1862 General Sherman received a letter from George B. McClellan, Major-General, Commanding U. S. Army, in which was stated that no attempt was to be made upon Savannah.[38]

Although he was sent appreciation for the amount of and importance of his services rendered, General Thomas West Sherman lost his command, and was sent a letter for his removal :

General Orders,   War Department, A. G. O.
No. 26   Washington, March 15, 1862

The States of South Carolina, Georgia, and Florida, with the expedition and forces now under Brig. Gen. T. W. Sherman, will constitute a military department, to be called the Department of the South, to be commanded by Major-General [David] Hunter.

By order of the Secretary of War:

L. [Lorenzo] Thomas
Adjutant-General.[39]

Following is an excerpt from the letter written on 1 April 1862 to Brigadier-General Viele on Daufuskie:

My dear General: I inclose you a copy of Major-General Hunter's order assigning me to the late command of General [T.W.] Sherman.

H. W. Benham
Brigadier-General, Commanding.[40]

General Benham received all of Sherman's charts, maps, plans, reports, money, official records, returns—everything appertaining to the expeditionary command in the First Division of the Department of the South.[41]

Under the command of Brigadier-Generals Hunter and Benham, and of Acting Brigadier-General Quincy A. Gillmore, final preparation was made to starve off and completely close all water routes and communications coming in to Fort Pulaski: gunboats were placed in Saint Augustine Creek; two companies of the Forty-sixth Regiment New York Volunteers, with two field pieces, were placed on board an old boat hulk anchored in Lazaretto Creek, cutting off boat communication from there; telegraphic communication to the fort was cut; because a gunboat and 18 Union men of the Forty-sixth New York Regiment had been captured by a large Confederate scouting party on 31 March on Wilmington Island, two regiments of troops were stationed there; and a gunboat was placed in Wilmington Narrows to aid in the blockade.[42]

Each battery had a service magazine capable of containing a supply of powder for two days of firing. The following 36 guns were manned, aimed, and ready to fire: twelve heavy 13-inch mortars, six heavy 10-inch columbiads, three heavy 8-inch columbiads, one 8-inch columbiad, five 30-pounder Parrotts, one 48-pounder James (old 24-pounder), two 84-pounder James (old 42 pounder), two 64-pounder James (old 32-pounder), and four 10-inch siege mortars.[43]

Fort Pulaski (not Savannah) was now bottled up and ready to be corked.

Siege of Fort Pulaski

Just after sunrise on 10 April 1862, Major General David Hunter, commanding the department, dispatched Lieut. J. H. Wilson of the Topographical Engineers, to Fort Pulaski, bearing a flag of truce and the following summons to surrender:

> Sir: I hereby demand of you the immediate surrender and restoration of Fort Pulaski to the authority and possession of the United States. This demand is made with a view to avoiding, if possible, the effusion of blood which must result from the bombardment and attach now in readiness to be opened.
>
> The number, caliber and completeness of the batteries surrounding you leave no doubt as to what must result in case of your refusal; and as the defense, however obstinate, must eventually succumb to the assailing force at my disposal, it is hoped you may see fit to avert the useless waste of life.

This communication will be carried to you under a flag of truce by Lieut. J. H. Wilson, U. S. Army, who is authorized to wait any period not exceeding thirty minutes from delivery for your answer.

I have the honor to be sir, very respectfully, your most obedient servant.

David Hunter,
Major-General, Commanding.[44]

To this demand Colonel Charles H. Olmstead sent a negative reply: "I was placed here to defend, not to surrender."[45] At a quarter past 8 that same morning, the first gun of the thirty-six was fired, followed by the remainder at fifteen-minute intervals for the next thirty hours. After eighteen hours of firing, the fort was breached in the southeast angle. As evening closed in, all the pieces ceased firing with the exception of two 13-inch mortars, one 10—inch mortar, and one 30-pounder Parrott, which were served throughout the night at intervals of fifteen to twenty minutes for each piece, to prevent repairs and to fatigue the garrison.[46]

To aid in firing the guns a detachment of one hundred seamen from the Navy had been kindly furnished off the Flagship *Wabash* by Flag-Officer Samuel Francis DuPont. A little after sunrise on Friday, 11 April 1863, all batteries again opened fire with decided effect, and shortly after noon an eight or ten-foot square hole had been made in the fort's seven-and-a-half foot thick walls. Preparation was being made for scaling-ladders to be placed and for men with guns and bayonets to pour through the opening when, at 2 P.M., a white flag was hoisted. The rebel flag, after filling out to the wind for a few minutes at half-mast, came slowly to the ground. The flag of the Union would soon be hoisted in its place.[47]

Major Charles G. Halpine, Captain A. B. Ely, and Acting General Quincy A. Gillmore were directed by Brigadier General Henry W. Benham to accept the surrender of the fort.[48] They were met on the inner drawbridge by Colonel Olmstead, who offered them his sword, bowing in a gesture of defeat.[49] However, in General Benham's report of 12 April 1862, he recommended that . . .

the commander of the fort, Col. Charles H. Olmstead, whose gallant conduct as an enemy and whose courtesy as a gentleman are entitled to all consideration, that, should you deem it proper, the courtesy of the return of his sword should be extended to him.[50]

The sick and wounded Confederate soldiers were exchanged for eighteen Union troops who had been captured in March on Wilmington Island. The officers and men of the fort were allowed to take with them all their private effects, such as clothing, bedding, books, etc., but this privilege did not include private weapons.[51]

The troops on Daufuskie were watching the bombardment of Fort Pulaski with much interest. Some had observed the shelling from atop the hill of Mary Dunn's Mongin Creek plantation while others had climbed large willow trees overhanging the water near the Mongin mansion at Bloody Point. When the firing ceased, throughout the day the shore was lined with excited soldiers: the fort was theirs.[52]

Big feasts were prepared of chicken, turkey, oysters, and vegetables brought from as far away as Hilton Head. Although the greatest celebration was at Fort Pulaski, everyone else, even those on Daufuskie, ate well and attended religious service conducted by the chaplains.[53]

"Perry's Saints" Help Garrison Fort Pulaski

The Forty-eighth New York Volunteers and Company G of the Third Rhode Island Volunteers were sent as the garrison force of Fort Pulaski.

Born in Ulster County, New York, James H. Perry graduated from West Point and in private life, when the war started, was a pastor of the Pacific Street Methodist-Episcopal Church in the city of Brooklyn. As the call went out for volunteers, he was one of the first to sign up. As companies formed he was the Colonel in command of the Forty-eighth New York State Volunteers that was soon to be known as "Perry's Saints," not that the whole regiment were saints, but because James H. Perry resigned as a pastor and took up a sword.[54]

While Colonel Perry was stationed at Fort Pulaski, on the 16-17 of June, 1862, a terrible storm prevailed along the coast during which a schooner was discovered on her beam ends on the bar off the west end of Cockspur Island, which was not far from the fort. With much difficulty the crew was rescued, but the vessel was a total wreck and its cargo, which consisted of sutler supplies, floated ashore on Tybee and Cockspur Islands. Cases and cases of claret (dry red wine) and champagne and barrels of beer and wine were too enticing to resist, and as a result, on 17 June many of the troops were inebriated and in a terrible state of demoralization. When Colonel Perry became aware

of the situation, guards were set along the shore to secure the cargo. He then applied the severest measures by confining the intoxicated ones to the guard-house and dungeon. After all of the alcoholic beverages were collected and locked up, order was restored. It was a probability that with all of the excitement and disorder, Colonel Perry was so upset that it brought on an attack the following day. On the afternoon of 18 June, Colonel Perry was writing at his desk when his pen suddenly fell from his hand, his head dropped, and he was gone: "the silver cord was loosed and the golden bowl was broken." He was respected and admired by all of his troops, and this was a sad day in the regiment. He was buried outside of Fort Pulaski, but later his body was removed to Cypress Hill Cemetery in Brooklyn.[55]

Thanksgiving Made a National Holiday

Jubilation and festivities over the capture of Fort Pulaski ran from April until fall, at which time General Hunter declared a Military Thanksgiving Day on 27 November.

George Washington had been the first to declare a Thanksgiving holiday in 1789. Observing the day was strictly a matter of state and local custom.

However, President Lincoln in 1863 issued a proclamation specifying that the holiday be on the last Thursday in November. Each president after him had to issue the same *annual* proclamation until 1941 when, under President Franklin Delano Roosevelt, the Thanksgiving holiday became law.[56]

Troops Returned to Daufuskie

With exception to the troops stationed at Fort Pulaski, most of the other men returned to Daufuskie where their duties were less severe than they had been. They enclosed their tents with poles and decorated them with moss and evergreens. The officers vied with each other in making their quarters attractive.[57]

Men from the Dunn Plantation would visit troops of the Forty-sixth New York, a German regiment stationed at Cooper River Landing. Anthony Scheelings, bugler of the Forty-eighth New York, was one of the most useful members of the company. With his little pack of dogs he roamed the woods from morning until evening parade, seldom returning without an abundance of appetizing game that he shared

among the messes with impartial liberality. Occasionally he would confront a rattlesnake, but with his gun and dogs he was more than a match for beast or reptile. But one day Scheelings returned from his usual ramblings with a very sad countenance. When asked what the problem was, all he could say was, "Mine leetle tog, mine leetle tog." Sometime later, when he had lost some of his grief, he explained that when his favorite little cur jumped across a creek it suddenly disappeared from sight. Soon afterwards he had seen a huge alligator whose movements were hastened by a shot from Sheelings' gun, but the "leetle tog" never returned.[58]

By July 1862 all of the troops had gradually left Daufuskie, with some heading for Fernandina and St. Augustine, Florida, while others left for Coosawhatchie, St. Helena, Edisto, Folly, James, and Morris Islands near Charleston.

Former Slaves Left Island

When Union troops landed on Daufuskie in 1861, all of the able-bodied former slaves (men, women, and children) left for Hilton Head and Beaufort, leaving only the old and sick. Over a year later none of them had returned.

Captain J. H. Mickler, commanding a battalion at Bluffton, South Carolina, visited Daufuskie with ten men from his company and five from Company B, Eleventh Regiment, South Carolina Volunteers. The following are excerpts from his report on 30 January 1863:

> . . . I proceeded on yesterday, the 29th instant to Daufuskie Island, where I succeeded in capturing 12 negroes, the only occupants of the island. As they proved to be old persons, several of them imbeciles, I did not think proper to remove them. An examination of three hours disclosed a remarkable accumulation of valuable bed furniture, clothing, provisions, dry goods, and sundries, besides silver and gold coin to the amount of $188, which latter I have turned over for the use of the people of Fredericksburg. I have also reported to the quartermaster's department 1 keg and 2 bags of nails, 172 pounds of bacon, 2 muskets and a shotgun, besides a small quantity of rope.
>
> . . . Having only two boats of limited capacity I was able to bring off only a small proportion of the spoils. The men however, succeeded in supplying themselves bountifully with many necessary articles of clothing, blankets, etc. For prudential reasons I did not think proper to burn what I was unable to remove.

The men all behaved well. The value of the articles removed is not less than $2,000.[59]

Zouave Soldiers in the Civil War

Zouave was the name of a Kabyle tribe of the Jurjura Mountains, Algeria, from whom the Zouaves were originally recruited. These Algerians were also members of a former infantry unit in the French Army, noted for their precision of its close-order drill and characterized by a colorful (red) Oriental uniform. Zouaves are also members of any military group having a similar uniform or members of any of various volunteer regiments in the American Civil War.[60]

During the Civil War there were 20,000 of these troops serving in the North and about half that many in the South. From Port Royal on 3 April 1862, General David Hunter wrote to the Honorable E. M. Stanton, Secretary of War, in Washington:

> . . . We shall do all that men can do with the force we have; but it distresses me to be in such a beautiful position for striking strong blows without the arms to strike. I beg that you will send us at once as many men as you think we can use to advantage, as all the officers in command report the re-enforcement of the enemy on their respective fronts.
>
> I most earnestly request that 50,000 muskets, with all the necessary accouterments, and 200 rounds for each piece, may be sent to me at once, with authority to arm such loyal men as I can find in the country, whenever, in my opinion, they can be used advantageously against the enemy.
>
> It is important that I should be able to know and distinguish these men at once, and for this purpose I respectfully request that 50,000 pairs of scarlet pantaloons may be sent me; and this is all the clothing I shall require for these people. . . .[61]

"The Little Iron Man"

A two-foot metal statue of an Algerian Zouave soldier was found on Daufuskie. Someone said that it had been seen in the white Mary Dunn Cemetery, but this has not been proven.

I first learned about this statue from Mrs. Bessie Futch who was the principal and one of two teachers at the Mary Fields Elementary (black) School. Knowing my concern about the history of the island, Mrs. Futch asked me if I knew anything about the "little iron man."

251

She said that she had been told that he had some sort of mystical prowess, because for each person who brought him in the house the wind would suddenly blow real hard, shutters would slam, and doors would open and shut; everyone who had possessed him became afraid and quickly threw him out.

I had not heard about this "little iron man," but I was surely going to find out about him. Paul Wilson, a young black man, lived at Cooper River where the stories about this little man had originated. He had helped Samuel Holmes with carpentry work and knew everyone here. Paul had only one eye, but he saw and was aware of everything that was going on on the island. Anyway, I asked him if he had ever heard of this "little iron man." He informed me that he had, that before his death Samuel Holmes was in possession of the little man. Sam would pull his boat as high on the river shore as he could get it, then tie the rope to a metal stake up on dry ground. Then he would stand this "little iron man" by the stake to scare anyone who threatened to steal his boat. Paul informed me that someone had beat up the "little iron man" and stolen Samuel's boat anyway, but that he knew about where to find the "little iron man." It wasn't long before Paul came to the house with the remains of the little man that he had discovered near the Cooper River Cemetery. He handed me the body of a statue made from some sort of metal that looks something like pewter, and the severed head that was bashed in, but he could not find the arms. It was true—someone thought that by destroying the statue its powers would be broken.

After examining the statue it could be plainly seen that it represents a French soldier because it has fleur-de-lis-like decorations on the baggy pantalooned uniform, and on the broken head is a fez with a tassel. The face looks foreign with a mustache and goatee. All of the statue's features are outstanding and have been expertly crafted in every detail. After some research it certainly suggests that the statue is a model of a Zouave soldier from Algeria. But where did it come from? Why was it brought here and who had it as a momento? These questions continue to remain unanswered.

Emancipation Proclamation

A proclamation issued by President Abraham Lincoln in September, 1862, became effective 1 January 1863, freeing the slaves in all

territory still at war with the Union. Slavery was abolished forever. The negroes were not only received and protected, but also the men were organized into regiments for service against their late masters.[62] Many registered for the First Regiment of South Carolina Volunteers, "although General Hunter in his rather odd way had 'recruited' soldiers for that at the point of a bayonet." The former slaves would now be paid for their labor. They could buy land as cheap as $1.25 per acre, build their own huts, plant their own gardens, and raise their own chickens and animals. They could live in government housing and their children could regularly attend school.[63]

Other Stories Concerning the Civil War

The British blockade runner, *Alliance* was seized by the crews off the USS *South Carolina* and *T. A. Ward* on 12 April 1864.[63] The *Alliance,* a handsome Clyde-built steamer with 2 engines and 3 stacks, grounded off Daufuskie Island with a cargo of soap, medicine, liquor, glass and salt. Drawing only 5-1/2 feet of water, she was piloted by John Makin, one of Savannah's most experienced pilots.[64]

•

(According to Mrs. Gillian White, there might be liquor remaining yet beneath the sands at Bloody Point. She was told that in the 1920s/1930s Gus Ohman would go there with a crony to play cards and gamble. They would run out of booze and Gus would take a long metal rod and poke it around on the beach and when he heard a "clinking" sound he would know that it was a bottle of liquor, then dig it up and they would drink it.)

•

The Yankee Invaders at Their Work

On Wednesday last, Mr. John Chaplin took with him seven negroes, and went in two boats to the plantation of his aunt, Mrs. [Mary] Dunn, on Daufuskie Island, for the purpose of bringing away such property as could be transported. On Wednesday night, he, with the negroes, occupied Mrs. D's dwelling, intending to leave when the tide favored in the morning. About two o'clock yesterday morning the door of the house was broken down by a party of ten Lincolnites, who captured Mr. Chaplin and five of the negroes, and conveyed them from the island in a boat. Two of the negroes escaped—one, who was sleeping in one of the

253

chambers, jumped from the second story window, and running to a point on the island, where he obtained a boat, came to the city yesterday morning. Before leaving the island, he saw the Yankees leave in their boat with Mr. Chaplin and the five negroes on board.

This is the manner in which Gen. Sherman proposes to give protection to private property.

Since writing the above, Paul, Mrs. Dunn's driver, who escaped from the cellar of her house when it was broken into yesterday morning, has arrived in the city. He states that on leaving his mistress' house he crossed over toward Mr. [John] Stoddard's place, Melrose, keeping himself concealed in the bushes. From his concealment, he saw a number of the enemy on Mr. Stoddard's premises directing the servants in driving up the cattle and horses. They had two mules and one of the plantation wagons to haul off their plunder, and one of the officers was mounted on a fine horse belonging to Mr. Stoddard. Paul thinks they carried off all the stock and the four negro men who had been on the place, who we understand, had been sent down by Mr. Stoddard to bring off the poultry and other property belonging to his negroes. Paul learned from the women on Mr. Stoddard's place that the Yankees were going to take possession of Dawfuskie Island, and that they would have a guard around it tonight. They asked many questions of the negroes about the neighboring island, who lived on them, etc. They also desire to know the distance of Fort Pulaski from Dawfuskie.[65]

Release of Mr. Chaplin by the Lincolnites

Mr. John Chaplin, whose capture by the Lincolnites, with five negroes on Daufuskie Island immediately after the taking of Port Royal, we mentioned at the time, returned to the city yesterday, with the negroes, having been released by Gen. Sherman on taking the oath not to bear arms against the United States.

The retaining of Mr. Chaplin, and the capture of the negroes, is evidently a stroke on the part of the Lincoln-raiders, by which they hope to induce the "loyal" citizens of Beaufort District to return to their homes and accept Yankee protection. They took pains to give Mr. Chaplin a large amount of information respecting their force, and the power and designs of the Lincoln Government, the dissemination of which they no doubt expect will be of advantage to them. We shall not give them the benefit of our circulation in communicating their empty boasts and lies to the people whom they were intended to lure and deceive.

We understand the Yankees are spreading themselves over the

Carolina islands, driving up and butchering the stock, digging the potatoes on the plantations and gathering the provisions, and appropriating to themselves whatever they can lay their hands on, without going out of the protection of their fleet.[66]

Faithful Negroes

We learn that the negroes of Mrs. [Mary] Dunn who had been captured by the Lincolnites with Mr. [John] Chaplin, on being released were persuaded by the Yankees to remain with them and receive wages. The faithful fellows replied that they preferred to go to their mistress. On getting away from the Yankees they would not even stop at the old homestead on Daufuskie for fear they would be seized again.[67]

Mary Dunn Petitions for Her Plantation

On 16 October 1865 Mary Dunn had Soloman Cohen, Esq., of Savannah, write the following petition for her to Provost Major Rufus Saxton:

> State of Georgia
> Burke County
> Waynesboro—
>
> > To Major Genl Saxton
> > Commanding & c.
>
> The Petition of Mrs. Mary Dunn respectfully showeth, that your Petitioner is a widow and is in her eightieth year and is the owner of a track of land on Dawfuskie Island in the State of South Carolina, containing about three hundred acres, and bounded on the north by Dawfuskie River and on all other sides by land now or lately belonging to John Stoddard and the estate of Mongin. That your Petitioner left Dawfuskie Island at the time of the Battle of Port Royal from fear alone, as she was old and unprotected. That said property never was "abandoned according to the Act of Congress, as she was not engaged in arms or otherwise in aiding or encouraging the rebellion." And your Petitioner further says that she had no son engaged in the rebellion, therefore, she respectfully prays an order restoring her said property to her.
>
> > /s/ Mary Dunn
>
> Sworn to me this
> 2nd day of October, 1865 ..../s/ Geo. F. Tallman
> > [His title is not legible.][68]

Mary Dunn's Request Denied

The document with a large *D* written on its face was returned to Soloman Cohen with this notation:

> State of Georgia
> Augusta, Ga.
> October 19, 1865.
>
> Respectfully returned to S. Cohen, Esq. Savannah, Ga. with the information that Maj. Genl. Howard, Commander, & c. personally directed me that the Sea Islands would remain under the immediate control of Provost Maj. Genl. Saxton to whom all applications in relation thereto will be addressed and forwarded at Charleston, S.C.
> My District is Confined to the Mainland of Georgia.
>
> > /s/ Davis Tillson
> > Brig. Gen. Vols. and A. [Acting]
> > A. [Assistant] Commander
> > State of Georgia.[69]

Mary Dunn did not get her land returned to her until sometime after 1867 for in Thurston Chase's Report from the Beaufort Tax Commissioner's Statement concerning Sea Island, S.C., Schools, April, 1867, this notation was made: "*Daufuskie*: A. [American] M. [Missionary] A. [Association] School—only the Dunn & Webb plantations belong to gov't."[70]

Daufuskians Who Served in the Civil War

Without a doubt, many white and black men served in the Civil War, but inquiries made to the older people now living only revealed a few names: James Peto Chaplin II (who volunteered at the age of fifteen) and Richard Fuller Fripp, Sr., age twenty, both of whom were white.

The black men who served were Bradley Mongin, Henry W. Green, Dennis Haynes, Cato McIntire, Sr., Marshall Miller, and Henry W. Green. Most of the former slaves joined either the 1st, 2nd, or 3rd Regiments of South Carolina Volunteers.

There's a little family history concerning James Peto Chaplin II. He was born 25 May 1845 on Ladies Island, but the family later moved to Daufuskie.

> When the War Between the States commenced, James Peto Chaplin II came from his home on Piney Island to Savannah to enlist. Being only

sixteen years of age, he was told by the commander of the Confederate troops that he was too young, to go back home. However, he joined the Savannah Cadets, a home-guard of young boys between the ages of 14 and 17 who were trained in military tactics to help defend the hometown. These boys were trained by Captain Richard Dennis Millen, who would have the distinction of being James Peto Chaplin's father-in-law at a later date.

After being in the Savannah Cadets for sometime, James P. Chaplin II left the Savannah area. He went to Beaufort, South Carolina, where on 16 February 1863, he enlisted in the Beaufort Volunteers with permission from his father, James Peto Chaplin, I. The Beaufort Volunteers was under the command of Captain Stephen Elliott, and later by Captain H. M. Stuart.

James Peto Chaplin II was in the Battle of Honey Hill, Coosawhatchie breast works, Pocotaligo, South Carolina. He also fought at Bennettsville, South Carolina. His last battle was at Greensboro, North Carolina, where he surrendered 26 April 1865.[71]

The only legal record found was the Muster Roll, Beaufort Volunteer Artillery, at the Surrender of the Battery under Lieut. General Joseph E. Johnson, at Greensboro, North Carolina, April, 1865. And the two names found listed on this Roll under the command of Captain H. M. Stuart are Privates James Peto Chaplin and Richard Fuller Fripp.

James Peto Chaplin was released from the War at nineteen years of age and was given the following document:

Greensboro, N.C.,
May 2nd. 1865

In accordance with the terms of the Military Convention, entered into on the twenty-sixth day of April, 1865, between General Joseph E. Johnston, Commanding the Confederate Army, and Major General W. T. Sherman, Commanding the United States Army in North Carolina, Private J. P. Chaplin, Stuarts Battery, has given his solemn obligation not to take up arms against the Government of the United States until properly released from this obligation; and is permitted to return to his home, not to be disturbed by the United States Authorities so long as he observes this obligation and obeys the laws in force where he may reside.

Fris T. Dow
Maj. & A Lg, USA
Special Commissioner

H. M. Stuart,
Captain C.S.C.,
Commanding[72]

The Spanish-American War 1898

Although this war was not felt on Daufuskie, it did touch the lives of two men: William Wiser Scouten, Sr., who served as a lieutenant in the Navy, Charleston, moving to the island in 1899, and Arthur Ashley Burn, Jr., who was to come to Daufuskie in 1913 as assistant lighthouse keeper.

Arthur, having volunteered for war service at the age of nineteen, was stationed a short time on Hilton Head and gives a personal account of his tenure, which includes the conditions at the Army Camp and happenings during two 1898 hurricanes:

I can enlighten you on the history of the sand Battery on Hilton Head, erected to defend Port Royal in 1898.

The Battery was about thirty ft. above sea level, consisting of 2-8" (two eight inch), modern rifles mounted on ancient carriages. From my point of view then and now, the fellow in front of them had a better chance of survival than the guys behind, there was no chance for recoil. We also had old Springfield single shot, and ancient ammunition, we tried it out on porpoises, the bullets did not go fifty feet.

Shortly after we were there, there was a hurricane Aug. 27-28 which leveled the Battery to the beach, blowing our tents to shreds.

Our Company was a detachment from 1st. Bat. Hy. Artillery, known now as Andersons Battery, we were 50 in number.

Malaria fever had on an average of 20 men in hospital at all times.

After the hurricane, we were ordered to Lands End, later known as Fort Fremont, which was finished after the War with Spain. There was a small 6" battery east of the main Fort at the time.

After we got to Lands End, we were visited by another hurricane which tore the new tents to shreds, we used the rags as best we could, then we put up barracks, which was a boon to fever-ridden, hungry men. Our food was the poorest possible, our allowance I believe was 12 cents per day, pay was $15.50 per mo.

We moved from Sullivans Island [to Hilton Head] on the steamer *Pilot Boy*. We stopped in Beaufort for a lighter loaded with supplies. The steamer was a side-wheeler, the 1st time I ever saw a side-wheeler tow.

The waters around Beaufort swarmed with tiny 5-ton flat boats, with negro operators diving and picking up tons of Phosphate rock from the river bottom and marshes.

The tramp steamer that took Dreyfus to Devils Island was anchored in the harbor, besides many 3 and 4 masts schooners loading with

phosphate rock and lumber. There were 2 or 3 Pilot boats, *The Addie, Sophie Amelia K.* and the *F. W. Shepper*, all sailing craft, for up to that time, all Pilot boats were sails.

The first hurricane blew 5 vessels on Bay Point Island, one on Hilton Head reef in front of our camp. The Capt. of the latter with Capt. Von Harten, were on the mail boat one Sat. Morning approaching the schooner, when the boat capsized drowning the three men. The Capt. of the mail boat, a colored man, was tangled in the sheet, the others were in the cabin. This tragedy was witnessed by our Co. which was being inspected on the beach.

There were two Monitors in the harbor in front of the Navy yard, *The Ampitrite & Miantonomore.* The dry dock was not completed as yet, the dredge was working night and day.

I shall now give you the names of the Detachment as my memory of fifty two years is getting thin:

1st Sergt., Herbert Moore	Sergt., Lee Clark
" Haskell Moore	Corpl., W. Bulcken
" Joe Mixon	" Ebe Rawls
" W. St. Julian Jervey	" ____ Weyman
" W. W. W. Winkler	
Musician: Henry Kuhne	
Cooks: Carsie Heiser	
____Hopkins, Canadian	
John Ortman	

Privates:

P. Y. Betha	Percy C. Blackman
Arthur A. Burn	Frank Carter Laffaucade
Henry Crosby	____ Crosby
David Cable	John Calder
____Groves	____ Harmon
____ King	Pat Knight
____ Koon	Oscar Limehouse
____ McDowell	____McKinnon, Canadian
John Ruggeiro	Lawrence S. Stein, Jr.
Halvor Svendsen	____ Von Spreckleson
Thornwell Wallace	____ Wallace, Beaufort
____ Zeigler	

Sorry, I cannot remember the other 12 names, if you publish, maybe others may write in and fill up the gap. If any send asbestos envelopes, notify me at once as I am especially interested in them.[73]

While Arthur was in the Army, there were certain secret passwords that were used when a soldier was on guard duty and another person approached his station. Arthur's favorite was this one:

"Halt! Who goes there?"

"Friend with a bottle."

"Approach, Friend, and draw the cork."[74]

To prevent them from having smallpox, vaccinations were given to each soldier. For some unknown reason many of the vaccinations were getting infected and a number of the men were having to have their arms amputated. Arthur was one of these men, and when the doctor informed him that his arm would have to be amputated, Arthur decided he would take a last swim while he had two arms. He played in the surf for an hour or more. The next morning when he reported to the doctor, the condition of the arm had improved immensely and the doctor asked Arthur what in the world had he done to it. Arthur replied that he had done nothing except to go swimming. The doctor was elated and said that the salt in the water was curing the infection. He immediately ordered all the men with infected arms to go swimming, which they did daily, causing their vaccinations to heal completely, with no more amputations.[75]

News of the war coming to an end called for a celebration. Arthur had never drank in his life, but on this night with everyone having champagne, he was forced to indulge. Not being aware that champagne was slow in making one inebriated, Arthur sipped a glass of the bubbly and felt nothing. It tasted pretty good, so he had another—then another. He went to bed that night and slept like a bear. When he waked up the next morning, he slipped on his shirt and pants, but when he bent over to put on his shoes, he fell smack on his face—drunk as a skunk. Because of Arthur's flushed face, his superiors thought that he was coming down with malaria or something equally as bad, and they sent him to sick bay. With all the good rest and attention, Arthur's hangover left in a couple of days. He was released with the doctor never knowing just what the problem really was. This experience was the beginning and the end of Arthur's drinking libation of any sort, and from that day forth he remained a teetotaler.

Wars on Foreign Soil

The last several wars were fought on other lands. Names of the following men who served were those who have cemetery headstones,

or are those who were remembered by William (Hamp) Bryan, Francis A. Burn, Sr., Miss Frances Jones, Mrs. William (Jo) Scouten, Jr., George C. Ward, Mrs. Geneva Bryan Wiley, and/or by personal contact to those now living. If your name, or that of your loved one, is not contained in this list, please forgive, as memory becomes evasive with time.

World War I

Men are listed with information from their headstones, followed by the name of the Daufuskie cemetery where they may be found, viz.:

Bryan, Arthur, Pvt., Vet. Hosp. (Maryfield)
Ferguson, Chance, Pvt., 548 Engrs. (Maryfield)
Hamilton, James, Co. B U. S. C. (Haig's Point)
Jenkins, Prophet, Pvt., 803 Co. Trans. Corp. (Cooper River)
Washington, Gabriel, Pvt., 1st Cl, 321 Serv. Bn. (Cooper River)

The following are among those who were remembered, but it can only be assumed that the majority of these men served in the Army:

Bacon, Dennis
Bryan, Abraham, Army
Graham, Adam
Haines, Moses
Holmes, Samuel, Army
Hudson, Buddy
Hudson, Irvin
Hudson, Jacob
Hudson, Rufus, Army
Procter, George (Snooks)

Robinson, Edward
Robinson, Henry
Scouten, George Gage, Messenger, Navy, Charleston
Scouten, William Wiser, Sr., Lt., Navy, Charleston
White, Andrew
Wiley, James
Wiley, Josey
Wiley, Josey

World War II

Bryan, James, Army, Germany
Bryan, William Henry (Sweet Boy), Army
Burn, Alfred Lance, S., Sgt., First Division (Red I) Twenty-sixth Infantry, Bronze Star, Germany (Mary Dunn Cemetery)
Burn, Francis Arthur, Sr., Oiler, Merchant Marines
Fripp, Marion, Pvt., Army
Goodwin, Barney Donald, Boatswain Mate 2nd Cl., Coast Guard
Goodwin, James Arthur, 1st Sgt. Rolling Fourth, Eighth Infantry, Germany
Gordon, Dennis, Tec 5—370 Infantry (Maryfield)

World War I, Charleston, S.C. 1918
Center Front: Rear Adm. F.E. Beatty
Center Rear: Lieut. William Wiser Scouten

The following inscription accompanied the photograph:

"To Lieut. W.W. Scouten USNRF
with pleasant recollections
and best wishes for the future.
/s/ F.E. Beatty
Rear Adm. Ret. U.S.N.
Cmdr 6th Naval Dist."

(Photograph courtesy Mrs. W.W. Scouten, Jr.)

Lieut. William Wiser Scouten, Sr., World War I
(Photograph courtesy Mrs. W.W. Scouten, Jr.)

S Sgt Alfred Lance Burn—First Division
26th Infantry WWII
September 5 1911—April 6 1989

Gordon, Leon
Graham, Major, Quartermaster, Cp., Army, Burma Road
Graves, Abraham, Merchant Marines
Hudson, Adam, Navy
Hudson, Leon
Hudson, Moses, Navy
Jenkins, Lawrence, Seaman, Navy
Jenkins, Samuel, Army
Mitchell, Lawrence, Army
Mitchell, Leon
Rivers, William (Prince), Army
Sanders, Thomas
Scouten, George Gage, Warrant Officer, Engineers, served on Dredge
   Hains, Guam, and Leyte Islands, Pacific
Simmons, Robert, Marines
Simmons, Walter, Jr., Pvt., Ninety-second Infanty Division
Simmons, Willis, Sr., Pvt., Thirty-first Infantry, Germany
Ward, Charles Edward, Buck Sgt., M.P. Division, Air Force, United
   States
Ward, George Calhoun, Ninth Division, 105th Field Artillery which
   gave direct support for the Forty-seventh Infantry, Germany
Ward, Norman Gary, Cp., Forty-seventh Infantry Division under
   General George Smith Patton's Third Army. (It was Gen. Patton
   who spoke to his men in essence: "I've heard you say that you joined
   the Army to give your life for your country. I'm here to tell you that
   you have the wrong attitude: Make your enemy give *his* life for *his*
   country.")
Wheelihan, Stewart Aloyiouis, Seaman, Navy, Pacific, PCE-893

The Korean War

Burn, Francis Arthur, Sr., Chief Petty Officer, Naval Reserve
Cook, Curtis Arthur, Boatswain Mate, 3d Cl., Coast Guard
Goodwin, James Arthur, 1st Sgt., Seventy-third Tank Battalion
Wheelihan, Stewart Aloyiouis, Boatswain Mate, 2nd Cl., Navy

The Vietnam Conflict

Bates, Francis Prevost, Warrant Officer I, Helicopter Pilot, Army
   National Guard, United States
Burn, Gene Anthony, Aviation Machinist Mate, 2d Cl., Naval Aviation,
   Atlantic

Burn, Robert Lancy, Air Craft Maintenance Supervisor (Civilian) Air America Inc., (CIA) Vietnam

Cook, Curtis Arthur, Boatswain Mate, 3d Cl., Coast Guard

Smith, Leonard Haskell (Sonny), Petty Officer, 2d Cl., Navigation, Naval Reserve, United States

Smith, Norman Jerry, Petty Officer, 2d Cl., Naval Reserve, C. B. Battalion, United States

Wheelihan, Stewart Aloyiouis, Boatswain Mate, 2nd Cl., Navy

NOTES

1. Starr, p. 57.
2. Murtie June Clark, _Loyalists in the Southern Campaign of the Revolutionary War_, 2 vols. (Baltimore: Genealogical Publishing Co., Inc., 1981), 1: 191; Starr, pp. 54-57.
3. _Royal Georgia Gazette_, 17 May 1781; Starr, p. 81.
4. Starr, p. 56.
5. Marchman-Anderson, pp. 10-12.
6. Holmgren, pp. 57-58.
7. _Royal Georgia Gazette_, 30 June 1782.
8. Robert N. Rosen, _A Short History of Charleston_ (San Francisco: Lexikos, 1982), p. 52.
9. Bill Killhour, "Lt. 'Marsh Rat' Marion becomes Gen. 'Swamp Fox'," _Beaufort Gazette_, 7 August 1988, p. 6-D.
10. Rosen, p. 53.
11. Ibid.
12. Ibid.
13. Edward T. James, ed. _Notable American Women 1607-1950, A Biographical Dictionary_, 3 vols. (Cambridge: The Belknap Press of Harvard University Press, 1971), 3: 198.
14. Ibid.
15. American Corporation, _The Encyclopedia Americana, The International Reference Work_, 30 vols. (New York: American Book-Stratford Press, Inc., 1956), 11: 314.
16. Ibid., p. 316.
17. Ibid.
18. National Urban League-Quasi-Judicial Agencies, _Dictionary of American History_, 7 vols. (New York: Charles Scribner's Sons, 1976), 5: 331.
19. _Encyclopedia Americana_, p. 316.
20. Ibid.
21. _Dictionary of American History_ , p. 331.
22. Ibid.; _Encyclopedia Americana_ , p. 316.
23. Holmgren, p. 69.
24. _Dictionary of American History_ , p. 388.
25. See Appendix XV for pictures of Confederate money.
26. United States Congress, _War of the Rebellion: A Compilation of the Official Records of the Union and Confederate Armies_, 4 series, 70 vols. (Washington: Government Printing Office, 1882), series I, 6:141, 171-72, 185; James M. Nichols, _Perry's Saints or The Fighting Parson's Regiment in the War of the Rebellion_ (Boston: D.

Lothrop and Company, 1886), pp. 74-75, 81, 100, 105.
27. *War of the Rebellion*, ser. 1, 6: 263.
28. Nichols, pp. 77-78.
29. Ibid.; D. Eldredge, Captain Third New Hampshire Vol. Inf., *1861-1865 The Third New Hampshire and All About It* (Boston: Press of E. B. Stillings & Company, 1893), pp. 119-23.
30. Nichols, pp. 79-80.
31. *War of the Rebellion*, ser. 1, 6:85, 141, 147, 150-51.
32. Ibid., p. 152.
33. Ibid., p. 153.
34. Ibid., p. 155.
35. Ibid.; Nichols, pp. 82, 87.
36. *War of Rebellion*, ser. 1, 6: 154.
37. Ibid.
38. Ibid., p. 225.
39. Ib id., p. 238; Eldredge, p. 127.
40. Ibid., p. 259.
41. Ibid., p. 258.
42. Ibid., pp. 136, 140, 154.
43. Ibid., pp. 154-55.
44. Ibid., pp. 134-35, 157.
45. Nicholas, p. 95.
46. *War of the Rebellion* , serv. 1, 6: 136-137, 158.
47. Ibid., pp. 136-137, 149, 167.
48. Ibid., p. 137.
49. Robert Carse, *Department of the South, Hilton Head in the Civil War* (Columbia: The State Printing Company, 1961), p. 126.
50. *War of the Rebellion*, ser. 1, 6: 138.
51. Ibid., pp. 139-40.
52. Nichols, p. 96.
53. Carse, pp. 126-27.
54. Nichols, pp. 19-25.
55. Nichols, pp. 112-16.
56. *Island Packet*, 27 November 1989, p. 10-A.
57. Nichols, p. 100.
58. Ibid., pp. 101-02.
59. *War of the Rebellion*, ser. 1, 14: 198-99.
60. *Webster's New World Dictionary*, 3rd college ed., s.v. "Zouave."
61. *War of the Rebellion*, ser. 1, 6: 263-64.
62. Nichols, pp. 104-05.
63. Carse, p. 82.
64. *Civil War Centennial*, 1861-1865 1961-1965.
65. *Daily Morning News*, 22 November 1861; Humphrey files
66. Ibid., 29 November 1861; Ibid.
67. Ibid., n. d., 1861; Ibid.
68. National Archives, RG 105, Records of the Bureau of Refugees, Freedmen and Abandoned Lands.
69. Ibid.
70. A. M. A. Archives, No. H6597, Fisk University, Nashville, Tennessee.

71. Humphrey files.

72. James Peto Chaplin II records; Humphrey files.

73. Letter of Arthur A. Burn, Sr., to N. B. Cooler, Hunting Island State Park, Frogmore, S. C., 30 January 1950.

74. Francis A. Burn, Sr., interview, 10 November 1989.

75. Miss Lillian Quinby interview, 4 May 1989.

8

RELIGION, CHURCHES, AND PRAISE HOUSES

Religion or a belief in a Supreme Being played a very important role in the life of the inhabitants of Daufuskie.

The Indians believed in the "Great Spirit."

When religious persecution of the Huguenots became intolerable, David Mongin's father entreated him and his brother Francis to leave France in 1725.

Contrary to the religion of the Empire and his Roman Catholic family, Phillip Martinangele had become a Protestant and was facing persecution when he fled Rome, Italy, circa 1740.

Black people having been sold or taken against their will from Africa and other places to be in bondage, never for one moment let the white man enslave their belief in a force that was bigger than they. Regardless of how they were treated, they never wavered from their inner will to live and worship their Lord Jesus. Their thoughts and what they had locked in their hearts were the only freedoms they had—the only things they possessed. A belief in their God and prayers to Him ultimately touched the hearts of those who could, and did—through circumstances—finally set them free.

The First Church Built on Daufuskie

The only record of an early church was of one built for white people; this is shown on a map that was made in 1806 for Mrs. Mary Ash Fraser by Hezekiah Roberts. This edifice could have been built by the Cockran, Ash, or Fraser families who were related—no one knows. The church was located on Melrose plantation on the south side of the Boundary Road that separates Melrose from Haig's Point. On the

269

opposite side of the church, or north side of Boundary Road (which would be by the eastern entrance to Haig's Point) was the pyramid crypt that held the bodies of several members of the Mongin family.

The denomination and name of the church remains an enigma. Perhaps two of the pastors who might have preached there were the Reverend Herman M. Blodgett who lived at Haig's Point and married a widow, Mrs. David John (Sarah) Mongin, in 1825; and/or the Reverend Alsop Park Vail Woodward, who married the daughter of Squire William Pope who bought Haig's Point from Blodgett in 1850. We do know that with these preachers and John Stoddard who lived at Melrose, all of these early plantation families were very devout Christian people.

How long the church stood by the Boundary Road is unknown, but it can be assumed that it was standing at the close of the Civil War. When the former slaves returned to the island sometime after 1867, the church was probably torn down and used in the construction of small houses built for and by them.

The white families who came after the war had their own boats and could have attended churches in Savannah.

Church Held in Little White School House

From a member of the Lane family it was learned that after the Daufuskie School was built for white children, circa 1913, the Reverend Wesley Avant, brother of Mrs. Hattie Avant Lane who lived at the Bloody Point mansion, preached in the school building every Sunday from 1915 until 1920, when the family moved from the island.[1]

After the departure of Wesley Avant and the Lanes, Arthur A. Burn and his second wife, Margaret, taught Sunday School from 1921 to 1925.

During 1936 to 1941 Brother George Washington Hutson, Savannah, Georgia, rode the steamer *Clivedon* on Sunday and had services at the Daufuskie School in the morning, and then he would preach for the black people at First Union in the afternoon. The preacher would sometimes bring along his wife Ethel and their children, Valeria, George, Doris, and Martha. One Sunday Mrs. Gary Ward would provide a big dinner for them and the following Sunday they would eat at Mrs. Jim Goodwin's house. When World War II started, the *Clivedon* stopped running, so Brother Hutson quit coming due to lack

270

of transportation, and too, many of the Daufuskie families left the island to work in the Savannah shipyard.

When teacher Daisy Langford was on the island from 1942-43, she taught Sunday School in the school building.

During the war the (white) Coast Guard men who were stationed at Melrose were invited by the black people to attend services at the First Union African Baptist Church at Maryfield. The black people were glad to share their church with these men who were serving their country, and the men were just as happy to be made welcome.

With the Daufuskie School closed and with no white preacher, the doors of the black church were opened to all (black and white) who wished to worship. Today, in 1991, all white people who desire may attend and become a member of the former all black church.

Praise Houses

The Negroes made up spirituals and sang as they hoed the cotton, rowed the boat, or dug the potatoes: "Come by heah, Lord, come by heah. . . . If'n ya pray right, Heab'n will be yor home, if'n ya ak right, Heab'n will be yor home. . . ." Their Saviour was as real to them as their master—and much more loving and kind.

When the slaves lived in their quarters they were permitted to have "shouts" at the cabin of the eldest Negro spiritual leader on the plantation. Then, small buildings approximately 15 x 20 feet in size, called Praise Houses, were built to accommodate the slave's spiritual needs. Here they had the chance, without interference, to freely express what they felt.

> No matter what the arrangements, it was here that the slave found in song and dance a unique aesthetic and spiritual release from his deadening toil, as well as his few slight opportunities for leadership and organization outside the realm of white domination.[2]

Shouts

A "shout" usually occurred in the early evening and if it happened to be on a Saturday it sometimes lasted all night.

To begin the shout, a light-wood fire would burn outside the door and one in the fireplace inside. Benches would be pushed against the wall.

The constant and ever-repeated refrain of some familiar hymn [spiritual] would bring up the dancers, and to the accompaniment of a "regular drumming of the feet and clapping of the hands" they would circle about, "winding monotonously round someone in the centre" while the excitement and intensity of the dance spread. The basic step was a shuffling movement of the feet. . . . It was accompanied by a vigorous hitching motion that agitated the entire upper body, "bringing out streams of perspiration." One observer commented on the endless variations of this dancing: "Some 'heel and toe' tumultuously, others merely tremble and stagger on, others stoop and rise, others whirl, others caper sideways, all keep steadily circling like dervishes. . . . Sometimes the dancing continued all night, and when the spell was at last broken it was "amid general sighing and laughing."[3]

Praise Houses on Daufuskie

When certain ones were asked when the Praise Houses were built on the island, the reply was: "We wuz bawn to 'em." Meaning: The Praise Houses were already built and standing when we were born.

There were four known Praise Houses here. One was across the branch on John Bryan's property (Mary Dunn Plantation); one was on the grounds of the First Union African Baptist Church (Maryfield Plantation); one was built (with permission) on Chaplin's property not far from the public landing (Benjie's Point Plantation); and one was in the church yard of Mt. Carmel Church No. 1 (Cooper River Plantation). These small houses were built for the convenience of the people living in that particular area. Inside were benches with no backs, a table that held a lamp and bible, and a wood heater. If they spent the night, soda biscuits (crackers) were eaten and coffee was brewed on the stove.

Children learned how to pray at an early age. It was required of students to attend Praise Houses after school on certain days so they could be taught how to sing spirituals, praise, and worship God.

Prayer meeting was held every Tuesday, Thursday, and Sunday night. "Sister Night" (just for the women) was held every Tuesday night in the Praise House. For some of those crossing the gaul to take a short cut to attend the Benjie's Point Praise House, a stack of palm fronds was built on one side of the gaul to light their way, with another

First Union African Baptist Church built circa 1885
(Now known as Union Baptist Church.)
(Photograph courtesy Mrs. Martha Hutton, 1989.)

Praise House—Union Baptist Church
The last existing Praise House on the Island, June 1990.

stack built on the opposite side. One stack would be lit while going to prayer meeting and the other stack would be lit on the way back. Some carried lanterns.

Baptism was held near the New River shore in front of Dick Fripps' store at Benjie's Point. Those who were to be baptized would change into white clothing in the Benjie's Point Praise House, then march down to the river, singing spirituals there and back.

First Union African Baptist Church

John Irwin Stoddard had received Maryfield Plantation in the distribution of the estate of his mother, Mrs. John (Mary Lavinia) Stoddard.

When the land was redeemed after the Civil War, John I. Stoddard had the plantation cut into lots and sold to the black people, most of whom were families of former slaves.[4] A group of the spiritual black men got together and on 29 January 1881, purchased Lot No. 18 (12 acres) in Maryfield Tract, for which they paid $82.00 and on which they would build the church. Names of the acting trustees on the deed are as follows: William J. Ficklin, Morris Hamilton, Doctor Morrel, Paris Myers, Richard Bryan, Edward Gibson, Nat Demery, Morris Emanuel, and Henry Williams.[5]

Apparently the church was built that year (1881) and in 1884 the church burned. Shortly thereafter a pleas for funds to rebuild and a notice of funds collected appeared in a Savannah newspaper:

> A letter to the editor requested that citizens donate to rebuild Church on Daufuskie Island. Letter written in behalf of ministers of Savannah.[6]
>
> At the Thanksgiving Union Service a large collection was taken up for the erection of a new colored Church in place of the one destroyed by fire on Daufuskie.[7]

The First Union African Baptist Church was built just south of where the burnt church stood. According to Hinson White, the man who built the edifice was Mingo Miller, father of Annie Crosby, who was married to Tom Crosby. The trustees did their share of the work as well.

Prior to 1880 the black people of Daufuskie were members of The Second Baptist Church, which was also known as the Old Fort Church

274

located on Houston Street in Savannah, Georgia. Deacon Isaac Houston accepted the call to the ministry and was ordained at The Second Baptist Church by the Board of Trustees of the Berean Association. The Reverend Houston also preached on Daufuskie.

Some of the First Union Church deacons were William Hudson, John Bryan, Mose Ficklin, Sippio Robinson, Joe Riley, Joe Grant, Robert Bryan, John Bryan, Jr., John Mongin, and Benjamin (Ben) Bryan.

Henry (Buddy) Hamilton would toll the church bell for Sunday morning services or to announce the death of a loved one on the island.

Doc Morrell was the music director. Mrs. Katie White Bryan played the organ for the choir and after she died, her daughter Isabell Bryan played for them.

Sunday School was at eleven in the morning; church service was at two in the afternoon; BYPU was at six; and Church again around eight at night.

On the second Sunday in each month members went to Savannah for the Lord's Supper.

On the second Sunday of August, in the midst of the great storm of 1893, row boats were returning from the church in Savannah to Daufuskie and were docking at the Bloody Point wharf. The water was so rough that the fourth boat was unable to make it, and two men were drowned. After this tragedy, a preacher was sent from Savannah to serve communion in the Daufuskie church.

Preachers Who Served the Daufuskie Church

There were several pastors who served after the Reverend Isaac Houston:

From the Berean Association: the Reverend Sims, Renera, Hudson, Richard H. Thomas, and W. W. Headen.

From Hilton Head and Daufuskie Island: The Reverend B. F. Jones, Peter W. Williams, Richard Bryan (the only true island-born pastor, and he preached every fourth Sunday), W. S. Scott, Willie Ford, and Frank Rubin Green.

One of the best loved preachers was the Reverend Richard H. Thomas from Savannah, Georgia, who was a teacher at Thunderbolt

College, now known as Savannah State. He would come to the island and serve communion on the second Sunday in each month. On the Friday of that week he would ride the *Attaquin, Clivedon,* or the *Pilot Boy* steamers (whichever was available) and stay with Mrs. Cynthia Bryan, wife of Backus Bryan. He would preach on Sunday around noon, serve communion, then preach again on Sunday night about 8 o'clock. On Monday he would return to Savannah on one of the steamers.

Mrs. Geneva Wiley fondly remembers the Reverend Thomas baptizing her in 1917. Mrs. Betty Brown recalls him as being a tall, fair-skin man. As a small child, when Betty saw the Reverend Thomas coming, she would run to meet him. He would pick her up in his arms and take her back home, as he would be spending the week end with the aunt with whom Betty lived. There were no screens then, so Betty would brush the flies away while the preacher ate his dinner. When very young, Betty also (along with twelve others) was baptized by the Reverend Thomas early one Sunday morning at Fripp's Landing.

The Church Was Filled on Sunday

During Sunday services, the church (including the balcony) would be filled to capacity. The building would resound with the voices of so many people harmonizing in song, or clapping their hands and tapping their feet.

There would be a revival once a year. Conventions would be held in the church and a Savannah steamer filled with people would come from Savannah. There would be so many present (two or three hundred) that the women on the island would have to cook in wash pots and serve on make-shift tables in the yard.

Sometimes on the third Sunday of the month the people at First Union African Baptist would go to Mt. Carmel No. 1 Church at Cooper River and join in their meeting to hear the Reverend Ham preach, or perhaps Mt. Carmel people would come down to First Union—they would swap around.

Offering Table and Close of Service

When the call for the offering was made, during the singing of a song, instead of ushers passing the plate, each person got up out of his

seat and went to the table in front of the pulpit and left their donation, then walked back to their seat. When the altar call was made and the service ended, the preacher stood in front of the table and as each person shook hands with him, they got in line by the side of the pastor until everyone who had attended church was standing in a long line by the pastor, which made every person not only shake hands with the pastor but also with everyone else who came to church.

A Wilderness Experience

To become a member of the church was not an easy matter. The first thing to do was to notify the preacher and deacons of your intention. They would then tell you that you had to pray and through a dream the Lord would show you the person in the church who would instruct and pray with you.

After the Lord showed you the person who would guide and direct you, you met again with the church officials and told them about your dream. If they accepted your story, then they would request that you and your instructor pray you through to the Lord.

When Johnny Hamilton was asked about this he said that he went in the "wilderness" (woods) to seek the Lord. The mosquitoes and gnats nearly ate him alive, but he finally prayed "through" and when he found the Lord, he felt so good—like he was walking on air, about three feet off the ground.

Once you "found the Lord," you then went back to the church officials and told them about your experience and how your instructor had prayed with you. They could usually tell by your face if you were telling the truth; you would be smiling and praising the Lord. If they accepted you, then you were baptized, which gave you the right to become a member.

These church officials would not take you at your word—you had to *prove* yourself; you had to give up all your bad habits, and act like you wanted to be "saved" before they would accept you into the church. You were required to go to prayer meeting, and if you missed two times, then you had to give account to the elders of the church.

The older generation on the island still think that persons who want to be church members should continue to seek the Lord through a "wilderness" experience.

The Council and Sister Trees

A big oak in the front of Lawrence and Maebell Jenkins' house was called the *Council Tree*. Following the service each Sunday, men who would be walking or riding their horses, cows, wagons, or carts, would gather under this tree and talk at length about the sermon, the church, their family, animals, oystering, or crops.

Across the opposite side and farther up the road was the *Sister Tree*. The women and children would get tired of waiting for the men, so they met under their tree (which was a big oak with three trunks) in the yard of Matilda Miller. They too talked and laughed about things that concern women—their husbands, sweethearts, children, sewing, and cooking—just a whole lot of "girl-talk."

Church Closes

In the late 1950s and throughout the 1960s, the church attendance continued to decline. The deacons tried to hold the church together, but after repeated attempts many were called from labor to their reward. This included the death of their pastor, the Reverend Frank Rubin Green, who had been coming over from Hilton Head. The doors of the First Union African Baptist Church were closed.

The Reverend Clarence L. Hanshew Opens Church

Manning Woods was the manager for Mr. G. H. Bostwick's Haig's Point plantation here on the island, but he was also a member of the First Baptist Church in Bluffton. Mr. Woods was aware of the church being closed on Daufuskie. It was through him in 1967 that the Bluffton church approached the Reverend Clarence Lee Hanshew, Director of Missions for the Savannah River Baptist Association, to begin some sort of worship service on the island.

The Bluffton Church Pastor, Bruce Newley, and layman Manning Woods, with the Reverend Hanshew, visited the island in February, 1968. They returned in March when the Reverend Newley preached his first sermon in the church. In April of 1968 they came to conduct services, but one week prior to their coming Dr. Martin Luther King, Jr., had been assassinated by a white man, so the church doors were locked. As the few who were present stood in the yard, the Reverend Hanshew said a short prayer, then the men left and returned to Bluffton.

Council Tree

After church services, the men would gather under the Council Tree to dispute important matters of the day. (Print courtesy of artist Christina Roth Bates, 19 July 1990.)

The first Vacation Bible School was held in Mary Fields School, July 1968. Rev. C. L. Hanshew extreme right. (Photograph courtesy of Thomas J. Brannon.)

Church services were then held in the school house. In July of 1968 the island experienced its first Vacation Bible School at Mary Fields Elementary. The Reverend Newley, the Reverend Hanshew, and his daughter Christine were the main ones who taught crafts and the Bible study class. (Every year since that time the Reverend Hanshew has seen that Daufuskie has had a Vacation Bible School.)

The Reverend Ron Cowart became the new pastor of First Baptist Church in Bluffton, and for a while he came to Daufuskie and conducted Sunday services in the Jane Hamilton School building at Cooper River. Then, Mrs. Sarah Grant opened the doors of First Union Baptist Church and invited the preachers back.

The deacons and other members of the church objected, but Sarah informed them that if God sent them, she would open the door for them and she didn't care if they were black or white, she was letting them preach in the church.

Rev. Ervin Greene New Pastor

In 1969 Ervin Greene of Ridgeland, a protegé of the Reverend Hanshew, joined the Reverend Cowart and the Reverend Hanshew as a summer missionary to Daufuskie. The Reverend Greene an-

Baptism of Edrina Washington and Emily Bryan, April, 1981. In the water by the public landing on New River is Rev. Ervin Greene on the right and Deacon Johnny Hamilton on the left. It was always customary for Deacon Hamilton to take his "staff" and probe for a sure footing before entering the water.

Above: Rev. Hanshew ringing the old church bell Sunday, 26 August 1984.

Left: Deacon Johnny Hamilton receiving an award from Rev. C.L. Hanshew, Sunday, 26 August1984.

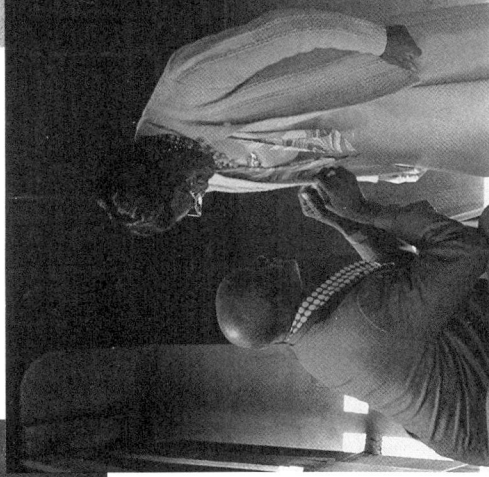

Right: Mr. Johnny Hamilton and Mrs. Sarah Grant, Easter 1972, inside the Union Baptist Church.

Rev. Clarence Lee Hanshew and Mrs. Sarah Grant, sitting on the porch of her home, 1973. (Photograph courtesy, Don Rutledge, Home Mission Board, Southern Baptist Convention, 1350 Spring Street NW, Atlanta, Georgia.)

Rev. C.L. Hanshew given a ride by Mr. Josephus Robinson, in his cart pulled by ox "John," circa 1968. (Photograph courtesy Don Rutledge, Home Mission Board, Southern Baptist Convention, 1350 Spring Street NW, Atlanta, Georgia.)

swered the call to be a minister in 1971.

Danny Atkinson, a Californian, came in the summer of 1975 as a summer missionary, then settled on the island.

The Reverend Cowart's obligations in Bluffton prevented him from returning to the island, so in 1976 First Union called the Reverend Ervin Greene as pastor. Danny served as a volunteer substitute when the Reverend Greene could not come.

Renovations Made on Church Building

In March of 1977 a group of young people worked to make repairs and repaint the church building. Many of these helpers were from the First Baptist Church of Opelika, Alabama, some of whom were also students at Auburn University, and other youths came from the First Baptist Church of Hilton Head, South Carolina. These volunteers were given housing on Hilton Head; transportation was supplied by members of First Baptist Church; and the paint was donated by Western Auto of Hilton Head.

A Church Wedding

The Reverend Greene performed the first wedding that the church had had in many years. On 20 September 1980 he officiated at the happy union of Miss Janice Stevens and Mr. Joseph Gordon. Others in the wedding party included Mrs. Ella Mae Stevens, mother of the bride; Mr. and Mrs. W. Gordon, parents of the groom; Miss Cynthia Stevens was the maid of honor; the best man was Mr. Danny Atkinson; and the bride was given away by Mr. Thomas Sanders. The reception was held in the pavilion near the public landing.

The Reverend Blake Holds Revival

A revival led by the Reverend J. Henry Blake of Charleston, South Carolina, was held in February, 1981. This was the first revival on Daufuskie in over twenty years.

The Reverend Greene had been appointed pastor of Brick Church at Penn Community Center at Frogmore. With this added responsibility it became very difficult for him to get to Daufuskie once a month. In 1983 Danny left the island.

More Repair Work on Church

In July, 1986, members of Spring Valley Baptist Church in Columbia spent four days on Daufuskie fixing up the church. They installed ceiling fans, reinforced the front porch, added new wiring and light fixtures, and built new restroom facilities out back.

The Reverend Hanshew continued to preach when the Reverend Greene could not be here.

The Reverend Marion C. Taylor New Minister

On various occasions the Reverend Marion C. Taylor had been a visiting pastor with the Reverend Greene and the Reverend Hanshew. It was in February, 1986, that members of First Union Baptist Church asked that the Reverend Taylor be their new pastor. The Reverend and Mrs. Taylor, who leads the singing, have been faithful in coming every second and fourth Sunday. The church is growing and the Reverend Taylor has baptized several new members in the cool waters at Cooper River Landing.

In 1987, as her missionary project, Miss Honey Johnson volunteered to serve as pianist.

Improvements Made on Church Building

On March 5-10, 1990, fourteen men from the Savannah Baptist Association, men on the island and others, volunteered their time to help restore the First Union Baptist Church. They poured concrete, insulated the ceiling, repaired flooring, installed electrical and plumbing fixtures, added new storm windows and leveled the sagging structure.

The week the workers were here, they slept on cots in the church and the Reverend Marion Taylor did the cooking—something he had not done since his Navy days. Men involved from the Ridgeland area were Alton Badget, Conner Finch, the Reverend C. L. Hanshew, Paul Hanshew, Bubba Lassiter, and Henry Simmons. A group from the Bel-Ridge Baptist Church of North Augusta were also part of the work crew.

The Melrose and Haig Point Cooperations were very helpful in providing materials and equipment.

Other needs of the building are the painting for both the interior

Attending Sunday Service—25 April 1982

Back Row: Rev. Marion C. Taylor, Danny Atkinson, Johnny Hamilton, Isaac Robinson, Lawrence Jenkins. *Second Row:* Claude Sharpe, Susie Smith, Mabell Jenkins, Ernestine Smith, Flossie Washington, Barbara Jenkins, Donald Jenkins, Emily Bryan. *First Row:* Sheila Robinson, Raymond Robinson, Michelle Smith, Nichole Smith, Katrina Williams, Larry Forrest, Jennifer Smith, Shawnta Washington, Eric Bryan.

and exterior and carpet for the floor, which will be accomplished on the next visit of the men from the Savannah River Baptist Association.

First Mount Carmel Church

Land for this church was purchased for 3.33^{1}/_{3}$ from Robert Pope on 14 May 1901:

> First Mount Carmel Baptist Church of Daufuskie Township of Hilton Head, Beaufort County in the state aforesaid [S.C.] all that piece and parcel of land situate and being on Daufuskie Island, Hilton Head Township, Beaufort County in the state aforesaid [S.C.]. Being also in Lot No. 14 as shown on map and surveyed by Mr. O. P. Law, February, 1884. Being also contained in said Lot No. (14) which lot is bounded on the North by outside high land line of the place and marsh, and Lot No. (13), South by Lot Nos. 13-15 & 20. East by Lots Nos. 21 and 22. West by Lots Nos. 11, 12-13 and 15 containing one task more or less (or 1/4 acre).

The church trustees listed on the deed are Richard Smalls, May Hamilton, and T. W. Crosby. The Notary Public is E. M. Pinckney.[8]

This church was an exact replica of First Union Baptist Church at Maryfield—only smaller. All of the people at Cooper River attended this church. Abe Mitchell and the Reverend Ham were two of the pastors who preached there.

When Thomas Stafford was asked about this church, he gave this account:

> Use to be some kinda good times dey. More praisin' n' singin' gwin on. A storm come tru and de Master turn dat church zactly round—de front door been facing Nort and when e stop, de front door wuz facing Sout. 'N de bad part wuz that de peoples were inside having church and de church turning wuz so smooth de peoples in de church didn't zactly know what happen 'til de service wuz over. A bunch been in de church dat day—Maggie Hudson, Lottie Rivers, Tina Miller—a heap been in dey dat day. De carpenter, Samuel Holmes n' some other mens jacked up de church and turn 'em back 'round agin like e auta be.

The church and the Praise House in the yard were used for school until 1940 when a storm tore both of them down.

Later a much smaller church was built on the same spot, but members gradually quit coming, the church closed, and in the 1960s rabbit hunters set the woods afire, which burned down the church.

Mt. Carmel Baptist Church No. 2
Cooper River, 1961

First Union
Baptist Church
March, 1968.

Present that Sunday were Mrs. Estella Hamilton, Jeanette Robinson, Margarite Washington, Edrina Washington, Janice Stevens, Willis Simmons, Joseph Simmons, Henry Simmons, Marion Green, Alfred Smith, Shirman Washington, Lenore Brown, Marie Robinson, Faye Robinson, Sally Ann Robinson, Cynthia Stevens, Mr. Johnny Hamilton. (Photograph: Billie Burn.)

In 1968, the Vista Volunteers, Henry and Rhea Netherton, used Mt. Carmel Church No. 2 as a library.

Second Mt. Carmel Baptist Church

After the storm tore the first church down, the members of First Mt. Carmel got together and bought land for another church. For $10.00 on 15 February 1941, a quarter of an acre of ground was purchased for Mt. Carmel Baptist Church No. 1 from Mary Holmes:

> ... All that parcel or lot of land known as part of the Paris Holmes Estate, more particularly bounded and described as follows to wit: to the North by lands of Beaufort County, to the West by the public road and on the South and East by the estate of Paris Holmes. And contains one-fourth (1/4) acre more or less being a part of Lot No. 33 survey made by O. P. Law in 1881. Located on Daufuskie Island, Hilton Head Township, Beaufort County, State of South Carolina.[9]

The only witness to the deed is Josephine Johnson with her husband, Malcolm Johnson, as the Notary Public.

Lumber and materials that could be salvaged from the First Mount Carmel was used to build the second church.

Cooper River people attended this church until it too was finally closed.

Library in Church

In 1968 Henry Netherton, the Vista Volunteer, made a library out of this second church. Through the Beaufort Library he had a boat load of old books and magazines brought over. He then hired a couple of girls—Vera Mae Moultrie and Vernetta Bryan—to sort out all the materials and place them on the church benches for display so the island residents could rent them like a regular library. It was short lived as it wasn't successful. Very few books were rented, so they were later hauled back to Beaufort.

At Cooper River, adjacent to the old Jane Hamilton School, the church still stands today. It has been sold, and now belongs to Mr. Don Mudd, Sea Oats Real Estate Company.

Seventh Day Adventists

All of the residents of the island were Baptist with the exception of one family who were Seventh Day Adventists. Refusing to allow their children to attend public schools or to attend the existing Baptist Churches, Mr. Arthur and his wife Beatrice Champion taught the

Bible and their lessons at home to their children, Miriam, Buster, and Charles. On Saturdays the people on the island who passed by their house could hear them singing religious songs.

Mrs. Champion and son Charles were killed in an automobile wreck on a trip to Florida.

The Champions lived at Cooper River above the present Mt. Carmel Baptist Church No. 2. In the 1960s one of their children, who was mentally disturbed, set fire to and burned down the house. The remaining family then moved off the island.[10]

Notes

1. Mrs. Myrtle Lane Marsh, daughter of George and Hattie Avant Lane, interview, 14 June 1988.

2. Willie Lee Rose, *Rehearsal for Reconstruction* (New York: Vintage Books, 1964), p. 91.

3. Ibid., p. 92.

4. Records of Beaufort, S. C., vol. 12, p. 260.

5. Ibid., Deed Book 13, pp. 491-92.

6. *Savannah Morning News*, 27 November 1884.

7. Ibid., 28 November 1884.

8. Beaufort County Courthouse, Deed Book 24, p. 258.

9. Ibid., Deed Book 57, p. 325.

10. Mrs. Louise Wilson interview 3 May 1990; Mrs. Agnes Simmons interview, 19 May 1990.

9

EDUCATION

Until 1860 Daufuskie was divided into several plantations. The children of these wealthy planters were either taught by private tutors or governesses or were instructed by their parents or sent to prestigious schools here or abroad.

Very few of the blacks ever received any education; therefore, until the American Civil War ended, there was no need for a school on the island.

All of the Sea Islands along the South Carolina coast were occupied by Union troops, November, 1861. With the exception of the old and sick, the black population left for Savannah, Hilton Head, or Beaufort. It wasn't until sometime after 11 May 1864 that the former slaves and their families returned. It was on this day that Colonel William H. Davis, One Hundred and Fourth Pennsylvania Infantry, headquartered on Hilton Head, sent the following report to Captain William L. M. Burger, Assistant Adjutant-General:

> Captain: . . . I left Hilton Head this morning on the armed transport *Croton* accompanied by the *Thomas Foulks* and the *Plato,* with 200 men from the Fifty-second and one hundred and fourth Pennsylvania Volunteers, under command of Lieut. Col. T. D. Hart, of the One hundred and fourth, to make a reconnaissance to Daufuskie Island. From Seabrook I sent the *Foulks* and *Plato* in advance, to steam around the island to prevent what forces the enemy might have upon it from leaving. I landed my forces at a wharf [Engineer's Wharf] which the enemy had partially destroyed, and leaving a sufficient number of men to protect the boat in case of attack, I sent the rest to skirmish through the island. Learning that there was some cotton on a plantation on the north part of the island, I proceeded there with a small party and

294

succeeded in collecting 90 bags, weighing about 4,000 pounds, which I brought away and caused to be turned over to the proper authorities at this place. None of the enemy were found upon the island, but Colonel Hart was informed by some colored people living on one of the plantations that a party of 6 armed rebels were there last night. The only inhabitants were *3 black women and 1 man, all very aged,* who remain on their late master's plantation, and who are reported as being almost destitute of food. I do not believe the enemy has at any time a greater force than a few pickets for observation. The *Plato* got aground late in the afternoon, where she was forced to lie until flood-tide. A detachment of 40 men was put on board to protect her in case she should be attacked by the enemy's boats.

I am under obligations to Captain Lane, late Government agent to this department, for information which led to my finding the cotton.[1]

School at Melrose

The exact date is unknown, but sometime after that May in 1864 the black people began returning to the island.

As early as 1862 the Freedmen's Bureau was sending teachers from Pennsylvania and Massachusetts and other states to islands around Beaufort. The American Missionary Association, Schools for Freedmen, sent to Daufuskie two white teachers, Ellen W. Douglas and Frances Littlefield. Not only were these women to teach school, but they were also required to be Christians and to teach Sabbath School as well. On one of the reports, their school began on 19 March 1867.[2] It is only an assumption (no proof) that perhaps their appearance was only to continue a school that had begun at an earlier date.

School was held at Melrose, either in the mansion or in one of the outside buildings and was called "Dawfuskie School." Classes were held for three hours each week day.[3]

There were no whites enrolled, but there were 85 black students, 52 males and 33 females. Forty of these students were over sixteen years of age. Night school was held for children and adults who could not attend during the day because of their having to work in the fields or having chores that had to be done.

The subjects taught in school were alphabet, reading, spelling, geography, arithmetic, writing, singing, and needlework. All of the students wrote on slates. No tuition was paid. There were eighty-eight enrolled in two Sabbath Schools which were probably held in the

white church, or in other buildings on Melrose property.

When the plantations were returned to their original owners, school at Melrose came to a close and the teachers had to leave. Esther W. Douglass wrote the following letter from Daufuskie to a Mr. W. E. Whiting, 2 May 1867:

> Dear Sir:
>
> I send you my account with the Association up to the close of last quarter. Please send what is due me by Mr. Pettibone. I feel that I have lost much time since I came south this time but it has been through no fault of mine and has been much harder for me than regular labor. We have a pleasant home here [Melrose] and are beginning to see some improvement in the people. Still I cannot but feel a little homesick when I think of the people we left. I received a letter last week from one of the men who was in my Bible class. He says they are keeping up the Sabbath and evening schools and praying every day for some way to open by which we may return. He says, "The children meet me when I come from the field, they are in such a hurry for school to begin."
>
> My address is the same as when I was at <Wild> Horn—Miss E. W. Douglass, Box 483, Savannah, Georgia.[4]

Confiscated Lands Sold to Finance Schools

Between 1863 and 1866, thirty-three "school farms" of 160 acres each (6000 acres in all) in St. Helena Parish were set aside from confiscated lands to finance schools for Negro children.

In 1866 Congress ordered the school farms of St. Helena's Parish and St. Luke's Parish to be sold at $10 an acre. The proceeds were to be applied for "support of schools, without distinction of color or race, on the islands in the parishes of St. Helena and St. Luke."[5]

Not until July 31, 1907, did the state treasurer of South Carolina, after an Act of Congress on Feb. 18, 1907, receive from the federal government $50,490 "for the use and support of free public schools in the parishes of St. Helena and St. Luke, in the counties of Beaufort and Hampton."[6]

However, there was a dispute over this as Congress was in error: only school farms had been designated from lands of St. Helena's Parish alone, and the money from this land should not have been shared with St. Luke's Parish.

In 1908, the General Assembly of the State of South Carolina enacted a bill for the investment of the $50,490 "in bonds or stock of the

State of South Carolina and to hold the same subject to the trust and uses in the said acts of Congress designated," with the interest going to the parishes.[7]

School Held in Praise Houses and Churches

Some financial appropriation had to have been made to pay tutors, for after the white teachers left Melrose, school was held in Praise Houses and any available empty house until two churches were built. The First African Union Baptist Church was built at Maryfield with a Praise House close by, and Mt. Carmel No. 1 Church was built at Cooper River, near another Praise House.

Maryfield Praise House

There were as many as 120 pupils that attended the school at the Maryfield Praise House which was inadequate, so students were also taught in the church. The church was used more for school than for religious services.[8]

Not all of the black children on the island were born of parents who were former slaves of Daufuskie plantation owners. Frances E. Jones' grandparents were Joseph and Margaret (Peggie) Gibson Michael; he had come from Charleston and she had come from St. Simon, Georgia. Jake Simmons, Sr., Nora Lawrence, and her son Johnny Hamilton had come from Hilton Head. Rose Brisbane's family had come from St. Helena; Margaret Locks' parents, Frederick and Elizabeth (Betsy) Locks, had come from St. Simon. John and Lula Allen Stafford had brought their family via Hilton Head and Bull's Island. From Albany, Georgia, came the Demerys, William Hudson and his sister Maggie. William became the father of Sarah, Cynthia, Rufus, William, and Hezikiah Hudson; Maggie married John Mongin and became the mother of Lillie Mongin Simmons and Carrie Mongin Miller. From Albany, Georgia, also came Ella Mae Grant Stevens' grandmother, Clara Lloyd. From Augusta, Georgia, came Josephine Jenkins. Abe Mitchell and Agnes Mitchell Simmons' father, Lawrence L. Mitchell, came from Albany, Georgia; their mother, Victoria (Mitchell) Mitchell, came from Hilton Head. Lawrence Jenkins' father, James Jenkins, came from St. Helena.

There is no way to list the hundreds of children who attended school at the Maryfield Praise House and Baptist Church, but some of those

early students were viz.: *Bentley*—Louvenia, Sarah, Sally, Willie; *Brisbane*—Liza; *Bright*—Betty; *Bryan*—Alfred, Bertha, Cornelia, Corrine, Cynthia, Elizabeth, Emiline, Geneva, John Bryan, Jr., Katy, William; *Demery*—Rebecca; *Drayton*—Angeline; *Ficklin*—Mose; *Gadson*—Flora; *Gibson*—Margaret; *Graves*—Elizabeth (Lizzie); *Hamilton*—Hannah, Marie; *Haynes*—Fanny, Gracie, Lottie, Moses, Tealie; *Holmes*—Isabell; *Hudson*—Cynthia, Matilda, Sarah, William; *Jenkins*—Eugenia, James, Lawrence, Sarah; *Jones*—Frances Elizabeth; *Locks*—Margaret; *Martin*—Johnny, Matilda; *Miller*—Ben, Chloe, Eliza, Jessie, Kit, Laura, Polly, Sheridan; *Mongin*—John; *Mordeci*—Lizzie; *Robinson*—Theresa; *Sanders*—Cornelia, Thomas; *Seems*—Bertha; *Simmons*—Jake; *White*—Katie; *Williams*—George, Maebell, Liddy, Phoebe, Pollyann.

The black teachers at the Maryfield Praise House and First African Union Baptist Church were Sam Reynolds, Andrew Reynolds, Richard Thomas; Maggie Robinson, Bertha Lee, Sarah Lee, and a Miss Jones were from Savannah; H. W. Washington, Samuel Hazel; a teacher from Beaufort by the name of Mrs. Cunningham, Frances Brown; Leontine Singleton from St. Helena (Hilton Head), and Miss Frances Elizabeth Jones, a former student and a native of Daufuskie.

There were only grades one through four. Some of the students liked school so much they would repeat those grades two or three times, or until they got too big to go to school.

A four-month school term lasted from 1 November to 28-29 February. Classes were held Monday through Friday from 9 A.M. to 4 P.M. Each morning about thirty minutes before time, one of the students would ring the church bell to notify everyone that there would be school that day, and not to be late.

On occasions when the ground was too wet or the weather too cold to plow their fields, the parents would pay the teacher's salary for an extra thirty days in order to extend the school term to five months. To get all of the farm work done it was necessary for the children to be at home for the planting in the Spring and for the "gathering" in the Fall.

The children played tag, hide-and-seek, jump rope, and baseball; they used a homemade ball made from old stockings and a stick for a bat.

From 1916 to the 1920s the Reverend Richard Thomas, the visiting preacher from Savannah, would come once a month to serve Com-

munion at the church and on this same visit he would have a spelling bee for the school children.[9]

In their lunch bucket, pail, pan, or bag, the children would bring a sweet potato, perhaps some fruit, a piece of fish or sweetbread, or maybe a biscuit—just whatever was left over from the table. Perhaps as a special treat a fortunate child would have a johnnycake purchased from the store. There were occasions they had nothing to carry for lunch. A well with a handpump supplied water.

Teachers punished the children by whipping them if they were late for school in the morning or if they did not get their lessons. Punishment also took the form of a whacking across the knuckles with a long black pointer stick if the children were at the blackboard and made a mistake in an arithmetic problem. For talking or being mischievous their hands were opened and given a few licks with a ruler or, in some instances, a small sassafras stick across the palms of the boys. Some had to stand in the corner of the room—perhaps on one foot.

Unless the grade was mastered, the child was not promoted. Some remained in one grade for as many as three years.

"Desks" in the Praise House were benches with no backs but with a place in front to put books. Slates and slate pencils were used. "Blackboards" were two, fourteen-inch wide boards, nailed across two-by-fours and painted black so that chalk could be used.

The School Census of 1921 lists these black students attending school on Daufuskie: *Bentley*—Abraham, Ella, Arthur, Eddie; *Brown*—Rosa; *Brisbane*—Agnes; *Ford*—David, Howard, Viola; *Grant*—Freddie, Joseph, Louie; *Gordon*—Dennis, James; *Graves*—Abraham; *Hamilton*—Eugene, Mabel, Henry, Mary Jane; *Holmes*—Leroy, Tilman, Herman; *Heyward*—Alice, Leathia, Arthur, Thelma; *Hudson*—Mirah; *Haynes*—Charlotte; *Johnson*—Ernest, Julia; *Martin*—Peter, Sylvia, Carrie; *Miller*—Wilhelmina, Kit, Thomas; *Mongin*—Lillie, Johnny, Hester; *Myers*—Josephine, Cely, Richard, Charles; *Robinson*—Charles, Susan, Willie, Theresa, Amelia, Gustave; *Smalls*—Bromice; *Walker*—David; *White*—Cerisa. (This list is continued in the Mary Fields Elementary segment.)

Mt. Carmel Church No. 1 Praise House

While children on the south end of the island were attending school at the Mary Field Praise House and Union Baptist Church, children

on the north end were attending school in the Praise House and Mt. Carmel Church No. 1 at Cooper River. All grades, rules, and regulations applied the same for both schools.

The teacher was J. D. Gaston (Mr. "Gasson") from St. Helena. Some of the students who attended school at Cooper River through the years were viz.: *Brown*—Louise; *Champion*—Joseph, Miriam; *Frazier*—Elizabeth; *Hamilton*—Johnny; *Holmes*—Bill, Christopher, Florence, Samuel, Toby; *Jenkins*—Ada, Bobby, Charlie, Crawford, Louise, Lottie, Prophet, Walter; *Joiner*—Gracie; *McIntyre*—Cato, Jr., Son; *Miller*—Gladys, Tina; *Mitchell*—Abe, Danny, Victoria; *Myers*—Bristol; *Reddick*—Clifford; *Riley*—Ben, Joseph; *Rivers*—Lottie, Prince; *Simmons*—Abraham, Alma, Mable, Patsy, Sammy; *Washington*—Gabe, Jake; *Wiley*—Richman.

There were times when a teacher was not available for Mt. Carmel No. 1 Praise House. When this happened the children at Cooper River would have to walk the four miles to the Mary Field Praise House until a teacher could be found.

After the storm of 1940 completely demolished Mt. Carmel Church No. 1, other arrangements had to be made for Cooper River children to go to school. (Continued in the Jane Hamilton School segment.)

Professor Daniel's Private School for Children

In the 1920s Professor John D. Daniels, a native of Jamaica, was sent by a mission in Pennsylvania to open a private school on Daufuskie. At first he was allowed to use the "Hall" in which to live and teach. (The "Hall" was short for the Oyster Society Hall—a building in which monthly meetings were held for all of those who worked in the oyster industry and who, having paid their dues, earned the privilege of being a member in this all black Society.)

The Professor taught summer and winter and charged ten cents per week per child. He later bought some property at Benjie's Point and built a house where he continued to live and teach. When he became very ill in 1927 his son came and took him off the island. He did not return.

There were other students, but only the names of these children were remembered who were taught by Professor Daniels: Eddie "B" Bentley, Lawrence Bryan, Lottie Bryan, Janie Gordon, Cynthia Hudson, Frances E. Jones, Vera Whaley, Ben, James, and Leroy Williams.

300

[Thanks and appreciation go to Miss Frances E. Jones, Mrs. Geneva Wiley, and Mr. Fred White for information concerning Professor Daniels.]

School for White Children

In the 1860s there were no white children on the island to attend the first freedmen's school. It was not until several years after the Civil War that young white couples settled on the island and had children. These children were either taught by their mothers or sent away to live with a relative in order to attend school—usually to Savannah.

As the number of children grew, and with parents who had neither the education nor the time to teach their children, teachers were sent and salaries paid by the School Department. As there were no Praise Houses or church buildings for white children in those early years, school was held in vacant houses. Location was not a factor—if the building was empty and available, it was used. Year after year the same building was used during each school term for free, unless the owner had the opportunity to rent it, then another building had to be found. Two of these black vacant houses that were used for school belonged to Frank Demery on Cooper River Road and Alice Bryant at Benjie's Point.

The first students to attend school from 1904-13 were as follows: *Cannon*—Daisy, Ernest; *Cetchovich*—Emil; *Chaplin*—Mary, Willie; *Fripp*—Claude, Laura; *Goodwin*—Benjamin Styles, Ethel, Ned, Oscar; *Scouten*—Gage; *White*—twins Alene and Allen, Hinson, George.

According to Hinson White, the pioneer teachers he remembers were Mrs. Stany Rivers and Mrs. Julia Cunningham. The teacher usually boarded with one of the parents. Hinson remembers Mrs. Rivers boarding with his folks who were living in the Bloody Point mansion at the time.

George White said that a teacher by the name of Mrs. Casey boarded with the Palmer family living in the old Bob Butler house at Benjie's Point. Mrs. Casey left before her term was up, as the kids were so bad she could not handle them.

George also well remembered the school term of 1910-11 that was held in the empty house of Alice Bryant at Benjie's Point. The teacher that year was Sarah Constable. She was a relative of and boarded with Albert and Evelyn Stoddard at Melrose. Sarah had long blonde hair,

blue eyes, and a pimply face. The boys really took a second look at her. To travel the six miles from Melrose to where school was held, Sarah wore khaki riding pants and rode a beautiful horse named Gertie.

Grades were one through seven; school was held Monday through Friday from 9 A.M. until 3 P.M. for nine months out of the year.

Their desks were old tables and chairs or anything that they could use to "make-do." The students had to furnish their own slates and slate pencils. There were no lights of any kind.

Lunches taken to school were foods left over from meals at home: a biscuit or piece of cornbread with fried fresh pork, sausage, or jelly and butter, a baked sweet potato, some fried chicken or a slice of cake, all wrapped in a section of brown paper, as newspaper was scarce. Some families had cows and the children brought fresh milk in glass canning jars or whiskey bottles. No one was allowed to go home to eat.

Sarah Constable had taught only the one term and part of the 1911-12 term when the Melrose mansion burned to the ground. Because she had no place to stay, Sarah had to quit teaching and return to Virginia where she had come from. Another teacher was hired to take her place.

Like the blacks, the white children had to help with the planting and harvesting as their parents could not afford to pay a hired person. George White said that he did not get to go to school much for he had to help his folks on the farm. He had such a little bit of "schooling" that he was really ashamed to write, even now, because his spelling and writing were so bad. He did like to go to school, though, and went every chance he got, just to get out of work. He spent so much time in the field picking cotton—picking cotton—that it seemed like all he ever did was—pick cotton. But, thank God, he said, the boll weevil killed it all by 1917 and he was glad, for it saved him a lot of misery not to have to pick cotton again.

First School Building on Island Built for White Children

On 22 January 1913, Richard Fuller Fripp, Jr., in the State of South Carolina and in the County of Beaufort, for the sum of $6.00, sold to the Trustees, School District No. 5 of Beaufort County, the following land for a school building:

> . . . All that parcel of land known as a part or tract of land known as a part of one acre of land belonging to R. F. Fripp, Jr., situated lying and

being in Hilton Head Township, County and State aforesaid and on Daufuskie Island and containing (1/4, one quarter of an acre) and bounded as follows—on the North by lands of R. F. Fripp, Jr., East by R. F. Fripp, Jr., South by Pender Hamilton and West by Public Road.

The deed was witnessed by J. W. White, Magistrate of Daufuskie, and by Elizabeth W. Medlock, step-daughter of Richard Fripp, Jr.

Known as Daufuskie School, the little white school house was built by carpenters from Bluffton, South Carolina: Ned Hodge, Berry Hutson, and Bill Hutson. While these men stayed on the island they boarded with the Jim White family living in the Bloody Point house.

A small building was erected in the back yard of the school that contained an outhouse for girls and boys with a wood shed separating the two. A well was driven in the front yard.

There would be no lights and a wood heater would keep them warm. Desks which contained ink wells and a storage place for books were installed. Slates and slate pencils would be used, but would have to be purchased by the students. In later years two blackboards would be mounted on opposite sides of the one window in the rear of the building and chalk would be furnished for the students.

School in the new building would open the fall of 1913. Arthur Ashley Burn had arrived that summer as assistant keeper at the Bloody Point lighthouse. The Burn children, Louise and Ashley, would be enrolled for that first term. Other students added to the class would be those who had become of school age or who had recently moved to the island: Bill Scouten and the James P. Chaplin, Jr., grandchildren, Bessie and Marion Wright.

Mrs. Myra Scouten—First Teacher for New School

William W. Scouten, Sr., had purchased Haig's Point Plantation in 1899. He and his wife, Myra, moved to the island shortly thereafter. When the new school building was completed, she became the first teacher.

Freeport was a part of Haig's Point. On Freeport was a house that the Scoutens rented to Ernest Cannon, whose wife had died prior to his moving to the island. Living with Ernest was his son Furney Cannon, with his wife and their two children, Ernest II and Daisy Cannon.

Charlie Sisson had moved in the Haig's Point lighthouse with his

Mrs. W.W. (Myra Gage) Scouten, Sr., Teacher (1927)
(Photograph courtesy Mrs. W. W. [Jo] Scouten, Jr)

wife and their two children, Frederick and Ruth Elizabeth (Beth) Sisson.

If it wasn't a school day, or should she have a light load, Mrs. Scouten was seen traveling the Cooper River Road in her buggy pulled by her pale red mare, Redwing. (Fred White said that by using her buggy, Mrs. Scouten got more M.P.H. —Miles Per Horse!)

But on school mornings Mrs. Scouten would ride in a big wagon pulled by her mule, Peggy. When Peggy got going she was hard to stop, because she was partially deaf. The two Sisson children would walk the short distance from the lighthouse and be waiting for Mrs. Scouten to board the wagon with her two sons, Gage and Bill. On the way they would pick up Ernest II and Daisy Cannon at Freeport.

It took an hour or more to drive the seven miles to school. Mrs. Scouten would travel the back way that the islanders referred to as the "Church Road," which would take them past the houses of Emily (Melia) Manuel and Frances Martin, on by the church and praise house, down by Peggy and Joseph Michael's. But before they reached Sipio Robinson's they made a right turn and rode down Swamp Road, which came out almost by William (Hamp) and Edna Bryan's, on past Cynthia and John Bryan's, Laura and George William's, Flora and William Heyward's, Leathia and Joseph Bryan's, then by the home of Beck and Arthur Heyward which led right onto the school grounds.

They traveled the same road each afternoon on the way to Haig's Point.

A Terrible Accident

On one such beautiful fall morning in 1914, when Bill Scouten was seven years old, the Cannon and Sisson children (plus Marion Wright, who doesn't recall just why he was with the group that morning) were with Mrs. Scouten (seven children in all) in the wagon riding merrily on their way to school. The birds were flitting through the trees; they saw a rabbit dash across the road in front of the mule and everyone shouted with glee. Squirrels were seen scampering about; trees on either side of the road looked so lovely dressed in their red, yellow, and orange leaves; a gentle breeze was blowing—everything was right with the world.

The wagon had just passed the house of a black lady, Emily (Melia) Manuel. Her land joined Melrose Plantation on the south and was the first cottage they saw each day. She was usually outside and greeted

them with a "Good morning," but on this particular day the house was shut up tight.

Charlie Medlock, a young white man and stepson of Dick Fripp, Jr., had decided at sunrise to ride Dick's dark brown mare, Baby, and go deer hunting. Not having any success on the hunt, he was returning to his home at Benjie's Point on New River. He rode out of the woods on the big road just as Mrs. Scouten and the children were passing by. He waved to them, and not being in a hurry, he followed along behind the wagon.

By this time the wagon had approached Frances Martin's house just above the church. They saw Emily Manuel walking down the road. (They later learned that she had been on her way to visit her daughter, Lizzie, who had married John Bryan and lived at "The Branch" on Mongin Creek.)

About the same instant they saw Emily, they heard the steamer *Pilot Boy* blow as it reached Benjie's Point. This side-wheeler always left Savannah early in the morning on its way to Beaufort, and it would return late in the afternoon of the same day.

The weather was a little on the chilly side, so Bill Scouten would jump out of the wagon bed to the ground, run a little ways, then, by putting his foot on the hub of the wheel, he would jump back in. He had done this several times, but this once Bill was not successful: when he put his foot on the hub to jump back into the wagon, his foot slid right through the spokes of the moving wheel.

Bill and the children screamed, but the mule was hard of hearing and it took awhile before Mrs. Scouten could pull back hard on the reins and stop Peggy. The wheel had gone round and round, breaking Bill's leg in several places.

Mrs. Scouten's first concern was to help her son. She got down out of the wagon as fast as she could, at the same time calling out pleadingly to Emily Manuel, "Mom Melia, Mom Melia, what am I going to do? What am I going to do?" She took Bill in her arms and hugged him close, tears streaming down her face.

Charlie Medlock saw what had happened, and jumped down quickly from his horse to help get Bill's leg out of the wheel. By this time Emily Manuel had reached the wagon and was busy taking off her apron to make a bandage. As Emily wrapped the apron around Bill's leg, she spoke reassuringly to Mrs. Scouten: "Chile, we jes gonna

William Wiser Scouten, Jr.
(Photograph courtesy Mrs.
W.W. [Jo] Scouten, Jr.)

do de bes we kin, and wid de hep ob de good Lawd Jesus, eberting gonna be aw rite."

They needed to get Bill off the island and to a doctor without further delay. Charlie remembered the *Pilot Boy* blowing just minutes before and realized that it would not tarry long at Benjie's Point. He knew that he would have to make haste to beat the boat to Haig's Point. As there was no dock there, small boats had to ferry passengers out into Cooper River to get aboard. Charlie jumped on his horse and rode as fast as he could to hold the boat until Mrs. Scouten could arrive.

Mrs. Scouten held her son in her arms in the back of the wagon while the other children sat about them with their big frightened eyes glued on Bill. Marion Wright had gone on home to his grandfather's at Chaplin's Landing. Young Gage Scouten took the reins and drove as carefully as he could so as not to jostle the wagon any more than he had to. The Cannon children hopped off the wagon as they passed the Freeport Road and walked on home, but the Sisson children continued to ride on to the Haig's Point landing.

Charlie Medlock had ridden his horse so hard and so fast, and the horse had gotten so hot and so lathered down that it foundered when it reached the river. Everyone thought it was dead. However, Charlie had arrived in time to hold the *Pilot Boy* and to tell its Captain, Tom Martin, what had happened. A bateau was waiting to transport the Scouten party to the waiting boat.

Bill was placed gently aboard and made as comfortable as possible. The captain turned the boat around and headed right back the way it

had come that morning in order to get to the nearest hospital. They had to travel twenty-one long miles and wait almost two miserable hours before they could reach the port of Savannah—an eternity for an injured child and an anxious mother.

Due to the delay in getting to the hospital, Bill's leg could not be saved. It was amputated just above the knee. Right away it became infected and more of the leg had to be removed, but everyone was so grateful that his life had been spared.

Back at School

The children waiting at school that day didn't know just what had happened, but they did know that the teacher had not arrived. They were so pleased that there would be no school, so they all walked back home. Later, of course, they were saddened when they learned about the accident.

Because of his youth, Bill's leg healed in no time and he was back in school. He could get about on his crutches almost as fast as the other boys could on their two good legs.[10]

Anecdotes to Accidents

Much later after the accident, two very interesting incidents occurred. One was related by Bill's wife, Jo Scouten:

> When the United States entered World War I, Bill's father, W. W. Scouten, Sr., was called back into active service (he had come out of the Spanish American War a Navy Lieutenant) and was stationed in Charleston. The family went with him and by this time Bill had graduated from using two crutches. When wounded soldiers and sailors were brought to the hospital and had a limb amputated, Bill was called in to teach them how to walk by using just one crutch.

The other incident took place on Daufuskie when Bill was about nineteen years of age. This story was submitted by Francis (Frank) A. Burn, Sr., as he was present at the time and declares it to be the "fact truth."

> This black man was being tried for killing some man's dog in a steel trap that he had set for a wild animal.
>
> Court was being held in the open pavilion at Benjie's Point Public Landing where the big steamers came in.
>
> Bill Scouten just happened to be down there that day and when he

found out what was going on, he burst in on the court session and in a very strong voice proclaimed that he was representing the defendant in the case.

Bill was a good actor and orator. Tapping his crutch for emphasis, he paraded back and forth, back and forth, in front of Magistrate Joe Hoskiss, who was presiding over the trial.

It took Bill thirty minutes to dramatically expound all the good traits and character of this man ... reliving the events that took place the time his leg got caught in the wagon wheel ... declaring that if it had not been for this man riding his horse to the Haig's Point landing and delaying the boat that day ... that he might not be alive today.

Judge Hoskiss was annoyed by Bill's action and long-winded speech, but was so impressed with his story (believing every word that was said) that he told the court he thought this was a terrible mistrial of justice, simply because the warrant had erroneously been dated and signed on Sunday, thus making it illegal. The case was dismissed, which freed the black man of the charges.

The only thing wrong with this whole episode was that Bill's story wasn't exactly true. The events had happened just as he had so meticulously proclaimed, but the black man was not the one who aided Bill in his distress—it was Charlie Medlock, a young white man.

Those who attended the trial could not question the story as they knew nothing about its authenticity. Bill just thought that the black guy was getting a raw deal, and, recognizing him as a friend, Bill wanted to help him out of his dilemma—which he did.

Mrs. Scouten Leaves—New Teacher Arrives

In 1918, when Mr. W. W. Scouten, Sr., was called back into active duty during World War I, the family moved with him to Charleston where he was stationed. A family by the name of Bunn moved into the Dick Fripp house at Benjie's Point and Mrs. Bunn became the new teacher.

Also moving to the island that year were the families of Westley Avant, George Lane, and Niva Harley. Those attending the school term of 1918-19 were the following: *Avant*—Luther; *Bunn*—Clarice, Henry; *Cetchovich*—Emil; *Goodwin*—Benjamin Styles (B.S.), Juanita; *Harley*—Audrey; *Lane*—Braddie, twins Corrine and Irene, twins Janie and Eugene, Leonard, Myrtle; *Palmer*—Charlsie, Lucille; *Saul*—

Norma. Mrs. Bunn taught only that one semester, then the family left the island.[11]

Miss Elizabeth (Betty) Medlock Teaches School

Bachelor Dick Fripp, Jr., son of Fuller and Margaret Fripp, Sr., married his first cousin Mary Fripp Medlock, who had two children, Charlie and Elizabeth (Betty) Medlock, by her former husband. Elizabeth Medlock began teaching the fall of 1919.[12]

School Census of 1921 for Daufuskie School

Those students whom Miss Elizabeth was teaching at the time were viz.: *Burn*—Arthur Ashley (fifteen years of age), Francis Arthur (six), Theodora Gertrude (thirteen); *Cetchovich*—Emil (seventeen); *Goodwin*—Juanita (nine), Barney (six), Benjamin (fourteen); *White*—twins Alene and Allen (fourteen), and Frederic (ten).

Former Student Admires Teacher

Miss Elizabeth was the only teacher that Fred White remembers. When asked about his school days he had this to say:

> Miss Elizabeth Medlock was a very good teacher. As the years went by, I realized more and more how unappreciative I, and most of us were, and I longed for an opportunity to apologize to her. I met her in Savannah in 1971, at the reception room on the day of a former student, Norman Ward's funeral. I was very grateful for the chance to tell her how sorry I was about taking so long to realize how nice she had really been.

Fred remembered the kindness and compassion of his special teacher by relating this incident:

> On some days, the students' dogs would follow them to school (like Mary's little lamb). I recall that on one cold winter's day we were about to freeze as the wood was wet and the stove wasn't putting out much heat, when Miss Elizabeth told us to let all the dogs come inside because the heat from their bodies would help to warm up the room. We kids couldn't get to the door fast enough to call in all the dogs.
>
> After much patting, hand licking and tail wagging, the dogs finally settled down and they did lend much comfort to us and to the room—strange but true.

310

Daufuskie School, circa 1930

(Left to right) James Goodwin, Lucy Goodwin, Charlsie Palmer, Ann Keenan, Barney Goodwin, Geraldine Ward, Calhoun Ward, Edward Ward, Nell Palmer, Norman Ward, Francis Burn, Leonella Burn.

When Fred was asked who furnished the wood for the heater in the one-room school, he remarked:

> I am not sure about the wood supply. It was probably donated and brought by some of the parents. But I do know we had to get it from some where since I'm positive there were not enough saplings on a quarter acre of school ground, nor enough dogs, to keep the room comfortable.

Miss Elizabeth Marries, Quits Teaching

Immediately following her marriage to Emil Cetchovich II in January, 1926, Miss Elizabeth quit teaching. Mrs. Oscar (Ann Keenan) Goodwin was hired to finish out Miss Elizabeth's school term that ended in June of that year.

Arthur A. Burn and Wife, Margaret, Substitute Teachers

Margaret Keenan Burn was usually the substitute teacher, but at times when she didn't feel up to it, Arthur taught in her place.

Mrs. Myra Scouten Returns as Teacher

Ann Keenan Goodwin had thoughts of being the permanent schoolmarm, but Mrs. Myra Scouten had returned to the island from Charleston and was given back her old job as teacher. Mrs. Scouten taught from the fall of 1926 until June, 1934, when Mr. Scouten became very ill and she was needed at home. During those last years Mrs. Scouten taught these other children: *Crosby*—Albert, Jeannette; *Bishop*—C.J., Hazel; *Bullard*—Hester; *Burn*—Leonella; *Cook*—Curtis; *Goodwin*—twins Lucy and James; *Hiott*—Archie, Grace, Lincoln, Teenchy; *Keenan*—Ann; *Palmer*—Nell; *Ward*—Ammie, Calhoun, Edward, Geraldine, Lillian, Norman; *White*—Annie.

Admiration of Former Teacher

Francis A. Burn remarked that Mrs. Scouten was a wonderful teacher:

> She read books that fascinated and held me spellbound—books by Shakespeare; *The Scarlet Peminal*, I can't remember the author; the *Three* [Four] *Crossings* by Winston Churchill; and others. I liked history and when Mrs. Scouten read about the French Revolution, the War of

Spain, and our Revolution, I was lost in time—I could see myself right there in the midst of the excitement—where it was all happening.

I was always disappointed when Mrs. Scouten stopped reading. I wanted her to keep on for she read with such emphasis and emotion, I could listen to her forever. She had a great impact on my life. Years later while serving in the Merchant Marines and the Navy, I was privileged to visit many of the far away places that she so graciously read to us about.

First Male Teacher

Following Mrs. Scouten, in August of 1934 Sheryl Hiott, the first male teacher, came to the island from Walterboro, South Carolina. He boarded awhile with Mrs. John (Juanita) Fripp who lived in the old Fuller Fripp house on New River. When she left the island, he stayed with Charlie and Pearl Palmer, who lived in the Bob Butler house near Ohman's store at Benjie's Point.

The Marchant family had moved to Daufuskie the summer of 1934 and would be farming at Melrose. David and Exie Harley Peth had brought their family to the island and rented the William Hudson home and opened Hudson's small store that had been closed for several years. Since their marriage in 1926, Emil and Elizabeth Cetchovich II now had a child of school age. Because of the increase of families, several new student were enrolled the fall of 1934: *Cetchovich*—Emil III; *Marchant*—Doris, Henry, James, Ruth; *Peth*—David, John, Thomas; *Stevens*—Jewel Rebecca (Mrs. Peth's daughter from a previous marriage.)

Sheryl Hiott taught only until the spring of 1935 when he resigned and a young Savannah lady, Julia Shriver (Shiver), came and finished out his term that ended in June. She did not return.

Edna Ingram Comes to Island

From Savannah came another young woman by the name of Edna Ingram, who taught school from August, 1935 to June, 1939. She boarded with Elizabeth and Emil Cetchovich II, who lived in the old Dick Fripp house at Benjie's Point.

Edna's twenty-eight students included other Cetchovich children, Emilie, Ralph, Walter, and Ida White.

Lunches Prepared at School

During the period from 1935-39 Jim Goodwin had an old Model T Ford truck. It had roll-up shades in the covered back to keep out the rain, and along the sides were seats for the kids. The Goodwin family lived in the Bloody Point mansion. Their married daughter, Juanita Goodwin Kennerly, lived with them and would drive the Goodwin children to school each morning in this old truck. Juanita would then prepare a hot lunch for all the school children from meal, flour, corn, butter, beans, and other commodities furnished by the government.

The meals were prepared in a small tin tool shed that had been built in the front yard of the school building. Squeezed into the small area was a two-burner kerosene stove and a small table that left barely enough room for Juanita to do the cooking.[13]

The parents furnished cooking utensils, plates, spoons, forks, drinking glasses, and cups. The children ate in the school room or sat on the porch steps or on a log in the yard. Sometimes, Gladys Marchant would come from Melrose and assist in serving the food.

Mrs. Jim (Lula Crosby) Goodwin was one of the school trustees. She saw that the children had an Easter egg hunt each year and special treats on other occasions. Graduation Day for the seventh graders was always looked forward to with anticipation and excitement. Guests were invited and there would be speeches, recitations, awards, and plenty of refreshments.[14]

Johnson Family Moves to Island

Gus Ohman, who had been the postmaster and owned the local grocery store, was leaving the island in 1938, following the death of his wife Edith. Malcolm and Josephine Johnson of Bluffton, South Carolina, had moved into the Ohman home. Josephine was to be the new postmaster and Malcolm came to farm and operate the Ohman store. They had two children, Georgia and Kenny Mack.

Edna Ingram Leaves Island—Mrs. Smoak Teaches

Edna was getting married to Sam Burroughs. After the school semester ended in June, 1939, Edna resigned her position and moved back to Savannah. Mrs. Katherine Smoak from Erhardt, South Carolina, became the new teacher in August of 1939. During her stay the

Daufuskie School circa 1939

Center back: Jim Goodwin. Next row: Mrs. Jim (Lula) Goodwin, Mrs. Katherine Smoak (teacher). Center row: Ammie Ward, Annie White, Emil Cetchovich III, Walter Cetchovich, Norman Ward. Front row: Curtis Cook, Ida White, Emilie Cetchovich, Lillian Ward, Ralph Cetchovich, Mr. Angus Fordham (superintendent of schools).

new students who enrolled were Marion Cetchovich, Georgia Johnson, and Kenny Mack Johnson.

That fall of 1939, Katherine's husband Preston Smoak was hunting with some other men. When he walked away from his stand, wearing a brown leather jacket, someone mistook him for a deer and shot him in the shoulder with a load of buckshot. This accident happened real early in the morning. Lance Burn took Mr. Smoak to Savannah in his boat, the *Dolphin*. The injury was not too serious. Following a short stay in the hospital, Mr. Smoak was released and back on the island.

The White School on the Decline

Families were leaving the island to work in the Savannah shipyard during World War II; children were graduating each year until 1945, when there were only two pupils remaining in school. From 1939 to 1945 the following white teachers taught in the little white school house:

> 1939-42: Mrs. Katherine Smoak, Erhardt, S.C.
> 1942-43: Mrs. Daisy Langford, Ridgeland, S.C.
> 1943-44: Mrs. Marie Perry, Ridgeland, S.C.
> 1944-45: Mrs. Ida Thomas, Fairfax, S.C.[15]

Before leaving for Savannah, Ida White's last teacher on the island was Mrs. Thomas. When Ida left, Georgia and Kenny Mack Johnson were the last children enrolled in school. Their parents, Malcolm and Josephine Johnson, were moving back to Bluffton. Mrs. Thomas moved right along with them and taught the children in their own home for the remainder of that semester, thus closing the Daufuskie School in 1945.

One Teacher—One Pupil

The school had been closed for three years when Gerald Yarborough came to live with his grandmother, Mrs. Gillian Ward, in 1948. He entered the First Grade that fall. The school department sent for a teacher, Mrs. Lola Merritt of Laurens, South Carolina. Mrs. Merritt came to the island and boarded with Fred and Mae Dierks at Benjie's Point.

Gerald only attended school that one year. As it was very boring, he and Mrs. Merritt took a lot of field trips which consisted mostly of

walks through the woods. After school was out in June, 1949, Gerald returned to Savannah to live with his mother, Mrs. Geraldine Yarborough Wheelihan, and Mrs. Merritt left the island.

Brabhams Move to Island

In the summer of 1949 William H. and Gertrude Brabham moved to Melrose to farm and raise cattle. Their five children, Mary Agnes, Clevy, Ollie, Johnny H., and Keewee, would all go to school that fall. Mrs. Merritt was sent for again, and this time when she returned she lived in the Sipio Robinson house.

The Brabhams remained until 1953, left the island, then returned in 1955. By this time Mr. Brabham had passed away and it was Mrs. Brabham and the children who lived at Melrose.

Mrs. Elsie Graves Getsinger was hired to teach the Brabham children. It was very difficult for them to attend school because Melrose was several miles away and the roads were flooded. At times the children would not even go home but would sleep in an old car near the school house all night so they would be on time for classes the next morning. Mrs. Getsinger taught one full term and part of another when in 1956 the Brabhams left the island for good, and Mrs. Getsinger returned to her home in Bluffton.[16]

Burn Family Returns to Island

The little school remained vacant until Lance and Billie Burn, with their son Gene, moved to the island from Ft. Lauderdale, Florida, arriving on 1 April 1959. Because the schools were segregated and there were no white children on the island, in order to complete his Fifth Grade semester, Gene attended May Howard School in Savannah until June, boarding with Mrs. Carol Noonan.

Lance had first come to the island in 1913 when his Dad, Arthur A. Burn, came as assistant Bloody Point Lighthouse keeper. After their marriage, Lance and Billie had moved to Daufuskie in 1935, leaving the island in October of 1939 when their second child, Bob, was six-months old. They had bought the Fuller Fripp place in 1947, but could never live on the island permanently because of economic reasons. They returned in 1959 and operated a business called "Jolly Shores." Most of their customers were weekend boaters that came mainly from Savannah.

Gene Burn would enter the Sixth Grade in August of 1959, so again Mrs. Lola Merritt was asked to return to the island. She accepted, and boarded with the Burn family until the one-room school building was turned into a doll-sized apartment for her, leaving just enough room for one desk. By this time the elementary schools on Daufuskie included the Eighth Grade.

School was not very interesting with one teacher and one pupil, but Mrs. Merritt would cook meals for herself and Gene, and they would take a lot of nature walks. Even though there was no one to play with and no competition, Gene was happy, for he was home, and he loved the island.

Williams Family Moves to Island

Gary and Gillian Ward had bought the old John Fripp place on New River in 1927. Mr. Ward had passed away in 1947. Their daughter, Lillian Ward, and Sefton Williams of Savannah, had married and had two sons. In 1959 the Williams built a restaurant on Lillian's property which she had received in the distribution of the Ward estate. In 1960 their son Gary enrolled in school for about five months, after which the business closed and the family moved back to Savannah.

Daufuskie School Permanently Closed in 1962

With the exception of the five months that Gary Williams attended school, there was only one teacher and one pupil for three years. Mrs. Merritt had taught Gene from August 1959 until June of 1962.

When Gene graduated it became front page news in South Carolina and Georgia papers.[17] The little white school house closed forever, never to function again as an institute of learning.

Daufuskie School Used as Dwelling for Black Teachers

In 1964 Mrs. Annie McDonald, principal of the black Mary Fields Elementary school, and her nephew Ronald Sanders, used the building for living quarters. When she left the island in 1967, Mrs. Julia Johnson, who succeeded Mrs. McDonald as principal, also resided in the white school building until she left in 1974.

318

Daufuskie School 1962
(Mrs. Lola Merritt, teacher; Gene Burn, graduate.)

Post Office in White School House

The U.S. Postal Service had awarded Nancy Levis a contract for the Daufuskie Island Community Post Office. With permission from the school department, Nancy used the school building for postal needs for a few months in 1987.

School Building an Office for Fire Department

Having no major repairs since 1960 and in very sad condition, the little school building stood as a stark reminder of children, of laughter, and of days gone by.

The Daufuskie Island Volunteer Fire Department has been established on the island. After the community was given permission to use the school building and the land in 1989, a large garage was erected on the back of the grounds to house the firetruck and equipment.

When Mrs. Lory Anderson-Kowalski was Chairman of Daufuskie Day in 1989, she collected over two thousand dollars in contributions

and donated it all to Dick Perkins, our volunteer fire chief, to purchase fire hoses and other accessories.

Again, with donations from islanders and various interested parties, Lory was responsible for implementing her plans to have the school repaired and used as an office for the fire department. Hired to do the carpenter work and painting, Robert L. (Bob) Burn completed the renovation in June, 1990.

To preserve this building—this little piece of history—so it can be used again by people is such a blessing and a happy ending for those who have such pleasant memories of getting their early education in this tiny white schoolhouse.

Mary Fields Elementary—Second School Built

Black children continued to attend school in the Maryfield Praise House and the First Union African Baptist Church until the 1930s, at which time the parents got together and under the umbrella of the church name they purchased two acres of land:

> In the State of South Carolina, County of Beaufort Know all men by these presents, that I, Frances Martin, Executor of the Estate of John Martin, who died intestate and appointed Francis Martin Executor, of Daufuskie Island, in the County of Beaufort, in the State aforesaid, for and in consideration of the sum of thirty-five ($35.00) dollars, to me paid by Union Baptist Church of Daufuskie Island, in the County of Beaufort, and the (receipt whereof is hereby acknowledged), have granted, bargained, sold and released, and by these presents do grant, bargain, sell and release unto the said Union Baptist Church, all that piece, parcel or lot of land known as part of the Estate of John Martin situated, lying and being on Daufuskie Island in the County of Beaufort and State of South Carolina, more particularly bounded and described as follows to with: to the *North* and *West* by the Estate of John Martin; to the *East*, by the Public Road; to *South* by the lands of Scipio Robinson and contain two (2) acres more or less.

This deed is signed by Executor, Frances Martin; witnessed by Edith C. Ohman and her brother, Joe Loper; Notary Public, Gus Ohman, dated 24 February 1930.[18]

To pay for the land the parents had given parties where they sold food, homemade ice cream, candy, and drinks. Once the land was purchased, they continued to earn and save money for a school building.

The parents met with Allen Paul, Superintendent of Beaufort County Public Schools, and were in agreement that the school department would pay half and the parents would pay half, which came to $400.00 each, or a total of $800.00 for a two-room schoolhouse.

It wasn't until 1933 that enough money had been saved and materials purchased to begin the building.

President Franklin D. Roosevelt had begun the Work Projects Administration (WPA) 1933-1943, to give federal relief to the unemployed. Paid by the government for this community project, these WPA workers on the island furnished the labor to build the school: Emil Cetchovich II was the foreman; Samuel Holmes was the head carpenter; Dennis Young, Sr., mixed cement and laid the brick work for the foundation pillars; Hinson White, Gabe Washington, Joe Riley, Albert (Bert) Gage, Henry (Lexie) Hamilton, Charlie Myers, and Bobby Jenkins helped in any area where they were needed.[19]

Like the Praise House, land that was purchased for the school was part of the Maryfield Plantation. When the new building was completed, the choice was to name the school Mary Fields Elementary.

From boards left over from the school building, the WPA workers made desks—some large, some small. Each homemade desk unit had a seat, a top to write on with a place to store books beneath. Outhouses were used and there was a shallow well with a handpump.

According to Miss Frances Elizabeth Jones, she only completed a few early grades at Maryfield Praise House and Union Church. She was sent to Savannah to complete grammar school, then on to Beach High. To be with her grandparents, Mr. and Mrs. Joseph Michael, and to take advantage of some extra-curricula studies, Miss Jones came back to Daufuskie and enrolled for summer courses (1926-1927) in the private school of Professor John D. Daniels. She attended Savannah State and completed her education with courses at South Carolina State College in Charleston. She began her teaching career in 1930 by replacing Leontine Singleton, who had left, while school was still being taught in the Maryfield Praise House and Union Church.

When Mary Fields Elementary opened in 1934, Miss Jones, with teacher Gertrude Byran, had a total of 108 students.[20] New regulations were that the school term would last for six months—from September until March. Grades would be one through six, and daily hours would be from 8:30 A.M. until 3:30 P.M. In 1935 the school went

to its present term of nine months, with grades one through eight.

The teachers always boarded with some of the parents or perhaps with a relative. Miss Jones lived with her Michael grandparents, and Gertrude Bryan stayed with her grandparents, Mr. and Mrs. Henry Williams.

For the first six years, Miss Jones taught grades four through eight. From her seventh year until she retired (1969), Miss Jones taught grades one through four.

In the beginning, slates and slate pencils were used; later came pencils and tablets. Books and supplies oft-times were slow in coming from the school department in Beaufort; therefore, a lot of reading work for the students was assigned from materials Miss Jones found in magazines like the *Greater Teacher Instructor* and *The Progressive Farmer*. Also used as sources of reading material were catalogues from Sears & Roebuck, Montgomery Ward, and Walter Fields.

To help with arithmetic problems, the teachers would cut from seed catalogues pictures of different fruits to show the students that one apple and one apple make two apples; or that one pear plus two pears equal three pears; or that four bananas, take away three bananas, equals one banana, etc.

From the Atlantic Coastline Calendars Miss Jones would cut out numerals and make math charts showing the children how to count to one hundred by 1s, 2s, 5s, and 10s. The teachers used whatever they had on hand or whatever was currently available to aid in educating the children.

The mothers decided they wanted to give their children a hot lunch at school each day. They purchased a kerosene stove and set it up in the corner of one of the school rooms. Vegetables came from their gardens, chickens from off their yards, and seafood out of the river. Flour, sugar, and other staple items they purchased from the store. The first cook was Elizabeth Mortiche who was paid $1.50 per month by the PTA (which had been formed along with the new school). Following Elizabeth, the next cook was Liza Hamilton.

In the mid 1950s the present kitchen, dining, and restrooms were blessed additions. A large wood-burning range was purchased for doing the cooking. A deep well was also drilled. By this time the educational department was responsible financially for the food and for any improvements made at the school.

322

In 1956 Mrs. Lizzie Bell (Della) Bentley Hamilton was hired as kitchen manager. Della kept the kitchen spotless. She scrubbed the aluminum pots and pans so clean they just shone. Mrs. Bessie L. Futch, teacher, made the comment that Della was the only person she had ever seen who timed the close of her workday by the amount of shine on her pots, and not by the hands on the clock.

Through the years, Fred H. Dierks, Danny (Fastman) Mitchell, and Hinson White were hired by the school department to supply wood for the cooking and for the two heaters that warmed the school rooms. (Later, air conditioners furnished both cold and heat.)

Other Teachers at Mary Fields

When teacher Gertrude Bryan left the island, many others taught with Miss Jones: Gladys Atkins, Gladys Myers, Eloise Brown, Ramey Williams, Lottie Tolbert, Prophet Dean Whitehead (no dates on the previous teachers); Annie Mae Huggins, 1958-1960. (It was Annie Mae who encouraged the children to attend high school on the mainland. Also, she was instrumental in getting the school department to give the students board money of $25.00 per month in lieu of transportation.) Other teachers included Charles Etta Weaver, 1960-1961; Bessie Futch, 1961-1964. (While Mrs. Futch taught, she and Miss Jones worked very hard each year to be assured that Daufuskie was well represented at the Fair in Beaufort. Weeks before, they would collect from the people canned glass jars of different kinds of vegetables, jellies, jams, honey, stalks of sugar cane, the choicest Irish and sweet potatoes, pumpkins, pecans, crafts—anything that the island produced was added to the booth at the fair. After Mrs. Futch left, Miss Jones continued to keep the Daufuskie booth at the Fair alive until she retired in 1969. Mrs. Futch returned to the island in 1965 to coordinate a summer program for the school children.) Annie McDonald was on the island from 1964-1967, and it was while Mrs. McDonald was principal, beginning in 1966, that the Head Start program was begun. Julia Johnson was teacher from 1967-1974.

School Integrated

From 1936 until June of 1969 Miss Jones had served as the lower grades teacher with the previously named principals who were black.

Desegregation was now being enforced; a white teacher had to be hired as there were no white children to integrate the school. After thirty-nine years of teaching, Miss Jones was retiring and the new white teacher would take her place.

Pat Conroy—First White Teacher

Pat Conroy began teaching in August of 1969. Mrs. Julia Johnson was the principal, but she taught grades one through four and Pat took grades five through eight.

Pat was the first white teacher and the first male teacher since Mary Fields Elementary had been built in 1934. After three days in school Pat was appalled that the children knew so little when he asked them questions about their birthday, about the island, the state, the president, and the ocean by our shore. What he did not know was that these children had been taught, but it was very difficult for them to retain what they had been told.

The students had printed a school paper. In the issue that came out in March, just prior to vacation and before Pat came in August, were the following articles:

Mary Fields Elementary

Pat Conroy's Room is on the right. (Photograph courtesy Mrs. Martha Hutton, 1988.)

Mary Fields Elementary School Room 1968

Left: Miss Frances Jones, teacher 1930-1969. Right: Mrs. Sarah Grant, PTA president.

Mary Fields Elementary Graduates 3 June 1968

Left to right: Laura Jenkins, Sylvia Stafford, Marion Green, Jeannette Robinson, Willis Simmons, Jr.

Daufuskie Is an Island

By: Janice Stevens, 8th Grade

Hello friends and neighbors! Daufuskie is an isolated island, located off the coast of South Carolina in Beaufort County. It has fertile soil and a mild climate. Daufuskie Island also has a beautiful beach located on the shores of the Atlantic Ocean.

Other bodies of water such as the Savannah River, New River, May river are polluted by the chemicals from Savannah, Georgia paper mills. Population at present is approximately 135—119 colored, 16 caucasian.

Ernest Washington Discovers George Washington

By: Margarite Washington, 7th Grade

Edvina: George Washington was President in 1492.

Margarite: No, Edvina, Columbus had just discovered America in 1492. George became President in 1789.

Edvina: Oh! Am I 297 years late?

Four Presidents Become Valentines

By: Rickey Lewis Stevens, 2nd Grade

We talked about four presidents. "George Washington is our First President of the United States of America," Ernest [Washington] said.

Barbara Ann [Jenkins] said, 'Nixon is our new president."

Johnson is our past president. Our teacher reminded us about Lincoln. For our valentine we pasted pictures of the four presidents that we talked about on a large red heart. They were our valentines.

Some of South Carolina Firsts

By: Edvina Washington, 8th Grade

1562-63—A light sailing vessel, the first ship built in America to cross the Atlantic, was built by Huguenots at Port Royal, S.C.

1712—The first state health officer in America was Gilbert Guttery of South Carolina.

1740—The first free school for Negroes in America was founded at Charles Town (Charleston) in S.C.

1776—South Carolina was the only state whose signers of the Declaration of Independence were all natives of the state and all college men, educated abroad.

Our Constitutional Heritage

By: Janice Stevens, 8th Grade

Amendment 15, adoped in 1870
Right of Suffrage
Section One: The Suffrage

"The right of Citizens of the United States to vote shall not be denied or abridged by the United States or any State on account of race, color, or previous condition of servitude."

This was passed after the Civil War and gave the freed slaves the right to vote. It is important in a democracy that all its citizens be able to choose freely the people who make their laws.[21]

Concerning the children not knowing their birth dates, Mrs. Sarah Grant, the midwife, was asked about this. Here is her reply:

When we children were coming up, our parents would not tell us our birthday. And when you got big enough to ask, they surely wouldn't tell you then for they thought you were too big for your britches and you didn't need to know. My Ma told me my birthday one time and I never forgot it, for I knew she would probably never tell me again.

It was and is a requirement of the teacher to see that each child produces a birth certificate prior to his or her entering the first grade.

Knowing their birthdays and many other things were irrelevant to the children on this island. They didn't care that it was the Atlantic Ocean—to them, it was "the beach." When they got out of a boat, they went "up on the hill," and could care less that it was called Daufuskie Island or that this was South Carolina.

Pat Conroy's students adored him for several reasons. Most of the children had a mother or grandmother in the home; Pat represented a male, or father-image to them. Because he did not believe in discipline and did not know what else to do with them when they became unruly, he loaded all eighteen of them into the jeep and took off to the beach or to the woods. Sometime they got hoes and rakes and went to the yard to dig and plant seeds to make a garden. They did not take books home at night as there was no homework required. Pat wrestled with the boys, played ball with them, and taught them how to play soccer (sometimes in the school room). They were introduced to classical music and loved Beethoven. He had them sing and he taped their voices on a recorder so they could hear how they sounded.

Pat had pictures of artist Pablo Picasso's naked women tacked up all around the room which absolutely petrified Mrs. Johnson when she saw them. He brought in artists and musicians in order to introduce the children to some of the beauty of the outside world of which they knew practically nothing.

These kids realized that they had a good thing going by having Pat give them lessons while wading on the beach or walking through the woods. This pleased them immensely—anything to get away from the confines of the school room—and they had so much fun learning. Such freedom and no spankings! They thought Pat was crazy, told him so, and called him "Conrack."

The PTA had always had a Halloween party for the children, but Pat saw that they were taken to Hilton Head and to Beaufort for their first trick-or-treat experience. Everyone had such a marvelous time.

They had been practicing for sometime, so prior to the Christmas holidays (1969), Pat had the children perform in *A Christmas Carol*, with him playing the part of Mr. Scrooge. The play was held in the old Mt. Carmel Church No. 2 at Cooper River, for it had enough benches (with no backs) to seat the crowd. Every person on Daufuskie was there; the room was packed. Pat's portrayal of Scrooge was outstanding and the children were just great. It was a thoroughly enjoyable evening for all.

Pat realized that the children had not been anywhere but perhaps to Savannah or Hilton Head, so right away he planned a trip and took all of them to Washington, D.C., in May of 1970. The kids enjoyed the big city so much that they didn't want to come back home. (It needs to be added that the places Pat carried the children to represented a lot of hard, dedicated, persistent work on his behalf. It took the involvement of monies, cars, buses and boats of the school department and personal friends to get the job successfully accomplished.)

Pat's graduating class in June of 1970 consisted of four students: Johnnie Mae Holmes, Jackie Robinson, Alfred Smith, and Margarite Washington.

Pat really liked the children, and when he returned to teach in August, 1970, on the very first day at school he discussed where they would go on another trip. Pat left the island and did not return, but left the Vista Volunteers, Jim and Vivian Strand, in charge of his class. Neither Mrs. Johnson nor the education department was informed as

to where he was. Pat had taken a consulting job in Ridgeland with a desegregation team from the University of South Carolina. With the money that was to be received, he intended to finance a trip for the children to Six Flags in Atlanta.

Before Pat's return in September, Beaufort County School Board Superintendent, Dr. Walter C. Trammell, had found out about his leave of absence without permission. As soon as Pat was back at school, Dr. Trammell called and fired him—followed by a letter for his dismissal.

Pat sued the school board for reinstatement. He came to the island and had a meeting with the parents and the children. A boycott of the school followed, and for several days the children refused to ride the school bus. After receiving threats that each parents could be fined $50 or serve 30 days in jail, Pat had a meeting in the Jane Hamilton School building at Cooper River and urged the parents to consider the best interest of everyone and see that the children returned to school; this the majority did.[22]

The first hearing for Pat's suit against the Beaufort County Board of Education was to be held in Hampton, South Carolina, 30 November 1970.

The hearing was postponed when it was learned that two of the lawyers involved in the case had conflicting criminal court cases, according to George G. Trask, one of Conroy's attorneys.[23]

The case was rescheduled and at the trial in January, 1971, Fourteenth Circuit Judge William L. Rhodes, Jr., upheld the school board's decision that Pat was fired and would not teach on Daufuskie again. (Pat did attend the June, 1971, graduation exercises at Mary Fields.)

The Water Is Wide by Pat Conroy

Pat had kept notes during the course of his stay and had written about his year's teaching experience while on the island. In June, 1972, his book, *The Water Is Wide*, was published. This became a best seller and later was made into a movie called "Conrack."

Pat came back to the island and gave Mrs. Susie Smith eighteen copies of his book for her to present one to each of his former students.[24]

Beaufort Library Provides Outreach Project

Beaufort Librarian, Mrs. J. E. (Jett) Ragsdale, Jr., coordinated a three-month Outreach pilot project that began the first week of April and ended the last of June, 1971, with Federal Library Services and Construction Act funds which would provide materials, equipment, and transportation to and from Daufuskie.

The project was held for approximately one hour twice weekly, usually after school, at the old Jane Hamilton School building at Cooper River. Sound filmstrips were shown, comic books, and some hardbound books were available to the group; suckers and potato chips were passed around between shows; and at the closing each day refreshments were served, consisting of cupcakes or cookies and Kool-Aid.

Those attending were school students; they were also allowed to bring their younger brothers and sisters, which accounted for about thirty children. At times a few adults accompanied Mrs. Ragsdale: Mrs. Margie E. Herron, from the State Library in Columbia, S.C.; Mrs. Johnette Edwards, one of the speakers at the Beaufort Public Library; Mrs. Karish, Director of the Peter Pan School for the Retarded in Beaufort County; and reporter Hallie Petterson.[26] Visiting the school the last day before graduation in June, 1971, and attending the Outreach activity was former teacher, Pat Conroy. Mrs. Sarah Grant, the local midwife, rarely missed a program and sat with a big switch in her hand, which no doubt accounted for the well-disciplined group of children. She absolutely refused to stay in the presence of a bunch of noisy, unruly children—she loved the children, but not the noise.

Furnishing transportation by water was Ed McTeer, game warden, who made only two trips. For the remainder of the project trips were furnished by a Hilton Head Harbor Marina charter boat captain, George Breen.

Assisting with land transportation were Lance and Billie Burn, with the school bus and Volkswagen, and Jim and Vivian Strand, with a pick-up truck. Vivian also baked the cupcakes, served the refreshments, and both Vistas helped with presenting the filmstrips or in any way that they could.

After the program ended the last of June in 1971, a party was held at the beach.

Despite the heat generated by having all of the windows blacked out in order for the film to show on the screen, the whole program came off quite well. A chance to see the wonderful stories on film, to receive free coloring and comic books, to enjoy the tasty refreshments, and the pure pleasure of being away from home and school and enjoying themselves, all added to the children learning a lot and having a great time as well.

A scaled-down version of the program was carried on during the summer of 1972 as part of the overall county Outreach project which was again Federally funded.[27]

Bicycles for the Children

In August of 1971 eleven bicycles were donated by Gamma Xi Omega Chapter of the Alpha Kappa Alpha national sorority of Charleston. One bike was given to each family with school-age children.

Mrs. Naomi Mackey was president of the chapter and Mrs. Katrina Buksha was the committee chairman, both of whom were from Charleston. The action to initiate the bicycle project was made through Dr. Walter C. Trammell, Beaufort County Superintendent of Education.[28]

Teachers Who Came After Pat

Following Pat's dismissal, Mike McEachern taught from September of 1970 until graduation in June of 1971.

> 1971-72: Bob Thompson
> 1972-73: Frank Smith (While here, he married Candis Kent.)
> 1973-74: Howard Johnson; John Marks

Howard Johnson was hired to teach the children in the fall of 1973. Johnson said that he was privately tutoring some children in England when he read about Pat and the Daufuskie School. He was hoping he would have the privilege of teaching here. Johnson's Daufuskie teaching career lasted exactly three days—from Wednesday, 21 August, through Friday, 23 August. He could not handle the children, left the island immediately after school was out that day, and hasn't been seen

Attendance at the Beaufort County Library Program

At Jane Hamilton School. Left to right: Sherman Washington (small child unknown), Julie Washington, Pat Conroy.

Left to right: Jerome, Donald, and Barbara Jenkins, Franklin Wiley, Jr., Joseph and Ernest Miller.

Vista Volunteers: Jim and Vivian Strand, at beach party.

(Pictures taken by Mrs. Betty [Jett] Ragsdale. Courtesy of Mrs. Julie Zachowski, director, Beaufort Library.)

333

since. John Marks came and taught from 26 August 1973 until 29 May 1974.

Mrs. Johnson became very ill and had to leave the island in July. Mr. Marks had no intention of teaching another term, but because Mrs. Johnson would not be returning, he agreed to teach until other teachers could be found.

When the school department advertised in newspapers throughout the south for a couple to teach at Mary Fields, newlyweds Jim and Carol Alberto of Charlotte, North Carolina, answered the call, and Mr. Marks left.[29] The Albertos began teaching in September, 1974, with Jim serving as the principal.

With Jim and Carol, the school department became more liberal. Prior to their coming, it had been the teachers' responsibility to find a place to board or live, and to furnish their own transportation on the island. Since the Albertos were the first *couple* to teach, for them the department brought a trailer, placed it on the school grounds, and sent a used vehicle so Jim could haul school supplies.

Several things of interest happened while Jim and Carol were teaching: there was a Halloween party at school every year, but the Albertos set the precedent of using the school bus for the children to have trick-or-treat by driving them to the home of each resident; in 1975 the old wood range was hauled out of the kitchen and a new large electric one was installed; in 1978 they were responsible for getting Mary Fields accredited by the Southern Association of Schools and Colleges. In May, 1981, with the aid of Pamm Tarchinski, coordinator for the South Carolina Arts Commission in the Hilton Head and Bluffton area, Shannon Wilkinson, free-lance writer and art director of *Southern World Magazine*, and others, *The Daufuskie Kids' Magazine* was published. Also in 1978 Julie Washington and Leon Bentley were given recognition for their vegetable gardening in the 4-H CLub. In August of 1981 the school became integrated with four white students, the first ever in the all-black school. These four were Nicholas and Rusty Batey, Jessica Murray, and Chad Wilson—all of whom left the island at the close of school in June, 1982. Nicholas, Rusty, and Jessica returned in January of 1983. Jessica left at Easter vacation and did not return, but Nicholas and Rusty stayed on until June, 1983, when they left the island.[30] In March of 1982, Jim and Carol became the proud parents of a little boy they named Zachary. Mrs.

334

H. V. (Betty) Bright-Brown had begun the Laura Bright Award in memory of her mother, by giving money each year to the graduating students, hopefully to encourage them to further their education. Betty granted these award from June, 1972, until the end of Jim and Carol's stay in June, 1987.

Sarah Grant's Children's Center

When Sister Ellen Robertson of St. Mary's Human Development Center at Pritchardville, near Bluffton, South Carolina, visited Daufuskie in October of 1977, she realized the need for the preschoolers to have some interaction and exposure to education before enrolling the first grade at Mary Fields Elementary School.

Available to Sister Ellen was a house trailer that the E.O.C. had brought to the island and placed on the school grounds to be used for educational purposes.

Named after the last midwife on the island, the Sarah Grant Children's Center opened 29 August 1978 with six children enrolled: two were infants, Erin Chapman and Samantha Robinson, children of the workers; and, ranging in age from two to five years, the other children included Eric Bryan, Sabra and Tyrone Robinson, and Katrina Williams. They were allowed to ride the regular school bus and eat school lunches.

Mrs. Mary Chapman, the lead teacher, had a bachelor's degree in Home Economics. Miss Jeannette Robinson, aide, had been trained at St. Mary's. The center not only offered care for the children, but also taught parenting skills, health care, and child management to the parents.[31]

Mrs. Chapman quit the center on 19 December 1978 with Sister Sharon Culhane (who was from Chicago and was living on the island), taking her place, 8 January 1979. In August, 1980, Sister Sharon was replaced by Danny Atkinson. From the lack of children—they were either moving away or entering the first grade—the center closed 27 May 1983. For a couple of years thereafter, the trailer was used as a Senior Citizen's Center.

Albertos Leave Island—Sister Sharon Teaches

In June, 1983, Jennifer Smith and Alberto Stevens were the last two students to graduate from the eighth grade. The Albertos left the

island shortly after graduation.

Sister Sharon Culhane, who had taught in the Sarah Grant Children's Center, left the island in 1980 and taught in a Hardeeville, S.C., School until June of 1983. She applied for and received the position that Jim and Carol had held at Mary Fields Elementary. Because Sister Sharon would be the only teacher (with Willis Simmons, Jr., as an aide), the school department sent the seventh and eighth grade children off the island.

Sister Sharon began her teaching career in August, 1983, with six students. She taught until June, 1988. During her stay many interesting things happened. In 1983 she took the class on a memorable field trip to the Riverbanks Zoo in Columbia, South Carolina. To help finance this trip, on Daufuskie Day the children sold popcorn and sandollars to tourists who rode the topless buses.[32] In 1985 the class went on an outing to Savannah, where they visited museums and the Show Biz Pizza Palace, the food there being the highlight of the whole trip. In 1986 the students were benefitted through International Paper adopting the school and donating $10,000, with the provision that the money be used for educational purposes.[33] Two computers were added to the classroom: an Apple IIc, complete with a color monitor and external disc drive, furnished by the Beaufort County School District, and an NEC PC-8012 computer, with two disc drives, monitor, printer, and enough software to run a small business, donated anonymously by a Hilton Head businessman in 1985. The computers were credited with improving students' test scores and general skills. Proof of this claim came in 1986 in the form of a teacher-incentive award for Sister Sharon and the school, awarded by the S. C. Department of Education. The award is presented annually to schools exhibiting outstanding teacher attendance, student attendance, and test scores.[34]

During her four-year stay, Sister Sharon did not have a public graduation program for her sixth-grade graduates in June, but she chose instead to have a private beach party for all of the students.

Sister Sharon resigned at the close of school in 1987 and accepted an assignment at a school in Kingstree, South Carolina, in Williamsburg County, where she continues happily to teach.

Mrs. Catherine Campbell, New Teacher

Mrs. Campbell, from Greenville, South Carolina, began teaching in August, 1987. In June of 1988, for the first time in four years, a graduation program was presented by Mrs. Campbell—Stephen Yarborough being the only graduate. Just about the whole island came, as it was something they had all looked forward to, especially the older people.

In September, 1988, Mrs. Mary Lou Werner, a former New York teacher, was hired to assist Mrs. Campbell, for now there would also be kindergarten children to contend with.

During the fall of 1988, Mrs. Campbell decided to revise *The Daufuskie Kids Magazine*. To discuss this possibility, in December she met with Shannon Wilkinson (who had conceived the idea, then edited and published the first magazine), Jan Lambrecht of the South Carolina Arts Commission, and Marilyn Bowler, a school supporter. Then, with the aid of Felton Eaddy, a creative writer with the South Carolina Arts Commission; Joan Kaufman, Van Sullivan, and Bill Littrell, who were responsible for the photographs; Mary "Stick" Carroll and Barbara Lisenby, who were in charge of art direction and production, the book was printed by Impressions, Hilton Head, and was on the market by May, 1989. Mrs. Campbell's plans are to have a revision of the magazine every two years.

Mrs. Campbell's Field Trips

In 1988 Mrs. Campbell took the children to the Epcot Center at Disney World, Orlando, Florida. In 1989 she took them to Columbia to visit the South Carolina State Capitol and other official buildings. In 1990 the children were taken to Maggie Valley in North Carolina. Chaperones, who were needed on these trips to assist Mrs. Campbell, were parents or other interested PTA members.

The 1989-1990 School Term

At the close of the school in June, 1990, Mrs. Campbell had taught eight little boys—no girls—and there will not be one to graduate: *Kindergarten*—Chase Henderson, Benjamin Jones, and Jason Letendre; *First Grade*—John Letendre and Rickey Stevens (the only black student); *Second Grade*—Josh Letendre; *Third Grade*—Johnny Barber and Travis Wilson.

Mrs. Ethel Mae Wiley remains the kitchen manager and has been in this role for the past twenty-one years. She began in 1969 when Pat Conroy started teaching at the school. There were times when she was sick or had to be away, and then Mrs. Janie Simmons, Mrs. Susie Smith, or Mrs. Albertha Stafford substituted for her.

Mrs. Flossie Washington is the school custodian and has been since 1967. She began the same time that Mrs. Julia Johnson was hired as principal. Mrs. Louvenia (Blossom) Robinson was the custodian prior to Flossie, with Blossom's daughter, Mrs. Lucille Robinson Smith, helping when Blossom was out due to illness.

School Bus Drivers

Mr. and Mrs. Fred (Mae) Dierks were the first to have a school bus contract, circa 1950. They were required to furnish gas and their own transportation, which was an open-end pick-up truck with a top and sides made of plywood. Jake Washington rode "shotgun" to help the children load and dismount, and to prevent a child from falling out of the back of the truck.

When the Dierks left the island in April of 1963, Billie and Lance Burn were awarded the contract. Their first "school bus" was a used, navy-blue laundry truck, converted with seats built down each side to hold the twenty-three children. They received the same $75.00 per month that the Dierks had been paid; this had to cover the cost of a vehicle and gas. Through the years they bought a regular big city bus from Mr. William Porter; then the school department sent over a small worn-out bus that was given to the Burns. The bus did not last very long, but they were responsible for the cost of all repairs. Because of the small amount received for driving the children, one could not afford to buy a decent vehicle. The school department was finally talked into furnishing gas and a small, brand-new bus that was sent to the island 27 September 1976, which is identical to the same one that is being used in 1990. Billie Burn drove the children from April, 1963, to June of 1981, and was receiving $200.00 per month after eighteen years and two months under contract.

From 1981 to 1990 the following persons drove the school bus:

1981-1982: Mrs. Emily Akins Burn
1982-1983: Mr. Willis Simmons, Jr.
1983-1987: Mrs. Ruby (Shorty) Smith

1987-1989: Mrs. Lucy Thompson
1989-1990: Ms Yvonne Wilson; Mrs. Joy Jones

Other Children Who Attended Mary Fields from 1934-1983

Brown—Lenore; *Bentley*—Albertha, Ethel, Hattie, Leon, Luvirn; *Bryan*—Annie Mae, Cleveland, Eric, Ernest, Everina, Georgia, Isabell, Joe Nathan, Joseph, Lillian, Margaret, Marie, Nick; *Clines*—Lashay, Liza, Mary; *Edwards*—Tieasha; *Ford*—Charlie; *Forrest*—Kenneth, Larry; *Fripp*—Marion; *Grant*—Ellie Mae, Ruby, Freddie, Jr.; *Graves*—Abraham, Jr., Elizabeth, Evelyn; *Green*—Marion; *Hamilton*—Henry, Jr., Linda; *Hazzard*—Melvin; *Holmes*—Arthur Lee, Evelyn; *Hudson*—Alice, Clarence, Hezekiah, Leon, Marie, Virgil, William, Willie Mae; *Jenkins*—Barbara, Eva Mae, Donald, Ethel, Jerome, Laura, Lawrence, Jr., Leonar, Rebecca; *King*—Darrell; *Mann*—Matthew; *Miller*—Ben, Carrie, Elizabeth, Emily, Joseph, Herbert, Rebecca; *Mitchell*—Elizabeth, Eva, Daniel, Fannie, Mirah; *Mongin*—George, Lucille; *Mordeci*—Francenia, Vinson; *Mountrie*—Melvin, Vera Mae; *Myers*—Elizabeth, Josephine; *Robinson*—Alma, Alphonzo, Annell, Jeannette, Jermaine, Linwood, twins Linda Marie and Louis Faye, Lucille, Rakenya, Raymond, Rosetta, Samantha, Sheila, Susie, Tanya, Theresa, Tyrone; *Rosemond*—Lorin; *Simmons*—Georgia Ann, Jake, Jr., Joseph, Luke, Ophelia, Sier, Willis, Willis, Jr., Walter; *Smalls*—Susie; *Smith*—Ernestine, Ethel Mae, Frankie, Jenewese, Jennifer, Michelle, Nicole; *Stafford*—Henrietta, Larceny, Lillian, Otis, Sylvia, Thomas, Jr.; *Stevens*—Alberto, Amelia, Bobby, Janice, Leroy, Rickey; *Thompson*—Rachel, Mamie Lynn, Trae; *Washington*—Beaulah, Edvina, Eleanor, Ernest, Henrietta, Jake, Jr., Julie, Lula, Lillie Mae, Mary, Rosalee, Shawnta; *Wiley*—Ben, Calvin, Elverine, Ernest, Henrietta, Franklin, Franklin, Jr., Joseph, Lawrence, Richman, Jr., William; *Williams*—James, Katrina, Maebell, Phoebe; *Wilson*—Paul, Yvonne; *Young*—Dennis, Jesse, Rebecca.

Jane Hamilton School

Mt. Carmel No. 1 Church and Praise House had been blown down in the 1940 storm. Because of this, the children at Cooper River had no place to attend school except to walk to Mary Fields Elementary. Because of the long distance and bad weather, it was very difficult for the children to get to school at all, therefore, it was necessary that a

339

school be built to accommodate them.

So the last school to be built on the island was at Cooper River in 1940. Mrs. Jane Hamilton had deeded to the Beaufort County Board of Education one-fourth acre of land for $1.00: bounded on the North by lands of Paris H. Holmes; East and South by lands of Robert Hamilton; and West by the public road.

The school was constructed by the same WPA workers who had built Mary Fields and they were also paid by the government. Mr. Arthur A. Burn supervised the work.[35] When completed, in honor of the land donor the building was called the Jane Hamilton School.

The two teachers were Christina White and Janie Mitchell. The names of a few of the students, viz.: *Hamilton*—Johnny, Jr.; *Holmes*—Katie Mae, Samuel, Jr.; *Jenkins*—Walter; *Knight*—Rachel; *Miller*—Gladys; *McIntyre*—Son; *Myers*—Leila; *Riley*—John, Lucille; *Stafford*—Flossie, Thomas; *Washington*—Lula, Susie; *Wilson*—Mildred, Paul; *Young*—Dennis, Jesse, Rebecca.

The school closed circa 1950 for lack of a teacher. When this happened, the children were bused by Mr. or Mrs. Dierks to Mary Fields Elementary.

Mrs. Jane Hamilton then made her home in the school building until she died there circa 1962. She is buried at Cooper River Cemetery.

The building was later used by different groups: Mrs. Rhea Netherton, a Vista Volunteer, used it for a children's craft shop; sometimes the Community Club Meetings, PTA parties, and Sunday church services were held in the building; the Beaufort Library held summer programs here; for awhile, Vista Volunteers Jim and Vivian Strand used it as a flea market for the clothes and food sent by different organizations; and for years it has been used for storage. It is now in need of repair.

The Daufuskie PTA

The Parent-Teacher Association was established when Mary Fields School was built in 1934. It was because of this organization that the school received many benefits.

The children were required to pay a tuition to enter school. According to the grade, some students had to pay as high as $8.00 per semester. Having to pay this tuition presented such a hardship for

parents who had as many as four or five children in school at one time that letters of complaint were sent to the school department. The tuition was removed and books and supplies were furnished for free.

When the Jane Hamilton School closed circa 1950, because of the long distance the children had to walk the PTA requested that the Cooper River children be bused to Mary Fields Elementary. The first transportation provided by Mr. and Mrs. Fred Dierks was only for those children who lived at Cooper River. Because the children living at Benjie's Point were within a short distance, they were required to walk to school each day. In later years there were so many bad cows running loose and such rainy weather in the winter that all the children were bussed.

In the 1960s Mrs. Sarah Grant was the PTA president; Mrs. Sarah Bryan was the secretary; and Mrs. Maebell Jenkins was the treasurer. In 1965 Billie Burn became the first white PTA member. New officers were elected every two years.

In 1990 the PTA officers were all white; President, Joe Letendre; Secretary, Terri Wilson; and Treasurer, Denise Henderson.

•

A little story told by Thomas Stafford was very interesting and relates perhaps why some black children might have been turned away from school.

In 1936, from Bull Island, Thomas had come to Daufuskie with his parents John and Lula Stafford, along with his brother Herbert and sister Flossie. The children had gone to school on Hilton Head prior to their attending the Mt. Carmel Church No. 1 and Praise House and Jane Hamilton Schools on Daufuskie.

Thomas was a natural-born story teller and intertwined in his tales he would throw in a "Great God" or two. When asked about his school days, he had this to say:

> Great God, when I bin to school on Hilton Head I ditn't git 'long wid dat teacher a tall. She hed uh stick fur de gurls which wuz small, an' uh sassafras stick fur de boys dat was bigger. She would lay ya han op'n n'giya six licks n'de right han n'five n'de lef han 'til ya could see bleed marks cross yor han.
>
> Den, she hav brik stack up inde corner uf de school room. She would purnish ya by puttin' 2 brikn'ya han, den make ya stan on one feet and

ya'd better keep ya balance or ya'd git it den fursho.

Ya couldn't tawk, ya couldn't git outa ya seat, ya couldn't do nuttin'! When I git to "Fuskie, I couldn't git 'long wid dem teachers either. Uh, huh, yeah, yes mam, so I decide ef'n dat's de way to git n'edgehucation—den I ain't want none—so I quit.

Notes

1. War of the Rebellion, ser. 1, 35:392-93, State Library, Columbia, South Carolina.
2. Teacher's Monthly School Report, May, 1867, A.M.A. Archives, No. H 6656, Fisk University, Nashville, Tennessee.
3. American Missionary Association, Schools for Freedmen, Teacher's Monthly Report, April, 1867, No. H 6572, Fisk University, Nashville, Tennessee. (See Appendix XVI).
4. A.M.A. Archives, No. H 6598; Fisk University, 17th Avenue N., Nashville, Tennessee, 37203.
5. Gerhard Spieler, "'School Farms' Proliferated in Area After Civil War," *Island Packet*, 24 February 1983.
6. Ibid.
7. Ibid.
8. William (Hamp) Bryan, interview 20 October 1983.
9. Mrs. H. V. (Betty Bright) Brown, Goldsboro, N. C., Mrs. Richman (Geneva Bryan) Wiley, telephone conversations, 28 March 1990.
10. To get the entire story about Bill's accident, phone calls and interviews were made to Mrs. Jo Scouten, George and Hinson White, Mrs. Geneva Wiley, and Capt. Marion T. Wright.
11. Mrs. Audrey Harley Clanton's letter, 8 November 1984.
12. Ibid.
13. Mrs. Juanita Goodwin Kennerly, interview 20 June 1988.
14. Francis A. Burn, interview 6 March 1990.
15. Mrs. Josephine Johnson's personal letter, 18 February 1982.
16. Mrs. Elsie Getsinger, interview by phone, 20 April 1988.
17. *State* (Columbia, S. C.), 3 June 1962, sec. A, p. 1; *Savannah* (Ga.) *Morning News*, 4 June 1962, sec. A, p. 1; *News and Courier* (Charleston, S. C.), 5 June, 1962, sec. A, p. 1.
18. Beaufort County Courthouse, Deed Book 47, p. 578.
19. Miss Frances Jones; Mrs. Geneva Wiley.
20. Miss Frances E. Jones, interview, 5 August 1985.
21. This little five-page paper was called "Daufuskie News," vol. one, 19 March 1969, written by the students under the supervision of Mrs. Julia Johnson and Miss Frances Jones, pp. 1, 3, 5.
22. *Beaufort Gazette*, 9 October 1970.
23. Ibid., 3 December 1970.
24. Mrs. Susie Smith, interview, 6 April 1990.
25. Pat Conroy's 18 students: *Holmes:* Johnnie Mae; *Hudson:* Virginia; *Jenkins:* Ronald, Stanley; *Robinson:* Carvin, David, Isaac, Jackie, Sallie Ann; *Simmons:*

Clarence, Ervin, Henry; *Smith:* Alfred, Joann, Soloman; *Stevens:* Cynthia; *Washington:* Margarite, Sherman.

26. Hallie Patterson, " 'Talking Book" Program is a Hit on Daufuskie," *Island Packet*, 3 June 1971.

27. A personal letter, pictures, and project materials received from Mrs. Julie Zachowski, Director, Beaufort County Library, 27 November 1979. (Julie was a replacement for the library position of Jett Ragsdale, who had left Beaufort and is now associated with the library in Martinsville, Va.).

28. *Beaufort Gazette*, 4 August 1971.

29. *Beaufort Gazette,* 6 September 1974.

30. Carol Owen Alberto's personal letter, 9 January 1984.

31. *Beaufort Gazette*, 4 September 1978.

32. Ibid., 25 August 1983.

33. Ibid., 7 August 1986.

34. *Island Packet*, 4 December 1986.

35. Verification by Francis A. Burn who visited his father at the school site in 1940.

10

FUNERALS AND CEMETERIES

Seeing that the dead have a decent burial is a very important segment of Daufuskie life. Although he was not an undertaker, Hinson A. White was a very useful assistant in shaving and helping dress a white male corpse. Black undertakers were Joseph Haynes, Mose Ficklin, Joseph Grant, and Sarah Grant. Each of them kept a supply of $100.00 caskets on hand at all times. Joe Grant was Sarah's husband and when he passed away in 1962, Sarah took his place and was the last undertaker on the island. She was already the midwife, which caused a person on the island to remark, "Granny bring 'em 'n she take 'em away." When Sarah ceased from her work, an undertaker had to be sent for from the mainland. He would come over and prepare the body right in the home. If a person died off the island, the body was sent to a funeral home then brought over on the *Clivedon* or the *Waving Girl* or whatever boat was available.

Sometimes a family could not afford to buy a casket. In this case a local carpenter was called upon to make a pine-box coffin which cost, if anything, very little.

At a person's death, the one officiating laid the body out in the home on a "cooling board" which was usually an ironing board. The body was bathed (the men shaved) and then dressed in their Sunday best clothes. Coffee grounds and turpentine were placed in the body cavities to prevent seepage and odors. If it was in the summer, the burial was usually the same day. But if the body was held over and the weather warm, the casket was placed on the front porch where there was plenty of air and a person stood guard all night. Of, if the body stayed inside, fans kept the body cool. "Wakes" were held each night prior to the burial. Relatives and friends would be present to mourn

the passing of a loved one. Food and drinks would be available to sustain them.

Persons digging the grave were usually friends of the family or in later years the county road workers among whom were Joseph Bryan, Daniel (Fastman) Mitchell, Clarence and Willis Simmons, Frankie Smith, and Thomas Stafford.

Customarily, the preacher conducted the funeral at the home, but if the body came from Savannah it was sometimes moved from the boat to the church, or in most cases, from the dock to the cemetery with a graveside service.

Following the service, in the early years, the casket was then placed in a wagon pulled by an oxen or horse. A procession of mourners walked behind the wagon and sung all the way to the cemetery. The casket was opened so that everyone could file past and see the loved one for the last time. Black and white people attended all funerals.

According to black tradition, before the body was placed in the ground, if there were a surviving child or grandchild, this child would be lifted over the casket so that the child would not fret for his parent or grandparent, and so that the spirit of the dead person wouldn't take the child to the grave with him or her. Facing the east, the casket was lowered into the ground and the dirt was rounded over the grave. A piece of oak limb was shoved into the ground as a head marker. All of the things that the person used during his/her illness was placed on the grave. Everything the dead needed would be right there, and they would have no reason to return for anything. Contents of the bottles of medicine were spilled and the bottles inverted; cups, saucers, tooth brushes, drinking or reading glasses, spoons, knives, forks, clocks, razors, false teeth, combs—all were sticking out and highly visible in this mound of dirt. Unless the funeral came from Savannah, floral arrangements were few.

Established during plantation days, there were actually eight cemeteries on the island. However, the pyramid-type vault for the (white) Mongin family at Haig's Point, by the eastern gate, was moved circa 1880 to Bonaventure Cemetery in Savannah, Georgia. Now there are seven cemeteries—one for white people known as the Mary Dunn Cemetery and six for the blacks. These six are: Bloody Point, Cooper River, Fripp, Haig's Point, Maryfield, and Webb. The two

largest and the most active have been the Cooper River and Maryfield Cemeteries.

There are two cemeteries on land that belonged to the Martinangele family: Mary Dunn Cemetery for the white people and the Fripp Cemetery for the blacks. The Fripp Cemetery was probably started by Mary Foster Martginangele to bury slaves after she purchased the property in 1762. Mary's daughter, Mary Martinangele Dunn, owned 300 acres of the family land which was known as Mary Dunn Plantation. Mary M. Dunn, in 1874, sold her 300 acre plantation, with the exception of the four acres (more or less) she stated as being a burial ground. She sold this property to her brother-in-law, William Fripp Chaplin, who had it surveyed in lots and sold. Fuller Fripp (a kind man) was in possession of the land that held the cemetery and continued to allow the black people to bury their dead, hence the name Fripp Cemetery. (William F. and Harriet Martinangele Chaplin were the grandparents of Fuller's wife, Margaret Chaplin Fripp.)

One interesting note is that all of the cemeteries border the water or marsh except the ones at Haig's Point and Webb Tract. There were no known cemeteries at Benjie's Point, Melrose, or Oak Ridge plantations. As ownership of the land changed, burial in most cemeteries ceased.

Several of the black people were consulted as to who is buried in which cemetery.[1] It is very difficult to try to remember the names of those who have been dead for so many years, but the following is the result of this inquiry. If anyone is omitted, it is only because that person's name could not be recalled. Some of the cemeteries have very few headstones.

Bloody Point Cemetery

This black cemetery is situated on the west side of Bloody Point by the waters of Mongin Creek. Many of the markers at this cemetery have been vandalized, and only four remain:

James Jones, Jr.
Born April 6 1886
Died October 16 1909
Sweet Be Thy Sleep

William [Dollar Bill] Bryant
Husband of Alice Bryant
Died October 21 1930
Age 52 Years

Grace Ficklin
Was born on Daufuskie
May 15 1874
Died February 5 1939
In Her Own Home
Age 65. At Rest

In Memory of Silas Bryan
Born January 10 1884
Died January 24 1945

Joseph Michael does not have a headstone, but his granddaughter Frances E. Jones states that he was born in 1865 and died 7 November 1933. Mr. Cleveland Bryan has a record of his little brother buried at Bloody Point: Thomas Bryan, Jr., born Friday, 12 May 1916—Died, Thursday, 3 Nov. 1916.

Names of the following black people could only be remembered but not their birth nor death dates:

Best: Florence
Brown: Isaac (Son)
Bryan: Martha; Nathanal; Robert, Jr., Silas, Sylvia, William
Hamilton: Morris, Pender
Heyward: Flora, Leotha
Jackson: George, London, Mary
Lee: Henrietta, Jimmy
Mongin: "Crab," Hezekiah (Kyah), Lemon (Robinson)
Robinson: Charles, Edward, Ollie
Walker: Hester, Simon.

Cooper River Cemetery

This black cemetery is situated on the west side of the plantation and borders the waters of Cooper River.

Following are the headstones that were found:

Janie Givens
B Feb 13 1906
D Nov 30 1943
Age 37

Lizzie McIntyre
B 1865
D Feb 27 1921
Age 56 Yrs

In Memory of N. Simmons
B Jan 31 1933
D Jul 24 1945

Willie Hudson
B Jun 6 1870
D Oct 28 1942

In Memory of
Cato McIntyre [II]
B Apr 20 1908
D May 27 1936
Age 28 Yrs

Lottie Carter
B Sep 6 1906
D Mar 3 1937
Age 31 Yrs

Tina Jenkins
B Jun 2 1883
D Jan 1 1941

Robert Hamilton
Age 66 (B 1851)
D Mar 31 1917

Prophet Jenkins
Georgia
803 Co Trans Corp
D Aug 28 1957

"My Beloved Husband"
Cato McIntyre [I]
B Apr 27 1847
D Oct 27 1919
"Resting with Jesus"

In Memory of Rebecca Chisolm
B Jul 4 1872
D Mar 1 1960
"At Rest"

In Memory of Elizabeth Riley
B Oct 27 1882
D Aug 13 1948

Gabriel Washington
South Carolina
Pvt 1cl
321 Serv. Bn
D Jun 11 1943

In Memory of
Benjiman Riley
B May 26 1916
D Jul 2 1939

There are two headstones with no inscriptions. The following are names remembered of ones with dates but no stone markers:

Brown, Derald, July 24, 1964—July 26, 1964
Hamilton, Jane, died 1962
Michael, Margaret (Peggy), May 30, 1865—April 17, 1963
Stafford, Charlease Marie (stillborn), Dec. 31, 1966
Washington, Agnes, Feb. 28, 1894—Aug. 22, 1971.
Washington, Lillie Mae (9 yrs old), 1954—1963
Wilson, Paul, March 27, 1927—Sept. 6, 1968.

The following have no dates or markers:

Brisbane: Charlotte
Brown: Jackson
Chisolm: Reverend
Grant: Priscilla
Hamilton: Bunkum, Lexi, Robert, Jr.

Houston: Jeremiah
Manuel: Amelia
Mitchell: Victoria
Riley: Joe; Julia

348

Fripp Cemetery

This black cemetery on Mary Dunn Plantation is located by the shore of New River on property that now belongs to a member of the Ward family. It was Mary Martinangele Dunn who had owned the last of her families' slaves. It is unknown whether any tombstones remain, but the following were either some of Mary's slaves or descendants of her former slaves:

Bryan: Abraham, Aleck, Baccus, Sr., Baccus, Jr., Ben, Biggam, Sr., Biggam, Jr., Clara, Cynthia, Ella, Ellen, Ernestine, Essie, Flora, Janie, Molly I, Molly II, Patsy, Paul, Richard

Holmes: Tom (Rose Brisbane's first husband)

Mack: Miriah Bryan (who was the cook for Fuller Fripp)

Haig's Point Cemetery

This black cemetery is just east of the Savannah Walk off Haig's Point Road, and contains these graves with markers:

John Stafford
1888—1944
He Kept the Faith

May Hamilton
Co. B.
21 U.S.C.I.

Kate Holmes
Born Barnwell, S.C.
July 4 1868
Dec 19 1945

In Memory
Elizabeth F. Holmes
Born Aug 3 1903
Died 1959

Doctor Mills
Born April 18 1866
Died Aug 17 1917

Mrs. Adres
Born 1834 (85 years old)
Died June 25 1919

In Memory of
Kattie Byers
1889—1950

In Memory
Samuel Holmes
Died June 8 1969

The following have small foot-markers provided by the funeral home:

Ida Holmes—Infant—Died, 1921
Ida Holmes—Teenager
Nora Lawrence—Died, 1956 (Mother of Johnny Hamilton)

List of names of persons buried with no markers but some dates remembered:

349

Stafford, Herbert, 1918—June 26 1968
Stafford, Lula, 1892—July 27 1964
Young, Tara "Missy," Aug 17 1893—Feb 23 1965

Frazier: Fred
Holmes: Theresa J., Rubin
Lawrence: Frank
Mills: Jim, Susie
Rivers: Dan, Prince
Simmons: Milton, Pink, Rufus
Smalls: Ben, Lucie, Maggie
Wiley: Jane
Williams: Margaret
Young: Leroy.

In the 1880 Haig's Point Census, these were listed according to color, sex, and age; most of them were former slaves and are probably buried in this cemetery:

Bryan: Louisa (BF 50)
Grant: Kilas (Father of Joe and Mose Grant), Mose, William (BM 1)
Gillard: Alick
Hamilton: Brister (BM 66)   *Small:* Samuel (BM 30)
Jenkins: Mary (BF 60)   *Spain:* Moses (BM 60)
Rogers: Lizzie   *Whig:* Tina (BF 40) [Tena Wigg]

Mongin-Stoddard
Pyramid-Type
Crypt Moved from
Haig's Point to
Bonaventure Ceme-
tery circa 1880.
(Photograph courtesy
Robert L. Marchman
III, 1989.)

Maryfield Cemetery

This black cemetery borders the marsh on the west side of Maryfield Plantation and near what is now known as Governor's Point. Being the most popular, it is also probably the largest black cemetery. There are a lot of markers here. Following is a list of those with dates:

BENTLEY:
Charley, Dec 31 1875—Mar 24 1944
Eddie, Feb 28 1909—June 15 1954
Janie, Apr 8 1908—Aug 8 1979
Mingo, May 26 1906—Sept 26 1936
Robert, Apr 10 1902—Feb 5 1953

BRYAN:
Alfred (Plue), Aug 1 1899—Dec 11 1941
Anthony William, Jan 26 1953—Mar 7 1956
Arthur, SC Pvt Vet Hosp Jan 6 1938
Elizabeth, May 4 1876—Apr 29 1963
John, Sr., May 1 1875—Nov 20 1962
John, Jr., Oct 16 1905—Apr 9 1946
Lawrence, Sr., July 28 1912—July 22 1938
Sarah, 1902—Aug 5 1982
Thomas, Nov 3 1888—July 26 1980
Vernetta, Feb 20 1949—Nov 24 1977
William (Hamp), 1901—Apr 22 1984

CROSBY
Annie, Dec 15 1866—Aug 26 1957

DEMERY
Albert, Feb 8 1926

FERGURSON
Chance, Jan 20 1890—Nov 11 1947, Ga Pvt. 548 Engrs WWI
Mrs. Pearl, May 16 1957

FIELDS
Helen C. Wesley, 1913—1951

GORDON
Dennis (NJ) Tec 5—370 Inf. WW II
June 3 1915—Sept 24 1944

GRANT
Cornelia, Mar 15 1895—Mar 10 1981

351

Freddie, Sr., May 6 1902—July 31 1987
Freddie, Jr., Mar 27 1935—Dec 25 1983
Joseph, Aug 2 1882—Feb 20 1962

HAMILTON
Henry, Sr., 1920—Jan 28 1967
Henry, Jr., July 24 1949—May 7 1980
Lizzie Bell, July 19 1919—Jan 12 1982
William, 1891—Jan 3 1974

HAYNES
Joseph, Jan 3 1866—Jan 5 1951

HEYWARD
Florence, Nov 19 1920—Feb 7 1964

HUDSON
Jacob, June 9 1890—Oct 11 1918
Marie, Sept 22 1915—Feb 29 1948

HOLMES
Louise, 1900—Mar 17 1970

JENKINS
Angeline, Mar 20 1875—Dec 10 1964

KELSON
Josephine M., Nov 4 1950

MILLER
Carrie, Apr 25 1900—Mar 19 1968
William, Sept 6 1895—Nov 15 1960

MORAN
Helen, 1911—1951

MYERS
Bell J., Oct 14 1883—Dec 14 1954
Joseph, June 10 1874—Feb 12 1955

ROBINSON
Louvenia (Blossom), June 10 1897—Jan 12 1982

SIMMONS
Jake, May 16 1903—June 26 1977
Sier (Si), Mar 24 1926—Sept 26 1986

STEVENS
Cornelia Sharon, Apr 19 1973—Apr 24 1973

WILEY
Benjamin, Oct 11 1935—Oct 31 1981
Lawrence, June 1 1928—Feb 14 1969
Richmond, July 5 1897—July 13 1972
Ruth Mae, Aug 11 1965—Mar 10 1966

WILLIAMS
George, May 10 1897—Feb 20 1960
Laura, Nov 23 1903—Mar 6 1960
Redix, Aug 3 1913—June 17 1941

A few names were remembered, but no dates:

Bentley: Sally
Demery: Frank
Grant: Hester
Graves: Sylvia
Haynes: Joseph, Maggie (Mongin)
Hudson: Chloe, William
Johnson: July, Lizzie
Jenkins: Abe
Lock: Betsy
Loyd: Sam, Susie
Miller: Aaron, Ben, Jesse, Kit, Liza, Marshall, Mingo, Phoebe
Mongin: Bradley, John, Lillie
Robinson: Sippio, Sr., Sippio, Jr.
Sanders: Chance, Clara

Webb Tract Cemetery

Webb seems to be the smallest of the black cemeteries. It is located just north of the present Hargray Telephone Company microwave on Cooper River Road and east of the gate on Webb Tract that leads down to Rabbit Point.

Two headstones were found but only one was inscribed: Robert Bryan, Born July 18, 1892, Died July 1, 1960.

Following are names of a few of the people who are buried here, with no dates. The source: thanks and appreciation to Mr. and Mrs. Hinson White, 20 March 1982.

Bacon: William
Bentley: Amelia
Bryan: Ben, Katie, Matilda
Jenkins: Virginia

McGraw: Hagar
Mordeci: Robert
White: Andrew, Daffney, Katie

Mary Dunn Cemetery

This is the only white cemetery and borders the marsh of Mongin Creek on the south side of the island. The second cemetery on the Mary Dunn Plantation, it contains 4.6 acres of land given by Mary Dunn to be used as a cemetery for her family.[2] However, in later years Mrs. Elizabeth Medlock Cetchovich, a relative of the Martinangele family, gave permission for other white people (who were not relatives) to be buried here.

The Chaplins cared for the cemetery grounds until they left the island, at which time they hired Mrs. Sarah Grant to care for the graves. When Ashley A. Burn was buried in 1926, his father Arthur A. Burn, his brother Francis A., and his sister Leonella kept the grounds clean.

At Mr. Ward's death in 1947, Mrs. Gillian Ward took over the job of beautifying the cemetery, planting flowers and trees, and keeping it in tip-top shape. Thanks to her, the cemetery did not revert to a jungle of growth.

Since the land of this cemetery completely cuts off the waterfront to the adjacent property on the north, in 1985 the owners took those of us who care for the cemetery to court to take the cemetery land which would give them access to the water and build a dock.

International Paper Realty Corporation of South Carolina needs to be thanked for letting their archaeologists and crew on three separate days lend a helping hand in locating three tabby graves eastward on the outside of the fenced-in area of the cemetery. On September 4-5, 1985, the following persons donated their time and effort in the actual work for which we thank them: Larry Lepionka, Colin Brooker, Mike Taylor, Ramona Grunden, Margaret Mellenger, and Joe Cavanagh. On January 4, 1986, we are indebted to the following who made every effort to locate grave sights on the south and west sides outside the cemetery fence: Lisa Lepionka, Joe Cavanagh, and Rickey Acres.

The land stayed in litigation for over a year and when it went to court on 5 January 1987, the judge ruled in our favor.[3] The cost to have the land surveyed and the lawyer's fee amounted to $11,000. With contributions through heirs, neighbors, and friends, the bill was finally paid.

354

Crypt and Tombstones, Mary Dunn Cemetery, 1962
(Photograph courtesy Bob East, New York City.)

The list of graves with markers:

BRANCH:
Alene, Oct 22 1907—June 19 1959

BURN:
Alfred Lance, Sept 5 1911—Apri 6 1989
Arthur Ashley, Nov 29 1878—Jan 20 1968
Ashley Arthur, Mar 26 1906—Feb 3 1926
Margaret Catherine Keenan, Jan 6 1897—Feb 26 1927

CETCHOVICH:
Katie, Oct 8 1907—Apr 1908

CHAPLIN:
Elizabeth M., Aug 31 1847—Aug 23 1849
Harriet L., Sept 27 1797—Aug 27 1830.

Listed in Harriet's tomb are her six children:

Francis, Died Dec 24 1815, Aged 18 days
Harriet M., Died Sept 30 1823, Aged 8 months
Infant Twins, Died Dec 18 1826, Aged 12 days
Philip, Died Aug 21 1828, Aged 3 years, 11 months
Elizabeth M. A., Died Aug 11 1830, Aged 16 years 4 months & 8 days
James Peto, Dec 18 1818—Aug 22 1865
Mary Caroline, Mar 11 1824—Mar 26 1891

DOWELL:
John J., Dec 14 1913—Jan 19 1914

DUNN:
Francis, 1777—Mar 21 1823 (46 yrs. old)
Mary, Dec 27 1785—Jul 6 1878

FRIPP:
Harriet, 1841—Nov 10 1912 (71 yrs. old)
John Francis, Sept 30 1869—Aug 11 1918
McNair C., 1951—Aug 17 1912 (61 yrs. old)
Mary H., Mar 3 1879—Apr 1 1891
Mary Ida, Jan 30 1869—Dec 5 1936
Margaret E., Nov 17 1843—Jan 15 1905
Milton J., Mar 31 1868—June 20 1911
Richard Fuller, Sr., Oct 1 1841—June 3 1922
Richard Fuller, Jr., May 24 1872—Mar16 1928

GREINER:
Hoke Smith, Sept 13 1909—Mar 29 1947

GRIMBALL:
Mary Ann, Dec 12 1791—Nov 6 1854
Paul, Oct 19 1767—Jun 5 1836
William P., Jan 16 1827—Jun 18 1847

JONES:
Æneas, Died in 1834 (29 years old)
Elizabeth, Died 1831 (51 years old)

MARTINANGELE:
Elizabeth, Jan 22 1765—Jan 1 1847
Isaac, Sr., Feb 10 1752—Apr 15 1796
Mary, Died 1790
Philip, Dec 28 1783—May 14 1852

OHMAN:
Edith L., Sept 29 1869—Jun 20 1937
Gustaf, Oct 28 1872 (Sweden), Oct 23 1950

PALPAL-LATOC:
Arthur Rene, May 17 1958—July 15 1976

PETO:
James, Nov 18 1821 (England), Died 1849

SMITH:
Ben H., Dec 20 1913—Sept 9 1982

WARD:
Edward Gary, Sept 22 1883—Nov 8 1947

WHITE:
Annie E., Feb 26 1870—Oct 17 1948
Hinson A., Dec 16 1899—Feb 3 1985
James W., Nov 5 1863—May 3 1948

The Martinangele Family

The brick crypt holds three members of the Martinangele family, but there is no record as to just who they are. Two metal caskets remain but a small wooden one deteriorated. The earlier tombstones in the cemetery represent a mother, Mary Martinangele, who died in 1790. Her son Isaac (1752-1796) married a widow, Elizabeth Godfrey (1762-1847). Elizabeth had been married to Anthony Godfrey who was killed by a rattlesnake on Daufuskie. Elizabeth and Anthony had one daughter, Elizabeth Ladson (1783-1831), who married William F.

Jones (who is not in this cemetery). Their son Æneas Jones (1805-1834) is listed on the tombstone with his mother.

Isaac and Elizabeth Godfrey Martinangele had six children, but only four are in this cemetery:

(1) Phillip III (1783-1852) who was a bachelor and killed by lightning on Daufuskie.

(2) Mary (1785-1878) who married Francis Dunn (1777-1823). They had no children.

(3) Mary Ann (1791-1878) who married twice. The first time she married James Peto (1793-1824). They had one daughter, Elizabeth Mary Peto who married William F. Chaplin, Jr., the son of Mary Ann's sister Harriet. Elizabeth and William Jr. are not buried here, but they had a little daughter, Elizabeth M. Chaplin (1847-1849), who is in the cemetery. Mary Ann married the second time to Paul Grimball (1767-1836). Mary Ann and Paul had three children: William P. Grimball (1827-1847) and two sons listed on Paul Grimball's tomb stone—B. Jenkins and Paul L. Grimball, 1836.

(4) Harriet (1797-1830) married widower William Fripp Chaplin (who is also not buried here). Harriet and William have seven children in this cemetery, six of whom are listed on her tombstone:

(1) Francis Chaplin, D. 21 Dec 1815, 18 days

(2) Harriet M. Chaplin, D. 30 Sept 1823, 8 mo

(3&4) Infant twins (no names) D. 18 Dec 1826, 12 days

(5) Philip Chaplin, D. 21 Aug 1832, 3 yrs 11 mo

(6) Elizabeth M.A. Chaplin, D. 11 Aug 1830, 16 yrs 4 mo 8 days

(7) James Peto Chaplin (1818-1865) was married to Mary Caroline Rhodes (1824-1891). Their children are Margaret E. Chaplin (1843-1905), who was married to Richard Fuller Fripp, Sr. (1841-1922), and Harriet L. Chaplin, who married Fuller's brother McNair Fripp (1851-1912). Harriet and McNair had no children.

Fuller and Margaret Fripp's three children in the cemetery, viz.:

(1) John Francis Fripp (1869-1918)

(2) Richard Fuller Fripp, Jr. (1872-1928) married his first cousin, Mary Ida Medlock Fripp, who died in 1936.

(3) Mary H. Fripp (1879-1891). Mary was an invalid during the entire twelve years of her life.

The Burn Family

The father is Arthur Ashley Burn (1878-1968). From Arthur's first marriage came these two sons: Ashley Arthur Burn (1906-1926), who, while working with the U. S. Geodetic Survey, drowned off Tampa Bay in Florida; and Alfred Lance Burn (1911-1989) who served in WW II and received the Bronze Star during the "Battle of the Bulge" in Germany.

Arthur A. Burn's second wife was Margaret Catherine Keenan Burn (1897-1927). Arthur and Margaret have a daughter Leonella Burn Padgett who was married to Hoke Smith Greiner (1909-1947).

Alfred L. Burn married Billie Smith from Columbus, Georgia. They have a daughter, June Crumley, whose son Arthur Rene Palpallatoc (1958-1976) died in a car accident in Savannah, Georgia. Billie Smith Burn's brother is Ben H. Smith (1913-1982).

The White Family

The father is James W. White (1863-1948); the mother is Annie E. White (1870-1948). Their children are Hinson Adam White (1899-1985); Clarence White (1905-1907); and Alene White Branch (1907-1959).

The Cetchovich Children

Katie Cetchovich (1907-1908) is the daughter of Mr. and Mrs. Emil Cetchovich, Sr. They also had another daughter Rosa, whose infant son John J. Dowell (1913-1914) is buried by Katie.

Mr. & Mrs. Gustaf Ohman

Gustaf (Gus) Ohman (1872-1950) was born in Sweden, coming to this country in a sailing vessel. When the ship docked in Charleston, Gus went A.W.O.L. and hid until the vessel set sail. He hung around the water, became employed in the lighthouse service, and was keeper at the Bloody Point lighthouse. Gus was married to Edith Loper (1869-1937) who was from Louisiana.

The Ward Grave

Edward Gary Ward (1883-1947) was from Awendaw, South Caro-

lina and worked on the dredge *Gilmer* out of Savannah. He had lived on Daufuskie with his family since 1923.

Graves with No Markers

Buried on the south side of the cemetery but having no markers is Ernest Cannon and his son Furney Cannon; both died in 1918.

Mrs. Hattie Avant Lane, born July 8, 1881, died, January 20, 1919, is buried west of Margaret Catherine Keenan Burn.

A Crosby infant baby (no name) circa 1934 is buried a little east of Hinson A. White.

When the archaeologists helped with the cemetery, three unknown tabby graves were discovered outside the fence on the east side.

Inside the cemetery is also an unknown tabby grave just west of James P. Chaplin and Harriet Chaplin.

Improvements Made to Cemetery

In February, 1990, the old fence wire and posts were removed with new materials taking their place. The posts are treated and guaranteed to last thirty-five years. The cemetery was also enlarged fourteen feet on the west side and five feet on the south side. Rather than the one large gate at the entrance, four gates were installed—one on either side. Robert L. (Bob) Burn was responsible for hauling the materials to the island in his boat, served as engineer in getting the plot squared, measured for the post holes and helped with stretching and tacking the wire. His wife Emily served as Bob's assistant. Others who helped with the project were Billie Burn, Francis Burn, Ruby (Shorty) Smith, Geraldine (Gerry) Wheelihan, and Stewart Wheelihan. Leonella Burn Padgett of Johns Island, South Carolina, contributed financially. Gerry Wheelihan was also responsible for getting five trees removed (two inside and three outside the fence) so there would be less trash and debris to pick up and prevent the dead trees from falling in the cemetery.

Shallow Well Dug for Mary Dunn Cemetery

Thanks and appreciation go to John Horry. On 8 May 1990 Horry Well-Pump Company, Ridgeland, South Carolina, furnished materials and drilled a thirty-five foot well for the convenience of watering

flowers in the cemetery. A hand pump was added. The water is tasty, clear, and so cool and refreshing. Not only for keeping the flowers alive, but the water will also be a blessing to many in times of a hurricane or when electricity fails.

Notes

1. Thanks and appreciation go to Mr. Cleveland Bryan, Mr. William (Hamp) Byrnes, Miss Frances E. Jones, Mrs. Janie Simmons, Mrs. Albertha Stafford, Mrs. Ella Mae Jenkins, Mrs. Geneva Wiley, and Mrs. Louise Wilson for their kindness in helping with the cemetery information.

2. Beaufort County Courthouse, Deed Book 9, p.11.

3. *Island Packet*, 30 August 1985, p. 1 A; *News & Courier,* 13 October 1985, p. 1 E; *Island Packet*, 5 January 1987, p. 1 A; *Island Packet*, 9 January 1987.

11

THE UNITED STATES MAIL

On July 26, 1775, members of the Second Continental Congress meeting at Philadelphia agreed... "that a Postmaster General be appointed for the United States, who shall hold his office at Philadelphia, and shall be allowed a salary of 1,000 dollars per annum. . . ."

That simple undramatic statement signaled the birth of the Post Office department, the predecessor of the U. S. Postal Service and the second oldest department or agency of the present United States of America.

It was more than a hundred years earlier, however, that the first official notice of a postal service had appeared in Colonial America. In 1639, the General Court of Massachusetts had designated Richard Fairbanks' tavern in Boston as the official repository for mail brought from or sent overseas (in line with a practice long used in England and other civilized nations), to use coffee houses and taverns as mail drops. For a full half century after the first regulation was approved in Massachusetts, post routes serving the colonies were operated by local authorities. In 1673 Governor Lovelace of New York established a monthly post between New York and Boston. The service was of short duration, but the postman's trail became the Boston Post Road—today's U.S. Route 1.

Pennsylvania's first post office was set up by William Penn in 1683. In the South, a private messenger service (usually slaves), connected and unified the huge plantations: a hogshead of tobacco was the penalty for failing to deliver mail to the next plantation.[1]

On 26 July 1775, Benjamin Franklin was appointed as the first Postmaster General under the Continental Congress.

Philadelphia was the seat of government and postal headquarters

until 1800, when the Post Office Department was moved to Washington, D.C. At that time all postal supplies, records, and equipment were carried in two wagons.[2]

Postmaster vs. Postmistress

The word Postmistress has been popping up in the news frequently, and it is wrong. Be it male or female, the word is Postmaster.

The origin is from a time when mail was attached to a post along a road for pickup, and from this, the establishment of the Post Roads. . . . Master was denoted as a skill, therefore, those who could master the Post Skills were called Postmasters. The word denotes skill, not gender as some suppose.[3]

(The same term applies to a woman at the helm of a ship—she is its Master.)

Ours Is the Best Postal System on Earth

Editor's Note: The following article is reproduced from the May 1973 issue of Arizona Highways Magazine:

EDITORIAL NOTE:

Don't knock it—ours is the best postal system on earth.

Did you know that in 1837 in America, pre-paid postage was not yet born? Letters were sent on "pay when delivered" basis at such exorbitant rates that people had to sell treasured possessions or borrow money to pay the postage for letters from their loved ones.

Cheap and uniform pre-paid postage rates were not a public reality until 1883.

Before, the postal system had all but died through private postal enterprise.

In 1792 local mail cost six cents per letter (C.O.D., of course). Letters going more than 450 miles were one dollar and more. By 1845 one needed a degree in math to compute postal rates.

For every letter composed of a single sheet of paper and conveyed not exceeding 30 miles, 6 cents; over 30 miles, but not exceeding 80 miles, 10 cents up to 25 cents for single sheet letters going over 400 miles. Then, when you mailed a letter of more than one sheet, you doubled, tripled, or quadrupled the rates according to the number of pages you enclosed! Since the letter was paid for upon arrival, recipients were often hesitant about doling out hard-to-come-by cash for their mail.

Imagine what a catastrophic situation would have evolved with all

our "sick humor cards" and so-called "junk" mail. It's no wonder that Black Market letter smuggling was a profitable business in the mid 1800s.

Today's postal rates are bargains when evaluated in realistic perspective. In 1918 when a dollar bought two days' groceries, air stamps were 24 cents. Today [May, 1973], with inflation and the devaluation of the dollar, air letters can be sent for 11 cents.

Stamps have made millionaires. When the first U.S. air mail stamp (24 cents) was issued [1918], a philatelist, W. T. Roby, bought a first-day issue full sheet of 100 stamps. He later discovered that the airplane on the stamp was pictured flying upside down. It proved to be the only sheet inserted the wrong way into the press. Roby's 24 cent investments are now worth more than $30,000 per stamp!

So, the next time you lick a stamp, think upon the romance, the wonder, and the reality of one of the greatest assets—the Postal Systems of the world. —J.S.[4]

The postage stamp was invented by Sir Rowland Hill, the Postmaster General of England, in 1840. However, the United States government did not adopt the stamp until 1847. Mailers had the option of sending their letters C.O.D. until 1855 when prepayment became compulsory.[5]

One-Ounce Postal Letter Increases

July 1, 1885—2 cents
Nov. 3, 1917—3 cents
July 1, 1919—2 cents
July 6, 1932—3 cents
Aug. 1, 1958—4 cents
Jan. 7, 1963—5 cents
Jan. 7, 1968—6 cents
May 16, 1971—8 cents
March 2, 1974—10 cents

Dec. 31, 1975—13 cents
May 29, 1978—15 cents
March 22, 1981—18 cents
Nov. 1, 1981—20 cents
Feb. 17, 1985—22 cents
April 3, 1988—25 cents
Feb. 3, 1991—29 cents

Improvements and Reforms in the Postal System

• Parcel Post began 1 January 1912
• Air Mail, 15 May 1918—abolished in 1977 as a separate rate category.
• Zip Code became a reality, 1 July 1963.

- U.S. Postal Service: On 12 August 1970, President Richard M. Nixon signed into law the Postal Reorganization Act, converting the U.S. Post Office Department into an independent establishment, the United States Postal Service.
- Postal Seal: Abandoning the old seal of a "post horse in speed, with mail bags and rider," when the U.S. Postal Service was established, a new seal was adopted featuring a bald eagle poised in flight that identifies today with anything connected with the Postal Service.[6]

Daufuskie Island Mail

The first mail to Daufuskie, no doubt came by sailing schooners and was delivered by hand through sea captains, relatives, or friends of the family.

Savannah was founded in 1733, therefore it can be assumed that a Post Office was one of its first establishments as mail was so vital personally and essential for business.

There were advertisements placed in newspapers, notifying the family there was mail for them at the Post Office.

In 1867 Miss Esther W. Douglass (one of the American Missionary Association teachers at Melrose) gave as her address: P.O. Box 483, Savannah, Georgia.[7]

Planters on the island had their own vessels, transporting cotton and produce to the wharfs in Savannah, making it convenient simultaneously to pick up their mail at the Post Office.

There was a black family of Jeffersons who lived at Melrose. The men helped with the farming and the women cooked, washed, and cleaned. James and Abraham Jefferson would take turns riding a horse to Benjie's Point in the 1890s and pick up the Stoddard mail from sacks that were left on the dock by the steamers, and take it back to Melrose.

Circa 1898-1909 mail was brought to the island Monday, Friday, and Sunday via the Beaufort-Savannah Line by boats like the *Pilot Boy, Louise, Attaquin, Merchant,* and *Clivedon.*

Mail sacks would be left on the dock for people to rummage through and find their mail. Because of its importance, to see the mail so carelessly handled disturbed Mrs. Evelyn Byrd Stoddard. Her son Albert H. Stoddard III graciously shared the following information

that his mother had told him over the years concerning the Daufuskie Post Office:

> She was married to Albert H. Stoddard, Jr., in October, 1909, and came to Daufuskie shortly thereafter to live at Melrose. She told me that when she arrived there was no post office on the island. The mail came from Savannah on the Savannah-Beaufort Line river board which had a regular scheduled run. In my recollections this boat ran three times a week in the summer making the round trip in one day, and twice a week in the winter, staying over night in Beaufort and returning to Savannah the next day. Anyhow, the mail was left on the dock in mail sacks and the island residents came to the landing to pick up their mail directly from the sacks. On the next trip around, the boat would pick up the sacks from the time before in which had been deposited any letters the islanders wanted posted. Needless to say, the arrival of the steamer was an important event to the island residents, and most of them met the boat in order to get mail, post letters, and just have a little outside diversion. If you were not there, your mail was left in the sack until you got there to pick it up unless you asked a friend or neighbor to pick yours up for you. There were considerably more white families on the island in those days than there are now, most of them living in the vicinity of the public landing. I don't know how long it was after she came to the island that the post office was established, but it was probably not too long after she arrived there in the fall of 1909. She has told me that she felt there should be a post office and she talked to several of the families that lived near the landing, trying to get one of them interested in taking it on. According to her, there were some feuds between some of the families and they didn't want to go to some of these places to get their mail or have the people they didn't like coming to their house to pick up mail. That is why she finally decided to take on the job herself and have the post office at Melrose, though this was certainly inconvenient for everyone on the island.[8]

First Post Office and Postmaster on Daufuskie

Mrs. Evelyn Byrd Stoddard was made the first Daufuskie Postmaster, 4 March 1911. The Post Office was in the tack room of the Melrose barn. The Postal Department furnished the few little supplies that were needed—such as cancelling stamp and stamp pad, but furnished no furniture or fixtures. There was no salary, only a commission on the sale of stamps that didn't bring in much revenue. This was probably

Right: Mrs. Evelyn Byrd Stoddard— First Postmaster, 1911-1915. (Photograph courtesy Albert H. Stoddard III, 1982.)

Below: First Post Office in Melrose Barn Tack Room. (Photograph courtesy Leon Bond, 1943.)

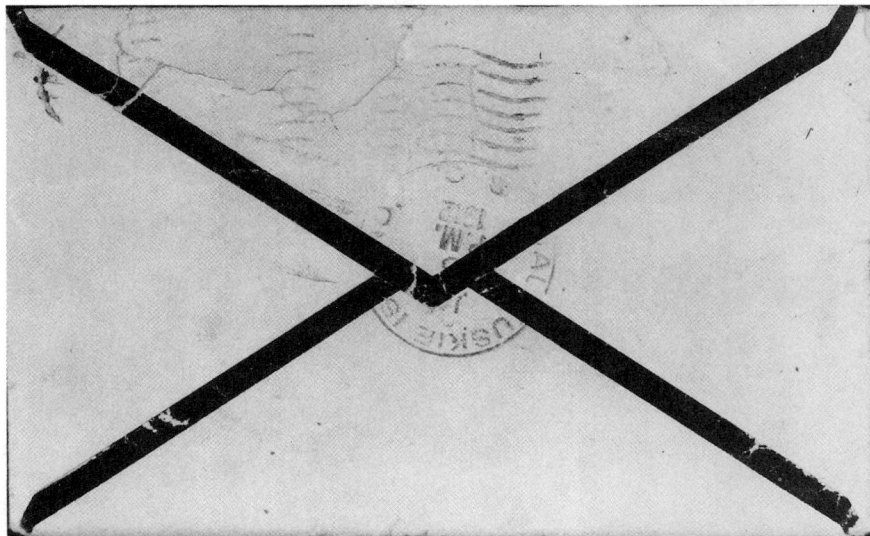

A Letter Dated January 3, 1912, Received at the Melrose Post Office

(Letter courtesy Albert H. Stoddard III, 1982.)

Please note the letter outlined in black. It was customary during that era that when a person died a letter was sent to loved ones and friends with a black edging. In fact, there was a song—"A Letter Edged in Black." Large black bows of wide ribbon (called drapes) were also tacked on the front door of the home. And black was the general color worn when attending a funeral.

the reason that no one was too interested in taking on the job.[9]

During the next four years the following men were involved with the mail:

Circa 1911-1916: Morris Hamilton, who ferried pears from June through August to Savannah for the Stoddards, would sometimes pick up the mail and bring it back to the Melrose Post Office for them.

During 1912-1913: The mail would come in on the steamers *Louise* or *Attaquin* three times a week. Riding horseback, Hinson White carried the mail from the Benjie's Point wharf to the Post Office at Melrose, then bringing the outgoing mail back, he would put it aboard the boat for the return trip to Savannah. For his services, Hinson was paid $3.00 per month.[10]

Mrs. Edith C. Ohman, Second Postmaster, 1915-1937. Gustaf (Gus) Ohman, Third Postmaster, 1937-1938. (1900 photograph courtesy Samuel Henry Rodgers, 1985.)

369

Bob Butler, who lived near Gus Ohman's store at Benjie's Point (and where Joe Loper later lived), had a son, Robbie, who would mostly walk (but sometimes ride a mule) the seven miles to Melrose and bring back mail for the colored people. For this, Robbie would charge 25 cents per family.[11]

Mrs. Evelyn B. Stoddard apparently gave up the Post Office in the spring of 1915, for it was at that time that William Robertson (who boarded with the Chaplin family) would go to Savannah in his launch, pick up the mail, and bring it back to Chaplin's Landing where the letters and packages would be distributed by James P. Chaplin, Jr., from his little store.[12]

Edith C. Ohman Postmaster

Gustaf (Gus) Ohman came to the island as the Bloody Point lighthouse keeper. He later had purchased some Benjie's Point land, built a store (1912), and had the first gasoline pump and the only light plant on Daufuskie. His wife, Edith C. (Loper) Ohman, was made Postmaster 26 August 1915. Gus built an additional section to the store just for the Post Office. Mail continued to come to the island three times weekly on the large steamers. But by the 1930s only the boat *Clivedon* was on the Savannah-Beaufort Line.

Edith with her postal duties and her brother Joe Loper managing the store, Gus was free to do what he liked best—to gamble and go fishing. He had a real nice boat, a car, and plenty of money. He was also known as the "king" of Daufuskie. He had gone fishing with two United States Presidents—Grover Cleveland when he fished at South Island, near Georgetown, South Carolina (circa 1895), and Herbert Clark Hoover off Hilton Head and Daufuskie (circa 1930).[13]

Gus Ohman Postmaster

Edith C. Ohman was the only Postmaster to die in office. On 20 June 1937 she had stepped out of the Post Office intending to go to their home, thirty feet away, when she fell to the ground with a cerebral hemorrhage, dying instantly.[14] Leonella L. Burn served as acting Postmaster from 15 July 1937 until Gus Ohman was confirmed as Postmaster 2 September 1937. Gus ran for the House of Representatives that year but lost. Without Edith the island was not the same, so Gus decided to leave.

Josephine Johnson Postmaster

Gus leased his store to Malcolm and Josephine Johnson who came from Prichardville (near Bluffton), South Carolina. Josephine became acting postmaster on 14 October 1938, confirmed on 26 October 1838. The *Clivedon* continued to bring the mail until its top decks burned in the early 1940s. (The hull was used as a barge to transport oil along the Savannah River during WW II.) A black man from the island became the mail carrier. Using his boat he brought the mail to and from Savannah three days a week, but now it came on Mondays, Wednesdays, and Fridays—no more Sunday mail delivery. Josephine served as Postmaster for almost seven years when she and Malcolm decided to leave and move to Bluffton, South Carolina.[15]

Left: Gustaf Ohman circa 1937, when he ran for the House of Representatives and lost. (Photograph courtesy Samuel Henry Rodgers, Sr.) Right: Leonella L. Burn, acting Postmaster following Mrs. Ohman's death, 15 July to 2 September, 1937. (Photograph [1937] courtesy Mrs. Leonella Burn Padgett.)

Above left: Gus Ohman and Mrs. Josephine Johnson, Fourth Postmaster, 1938-1945. Right: Ohman's Store and Post Office. Note gas pump on left (photograph [1938] courtesy Mrs. Josephine Johnson.)

Gus Ohman's Store and Post Office circa 1938

Left to right: Mr. Davis (worked for pulpwood company), Daisy Miller, Ida White, Mrs. Josephine Johnson (Postmaster), Annie White, Fred Frazier, Mrs. Annie (Nanna) Crosby, Geechee Brown (seated). On porch left: Mrs. Marie Perry (the white school teacher). Right: Mrs. Lou Godwin, school trustee. Photograph courtesy Mrs. Ida White Tatum.)

Left: William (Geechee) Brown with Georgia Johnson sitting by Gus Ohman's first gas pump. Right: Geechee Brown with his dancing, wooden doll sitting on the Post Office/store porch 1938 (Photographs courtesy Mrs. Josephine Johnson.)

Mrs. Mary Meyer Dierks Postmaster

A native of Hanover Germany, Fred Henry Dierks had entered this country via Ellis Island in 1914. He married a German girl, Mary

Mrs. Mary M. Dierks, Fifth Postmaster, 1945-1947, 1956-1963. Fred Dierks, Sixth Postmaster, 1947-1956. (Photograph [1945] courtesy Mrs. Ida White Tatum.)

(May) Catherine Meyer. The couple, making their home in Savannah, operated a successful restaurant on the corner of East Board and Bay Streets. With friends they had visited Daufuskie Island, had taken a liking to it, and bought some property, circa 1942, from the Cetchovich family at Benjie's Point on New River. Their land surrounded the county property that had a dock and pavilion. In previous years the *Clivedon* would come from Savannah with passengers and a live band. The boat would tie to the public wharf and everyone would have a fine time dancing, eating deviled crabs and other good foods. The Dierks exchanged an equal portion of their northern property with the county so that the Dierks' property would be all in one piece. The county did not replace a pavilion on the new property, but did build a dock.

Mrs. Mary M. Dierks assumed charge as Postmaster on 9 May 1945, confirmed on 24 September 1945. Until the Dierks built on their property, Gus Ohman let them rent his store and Post Office space.

Mr. Dierks had his own boat and since he had to pick up store supplies anyway, it was easier to have the mail switched from Savannah to the Bluffton Post Office.

Fred Henry Dierks Postmaster

Because of personal reasons, Mr. Dierks became Postmaster, assuming charge 7 October 1947.[16] With the exception of Joe Joyce

Dierks' Post Office and General Store 1945-1963. Mrs. Mary M. Dierks, Mr. Fred M. Dierks. (Photograph courtesy Mrs. Joann Dierks Yarbrough. This picture appeared in an article about Daufuskie, *News and Courier*, Charleston, S.C., 30 November 1958.)

carrying the mail for Mr. Dierks during 1953-1954, Mr. Dierks was responsible for mail the other years.[17] Mail days continued to be Mondays, Wednesdays, and Fridays.

Mary M. Dierks Postmaster Second Time

Due to Mr. Dierks' health, again Mrs. Dierks was acting Postmaster 27 January 1956, confirmed on 11 March 1956. Jake Washington was now helping Mr. Dierks haul freight and the mail. Mrs. Dierks remained the postmaster until 15 March 1963, when they decided to retire and move back to Savannah. While living on the island, the Dierks provided many services. He was magistrate, road crew supervisor, operator of the sheriff's ship-to-shore battery radio, and he held the voting precinct at their store. They provided a vehicle that Mrs. Dierks used as a school bus. In order to catch the river traffic, they also operated "Twin Oaks," a small snack and drink bar that Mr. Dierks

and his son-in-law, R. Gene Yarbrough, had built near their dock.

In August of 1959 the Dierks permitted the Savannah Beach Marine Reserve Squadron to sponsor a Father-Son outing on their New River property. The camping of sixty-five boys lasted six days with swimming, nature walks to the beach, and classes in first aid, woods safety, island history, and water safety.

Some of the leaders for this outing were Perry Soloman, Jimmie Hernandez, Jim McHugh, and chaplain, the Reverend Charles Webster. A few of the boys were Jim Hernandez, Johnnie Hosti, Kenneth King, George Rentigers, Berty Ussery, Randy Ussery, and Wayne Yeo.[18]

Mrs. Billie K. (Smith) Burn Postmaster

After living five years in Ft. Lauderdale, Florida, Lance and Billie Burn had returned to live permanently on the island 1 April 1959. In August of that year they began operating their own business called

U.S. Post Office, Daufuskie Island, S.C.—January 1968. Postmaster Billie Burn, Assistant Postmaster Lance Burn. (Photograph may be seen in *The Baptist Courier*, Greenville, S.C., 14 March 1968.)

Above: Lance Burn and Senator Strom Thurmond silhouetted against the Daufuskie Post Office, 28 August 1973. Below: Postmaster Billie Burn and Senator Strom Thurmond, U.S. Post Office, Daufuskie Island, S.C., 28 August 1973.

Mrs. Billie K. Burn,
Seventh Postmaster,
1963-1984.

"Jolly Shores," serving oysters, shrimp, deviled crabs, hamburgers, and drinks to boaters who frequented Daufuskie during weekends.

Billie assumed charge as Postmaster 15 March 1963, using one of the rooms in their business as the Post Office. When Postal Inspector J. W. Gabbert closed out Mrs. Dierks and helped move the Post Office equipment and supplies to the Burn's place, he learned that we only received mail three days a week. He remarked that we should not be punished just because we were isolated, so he went about getting us mail five days a week—Monday through Friday.

Lance Burn was assistant Postmaster. Hours of the Post Office depended upon its revenue, which allowed the Daufuskie Post Office to be opened three hours daily. Salary was based on receipts generated by stamp sales and money order fees.

Billie provided a vehicle and drove the black children to Mary Fields Elementary. She also carried the mail daily on her school bus which provided the island with free mail delivery service nine months out of each of the eighteen years that she drove the children.

With the Dierks leaving the island and closing the store, Jake Washington was awarded the mail messenger contract and every day that he went to Bluffton for the mail, he was loaded down with little grocery orders for the people of Daufuskie.

Lance Burn was substitute mail messenger when Jake's boat would break down. But when Jake became ill, circa 1972, and had to leave the island for a year, Lance was awarded the mail contract and carried the mail from Bluffton and then from Savannah until he retired in 30 June 1984.

In 1970, when Pat Conroy was relieved of his job as teacher at Mary Fields Elementary, in order to help Mrs. Julia Johnson keep the school open the two months it took to settle the case, Billie Burn volunteered her services to substitute for Pat's class—with permission from the Post Office and Beaufort County Educational Departments.

Because of her husband's illness, Billie Burn retired 30 March 1984 with 21 years of service. After 73 years, she was the last of the Postmasters. All small Post Offices were being discontinued and at her retirement the future Daufuskie Post Office would be let out under three-year contract bids.

Summary of Daufuskie Postmasters

Mrs. Evelyn B. Stoddard	March 4, 1911
Mrs. Edith C. Ohman	August 26, 1915
Miss Leonella L. Burn	July 25, 1937 (Acting)
Gustaf (Gus) Ohman	September 2, 1937 (Confirmed)
Mrs. Josephine Johnson	October 14, 1938 (Acting)
	October 26, 1938 (Confirmed)
Mrs. Mary M. Dierks	May 9, 1945 (Assumed Charge)
	September 24, 1945 (Confirmed)
Fred Henry Dierks	October 7, 1947 (Assumed Charge)
Mrs. Mary M. Dierks	January 27, 1956 (Acting)
	March 11, 1956 (Confirmed)
Mrs. Billie Kay Burn	March 15, 1963 (Assumed Charge)
	March 30, 1984 (Retired)[19]

Contract Post Office Persons

Mrs. Christina Bates	March 31, 1984
Miss Kerry Gedge	December 3, 1984

Mrs. Nancy Levis   January 11, 1986
Mrs. Lory Anderson-Kowalski   August 11, 1987
Mrs. Henrietta Canty   October 10, 1987

What is the difference between a Postmaster and a contract postal person? The Postmaster was responsible for all the daily bookkeeping and records pertaining to Postal operations, while a contract postal person is only accountable for the daily sale of stamps, money orders, and fees—with an accountant at a larger office doing all of the bookkeeping. The one thing in common is that both had to provide a building for postal equipment and activities.

When Lance Burn retired in 1984, Francis P. (Bud) Bates was awarded the mail messenger contract and has been carrying the mail since then to Hilton Head, South Carolina.

Notes

1. United States Postal Service, History of the U. S. Postal Service 1775-1982 (Washington: Government Printing Office, Publication 100, April, 1983), p. 1.
2. Ibid., p. 2.
3. Mary Carter, Iowa ed., "Know Your Terms," Postmaster Advocate, September, 1983.
4. U. S. Postal Service, Regional Bulletin, Vol. 3, No. 23, 7 June 1973, p. 3.
5. The American Educator Encyclopedia, 1948 ed., s.v. "Postage Stamps."
6. History of the U. S. Postal Service 1772-1982, pp. 6, 8 9, 11, 12.
7. See Appendix XVII.
8. Personal letter, Albert H. Stoddard III, 3 April 1972.
9. Ibid.
10. George White, personal file.
11. Mrs. Sarah Grant interview, 9 June 1975.
12. George White
13. Chlotilde R. Martin, "Mail Boat Comes 3 Times Weekly," News and Courier (Charleston), 28 May 1933, pp. 3, 9-B.
14. Francis A. Burn was present when Mrs. Ohman fell.
15. Mrs. Josephine Johnson interview 3 July 1990.
16. Mrs. Johannah (Joann) Dierks Yarbrough interview, 6 July 1990. (Joann is the only child of Mr. and Mrs. Fred H. Dierks. Living with an aunt, Joann attended Savannah schools, visiting the island on weekends and holidays.)
17. Joe Joyce interview, 6 July 1990.
18. John V. Burke, "Roughing It on Daufuskie, Lads Have More Fun than Dads on All-Week Camp," *Savannah Morning News*, 9 August 1959, p. 6D. (Material compliments: Mrs. Joann Dierks Yarbrough, 17 July 1990.)
19. United States of America, General Services Administration, National Archives and Records Service, Washington, DC 20408.

12

TRANSPORTATION

From Indian dugout canoes to sailing schooners, to sail boats, bateaus, launches, yachts and steamers, Daufuskie people have always had to rely on some sort of water transportation.

The *Savannah Morning News* brings these reports concerning boat transportation to the island:

6-29-1874

Members of the Second African Baptist Church proceeded to Daufuskie on steamer *Carrie* for the purpose of witnessing the baptism of several members.

6-30-1874

The fine steamship *Carrie*, under command of the efficient and popular Captain Joe Smith, will leave for Daufuskie this morning with an excursion party, under charge of the Rev. Father Patrick Knaresboro, and including the Sisters of Mercy.

10-6-1875

The steamship *Cleopatra* bought out for Henry Mongin Stoddard, Esq. a steam yacht called the *Spitfire* of Bloody Point built by Herreshoff Mfg. Company of Bristol to N.Y. The *Spitfire* is intended for the owner's private use between Savannah and his place on Daufuskie Island.

2-10-1878

The *City of Bridgeton* was making a round trip to Daufuskie Island around Tybee with no stop there—50 cents per person.

Freight and Passenger Boats to Daufuskie

In the later part of the 1800s and the early 1900s the whole island was farmed. Pears, pecans, produce, and freight had to be shipped to

381

the mainland—either to Savannah, Bluffton, or Beaufort—and as far away as Charleston. Sometimes there were as many as five steamships a day either docking at "Palmetto Park" (the pavilion of Richard Fuller Fripp, Sr.) or the public landing, or anchoring off shore. Passengers could ride any boat, in any direction, and as often during the day as they chose, for passage of 25 cents per trip. Daufuskie was a beehive of activity.

Following are names of some of those early boats and please bear in mind that the same captain would change to another vessel when the one he was working on burned, sank, or was sold:

The *Planter* tied up to Fuller Fripp's dock and would stay until the next day in order for the boat to be loaded with pears and produce. The captain would rent the cottage of John F. Fripp for the overnight stay while the crew could rent rooms over Fuller Fripp's liquor store where brawls were sometimes frequent.

The *Clifton* (Captain Johnny Jessley) was a side-wheeler with two decks and a pilot house on top. This boat went aground in front of Roger Pinckney's house on Beaufort River. Today, at low tide, the remains of the boiler are still visible.

The *Seagate* (Captain Rossignol), a single-screw boat.

The *Bertha* and *Doretta*. (Only the names are remembered.)

The *Attaquin* (Captain Ratcliff; Captain Conner), a steamer, 80' long, two decks, was sold and replaced with the *Isabella*.

The *Isabella* (Captain Conner) was a diesel boat.

The *Hilderguard* (Captain Henderson), 80 feet long, two decks.

The *St. John* (Captain Haddin), a steamer 120 feet long, four decks, 1400 passengers, with meals served on board. The largest boat that ever came to Daufuskie. Lance Burn was in Savannah's Bethesda Orphanage from 1915-1923 and on special occasions he would catch this boat to visit his folks on Daufuskie.

The *Idabelle* (Captain Gibb Conner) two decks. It was running in a fog when it hit a light, knocking it down near the dock.

The *Louise* (Captain Sinclair; Captain Peck), 80 feet long, two decks, side-wheeler.

The *St. Clair* (Captain Peck), 80 feet long with paddle wheel in stern.

The *Pilot Boy* (Captain Crawford; Captain Tom Martin) 100 feet

long, two decks, a side-wheeler with a "walking beam." There was a huge beam over the top of the boat with big chains that went through the deck that turned the paddles. The "walking beam" worked somewhat on the order of the wheels on a train. The beam would go down on one side, then up on the other side, while turning the paddle wheels, thus getting its name "walking beam." This boat would bring as many as 500 people to church conventions or revivals on Daufuskie. It would come once—or sometimes twice—a week. Roger Pinckney thinks the *Pilot Boy* was damaged during the 1893 hurricane, repaired, and put back on the line. We do know that it was making runs to Daufuskie in 1914 when it carried Bill Scouten to Savannah after he got his leg caught in the wagon wheel. George White had heard that the boat was supposed to have sunk off the Florida coast and was replaced with the *Merchant*.

The *Merchant* (Captain Tom Martin), 100 feet long, steamer, three decks. It was a fast boat and ran consistently, making trips to Beaufort every two weeks. When a lad, according to Niels Christensen, he would ride this boat from Beaufort to Savannah during 1921-1922. At that time the crew on the boat was Captain Croufut, Captain Butler, chief engineer Harry Burr, and mate John Polite.

The *Isabelle* (George Conner was the captain and his brother was the engineer), 65 feet long, two decks, a small gasoline work boat. The *Isabelle* burned between Daufuskie and Bluffton circa 1929.

The *Imogene* (Captain McDonald), owned by the Wilkins Company, had one deck and a cabin—from Savannah to Daufuskie on Monday, loaded up with pears and produce, and back to Savannah on Tuesday. This boat also went as far as St. Helena.

The *Islander*, 2 decks plus a pilot house on top.

The *Clivedon*, 100 feet or more long with three decks. Built in 1890 at Matthews Bluff in Hampton County, she was a broad-beamed side-wheeler with a hull of charcoal iron. In 1908 her owner, George Beach, converted her into a steamer, single-screw. She would bring as many as 500 people to attend the Daufuskie First Union African Baptist Church. She traveled from Savannah to Beaufort three times a week—Tuesday, Friday, and Sunday—dropping off and picking up the mail as she passed Daufuskie. Her owners in the late 1920s and early 1930s were Butler and Ball. A round-trip ticket from Daufuskie to Beaufort, with stops at Hilton Head and Parris Island, cost $1.00. According to George White (1985), the *Clivedon* had many captains. There were more, but the ones he could remember were Rossignol, Hensworth, Crawford, Charles

Butler, and John Polite. From the files of Roger Pinckney, Beaufort (6 August 1990), her last owner was S. Tarver and her last captain was D. D. Hallman. The *Clivedon* burned to the hull and her documents surrendered in 1944. The *Clivedon* had been on the Savannah-Beaufort line for 36 years, thus closing the era of the big steamers. However, that was not the end of her. Shortly after she burned she was outfitted as an oil and freight barge, operating up and down the Savannah River.[1]

Cetchovich Boat Service

Emil Cetchovich, Sr., operated an oyster shucking factory at Benjie's Point. For transportation in getting his oysters to L. P. Maggioni Company in Savannah during the 1930s, his boat, the *Zessene*, was operated by his son Emil Cetchovich, Jr., who would make several trips a week. Passengers were allowed to ride the boat for 50 cents each way, paying 10 cents per bag or box of groceries.

Sugar Boats

Also in the 1930s there were two boats, the *Tomoca* and the *Russell*, that carried sugar from Savannah to Charleston and possibly to parts beyond. These boats did not carry passengers, but if they passed you rowing or broken down they would take you aboard to sit in their cabin while they towed your boat to wherever you needed to go. They were a blessing to many people traveling the waterways.

Charlie Simmons' Boats from Hilton Head

In 1927 Charlie Simmons, Sr., bought *Lola*, his first boat—30 feet long and powered by a 15 HP gasoline engine. Three times a week he would make trips to Savannah, picking up freight and passengers (going and coming) from Daufuskie. He would have produce, oysters, clams, turkeys, pecans, chicken coops filled with chickens poking their heads out between the slats—anything that had to be sold in the Savannah market, he carried it on his boat.

The *Lola* proved to be too small. Charlie purchased the *Edgar Hearst*, making the same trips to Savannah with freight and passengers, never forgetting the residents of Daufuskie. He also made a Saturday run which the island people enjoyed as they could go to Savannah and be back home all in the same day without taking time off from their regular work.

Charlie's last boat was the *Alligator*, which stayed on the Hilton Head-Savannah run during the late 1940s and early 1950s. Building of the Hilton Head bridges in 1956 put a halt to Charlie's freight-boat days.[2] However, for many years he continued to bring a barge to Daufuskie to transport cattle from the island to the market via Hilton Head. The last time he removed cows from Daufuskie was circa 1986, when the golf course at Haig's Point was completed. What happened was that there had been an agreement among the island people: Cows would be let out November 1 and taken up April 1. Hardly anyone had fences for their gardens, so, after the sweet potatoes were dug, on November 1 the cows were let out on the island to run free. Then, on April 1, when it was time to plant gardens, the cows were all herded up and each one staked out on a rope or kept in contained areas on the owner's property.

When the cows were let out after the golf course was built, they headed straight to Haig's Point to eat the green succulent grass. Unable to pay fines or to meet the cost of supporting the cows during the winter, the owners were forced to sell their cows. This was the first negative result of development.

Boats Following the War

When the *Clivedon* burned it threw the burden of transportation on each individual. During World War II a few men joined the service while several residents left Daufuskie, moved to Savannah, and worked in the shipyard until the war was over.

The first boat coming from Savannah after the war was the *Bessie M. Lewis*—a two-decker, between 50-60 feet long. This boat (rebuilt by Robbie Chaplin) was operated by its owners, a Captain Brown with William T. Perry as the engineer. John Polite was the mate.

This was the last boat that made regular scheduled trips to Daufuskie, but this did not last long for by this time there was little farming done and just about everyone on Daufuskie had boats that ran by gasoline powered outboard motors, although some did have small launches with inboards.

Cap'n Sam's River Street Fleet

The first boat that Sam Stevens put on the Savannah line in the early 1950s was the *Visitor*, a boat that carried approximately 75 passengers,

making excursion trips to Daufuskie and Hilton Head. His next boat was the *Waving Girl*, a rather fast two-decker, 317 passengers, which ran to Daufuskie without a schedule, but which made excursion cruises, usually arriving at Daufuskie around 10:30 P.M. It also came on Saturday and Sunday afternoons between 2 and 3 P.M. This boat was the most popular and was chartered when there was a Daufuskie funeral.

As his business grew, Sam Stevens added another boat to his fleet: the *Cap'n Sam*, a 110-foot, four-decker, stern-paddle-wheeler that traveled rather slow but carried from 350 to 375 passengers.

For smaller jobs Sam also had the *Miss Savannah*, approximately 48 feet long and carrying 49 passengers. He also had the *River Queen*, an open, two-decker with an esthetic paddle wheel on the stern. It carried 150 passengers.

With space available Daufuskie people could pay the going fare of $7.00 to $10.00 and ride any of Sam's boats, coming from or going to Savannah. Too sad, because of debts and IRS problems, in 1990 all of Sam's boats were confiscated and sold.

The Fripp Bateau

All during the large steamer and boat era, in order to work or take produce, oysters, fish or crabs to Tybee or Savannah, men of Daufuskie relied on their own little sail boats and rowed their bateaus. One of the best known was the "Fripp Bateau." You were just nobody unless you owned one of these boats.

James P. Chaplin, Sr., son of Harriet Martinangele Chaplin, owned Piney Islands Plantation. He had a daughter, Margaret, and a son, James P., Jr. Richard Fuller Fripp, Sr., from Morgan Island near Beaufort, had served in the Civil War and met James, Jr., who was in the same regiment. They became good friends and when Fuller Fripp was invited to visit the Chaplins, he met Margaret, fell in love, married, and lived on the Chaplin plantation for a spell.

In 1874 James P. Chaplin, Sr.'s, father, William Fripp Chaplin, had purchased the plantation of his sister-in-law, Mary Martinangele Dunn, and had the land cut up into lots. Through Margaret, Fuller purchased 80 acres of this land which bordered New River and Mongin Creek. It was on New River where Fuller built a house and

began his boat building business. His boats varied in size up to 22 feet in length and all of them had a skeg.

After talking to William (Hamp) Bryan, who was familiar with this boat, it was learned that the characteristic that made the Fripp bateau so special was that it cleared the water on the bow and stern; the run of the bottom of the boat was brought clear of the surface when loaded, so that no part of the transom was immersed, thereby eliminating the drag which would have been created by a partially immersed transom.

When Fuller's sons, Dick Fripp, Jr., and John F., became of age, they helped their father build these boats. The Fripps remained in the boat business until John's death in 1918, Fuller's death in 1922, and Richard, Jr's., death in 1928. So well built were the Fripp bateaus that some were still around in the 1940s.

James Peto Chaplin, Jr., was also a boat builder but he had his own method of building boats. Being in ill health, he left the island and died in Savannah in 1919.

Lance Burn's Boat *Dandy*

The *Dandy* was a 33-foot-long boat with a 14-foot beam, powered by a 120 HP Gas Screw motor. The cabin was large and airy with an overhead clearance of seven feet—the perfect boat to haul passengers and freight for Daufuskie.

Lance Burn and his eleven-year-old son, Gene, rode the *Dandy* from Ft. Lauderdale up the Intracoastal Waterway arriving at Daufuskie on 1 April 1959. The trip had taken them a week, but by not being in a hurry they had thoroughly enjoyed seeing the sights along the way.

As soon as the *Dandy* reached Daufuskie, she began her twice-weekly trips to Savannah on each Tuesday and Friday. Her cabin was filled with passengers and her stern was loaded with feed and groceries. Passage was $1.50 each way, plus freight of 25 cents per grocery bag and 50 cents for a sack of feed. During her five-year run the *Dandy* brought 13 vehicles to the island. She was so wide that a car/truck fit perfectly crosswise her stern. Owners paid a freight price of $25.00 per car. In 1964 when the *Dandy* needed repairs and became disabled, she was pulled up by the shoreline near the Burn's dock where she remained through the years and slowly deteriorated.

EOC Boat the *Miss Frances Jones*

In 1963, State Economic Coordinator Townes Holland had visited Daufuskie and saw the potential of the island building itself up by linking it to the mainland, either by boat or causeway.

Providing a boat was the cheapest way out. Through Mr. Holland's working with Ervin Berry, Executive Director of Beaufort-Jasper County Economic Opportunity Commission (EOC), and with Lance Burn, the EOC Director on Daufuskie, and with others, a trip was made to Wilmington, North Carolina, August, 1967, to find a boat through the General Services Administration that would be suitable for Daufuskie.[3] Their visit was a success, and on 14 February 1968 the *Miss Frances Jones*, a small Navy, Higgins, Personnel Landing Craft with its motor overhauled and its hull painted gray, came to Daufuskie and tied up at William (Bill) Porter's dock on New River. Miss Frances Jones, after whom the boat was named, and one of the two teachers at Mary Fields Elementary, had her class make a number of large red valentines. When they arrived at the boat, the children were instructed to place all of the big red hearts on the floor of the outside deck. The people on the island were elated. It was the first boat in history at their personal disposal whereby they could go to Savannah and return to Daufuskie daily, free of charge.

The boat made runs, Monday through Saturday, to Savannah, with the crew working 48 hours per week. It made limited trips to Bluffton. Salaries being paid through EOC funds did not include pay for overtime. Therefore, when it was learned that they could only work 40 hours a week, the crew took Wednesdays off but ran the other days except Sunday. Robert Lewis began as captain of the boat, with Willis Simmons, Sr., later taking charge. Thomas Stafford and Walter Joseph Bryan were the first and second mates. Salaries were paid through EOC funds.

The boat ran until circa 1972. Not willing to spend large sums of money on major motor repairs that were too costly for the bad shape of the hull, the boat was laid to rest.

However, the island was blessed again and through the efforts of Thomas Barnwell, Jr., Assistant Beaufort-Jasper EOC Director, Senator Strom Thurmond, and the New Director of Beaufort-Jasper EOC, Charlie Simmons, Jr., the boat *Strom Thurmond* was presented

to the island residents on Tuesday, 28 August 1973. This vessel was a 36-foot Army launch, like new, and it rode comfortably.[4] It lasted a few years until cut-backs in government funds caused the Daufuskie boat program to fold, which put the men of the island back in their own little boats making runs to Savannah.

School Boats

Daily boat trips off the island for students in the fifth grade and above began with the 1987-88 school term.

The Beaufort County Board of Education advertised for a contract bid to transport school children Monday through Friday to Jenkins Island dock, where the students were to be met by buses which would take them to their prospective schools. Wick Scurry was awarded this first contract, leaving from his Cooper River dock, carrying the children on the *Calibogue* and at times in a smaller, open speedboat.

Operating from the Cooper River (Melrose) Landing Marina, Islands Charter Service, Inc., with Ed Richards as owner/captain, was awarded the second school-boat contract for the 1988-89 term, using his boat, the *Mary C.* Ed had one deck hand.

The third contract for the term of 1989-90 was given to Sam Stevens, Savannah, Georgia, who used his boat the *Miss Savannah*, hiring Maurice Canty as captain and one deck hand. This boat would leave from Savannah, pick up the children at the New River public landing on Daufuskie at 6:30 A.M., go by Jack Rowe and Buck Islands, let the children off at Jenkins Island where the boat and crew spent the entire day. The children would board the boat at 3:30 P.M. for the return trip, reaching Daufuskie at 4:30. The boat would be back in Savannah by 6 P.M. With too many breakdowns and problems which caused the children to miss early classes, the *Miss Savannah* lost out a few months short of her contract.

As a result, Captain Ed Richards of the *Mary C.* was awarded a five-year contract, which enabled him to complete the 1989-1990 school term that ended in June, 1990.

During school days Daufuskie residents were allowed to ride the *Miss Savannah* and the *Mary C.* and bring their freight for free. Since vacation time Beaufort County Council has paid for the *Mary C.* to provide free transportation for the residents to Jenkins Island on Mondays and Fridays.

Unless the contract changes, for the next five years, when school resumes on 4 September 1990, the residents of Daufuskie will be permitted to ride the *Mary C.* daily with Captain Ed and the students.

Notes

1. Complete reliance on the memory of Daufuskie people, and others familiar with the island, made the names of these steamers and boats possible. Length of boats and the number of passengers were given to the best of their knowledge. Thanks and appreciation to A. Lance Burn, Francis A. Burn, Sr., Emil Cetchovich II, Niels Christensen, Gilbert J. Maggioni, Roger Pinckney, Fred and George White, and Mrs. Geneva Wiley.

2. Fran Smith, "The Way It Was—For 56 Years, He's Been Island's Link to Mainland," *Island Packet*, 22 September 1983, pp. 1A, 17A.

3. EOC South East Region Newsletter, Vol. 2, No. 8, August, 1967, pp. 6,7.

4. Bill Wright, "Daufuskie Boat Launched, Thurmond Visits Island," Beaufort *Gazette*, 29 August 1973; *Island Packet*, 6 September 1973.

River Street, Savannah, Georgia, circa 1900
(Photograph courtesy Mr. Gilbert J. Maggioni.)

Steamer *Merchant* circa 1915—Savannah-Beaufort Line
(Photograph courtesy Mrs. Harriet Butler Eyler, Savannah, Ga., and Mr. Gilbert J. Maggioni, Lady's Island, S.C.)

Steamer *Clivedon* in New River circa 1915

(Photograph courtesy Mrs. Harriet Butler Eyler, Savannah, Ga., and Mr. Gilbert J. Maggioni, Lady's Island, S.C.)

Off-loading Excursions at Daufuskie Island, S.C., circa 1915

Side-wheel steamer *Attaquin*, outboard; screw steamer *Clivedon*, center; side-wheel steamer *Pilot Boy*, inboard. (Photograph courtesy Mrs. Harriet Butler Eyler, Savannah, Ga., and Mr. Gilbert J. Maggioni, Lady's Island, S.C.)

Above: *Isabelle*, circa 1925. Below: *Isabelle*, Daufuskie Dock circa 1924. Lucille Palmer, Juanita Goodwin, Mary I. (Mamie) Fripp, Pearl Fripp, Lula Goodwin, Barney Goodwin, Nell Palmer, James Goodwin, Juanita Fripp, Agnes Palmer White, Hinson White, William (Hamp) Bryan. All are not identified. (Photographs courtesy Mrs. Ida White-Tatum.)

Attaquin and *Louise* circa 1918—Docked at Palmetto Bluff
(Photograph courtesy Mrs. Betsy Caldwell, Bluffton Historical Preservation Society, Inc.)

Clifton circa 1900

The *Clifton* wrecked in front of Roger Pinckney's house in Beaufort River about 1910. The boiler of the vessel remains visible at low tide. (Photograph courtesy Mr. Roger Pinckney.)

Islander circa 1920, at Beaufort Dock
(Photograph courtesy Mr. Roger Pinckney.)

Clivedon circa 1930—Docked at Palmetto Bluff
(Photograph courtesy Mr. Roger Pinckney.)

Front and back of the ticket to ride the *Clivedon*, circa 1936. (Ticket courtesy Mrs. Josephine Johnson.)

The Fuller Fripp house on "The Fripp Place." Sitting on the front porch left to right: Richard Fuller Fripp, Sr., his wife Margaret, their three children— John Francis, Margaret (Pearl), and Richard Fuller, Jr., circa 1895. (Photograph courtesy Mrs. Joy Fripp Canady, Columbus, Georgia.)

Richard Fuller Fripp, Sr., circa 1900. He often wore the ends of his moustache wrapped around his ears. (Photograph courtesy Mrs. Joy Fripp Canady, Columbus, Georgia.)

"Chaplin's Landing" boat house, circa 1900. Left to right: James P. Chaplin, Jr. (father); children: William Francis, Robert Lee (standing on tree log), Georgia, Virginia, Mary, and James P. III (leaning against tree). (Photograph courtesy David Humphrey, Savannah.)

James Peto Chaplin, Jr., at "Chaplin"s Landing," standing near his oyster house and a boat that he built, circa 1910. (Photograph courtesy David Humphrey, Savannah.)

Above: Waiting for the steamer, circa 1906. James P. Chaplin, Jr. (with packages), Mary Chaplin (daughter), Mrs. James P. (Lou) Chaplin, Jr. (Photograph courtesy Mr. David Humphrey.) Left: the *Bessie M. Lewis*, circa 1947. (Photograph courtesy Mrs. Ida White-Tatum.)

403

The *Miss Frances Jones*, 14 February 1968.

Valentines placed by school children on deck of the *Miss Frances Jones*, 14 February 1968.

Boat *Miss Frances Jones* on the way home from Savannah, circa 1968. Left to right: Captain Robert Lewis, Henry Netherton, Rhea Netherton, Viola Bryan, Mrs. Ella Mae Stevens.

13

DAUFUSKIE ECONOMY

Surrounded by waters teeming with seafood, Daufuskie has woods abundant with wild game, and sandy type soil that produces a bountiful supply of vegetables and fruit. It would be very difficult to starve anyone who chose to live on the Island. The Indians sustained themselves out of the sea and off the land for thousands of years. It wasn't until foreigners (such as Indian traders) came, bringing guns, tools, clothing, etc.—things that were all new to the Indian—that the natives began to trap more animals for their furs, to kill more deer for their hides, and to plant more corn, in order to trade for those things that they saw and wanted.

Traders were the first white people to accumulate fortunes by charging Indians exorbitant prices for their wares. Bushels of corn were required for the purchase of some sort of cheap trinket or item; for unpaid rum bills young kidnapped Indian braves were accepted and sold into the West Indies slave trade; and many fur pelts or deer hides were needed to purchase an axe or piece of clothing.

Abuses and ill treatment by the traders became the major factor in the Yemassee War of 1715, which the Indians lost and which drove them from Daufuskie forever. The island was depopulated for over a decade, but the reopening of the land office in 1731 and the settlement of Savannah in 1733 brought new property owners to Daufuskie.[1]

With water as a barrier, Daufuskie provided a natural pasture, requiring little or no fencing and a bounty of marsh grass which eliminated the need of salt licks. From the 1730s to 1740s the first landowners relied on ranch farming. In the 1750s they shifted to the planting of indigo which proved to be more profitable than raising

cattle; by 1770 they were committed to it. Proof of dependence on indigo farming is found in newspaper advertisements for Daufuskie land sales. One tract was described as "exceeding good for corn and indigo," while, at a later date, a 500-acre tract was listed as "valuable for . . . indigo and provisions."[2]

(Tradition has it that men who could afford large plantations of indigo were referred to as "Blue Bloods.")

One odd thing about producing dye from indigo plants was that the process required human urine as a catalyst, which became rather smelly. As the indigo neared harvest time, wooden tubs in which to collect their urine were placed near slave quarters of the plantation. (The use of potash as a catalyst eventually replaced this primitive method.) The indigo operation was kept at a distance from the residential areas of the plantation where prevailing winds would carry the foul odor away from its living quarters.[3] Indigo was grown successfully until 1800. (Wild plants continue to be found on the island.)

An economic source in the late 1760s was through Robert Watts, who maintained a shipyard on his Bloody Point tract. Lumber to build his large vessels came from his personal live oak grove.

Due to the salinity of the water, rice was never grown commercially on the island. For private use only small patches were planted in the tupelo swamp or fresh water areas down the center of the island that some of the black people referred to as "the gaul." Plucking the rice in its milky stage, ricebirds eventually became so numerous that the growing of any rice finally ceased.

In the 1800s cotton had replaced indigo as a cash crop. Plantation owners became extremely wealthy as their slaves produced more and more cotton. However, planting of the crop virtually stopped with the Civil War. Because there were no slaves to work the fields, cotton crops were grown less and less until in 1916 the boll weevil, which had migrated from Mexico, killed it all.[4] Other than small patches grown for personal use, Jim White and family, who were sharecroppers at Melrose in 1918, were probably the last to plant cotton on Daufuskie.

Before the turn of the century all of the former slaves had purchased a little piece of land, built themselves houses, and were planting gardens. If the family was large, in order to grow enough provisions, they rented tasks (one-fourth acre at 25 cents) from plan-

tation owners, a few of whom resided in Savannah. Sometimes there would be such a demand that there was scarcely enough tasks of land to go around. If they didn't want to utilize one of the big steamers that came daily, laden with produce, chickens, turkeys, fruits, and a variety of seafoods, islanders would sail their boats to Savannah and sell their products at the old City Market.

Although things got rough following the Civil War, from jobs on and off the island and from resources among themselves, needs of the people were provided for in different ways.

Black women cleaned, cooked, and/or washed for white families on the island, or worked as domestics in Savannah or on Tybee Island.

A few of the men (black and white) found employment at the Quarantine Station near Ft. Pulaski. Others worked on the Corps of Engineers' dredges like the *Henry Bacon, Creighton, Cumberland, DeWitt Clinton, Gilmer, Morgan, Pascagoula,* and the *Welatka.* The two sea-going dredges were the Calebra and the Dan C. Kingman. A sad thing happened to the Gilmer in 1931. It sunk in 30 feet of water just south of Field's Cut on the Elba Island side of Savannah River. When it went down, it drowned twenty-six-year-old Thomas Lee Harley, who was third engineer and who had lived on Daufuskie with his parents in the 1920s.[5]

Black carpenters on the island were Charlie Bentley, Joe Bryan, Paul Bryan, Joe Champion, William Crosby, Lexie Hamilton, Samuel Holmes, William Hudson, and Frank Lawrence. For the price of labor, one of these carpenters would charge $75 to build a small four-room house.

Assisting Dick Fripp in the boatbuilding business were William "Geechee" Brown, Thomas Crosby, Bobby Jenkins, Frank Jenkins, Ben Miller, and Gabe Washington.

Fanner-baskets, used to winnow chaff from rice, were made from local bulrush or pine needles, laced with strips of palmetto. Those who made these and other types of baskets were Brister Brown, George Jenkins, Dennis Haynes, Toby Holmes, Victoria Mitchell, and Walter (Plummey) Simmons. Jimmie Lee made baskets of white oak strips.

Dennis Haynes, Joseph Michael, and William Hudson had corn grinders and would grind meal or grits for their families and friends.

Bun Small and a Mr. Wright had cane grinding mills that took a mule or oxen to grind stalks of sugar cane to get the juice that was

Dredges, Savannah River, circa 1930s

Morgan
(Photograph courtesy Mrs. Ida White-Tatum.)

Creighton
(Photograph courtesy Mrs. Ida White-Tatum.)

Dredge and Tow Boats Along Savannah River circa 1930s

Quarterboat—Towboat
(Photographs courtesy Mrs. Ida White-Tatum.)

boiled down to make syrup. Sometimes the children were allowed to visit the mill and drink some of the juice.

Cast nets, used to catch shrimp and mullet, were hand made by most of the men on the island, but John Bryan and Thomas Stafford probably made more of these nets than anyone else.

In the early years, with the use of small bateaus, crabs were caught on 500 to 1000-foot crab lines that were tied every couple of feet with a piece of bull nose. The bait was furnished by the company that sent a shrimp boat to the island to pick up barrels of live crabs, taking them to Savannah. In the 1970s crab lines were abandoned for crab traps approximately 3' by 3' made from an iron rod frame covered with chicken wire.

Daufuskie Deviled Crabs

In the 1920s the famous Daufuskie deviled crab was born. It was Mrs. Kizsie Bryan, wife of Sam Bryan, who began making these crabs, selling them to visitors coming in on boat excursions or church picnics. Then Kizsie taught Mrs. Susie "Muffet" Smith.[6] From Susie, the idea spread over the island and soon all of the women were selling deviled crabs. The ingredients used besides crab meat might be celery, bell pepper, onions, or a bit of sweet relish. To hold the mixture together, some use Ritz crackers, soda biscuits, or bread crumbs, with a little mayonnaise. Seasoning besides salt and pepper could be a dash of hot sauce or lemon juice. Baked to perfection in original crab backs (barks), each woman's deviled crabs are individual in taste, with some being mild and others being very hot. The price of a deviled crab began at 15 cents; today the cost is $4.00 or more.

Gathering Turpentine

The turpentine industry flourished circa 1918 to the mid-1930s. Savannah wharfs were filled with barrel after barrel of sticky pine gum. Those who participated in the program made rows of deep cuts in the bark of a pine tree in the shape of a V, resembling the backbone of a fish, in order for the resin to flow into small clay pots that hung just below the point made by these cuts. Several years ago, some of these clay pots were found on Pine Island, left there by the Chaplin family, who owned Piney Islands plantation.

411

Tending a Crabline circa 1920-1970s
(Courtesy of artist Christina Roth Bates.)

Decorative Labels, Fruitland Farm, Daufuskie Island, S.C.
(Labels courtesy Claude Fripp, son of Mrs. John Fripp.)

Fruitland Farm Cannery

Between 1916-1918 Mrs. John (Juanita) Fripp and daughter Laura operated Fruitland Farm, the only fruit and vegetable cannery ever on the island. The two women prepared the food from their own garden and orchard, then processed the tin cans in a homemade boiler in the backyard of the Fuller Fripp home. In his store at Benjie's Point, Dick Fripp, Jr., displayed the decorative labeled cans of pears, figs, and tomatoes.[7]

Daufuskie Magistrates

The South Carolina governor appoints Daufuskie magistrates. The first two men known to hold this position were Joe Hoskiss and then James "Jim" W. White. Just when their appointments began is unknown, but Jim White served until 1935. After Mr. White the follow-

Magistrate James W. White and Horse "Billy," circa 1940
(Photograph courtesy Mrs. Ida White-Tatum.)

414

Magistrate Alfred L. Burn, Senator Strom Thurmond, silhouetted in front of the Daufuskie Post Office, 28 August 1973.

Judge Francis A. Burn, Sr., appointed magistrate of Daufuskie, 13 April 1988, by Governor Carroll Campbell. (Photograph courtesy Judge Burn.)

Left: Jim Goodwin and Malcolm Johnson, circa 1939. Daufuskie Pavilion in background. (Photograph courtesy Mrs. Josephine Johnson.) Below: Constable Hinson A. White and horse Daisy, circa 1939. (Photograph courtesy Mrs. Ida White-Tatum.)

ing men were magistrates according to a vaguely kept record book, "Docket & Report of Magistrates," that was begun by W. W. Scouten in 1935:

> William Wiser Scouten, Sr.: 26 November 1935–circa 1939
> James "Jim" W. White: 1940–1948 (2nd appointment)
> Fred Henry Dierks: 28 September 1948–5 December 1949
> Arthur Ashley Burn: 5 December 1949–23 August 1954
> Fred Henry Dierks: 23 August 1954–21 January 1961 (2nd appointment)
> Arthur Ashley Burn: 21 January 1961–21 January 1965 (2nd appointment)
> Clifford Marcus Boyd: 21 January 1965–21 August 1966 (Arthur A. Burn's grandson)
> Alfred Lance Burn: 1 September 1966–30 June 1977 (Arthur A. Burn's son)

Lance Burn received a salary of $50.00 per month. Following his resignation the magistrate office remained closed until his half brother, Francis Arthur Burn, Sr., was appointed to that position 14 April 1988.

Constables

James W. White was appointed constable under magistrate W. W; Scouten, 27 January 1936, serving until 1937. James "Jim" H. Goodwin was constable from 1937 to 1941. Hinson Adam White served as constable under his father, J. W. White—and all the other magistrates from 1941 to circa 1972 when it was decided that the position of constable was no longer necessary.

Midwives

In the early years midwives earned money fairly regularly as there were plenty of young women having babies. The first of these midwives were trained by their mothers and the later ones received training from a county nurse.

The midwife would attend the woman at delivery. Then for the next nine days she would come to the house, bathe the mother and baby, and if necessary cook meals, wash their clothes, perhaps straighten the house a bit—all for the sum of $25.00.

Midwives were Marchele Bentley, Molly Bryan, Rose Brisbane, Lizzie Butler, Cornelia "Lemon" Grant, Sarah Hudson Grant, Lizzie

House of Mrs. Sarah Hudson Grant (1987). Sarah was the midwife, undertaker, Sunday School president, PTA president. She bought this house from Fuller Fripp for $15, had it moved and rebuilt for $25. H. Emmett McCracken, superintendent of Beaufort County Schools, called her "Mayor of Daufuskie." (Photograph courtesy Pamela Brooks.)

Johnson, Susan Lloyd, Mae Pryor, and Susie "Muffet" Smith.

Sarah Hudson Grant was the last midwife. She had begun in 1932 "birthing babies." At that time she bought from Jim Goodwin a one-seated buggy to which she hitched her big black horse *Tillman* (named for the South Carolina governor). When she was brought word that it was "time" for the delivery of one of her patients, she would get her little black bag with its tiny scale, soap, thread, scissors, gauze, etc., hitch up *Tillman,*

and ride wherever she had to go. The last baby Sarah delivered was Alberto Stevens, born 18 January 1969, to Mrs. Ella Mae Stevens.

During her 37 years Sarah had "grannied" over 130 babies. Times were changing and no longer could a woman be a midwife. Prospective mothers were forced to visit a doctor on the mainland and admitted to the hospital for delivery.

Lumber Companies

From 1916-1920 the Hilton-Dodge Lumber Company furnished jobs on Daufuskie; in the 1930s there was a pulpwood company; and in the late 1940s Otis Perkins Lumber Company was cutting timber.

WPA and CCC Camps

During the depression years of 1938-1943, the WPA (Works Project Administration) furnished jobs on the island for the older adult while the young men were sent off the island to CCC camps (Civilian Conservation Corps).

Whiskey Stills

Also during the depression, several families made moonshine whiskey (the very best) selling it to each other, to visitors arriving on boats at the public landing, to the soldiers at Ft. Screven near Tybee, or to eating joints on Bay Street in Savannah. Many made wine and some made homebrew. What couldn't be sold, members of the family helped to consume—sometimes causing many domestic fights.

Fishing and Fishing Drops

Fishing was another way that boosted the economy of most islanders: seine nets were used on the beach while gillnets were used in the

creeks and along the shore of islands around Daufuskie. Baited only with pieces of dead shrimp, mullet, or live fiddler crabs, handlines were used off the dock or in a boat, wherever the fish were biting. There were no rods and reels in those days. With a lantern at night many fish were caught by gigging. It was necessary to be familiar with the tides when using a gill net or handline. Following are names of some of the best known fishing drops familiar to all old-timers of Daufuskie: Beacon Creek, Big House, Buck Dam, Bloody Point Beach, Cockspur Light, Freeport, Gaskin Banks, Gaynor's Bank, Haig's Point Landing, Jack Rowe, Jettys (North and South), Long Island, Melrose Beach, Oak Ridge (on Mongin Creek), Papy Burn's Landing, Public Landing, Robinson Island, Salt Pond, Tea Kettle, Turtle Island Beach, Venus Point.[8]

Shrimping

Tons of shrimp were caught by casting in the creeks or by nets pulled behind either small or large boats that had to drag for shrimp in the sounds.

County Work

Through the County Supervisor Herbert Attaway (1950s–1960s) and Public Works Directors C. Charles "Chink" Haigh (1962-1990) and E. M. Russell, Jr. (1 July 1990), jobs have been provided for a crew of five to ten men—cutting the bushes by the side of the roads; keeping the ditches clear to drain the land for gardens; grade and repair holes in roads with oyster shells; clean up the debris caused by storms; put up stop signs, grade the roads and recently to handle trash dumpsters. Field Manager Luke Inabinett, working under the direction of Mr. Haigh and Mr. Russell, has seen that all of the tools and equipment needed for the roadwork has gotten to the men on the island. Road supervisors on Daufuskie have been Jim Goodwin, Arthur A. Burn, Fred H. Dierks, Hinson A. White, A. Lance Burn, Ben H. Smith, Leonard H. "Sonny" Smith, Clarence Simmons, and Gary Ward.

S.C. Electric and Gas Company

Beginning in May of 1952, Irvin Tavel from Edisto Beach, South Carolina, began clearing the right-of-way for the South Carolina

Electric and Gas Company in order to bring electricity to Daufuskie. Mr. Tavel's work force consisted of island men with Arthur A. Burn as supervisor. The first work was completed 14 August that year. However, every few years Mr. Tavel would return and hire the same men to keep trees and bushes cleared away under the wires.[9]

Trapping

Several of the men supplemented their incomes during the winter by trapping animals. Skins of otter, mink, 'possum and 'coon brought good prices at Jake Kirshner Furs in Savannah. In the 1970s Lance Burn and Jake Simmons were the last two Daufuskie trappers.

Islander Gets City Job

Daufuskie Islander Richmond Wiley, who had worked at one time as a deckhand on an engineering dredge, was given an unusual job by the city of Savannah in 1955. Mayor W. Lee Mingledorff, Jr., referred to Richmond as the "Commodore of the Savannah Navy." Richmond performed the city's only water-borne service in a 12-foot bateau. He searched the harbor five days a week, from 8:00 A.M. until 4:30 P.M., clearing driftwood or other flotsam that might represent a hazard for shipping, between the Seaboard Air Line Railroad bridge to the Standard Oil docks—on both sides of the river. For this work Richmond was paid $185 a month and furnished a boat and motor. He lived in Savannah during the week, but on weekends he would travel in his own boat to visit his wife, Geneva, and their ten children on Daufuskie. Harbormaster Joseph A. Power, Richmond's boss, had remarked that the Savannah Navy might be small, but it was dependable. Richmond was devoted to his job, providing excellent service until shortly before his death in 1972, at the age of seventy-two.[10]

Santa Cruz College Students

In the late 1960s and during the 1970s Professor J. Herman Blake, of Oaks College in Santa Cruz, California, sent two white male students each college quarter to board with a black family on Daufuskie. Professor Blake paid $40 per week for each student during their stay. While these young men were here they helped in many ways, but mainly with the school children in formulating a small school newspa-

421

Mrs. Viola Bryan with two students, (left) Doug Brown and (right) Alan Fisher, who were sent to Daufuskie by Professor J. Herman Blake, Oaks College, Santa Cruz, CA, 1968.

Circa 1983. Home of Mrs. Viola Bryan where Pat Conroy lived. Later owned by Professor J. Herman Blake, the house burned Christmas 1983. (Photograph courtesy Mrs. Martha Hutton.)

per. The first two students were Doug Brown and Alan Fisher, who boarded with Mrs. Viola Bryan. She wanted to earn money to add a bathroom to her home. Viola had made the remark that if she never lived long enough to enjoy it, she still wanted an inside bathroom. She got her wish, the bathroom was added, all of the fixtures were in place, but she died 26 August 1969 before the water lines and plumbing were completed. She did not have the pleasure of using the bathroom that she had worked so very hard to get. Pat Conroy rented the house for awhile and others lived there. Professor Blake loved the island and sometimes after Viola's death, he purchased the house from her heirs. He came as often as he could spending many pleasant trips here. He brought several guests with him, one of whom was Alex Haley, who wrote *Roots*.

Following the graduation of three of Pat Conroy's former students, Cynthia Stevens, Jackie Robinson, and Ervin Simmons, Professor Blake made it possible for them to attend Oaks College at Santa Cruz, with all expenses paid. The first two returned home after a couple of years, but Ervin remained and graduated.

The professor's house burned to the ground Christmas 1983. He was so hurt over this loss and not having any place to stay that he rarely returned to the island, and now has the land up for sale.

Tourist Boats

From 1978 to 1980 Skip Hoagland in his boat *Island Skimmer*, was the first to provide service for tourists to the island from Hilton Head. Skip's boat had a top but was otherwise open, 40 feet long, and held 49 passengers. It was unique in that it had an oriental look and was adorned with beautiful hanging baskets of ferns.[11]

Skip was followed by Stan and Sally Maurer's *Vagabond Cruises* in 1979 with their boats *Adventure* and *Vagabond,* which carry 150 passengers each. *The Drifter* and *Gypsy* were on the line but they have been sold. Operating from Hilton Head, the Maurers have the *Vagabond* with their son, Mark, now making tours with the *Adventure.* Both provide good, dependable service.[12]

Karen Bona spearheaded a tourist company in 1985 known as the *Daufuskie Seafari,* along with her partner Eddie Odom. They operate from Hilton Head, with Eddie giving private bus tours on Daufuskie. They have been very successful and continue with their tours.[13]

All parties who brought tourists have had Daufuskie buses (some with tops, some without) using Daufuskie drivers, giving short guided tours with a person on board who relates some of the history of the island as they ride the dusty roads. The tourist trade is seasonal—from March 1 to November 1.

Melrose Landing

Situated on Cooper River, Melrose Landing has a nice dock with rental docking space, a store stocked with the usual for boaters and campers, plus they have gasoline for Daufuskie cars and trucks. Hundreds of workers and the school children disembark from boats that dock at this landing. It is a very busy place and hires several people.

Freeport Landing

Also on Cooper River, Wick Scurry's Freeport Landing (known as the "Gateway to Daufuskie") is the island's only public marina. Wick services and provides storage space for boats. He has a store that caters to the tourist trade—all of which provides jobs for several workers.

•

Since development began in the mid-1980s, there has been a variety of jobs available to anyone needing employment. Not only is everyone on the island working who wants a job, but hundreds of workers (many out of state) pour in on boats daily from Hilton Head and Savannah. The economy of the island is booming.

Notes

1. Starr, p. ii.

2. Ibid., p. 44; *Georgia Gazette*, 2 February 1768; *City Gazette and Daily Advertiser* (Charleston), 16 April 1795.

3. Printed in Honor of the Bicentennial of the United States, Indigo in America (Parsippany, New Jersey: BASF Wyandotte Corporation, 1976), p. 11. (Booklet courtesy: Mrs. Joann Dierks Yarbrough.)

4. The first boll weevil caught in South Carolina was from a plantation on Daufuskie in 1916 by George M. Anderson, Entomologist, Clemson University. The specimen is on exhibit at the Pendleton Museum, Pendleton, S.C. The second boll weevil specimen was also caught on Daufuskie in 1916 and remains in the Clemson University Entomological Collection. Thanks and appreciation for their personal

425

letters: John C. Morse, Professor, Clemson University, 14 February 1985; Miss Frances McAlister, Six Mile, S. C., 8 March 1985; and for calling attention to the Daufuskie boll weevils in the first place, thanks to Mr. Ragnar E. Anderson, Clemson, S.C., 31 January 1985.

5. *Savannah Morning News/Press*, 14 September 1931. (Thanks to Mrs. Audrey Harley Clanton, sister of Lee Harley, for a copy of the article and information.) It seemed the *Gilmer* was "cursed." It was raised to the surface and was being towed by the *Dan C. Kingman* (a sea-going dredge) to a northern port (possibly Charleston) for repairs. When the tow got off shore, the weather became really bad and when the *Gilmer* started sinking, its tow-line was cut from the *Kingman* and it sank—again, where it remains.

6. Mrs. Geneva Wiley interview, 14 August 1990.

7. Mrs. Laura Timmons interview, 12 June 1984.

8. Names of fishing drops were provided by Lance Burn and Mrs. Gillian Ward-White.

9. Arthur A. Burn's daily record of 1952-1953; Mrs. Irvin (Virginia) Tavel, Edisto, personal letter, 19 September 1990.

10. Patrick Kelly, "Skipper of City's Navy," *Savannah Morning News*, 17 June 1959. Thanks to Mrs. Joann Dierks Yarbrough for sharing the article, 25 July 1990.

11. Skip Hoagland telephone conversation, 20 September 1990.

12. Sally Maurer interview, 19 September 1990.

13. Eddie Odom telephone conversation 18 September 1990.

The Old Market House, Savannah, Georgia. (Anonymous: circa 1900-1910.)

Old City Market, Savannah, Georgia, circa 1900-1915. (Photograph courtesy Mr. Gilbert J. Maggioni.)

14

THE OYSTER INDUSTRY

L ush, and the tastiest on the east coast, oysters were plentiful around Daufuskie and neighboring islands. Oystering became the only industry that Daufuskie ever had, providing work for the Daufuskie people from the 1880s to 1959. During those years oyster leases were granted to different ones who applied to the State Board of Fisheries. The earliest Daufuskie record found thus far is dated 21 March 1896, from the Office of Secretary of State (D. H. Tompkins), Department of Public Lands, Columbia, S. C., with 87 acres leased to Richard Fuller Fripp, Sr., for $15.15 per annum and 90 acres leased to James Peto Chaplin, Jr., for $21.50 per annum.[1]

A small oyster shucking factory had been operated by James P. Chaplin, Jr., and perhaps a few oysters had been opened for E. V. Toomer, but it was a man named Maggioni who brought a full-scaled oyster business to Daufuskie.

L.P. Maggioni Company

Luigi Paoli Maggioni was born in Genoa, Italy. Contrary to his wishes, but forced by the Italian tradition that a father control the future occupation of his son, Luigi was enrolled at a seminary to become a priest.

It didn't take him long to find out that studying for the priesthood was not to his liking. One day Luigi Paoli could stand it no longer. He jumped out of the window of the seminary and boarded the first schooner tied to the dock. Signing on as cabin boy, he sailed to America, being shipwrecked off the west coast of Florida. Working his way to Jacksonville, he met and married an Italian girl, Natalia Bettelini.

429

They began by selling small gadgets and pencils, later moving to Isle of Hope near Savannah, to sell their wares. Luigi's brother, who had joined them in America, was skilled at making kites and other items which were sold in their store. Shortly, seafood from local fishermen was added to the merchandise.

The seafood proved to be such a popular commodity that the need to expand forced the business to move to the city of Savannah—thus the beginning of the L. P. Maggioni seafood industry in 1870.[2]

In the 1880s Maggioni had the opportunity to lease oyster beds in Florida, Georgia, and South Carolina. This opened up a whole new field—economically helping hundreds of workers and netting the company a nice profit.

Oyster Cannery on Daufuskie

All of the older black people now living on the island were born between 1903 and 1905. They grew up knowing about and working in Emil Cetchovich's oyster shucking factory, but when asked if there had been an oyster cannery here, the answer would be "no." Little wonder, since the cannery was here and gone about the time they were born, and apparently knowledge of it was not handed down by their parents.

It wasn't until August, 1990, that it was learned that a cannery had been on Daufuskie. Roger Pinckney was the Beaufort County Coroner for thirty-three years and is now in the process of writing a book about his experiences. He called and during our discussion Roger asked if I knew that an oyster cannery had been on Daufuskie. I said no, that no one on the island remembers a cannery being here. Roger said, "Well, there was, for my friend has pictures proving it."

My ears perked up and a bell in my head went "Bong!" "Who is this man?" I wanted to know. "Please set up an appointment so that I might meet him and have a look at these pictures."

So, on Monday, 6 August 1990, I boarded the school boat, *Mary C.,* at 6:40 A.M., arriving at Jenkins Island on Hilton Head at 7:30, then drove to Roger's house in Beaufort to pick him up, as our appointment was at 10 o'clock on Lady's Island.

On the way my adrenaline was flowing a mile a minute; I could hardly contain myself. When we arrived, Gilbert J. Maggioni and his lovely wife Lucille came out on the porch and Roger introduced us.

We were invited into the dining room where I was shown the pictures that Roger had told me about. By this time I was chomping at the bits.

Yes, the pictures were of Daufuskie because the James P. Chaplin dock could be seen and other areas in the background could be identified as being near the public landing on New River. I was ecstatic!

Gilbert was so kind as to have copies made and on 22 August 1990 I returned to see him and Lucille and to pick up the pictures. No one can understand the joy that I felt; I couldn't believe that I now held in my hands pictures revealing that part of the past that might have been buried to Daufuskie people forever, had it not been through the kindness of Mr. Roger Pinckney and Mr. and Mrs. Gilbert Joseph Maggioni, to whom I shall ever be grateful.

The Maggioni pictures that you see in this segment were taken sometime between 1893 to 1903 by Gilbert's father, Joseph Onorato Maggioni, who, with his brother Gilbert Phillip Maggioni, worked with their father, L. P. Maggioni, in the Daufuskie oyster operation.

Maggioni and Company

L. P. Maggioni leased from Minus Sanders his Benjie's Point, New River land, on which Maggioni & Company built an oyster canning factory in 1893. This was a big outfit with a huge loading-dock area, several buildings, a boiler shed, and three sets of tracks on which the eight-foot iron-slot cars (filled with oysters) would be moved into the steamer.

Other black and white workers were brought to the island from Savannah and Hilton Head. The men would do the picking (gathering) of the oysters while the women and children would do the shucking (opening).

Daufuski Oysters (minus the "e" in Daufuskie) became the Maggioni brand name. The labels placed on the cans were/are blood-red with the trademark of an Indian Head adorned with a beautiful, feathered war bonnet. (These oysters may be found on shelves of the supermarkets today, but they do not contain oysters from Daufuskie.)

Oyster boats were built to use a sail. They had wide beams and shallow bottoms that drew very little water which permitted them to get close to the oyster beds on low tide.

While the cannery was on the island, tons of oysters were opened

Daufuski

BRAND

OYSTERS

NET WT.
8 OZ.
226 g

DISTRIBUTED BY
L. P. MAGGIONI
& CO.,
P.O. BOX 1748
SAVANNAH,
GA. 31402
PRODUCT OF
U.S.A.

INGREDIENTS: OYSTERS, WATER, SALT.

0   41438 00011

Daufuski

BRAND

ATLANTIC COVE OYSTERS

OYSTER STEW

1 can (8 oz.) Daufuski   3 teaspoons butter
Oysters, drained   Salt and white pepper
3 cups milk   Chopped parsley or paprika
Combine Oysters, milk and butter in a medium sized saucepan and bring
to the simmering point. Season to taste with salt and pepper and serve immediately with a sprinkle of parsley or a dash of paprika. Makes 2-3 servings.

SAUTÉED OYSTERS AND EGGS

1 can (8 oz.) Daufuski Oysters   1 tablespoon butter or bacon fat
Dash of curry powder or garlic salt
Drain Oysters well and add to melted fat in a small frying pan. Heat
thoroughly and add a dash of curry powder or garlic salt. Serve on
scrambled eggs or buttered toast. Garnish with sprig of parsley or water
cress and serve with sliced tomato. Makes 2 servings.

ATTENTION: SHELL PARTICLES MAY NORMALLY BE ENCOUNTERED IN
THIS PRODUCT. EXAMINE WITH CARE BEFORE USING.

5660-DA-0300
2-1/2 X 8-3/4 - 1/2 LAP

L. P. Maggioni & Co., Oyster Can Label
(Courtesy Mr. L. Paul Maggioni.)

each day, piling oysters shells as high as ten to twelve feet around the dock.

Where live oysters were gathered, dead oyster shells would be scattered to replace them in order to permit baby oysters a foundation on which to grow.

The cannery was removed from Daufuskie in 1903. Management of the remaining oyster industry now left on the island continued to be handled by the Maggioni Company, with the oysters being sent to Savannah or the cannery at Port Royal.

Several Maggioni buildings remained on the island; a long shotgun one that had 12-15 rooms was referred to as the "Hickey" house.

On 31 August 1912, Minus Sanders sold for $600.00 the property "now occupied by the Maggioni Company" to Emil Cetchovich, who made a down payment of $100.00, with the balance to be paid "on or before the first of February 1913," with the understanding that Minus would have one year in which to remove all buildings, fences, wires, posts, and everything that he had on said lot "except the trees."[3] Emil Cetchovich didn't wait that long; he paid the balance 29 September 1912.[4]

(Up to this point it was always believed that back in the 1890s Maggioni leased Emil Cetchovich's land on which the cannery was built. But according to the sale of said property from Minus Sanders to Cetchovich, it is evident that Maggioni leased land from Minus. No Record.)

Emil Cetchovich

The Cetchovich family lived in Vienna, Austria. They had two sons, Rafael and Emanuel. Rafael wanted to come to America. With his parent's consent and with a job on one of the sailing schooners, he left Austria and arrived in New York in the 1880s.

Rafael stayed so long without returning home that his mother became very worried. Knowing the name of the vessel on which he had sailed, Mrs. Cetchovich sent her other son, Emanuel (Emil), to look for Rafael and bring him back.

When Emil got to New York, he found his brother. But, with plenty of work and liking America, he too stayed, never returning to Austria. The two young men left New York on a boat that took them to San Francisco. Working there for a while they then found passage on a

ship coming to the east, which landed them in Savannah.

Ravanel Rice Enterprises was operated by a man named Marshall who lived on Rose Island. Emil and Rafael found employment on their boat that carried rice from Savannah to Charleston. Pee Wee Toomer was the rice boat captain.

Louisa Scouten from Amsterdam, Holland, had come to America in the 1880s to attend the New York World's Fair. After visiting the fair, she chose to stay in America. She found work, then later married a man by the name of Benny. They had one little daughter, Rosa. Benny worked along the water and brought the family to Savannah. He, too, found employment with Ravanel Rice Enterprises.

Becoming friends, Emil Cetchovich (single, and sometimes lonely) would be invited on many occasions to have dinner with the Bennys. When Benny died from a fever, Emil continued to visit Louisa and her daughter. Their friendship blossomed into romance with Emil and Louisa being married circa 1899.[5]

Having to pass Daufuskie on the way to deliver rice to Charleston, Emil probably stopped at the Maggioni oyster dock and got acquainted. Or perhaps he worked on one of their boats. At any rate, he

Mr. and Mrs. Emil Cetchovich, Sr., circa 1939. Their two-story house can be seen in the background. (Photograph courtesy Mr. James [Jimmy] Hopkins.)

visited the island and liked it so well that this is where he decided to settle down.

Bringing Louisa and Rosa with him, they lived in part of the "Hickey House" for a while, then rented a two-room house from Liza Jones until they could build a home of their own. Their son Emil, Jr., was born in 1904 and little daughter Katie in 1907. She died in 1908 and is buried in the Mary Dunn Cemetery. When he became an adult, Emil, Jr., began helping his father in the oyster business. (He died in Savannah, 1989.)

Oyster-Shucking Factory

After Emil Cetchovich, Sr., purchased the land, he leased it in 1917 to "G. Phillip Maggioni and Joseph O. Maggioni a pair of copartners doing business under the name and style of Maggioni & Company of Savannah, Georgia."[6]

Two Daufuskie oyster ground leases were granted the Maggioni brothers, 2 October 1919: one from Emil Cetchovich for 135 acres along New River, the second from Louisa E. Cetchovich for "500 acres of water and marshland suitable for oyster culture, situated at Daufuskie Island."[7]

Emil, Sr., began operating an oyster-shucking factory for the Maggioni Company. Manny Hubbard drove the piling. The oyster company furnished the lumber and other materials to construct a wharf and a factory building 100 feet long and 45-50 feet wide, with thirty-six 2-1/2' x 2-1/2' stalls. Stalls were simply a shelf built like a seat in an outhouse except with larger holes. A wide board in between the openings would hold a "cracker" used by the women to break off the lip of the oyster to open it more easily, then flip the shells to fall to the shoreline below. The pile of empty shells would get so high that a wheel barrow would have to be used to haul them away.

Oysters were gathered only during the months with an "r"—beginning in September, and ending in the spring, in April. During the hot summer months, the oysters would turn "milky" from spawning and were allowed to rest.

It took only two tools to open oysters: a metal oyster knife and a cracker (which was simply a short piece of metal that could be a piece of spring from an old wagon seat, or a wide file, stuck in a six-inch long block of wood, six or eight inches in diameter.)

If it was a sunny day, the women would take their "cracker" outside the factory, sit on a box or log on the dead shells, and open oysters. To hold the oyster and prevent cutting themselves, they used an old rag or glove on their left hand. Protecting their clothing, they would wear an apron or a crocus bag thrown across their lap. They would have to dress warm for it was cold near the water. (Some of the women stated in later life that their limbs and joints ached from getting so cold while opening oysters for all those years.)

With breakfast to cook and children to get to school, the women hardly ever showed up at the factory until around 9 o'clock each morning, then worked late into the evening.

Usually, a wife would open oysters that her husband had brought in. But sometimes a woman would not have a husband who picked oysters (he might have a job on the dredge or at the Quarantine Station), so she would shuck oysters for any man who had more than his wife could handle. That is why a man welcomed other women helping his wife to do the shucking—the more oysters, the more money that was made by all. A woman shucking oysters for a man other than her husband received pay for half the shucking price.

Oyster knife on "cracker."

For picking oysters, the company would supply the men with oyster tongs and shovels, a bateau, or whatever they needed. With their long-handled tongs the men could grapple for oysters in deeper water. They had only one low tide a day, and when the tide was low in the afternoon causing the men to get back too late for a shucker to open their oysters, there was a small extra building near the factory where the oysters could be stored overnight. Every man could identify his pile of oysters.

Oysters were gathered all winter, but during the summer the men would be putting out seed-oysters and planting empty shells for the young oysters to grow on.

With the exception of the ocean side with its pounding surf, oysters were plentiful all around the remainder of the island. Over a period of time, in order to make it convenient for the black people to be near their home and protect them from the weather, several oyster-shucking shacks were built near the shore on different persons' land.

Two were built on the northshore at Cooper River, one on lands of Cato McIntyre, and one at Robert Jenkins' place. Another was at a small settlement where Dick Washington lived on Webb Tract, called "Rabbit Point." One oyster-shucking shack was on John Mongin's Maryfield property, referred to as "up in that corner." Two were built on the westside at Dick Fripp's Benjie's Point place on New River. On the southside, facing Mongin Creek, three were located: one at John Bryan's, called the "Branch"; one at "Jimmie Lee's Landing" (where the Hilton-Dodge train crew would throw logs to raft or pile them aboard water barges); and another at Arthur A. Burn's "Little Place" that the black people referred to as "Oak Ridge." With all the oyster shells along the Haig's Point shore, there was probably one up there, too.

The oyster shelters were simply built, with walls, a door, a few windows, and a shed roof, approximately 10' x 12' in size, built near the water so the shells could fall through openings and go overboard. They also had an old wood heater as the winters were extremely cold. Oysters were only opened during daylight hours as there was no electricity. It was also agreed that half of the oyster shells would remain on the property of the landowner, which was a great help in preventing erosion.

The pickers and shuckers worked together, thus the need for a fast shucker was important for the money received from a gallon of oysters was divided equally between them. A fast shucker would open six to eight gallons of oysters a day while the average shucker opened three gallons. A form with holes was used to move the oysters over them to separate the sizes. For opening a gallon of standard sized oysters, the price was 45 cents and for selects, 55 cents. In the 1930s oysters were bringing $1.05 per gallon.[8]

Emil, Sr., had a horse and wagon that he used to travel to "Rabbit Point" and Cooper River to collect all the oysters that had been shucked. Oysters from The Branch, Jimmy Lee's, and Oak Ridge,

were carried to Benjie's Point by sailboat, ox-cart, or wagon—whatever was available.

On certain occasions some of the people opening oysters on the river bank above the Cooper River oyster shacks would miss Emil's wagon and would have to carry buckets of oysters on their heads the five miles to Benjie's Point and get paid ten cents a bucket.[9]

In the early years Henry Bryan would be paid $4.00 per night or about $35.00 per week for sailing the oysters to town in a Fripp boat named *Spider*, which was about twenty-two feet long and eight feet wide. It took all night to make the trip to Savannah and be back to the island the next day in time to carry another load.[10]

Leonard Jackson was hired to keep records, wash, measure, sort, then pack the oysters in gallon tin cans and store them on ice in a large chest-type cooler. He then saw that they were loaded on Henry Bryan's boat to be sailed to Savannah during the night.

Henry Bryan quit, then Henry Graham was hired to sail the oysters nightly, until he got shot by Rebecca Godman and died.

In the 1920s Emil Cetchovich, Sr., did not renew the Maggioni land-lease on his property, but started an oyster-shucking business of his own. It was his son, Emil, Jr., who carried the oysters—as many as 600 gallons a week—to the L. P. Maggioni Company in Savannah. He, too, would haul oysters at night and passengers in the daytime. On his return trips from Savannah, Emil, Jr., would bring back passengers, blocks of ice, supplies for their small store, and a lot of freight. Through the years the boats that the Cetchovichs owned were the *Priscilla, Zesseen, Jess Isle*, and the *Katie E.*[11]

(Emil Cetchovich, Jr., related this little story about one of his trips to Savannah: They had finished loading oysters, all the passengers were aboard, and the *Zesseen* had taken off from the dock. The weather was stormy; the wind was blowing a gale and the water was rough. When they got out of New River and into Walls Cut, a big puff of wind blew them high and dry—smack out of the water near Marker 42. Being frightened, everyone screamed but no one was hurt. They were so far up on the hill that the men had to get in a bateau, which Emil had been towing, return to the island, get their bateaus, shovels, and picks, and dig the forty-foot *Zesseen* out of the mud to get it back in the water.)

Oysters on the Decline

The oyster business in 1937 was on the decline "and went to the devil," so said Emil Cetchovich, Jr. The reason for the decline? He said the WPA, the Welfare, and the NRA (National Recovery Administration) were paying the workers more money than they could make working for him. Members of the Oyster Society had met in the church and voted against raking and shucking oysters any more. Emil said most of them quit and did nothing but receive a small check each month.

Oyster Factory Closes—Cetchovichs Leave Island

World War II commenced and with no help available the oyster-shucking factory closed. The older Cetchovichs were beginning to be in ill health and left the island circa 1942. They sold their place in 1945 to Fred and Mae Dierks.

Junior Graves Opens Oyster House

With permission to build on the Benjie's Point property of Mr. Fred H. Dierks, circa 1947, Junior Graves built a dock, a concrete-block

Junior Graves' Oyster-Shucking House.

Circa 1952. The last one on Daufuskie. Small house on left where pickers stored oysters overnight. (Photograph courtesy Mrs. Ida White-Tatum.)

439

oyster-shucking house with stalls, and a small receiving house, for the men to store their oysters in overnight.[12]

Junior's brother Woodrow (Woody) Graves and his wife Elsie managed the operation. In the 1940s-50s Woody hired Hinson A. White to oversee the washing, sorting, and packing of the oysters. One hundred gallons were shucked weekly with Woody carrying them to Bluffton until Jake Washington began carrying the mail for Mr. Dierks. Then Jake would carry the oysters three days a week on his mail run.

Oysters Polluted

In the early 1950s, South Carolina health officials warned Junior Graves that oysters on the south side of Daufuskie (which included Mongin Creek and the south branch of New River) were being polluted by contaminated waters of the Savannah River.

Mrs. Geraldine Wheelihan Manages Oyster House

In 1956 Hinson White quit the oyster business to supervise the road work on the island for the County. Gerry Wheelihan now managed the oyster house for Junior Graves. Two hundred gallons of oysters were being opened weekly. By this time shuckers were receiving $1.50 per gallon for standards and $1.60 for selects. On the market oysters were selling for four or five dollars a gallon.

Twice a week Gerry would carry oysters to Bluffton in her sixteen-foot bateau, powered by two, 10-HP Wizard outboard motors. A truck would meet her and take the oysters to the Maggioni factory in Savannah.

Oysters Dumped Overboard

Pickers were warned against gathering polluted oysters, but the Health Department had not posted any signs to this effect. There was no visible evidence that anything was wrong with the oysters until they were allowed to sit overnight. By the next morning they would smell terrible and turn pink or bloody looking. (Later diagnosed as "Pink Yeast.")

Gerry was not aware of this as the gallon cans and lids were tin and once the oysters were packed they remained on ice and were not opened until they reached the factory.

One day she was asked to report to the Savannah factory and was shown the polluted oysters for the first time. Ninety-six gallons had turned "pink" and had to be dumped overboard. She was informed that a good oyster washed in the same water as a polluted one would become contaminated. From that time on Gerry had to work more closely with the pickers to keep them away from the polluted areas and to make certain that polluted oysters did not leave the island.

Oyster House Closes

By 1959 the polluted waters had contaminated all the oyster beds on the island's south and west sides, through Rams Horn Creek up to, but not including, Cooper River.

Pickers were having too far to row to get the few good oysters left, and the shuckers were not getting enough oysters to keep them busy. So, the oyster house closed permanently in 1959.

An era had passed. After nearly seventy years no more oyster shucking would be done on Daufuskie.

Names of Pickers and Shuckers

Too many years have passed for the present generation to recall all who worked as pickers and shuckers during the oyster era. But it is only fitting to honor those who worked so hard and long in the cold winters to keep alive the only industry that Daufuskie ever had.

PICKERS:
Bentley: Charlie, Mingo
Brisbane: Dan, Peter, Richard
Brown: David, William (Gee Chee)
Bryan: Alfred, Backum, Backus, John, John, Jr.
Fripp: John
Grant: Cooley, Joe
Graves: Isaiah
Hamilton: Henry, James, Johnny Morris, William (Donkey)
Holmes: Samuel, Tom
Hudson: Rufus, William
Jenkins: Frankie, George, Robert

Miller: Boise, Clifford, Frank, Kit
Mitchell: Abe
Robinson: Josephus (Two-Time), Sipio
Simmons: Jake, Walter
Washington: Gabriel
Williams: George

SHUCKERS
Bentley: Amelia, Pet, Sally
Brisbane: Phyllis, Rebecca, Rose
Brown: Beck, Daisy, Marie
Bryan: Cynthia, Georgia, Leether, Lillie, Lizzie, Polly Ann, Sarah (Edna), Viola

Grant: Alice, Cornelia (Lemon), Sarah
Graves: Sylvia
Hamilton: Estella (Stella), Jane, Lizzie Bell (Della), Pender
Heyward: Flora
Holmes: Dove
Hudson: Missy
Jenkins: Angeline, Missy, Virginia
Lawrence: Nora
Locke: Betsy

McGraw: Hagar
Miller: Carrie, Geneva, Lena
Myers: Bell
Simmons: Agnes, Lillie
Robinson: Albertha, Louvenia (Blossom), Susie
Smith: Susie (Muffet)
Stafford: Hattie, Lula
Washington: Agnes
Wiley: Geneva
Williams: Laura
Wilson: Lissie, Sally.[14]

Fate of the Last Oyster House

When the oyster business closed the block oyster house belonged to Fred Dierks for the use of his land. Fred and Mae left the island in 1963 and subsequently both passed away, leaving their only child, Joann Dierks Yarbrough, to inherit the property.

Erosion claimed the small concrete-block receiving house near the dock. In the 1970s Joann had the remains of the old block oyster house torn down and let the Strojny family build a summer cottage close to the same spot.

Oyster Condition in 1990

In the 1970s the city of Savannah constructed a sewerage treatment plant to purify the water that would be discharged into the Savannah River. Union Camp Paper Company and other industries were also compelled to clean up the waste water they were dumping into the river.

Daufuskie was hoping that after several years the water would be purified sufficiently to allow the oysters to make a comeback. This has not proven so.

The water was polluted so completely from the Savannah River and with the aggravation of fuel from boat marinas, plus housing developments, the oysters have almost been exhausted. Only a few edible ones remain at Cooper River and at Freeport Creek between Haig Point and Melrose.

Oyster shells gracing the shoreline around the island are the only

visible evidence that an oyster business ever existed. They, too, will soon be gone.

Today there are no longer any "select" (single) oysters in Beaufort County—only "standard" in size.

L. P. Maggioni Company in Savannah now sells only canned oysters (none raw in the gallon, nor shell oysters) and their company in Beaufort sells only bags of oysters in the shell—over fifty pounds for $16.00.[15]

Notes

1. Mrs. Joy Fripp Canady, Columbus, Ga., personal files, 15 April 1983.

2. Mr. L. Paul Maggioni, Savannah, Ga., interview 29 September 1983; Fran Smith, "Maggioni Family Still Harvest Seafood," *Packet*, 1 July 1982; Gerhard Spieler, "County Has Only Steam Oyster Cannery," *Beaufort Gazette*, 16 September 1986.

3. Beaufort County Courthouse, Deed Book 30, p. 449.

4. Ibid., p. 456.

5. Emil Cetchovich, interview, 6 September 1984.

6. Beaufort County Records, Clerk of R. M. C. & C. C. P. & G. S., Lease Book 2, p. 66. (This was the former lease of J. P. Chaplin, Daufuskie, 1 September 1914.)

7. Ibid., Lease Book 1, pp. 176-180. (This was the former lease of E. V. Toomer, Hilton Head, 12 November 1914.)

8. Emil Cetchovich, Jr.

9. Johnny Hamilton interview, 5 May 1985.

10. Emil Cetchovich, Jr.

11. Ibid.

12. Mrs. Joann Dierks Yarbrough.

13. Mrs. Geraldine Wheelihan interview, 10 June 1990.

14. For the names of the pickers and shuckers, thanks and appreciation go to Mr. Johnny Hamilton, Mrs. Lillie Simmons, Mr. Hinson A. White, and Mrs. Geneva Wiley.

15. A personal telephone call to both the Savannah and Beaufort L. P. Maggioni Companies, 26 October 1990.

OYSTER SHACKS

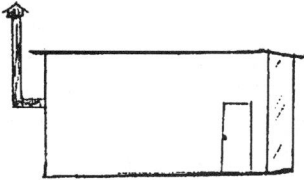

Front view

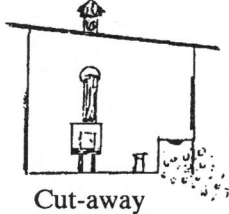

Cut-away
side view

Back view

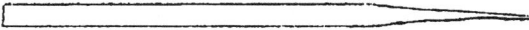

Side view

Top view

TOOLS

Oyster Knife

Oyster Cracker

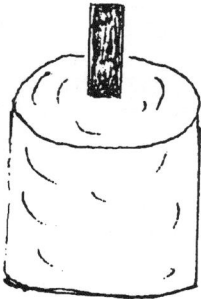

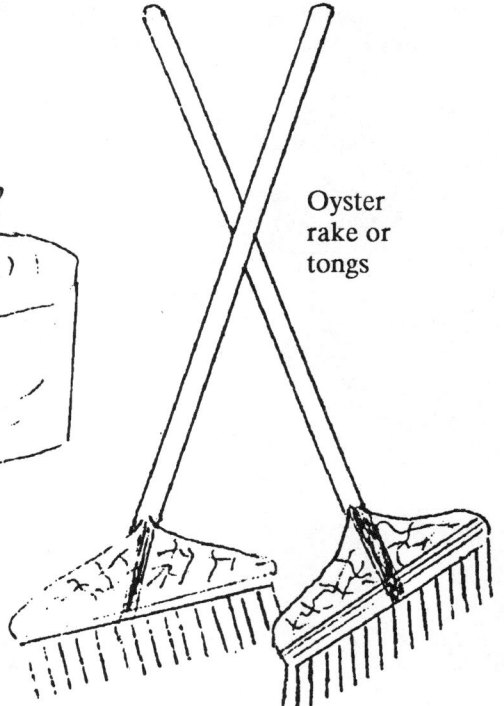

Oyster
rake or
tongs

Front
view

Side
view

"The Breakers"
John L. Wall sitting on steps. (Photograph courtesy Mr. Gilbert J. Maggioni.)

Fireman Jim in Boiler Room

Oyster Worker and Family
(Photographs courtesy Mr. Gilbert J. Maggioni.)

446

Oyster Steaming Crew
Ernie W. Dufloque right front. Others unknown. (Photographs courtesy Mr. Gilbert J. Maggioni.)

Maggioni workers left to right: Lee Gilford, John L. Wall, Walee E. Park, Unknown, Ernie W. Dufloque, Tom Gilford; front, Adam Fisher.

(Photographs courtesy Mr. Gilbert Maggioni.)

L.P. Maggioni Work Boat—Captain Raderick in Pilot House

Looking northward, note J.P. Chaplin wharf in background. Note boxes of canned oysters stacked on dock, lower left.

(Photographs courtesy Mr. Gilbert J. Maggioni.)

Side Looking Northward

Maggioni and Company from Wharf

(Photographs courtesy Mr. Gilbert J. Maggioni.)

Northern View

Oyster Cannery on Daufuskie
(Photographs courtesy Mr. Gilbert J. Maggioni.)

River View of Operation

Aunt Elsie, Housekeeper and Cook
(Photograph courtesy Mr. Gilbert J. Maggioni.)

Nick Aprea (standing), Gilbert Phillip Maggioni (right), man on the
left and black boy, names unknown. (Photograph courtesy Mr. Gilbert J.
Maggioni.)

Unknown young people having a Daufuskie oyster roast. (Photograph courtesy Mr. Gilbert J. Maggioni.)

Unknown Young People Having Fun on Daufuskie
(Photographs courtesy Mr. Gilbert J. Maggioni.)

15

STORMS AND
OTHER PHENOMENA

Cyclone, storm, hurricane—by whatever name it is called—
sends chills up and down the spine of anyone who has weathered one. Situated "on a northwestern edge of a major hurricane
'corridor' which originates in the Atlantic Ocean just above the
Equator," South Carolina, about once every four years, has been
visited and affected by tropical storms.[1]

"The concave South Carolina coastline and broad shelf act as a
funnel and make the tides rise higher here, to heights of seven to nine
feet."[2]

Only a few of the many storms have done any real damage on
Daufuskie. With no communication in the early years, storms just
sneaked up on Daufuskie residents. They only knew that when the
wind blew in gusts and the rains came in sheets, a storm was descend-
ing upon them. With no time for preparation, under the circumstances
they did the best they could to secure their homes and protect their
animals. Because it was so remote, news of a catastrophe on the island
did not reach the mainland until sometimes days after it happened.

Tornadoes have ripped through the island many times without
anyone's knowledge until someone noticed the line of trees that had
been leveled in its path. A tornado in 1927 removed Pender Hamilton's
house from its wooden pillars and sat it on the ground.

There's no one on the island to recall, but without a doubt Daufuskie
felt the effects of the 1886 Charleston earthquake. At 1:12 A.M., 3
August 1959, the house shook, the cups in the cupboard and the
window panes rattled something fierce from the effects of a New
Jersey earthquake.[3]

456

Although a storm has been reported as early as May (1934) and as late as October (1792), the majority of them arrive during August and September. It was in 1954 that hurricanes began to carry a female name—until the Women's Lib movement when male names were also included. (In jest, a person asked, "Do you know why storms are called 'hurricanes'?" The answer: "Because, whoever heard of a 'himmicane'?")

The island might have gotten some of the wind and rain from several others, but the actual storms that have affected Daufuskie to any degree have been the cyclone of August 27th and 28th, 1893; the hurricane of 1940; Gracie, September 29, 1959; and David, September 4th and 5th, 1979.

The 1893 Cyclone

There were three storms in 1893: one on June 16, another August 27-28, and the third October 13, but the one in August was the most severe with 140 mile winds. In fact, it was so bad that it will go down in history as the worst storm ever to hit South Carolina, including Hugo on September 21-22, 1989.

There was an 18 to 20-foot surge, but it did not completely inundate Daufuskie because it is higher than other islands in the area.

On Daufuskie the Bloody Point Lighthouse near the beach was damaged and some of the smaller buildings were swept off their footing, but were later retrieved. Keeper Robert A. Sisson did not report on the severity of the storm, but was reimbursed by the lighthouse department for food and clothing that was damaged or swept away. (See Bloody Point Lighthouse section.)

At Melrose, Bertie Stoddard was at home alone. When the storm progressed he went to the attic and lay flat on the floor until it was over. The house stood firm but the lovely gardens were completely destroyed. They later were replanted but were never the same.

The house at Bloody Point also weathered the storm, but the flower gardens were were also completely destroyed.

There were not any stories handed down among the black people; therefore the storm to them was probably no different from any other that had hit the island.

At Coosaw Island "there was a schooner drawing fourteen feet of

Melrose after the 1893 Storm

All of the flower gardens were destroyed. (Photograph courtesy Mr. Albert H. Stoddard III.)

Pilot Boy

Boats washed ashore in Beaufort during 1893 storm. (Photograph courtesy Mr. Roger Pinckney.)

water loading at the Pacific Mines that was carried three miles over the marsh. . . . The tide must have been between twelve and eighteen feet above mean high tide. . . . One of the Coosaw tug boats was near Gardner's Corner, about five miles inland."[4]

Miss C. Mabel Burn, a Beaufort teacher and cousin of Arthur A. Burn on Daufuskie, gave a first-hand account of this storm:

In 1893, we [in Beaufort] had the most terrible hurricane that this coast has experienced in a very long time.

It was Sunday, August 27th, 1893. We all went to church, but it began to rain, and we hurried home.

All day the wind blew in gusts and rain fell. As evening came on the wind blew harder. Tide was due to be high about 5 P.M. and should have been low water about midnight, but as night settled down, the wind increased in velocity and the tide was held up and could not fall, so the next tide piled on top of the first, and by midnight the ocean had come in over St. Helena and Lady's Island and flooded Beaufort. The wind grew higher and higher, until it reached 125 miles per hour.

The waves of the sea dashed against houses and on the Point where we were living, all small houses were washed away; not one was left standing when morning came.

Around 1 A.M. there was a furious ringing of our door bell, and a tall negro man we knew asked if he might bring women and children to our front porch as all their houses were gone, and they had them in boats seeking shelter. My father said, "No, the piazza is about to go as it is only held up by one column. Bring them into the house." So in a room used as a private school room, and equipped with benches and chairs they were sheltered the rest of the night. Three trips of the big ferry boat were made, bringing 12 to 15 people each trip, so we had around 30 people sheltered for the night. They had lost everything they possessed except what was on their backs. When morning came, two old colored people, man and wife, were drowned. One lay at our front door, the other the back.

The wind came from the east, so I stood at the west windows and watched what was taking place. Huge waves dashed against the causeway near the house, and the wind cut them off and carried the water far back in town. All night this kept up.

Way in the worst of the storm we heard a crash. Boards from a house on the next corner from ours, probably 200 feet away, had been torn off and driven end ways through the side of our house. The house was so badly ruined we had to leave it when the storm was over.

Toward 5 A.M. the wind began to abate, and when daylight came, it was over. But what a wreck.

The water front was a shambles. The cotton gin of George Waterhouse was entirely demolished. The two great boilers were carried by the waves and landed against the bluff in front of the Sea Island Hotel.

The Steamer *Clifton,* a steam boat which operated between Beaufort and Savannah, was carried by the waves to the bend beyond the Court House and placed right against the bluff. A deep channel had to be dug in order to get her afloat after the storm passed.

Capt. George Crofut saved his tug boat by running with the wind and putting the boat against the bluff in front of the court house. This too, had to be dug out after the storm passed.

All goods stored in the basements of the stores on the water front were lost, unless merchants took warning on the approach of the storm and removed them to higher ground.

Roofs of the stores were torn off and Bay Street a shambles. Every street in town was piled as high as the house tops with uprooted trees, demolished houses, household furniture, etc. It was impossible to get through the streets without climbing over and under debris.

As almost all houses depended on cistern water for the homes. They were under the houses and filled with water by gutters from the roofs when it rained. Those were now full of salt water and none could be used. We had a bad time. The water we had to depend on was from a well owned by Capt. C. C. Townsend who was mayor of the city at the time, and so we got small buckets or jars from him until the cisterns could be cleaned out and the rain refilled them.

For weeks fires were kept burning in the streets and dead bodies of dogs, chickens, etc., were flung in and burned for they could not be buried.

Miss Clara Barton and the Red Cross came and lent all the aid they could to relieve the distress, and this was very valuable to the helpless.

Communication with the outside world was cut off, as of course we had no electricity nor telephones, so relatives from other places were much distressed until rail or boat communication could be resumed.

There was only one white person lost that I remember of. It was Dr. Hazel, brother of Mrs. Susan Rice. He was quarantine doctor on Parris Island at the outgoing sea depot, and he was drowned. We understood he lost his life in an effort to save the lives of two negro boys. There was much difficulty in getting the body to the Baptist cemetery, as streets were piled high with debris, but by many windings and sending men

ahead with axes to cut the debris of trees, etc., the hearse finally made it and he was buried.

But on St. Helena and Lady's Island hundreds of people were drowned, almost entirely negro, for they had no way to escape, and the people of Beaufort town could not get to them, as there was no bridge to cross the river, boats only could be used, and these were a wreck and sunken so not available.

For weeks men hunted these islands for the bodies, and when found buried them at once, for no funerals could be held.

Well, finally all was over and Beaufort picked up and started over again.

And on September 29th, 1959, we were still here to undergo hurricane "Gracie" who did her best to demolish us, but she failed and we are still on hand and getting back to normal. "Gracie" did not have the help of the ocean that 1893 did, so she did her best but the ocean did not help her.[5]

The Hurricane of 1940

This storm did more damage to Daufuskie than any other recorded since 1893. Usually, perhaps part of a roof is blown off or a few trees uprooted, but this storm on 10 August 1940, with its 130-mile winds, destroyed Mt. Carmel Church No. 1 and Praise House at Cooper River. It played havoc over the entire island and blew down so many trees, making some of the roads impassable.

Malcolm and Josephine Johnson operated Gus Ohman's Benjie's Point store and she was the postmaster. Josephine related her story concerning this storm: Sunday was a big day—the boat *Clivedon* brought the mail twice on the Sabbath—once at 11 in the morning coming from Savannah on its way to Beaufort, and again at 6:30 in the afternoon on its way back.

In order to conserve time, the captain of the boat usually blew his whistle when he came out of Fields Cut so that Josephine could have the mail down to the dock when he arrived. On the morning of Sunday, 10 August 1940, Malcolm and Josephine had waked up to a dreary, rainy day and by 9:30 the wind had picked up and the rain was pouring down. At the usual time, Josephine did not hear the boat blow and wondered why, but she went ahead and put the mail in the sacks anyway so she would be ready. Realizing that for some reason the boat

would be late, she sat down in the post office section of the store and started crocheting on a tablecloth she was making. Turning on the radio, it was then that she heard the announcement of a hurricane with 90 mph winds that would come ashore at noon on the high spring tide, between Savannah and Beaufort. They wanted to leave in their boat for Bluffton but it was too late for that. The water was so rough, and with the tide rising so quickly, lines were being snapped and boats were getting away. Malcolm rode through the island telling everyone about the storm.

By this time the pigeon houses were blown down, Coca Cola crates that had been stacked on the back porch of the store were flying through the air, and gasoline drums were being blown about. It blew the roof off the storage building, ruining feed, sugar, flour, grits, meal—all of the store supplies. The pony stable collapsed, everywhere trees were being uprooted, and debris was flying through the air.

The store was less than a quarter of a mile from New River and was between two and three feet off the ground, but with the tide 12-14 feet above normal and heavy rains, water was coming in the door of the store. An oak tree went through the screened side porch of their house. When part of the roof blew off the store there came a lull and they made their way through the tree limbs and went to the house, which was nearby. The radio and Delco were gone, so they had no way of knowing what was happening.

The storm came back that evening. They remained in the house, putting mattresses on the floor in a hall that had no windows, huddling there for the remainder of the night, while they heard things being tossed about outside.

At daylight on Monday morning, 11 August, they could not believe what they saw. Fallen trees, roofing tin, debris was everywhere. Everyone on the island had been spared, but it was a living nightmare and one they hoped that they would never have to go through again.

Malcolm was farming and pasturing his cows at Melrose. There was an old barn up there for the animals to get in out of the weather. They just knew that the building had blown down on top of them and killed them all. But when Malcolm saddled up his horse and rode up there, all the cows were fine and the building was still standing.[6]

463

"Gracie" in 1959

Gracie came in on Tuesday, 29 September 1959, with 120-mile winds that were terrific, damaged some roofs, blew down some trees, tore up docks, strewed tons of debris, but other than that, little damage was done. The tide was low so there was no flooding.

Other Hurricanes

Daufuskie got some wind from David, 4 September 1979, with maybe a tree or two down, but nothing serious. The sample applies to other storms that have come since then, including Hugo, 21-22 September 1989—no real damage was done.

Freeze of 1950

On Friday, 24 November 1950, the weather was warm, everyone on Daufuskie was in his or her shirt sleeves, busy with everyday activities. They went to bed that night, but before daylight a cold wave had crept in to the coast, driving the temperature down to 19 degrees. The island had no electricity and only a few had battery-operated radios. Because it was so warm, no one bothered to turn on the radio to listen to the news.

Arthur A. "Papy" Burn was one of those who had a 500-gallon tank of water, and that very afternoon he, his daughter Teddy, and her husband Frank Beard had just completed Papy's new bathroom. To celebrate the occasion, each of them took a bath and went to bed. They remembered they had reached for extra covering during the night, but thought nothing of it. The next morning, Saturday, the 25th of November, when everyone got out of bed it was so-o-o-o cold! They found every water pipe frozen and the commode had burst. Papy Burn was fit to be tied. He was a cursing man anyway, but he was so mad the things he said that morning almost thawed the pipes and curled them up. But that wasn't all. He also had two cars with "busted" blocks. Papy started in again. When he ran out of curse words, he made up some new ones.

Very few people had running water, so frozen pipes were not their problem. However, every car, truck, and tractor on the island never ran again; the blocks had burst in all of them. In Savannah, 2500 cars had frozen; the weather had slipped up on them, too!

464

The First Big Snow

The winter of 1968 brought the island's first big snow with at least six inches remaining on the ground for several days. It was also the most snow the black people had ever seen. Some of them were so scared and started praying; they thought the world was coming to an end.

Total Eclipse of the Sun

Near 2 P.M., Saturday, 7 March 1970, Daufuskie experienced a total eclipse of the sun (the moon came between the sun and the earth). There was complete darkness for only a short while, then it was all over. It was eerie and real weird. Nothing like that had ever been seen in this part of the country before, and will probably never happen again.[7]

Another Freeze

On Christmas, 1983, another freeze hit Beaufort County, but this time it was a different story for Daufuskie. Being forewarned by TV and radio made a big difference. With anti-freeze in radiators or draining the water out of the blocks, no cars were frozen. However, with eleven-degree weather, some water pipes did burst.

Sprinkler systems and water pipes thawing out all over the County caused much damage, especially in condos where the water leaked from one story to the next, causing ceilings to fall, furniture to become ruined, and carpets to be soaked and ruined. There was more damage caused by the freeze than by most hurricanes.[8]

First White Christmas

Between the 24th and 26th of December 1989, six to eight inches of snow fell on Daufuskie, making it our first white Christmas in history. The temperature hovered around twelve degrees, which counted for the snow lasting over a week. It was beautiful. Everyone had a big time making snow men, throwing snowballs, and eating snow cones.[9]

Notes

1. Dr. Laylon Wayne Jordan, "A History of Storms on the South Carolina Coast," Department of History, College of Charleston, p. 2.

465

2. Don Grush, "Ominous Implications Heard in Island Speeches," *Island Packet*, Friday, 2 March 1984.

3. Cliff Sewell, *Savannah Now and Then* (Savannah: The Printcraft Press, Inc., 1974) p. 85.

4. *The State*, 3 September 1893; *News & Courier* , 7 December 1893.

5. Certified, a correct personal experience of the 1893 and 1959 storms of Beaufort County by Miss C. Mabel Burn, 3 November 1959.

6. Mrs. Josephine Johnson interview, 14 September 1990; Fran Smith, "Mrs. Johnson Remembers A Hurricane," *Island Packet*, Tuesday, 7 September 1976.

7. *Beaufort Gazette*, Thursday, 12 March 1970.

8. *Packet*, Wednesday, 4 January 1984.

9. *Beaufort Gazette*, Friday, 4 December 1989.

16

FIRSTS, EVENTS,
AND HAPPENINGS

In 1908 Henry Ford introduced the Model-T to the market at a basic cost of $850. The first car to arrive on Daufuskie was a Model-T Ford belonging to Birdie Stoddard who owned Melrose. The vintage is unknown, but it had to be one prior to 1918 for the family left the island that year.

Ohman's Store

Situated near the public landing at Benjie's Point, Gus Ohman's store, built 1910-1912, was probably the most popular one on the island. He had everything a country person could want, but the most sought-after item was what the clerk, Joe Loper, called "a slash" and sold for 8 cents.

To prepare a "slash" Joe would take his sharp butcher knife (Francis A. Burn said he could see him now) and right down the center, through the wrapper, he would cut out a plug from a 5 cent loaf of bread, being careful not to cut through the bottom. Holding the plug in his left hand, he would place the loaf under the spigot of the syrup barrel and let 3 cents worth of syrup run in the cavity. Joe would then place the plug back in the bread, wrap it all up in a piece of brown store paper, tie it with some white string, then pass it over the counter to the customer. Many a working person had a "slash" for lunch or one was bought as a treat to munch on while walking down the road.

Other Establishments

There had been many stores on the island but the last two country stores belonged to Fred and Mae Dierks at Benjie's Point and Samuel Holmes at Cooper River.

Opening in the early 1960s to catch the riverboat trade were beer stops that might have oyster roasts, with some providing foods like crabburgers, hamburgers, hotdogs, boiled shrimp, or chicken and dumplings. On New River was Fred H. Dierks' place called Twin Oaks at Benjie's Point; Sefton Williams' place, where John Fripp lived at one time; and Jolly Shores, operated by Lance Burn at the old Fuller Fripp place. Sam Stevens' Night Club was located at Cooper River. By 1965 all of them had closed except Sam Stevens who continued to operate until the 1980s. The reason Sam stayed open so long was that he brought most of his customers on his own boats from Savannah, while the others had to depend on limited river traffic, which wasn't enough to sustain them.

First Aid

In the early 1900s there were "angels of mercy." These were people who lived on Daufuskie and cared enough to help in time of need. One such person was Harriet Chaplin Fripp, wife of McNair Fripp. The black people called her "Miss Halley." She lived with her husband in a cottage on the property of Dick Fripp, Jr., at Benjie's Point. "Miss Halley" was always available at any time day or night.

After "Miss Halley" died in 1912, her relative, Elizabeth Medlock (later Cetchovich) took her place in helping with the injured and the sick.

Animal-Dipping Vats

Cows and horses on the island had problems with flies, ticks, and fleas. The Beaufort County Health Department in the 1920s had two dipping vats built on the island. These remain today—one on the property of John Fripp (now Ward property) and the other at Gus Ohman's (now Mobley's place). These vats were formed of poured concrete, made deep on one end where the animal entered the vat, while on the other end was a ramp which the animal could walk up to get out. The vats were filled with water and chemicals that would kill the parasites and discourage the flies for awhile.

Social and Welfare Workers

During the 1930s a Mrs. Platt was the social worker who took care of their needs and especially saw that commodities were given to families who were hungry.

Mary Frances Horton served as the Welfare worker during the late 1940s and early 1950s. Welfare checks were being given in the amount of about $15 per month to families who were in need. Emil Cetchovich remarked that the oyster business began failing by 1939 when his help got more money from welfare than they received while working for him.

First Form of Communication

In the early 1940s Mr. Fred H. Dierks was given a sheriff's battery-operated ship-to-shore radio, to be kept in his store on New River to insure a prompt response should anyone get sick or hurt or if a death had occurred. Many of the early calls were from Beaufort Sheriff J. E. McTeer stating that he had reports of a whiskey still on Daufuskie. If he got more than one complaint, the sheriff would be compelled to make a trip to the island. He would come over, borrow Mr. Dierks' vehicle to find the still, using axes to smash it to pieces. No one would ever get caught making whiskey for they would get wind of the sheriff's coming and would be on their way to Savannah to buy more brass tubing to get back in business as soon as he left the island.

When electricity came, Mr. Dierks' battery radio was exchanged for an electric one. He kept it until 1963 when he and Mrs. Dierks moved to Savannah. The radio was then turned over to Lance and Billie Burn at Jolly Shores, and was removed from their premises in 1984.

First Electricity

In 1951 the South Carolina Electric and Gas Company in Ridgeland had the necessary land easements signed by those residents across whose property the telephone poles and wires would be placed.

From May until August of 1952 Mr. Irvin Tavel, Edisto Beach, was responsible for having the right-of-way cut.

Immediately following the clearing of the line the electric company brought men to erect the poles and string the wire. Some of the black men boarded with black families on the island. The majority of the white workers boarded with Geraldine Wheelihan who operated Gus Ohman's old store and lived in his former house at Benjie's Point.

Where the men slept Gerry designated as "the bull pen." She provided food and lodging for them during the week, but on weekends the men would return to their perspective homes, then back on the

469

island early Monday morning. Hattie Hamilton Stafford helped Gerry with the cooking and cleaning.

Not one house on the island had been previously wired for electricity, which now was the responsibility of each home owner. By July, 1953, everyone on the island had electricity for the first time.

Nurse on Island

Mrs. Anne Pitts, R.N., was sent by the South Carolina State Board of Health to make visits on the island circa 1950s-1980s. She would come to the island when she was needed, frequently by helicopter, arriving on the island at 10 A.M. and leaving at 3:30 P.M. She also came by boat through the courtesy of Sam Stevens, Joe Joyce, Chief Toomer, Clarence Hodge, and sometimes she would ride with the doctor on a Naval Hospital boat that had the necessary equipment to make X-rays of people with possible lung problems. She worked mainly with the midwife, Sarah Grant, and her patients, but Mrs. Pitts made routine examinations of those with sore throats, took blood pressures, and bandaged injuries, but unless Dr. Donald Gatch, or another doctor, accompanied her, she was limited as to what she could do.

Geraldine Wheelihan was operating the old Gus Ohman store and allowed Mrs. Pitts to examine her patients on a table in the former post office section. Since the store was near the dock, it saved time and was more convenient for the people to come there rather than have Mrs. Pitts visit them. Of course, Gerry always gave a helping hand if she was needed and provided transportation for Mrs. Pitts to visit anyone in their home should they be too sick to come to the store.[1]

Polio Vaccine

At Mary Fields Elementary in May of 1963, Mrs. Anne Pitts and her aids gave the Salk Polio Vaccine on a cube of sugar to everyone on the island.[2] Through these past eighty years there has been only one known case of polio on Daufuskie, but possibly there was a second.

Emergency Medical Service

Since Geraldine Wheelihan had worked with Mrs. Pitts, in 1965 Paul Holmes, Captain of the Hilton Head Rescue Squad, came to the island and gave Gerry First Aid instructions. She was then authorized

to help with minor injuries or complaints on the island, using a personal truck for transportation. In 1967 Paul returned to the island, teaching a class in First Aid to several who were interested. Gerry helped with this class. Because she was dedicated to the work and had a strong desire to help in the community, by 1970 she was chosen as volunteer director of the Daufuskie EMS. The first ambulance she was given to use was small, but the others have been large and fully equipped to take care of any emergency. She also has a walkie-talkie that is constantly her companion.

Gerry's assistant is her son, Gerald M. Yarborough. On occasion they have attended several classes to be trained in special fields that have made them better qualified to serve.

International Paper has permitted them to ride on any of their Haig Point boats to transport patients to Hilton Head.

Beaufort-Jasper Comprehensive Health Services

BJCHS through Mr. Thomas C. Barnell, Jr., brought aid to Daufuskie residents in the 1970s. Miss Frances Jones and Miss Mary Washington were the first to work with the program in visiting patients and filling out the proper forms in getting them to the clinic at Chelsea.

First Telephone

In October, 1972, to those who wanted them, the first free telephones were installed and free service was granted by Joseph Limerick, Jr., president of the newly formed Coastal Carolina Utilities, Inc.

Joe was challenged by Hargray Telephone Company which in 1954 had been granted a PSC certificate to provide service to the island. Hargray had not provided service, stating that it was not economically feasible.

To be supportive of Joe, on Monday, 18 December 1972, eight-five island residents (mostly black) rode buses to Columbia, staying overnight, to testify in his behalf before the South Carolina Public Service Commission: they wanted phone service from no one but Joe. However, after a thirty-day deliberation by the SCPSC, on 14 March 1973, Hargray won the case but was required to furnish telephone service to the island within ninety days. This they did, through a microwave and by using underground cable.[3]

471

On 10 June 1973 there were eleven resident phones and a public phone near the county dock.

The first telephone book for Daufuskie was 6-1/2 X 9-1/2 inches in size. It came out in 1974 with twenty-two telephone numbers listed.

In 1990 the telephone directory measures 9 x 11 inches and contains 196 Daufuskie telephone numbers.

Voting

Voting in the early 1900s was done in the front yard at Gus Ohman's store. "Poll Tax" of $1.00 was prerequisite by a voter in order to participate in an election. When poll taxes were not paid, the men were fined, paying it off by working on the County roads.

On Daufuskie the court wanted the men to go to Beaufort to work off their fines, but Jim Goodwin, who was the road supervisor, informed the men that there were no shade trees in Beaufort where they had to work, so they were allowed to work out their fines on Daufuskie roads.

In South Carolina the poll tax was abolished 23 January 1964, when the 24th Amendment to the Constitution outlawed payment of the tax.[4]

When Arthur A. Burn came to the island in 1913 there were 600 black people but only 53 white male voters—the blacks would not and the women were not allowed to vote.

Black men had been granted the privilege to vote when they were freed by the Emancipation Proclamation by President Abraham Lincoln; this became effective 1 January 1863, but it was not until 26 August 1920 when the 19th Amendment to the Constitution became law that women gained the right to vote.[5] Indians were not allowed to vote until 1924.

On Daufuskie there were no fancy voting machines with levers to pull by numbers. A ballot was simply marked with a pencil while sitting at a table or bench placed in the yard, under the shade of a low-hanging branch of a live oak tree.

Back in the early days the voting was done on a Tuesday, but the results could not be sent into Beaufort until Friday when the steamer *Clivedon* came, which was the island's only means of communication.

In 1934 Daufuskie's late vote count prevented a runoff for Beaufort

472

County Auditor. All 12 votes went to Gary Black, giving him the victory.

After Mr. Ohman left the island, Malcolm and Josephine operated his store and post office. It was they who held the voting precinct from 1938 to 1945. When they moved back to Bluffton in 1945, the voting precinct was put in the hands of Fred H. and Mae Dierks, who shortly thereafter were given a sheriff's radio. They too had voters marking their ballots at tables or benches under shade trees in the yard, or inside the store if the weather was inclement.

But things were now changed—voters were hurried to the poll by truck, wagon, or ox cart to cast their votes so that returns could be tallied and the managers go home. The results were *called* into the Beaufort sheriff, sometimes as early as 9:30 A.M. on election day.

With the island now equipped with a radio, a different situation occurred when Mr. Black ran for auditor in 1954: early on election day the island radioed that it had cast a big margin for Mr. Black. His opponent charged that this report started a rush to the Black "Bandwagon."

It was discovered that early ballot totals sent to Beaufort via the radio had a decisive effect on the other voters of the County. "As Daufuskie votes—so votes the County."

Those running for office started complaining, but it wasn't until circa 1962 that early reporting of returns was stopped. Daufuskie could not send in a report until the poles closed at 7 P.M. With so few votes, Daufuskie continued to be the first to call in their voting totals.[6]

South Carolina Governor James F. Byrnes visited the island in 1960 to see the place that played such an important role in one of his early political campaigns by reporting late and giving him enough votes to prevent a runoff. It was also a good time for him to visit his old classmate Arthur A. Burn.

The only way to vote was to register, which had to be done in Beaufort. In 1959, when Lance and Billie Burn returned to the island to operate their business, Jolly Shores, they found out that a good number of black people would like to vote but had no way to get to Beaufort. The Burns had brought their boat *Dandy* with them when they came from Ft. Lauderdale, so they loaded up twenty-one black women and men aboard and took them to Savannah. After arriving

there, Geraldine Wheelihan and Billie Burn made several trips to Beaufort to register them to vote. Using only a two-seated car, and despite a flat tire and other delays, finally everyone was registered and back on the island before dark.

Later, the County sent a voter registration team to the island to save the people the misery of having to go all the way to Beaufort.

From 1960 to 1962, Billie Burn as manager, Hinson White as clerk, and Viola Bryan and Sarah Grant as box managers supervised the voting at Jolly Shores. In 1963 when Billie was made postmaster, it was against Postal policy for her to participate in the voting process.

Clifford Boyd accepted the responsibility as voting manager from 1964 to 1968, with Hinson, Viola, and Sarah working with him, but the precinct was held at the Mary Fields Elementary School. The radio was at Jolly Shores so when the votes were tabulated after 7 P.M., Clifford would bring the results to Billie and she would phone them in to the Beaufort sheriff's office.

Clifford left the island in 1969 and Geraldine and Stewart Wheelihan inherited the job of running the voting precinct which they held at Jane Hamilton school at Cooper River. Ballots were marked in a small, self-standing wooden booth with a curtain across the front. having no water or electricity made this building very undesirable and miserable. Before the next election the Wheelihans returned to Mary Fields Elementary with all of its conveniences.

Sometimes if the election is going to be a close one, poll watchers will be present. Usually the blacks vote in a Democratic block whereas most of the whites vote on an individual basis for the person they think better qualified.

Telephones came to the island in 1973 which gave Gerry the opportunity to call in her own results of the elections.

In 1990 Gerry Wheelihan continues to manage the voting precinct with 67 registered voters. Stewart Wheelihan serves as clerk with Ella Mae Stevens and Agnes Simmons as box managers. In the past, when needed, Mrs. Gillian White has served as a box manager. If there are more than two voting boxes, another manager is hired.

Geraldine, having served as Committee Person, has attended political meetings in Beaufort and Columbia.

Normally, we have had only Democratic precincts, but with all of

the new people who have come to the island, for a couple of times the Republicans have also had theirs.

Secret Orders

There were three secret lodges or orders on Daufuskie. Officials from Savannah came to instruct the people in getting them organized and set up.

1. *The Oyster Union Society.* This was begun in October of 1919 to financially benefit the oyster gatherers and shuckers when they were sick or disabled and couldn't work.

2. *The Knights of Pythias "Pity"* was begun in 1916 and ended circa 1934.

3. *The Odd Fellows*—started in 1927, ended circa 1930.[7]

Once the organizations were established, meetings were held once a month in the Maryfield Praise House on the grounds of the First Union African Baptist Church. There were few in the beginning but grew to approximately fifty members. Dues were $1.00 per month.

They needed a building of their own and found out that the James P. Chaplin, Jr., two-story house was vacant and for sale, and the Chaplins also had a piece of land that the members could buy. So, from Mrs. J. P. Chaplin, 8 March 1921, the Union Sisters and Brothers bought the house and one task (1/4 acre) of land.[8]

> We brake 'em down 'n mov'em boad by boad on we task of ground. Older mens like Charlie Bentley, Josepheus Robinson, Joe Riley, and William Hudson brok 'em down and younger mens like Johnny Hamilton and Willie Bentley draw nails. Winda sheets wuz taken out and replaced.

After the building was reassembled, it was known as the "Hall," and the members continued to meet once a month.

The *Oyster Society* met downstairs of the meeting Hall. Women were included in this organization and were afraid to go up the stairs where all the shenanigans were going on.

The *Knights of Pythias* and the *Odd Fellows,* being strictly for the men, held their meeting upstairs. They had some funny things taking place that were boisterous and scared the women, especially on "nition" night that was sometimes really wild.

New members would have to go through an initiation process, one of the tests being to view a "dead man." A small casket that one of the carpenters had made was lined with pine straw. They fashioned a man's "head" using moss as his hair. Then the whole thing inside was covered with a white sheet with just the "head" showing, with maybe a little catsup scattered about as "blood." The member would be brought in blindfolded, then after much ado as to how the "man" had been butchered with an axe—the whole gory bit—they would open the casket, take off the blindfold, and see the reaction of the member, followed by much backslapping and merriment.

Another thing they required in the initiation was to have a member jump on a triangular board with dozens of "nails" with their pointed ends sticking upward. The joke was that the "nails" were black rubber that looked like nails, but the member did not know this. While the regular members were guffawing and jeering at him, it would take him awhile to get up enough nerve to run and jump on these so called "nails." With enough libation, he would finally throw caution to the wind and away he would go, only to find to his delightful surprise that when he landed on the nails they were soft and were not the real thing. (The "coffin" and the triangle with the "nails" remain on the island.) A few of the male members were Charlie and Jimmy Bentley, David Brown, Ben and William Bryan, Joe Haynes, Frank and George Jenkins, McKinley and Rufus Hudson, Morris Hamilton, Charlie Myers, Joe Riley, and Josepheus Robinson.

The members of all the orders would have parties and sell shrimp, crabs, and have oyster roasts—anything to make money for the treasury. When someone became ill, they were given money to help with medicine, doctor bills, or to the family should there be a funeral.

The Oyster Society outlasted the other two. Through the years, with members gradually dying, by 1980 there were so few members that the treasury money was divided equally among those who were still living. The "Hall" and land were sold circa 1981 to Jim and Dorothy Thompson of Savannah, and the Society was no more. Some of its members were Marie Brown, Charlie and Sally Bentley, Georgia, Sarah, Viola, and William Bryan, Cornelia (Lemon) and Sarah Grant, Johnny and Stella Hamilton, Missy Hudson, Maggie Haynes, Frances E. Jones, Nora Lawrence, Gracie Miller, Lavinia (Blossom)

and Josepheus Robinson, Jake and Lillie Simmons, and Geneva Wiley.

Voodoo

Voodoo in the beginning was a good thing, according to Jo Ann McShane Jennings (known as Lady Bishop in the voodoo world) and she continues to believe that it is.

She calls voodoo . . .

an African science tied with the laws of nature, dealing with spirits and the saints." She also refers to it as a religion, deriving its name from *vodum*, which means "spirits" in some African dialects. Different spirits, she says, are sought to answer different needs.

The primary purpose of voodoo is healing with herbs, prayers, rituals, and spiritual intercession," she says. Too many people correlate voodoo with pins and needles stuck in dolls to create pain and suffering. That is witchcraft, not voodoo. But it can be an extension of voodoo in the hands of a person who was evil to begin with.[9]

According to Ms. Jennings, it is apparent that voodoo was perverted to mean "hoodoo" by an evil person who put it to work for harm by using hexes, evil-eye, or "root medicine."

Ramsey Mellette, Jr., M.D., medical director of the S.C. Consortium of Community Teaching Hospitals, states ". . . that the Lowcountry version of voo-doo originated in Africa. One reason it persisted in the New World was that it was one thing that masters could not take away from slaves."[10]

It is sad to say that there were several voodoo persons on Daufuskie who meant harm, but they have either moved away or died. It is hoped that there is no one who practices it here now.

Recreation—Entertainment

Daufuskie's greatest asset has been its dock, the hub around which the island has revolved. Since before the turn of the century the only recreation available was to be at the wharf and watch the steamers come in. To see firsthand who was coming or going, what they were wearing, or what new piece of furniture they brought over on the boat was the highlight of everyone's day.

In the 1930s there were two black men, Joe Grant and Joe Riley,

who would box. The folks would make money bets and some would go home happy with a few extra bucks in their pockets. And Emil Cetchovich (white) and Prophet Jenkins (black) would wrestle. Prophet would throw Emil over his shoulders and make Emil "bull fightin' mad" and the crowd would go wild.

Also in the 'thirties the County had built a pavilion at the public landing. The *Clivedon* would come in with a hoard of people and a band. The music would entice the crowd to begin dancing and with plenty of good food, beer, wine, and moonshine, everyone had a ball.

The PTA has several entertaining programs during the year with Halloween night and Graduation Day exercises being well attended.

In the last few years, with the new development and an increase in population, perhaps there might be an occasional birthday, beach party or Christmas party, a barbecue, or an oyster roast.

So many leave the island and go to the mainland for recreation or entertainment—tennis, theatre, or whatever.

Geodetic Survey

Sometime in the spring of 1963 the U.S. Geodetic Survey team drilled a well, over 400 feet deep, at Haig's Point. The purpose of the well was to keep a close watch on the salinity of the water, and, with its seismograph, to produce a record should an earthquake occur.

From 2 July 1963 to 22 August 1966, once a month, a Mr. Odum from Savannah would stop by Jolly Shores and use the vehicle of Lance Burn to ride to the well and check it out. For the use of his car Lance was paid $3.00 per trip.

When Anchorage, Alaska, had a terrible earthquake on 27 March 1964, it registered in the Haig's Point well.

Daufuskie Island Community Improvement Club

Two years prior to its inception, Mr. Thomas C. Barnwell, Jr., would come to Daufuskie and stop at Samuel Holmes at Cooper River to borrow his horse "Friendship." Mr. Barnwell would ride bareback over the island to talk with each householder concerning everyone getting together and forming a community group whereby we could act as one body, representing the needs of all the people. This would also give some clout in future decisions to be made for programs or projects that might be made available for the island.

478

Mr. William (Hamp) Bryan and Mrs. William (Sarah) Bryan 1968. Hamp was chairman of the Daufuskie Island Community Improvement Club from 1966 until his death in 1984. Sarah was very active in the PTA and the First Union African Baptist Church.

Through much effort on the part of State Coordinator, William K. March, Mr. Barnwell and others of the Office of Economic Opportunity, on 22 June 1965 the State of South Carolina issued a Certificate of Incorporation to the *Daufuskie Island Community Improvement Club.*

When we arrived at the first meeting they were not elected, but the names of the following officers were found already written on the blackboard: Chairman, Clifford Boyd; Co-Chairman, William (Hamp) Byran; Secretary, Billie Burn; Asst. Secretary, Frances E. Jones; Treasurer, Viola Bryan; Treasurer, Samuel Holmes; Finance, Alice Grant; Ways and Means, Thomas Bryan. We agreed to meet the first Wednesday in each month.

Clifford Boyd left the island in 1969. William Bryan taking his place as chairman served until his death in 1984, when Sister Sharon Culhane became chairman. Following her was John Wampler, Sally Ann Coleman, then Yvonne Wilson.

At Viola Bryan's death in 1969, Billie Burn acted as Secretary-Treasurer. Billie resigned in 1986 after serving twenty-one years. Mrs. Sylvia Wampler volunteered as secretary, followed by Yvonne Wilson, then Chip Lewis.

After Billie, Mrs. Janie Simmons became treasurer, then she resigned and Mr. Lawrence Jenkins now serves as treasurer.

Miss Frances E. Jones had moved to Hilton Head although she continued to attend the monthly meetings. Her position was dissolved in 1986. The remainder of the original officers are all dead.

Through the years many programs and benefits have been given to the island through the Club leadership.

Titanium Drilling

A company that came to the island to drill for titanium on 23 March 1969 made a core test in the yard of Miss Frances E. Jones, who had given them permission to do so.

As the drilling progressed, the contents of the core was laid out on the ground. This proved very interesting with its different layers and colors of sand, clay, and shells. Lance Burn thought it noteworthy for the company to make a list of materials found at different depths. Here is the soil level information they shared with him:

20 feet—sand
26 " —sand and broken shells
33 " —sand and broken seashells
41 " —15% sand; 85% gray clay
47 " —10% clay; 25% shell; 65% sand
51 " —15% sand; 85% clay
57 " —Top Hawthorne formation; 15 million years old
60 " —85% sand; 15% clay
66 " —40% sand; 60% clay
70 " —15% sand; 25% phosphate; 60% clay
73 " —same
75 " —10% sand; 15% phosphate; 75% clay
79 " —10% sand; 25% phosphate; 65% clay
$79^1/2$ "—sandy limestone

Vista Volunteers

From Berkeley, California, Mr. and Mrs. Henry Netherton were VISTA Volunteers (Volunteers in Service to America) who were sent to Beaufort County to serve on Daufuskie. They had arrived in Beaufort, living in a hotel where they remained for three weeks, waiting for permission from the governor to depart for the island.

Thinking that VISTA workers arrived in the state without his authority, South Carolina Governor Robert McNair refused to have them admitted, asking Peace Corps Director Sergeant Shriver to have them withdrawn immediately from Beaufort County, stating that they were not needed here, in Dorchester, nor in any other county in the state.

Governor McNair had previously signed a letter approving the VISTA program for South Carolina and apparently had forgotten about it. The governor sent South Carolina anti-poverty coordinator Townes Holland to Daufuskie to investigate the whole situation. Mr. Holland then met with Glenn Blackburn, director of the VISTA program, for a discussion of the matter. Their report was accepted favorably and the Nethertons were allowed to remain.

Henry and Rhea Netherton arrived on Sunday, 19 September 1965, and stayed until 26 August 1969. They were to stay only one year and wound up staying four. They helped the island in so many ways: Social Security benefits for the self-employed; Social Security benefits for

older people as well as young widows who did not know that through their dead husband's Social Security they could get financial aid for themselves and their children; they worked with the children during summer vacation in the Neighborhood Youth Corps, supervising them in making road signs, raking the church and school yards, cutting weeds and picking up trash along the roads—just anything that Mr. Netherton could think of to keep them busy.

They also had VISTA School in Dierks' place at Benjie's Point. Here they learned how to make crafts; books were available to read and games were played.

They did such a wonderful job that the islanders wanted the Nethertons to continue on indefinitely, but having served for four years they were not allowed to extend their stay any further.[11]

Following the Nethertons' departure, Jim and Vivian Strand came as VISTA Volunteers, September, 1969, serving only one year, leaving in August, 1970.

Santa Claus Comes by Boat

Arriving in two boats on 23 December 1970, forty Middle High School students from Charleston played Santa Claus to equally as many young children on Daufuskie. The colorful presents brought smiles to the faces of the Daufuskie children, but their greatest gift was in seeing their beloved former teacher, Pat Conroy, step off the boat. (Pat had been dismissed by the school department in September.)

The idea for the project originated in an Afro-American Club at Middleton High, after Mrs. Katrina Buksha, club sponsor, and another teacher, Marion Toatley, having read an article about Daufuskie in the *Evening Post*. News of the project soon spread over the school and all of the students became involved.

After two weeks of buying and wrapping over 200 gifts, the group drove to Hilton Head where they found that Daufuskie was so isolated it was very difficult to reach. Refused boat transportation from the Coast Guard and Navy, as well as a helicopter from the Air Force, they made a telephone call to Orion Hack on Hilton Head which produced positive results.

Within thirty minutes they had found two boat persons who would transport the biracial group to the island: Allen L. Engelhardt, a Connecticut Yankee and retired South American mining engineer,

with his fast cruiser *La Bundancia* and a Hilton Head trawler, *Capt. Dave*, owned by David Jones and skippered by Capt. James Murray.

Having reached the Cooper River dock, the black Santa, Middleton High senior Jerry Fields, greeted the island children. Presents were given out, refreshments enjoyed, and during their visit the Santa from Middleton High met and took an ox-cart ride with Daufuskie's black Santa, Johnny Hamilton. Misty-eyed when it became time to depart, all involved had had an unforgettable day.[12]

First Prefab Houses

In 1975 there were three prefab houses brought to the island through the Farmers Home Administration Program. These two and three bedroom houses cost under $20,000 with small monthly payments to be paid off over a 20-year period.

The houses were made in two sections and were brought over on a barge by Butler Construction Company out of Savannah. Owner of the company, Mr. James B. Butler, came personally to see that the block foundations were built, the plumbing installed, and the houses made ready for occupancy.

Those who were the recipients of these houses were Mrs. Janie Bentley, William and Stella Hamilton, and Mrs. Ella Mae Stevens.

Wells from B-JCHS

The majority of homes on the island had a shallow well with a hand pump. In 1975 Beaufort-Jasper Comprehensive Health Services, with Sargent Drake as supervisor, did something about this and had seven deep wells dug in various places about the island in order to have running water for everyone who desired it. (Said wells, with electric pumps, continue to operate in 1990.)

Daufuskie Island Co-Op

There was no store on the island and having to travel to Savannah or Hilton Head for food and other necessities became quite a chore. Recognizing our plight, in January 1975 a grant of $19,000 was given by the National Catholic Bishops' Campaign (CHD) for a cooperative and dry goods store on Daufuskie. Beaufort-Jasper Comprehensive Health Services, Inc., was the administrative agency that received this Daufuskie grant.[13]

Mr. Emory Campbell was chosen as coordinator, being account-able for the funds and for the supervision of the construction of the building. Workers from B-JCHS supplied the labor.

The CHD granted additional sums that amounted in all to over $33,000. The additional funds were used to stock the store and pay utility and insurance costs, while CETA provided funds and training for two full-time positions—manager Bud Bates and sales clerk Edrina Washington.

With everything completed and the store stocked, a grand opening was held 6 December 1975, with Governor James B. Edwards present to do the honor of cutting the ribbon. With these festivities, the Daufuskie Island Co-Op was born.

(Shortly thereafter, the pavilion was built.)

After five years of operation, CETA cut back funds, the manager and clerk were forced to quit, and this turned the Co-Op over to Daufuskie residents. The store operated for a while, but with little funds, poor management, and owing $10,000 to IRS and the S. C. Tax Commission, it was placed under Chapter 11 of the Bankruptcy Court and closed in June, 1985.

Agreeing to pay off the $10,000 in lieu of rent, Mr. Roy Prescott, owner of two restaurants on Hilton Head, leased the store and pavilion 1 September 1985, operating under the name of Remy's. Mr. Mike Hartle was hired as manager. The Co-Op was debt free when Mr. Prescott's five-year lease expired, 30 August 1990.

The store and pavilion, since 1 September 1990, have been under the new management of Roosevelt Brownlee and Tina Kohout. They have many things to work out before the store is in full swing with cleaning, painting, repairing, and remodeling. But if the store reflects their interest, dedication, and hard work, it will prove very successful. The new name chosen for the establishment is Ujima's, an African name meaning "collective responsibility" in Swahili.

Daufuskie Day

Through the combined efforts of Mr. Emory Campbell, Mr. Thomas Barnwell, and others, the first Daufuskie Day was held in June, 1976. Its main purpose was to help economically every interested individual on Daufuskie and at the same time let outsiders have a look at our beautiful island. Each island person or family and artists from

the mainland would have a booth with their crafts or food, art work, T-shirts, and jewelry. Cappy the Clown would do face painting and for the past two years we have had a dunking booth.

As soon as guests arrive a program will begin with a notable person as a guest speaker, followed by other speakers, then a brief history of the island is read. For entertainment there has been a group of children who have performed as dancers.

The majority of the time there have been four large boats involved in bringing passengers: Sam Stevens' Savannah boats the *Waving Girl* and the *Cap'n Sam*, and Stan, Sally, and Mark Maurer's Hilton Head boats the *Vagabond* and the *Adventure*. Twenty or more private boats come and anchor out along the shore near the public landing. The Maurers also have two large topless buses used to give short tours over the island.

June, 1990, marked the fourteenth year of Daufuskie Day. Each year the crowds get bigger and bigger, some coming from as far away as New York. And each year a different person acts as chairman, seeing that boats are made available, boat tickets printed, advertisements made in newspapers, on radios, and TV; choosing a person as a guest speaker—all the thousand and one things needed to make the day successful. Then pray that it doesn't rain! Hopefully, this will continue for years to come.

Bathrooms Airlifted to Daufuskie

With running water available few on the island had indoor bathrooms. Through B-JCHS and Jasper Career Education Center, in 1981 this was remedied:

> When they enlisted, these Marines weren't told they would be delivering bathrooms. But they will. Tomorrow morning, three mobile bathrooms will be airlifted to the public dock on Daufuskie Island from the Beaufort-Jasper Comprehensive Health Service, the Career Education Center, and United Way.
>
> "The project started off as someone's wild idea," said Leonard Kaye, director of health care services at B-JCHS.
>
> Kaye said approximately 50 percent of the Daufuskie Island residents don't have indoor bathrooms. The three residents were selected by B-JCHS on the basis of medical need and income, he said.
>
> United Way provided the funding and approximately 90 students of

the education center's building construction/plumbing/electricity classes built the bathrooms, according to Don Bateman, principal.[14] (Two additional bathrooms were airlifted in June, 1986.)

These bathrooms, approximately 8 x 10 feet, were complete with hotwater heaters. Watching them swinging by metal cables beneath these huge helicopters was quite entertaining and brought many islanders to gaze at them.

Daufuskie Island on National Register

At the request of South Carolina Coastal Commission and Beaufort County through the South Carolina Department of Archives and History, Rebecca Starr, an American history student at the University of South Carolina in Columbia, and Charles Lowe, an architectural analyst and representative of the South Carolina Commission, came to the island in March, 1981, and photographed every house, building, and structure, gathering pertinent information concerning their size, shape, and the materials used to construct them.

Before the end of 1981 with the information gathered by Charles Lowe and herself, Rebecca Starr submitted a National Register of Historic Places Inventory-Nomination Form to the U.S. Department of the Interior, Heritage Conservation and Recreation Service, Washington, D.C., and in the week of June 20, 1982, Daufuskie was accepted on the National Register of Historical Places.

New Businesses

Calibogue Shrimp Company, operated by Francis A. Burn, came to the island in 1977.

The United Parcel Service (UPS) office was first set up on the island by Mrs. Geraldine Wheelihan; her first packages were received on 20 August 1981. Mr. Franklin Wiley would bring the packages in his boat from Hilton Head, then Mrs. Wheelihan would see that they were delivered on the island. Following Mr. Wiley, Captain and Mrs. John Wampler were responsible for bringing the packages in their boat, and now Captain Ed Richard brings them over on his boat, the *Mary C.*

Bud Bates Realty Inc. in 1981 became the first one of its kind on the island.

In 1982 our first physician, Dr. Peter Frank, opened his *Daufuskie*

Medical Center.

Our only resident artist, Mrs. Christina Roth Bates, hung out her *Christina Bates Studio* shingle in 1982.Her beautiful prints of island-ers' lost occupations have brought them to life again.

In 1985 there was *Billie Burn Books 'N Crafts*.

Mrs. Sylvia Wampler's *Southern Shirtique* was opened in 1986. Mrs. Wampler, with her artistic talent, prints her own T-shirts. With her "store" on wheels, Sylvia is always at the dock, selling her shirts and other Daufuskie souvenirs to tourists who come to the island by boat loads.

In 1986 real estate broker John Wampler hung out his *Captain John's Realty* sign.

Ed Richards, in August 1987, started his *Islands Charter Service, Inc.*

Don Mudd's *Sea Oats Real Estate Company* opened in 1987.

Thrift Construction Company, began circa 1987-1988 by Paul Thrift.

Daufuskie Woodworks operated by Richard Lahr was opened in 1988. If beautiful custom work is what you need, Richard is the one who can do it for you.

Steve Joyner's *Steve's Custom Electric* opened in 1989.

Firsts

The first book written *about* Daufuskie, its school, and the students was *The Water is Wide*, by teacher Pat Conroy in 1972.

The first *Booklet* published *by* a Daufuskie person, "Visitors Guide to Daufuskie Island," by Robert L. Burn, was published in 1981.

The first *book* published *by* a Daufuskian was a history/cooking book entitled *Stirrin' the Pots on Daufuskie,* by Billie Burn, 1985.

STOP signs were first put up on the island by county workers, 27-30 April, 1986.

The first 25 mph SPEED signs were placed near the school area on 8 May 1986.

Several trash dumpsters were situated about over the island in the spring of 1990.

Citadel Cadets Drift to Bloody Point

It all started on Sunday, 23 April 1967, when three eighteen-year-old freshmen Citadel cadets decided to go fishing off the Charleston

harbor. James W. Breazeale, Jr., of Charleston, Richard E. Belles of Massachusetts, and Roger Meyers of Pine Bluff, Arkansas, left in their sixteen-foot Boston Whaler to follow the *Mustang*, a fishing vessel that they thought would lead them to where the big fish were, according to an ad they had read in the paper.

After they got out there the water was looking pretty rough, so they decided they had better go back in. In doing so, they lost sight of the *Mustang*, and with the rough water lost their bearing. They had a compass but read it wrong, taking a southwesterly course. Not seeing any shoreline, they eventually ran out of gas and were at the mercy of the sea. When they had not returned to port by Sunday night, a call from the Citadel triggered a massive search.

The 95-foot cutter *Cape Morgan* began an offshore search about 10 P.M. Sunday, followed early Monday morning by a force of military personnel and civilian volunteers. Aircraft flew in from New York to St. Petersburg, Florida.

The cadets saw two jets streak overhead on Monday, and on Tuesday they counted twenty planes and helicopters, but none spotted them.

The nights were cold with twenty-foot waves that tossed them about. Clad only in swim suits and T-shirts, they huddled together to keep warm. Their food consisted of three soft drinks, four slices of bread, and some peanut butter.

Finally, drifting in at Daufuskie's Bloody Point on the morning of Wednesday the 26th, they secured their boat, walking until they came to the Mary Fields Elementary School, an approximate distance of two miles.

In the meantime Billie Burn had heard the early news that Wednesday morning; had the cadets not been found, a fleet of helicopters was to take off at 9 A.M. Having made her appointed rounds, she reached the school about 8:20 to disperse the school students and saw, there on the school grounds, three young men, their legs and faces badly sunburned. One was holding a bread wrapper with two heels of bread, while another clutched a large glass jar which held a few tablespoons of peanut butter.

They came up to the open door of the bus and Billie asked, "You're not—?" They said, "Yes, we are." She could not believe that these cadets had drifted this far. "Am I glad to see you! They are looking for

you by air and by sea," she said. "In fact, I need to get you home so I can stop a fleet of helicopters that are to take off in just a few minutes."

Upon their arrival at Jolly Shores, a quick call via the two-way radio notified the Beaufort County sheriff that the cadets were safe on Daufuskie, thus calling off the search.

Lance and Billie Burn prepared breakfast for the three men, then made them as comfortable as possible until the sheriff's boat could arrive.

After much confusion and getting their boat from Bloody Point, the cadets were safely transported to Beaufort by Deputy Sheriff G. J. Buck Debruhl.[15]

Ironic as it may seem, back at the Citadel Cadet Pat Conroy and other staff members of the *Shako*, the campus literary magazine, had written an underground letter concerning an injustice in the discipline dished out to a cadet for an infraction, while at the same time a company commander went scot free for having done something worse. Copies of the letter were conveniently found on the mess hall tables before evening formation.

After reading the letter there was chaos in the mess hall; all the copies were to be collected and destroyed. But because the letter generated enough debate, it acted as a catalyst to force the administration to appoint a board to review the case. As a result the commander was reduced to a private, with no other punishment, which the cadets thought was not enough.

Having given it some thought, *The Boo* had just about traced the penning of the letter down to Pat and his cohorts, getting ready to lower the boom on them, when a week after the letter appeared the Citadel's three young men became lost at sea. All attention was then turned to the safety of the cadets, with the "letter" incident seeming minimal and being quickly forgotten.[16]

For their small part in the rescue efforts, Lance and Billie received the following in a personal letter from The Citadel's president, dated 27 April 1967:

> Dear Mr. and Mrs. Lance Burn: You played an important role in the return to The Citadel of our three lost cadets. We are deeply grateful to you for your assistance in this matter, and the cadets have expressed their appreciation for the hospitality which you showed them and your prompt action in making their whereabouts known here.

Robert L. (Bob) Burn and His Blue Gypsy 1972
(Photograph courtesy R.L. Burn.)

490

The breakfast you gave them was the first "square meal" they had had since they were lost and they all remember it in a special way. They wished to be remembered to you and all of us at The Citadel recognize that you rendered valuable service in looking after these young men for us until they began their return to The Citadel, where, as you well imagine, they were received most enthusiastically by their parents, friends, and fellow cadets. Sincerely, /s/ Hugh P. Harris.

Daufuskie Sailor Crosses Atlantic

In June of 1972 Robert Lancy Burn entered the Observer Singlehanded Transatlantic Race from Plymouth, England, to Newport, Rhode Island, a race sponsored by the Royal Western Yacht Club.

Bob had a childhood dream, passed on from his grandfather Arthur A. Burn, of owning his own sailboat and making a long ocean voyage.

While in the U.S. Army in the 1960s he taught himself celestial navigation and began looking for his dreamboat. He quickly learned that money was the big hurdle to overcome, a seagoing boat was expensive!

Following his tour of duty he attended Northrop Institute of Technology, Inglewood, California, and obtained his FAA airframe and power plant licenses. He was immediately hired by Air America, spending just over five years in Viet Nam as an aircraft maintenance supervisor.

By 1971 he had accumulated enough money to buy the boat, which he had located in his travels in Copenhagen, Denmark. This was a *Great Dane 28* built by Klaus Baess.

Bob resigned his position with Air America and flew to Denmark. With a longtime friend the two set sail from Copenhagen, 4 April 1971.

Surviving shipwreck and storm, within the next thirteen months Bob sailed the Atlantic three times, the last crossing being his solo in the O.S.T.A.R.

During the planning stages of his voyage Bob gained tremendous respect for those who originated the regatta. To meet those men was his main objective for entering the race. He had the pleasure of being introduced to Sir Francis Chichester, but the famous sailor became ill at the very beginning and had to turn back; sadly, he died before the race was over.

After thirty-nine days at sea, Bob reached Newport, Rhode Island, finishing second on handicap. His *Blue Gipsy* was the twenty-fifth boat to cross the finish line out of the fifty-nine starters.[17]

So that everyone can enjoy reading about his labor of love, the wreck, the hardship of storms at sea—all of his thrilling sailing adventures—watch for his forthcoming book *The Long Voyage Home*.

Notes

1. Mrs. Jo (Anne) Pitts, Bluffton, S. C., telephone interview, 2 October 1990; Mrs. Geraldine Wheelihan, interview 2 October 1990.

2. Mrs. Pitts.

3. *Beaufort Gazette*, 20 December 1972; *Island Packet*, 20 March 1973; Ibid., 6 September 1985.

4. *Beaufort Gazette*, 11 January 1989.

5. *Island Packet*, 16 August 1985; *Beaufort Gazette*, 26 August 1986.

6. Tom Laughlin, "Daufuskie: First to Report Votes," *State*, 12 June 1966.

7. Mr. William (Hamp) Bryan interview 10 May 1982.

8. Beaufort County Courthouse, Deed Book 41, p. 80.

9. *Island Packet*, 18 June 1987.

10. Lucy Cobb, "Doctors learn how to combat 'evil eye' and stop 'haints'," *Island Packet*, 29 August 1984. Suggested reading concerning witchcraft: Sheriff J. E. McTeer, *Fifty Years As A Witch Doctor*, (Beaufort: Beaufort Book Company, 1976).

11. *State*, 3 September 1965; *News & Courier*, 3 September 1965; *Savannah Morning News*, 5 September 1965; Ibid., 22 September 1965.

12. Jack LeLand, "Santa Claus Travels By Trawler, Oxcart," *Evening Post* , 24 December 1970.

13. *Island Packet*, 2 January 1975.

14. *Beaufort Gazette*, 21 April 1981.

15. *News and Courier*, Thursday, 27 April 1967.

16. Donald Patrick Conroy, *The Boo* (Verona, Virginia: McClure Press, 1970), pp. 148-161.

17. Bessie Hockstra, "Daufuskie Islander Sails Across Ocean," *Beaufort Gazette*, 29 July 1971; Ibid., 9 September 1971; Ibid., 6 August 1972; Jim Littlejohn, "An Interview with Bob Lancy Burn," *Island Events*, 4-10 May 1985; Ibid., 11-17 May 1985.

17

POEMS BY BELOVED FRIENDS

After the Kehoe/Cummings partnership purchased the Bloody Point Lighthouse from Arthur A. Burn, Dr. Wayne Lee Cummings, the husband of Mary Kehoe Cummings, wrote this poem about the place, circa 1966:

Ye
Olde
Lighthouse

DAUFUSKIE ISLAND
SOUTH CAROLINA

By: Wayne E. Cummings

Ye olde Lighthouse down by the sea,
In days of old reflected beams for me;
Once standing so brave by the deep blue sea,
Then moved inland to protect you for me.

Ye olde Lighthouse once by the sea,
Now reflecting thoughts through me;
Where once I dreamed of wonders by the sea,
At last fullfilled in owning you for me.

Ye olde Lighthouse now inland from the sea,
Filled with laughter by my family and me;
Together we stand looking toward the sea,
A noble end to thee from me.

493

Being spiritually led to help in the First African Union Baptist Church, in 1976 Mrs. Mildred Rosemond came from Fresno, California, bringing her son, Lorin, with her.

Lorin attended Mary Fields Elementary graduating in June of 1977. I drove the school bus and picked up everyone to attend church on Sunday. It was Mother's Day, 8 May 1977, and when Lorin got on the bus he handed me a folded sheet of paper. After I arrived home from the service that day I opened the note, and to my surprise he had written a poem just for me:

To My Special Mom

Each and every morning as I board the bus
Your smile touches my heart
And it's always happy as we part.
You're like a lilly (sic) of the valley
A bright morning star
Though I already have a mother
I have a special Mom too
And Mrs. Burn that special Mom is you.
Happy Mother's Day /s/ Lorin Rosemond

The preachers of First Union African Baptist Church had permission to tie to our dock to stay all day or a week during Vacation Bible School. Many, many times after Lance Burn had made sure their boat was secured to the dock, the preacher and party would mosey on up to the house where cake and coffee would be waiting for them. Or perhaps Lance had gone shrimping and would present them with a generous package of shrimp or fish to take home—or maybe the pears were ripe to share.

Rev. Greene's lovely wife Ardell was often in the party. On 23 September 1977 we received this note from them:

Mr. & Mrs. Burn: This poem is an effort to let you know how much we appreciate the things you do for us. Love, /s/ Ervin & Ardell

To Mr. & Mrs. Burn By Ardell Greene

There are folks who live by the riverside
Whom I write about with great pride
These two are man and wife
Two of the sweetest persons we've come to know in our life
They'll give you some of their best food

494

And they're forever in a friendly mood
They always perform some friendly task
And you can tell it's not under a mask
The kindness comes from the bottom of their soul
Their smiles play a dramatic role
Time will tell and by faith you can see
The Burns in Heaven with you and me
Shrimp, pears and fish they give
So a family of four might live
It's these two that God will bless
No doubt about it, Oh Yes!

Harriette Boyd is a sister-in-law of Gracie Boyd who came to the island to live in the 1970s. Harriette lives in Columbia and every time she finds an article concerning Daufuskie she rushes it on to me—or, she might bring it, as she visited Gracie as often as she could. Harriette's love for Daufuskie is almost as profound as ours and at times she would attend church. Following are the thoughts that she expressed in 1983:

To live happily at Daufuskie
You must have the soul of a poet
The mind of a philosopher
The simple tastes of a hermit
And a good jeep!

Just north of the Bloody Point lighthouse on Oakridge, Thursday, 30 December 1982, a four-placement, single-engine Piper Cherokee 180, with only the pilot on board, for some reason dropped down too low, hitting the tops of trees and literally exploding the plane and the pilot. Searching through the strewn wreckage, about nine pounds of cocaine were found.[1]

Then, later, a former resident of Daufuskie was caught and sent to prison for dealing in drugs.

Following these accounts and being so inclined, Douglas William Cooper of Charleston, who married Sandra (Francis and Ethel Burn, Sr.'s, daughter) wrote this poem circa 1984:

I didn't have much of a future
And really not much hope
But I had me a rundown shrimper
So I got me a load of dope.

495

I headed into Charleston
A port city by the sea
But somebody sent them a message
And the Narcs were waiting for me.
Well, the judge didn't take it kindly
And gave me six years in jail
But I had a slick city lawyer
Who got me out on a ten dollar bail.
Well I left the city of Charleston
And I sailed the seven seas
Till I bought some land on an island
By the name of Da fus key
Well the locals on the island
Like Billie, Frank, and Lance
They didn't take a likin to me
And said I'd lose my pants.
But now the future is much brighter
And I'm making money left and right
Cause while they're shrimping in the daytime
I'm running drugs at night!

Notes

1. David Stacks, "One Dies in Crash of Plane," *Beaufort Gazette*, 30 December 1982.

18

DAUFUSKIE MEMORIES

David Humphrey, a great grandson of James P. Chaplin, Jr., has been collecting family history and shares the following stories written by his uncle, Captain Marion Thomas Wright, grandson of J. P. Chaplin, Jr., and a former captain on several tugs of the Atlantic Towing Company on River Street in Savannah. David adds these comments concerning the stories:

> . . . the recollections of a simpler and more beautiful time. A time when people had more time, and a lot more respect for each other. A time when love and compassion were the threads that held together families, friends, and neighbors.
>
> The stories . . . are about life on Daufuskie Island, South Carolina in the latter 1800s and early 1900s. . . . To the reader of these beautiful stories, it is asked by the compiler that they be read with respect and understanding for the revered loved ones, who although have gone on, are not forgotten.[1]

Life on Daufuskie Island #1

On the Sabbath, the entire [Chaplin] family would prepare to go to church. My grandmother was a very religious woman, and she had no patience with dawdlers, and was prompt to let them know of her displeasure. My grandfather would be out in the stable hitching-up the mare to the family buckboard, in which we were transported to the church grounds.

My grandfather would always drive the buckboard, but never joined his family in going inside of the church. He claimed that God had given all human beings a conscience, which was a small part of God Himself. So, all people knew right from wrong—to simply live by the Golden Rule: "Do unto others as you would have them do unto you." My

grandfather did not really believe in paying anyone for preaching the gospel. He believed that this should be a great honor to anyone, and, that a preacher should work the same as any other person for his living.

So, while the rest of the family went inside to listen to the gospel, my grandfather sat outside under the large oak trees and would read his Bible. When church was over and farewells were said, as this was part of their [our] social life also, we would load up in the wagon, and Grandfather Chaplin would drive the family back home. My dear old Grandmother Chaplin was a very good person and a firm believer that you earned whatever you received in this old world. And, she set an example by hard work and long hours. She was in reality the backbone of our family, as most of her sons and daughters would agree. Her day started long before sunrise and ended long after sunset.

She supervised the preparation of the meals, the laundry, the making of soap by cooking the animal fat saved from time to time. She, of course made her own potash by saving the ashes from the fireplace and adding other necessary ingredients, including soft rain water to the finished soap product. She gathered eggs daily from the nests of her Rhode Island hens and other breeds. Some of the eggs were used for our meals, and some were sold at my grandfather's store.

I can remember the orchards of apples, pears, peaches, scuppernong grapes, mulberry trees, walnuts, and hickory nuts (the meat is as sweet as any, a taste all its own).

My grandfather was widely known for having a "green thumb," as every plant he tended seemed to bear fruit. His system of planting has been used by the farmers of the universe for untold ages. His planting took place on favorable stages of the moon. Peas, beans, and other vegetables were the ones he was particularly careful to plant as close to the stages of the moon as possible. How many people know that the ocean tides are primarily controlled by planet moon, and that our own planet earth is controlled partly by the magnetic pull of gravity from the moon? The plant life on our earth is likewise affected. Most farmers and sailors learn these facts at an early age because magnetic attraction affects their professional lives. Very few city dwellers, however, ever study or read about this relationship.

Capt. Jim Chaplin (James P. Chaplin II), as he was known by all the inhabitants of the island was a very unusual man. Besides the vegetable farm that he worked himself, he was also active in many other fields. He maintained an oyster shucking plant (oyster factory) where the employees separated the oyster from the shell. They then placed the oysters in a gallon can (this method was known as wet packing) as there were no

498

ice plants on Daufuskie Island in 1914. All ice was shipped to the island packed in sawdust for insulation from Savannah. The oysters required great care to prevent them from spoiling. The arrival of the excursion boat on time was another important factor in my grandfather's business.

There was a commissary (or company store) operated by him. I believe, from my Grandmother Chaplin's remarks at times, that this business venture was not quite as successful as the oyster business. A customer was issued goods from the store against his earnings or credit. Sometimes a customer, having not worked, due to bad weather or illness, or some other valid reason, would not have any credits to draw against.

But this small and trivial fact would not discourage my grandfather, if he knew the family was truly in need, from letting them have goods anyway. But, of course, this was considered bad business by my grandmother, and she never hesitated to inform my generous grandfather of his chances of going bankrupt. It was no family secret that the store was in the red, the goods were gone, and no money to buy more. These were very critical times, but, just when things looked the worst, someone always came in and paid something on their account. These little payments helped my grandfather over the hurdle, time and time again. I was a witness to similar happenings.

Now years later, I am fully convinced that my Grandfather Chaplin was a very rich man, not in worldly goods, but in the ways that count. He gave to the hungry, and in turn, he himself was fed by their love and respect. I would agree with my dear grandmother that he was not a business man in the sense that the word implies, but he was something better. He was a warm hearted, gentle person who really cared for his fellow man. He was called out at all hours of the day and night to advise on many matters, ranging from a gestation period of a sow to the treatment of a human being. Between my grandfather and grandmother, their knowledge of medicine on Daufuskie was rated very highly as was their prompt attention and attendance to the sick.

I was a witness of the medical ability of my grandfather on one occasion: a newborn calf had hooked a young colt in the stomach causing the intestines of the colt to protrude from its stomach. My grandfather threw the colt to the ground, and then ordered me to go tell my grandmother to bring a basin of warm water, bottle of ether, and some clean linen. I watched as my grandfather put the animal to sleep, cleaned and replaced the entrails, and then take a silk thread and needle and sew up the wound. After this, he placed clean dressing over the wound.

I also remember one time when I was four years old that I was playing pirate when I slipped and fell into an old schooner cabin that had glass windows and cut my leg very badly. The cut was so deep that the tendons and the bone were visible to the naked eye. My grandfather and grandmother chloroformed me and sewed my wound up. The scar will always be on my leg. It is a good twelve inches now. It is estimated, judging by the passage of some sixty years, that the wound was approximately two-thirds the length of my leg. The cut, however, healed without any complications.

Life on Daufuskie Island #2

My childhood memories of Daufuskie Island bring to mind stories of my grandfather James Peto Chaplin's hunting companion—Gus Ohman, who was a store keeper and, his wife, Edith, and his horse, Champion. . . .

In the year 1912, my father, Captain Harry Vivian Wright, died—a tragedy that changed the course of his children's lives. The death of my father left a void in my life, but not for long. My grandfather, already burdened with the responsibility of supporting eleven people on $85.00 a month, took over the duties of my father we children had lost.

I was my grandfather's shadow and followed him everywhere he went. The only exception being his weekly poker game with Gus Ohman and others. I was excluded due to my youth.

In the year 1912 Gus Ohman owned and operated the largest general store on the island. He also charged the highest prices for his wares, especially to the colored families that were hard pressed for cash as they often had to charge their meager supplies until the end of the month, and sometimes even for a longer period. It was customary to charge a small percent for credit, but. . . .

Gus Ohman's high prices to the Negro families that traded at his store were well known to most of the white families on the island. But only my grandfather, who disliked an injustice, was outspoken enough to bring the subject up with Gus Ohman, who was a very powerful built man with an uncontrollable temper.

My grandfather and Gus Ohman were companions of many a deer hunt, both were avid lovers of the hunt and crack marksmen, and, had a mutual respect for each other.

However, they had their differences of opinion concerning the political and local affairs of the island. My grandfather maintained that the Negroes of the island, due to their lack of an education, were exploited. Gus Ohman, on the other hand, claimed their ignorance was

due to a lack of ambition to better one's self. As in his case, when he first came to America [from Sweden] as a boy, while working twelve hours a day, he had taught himself the English language at night. My earliest memories of these debates were pleasant as both men were well versed in the English language. And, as the argument grew warmer, Gus would revert to his mother's tongue. Most of the arguments would end on a friendly note, and both would discuss plans for their next deer hunt.

Gus Ohman owned a very beautiful and powerful horse named Champion. Champion was often used in stud service with my grandfather's mares. This was a profitable enterprise for both men and they knew it. Their heated debate never once threatened this business relationship.

My grandfather was born on Lady's Island, South Carolina in 1845. He was one of four children. One child died at a very young age. The other two being girls. He helped support his father and mother by hunting and trapping—often sleeping on the ground in front of a camp fire.

I was only ten years of age when my revered grandfather died in the month of August 1919. His death was so peaceful that I, a little boy full of energy and enthusiasm for life, never fully realized what was happening to his wonderful grandfather.

My grandfather was critically injured several years before his death by a young high-strung stallion. While attempting to keep it from trampling my grandmother's rose garden, he reared up striking my grandfather in the chest, knocking him to the ground and still excited, stepped on his chest. This caused severe damage to his chest from which he never recovered.

As we lived on an island that was completely cut off from the mainland, the only regular transportation was a river steamboat called the *Pilot Boy*. It made the run to the island once a day around noon, and then was secured to a dock in Savannah for the night. The only other means of transportation was by row boat or sailboat, and this was a very slow method of transporting an injured person to a hospital or doctor over twenty miles away. This, however, was the only transit system that my relatives had. Thus, my grandfather was wrapped in heavy blankets and carefully placed in a large fishing dory well for ward in the under decking to protect him from the spray and weather. This dory was often used for fishing off shore when fish were scarce locally. It was fully equipped with main sail and jib with center board. Its purpose was to keep the sailing vessel from making excessive leeway when working to windward.

501

I was given permission to make the trip with my grandfather only after much pleading that I would be near to him and watch over him and keep him covered with the blankets. The passage to Savannah took four and a half hours and much of that time I was cold and miserable due to a light rain that had started to fall just as we were leaving the island.

The doctor, a former army surgeon who had been wounded at the Battle of Honey Hill, South Carolina during the War Between the States, and had been in the same regiment as my grandfather, knew that the injury was a serious one. He wanted my grandfather to go to the hospital at once, but my grandfather was a very obstinate person at times and this was one of the times. He was carried to his daughter's house (Georgia Padgett) where he stayed for a few days to get his "strength back" as he so often said. Less than a week later, my grandfather was back on his beloved island of Daufuskie.

The doctor that examined my grandfather the day of the injury predicted that he would not live more than three months in his present condition. My grandfather laughed when told this and he replied, "I'll live for more than five times that long." And he did! Almost two years to the day he died in his own bed in his own home, but not on his beloved Daufuskie, but rather, at his new home in Savannah at 520 East 33rd Street. It was a small house that he had bought for my grandmother.

The day of his death was so earth-shaking to his young grandson that it was sometime before I could even talk about his passing, and even then for a short time only. My grandfather had been confined to his bed the last two weeks of his life, due to his weakened condition. My grandmother tended to her husband tirelessly until she, being an elderly person herself, gave out. My mother, Virginia Susan Chaplin Wright, would take over nursing duties until my grandmother rested up. During his illness he was an ideal patient. He appreciated the care and love he was the object of, thanking each and every one for the services they had performed for him. This was in keeping with his character. Not one of his children had ever heard him utter one word of profanity. His favorite words when aggravated were, "Blast it all."

My grandfather had called all of his children to his bedside when he realized that his earthly days were numbered, as there were still some important things to be done. His sons were standing on the right hand side of his bed, and his daughters were standing on the left side of his bed. He talked in a low but firm voice explaining what had to be done. My grandfather told his children that he was selling Pine Island, and that it was a valuable piece of property that would some day be worth a top price on the real estate market. But since there had been some argu-

ments among his children as to whom the island would go to, he was selling the island. The money from the sale would be put in trust for his wife, their mother, to live on. The rest of the "Chaplin Tract" would be divided into equal shares to be held or sold as the owner desired. . . .

. . . During the discussion of the division of the property, he said, "I would advise all of you to hold on to this property as some day it will bring a very handsome profit. This property has been in my family for six generations. My great grandfather owned this land at one time. A man who owns a piece of land and works with his hands to bring forth a crop is as close to God as he will ever get here on earth. Don't forget what I have said."

He was weary from talking to an audience who could not see beyond the four walls of the room that they had been standing in. He closed his eyes while listening to the strains of music from the hymn "That Old Time Religion" which he had requested my sister, Vivian, to play on the phonograph for him. It is not certain just what minute my grandfather died, however, in my opinion, he was looking out of a window into another world while preparing to depart this one. The smile on his face would lead me to believe that he saw something green and beautiful, and like most farmers, he wanted to know who tended the fields.

When my father died at thirty-two years of age, he left me a gold watch. But when my grandfather died, he left me a way of life.[2]

•

Mrs. Katie Swindell of Savannah was a dear friend to Dick and Mary Ida Fripp on Daufuskie. Upon invitation, Mrs. Swindell would bring along her young daughter, Beth, to enjoy the breeze, the beach, and the gracious hospitality of the Fripps.

It was Beth, now Mrs. Beth Swindell Shirley, who was so kind as to share an account of her numerous visits to the island.[3]

Daufuskie

As a seventy-seven-year-old woman, one's mind is frequently returning to scenes and memories of "bygone"days; at this point, that is exactly what is happening to me—and they are particularly happy for they are centered on Daufuskie Island, a place where I spent, as a visitor, many happy childhood days.

Mary Ida Fripp (we called her "Aunt Mamie," although there was no blood relationship) and her husband, Richard Fripp, Jr. ("Uncle Dick"— still no relationship), and my mother, Katie Swindell, had been close

friends for years—even during the years when "Aunt Mamie" was Mrs. Charlie H. Medlock. Her daughter, Betty, even lived with us in our Savannah home for a short time. That was not too long after "Uncle Dick" and "Aunt Mamie" were first married [1906], hence our frequent visits to their home on Daufuskie.

And what memorable visits they were!!! Even now I can see in my mind's "eye" their lovely sprawling island home on the Inlet [New River]. On one side {south}, and a little to the front of it, stood the small cottage in which "Aunt Pearl," Uncle Dick's sister, lived. On the other side [north] of their home, a few feet farther away, stood Uncle Dick's country store. And oh my, the wonderful odors that old store contained—mixed odors of coffee beans, spices, leather goods, sugars and honey. And then, there were materials of cloth, dry goods—well, everything from kegs of nails to straight pins!!! Quite a few of my happy moments, as a child, were spent in that store.

It was on Daufuskie that I learned to ride horseback—and what a thrill that was! The only problem was that the first time out on that horse's back, she bolted when some small animal in the road jumped up at her—and away we flew—stopping only at a gate, leaving me clinging to her side. What a fright that was—but, it didn't deter me, I climbed back on her after she had quieted down. We turned and went back down the road to the beach and Bloody Point. We travelled that road many a time.

In going this route we would pass the little school house in which Aunt Mamie's daughter, Betty, taught for awhile. In fact, it was while she was teaching there she met and later married Emil Cetchovich, Jr. By the way, when Betty would be visiting us at our old homeplace in Savannah—Emil and Betty would do some "high powered" courting on our front porch! Speaking further of Betty, she saved her mother's life one time, while there on Daufuskie: "Aunt Mamie" was carrying an old-fashioned, white pitcher filled with water from the kitchen to one of the bedrooms, when she tripped and fell. The pitcher broke and her throat hit one of the jagged pieces and cut it rather severely. Betty heard the crash, rushed to her mother and saw she was bleeding. Betty dashed out and under the house, grabbing handfulls of cobwebs—rushed back to her mother and plastered the wound with the cobwebs to stanch the blood—which it did after several applications. We were told later that the doctor said that stopping the bleeding saved Aunt Mamie's life.

A final memory of my childhood days on Daufuskie: The First Baptist Church in Savannah, of which I was a member, had several of their annual Sunday School picnics on Daufuskie. How well I remem-

ber the long tables loaded down to the "groaning point" with all kinds of "yummy, yum, yum" foods and barrels of lemonade. I can see now the men and boys playing softball or throwing horseshoes; we girls playing "hide-and-go-seek," or tag—or both groups having "crocus sack" races; all the while the women sat around indulging in "woman talk." Oh, yes, those were the days that made wonderful memories!!!

Notes

1. David Humphrey's personal files, 11 April 1986.
2. Captain Marion Wright who wrote about his grandfather, J. P. Chaplin, Jr., resides in Tampa, Florida.
3. Personal letter of Mrs. Beth S. Shirley, Wauchula, Florida, 7 December 1987.

19

AN IMAGINARY JOURNEY

There is no way that the history of Daufuskie can be written without including Savannah, Georgia. From the time of its founding in 1733, people of Daufuskie have depended upon Savannah for everything—from nails to banking.

With mansions on Daufuskie, the early 1700 planters also owned townhouses in Savannah and warehouses along the river front. They made trips to Savannah in their sailing vessels.

People on other islands, without bridges, from Hilton Head to Beaufort, depended upon Savannah—it was their "trading post" too. The waters have always been their roads.

For over a half-century all of the older people on Daufuskie have taken the same trip by boat to Savannah to tend to business, shop, or sell their wares. A way was always made to travel the thirty-four-mile round-trip to get to "town" as Savannah was called. Up on the flood and back on the ebb—some caught the steamers, some rowed (taking nine hours there and back), while others sailed in oyster bateaus. It was better to be in town early in the morning so that shopping could be completed and back down to River Street in order to load up while the tide was high. Loading on low tide was almost an impossibility. To catch the ebb tide from 2 to 3 o'clock in the afternoon would put you back on the island, unloaded, and home before dark.

When we went to "town" in Papy Burn's launch, *Laura* (which took us almost two hours), the closest place to tie up at the river and be near the city was at Barnard Street dockage area—and often filled with Daufuskie bateaus, oyster boats with sails, and small launches. The only accommodations available to get up the bluff to spend our money in Savannah was a set of wooden steps, slimy from silt and oil (which

once caused Mae Dierks and Addie Burn to slide overboard) and an old iron ladder used on low tide, which exposed the huge culverts that spewed out raw sewerage into the river. Climbing down this ladder with parcels proved very difficult. (How Daufuskie teacher Frances E. Jones made it with her crippled leg is beyond me, but she did.) Every obstacle and obnoxious odor would be overcome and overlooked, just to get to Savannah to see a movie or buy an ice cream cone. We all loved Daufuskie, but it was nice to get away for a day and be in the midst of all the noise, sights, and smells of city life.

Usually, the first person we saw at Barnard and River Streets was black, barefoot "Maggie" who would be fishing with a handline from the rotting pier and occasionally pulling up a big-mouthed catfish. Then there was black "Nappy" (affectionately referred to as "Captain of the Port") who was forever there to help with lines in tying up our boat or eager to assist with loading and unloading freight. And the Gallovitch boys, Frank, Clarence, Earl, and John, were always present to lend a hand wherever needed.

There would be lone venders walking the streets pushing their handcarts filled with vegetables, shrimp, and crabs. "Getcha fresh collard greens, fresh shrimps, fresh biled crabs or biled peanuts 5 cents a bag," they would be hawking.

The old city market on Barnard between Bryan and Congress Streets would be a hub of activity—wagons and trucks loaded with produce parked all around outside with stalls inside of seafoods of all kinds, fresh vegetables, cut flowers—anything you wanted. Black people would be sitting around shelling fresh butter beans or field peas in their fanner baskets. And in the basement floor of the market, for 50 cents you could buy a big fish dinner. There was an open fruit stand, just across from the market on Barnard Street, not far from Kress' Five and Dime store, where you could buy every kind of fruit and nut imaginable.

The market was torn down and replaced with a parking garage. All of the businesses have closed or left, with the exception of one—Frank C. Mathews Seafood—it still remains in the same spot since the 1930s, on Barnard between Congress and St. Julian Streets.

And down at the river, the little tugboat, *The Island Girl,* would swish her little self back and forth, shuttling workers and passengers from the Savannah wharf to one on Hutchinson Island. This little boat

went back and forth (circa 1924-1954) until the Talmadge Bridge was built.

I thought it appropriate to take you, the reader, on an imaginary journey to point out places and things of interest in Savannah and down the water route as Daufuskians have done, yeh, these many years. Many of the buildings do not exist today, but along the way you will be brought back in time to things and places as they were "back when," So, with that in mind, let's begin this most fascinating tour of Savannah and the voyage to Daufuskie.

•

The year is anytime between 1850 and 1965. From the livery stables in Savannah, we have rented a carriage drawn by two magnificent black horses. To accompany us and handle the horses will be Moses, the livery stable's most trusted driver. We will tour the city, then go to the Abercorn Street wharf on the Savannah River where we will board a lovely sailing vessel that will take us to Bloody Point on Daufuskie for lunch.

It is late October and a twinge of autumn is in the air. We've had to rise early as there is so much to do and see on this beautiful, crisp day. So, tuck the lap blanket around your legs to keep you snug and warm, and let's be on our way.

The first place to see is on Chippewa Square, 17 W. McDonough Street, the townhouse of Mr. John Stoddard. The house, built by silversmith Moses Eastman, was begun in 1844 and bought by Mr. Stoddard in 1848.

Mr. Stoddard lived here with his wife, Mary Lavinia, spending summers at Melrose on Daufuskie. Following his wife's death in 1865, their daughter Mary Helen lived here with her husband John L. Hardee, until 1893 when the house was sold. The house is now occupied by the Atlantic Mutual Fire Insurance Company.[1]

Now look just across the street at Nos. 19 through 25 on W. St. Julian. These massive row-houses were built by John Stoddard in 1854. The house at 15 W. St. Julian was built by John in 1867.[2]

A fascinating place you must see is the Green-Meldrin House on Bull Street facing Madison Square (1. W. Macon Street). The house is now used as a Parish House by St. John's Church. It was completed in 1861 by Charles Green, whose son Benjamin Green married

508

Isabelle Stoddard, daughter of John and Mary Lavinia Stoddard. Isabelle owned and cut into lots Benjie's Point Plantation on Daufuskie.

General William Tecumseh Sherman established his headquarters in the Green House during the Civil War and probably from this house he penned the note on 22 December 1864, giving President Lincoln the City of Savannah for a Christmas present.[3] This house is now open to the public and is so beautiful inside—please pay it a visit.

We'll take a quick ride to 207-209 W. Jones to see the Jesse Mount double-house, built in 1852. Jesse was a Philadelphia lawyer and merchant, coming to Savannah in about 1820. On 20 December 1820, he became the third husband of Love Martinangele, daughter of Isaac and Elizabeth Martinangele of Daufuskie. Jesse and Love had one child, Amanda Elizabeth, born circa 1820-1821. Amanda married Charles J. Zittrouer on 9 May 1839. They had two daughters, Sarah Rebecca and Jessie Amanda Zittrouer.

Jesse had also owned the house at 122 W. Jones and another home in South Carolina, therefore, it isn't certain in just which one of them this incident occurred. On the wall of the sitting room hung this life-sized portrait of his eighteen-month-old granddaughter, Sarah Rebecca. The beautiful 1841 oil painting was the work of artist F. R. Street. During the Civil War, Yankees entered Jesse's home, and upon seeing the portrait one soldier pierced it through with his bayonet, removing it from the wall and handing it over to the slaves to "decorate their cabins." Following the soldiers departure, the slaves graciously returned the picture to the family.[4]

We must hurry as we do want to be at the river front on time. We'll go quickly to visit 24 E. Habersham Street, the John David Mongin "capital dwelling house" built in 1797. You know that he owned several plantations on Daufuskie.

After John David sold the townhouse to Edward Swarbreck, it was visited by Lafayette in 1825. The house next belonged to Christ Church and was used as a hospital during Savannah's last epidemic of yellow fever in 1876.[5]

We don't want to miss a thing; we've just passed the Mongin house. We will now take a right turn off Habersham and at 419 E. St. Julian Street we'll see the Squire Pope townhouse built in 1810. I'm sure that you recall that Squire Pope owned Daufuskie's Haig's Point which he purchased from the Reverend Herman Blodgett in 1850.

We need to take a short trip down Broughton Street to get on Abercorn, which will take us to Bay Street and on to the river.

See the lamp-lighter pulling the street lights down by their chains? He will hoist the lights back up the lamp post to relight tonight, but before he does he will extinguish the flame, clean the shade, trim the wick, and fill the lamp with oil. The merchants are opening their stores, getting ready for a busy day. There are several carriages and wagons in the streets. Couples with valises are leaving the hotel; perhaps they will catch an early boat. It is so exciting to see the hustle and bustle of a town beginning to wake up in the morning.

We're now on E. Bay Street. Take a look at the Stoddard warehouses—Number 12 Building, 42 E. Bay, was built sometime between 1859 and 1876; Numbers 208, 230 E. Bay, were built 1858-59; and 216 E. Bay was built circa 1875.[6]

We've just left Bay Street and are now riding the narrow passage to the river. I love to hear the clip-clop of the horses hooves on the cobblestones.

Did you know that the Savannah River has had other Indian names? Its final name was given it from the Shawnee or Savannah Indians who in the 1680s drove out the Westo Indians who were in possession of a large portion of the lower river land. Did you also know that by 1740 Augusta had become a good-sized town, and that the first freight hauled between Savannah and Augusta was carried by poleboats? The name was derived from the fact that boats were "poled" or pushed up and down stream using long poles and some hefty, robust men. These poleboats were used until 1816 when the first steam boat *Enterprise* made its maiden voyage from Savannah to Augusta.[7]

Well, here were are at the river front. There are a number of vessels at dockside with several anchored out in the channel. Smell that heavenly, spicy aroma wafting out from the hold of that East Indies schooner with its cargo of cinnamon, nutmeg, cloves, and peppers! The lovely fragrance has permeated the air clear up to Broughton Street.

Let me tell you a very interesting story. Had we been here at the river front on a morning in 1740, we would have seen a very sick man being carried aboard his vessel. A terrible thing had happened to him:

510

Mr Charles Odingsell, an inhabitant of South Carolina, had been a great benefactor to the infant colony of Georgia. Having come to Savannah to see how the Colony was succeeding, being abroad some-time after it was night as he was going to his lodging, was taken up in the street for a stroller, carried to the Guard House and threatened with the STOCK AND WHIPPING POST—the terror and fright of which—threw him into a high fever. He was carried aboard his boat in order to be sent home and died in the way somewhere about Dawfuskee Sound.[8]

There has been found no record of proof that this man was a relative nor in any way connected, but a Charles Odingsell was the third husband of Sarah Ash-Livingston-Odingsell. The Livingston-Ash children were heirs of former lands of Haig's Point, Freeport, Cooper River, Newburgh (Webb Tract), Melrose, Maryfield, and Oak Ridge Plantations on Daufuskie.

Here we are at the wharf where our sailboat is waiting. Thank you, Moses, you were a superb driver. Now, everyone carefully step down out of the carriage so Moses can drive it and those wonderful horses back to the Savannah stables.

Please hurry, as I see the boat lines are being loosed from the dock. The tide is ebbing and will be in our favor. Everyone safely aboard? Good. I insist that you remain on deck—it will be to your advantage in viewing the whole panorama while we leisurely sail down the river.

As we are traveling, points of interest will be brought to your attention. More emphasis will be placed on those connected in any way to Daufuskie or its people.

Just below the city on your right are the Brewton Hill (Bruton Hall) rice fields of George Haig. Mr. Haig had purchased 490 acres of land from Rebecca Motte and Charles Pinckney in 1789. Haig died in 1791. But his son, Dr. George Haig, is seen in possession of land in the same area on an 1833 map.[9] The Haigs were also owners of Haig's Point on Daufuskie, after whom the plantation was named.

Either on part of the former Haig's Rice Field, or near it, was the Southeastern Shipbuilding Corporation. During World War II this company built 88 liberty ships, one of which—Number 30—was named the *S. S. Florence Martus*, in honor of the famous "Waving Girl."[10] Many Daufuskians worked at the shipyard all through the war years: Arthur A. Burn, Hoke Greiner, Gary and Gillian Ward, and Flossie Washington, to name a few.

Remains of the cradles that held the ships while they were being built are still visible today. Visit them by turning north off East President Street onto Wahlstrom Drive; that will take you down to the Savannah River where the Hardaway Company occupies the old shipyard area.

As you can see we are coming up to Ft. Jackson on the starboard side. But before we do, right in front of the entrance to the mote, known as Five Fathom Hole, on 24 December 1864, a Confederate Navy vessel, the first of the ironclads built in Savannah (the *C.S.S. Georgia*) was sunk to prevent its capture as Sherman's army approached Savannah. There have been thoughts of bringing it up, but the vessel continues to remain in its watery grave.

Ft. Jackson was built in 1811 and named after James Jackson (1757-1806), Revolutionary soldier, Governor of Georgia, and a United States Senator. While the Fort was being built, two slaves, Isaac and William, owned by F. G. Champion, worked as boatmen and were paid $30.00 each per month. John Godfrey, a blacksmith, was paid $2.00 per day.[11]

All vessels entering the Savannah River were directed to Ft. Jackson to be inspected by the U.S. Health Officer there.[12]

The Fort was occupied by State troops in 1861 following Georgia's secession from the Union, and by Union troops in 1862 during the Civil War. After the Civil War the name of the Fort was changed to Fort Oglethorpe and remained so until the early twentieth century. In 1905 the War Department turned it over to the Army Engineer Department.

For years the Fort was abandoned, and when in the 1930s we would pass it as we traveled to the city, it was overgrown with trees and bushes and was so dark and forbidding it could not be recognized as being anything.

It was refreshing to know that in 1951 the land on which the Fort was built (Salters Island), was purchased by the American Cyanamid Company, who in 1958 deeded Fort Jackson and approximately seven acres of land to the State of Georgia for development by the Georgia Historical Commission. Fort Jackson also had a range light whose keeper was Daniel Z. Duncan, taking oath 15 December 1888 at a salary of $600.00 per annum. Gustaf (Gus) Ohman was also keeper at this light at one time. This is an interesting place to see, but might be

closed on certain days, so call before you decide to visit.[13]

We are now approaching Elba Island, which lies between North and South Channels. The North Channel was chosen as the Savannah River, because it had much deeper water and was suitable for sailing and other large vessels. As we bear to port around Elba Island, the bend in the river almost makes a "corner" and has always been referred to by Daufuskians as Proctor's Corner. I checked into this to find out why the people called this so (and still do), and who was this "Proctor" person? So far, his first name has not been disclosed; only the name "Col. Proctor" has been found.[14] On the South Carolina side across from Elba Island, Colonel Proctor had 800 acres of land, a home, several out buildings, and he grew rice on his plantation.[15] During the Civil War the buildings were burned and artillery batteries were located in the vicinity. The chimneys remained standing for a spell. By 1896 the rice fields were indicated as being abandoned. However, in the 1930s and 40s a Mr. Pinckney had a huge truck-farm there. On our trips up the river, we would see him in his open passenger boat, with a top, transporting workers to and from Savannah to tend the fields. Apparently the encroachment of salt water eventually destroyed any use of that land.

Look on your starboard side—a most interesting place is coming up on Elba Island—*The Waving Girl* Light Station. On 3 March 1881 funds were appropriated by an act of Congress for the purpose of lighting the Savannah River between the mouth of the river and the city of Savannah. Two beacons were erected for such a purpose on Elba Island in 1884. A keeper's dwelling was built in 1887 at a cost of $3500. The first keeper was James Kelley, a native of Georgia, appointed 3 October 1884, removed 17 September 1887—salary $720.00 per annum.[16]

George W. Martus was born in the District of Columbia in 1861. His famous sister, Florence, was born 8 August 1868 in the home of an officer of Fort Pulaski, just outside the Fort walls on Cockspur Island. Their father was a soldier at Fort Pulaski. George was only eighteen years of age when he became keeper at the Cockspur Island Lighthouse, shortly thereafter being transferred to the Elba Island light.

Their parents had died, so when George was made keeper at the Elba Island lighthouse in 1887, Florence made the move with him so she could keep house and do the cooking for her brother.

Florence began waving at every boat that passed—a white cloth by day, a lantern by night. Then the vessel would salute her in return with three blasts from its whistle.

It didn't take long for a romantic rumor to begin: Legend has it that her sweetheart left with a promise to come back one day. She vowed she would wave at every ship until his return—but he never came back. The Elba Station now became known as *The Waving Girl.* Sailors from ships all over the world waved at her as they passed.

In 1931, when George W. Martus reached 70 years of age, he retired. With both leaving the island, George and Florence tried to live in Savannah for awhile but found it too crowded. They then moved to a white cottage at Bona Bella, near Isle of Hope, where they had more space and were closer to the water.[17]

The well known World War II journalist Ernie Pyle had heard about *The Waving Girl.* He came to Savannah, found out where Florence lived, then went to her home for an interview. In the course of conversation Ernie asked her, "Now, please don't mind me asking this, but is that legend true about your sweetheart going away and never coming back? Is that why you waved at ships?"

"Oh, that old stuff!" She said it sort of testily. She didn't say whether it was true or not, and Ernie Pyle couldn't tell from her tone. "Why I was born and raised right down at the mouth of the river, and we knew all the local tug-boat and schooner captains, and it was only natural that I should wave at them when they passed. And then I just got to waving at everybody."

Florence told Ernie Pyle that she had kept a diary the years they had lived on Elba Island. She had not only written things about their daily activities but had also recorded the name of every boat and where it was from—possibly 50,000 ships or more. The ledger filled four large volumes. In sorting out all her stuff in getting ready to move, she came across the diaries and thought to herself, "The young people nowadays don't want to read any of this old junk. It'll just collect dust." So she threw them in the fire! The daily records of forty-four years, kept in her own hand, gone up in smoke in two minutes.

Then Ernie Pyle said to her, "If I knew you better I'd give you a great big kick."

Florence laughed, and her reply was, "Well, I guess you ought to."[18]

On 31 May 1931, replacing George W. Martus at *The Waving Girl*

Station was Theodore T. Gilliard. He and his wife were from North Carolina. He was a tall, slender, weather-beaten man and she was a short, hefty blonde. Being left alone most of the time, she was also a talker. That was such a lonely place that when you did see someone, you talked their ears off.

Lance Burn was tending lights around Daufuskie. When the Gilliards planned a vacation in February 1939, Lance was instructed to be the relief keeper for the thirty days they would be gone. Our little daughter June was almost three, and I was expecting our second child (Robert L. Burn, called Bob). Since Mrs. Gilliard waved at each ship day and night, it became my duty to follow the same tradition. I waved a white towel by day, a lantern by night. After a few nights we got tired of hopping up and down, and left the lighted lantern on the window ledge. Some of the horns on those boats were so loud that their three blasts just about blew us out of bed. There was not a comfortable chair in the whole place, so for thirty miserable days I was *The Waving Girl*.

The Gilliards remained at the Elba Island lighthouse until 1943 when it was discontinued and the Coast Guard took over the lights.

On her seventieth birthday, 7 August 1938, Florence Martus was given a birthday party at Fort Pulaski on Cockspur Island by the Propeller Club, Port of Savannah. Her giant birthday cake was adorned with a replica of the home of Elba Island from which she had waved to so many passing ships. Three thousand people attended the celebration. The Club's General Chairman, Edward A. Dutton, introduced the distinguished guests: Robert M. Hitch, Mayor of Savannah and Congressman Hugh Peterson. President of the Propeller Club, Samuel A. Cann, introduced Miss Florence Martus; and presentation of the birthday cake and gifts was given by Mrs. J. Roger Cohan, President, Women's Organization for the Advancement of the American Merchant Marine.[19]

Florence Martus died 8 February 1943. Her body was buried near her brother George W. Martus, who had preceded her in 1939. They both are buried at Laurel Grove Cemetery.

The Waving Girl lighthouse remained vacant for years. The date palm tree that produced edible fruit and grew by the east porch had died. Large trees and underbrush had almost hidden the house from the river. Rabbit hunters (circa 1949) set the grass afire and burned the house to the ground. Encroachment of the sea claimed where the

The Waving Girl Station on Elba Island in Savannah River, circa 1930
(Photograph courtesy Mrs. Ida White-Tatum.)

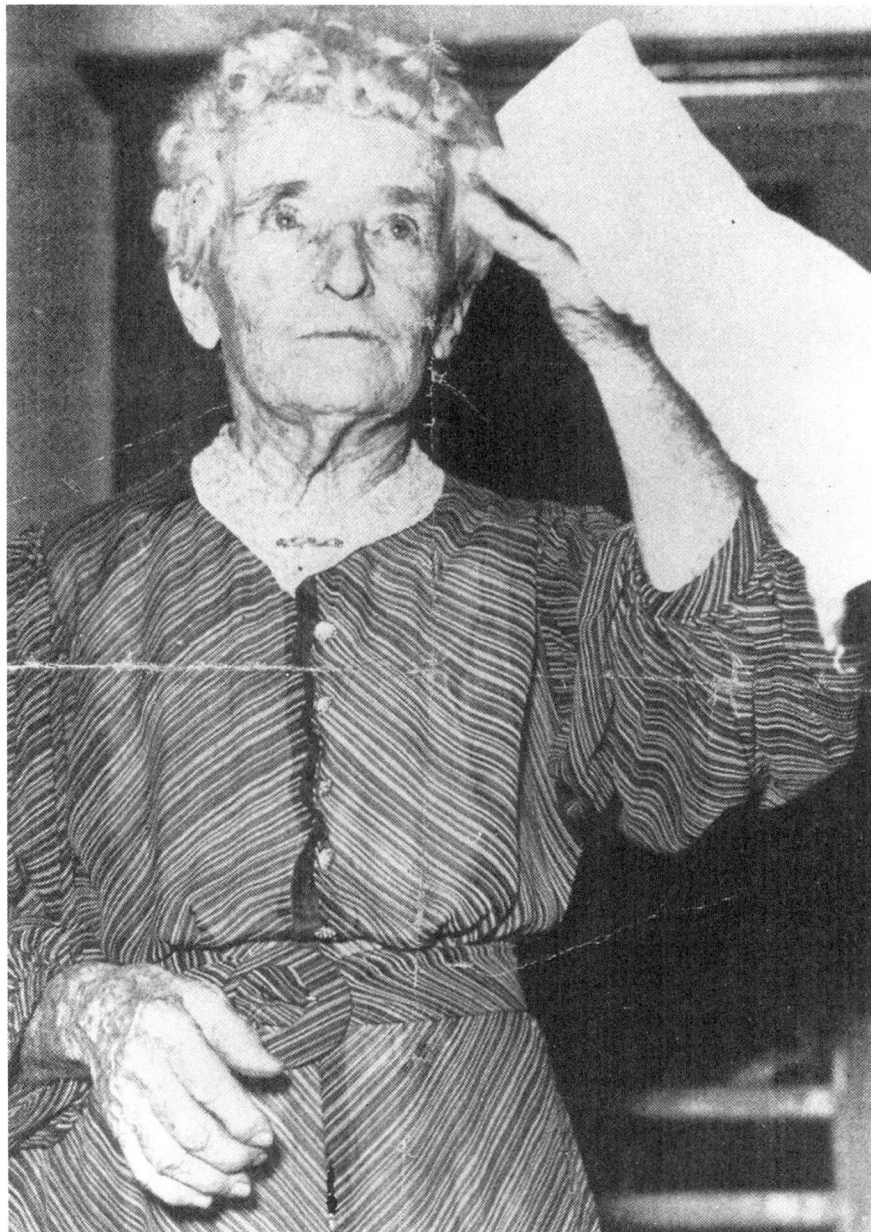

Florence Martus—"The Waving Girl"

Photograph from program of the birthday party given Florence at Ft. Pulaski by The Propeller Club, 7 August 1938. She was 69 years old at the time. (Compliments Gene A. Burn.)

house once stood. Having been at the back of the house, the cistern for years was exposed on the shore. Finally, there was nothing left.

But Florence Martus was not forgotten. A liberty ship was named after her and a statue of her and one of her several collie dogs stands on River Street. She continues to wave at each ship that passes.

Just below *The Waving Girl* Station is Elba Island Cut. For years, vessels traveling the Intracoastal Waterway had to go up the Savannah River to South Channel, then come all the way back down South Channel to St. Augustine Creek. This cut across Elba Island was made sometime between 1940 and 1947 which made a five or six mile shortcut, saving time and gas for all boats in years to come.

On your left is Fields Cut. This was known as Mud Creek during the Civil War and was not navigable except on high tide when only shallow-bottomed boats could make it through. Sometime after the war it was dredged for passage of all sized boats.

Normally, we would take Fields Cut to Daufuskie, but today we are going on down Savannah River, like the sailing schooners had to go years ago, for there are other sights that I want to recall and tell you about.

Coming up on your left is Venus Point light and dwelling on Jones Island. The keepers here were Charles Sisson, 7 August 1893, Salary: $700.00 per annum; First Assistant, Fred G. Sisson, 3 August 1896, Salary: $300.00 per year; Assistant Gustaf Ohman, 16 August 1896, Salary: $300.00 per annum. Gus was paid as a laborer prior to the oath.[20]

Again, on the starboard side, we are approaching one of the most interesting and busy pieces of land along the river—Cockspur Island.

The first thing that comes into view is the dock and building that belongs to the Savannah Pilots' Association where the pilots stay who guide the big vessels into port.

Next to this was the Tybee Knoll Cut Light Station. This Station was a duplex house for the keeper and his assistant. The building had a light tower built right into the house (something like the Haig's Point lighthouse on Daufuskie). In the 1920s, Ed Floyd was the keeper and Arthur A.Burn was his assistant. After them came Keeper Fahey and his Assistant Don Goodwin (formerly from Daufuskie).[21] These two remained at the lighthouse until it was discontinued in the 1940s. What happened to the house is unknown, but there is nothing left of it today.

Traveling down the river a short way from the lighthouse was the Quarantine Station. There was a nice dock, a small hospital, and other buildings where Dr. Lindley and Dr. Brown and their attendants were housed.

Several Daufuskie men worked at the Quarantine and retired from there, two of whom were Robert Bryan and Thomas Bryan. When William (Bill) Timmons worked there as an assistant, one of the doctors liked to hunt coons and had several hound dogs that slept under the buildings, which were high off the ground. Fleas became so prevalent that Bill was instructed to hose down under the buildings to keep down the population of the fleas, as they could not breed in sand that was wet.[22]

Prior to being on Cockspur Island the Quarantine Station was known as Lazaretto Camp, a very popular place over 150 years ago, situated on the back side of Tybee Island in 1749. The word "lazaretto" means "Quarantine Station."[23]

The early shipping industry was a very dangerous undertaking. Often ships would visit a port, pick up an infectious disease, then transmit that disease to the next port. If a ship was suspected of carrying a disease, the boat was boarded by officers from the quarantine at the Lazaretto Camp and the situation was taken care of. Lazaretto Creek is named for this Camp.

For a brief time in the mid 1800s, the Camp was moved to Thunderbolt, where it picked up the nickname of the "Pest Hole." It wasn't the most popular place around.

Then in 1885 the Quarantine was established on Cockspur Island, where a small hospital and several buildings were constructed. The quarantine remained here until it was discontinued in the 1940s. Bill Timmons was one of the assistants transferred to the station in Charleston.

We are now coming up on Fort Pulaski on the right. This fort was begun in 1829. Two others had stood about on the same spot: Fort George, dismantled by patriots in 1776, and Fort Greene, destroyed in the hurricane of 1804.[24]

But the forts are not my main concern at this point. The parade grounds of Fort Pulaski were often used for duels. One of much interest was fought by John Joshua Chaplin, born 1826 or 1828, the youngest son of William Fripp and Harriet Martinangele Chaplin of Daufuskie.

519

On 22 October 1855, a duel was fought at Fort Pulaski between John Chaplin, of South Carolina, ex-lieutenant in the United States Navy, and his brother-in-law, Dr. Kirk, of Savannah. Three shots were exchanged. On the last fire, Doctor Kirk was killed. Chaplin was slightly wounded in the foot. The statement was made that Chaplin fired his first shot in the air, but Dr. Kirk refused to acknowledge this gracious act with a reconciliation, and forfeited his life.[25]

Just beyond Fort Pulaski walls on the east, built on an oyster shell pile and mud, is Cockspur Island Lighthouse. According to the National Archives in Washington, D.C., a lighthouse was built on this spot as early as 1827, but the one now standing was built in 1848-1849 by Savannah builder John Norris, who won the contract and constructed a tower of brick and mortar 46 feet high and 16 feet wide at the base. This light used a sperm or whale oil flame to signal mariners. A cottage was built nearby for a keeper and an assistant. Total cost of lighthouse and cottage was $2,670.[26]

The Cockspur light was build simultaneously with a sister light on Oyster Bed Island Lighthouse. The Cockspur light ushered ships into the then-used South Channel and tended by the keeper, while the Oyster Bed light was placed in the North Channel (as part of the Jones Island system of lights) and tended by the assistant keeper.

Keepers of the Cockspur Lighthouse:

John H. Lightburn, 1849.
Cornelius Maher, 1851, who tried to help someone in trouble, the boat capsized, and drowned the keeper in 1853.
Mrs. Mary Maher (the keeper's widow) 1853-1856.
Thomas Quinfiven was made keeper in June, 1856, and was dead from a fever by October. He was 29 years old.
Patrick Eagan, 1856-1857.
Thomas Flood, 1857-1861. His duties were interrupted by the Civil War.

The lighthouse lay dormant during the war. But following the war there were other keepers:

Thomas Flood was reappointed, serving until 1869.
Patrick Eagan, again in 1869-1877. Eagan and his sons operated the lighthouse as a family affair. During 1871, death claimed one of Eagan's sons. There had been several storms and during one Eagan and his two "under age" sons (Michael and Thomas) were journeying to light the Cockspur tower when their boat overturned. They were blown with the

In the front yard of dwelling, Fort Pulaski's parapet wall. Left to right: Claude F. Fripp and Lance Burn, circa 1916. A ward of Mrs. John Fripp (Claude's mother), Lance remarked that every cannon ball he found, he rolled it over the wall of the Fort and was responsible for half the cannon balls found there. William Timmons worked at the Quarantine Station and was married to Claude's sister, Laura Fripp. Claude also worked at the Quarantine and boarded with Bill and Laura. They lived in this house for two years, circa 1916-1918. By trade, Lance became a plasterer, and in 1936, when repairs were being made to open Ft. Pulaski to the public, he and Percy Jones plastered the dungeon.

Cockspur Lighthouse keeper's quarters built on parapet wall, Fort Pulaski. This house was struck by lightning so many times, it was finally destroyed. (Photographer anonymous.)

capsized boat to Daufuskie Island where the father and Michael were rescued the next day, but the body of young Thomas was never found.

Charles Poland, 1877. While he and his wife were living there, the keeper's cottage was struck by lightning which wrecked the house and gave them quite a shock. The hurricane of 1881 blew the cottage away.

George Washington Martus, 1881. He served until 1886 when he was appointed keeper at the Elba Island Lighthouse where he moved with his sister, Florence, who became the *Waving Girl.*

Jerimiah Keane, 1886. The hurricane of 1891 no doubt inundated the Cockspur Lighthouse, because the Fort Pulaski parade ground was covered with five feet of water. Following this hurricane, for safety a two-story keeper's house was built on top the parapet of the Fort. By this time the Fort had been abandoned.

Gustaf Ohman, 1901. He was the last one serving until the light was discontinued in 1909 when traffic on South Channel had dwindled in favor of the North Channel, or Savannah River. The Cockspur tower continued to serve as a harbor beacon until it was abandoned in 1949 by the Coast Guard.[27]

We are now veering around Oyster Bed Island Lighthouse that will lead us into Wright River. As we leave Wright River and make a starboard turn there is a short channel known as Walls Cut that proves rather interesting. During plantation days this cut frequently filled with mud to the point that passage of ships was almost impossible. In order to alleviate this condition, the following petition was presented by the planters:

1800
State of South Carolina
To the Honorable President of the Senate of the said State

The petition of the several inhabitants of May River Neck, the Islands of Hilton Head, Daufuskie, Bull's & Savages in the Parish of St. Lukes and State aforesaid, humbly sheweth, that your petitioners view with much concern the probability of an obstruction of safe continuous betwixt the inhabitants of the Sea Coast in the Parish aforesaid and the City of Savannah in the State of Georgia; by the daily filling up of the Cut commonly called Walles Cut. And as your Petitioner as well as the Community at large have heretofore reaped & must continue to reap considerable advantage from a speedy & safe communication betwixt the two States by means of the said Cut; and it appearing to your petitioners that no Law heretofore pafsed by preceding legislatures has

been sufficient for effectually opening the same. Your petitioners therefore humbly pray that the Honorable House of Senate will in their present sefsion concur with the Honorable House of Representatives in pafsing an Act requiring the several inhabitants of May River Neck, as well as the inhabitants of the Islands of Hilton Head, Daufuskie, Bull's & Savages with their respective male slaves that are liable to work on the public roads, to work on said Cut, not more than six days in every two years, until compleated (sic), by which means your petitioners will be enabled to keep their public roads in good repair & gradually open the said Cut to the great benefit of your petitioners & the Community at large.[28]

After leaving Walls Cut you now enter New River. If you make a starboard turn into New River, it will take you to Bloody Point. If you live near the public landing at Benjie's Point or perhaps at Cooper River, you will take a port turn in New River. For those living on Mongin Creek, a starboard turn from New River into this Creek will take you home.

Our voyage to Daufuskie has ended. It has been a lovely, eventful day. We will head for Bloody Point and have a delicious lunch, walk the beach for a spell, perhaps find a few shells, then make our way back to Savannah.

Hopefully you have enjoyed your trip to Daufuskie and have a better knowledge of the sights that we have been privileged to see through the years. It was my pleasure to be your guide.

Notes

1. Information about the house came from the Atlantic Mutual Fire Insurance office, 12 June 1989.
2. Mr. Albert H. Stoddard III.
3. *Sojourn in Savannah*, a guidebook with a map of Historic Savannah, may be purchased at the Georgia Historical Society on Whitaker Street.
4. Mrs. Sophia Wells Barnes, Savannah, personal files, 12 October 1986. Being a close relative, the bayonet-pierced portrait now hangs on Sophia's living room wall.
5. Walter C. Hartridge.
6. Mr. Albert H. Stoddard III.
7. Ruby A. Rahn, *River Highway for Trade, The Savannah* (Savannah: U.S. Army Engineer District, Corps of Engineers, June 1968), pp. 12, 13, 19, 10. Book shared through the courtesy of Mr. Walter S. Schaaf, U. S. Engineers, 20 May 1986.
8. *S. C. Historical and Gen. Magazine* , 23, pp. 150-51; *Narrative of the Colony of Georgia.* (Charles Town: P. Timothy, 1741), p. 35.
9. M. L. Granger, *Savannah Harbor, Its Origin and Development 1733—1890* (Savannah: U. S. Army Engineer District, Corps of Engineers, Savannah, Georgia,

November 1968), Chart of the Savannah River, 1833, p. 54; Mary Granger, *Savannah River Plantations* (Savannah: Georgia Historical Society, 1947), pp. 32, 46-49.

10. Georgia Historical Society, Savannah, *Ships Miscellaneous*, pp. 148-49; *Savannah Evening Press*, 27 September 1943.

11. All of this information may be found in pamphlets obtained at the Fort.

12. Quarantine Notice, *Savannah Gazette*, 4 November 1811.

13. Most of this information may be obtained from pamphlets at the Fort.

14. An Early Hand Drawn Map of S. C. Plantations on the Savannah Back River—Many of whose owners had summer houses in St. Luke's Parish. (Also including some plantations on Georgia side of the Savannah River). Map purchased through the courtesy of The Bluffton Historical Preservation Society, Inc., 25 October 1988.

15. Index Map, Savannah River, Ga., Showing Works Constructed from 1804 to 1896. Also location of Rice Plantations now under cultivation and those abandoned. Map shared through the courtesy of Mr. Walter S. Schaaf, U. S. Engineers, Savannah, 20 May 1986.

16. Coast Guard Group #26.

17. *Washington Herald*, 12 June 1931.

18. *The Washington Daily News*, 21 February 1936. A copy of the article was sent through the courtesy of the National Archives, Lighthouse Clipping File, "Elba Island Light Range, Ga, 6th District," Group #26. Ernest (Ernie) Taylor Pyle, U. S. journalist, born 1900-1945, was killed by a Japanese sniper's bullet on the tiny Island of Le Shima in April of 1945, 20 days before the Germans surrendered. Ernie is buried at the Punch Bowl, Oahu, Hawaii.

19. The Propeller Club, Birthday Party for Miss Florence Martus, "The Waving Girl," Program, 7 August 1938; Thomas L. Stokes, *The Savannah* (New York: Rinehart & Co., 1951), pp. 364-76; Elinor De Wire," The Women of the Lights." *The Adventure of the American Past, American History Illustrated* (February 1987): 48.

20. Group #26.

21. Francis A. Burn, Sr. interview 4 March 1990.

22. Mrs. William (Laura) Timmons, interview, 24 June 1982.

23. Gerhard Spieler, "Marine Quarantine Stations on S. C. Coast Date Back to 1698,"*Beaufort Gazette*, 21 March 1988.

24. Eva J. Barrington, "Historic Acts on Cockspur are Recalled," *Savannah Morning News,* 7 November 1950; Trudy Yates, "Fort Pulaski the Third Such Edifice on Cockspur Island," *Island Packet,* 12 October 1983.

25. Thomas Gamble, *Savannah Duels and Duellists 1733-1877*, (Savannah: Review Publishing & Printing Company, 1925), p. 211. Copy shared courtesy Mr. David Humphrey, Savannah.

26. Gary Mikell, "Lonely Lighthouse Has Survival Instinct," *Savannah Morning News & Evening Press*, 3 July 1977.

27. Ibid.

28. General Assembly Petition #120-l800, S. C. Department of Archives and History, Columbia, S. C.

Billie Burn

Billie Smith Burn, born in Monroe, Tennessee; schooled in Columbus, Georgia, attended Draughons Business College, Savannah; worked as a secretary for Union Camp Corporation, Savannah, in the 1950s; employed as estimator for the Union Plastering Company, Fort Lauderdale, Florida, 1955–1959; from 1963 to 1984 was postmaster of Daufuskie and, for almost as many years, the Mary Fields School bus driver.

She was the first white member and the PTA treasurer, 1963–1977; secretary-treasurer of the Daufuskie Island Community Improvement Club from 1965 to 1986; registrar (births and deaths), 1963–1986; president of the store Co-op in 1985 and chairman of the "Daufuskie Day" for that year. She attends the Union Baptist Church and participates in many community activities.

Her first publication was a "Mary Dunn Cemetery" booklet printed in 1983 by the Atlantic Printing Company, Savannah. Her first book was *Stirrin' the Pots on Daufuskie*, printed in 1985 by Impressions Printing Company, Hilton Head—with its fourth printing made in 1990 and representing a total of 12,500 copies.

Her husband, Lance Burn, died in 1989. She continues to reside on Daufuskie, where her son Bob and his wife Emily live nearby. Contact her: Billie Burn, P.O. Box 29, Daufuskie Island, S.C. 29915.

The Burn Family—1980

Left to right: Billie, Bob, June B. Crumley, Gene, and Lance.

Appendix I
Translation
A Road for Daufuskie

1805-/3/01

State of South Carolina
Parish of St. Luke

To the Honorable Speaker and other members of the House of Representatives of the State aforesaid.

The Petition of the subscribers, inhabitants of the Island of Daufuskie and other inhabitants of the Parish aforesaid Humbly sheweth, that the inhabitants of the Island of Daufuskie, labor under great inconvenience for want of a Road established by law through said Island, whereby they might have free intercourse to and from a landing which would greatly facilitate their attendances at a place of worship and their muster-field—

It is with much concern your Petitioners have to state that only of late this right of free intercourse through the Island has been denied to the Inhabitants thereof, and that fences have been erected for the purpose of impeading their usual communication, which has tended not only to render the duty of a Patrol difficult and ineffectual, but has also divested a portion of the free citizens of our State of priviledges heretofore exercised and enjoyed.

Your Petitioners therefore, relying upon the justice of your Honorable Body, Humbly pray that you will appoint Commissioners for the purpose of laying out a Road through said Island by which means the former intercourse of the inhabitants thereof will be an established way to enable them to perform their duties required by the precepts of Religion, and the laws of the State and your Petitioners will ever pray—

2 October 1805

(Signatures listed.)

Phillip Martinangele

John D. Mongin

529

Appendix II
DAVID MONGIN
Pedigree Chart

(No. 1)
5. David Mongin

GREAT-GREAT GRANDFATHER
BORN
WHERE France
WHEN MARRIED 4 Sept 1726
DIED 22 Nov 1770
WHERE Charleston

Persille Dair d. 1747

GREAT-GREAT GRANDMOTHER

OTHER WIVES
(2) Elizabeth Edwards
m. 1749 d. 1759
(3) Mary Ann Burgoyne? Bekin?
m. 1765
No children

(No. 2)
4. David John I

GREAT GRANDFATHER
BORN 1739
WHERE England
WHEN MARRIED 1762
DIED 1815
WHERE Charleston

Sarah Grimkie

GREAT GRANDMOTHER

(No. 3)
3. John David

PATERNAL GRANDFATHER
BORN 1763
WHERE S May River
WHEN MARRIED 1790
DIED 14 Nov 1833
WHERE S May River

Sarah Watts d. 1816

PATERNAL GRANDMOTHER

OTHER WIVES
(2) Ann Harrison
m. 1823 d. 1850
No children

(No. 4)
2. David John II

FATHER
BORN 1791
WHERE S May River
WHEN MARRIED c. 1818
DIED 1823
WHERE Daufuskie

Sarah Irwin d. 1833

MOTHER
(2) HUSBAND
Rev. Herman M. Blodgett
WHEN MARRIED 1825
CHILDREN
Benjamin, Joseph, Sarah M. Blodgett.
All children dead by 1840.

(No. 5)
1. Mary Lavinia

BORN Feb 1819
WHERE Daufuskie
WHEN MARRIED 7 Jan 1836
DIED 22 Feb 1865
WHERE Savannah Ga

John Stoddard

NAME OF HUSBAND OR WIFE
BORN 11 Mar 1809
DIED 25 Jul 1879

In order to better understand,
DAVIDS are listed as generations
one (No. 1) through four (No. 4).

Appendix III: Family Group Record

DAVID MONGIN and PERSILLE DAIR (No. 1 Wife)

HUSBAND—DAVID MONGIN (No. 1)

VITAL DATA	DAY MONTH YEAR	CITY, TOWN or PLACE	COUNTY or PROVINCE	STATE or COUNTRY
Birth	1690			France
Marriage	4 Sept 1726	Soho Square	London	England
Death	23 Nov 1770	Charleston	Charleston	South Carolina
Burial	Huguenot Churchyard, Charleston, South Carolina			
Husband's father			Husband's mother	
Other wives, if any:				

WIFE—PERSILLE DAIR

VITAL DATA	DAY MONTH YEAR	CITY, TOWN or PLACE	COUNTY or PROVINCE	STATE or COUNTRY
Birth				
Death	6 Aug 1747	Soho Square	London	England
Burial	Westminster Abbey, London, England (no proof)			
Wife's father			Wife's mother	
Other husband's, if any				

SEX	CHILDREN'S NAMES IN FULL	DATA	DATE	LOCATION
F	1. Elizabeth (twin)	Birth	19 Sept 1728	London, England
		Marriage		
		Death		London, England
	Full name of spouse: Robert Harvey	Burial		
		Children		
F	2. Margaret (twin)	Birth	19 Sept 1728	London, England
		Marriage		
		Death	20 Oct 1728	London, England
	Full name of spouse	Burial	Westminster Abbey	
		Children		
F	3. Frances	Birth	20 Nov 1730	London, England
		Marriage		
		Death	30 Nov 1730	London, England
	Full name of spouse	Burial	Westminster Abbey	
		Children		
F	4. Mary Persille	Birth	14 Dec 1735	London, England
		Marriage		
		Death	20 Dec 1735	London, England
	Full name of spouse	Burial	Westminster Abbey	
		Children		
M	5. David John	Birth	4 Mar 1739	London, England
		Marriage	1762	Charleston, South Carolina
		Death	1815	Charleston, South Carolina
	Full name of spouse: Sarah Grimkie	Burial	Charleston, South Carolina	
		Children		
F	6. Jane Mary	Birth	3 Aug 1741	London, England
		Marriage	1773	Walnut Grove, S May River, SC
		Death		
	Full name of spouse: John Middleton	Burial		
		Children		

In August 1747 David Mongin (No. 1), with his surviving children, Elizabeth, David John, and Jane Mary, embarked from Liverpool for America. Information: Mongin files of Mrs. Charles Ellis II, Robert L. Marchman III, and Ben Anderson, Jr.

531

Appendix III (cont.): Family Group Record

DAVID MONGIN and ELIZABETH EDWARDS (No. 2 Wife)

HUSBAND—DAVID MONGIN (No. 1)				
VITAL DATA	DAY MONTH YEAR	CITY, TOWN or PLACE	COUNTY or PROVINCE	STATE or COUNTRY
Birth	1690			France
Marriage	23 Dec 1749	Princeton	Mercer	New Jersey
Death	23 Nov 1770	Charleston	Charleston	South Carolina
Burial	Huguenot Churchyard, Charleston, South Carolina (no proof)			
Husband's father:			Husband's mother:	
Other wives, if any: (No. 3 wife—Mary Ann Bourguin, sister of John Lewis Bourguin, no children				

WIFE—ELIZABETH EDWARDS				
VITAL DATA	DAY MONTH YEAR	CITY, TOWN or PLACE	COUNTY or PROVINCE	STATE or COUNTRY
Birth	1732	Princeton	Mercer	New Jersey
Death	8 Dec 1759			
Burial	*Record of the Mongin Family*, p. 6, states that she is buried on Daufuskie.			
Wife's father: Jonathan Edwards			Wife's mother: Sarah Pierrepont	
Other husband's, if any				

SEX	CHILDREN'S NAMES IN FULL	DATA	DATE	LOCATION
M	1. William Edwards	Birth	6 Jan 1750	Walnut Grove, S. May River
		Marriage	25 May 1783	
		Death		
	Full name of spouse Margaret M. Pendarvis	Burial		
		Children		
F	2. Mary Jane	Birth	8 May 1753	Walnut Grove, S. May River
		Marriage	26 Sep 1771	Walnut Grove, S. May River
		Death		(The couple sailed for
	Full name of spouse Sir William Godfrey	Burial		England the next day.)
		Children		
M	3. Thomas Jones	Birth	10 Aug 1755	Walnut Grove, S. May River
		Marriage		
		Death	1762	Daufuskie Island
	Full name of spouse	Burial		Daufuskie Island
		Children		
M	4. John Andrew	Birth	15 Oct 1758	Walnut Grove, S. May River
		Marriage	23 Nov 1786	Hilton Head, South Carolina
		Death		
	Full name of spouse Martha Bull	Children	Daughter Catherine married Edward Stafford,	
			7 Apr 1831, S. May River, no children	
5.	Birth			
		Marriage		
		Death		
	Full name of spouse	Burial		
		Children		
6.		Birth		
		Marriage		
		Death		
	Full name of spouse John Middleton	Burial		
		Children		

Appendix IV: Family Group Record

DAVID JOHN MONGIN I and SARAH GRIMKIE

HUSBAND—DAVID JOHN MONGIN I (No. 2)

VITAL DATA	DAY MONTH YEAR	CITY, TOWN or PLACE	COUNTY or PROVINCE	STATE or COUNTRY
Birth	4 Mar 1739	London		England
Marriage	1762	Walnut Grove	S. May River	South Carolina
Death	1815	Charleston		South Carolina
Burial				

Husband's father: David Mongin (No. 1)   Husband's mother: Persille Dair

Other wives, if any:

WIFE—SARAH GRIMKIE

VITAL DATA	DAY MONTH YEAR	CITY, TOWN or PLACE	COUNTY or PROVINCE	STATE or COUNTRY
Birth				
Death				
Burial				

Wife's father   Wife's mother

Other husband's, if any

SEX	CHILDREN'S NAMES IN FULL	DATA	DATE	LOCATION
M	1. John David	Birth	1763	Walnut Grove, S. May River
		Marriage	1790	Walnut Grove, S. May River
		Death	14 Nov 1833	Walnut Grove, S. May River
	Full name of spouse Sarah Watts d. 1816	Burial	Bonaventure Cemetery, Savannah, Georgia	
		Children		
F	2. Catherine	Birth	1765	Walnut Grove, S. May River
		Marriage		
		Death		
	Full name of spouse James Smith	Burial		
		Children	James Mongin, David John, and William Smith	
M	3. Daniel William	Birth	1768	Walnut Grove, S. May River
		Marriage	1798	
		Death		
	Full name of spouse Schepelia Rivers	Burial		
		Children	John David, Susan Frances, Louisa, and Mary Mongin	
F	4. Margaret	Birth	1771	Walnut Grove, S. May River
		Marriage		
		Death		
	Full name of spouse William P. Gray	Burial		
		Children	None listed	
M	5. Richard*	Birth	1774	Walnut Grove, S. May River
		Marriage		
		Death		
	Full name of spouse	Burial		
		Children		
	6.	Birth		
		Marriage		
		Death		
	Full name of spouse	Burial		
		Children		

*Richard Mongin was murdered by his slaves at his plantation (No. 8) on S. May River. The slave shot his master down in the doorway after supper with his master's own gun. He expiated his crime on the Gibbet by a roadside, afterwards known as Gibbet Road, S.C. Richard Mongin never married, being quite a young man when killed. (*Record of the Mongin Family*, p. 7.)

Appendix V: Family Group Record

JOHN DAVID MONGIN and SARAH WATTS

HUSBAND—JOHN DAVID MONGIN I (No. 3, known as "Money Mongin")					
VITAL DATA	DAY MONTH YEAR	CITY, TOWN or PLACE	COUNTY or PROVINCE	STATE or COUNTRY	
Birth	1763	S. May River	Beaufort	South Carolina	
Marriage	1790				
Death	14 Nov 1833	S. May River	Beaufort	South Carolina	
Burial	Bonaventure Cemetery, Savannah, Georgia				
Husband's father: David John Mongin I (No. 2)			Husband's mother: Sarah Grimkie		
Other wives, if any: Ann Harrison, m. 1823, d. 1850					

WIFE—SARAH WATTS				
VITAL DATA	DAY MONTH YEAR	CITY, TOWN or PLACE	COUNTY or PROVINCE	STATE or COUNTRY
Birth				
Death	1816			
Burial	Buried on Daufuskie, her body was later moved to Bonaventure Cemetery in Savannah.			

Wife's father				Wife's mother	
Other husband's, if any					

SEX	CHILDREN'S NAMES IN FULL	DATA	DATE		LOCATION
M	1. David John II	Birth	1791		
		Marriage	1812		
	Full name of spouse	Death	1823		Daufuskie
	Sarah Irwin	Burial	Bonaventure Cemetery, Savannah, Georgia		
F	2. *Mary Ann Taylor Mongin		After David's death, Sarah Irwin Mongin married in 1825 to Rev. Herman M. Blodgett. Sarah and Rev. Blodgett had three children: Benjamin, Joseph, and Sarah M. All three were dead by 1840. Buried in Bonaventure Cemetery, Savannah, Georgia. Not aware of any surviving children.		

*Mentioned and sharing in his will, Mary Ann is stated by John David to be an adopted daughter.

Appendix VI: Family Group Record

DAVID JOHN MONGIN II AND SARAH IRWIN

HUSBAND—DAVID JOHN MONGIN (No. 4)

VITAL DATA	DAY MONTH YEAR	CITY, TOWN or PLACE	COUNTY or PROVINCE	STATE or COUNTRY
Birth	1791	S. May River	Beaufort	South Carolina
Marriage	1811-1812			
Death	1823			
Burial	Bonaventure Cemetery, Savannah, Georgia			

Husband's father: John David Mongin (No. 3) Husband's mother: Sarah Watts

Other wives, if any:

WIFE—SARAH IRWIN*

VITAL DATA	DAY MONTH YEAR	CITY, TOWN or PLACE	COUNTY or PROVINCE	STATE or COUNTRY
Birth				
Death	8 Oct 1833	Daufuskie	Beaufort	South Carolina
Burial	Bonaventure Cemetery, Savannah, Georgia			

Wife's father: Wife's mother:

Other husband's, if any

SEX	CHILDREN'S NAMES IN FULL	DATA	DATE	LOCATION
M	1. Edmund W.	Birth		Daufuskie
		Marriage		
		Death	1813	Daufuskie
	Full name of spouse	Burial		Daufuskie. Later moved to Bonaventure Cemetery
M	2. David John	Birth		Daufuskie
		Marriage		
		Death	1815	Daufuskie
	Full name of spouse	Burial		Daufuskie. Later moved to Bonaventure Cemetery
F	3. Jane J.	Birth		Daufuskie
		Marriage		
		Death	1821	Daufuskie
	Full name of spouse	Burial		Daufuskie. Later moved to Bonaventure Cemetery
M	4. William Henry	Birth	Jan 1816	
		Marriage	1836	Savannah, Georgia
		Death	1 Sep 1851	Savannah, Georgia
	Full name of spouse Isbella Rae Habersham	Burial		Bonaventure Cemetery, Savannah, Georgia
		Children	None	
F	5. Mary Lavinia (twin)	Birth	Feb 1819	
		Marriage	7 Jan 1836	Paris, France
		Death	22 Feb 1865	Savannah, Georgia
	Full name of spouse John Stoddard	Burial		Bonaventure Cemetery, Savannah, Georgia
		Children		
	6. Sarah (twin)	Birth	Feb 1819	Daufuskie
		Marriage		
		Death	1822	Daufuskie
	Full name of spouse	Burial		Daufuskie. Later moved to Bonaventure Cemetery

*Sarah Irwin-Mongin-Blodgett Obituary, *Daily Georgian*, 11 October 1833, p. 2, col. 5.

Appendix VII

Mongin-Stoddard Vault—Bonaventure Cemetery

For those who want to visit the Mongin/Blodgett vault, Bonaventure Cemetery, Savannah, Georgia, take the road that leads near the water's edge. The vault is built like an Egyptian pyramid and has inscribed at the top: "In Memory of John D. Mongin [No. 3] died November 14, 1833, Aged 73 years." At the bottom of the vault is a stone tablet inscribed:

Mrs. Sarah [Watts] Mongin	1816—Wife of John David Mongin (No. 3)
David John Mongin [No. 4]	1823—Son of John David Mongin (No. 3) and Sarah Watts
Mrs. Sarah [Irwin] Blodgett	1833—Wife of David John Mongin (No. 4)
Edmund W. Mongin	1813—Son of David John Mongin (No. 4) and Sarah Irwin
David J. Mongin, Jr.	1815—Son of David John Mongin (No. 4) and Sarah Irwin
Jane J. Mongin	1821—Daughter of David John Mongin (No. 4) and Sarah Irwin
Sarah Mongin	1822—Daughter of David John Mongin (No. 4) and Sarah Irwin and twin to Mary Lavinia
Benjamin Blodgett	1827—Son of Sarah Irwin Mongin Blodgett and Herman M. Blodgett
Joseph Blodgett	1831—Son of Sarah Irwin Mongin Blodgett and Herman M. Blodgett
Sarah M. Blodgett	1840—Daughter of Sarah Irwin Mongin Blodgett and Herman M. Blodgett

This Mongin/Blodgett vault was originally on Haig's Point (facing south), just inside the Boundary Road gate on the left side of the avenue of oaks that led to the Haig's Point house. The vault faced the only white church on the island that was just across the Boundary Road that separated Haig's Point from Melrose. The church was either burned during the Civil War or was taken down to construct homes for the free slaves.

Appendix VIII: Family Group Record
JOHN STODDARD AND MARY LAVINIA MONGIN

HUSBAND—JOHN STODDARD					
VITAL DATA	DAY MONTH YEAR		CITY, TOWN or PLACE	COUNTY or PROVINCE	STATE or COUNTRY
Birth	11 Mar 1809		Northampton	Hampshire	Massachusetts
Marriage	7 Jan 1836		Paris		France
Death	25 Jul 1879		Savannah	Chatham	Georgia
Burial	Bonaventure Cemetery, Savannah, Georgia				
Husband's father: Solomon Stoddard (1771-1860)				Husband's mother: Mary Tappan (1771-1852)	
Other wives, if any:					

WIFE—MARY LAVINIA MONGIN (NO. 5)					
VITAL DATA	DAY MONTH YEAR		CITY, TOWN or PLACE	COUNTY or PROVINCE	STATE or COUNTRY
Birth	Feb 1819		Daufuskie	Beaufort	South Carolina
Death	22 Feb 1865		Savannah	Chatham	Georgia
Burial	Bonaventure Cemetery, Savannah, Georgia				
Wife's father: David John Mongin II (No. 4)				Wife's mother: Sarah Irwin	
Other husband's, if any					

SEX	CHILDREN'S NAMES IN FULL	DATA	DATE	LOCATION
F	1. Mary Helen	Birth	4 Jan 1837	London, England
		Marriage	5 Feb 1861	Savannah, Georgia
		Death	19 May 1914	Savannah, Georgia
	Full name of spouse John L. Hardee	Burial	Bonaventure Cemetery, Savannah, Georgia	
		Children		
M	2. Albert Henry	Birth	Feb 1838	Savannah, Georgia
	Full name of spouse	Marriage	1865	
	(1) Elizabeth Hamilton	Death	21 Sep 1918	
	(2) Leila Pegram	Burial	Bonaventure Cemetery, Savannah, Georgia	
	m. Nov 1880, N.Y.		Elizabeth Hamilton died 1 April 1873	
F	3. Isabelle	Birth	31 Jan 1840	Savannah, Georgia
	Full name of spouse	Marriage	11 Nov 1860	Savannah, Georgia
	(1) Benjamin Green d. 1865	Death	1927	Savannah, Georgia
	(2) Maj. Wm. D. Waples	Burial	Bonaventure Cemetery, Savannah, Georgia	
	m. 6 Feb. 1872 d. 1891	Children		
M	4. John Irwin	Birth	13 Jul 1843	
		Marriage		Savannah, Georgia
		Death	1924	
	Full name of spouse Agnes Sorell	Burial	Bonaventure Cemetery, Savannah, Georgia	
		Children		
M	5. Henry (Harry) Mongin	Birth	24 Jan 1846	Savannah, Georgia
		Marriage		
		Death	1905	
	Full name of spouse Mary Soullard	Burial	Bonaventure Cemetery, Savannah, Georgia	
		Children		
	6.	Birth		
		Marriage		
		Death		
	Full name of spouse	Burial		

Appendix IX: Family Group Record

PHILLIP MARTINANGELE AND MARY FOSTER[1]

HUSBAND—PHILLIP MARTINANGELE

VITAL DATA	DAY MONTH YEAR	CITY, TOWN or PLACE	COUNTY or PROVINCE	STATE or COUNTRY
Birth	Circa 1720	Rome		Italy
Marriage	9 May 1743	Beaufort	St. Helena's Parish	South Carolina
Death	1760/61	Port Royal Island	Beaufort/Granville	South Carolina
	Came to America c. 1740			

Husband's father: Husband's mother:

Other wives, if any:

WIFE—MARY FOSTER

VITAL DATA	DAY MONTH YEAR	CITY, TOWN or PLACE	COUNTY or PROVINCE	STATE or COUNTRY
Birth				
Death	2 April 1790	Daufuskie	Beaufort/Granville[2]	South Carolina
Burial	Mary Dunn Cemetery, Daufuskie			

Wife's father: Wife's mother:

Other husband's, if any

SEX	CHILDREN'S NAMES IN FULL	DATA	DATE	LOCATION
M	1. Francis	Birth	2 Feb 1744	Port Royal Island, S.C.
		Marriage		
		Death	after 1772	
	Full name of spouse	Burial		
			Baptized 28 May 1744, St. Helena's Parish	
F	2. Mary	Birth	16 Dec 1745	Port Royal Island, S.C.
		Marriage	5 May 1767	
		Death	1812	McIntosh County, Georgia
	Full name of spouse John Hopkins	Burial	Her son supposedly brought her body back to Daufuskie and buried her with her parents.	
M	3. Phillip, Jr.	Birth	20 Nov 1747	Port Royal Island, S.C.
		Marriage		
		Death	Dec 1781	Daufuskie Island, S.C.
	Full name of spouse Elizabeth (?)	Burial	Possibly on Daufuskie, but no proof.	
		Children		
M	4. Thomas	Birth	1749	Port Royal Island, S.C.
		Marriage		
		Death		
	Full name of spouse	Burial		
		Children		
F	5. Margaret	Birth	1750	Port Royal Island, S.C.
		Marriage	1781	
	Full name of spouse	Death	6 Feb 1808	
	1 Richard Pendarvis 2 William Edwards Mongin		Richard was murdered 1781. She married William 25 May 1783. He died 1814.	
	6. Simeon	Birth	prior 1761	Port Royal Island, S.C.
		Marriage	14 Feb 1785	
	Full name of spouse	Death		
	Love Tucker-Henning-Rowland	Burial		
		Children	None	

continued on next page

Appendix IX: Family Group Record

PHILLIP MARTINANGELE AND MARY FOSTER[1] (cont.)

HUSBAND—PHILLIP MARTINANGELE					
VITAL DATA	DAY MONTH YEAR		CITY, TOWN or PLACE	COUNTY or PROVINCE	STATE or COUNTRY
Birth	Circa 1720		Rome		Italy
Marriage	9 May 1743		Beaufort	St. Helena's Parish	South Carolina
Death	1760/61		Port Royal Island	Beaufort/Granville	South Carolina
	Came to America c. 1740				
Husband's father:				Husband's mother:	
Other wives, if any:					

WIFE—MARY FOSTER					
VITAL DATA	DAY MONTH YEAR		CITY, TOWN or PLACE	COUNTY or PROVINCE	STATE or COUNTRY
Birth					
Death	2 April 1790		Daufuskie	Beaufort/Granville[2]	South Carolina
Burial	Mary Dunn Cemetery, Daufuskie				
Wife's father:				Wife's mother:	
Other husband's, if any					

SEX	CHILDREN'S NAMES IN FULL	DATA	DATE	LOCATION	
M	7. Isaac	Birth	1 Aug 1752	Port Royal Island, S.C.	
		Marriage	20 Mar 1782		
	Full name of spouse	Death	15 Apr 1796	Daufuskie Island, S.C.	
	Elizabeth Conyers Ladson	Burial	Mary Dunn Cemetery, Daufuskie		
	widow of Anthony Godfrey	Children			
M	8. Abraham	Birth	20 Jul 1754	Port Royal Island, S.C.	
		Marriage	Could have married both wives in the Bahamas.		
	Full name of spouse	Death			
	1 Lady Elizabeth Yard(?)	Children	Wife No. 1—one child, Elizabeth		
	2 Unknown		Wife No. 2—two children, Ellen and Margaret		

1. Anderson Genealogy, n.p.: "St. Helena's Parish Register," *South Carolina Historical Magazine*, vol. 23 (July 1922), pp. 132-36, 139; Minutes of Vestry of St. Helena's Parish; Epitaphs, Mary Dunn Cemetery, Daufuskie Island; Chaplin Family Bible; Rev. Robert E.H. Peeples, president, Hilton Head Historical Society.

2. This county was called Granville for Proprietor Lord Granville. The Duke of Beaufort succeeded him in 1709. In 1711, the newly laid-out town of Beaufort, the river and county were named in his honor. Ref: Claude Henry Neuffer, *Names in South Carolina*, 30 vols. (Columbia, published annually by the Department of English, University of South Carolina, Winter, 1970), vol. 17, p. 49.

Appendix X: Family Group Record

ISAAC MARTINANGELE AND ELIZABETH C.L. GODFREY

HUSBAND—ISAAC MARTINANGELE

VITAL DATA	DAY MONTH YEAR	CITY, TOWN or PLACE	COUNTY or PROVINCE	STATE or COUNTRY
Birth	1752			
Marriage	20 Aug 1782			
Death	15 Apr 1796	Daufuskie Island	Granville	South Carolina
Burial	Mary Dunn Cemetery			

Husband's father: Phillip Martinangele, Sr. Husband's mother: Mary Foster

Other wives, if any:

WIFE—ELIZABETH CONYERS LADSON GODFREY

VITAL DATA	DAY MONTH YEAR	CITY, TOWN or PLACE	COUNTY or PROVINCE	STATE or COUNTRY
Birth	11 Dec 1763			
Death	1 Jan 1847			
Burial	Mary Dunn Cemetery, Daufuskie Island			

Wife's father: Wife's mother:

Other husband's, if any

SEX	CHILDREN'S NAMES IN FULL	DATA	DATE	LOCATION
M	1. Phillip III	Birth	28 Dec 1783	Daufuskie Island, S.C.
		Marriage		
		Death	14 May 1852	Killed by lightning
	Full name of spouse	Burial	Mary Dunn Cemetery, Daufuskie, S.C.	
	Bachelor	Children		
F	2. Mary	Birth	27 Dec 1785	Daufuskie Island, S.C.
		Marriage	7 Feb 1807	
		Death	6 Jul 1878	
	Full name of spouse	Burial	Mary Dunn Cemetery, Daufuskie Island	
	Francis Dunn	Children		
F	3. Love	Birth	30 Jan 1788	Daufuskie Island, S.C.
	Full name of spouse	Marriage		
	(1) Mr. Mead	Death		
	(2) Mr. Forsythe	Burial		
	(3) Jesse Mount	Children	Amanda Mount	
M	4. Isaac, Jr.	Birth	2 May 1790	Daufuskie Island, S.C.
		Marriage	No record	
		Death	No record	
	Full name of spouse	Burial		
		Children		
F	5. Mary Ann	Birth	12 Dec 1791	Daufuskie Island, S.C.
		Marriage	17 Dec 1818	
	Full name of spouse	Death	6 Nov 1854	
	(1) James Peto	Burial	Mary Dunn Demetery, Daufuskie Island	
	(2) Paul Grimball	Children		
F	6. Harriet	Birth	1 Oct 1796	Port Royal Island, S.C.
		Marriage	1811	
		Death	27 Aug 1830	
	Full name of spouse	Burial	Mary Dunn Cemetery, Daufuskie Island	
	William F. Chaplin	Children		

Elizabeth was the widow of Anthony Godfrey who died from a rattlesnake bite on Daufuskie. Their daughter, Elizabeth Ladson Godfrey, b. 1783 (m. Wm. E. Jones), d. 1834, buried Mary Dunn Cemetery.

Appendix XI

Perhaps methods similar to these were used to preserve meat on the plantations.[1]

Mr. Bert Stoddard's Recipe
CORNED BEEF

(For 100 lbs.)
8 lbs. of salt
2 ozs. saltpeter
2 lbs. sugar
Enough water to cover the beef

Boil salt, sugar, saltpeter and water together until all are dissolved. Let cool—pour over beef packed in barrel.

Garland Rice Recipe
GOOD HAMS, SUGAR CURED

To a 200 lb hog dressed:
1 lbs. brown sugar
1-1/4 ozs. saltpeter
10 lbs. coarse salt
2 ozs. black pepper

Chill whole hog overnight. Cut up next morning, putting each piece by itself—meat side up and rub with salt. Let stand 24 hrs., brush off all salt and rub with salt, sugar, etc. Pack in barrel—meat side up. Let stay in brine 3 to 6 weeks, hang and let dry. Smoke with corn cobs and hickory chips—not too much—then wash in boiling water. Wrap in brown paper, sew up in cloth, pack closely in a box or barrel and sift ashes over it.

1. Billie Burn, *Stirrin' The Pots On Daufuskie* (Hilton Head: Impressions Printing Company, 1985), p. 10.

Appendix XII

Old Ash Hopper Days

In grandmother's day I remember well,
    When the soap supply ran low,
The ash hopper stood near the old back gate,
    And was filled to the overflow.

With ashes of wood from the kitchen stove,
    And rain water poured on top,
Before very long on a sunny morn
    The lye would begin to drop.

Each "batch" was drawn as need required,
    And observed in its every phase;
Its strength was obviously great enough
    When an egg to the top would raise.

So well I remember my brother Bob;
    His heart wasn't in it I fear—
Making his way with pail in hand
    To the hopper that stood in the rear.

He wished himself in pleasanter scenes,
  As the task he undertook,
Building a 'dream city' far away
  Or dropping a line in the brook.

Chagrined at the irksome task at hand,
  As mother stood by the door,
A "million gallons" it seemed he'd bought
  And all she could say was "more."

Resentment mounted—his face was flushed,
  This thing he could not endure,
He glanced at the high yard fence between,
  And felt in a measure secure.

With the ugliest face he could possibly make
  His evils he'd recompense,
But such a mistake he shouldn't have made
  She fairly flew over the fence.

She spared not the rod, yet with kindness she spoke;
  'Twas because of her love and all such,
Until deep in his soul he did solemnly wish
  That she never loved him so much.

Hardly a springtime came and went
  Since the ash hopper days of yore,
That mother didn't relate the tale,
  As she stood by the kitchen door.

Now our soaps are packaged in colors bright,
  And dissolve at the water's touch,
But I'll always remember the good old days,
  When lye soap was used so much.

                                        Anonymous

Appendix XIII

Following is a list of seventy-two (72) slaves and their worth according to the appraisal of William Henry Mongin's estate as of 31 December 1851.[1]

1.	John Russell	$450.00	37.	Doll	$350.00
2.	Charity	$600.00	38.	Lydia	$250.00
3.	Stephen	$250.00	39.	Lucy	$600.00
4.	Jimmy	$200.00	40.	Cumsey	$200.00
5.	Braddock	$100.00	41.	Gilbert	$100.00
6.	Amy	$600.00	42.	Old Bob	$100.00
7.	Polly &		43.	Archie	$700.00
8.	Child	$150.00	44.	Auber	$500.00
9.	Moses	$700.00	45.	Chloe	$600.00
10.	Cumba	$600.00	46.	Louisiana	$300.00
11.	Fatima	$300.00	47.	Hester	$200.00
12.	Harry	$600.00	48.	Melissa	$500.00
13.	Sally	$600.00	49.	Henry	$450.00
14.	Susannah	$500.00	50.	Rose	$350.00
15.	Charlotte	$350.00	51.	Lazarus	$300.00
16.	Eliza	$300.00	52.	Matilda	$250.00
17.	Lucy	$250.00	53.	Bob	$200.00
18.	Fatima	$200.00	54.	John	$600.00
19.	Grace	$200.00	55.	Renty	$400.00
20.	Hester	$600.00	56.	Judy	$600.00
21.	Gabriel	$250.00	57.	Maria	$350.00
22.	Jane	$600.00	58.	Diana	$250.00
23.	Sarah	$150.00	59.	Louisa	$200.00
24.	Davy	$100.00	60.	Harry	$700.00
25.	Patrick	$700.00	61.	Henry	$1000.00
26.	Gom	$700.00	62.	Peter	$600.00
27.	Clarineta	$600.00	63.	Hannah	$600.00
28.	Rebecca	$500.00	64.	Simon	$1000.00
29.	Old Scipio	$200.00	65.	Philis	$600.00
30.	Billy	$600.00	66.	Davis	$450.00
31.	Judy	$600.00	67.	Bess	$250.00
32.	Rachard	$300.00	68.	Betty	$100.00
33.	Minty	$250.00	69.	Paul	$500.00
34.	Child of Amy (No. 1)	$150.00	70.	Morris	$450.00
35.	Daniel	$100.00	71.	Dick	$100.00
36.	Jacob	$500.00	72.	Mack	$100.00

1. Probate Judge Office, Savannah, Georgia, #323.

Appendix XIV

Gullah Words and Phrases

The word Gullah is derived from three possible sources: (1) *Angola* in Africa, where the choice slaves came from, (2) *Golas*, the name of a group of Liberians who lived on the West Coast of Africa between Sierra Leone and the Ivory Coast, and (3) *Gwalla*, a powerful tribe of Cammi or Comi Negroes in the French Congo.[1]

Following is some of the quaint Gullah spoken while conversing with different ones on the island. It is not listed here to embarrass anyone, but retained as a permanent record for all to enjoy.

Gullah is fast disappearing as the older folk who used it are dying, and children of each new generation are growing up without ever having heard it spoken. Like the passing of the cow and cart, Daufuskie will never be the same when strains of Gullah have completely vanished.

Baby hab e fus peg—baby has its first tooth
Mout mek yu backside lib high—don't sass and keep gossip to yourself or somebody might give you a whipping
Frum de time de dew cum t dayclean—from early evening until daylight the next morning
Fishning—going fishing
Screem—screen
Winda sheet—a frame of glass window panes
Carbon a cigarettes—carton of cigarettes
Citus & Sutum Bank—Citizens & Southern Bank
Ever-rue—Evinrude (outboard motor)
Will da circus bees unbrokeen—will the circle be unbroken
Ditn tink she wana awfago—didn't think she wanted all to go
Tinning—tin to fix the roof
Ketch de fire—start a fire
E ain bin huh gin—he hasn't returned since he left
She bin ta we house—she was at our house
Hissory—history
De jail lease um—he was released from jail
Scrapiron—moonshine whiskey
Ax or hoe stick—axe or hoe handle
Time ober—time passed quickly
Dey wide um up—they divided them up

E tuh wicket—he is too wicked

Lim em up—prune the dead branches off the tree

Trash da pecans—take a cane pole and thrash the branches so the pecans will fall to the ground

Azaretic—arthritis

E got e long ah—he wants everything he sees

Ah bin telum—I've been telling them

She got e short ah—she wants very little she sees

Tro e ah oberdefence—look over the fence (at my garden)

Hep—help

Awfis—office

Up dawinda —push the window up

Ratchuh—right here

Seperate tank—ceptic tank

Recepteral tank—ceptic tank

E du betta nex tym gin—if he has the opportunity, he will do better the next time

Abuse ya out—to curse you out

Don know what e be gwin tuh do fa troot—to tell you the truth, I don't know what he is going to do

Ya ol man ben een de crick?—has your husband been shrimping or fishing?

Yesen, e be stron, e got a 144 frame—yes mam, his body is strong and holding up good for his 72 years

Islant luminated wid ol peoples—the island is blessed because of the christian wisdom of its older citizens

E voke me—he provoked me

Dem em—condemned them

She vorse um—she divorced her husband

She ain take it—she hasn't learned yet

She een de mercy room—she is in the emergency room

House gone in—the house is so old it has fallen down

Broke um down—the house was taken down piece by piece and removed to another area and rebuilt

Ankerhawl—alcohol

Don't wait until you get a whole lot of something to share, share out of the little that you have—(older wisdom)

Eber ting n de milk ain white—somebody is not being honest in the situation, something crooked going on

Han go, han cum—give and it will come back to you

Borrowed horse gits sic queek—when something is borrowed, usually

546

something happens to it where it will either have to be replaced or repaired

'Fuskie gittin lo down, gwine up one feet cum back sree—can't get ahead for going backwards

Quiet calf gits de mos milk—when a calf is sucking quietly, it is getting more milk than if it ran from side to side of its mother

Eber did bin—that's the way it has always been

Me mind goes all about—I think about many things

Me mind jest don be wid me, it lef me—my memory is bad

Draw a cup uh coffee—make a cup of coffee

Tank Jesus, de storm pass 'Fuskie by—the storm did not come to the Island

House sharks—people who come in old houses and steal things

Possum bin outa dem big woods n be dead bfo me front doe—a possum came out of the woods and died at my front door

Lecket—collect it

Pot salt—coarse salt

Ain nected up yet—it hasn't been connected yet

Bozz—a gap or gate opening

Perenna—marina

Wreck it—direct it

Thornato—tornado

Wese born ta de praise house n church—don't know when they were built, they were here when we were born

De jessie-maes is bloomin—the yellow jasmine are blooming

Beat de boy down lo—really put a beating on the boy

Ponouncement—announcement

Spoon arn—smoothing iron, an old iron that is heated on the stove to iron clothes

Extrasizing—exercising

E een tension care—he is in intensive care at the hospital

Gaaden gone een—plants are all dead

Tigan well—artesian well

Father govermint—United States government

Robbersarry—commissary

Keep ya tongue een ya teet—keep your tongue in your teeth; shut your mouth; don't repeat what I just told you

Critter—cow

She been ta tawk witem—she went to talk with them

Put fire een ya feet—run real fast, hurry

Willful wase mek a wishful wont—waste deliberately and you will live to wish you had it back

Blaze em out—cursed him out

Dey naked de boat—they stole everything off the boat

Peanuts black-up een de field—peanuts rot in the field

Shawt patience—short patience means a bad temper

Own da hill—left the dock or boat and gone up on dry ground

Roach liver and roast liver—cirrhosis of the liver

De sickest ain always da dearest—is what they say when a well person suddenly dies who has been caring for the sick

Haint blue—shutters, trim on doors and windows were painted blue (Blue is the color of heaven, the devil would be scared away and would not enter a blue opening of a house. Haints are creatures of the darkness; don't work during the day.)

Pump suckers—leather washers for a hand water pump used on a shallow well

Tank God fer brett n body—thank God for breath and body

Ef life las—if life lasts (to see another day)

People teefing Hall money—people are stealing the dues money collected by the Oyster Society

She putt her bess on da outside—she is sick but she smiles and makes everyone think she is okay

•

Wycliff Bible Translators, Pat and Claude Sharpe, Beaufort, together with the Reverend Ervin Green, pastor at Brick Baptist Church, Frogmore, and Ronald Daise, author, are translating the Bible into Gullah. They have completed selected Psalms and parts of Luke. A sample of their work appeared in one of our local newspapers. From the King James Version, Luke 2:16 in English:

"And they came with haste, and found Mary and Joseph and the baby lying in a manager."

The same passage in Gullah: "Now den, de shepud mekace en gone to Betlam fa luk. Dey, dey done fin Mary en Josuf en de Chile. En dat Chile leddown een a trough." [2]

•

I've been in their company many times and it is true: when families on the island, who speak Gullah, get together and carry on a regular conversation, an outsider cannot understand a word they are saying. It sounds like another foreign language.

1. Reed Smith, *Gullah* (Columbia: University of South Carolina Press, 1926; reprint ed., Columbia: Harold S. Reeves, 1967), p. 4, n. 2.

2. "Christmas Story to be Read in Gullah," *Beaufort Gazette*, 13 December 1985, sec. A, p. 10.

Appendix XV

Beufat S C
Affid Ruly
Filed 16 Aly 1882 and
Recorded in Vol 13 page
24 —   S. J. Baumfield
                    Ruly

Site of
Rear Beacon
5 acres

Sites for Beacons
of the
Bloody Point Range,
Daufuskie Island, So. Ca.

Scale 300 ft. to 1 Inch.

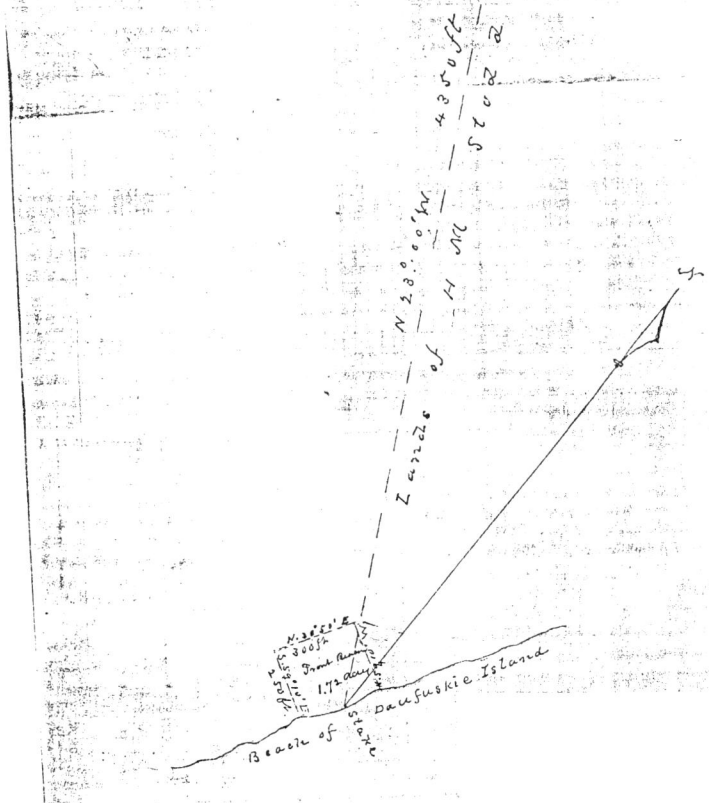

N 23°.00'. W
Lands of — H. M
435 0 ft

N 23°00' E
300 ft
Front Range
1.72 days
Beacon of stake
Daufuskie Island

Appendix XVI

Confederate Money

Appendix XVII

Melrose School Reports

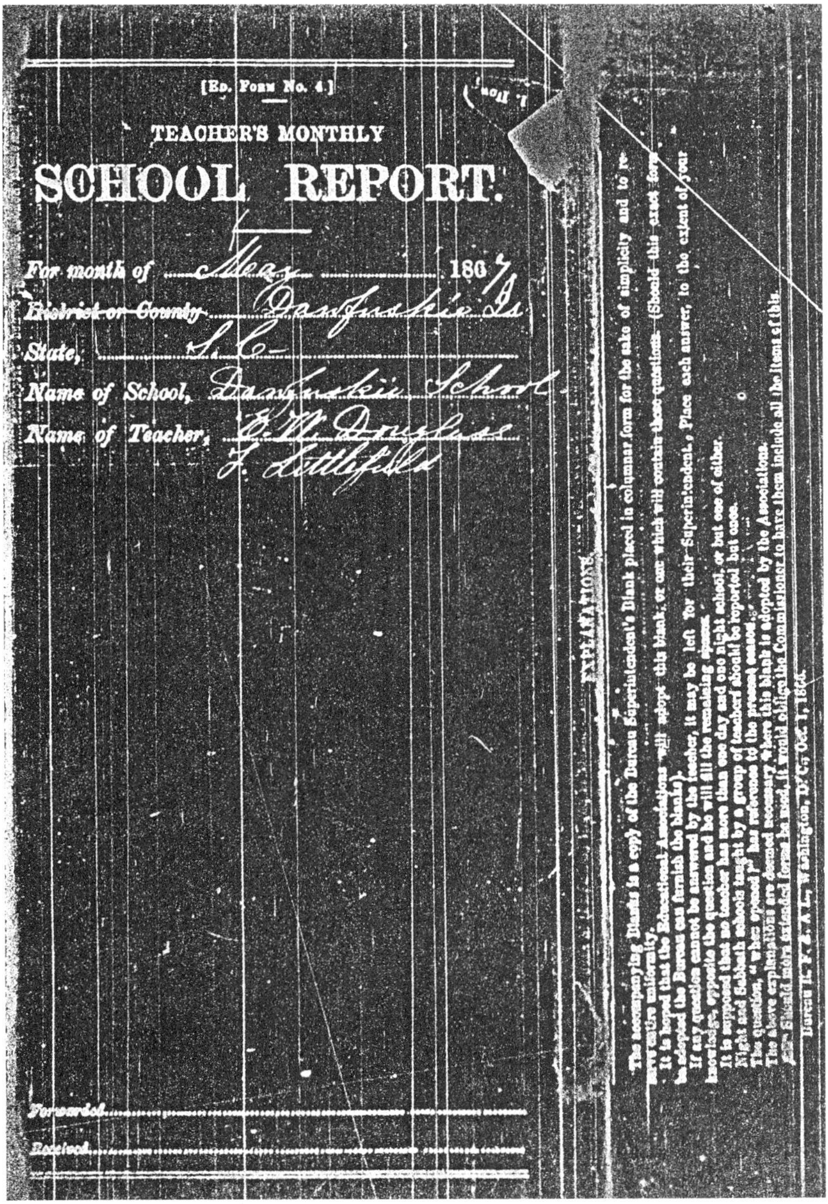

[Ed. Form No. 4.]

TEACHER'S MONTHLY

SCHOOL REPORT.

For month of May 1867

~~District or County~~ Dawfuskie Is

State, S. C.

Name of School, Dawfuskie School

Name of Teacher, E. M. Douglass
F. Littlefield

Forwarded............

Received............

EXPLANATIONS.

The accompanying Blanks is a copy of the Bureau Superintendent's Blank placed in columnar form for the sake of simplicity and to reserve entire uniformity.

It is hoped that the Educational Associations will adopt this blank, or one which will contain these questions. (Should this exact form be adopted the Bureau can furnish the blanks).

If any question cannot be answered by the teacher, it may be left for their Superintendent. Place each answer, to the extent of your knowledge, opposite the question and he will fill the remaining spaces.

It is supposed that no teacher has more than one day and one night school, or but one of either.

Night and Sabbath schools taught by a group of teachers should be reported but once.

The question, "when opened?" has reference to the present season.

The above explanations are deemed necessary where this blank is adopted by the Associations.

☞ Should more extended forms be used, it would oblige the Commissioner to have them include all the items of this.

Bureau R. F. & A. L., Washington, D. C., Oct. 1, 1866.

American Missionary Association,

SCHOOLS FOR FREEDMEN.

TEACHER'S MONTHLY REPORT.

Name of Teacher, *E. W. Douglass & F. Littlefield*

in the school called *Daufuskie School*

at *Melrose*   County (or Parish) of *Daufuskie Island, S.C.*

State of *S. Carolina*   for Month of *April* 186 7

No. of days the school was kept during the calender month,	21	No. of hours each day, 3
If absent any number of days, how many?	0	Cause? 0
" " " hours, "	0	Cause? 0
No. of different pupils, 42	New 0	No. transferred from other schools, 0 Average attendance, 34
No. of males, 25	No. females, 17	No. adults (over 18), 1 No. white, 0
No. in Primary studies, 47	Intermediate, 0	Advanced, 0
No. who write, on slates only 25		do. with pen, 0

Is Singing taught in school? *Yes*   Calisthenics or Gymnastics? *No*

No. sessions in Night school, 17   Name of the school, *Daufuskie*   Average attendance, 31

" " Sabbath school, 4   "   40 children

" " adults 3   "   27 adult

Amount, if any, received for tuition, 0

No. of visits made in colored families, 3.5

No. of Bibles distributed, 0   No. of Testaments, 1

No. of Books,   Tracts and Papers, 2.75

No. of families in which you have engaged in religious services, either by reading the Scriptures, singing, or prayer,

No. of hopeful conversions, if any, during the month,

Items for Freedmen's Bureau, not given above :

No. in Alphabet, 32   Who spell and read in easy lessons, 37   In advanced readers,

In Geography, 2   In Arithmetic, 5   In higher branches, 0

No. free before the War, 0

[Ep. Form, No. 4.]

TEACHER'S MONTHLY SCHOOL REPORT,

For the Month of May 1867.

☞ A School under the distinct control of one Teacher, or a Teacher with one assistant, is to be reported as one School.
☞ To be forwarded as soon as possible after the 1st of each month.

Number of Day-Schools	1
Number of Night-Schools	
Location, and Name of School	Daufuskie Island. S.C.
When opened	Jany 19
Societies, &c., Patrons	A. M. A.
Number of Schools sustained by freedmen	0
Number of Schools sustained in part by freedmen	0
Number of teachers transported by Bureau	
Number of School buildings owned by freedmen	0
Number of School buildings furnished by Bureau	
Whole number of teachers	2
Whole number of pupils enrolled	55
Number of pupils enrolled last report	56
Number left school this month	6
Number of new scholars this month	5
Average attendance	35
Number of pupils paying tuition	0
Number of White pupils	
Number always present	8
Number always punctual	
Number over 16 years of age	40
Number in Alphabet	12
Number who spell and read easy lessons	21
Number of advanced readers	4
Number in geography	9
Number in arithmetic	
Number in higher branches	
Number in writing	All will on slates
Number on needlework	14
Number free before the war	2
Number of Sabbath Schools	
Number of pupils in Sabbath Schools	88

White 2 Colored 0
Male 27 Female 28

To these questions give exact, or approximate answers.

1. How many of above Schools are graded? .... How many grades? ....
2. How many Day or Night Schools, within your knowledge, not reported above? .... Number of pupils (estimated) in such Schools? ....
3. How many Teachers in the above Day or Night Schools? .... White, ... Colored, ...
4. How many Sabbath-Schools, within your knowledge, and not reported above? .... Number of pupils (estimated) in such Schools? ....
5. How many Teachers in the above Sabbath-Schools? .... White, ... Colored, ...
6. How many Industrial Schools? .... Whole number of pupils in all? .... State the kind of work done, ...
7. Whole amount of tuition paid by the Freedmen during the month, ...
8. Whole amount of expenses for the above Schools by the Bureau for the month, ...
9. Grand total of expense per month for support of above schools by all parties, ...
10. Whole number of High or Normal Schools, ... How many pupils in all? ....
11. Remarks The above report includes that for Night School

Bibliography

Published

Bierer, Bert W. *Indians and Artifacts in the Southeast*, Columbia: Bierer Publishing Company, 1980.

Botume, Elizabeth Hyde. *First Days Amongst The Contrabands.* Boston: Lee and Shepard Publishers, 1893.

Carse, Robert. *Department of the South, Hilton Head Island in the Civil War.* Columbia: The State Printing Company, 1961.

Clark, Murtie June. *Loyalists in the Southern Campaign of the Revolutionary War*, 2 vols. Baltimore: Genealogical Publishing Company, 1981.

Coldham, Peter Wilton. *American Loyalist Claims*, 13 vols. Washington: National Genealogical Society, 1980.

Conroy, Ronald Patrick. *The Boo.* Verona, Virginia: McClure Press, 1970.

Cooper, Thomas and David J. McCord, eds. *The Statutes at Large of South Carolina*, 10 vols. Columbia: A. S. Johnson, 1841.

Coulter, E. Merton. *Georgia's Disputed Ruins.* Chapel Hill: University of N. C. Press, 1937.

Cram, Mildred. *Old Seaport Towns of the South.* New York: Dodd, Mead & Company, 1917.

Crary, Catherine S. *The Price of Liberty, Tory Writings from the Revolution Era.* New York: McGraw-Hill Book Company, 1973.

Crum, Mason. *Gullah, Negro Life in the Carolina Sea Islands.* Durham: Duke University Press, 1940.

Daise, Donald. *Reminiscences of Sea Island Heritage.* Orangeburg: Sandlapper Publishing Company, 1986.

Davidson, Chalmers Gaston. *The Last Foray, The South Carolina Planters of 1860: A Sociological Study.* Columbia: University of South Carolina Press, 1971.

Eldredge, D. *1861-1865, The Third New Hampshire and All About It.* Boston: Press of E. B. Stillings & Company, 1893.

Fleetwood, Rusty. *Tidecraft, The Boats of Lower South Carolina and Georgia.* Savannah: Coastal Heritage Society, 1982.

Gamble, Thomas. *Savannah Duels & Duellists 1733-1977.* Savannah: Review Publishing & Printing Company, 1925.

Granger, Mary. *Savannah River Plantations.* Savannah: The Georgia Historical Society, 1947.

Granger, M. L. *Savannah Harbor, Its Origin and Development 1733-1890.* Savannah: U. S. Engineers Corps, 1968.

Graydon, Nell S. *Tales of Beaufort.* Beaufort: Beaufort Book Shop, Inc., 1963.

Hartridge, Walter C. *John David Mongin's 'Capital Dwelling House' on Warren Square*. Savannah: by the author, n.d.

Holcomb, Brent. *Marriage and Death Notices From Charleston Observer, 1817-1845*. Greenville: A Press, Inc., 1980.

Holland, Rupert Sargent. *Letters and Diary of Laura Matilda Towne, Written from the Sea Islands of South Carolina 1862-1884*. Cambridge, Mass.: Riverside Press, 1912.

Holmgren, Virginia. *Hilton Head: A Sea Island Chronicle*. Hilton Head: Hilton Head Island Publishing Company, 1959.

Ivers, Larry E. *Colonial Forts of South Carolina, 1670-1775*. Columbia: University of South Carolina Press, 1970.

James, Edward T. *Notable American Women 1607-1950*, 3 vols. Cambridge: The Belknap Press of Harvard University Press, 1971.

Jarrold and Sons Limited. *Westminster Abbey Official Guide*. Norwich, Great Britain: by author, Ltd., Revised Edition, 1988.

Johnson, Arnold Burgess. *The Modern Light-House Service*. Washington: Government Printing Office, 1889.

Johnson, Gion Griffis. *A Social History of the Sea Islands*. Chapel Hill: The University of North Carolina Press, 1930; reprint, New York: Negro University Press (A Division of Greenwood Publishing Corp.), 1969.

Killion, Ronal G. and Charles T. Waller. *Georgia and the Revolution*. Atlanta: Cherokee Publishing Company, 1975.

Martin, Josephine W., editor. *"Dear Sister." Letters Written on Hilton Head, 1867*. Beaufort: Beaufort Book Company, 1977.

McAllister, [Samuel] Ward. *Society as I Have Found It*. New York: Arno Press, Reprint Edition, 1975.

McCrady, Edward. *The History of South Carolina Under the Proprietary Government, 1670-1719*. New York: MacMillan Company, 1897.

_____. *The History of South Carolina Under the Royal Government, 1719-1776*. New York: MacMillan Company, 1899.

Merchants & Miners Transportation Company. *Tales of the Coast*. Baltimore, Md.: by author, 1927.

Miller, Annie Elizabeth. *Our Family Circle*. Linden, Tennessee: Continental Book Company, 1975.

Milling, Chapman J. *Red Carolinians*. Chapel Hill: University of North Carolina Press, 1940.

Mitchie, James L. *An Archaeological Reconnaissance Survey of the Haig Point, Webb, and Oak Ridge Tracts, Daufuskie Island, South Carolina*. Columbia: University of South Carolina Institute of Archeology and Anthropology, 1983.

556

Myers, Robert Manson. *Children of Pride.* New Haven and London: Yale University Press, 1972.

New York Observer. Obituary of John Stoddard, 7 July 1879.

Neuffer, Claude Henry. *Names in South Carolina.* Spartanburg: The Reprint Company, thirty-year, annual publication, 1954-83.

Nichols, James M. *Perry's Saints or the Fighting Parson's Regiment in the War of the Rebellion.* Boston: D. Lothrop and Company, 1886.

Peel, Mrs. William Lawson, ed. *Historical Collections of the Joseph Habersham Chapter, Daughters of the American Revolution.* Baltimore: Genealogical Publishing Company, 1968.

Ploski, Harry A. *The Afro-American (Fourth Edition).* New York: Bellwether Publishing Company, Inc., 1983.

Raboteau, Albert J. *Slave Religion, The Invisible Institution in the Antebellum South.* New York: Oxford University Press, 1978.

Rahn, Ruby A. *River Highway For Trade, The Savannah.* Savannah: U. S. Corps of Engineers, June 1968.

Ramsey, David, M.D. *Ramsey's History of South Carolina From Its Settlement in 1670 to the Year 1808.* Newberry: Walker, Evans & Company, Charleston, 1858.

Rauers, Betty and Franklin Taub. *Sojourn In Savannah.* Savannah: Printcraft Press, 1968.

Rogers, George C., Jr., et al., eds. *The Papers of Henry Laurens,* 9 vols. Columbia: University of South Carolina Press, 1968-1981.

Rose, Willie Lee. *Rehearsal for Reconstruction, The Port Royal Experiment.* New York: Vintage Books, A Division of Random House, 1964.

Rosen, Robert N. *A Short History of Charleston.* San Francisco: Lexikos, 1982.

Sale, Edith Tunis. *Old Time Belles and Cavaliers.* Philadelphia and London: J. B. Lippincott Company, 1912.

Salley, A. S., Jr. *Minutes of the Vestry of St. Helena's Parish, South Carolina, 1726-1812.* Columbia: The State Company, 1919.

Salley, A. S., Jr., and R. N. Cholas Olsberg. *Warrants for Land in South Carolina, 1672-1711.* Columbia: University of South Carolina Press, 1973.

Scribner Charles' Sons. *Dictionary of American History,* 7 vols. New York: by author, 1976.

Sewell, Cliff. *Savannah Now and Then.* Savannah: The Printcraft Press, Inc., 1974.

St. Simons Public Library. *Old Mill Days.* St. Simons, Ga.: Glover Printing Company, 1976.

Stoddard, Albert H. II. *Gullah Tales and Anecdotes of South Carolina Sea Islands.* Savannah: by the author, 1940.

_____. *How Buh Wasp Got His Small Waist.* Savannah: by the author, 1941.

Stoddard, Charles and Elijah W. Stoddard, comps. *Anthony Stoddard, of Boston, Mass., and His Descendants: A Genealogy.* New York: J. M. Bradstreet & Sons, 1865.

Trinkley, Mike, Ph.D., ed. *Archaeological Investigations at Haig Point, Webb, and Oak Ridge, Daufuskie Island, Beaufort County, South Carolina.* Columbia: Chicora Foundation Research, Series 15, 1989.

United States Congress. *War of the Rebellion: a Compilation of the Official Records of the Union and Confederate Armies,* 70 vols. Washington: Government Printing Office, 1882.

Wood, Virginia Steele. *Live Oaking, Southern Timber for Tall Ships.* Boston: Northeastern University Press, 1981.

Wright, Gavin. *Old South, New South.* New York: Basic Books, Inc., 1986.

Unpublished Manuscripts

Atlanta, Georgia. "Record of the Edwards Family of New England Connected with the Mongin Family of South Carolina, by Marriage. Copied from the life of Rev. Jonathan Edwards, the greatest divine that has ever lived in the United States of America." Typescript. In possession of Robert L. Marchman, III.

Beaufort, S. C. Beaufort County Library. Dr. James Stuart. "Christmas on the Plantation." A gift to the Beaufort Township Library from Mrs. Ruth Rhett Holmes. unpublished typescript, n. d. Reference at Library: "VF Beaufort County—Stuart Family."

Columbia, S. C. South Carolina Department of Archives and History. Colonial Plats and Royal Land Grants, 1695-1776.

_____. Barnwell, John. "Map of Southeastern America," (Circa 1722)

_____. *The South Carolina Gazette.*

Peoria, Illinois. "Leaves From the Martinangele Family." Typescript. In possession of Ben Anderson, Jr.

Savannah, Georgia. Georgia Historical Society. *Columbian Museum & Savannah Advertiser,* 1796-1798 (Microfilm). Unpublished index.

_____. Jeremiah Evarts' Diary, 1822.

_____. *Republican & Savannah Evening Ledger*

_____. *Royal Georgia Gazette.*

_____. The Diary (Journal) of the Reverend John Jochim Zubly, from a transcript made by Mrs. Lilla M. Hawes.

Savannah, Georgia. "Record of the Martinangele Family Connected with

the Mongins of South Carolina, copied 1899." Typescript. In possession of Mrs. Charles (Katharine) Ellis II.

_____. "Diary of John Michael Doyle, 1881-1883," Typescript. In possession of Charles A. Lebey.

_____. "Record of the Mongin Family Copied From the Family Bible of David Mongin, Sr." Typescript. Charles A. Lebey.

_____. William Green Family Bible Records, and the Love Green Martinangele lease document, Charles A. Lebey.

_____. U. S. Engineers Maps of Savannah River, 1833 and 1855.

Theses and Interviews

Cetchovich, Emil II. Savannah, Georgia. Interview. 6 September 1984.

Maggioni, Gilbert J. Lady's Island, S. C. Interview. 14 August 1990.

Maggioni, Paul. Savannah, Georgia. Interview. 29 September 1983.

Starr, Rebecca Kirk. "A Place Called Daufuskie: Island Bridge to Georgia, 1510-1830." M. A. Thesis, Department of History, University of South Carolina, 1984.

Stoddard, Albert H. III. Savannah, Georgia. interview. 18 July 1982.

Articles

Dewire, Elinor. "Women of the Lights." *The Adventure of the American Past, American History Illustrated.* (February 1987): 48.

Ivers, Larry E. "Scouting the Inland Passage, 1685-1737." *South Carolina Historical Magazine* 73 (July 1972): 117-129.

Timothy, P. "Narrative of the Colony of Georgia," *South Carolina Historical and Genealogy Magazine* 23 (1941): 150-51.

Weir, Robert M. "Muster Rolls of the South Carolina Granville and Colleton County Regiments of Militia, 1756." *South Carolina Historical Magazine* 70 (October 1969): 226-239.

INDEX

Craft, Lee [John Leaycraft], 234
Craft, Lee, 45
Craven, Charles, Governor, 14
Crawford, Captain, 382, 383
Creek, 3
Creeks, 3, 14, 20, 21
Creighton, 166, 408, 409
Crofut, George, Captain, 461
Crosby, Albert, 312
Crosby, Annie (Nanna), 372
Crosby, Annie, 274, 351
Crosby, Henry, 259
Crosby, Jeannette, 312
Crosby, T. W., 289
Crosby, Thomas, 408
Crosby, Tom, 274
Crosby, William, 408
Crosby, _____, 259
Croton, 294
Crouch, 208
Croufut, Captain, 383
Crumley, June Burn, 359
Culhane, Sister Sharon, 335, 336, 480
Cumberland, 408
Cummings, Mary Kehoe, 220, 493
Cummings, Wayne Lee, Dr., 493
Cunningham, Julia, 301
Cunningham, _____, Mrs., 298
Cusabo, 21, 210
Cypress Hill Cemetery, 249

Daddy January, 71
Daddy Moses, 72
Dade County, Florida, 198
Dair, Persille, 30, 530, 531, 533
Dandy, 387, 473
Daniel, Robert, 77, 78
Daniels, Professor John D., 300, 301, 321
Darien, Georgia, 44, 170, 173
Daufafuskie, 3
Daufuskie Creek, 15
"Daufuskie Fight," 16
Daufuskie Island (U.S. Post Office), 377
Daufuskie Island (mail service), 365
Daufuskie Island, 45, 48, 92, 108, 319, 394
Daufuskie Lighthouse, 220
Daufuskie Picnic, 146
Daufuskie School, 91, 271, 303, 311
Daufuskie, 1, 2, 3, 4, 5, 6, 8, 10, 13, 16, 19, 27, 31, 34, 35, 41, 42, 43, 44, 46, 47, 49, 50, 51, 52, 53, 54, 58, 62, 63, 64, 66, 70, 74, 75, 77, 78, 81, 82, 90, 95, 96, 99, 100, 110, 113, 117, 125, 126, 130, 133, 134, 138, 139, 143, 144, 155, 156, 157, 160, 166, 167, 170, 175, 202, 208, 235, 239, 241, 275, 383, 523

Davant, Charles, 234, 235
David, 464
Davids, Isaac, 233
Davies, Edward Thomas Lloyd, 166
Davies, Edward, 46
Davis, William H., Colonel, 294
Dawffus Tee Island, 2
Dawfuskie Island, 39, 255
"Dawfuskie School," 295
Dawson, Christopher, 39
Day, Nicholas, 13, 77
De Martinangel, Margaret, 233
De Martinangel, Philip, 233
De Martinangel, Phillip, 45
De Martinangelo, Prince Filippo, 38
DeVeaux, Andrew, Major, 232
DeWitt Clinton, 408
Debruhl, Sheriff G. J. Buck, 489
Defusky Island, S. Carolina, 46
Demery(s) family, 297
Demery, Albert, 351
Demery, Frank, 301, 353
Demery, Nat, 274
Demery, Rebecca, 298
Dennis (slave), 115
Dennis family, 124
Derst, Elizabeth (Bettye), 50
Derst, Elizabeth Courtenay Morgan (Mrs. E.J.), 57
Deutsch, Morton, 157, 158, 159, 160, 164, 167
Devils Island, 258
Diar, Persille, 26
Dick Fripp's Store, 274
Dick, houseboy, 73, 74
Dickinson, Richard W., the Rev., 83
Dierks, Fred Henry, 316, 323, 338, 340, 341, 374, 375, 379, 417, 420, 439, 442, 467, 468, 469, 473,
Dierks, Fred M., 375
Dierks, Fred and Mae, 316, 338, 340, 341, 439, 467
Dierks, Mary Meyer (May/Mae; Mrs. Fred H.), 316, 338, 340, 341, 374, 375, 378, 379, 439, 467, 473, 507
Diller Woods, 177
Diller, Elizabeth A., 177, 179
Diller, William E., Dr., 155, 177, 178
Dirk, _____, Dr., 520
Dodge, Meigs & Company, 170
Dodge, Norman W., 170
Dooley, Tip, 131
Dorbins, John, 134
Doretta, 382
Dougherty, 233

Hermitage, the, 63
Hernandez, Jim, 376
Hernandez, Jimmie, 376
Herreshoff Meft. Company, 144
Herron, Margie E., 331
Heyward, Alice, 299
Heyward, Arthur, 299
Heyward, Beck and Arthur, 305
Heyward, Flora and William, 305
Heyward, Flora, 347, 442
Heyward, Leathia, 299
Heyward, Leotha, 347
Heyward, Thelma, 299
Heyward, Thomas, Jr., 236
Hiawatha, Kansas, 89
High Point, 44
Hilden, Samuel, 2, 13, 77, 134
Hilderguard, 382
Hill, Joseph, 232
Hilton & Dodge Lumber Company, 170, 175
Hilton Head Cemetery, 88
Hilton Head Historical Society, 46, 181
Hilton Head Island, 39
Hilton Head, 4, 16, 31, 52, 84, 110, 112, 113, 128, 130, 131, 133, 175, 176, 188, 206, 215, 217, 220, 232, 233, 234, 239, 240, 248, 250, 258, 259, 275, 278, 294, 297, 298, 329, 331, 334, 336, 337, 341, 370, 383, 385, 424, 425, 431, 471, 480, 482, 486, 506, 523
Hilton, Joseph, 170
Hilton-Dodge Lumber Company, 419
Hilton-Dodge Lumber Train, 170
Hiott, Archie, 312
Hiott, Grace, 312
Hiott, Lincoln, 312
Hiott, Sheryl, 313
Hiott, Teenchy, 312
Hitch, Robert M., Mayor, 515
Hoagland, Skip, 424, 426
Hobbs, Lester, 129, 131
Hoboken, New Jersey, 43
Hodge, Clarence, 470
Hodge, Ned, 303
Hogg Plantation, 94
Holcombe, Henry, The Reverend, 46
Holland, Townes, 481
Holmes, Arthur Lee, 339
Holmes, Bill, 300
Holmes, Christopher, 300
Holmes, Dove, 442
Holmes, Elizabeth F., 349
Holmes, Evelyn, 339
Holmes, Fannie Brown, 175, 176
Holmes, Florence, 300

Holmes, Herman, 299
Holmes, Ida, 349
Holmes, Isabell, 298
Holmes, Johnnie Mae, 329, 342
Holmes, Kate, 349
Holmes, Katie Mae, 340
Holmes, Leroy, 299
Holmes, Louise, 352
Holmes, Mary, 292
Holmes, Paris H., 340
Holmes, Paris, 292
Holmes, Paul, Captain, 470, 471
Holmes, Rubin, 350
Holmes, Ruth Rhett, 76
Holmes, Samuel, 252, 261, 289, 300, 321, 349, 408, 441, 467, 478, 480
Holmes, Samuel, Jr., 340
Holmes, Theresa J., 350
Holmes, Tilman, 299
Holmes, Toby and Kate, 173
Holmes, Toby, 300, 408
Holmes, Tom, 349, 441
Honey Hill, Battle of, 257
Hopkins, Alex S., Jr., 48, 49, 52, 54, 56, 57
Hopkins, Francis, 42, 43, 49, 54, 79, 81
Hopkins, Francis, General, 43
Hopkins, James (Jimmy), 434
Hopkins, John (family), 235
Hopkins, John Livingston, 43, 79
Hopkins, John Livingston, Colonel, 43, 44
Hopkins, John Livingston, Jr., 44
Hopkins, John, 41, 42, 48, 49
Hopkins, John, and Mary Martinangele, 79
Hopkins, Mary M. (Martinangele), 8
Hopkins, Mary M., 49
Hopkins, Mary Martinangele, 42, 43, 48, 160
Hopkins, W. Cabell (Frances Fullerton), Mrs., 56
Hopkins, _____, 259
Horace (slave), 115
Horry, John, 360
Horton, Mary Frances, 469
Hoskiss, Ed, 126
Hoskiss, Joe, 126, 309
Hoskiss, Liza, 126
Hosti, Johnie, 376
Hostwick, George H., 176
Houston, Isaac, the Reverend, 275
Houston, Jeremiah, 348
Hover, Susan, 45
Howard, _____, Major General, 115, 256
Howell, Evan Park, 89
Hubbard, Manny, 435
Hudson, Adam, 265
Hudson, Alice, 339

574

U.S. Post Office, 363
Union Army, 144, 165, 179
Union Baptist Church of Daufuskie Island, 320
Union Baptist Church, 171, 273
Union Camp Paper Company, 442
Union, 109, 112, 169
United Coal Company, 167
United States Maritime Service, 92
University of Edinburgh, 82
University of Georgia, 49
University of Virginia, 120
Upham, James, 238
Ussery, Berty, 376
Ussery, Randy, 376

Vagabond Cruises, 424
Vagabond, 424, 485
Van Pelt, P. S., D.D., The Reverend, 30
Varner, Elizabeth, 82
Vaughan, William H., 176
Venus Point, 88, 212, 213, 242, 243, 420, 518
Viele, Egbert L., Brigadier General, 240, 245
Viele, Egbert L., General, 109, 112
Vietnam Conflict, 265
Virginia (slave), 115
Virginia, 15
Visitor, 385
Von Harten, Captain, 259
Von Spreckleson, _____, 259

Waccamaw, 21
Waddell, Senator James M., Jr., 189, 190
Walker, David, 299
Walker, Hester, 347
Walker, Simn, 347
Wall's Cut, 242
Wall, John L., 445, 448
Wall, John L., Adj. Captain, 227
Wallace, Thornwell, 259
Wallace, _____, 259
Walls Cut, 438, 523, 524
Walnut Grove Plantation, 27, 29, 30, 33
Walnut Grove, 31, 35, 51, 139
Walterboro, South Carolina, 313
Wampler, Captain and Mrs. John, 486
Wampler, John, 480, 487
Wampler, Sylvia, 480, 487
Wando, 22
Waples, William D., Major, 180
War Between the States, 144
War of the Rebellion, 240
War of 1812, 139
Ward family, 349

Ward, Ammie, 312, 315
Ward, Calhoun, 311, 312
Ward, Charles Edward, 265
Ward, Edward Gary, 357, 359
Ward, Edward, 311, 312
Ward, Gary and Gillian, 318, 511
Ward, Gary, 420
Ward, Gary, Mrs., 270
Ward, George C., 261
Ward, George Calhoun, 265
Ward, Geraldine, 311, 312
Ward, Gillian White, 165
Ward, Gillian, 354
Ward, Gillian, Mrs., 316
Ward, Lillian, 312, 315, 318
Ward, Norman, 310, 311, 312, 315
Ward, Norman Gary, 265
Waring, A. J., Dr., 1
Waring, Martha G., 146
Wars, Their Impact on Daufuskie, 232
Washington (state of), 22
Washington, Agnes, 348, 442
Washington, Beaulah, 339
Washington, D.C., 207
Washington, Dick, 437
Washington, Edrina, 282, 290
Washington, Edvina, 327, 339
Washington, Eleanor, 339
Washington, Ernest, 339
Washington, Flossie, 288, 338, 511
Washington, Gabe, 173, 300, 321, 408
Washington, Gabriel, 261, 348, 441
Washington, George, 237
Washington, George, General, 238
Washington, George, President, 249
Washington, H. W., 298
Washington, Henrietta, 339
Washington, Jake, 300, 338, 375, 379, 440
Washington, Jake, Jr., 339
Washington, Julie, 333, 334, 339
Washington, Lillie Mae, 339, 348
Washington, Lula, 339, 340
Washington, Margarite, 290, 327, 329, 343
Washington, Mary, 339, 471
Washington, Rosalee, 339
Washington, Shawnta, 288, 339
Washington, Sherman, 290, 333, 343
Washington, Susie, 340
Wateree, 21
Waterhouse, George, 461
Watts, Charles, 49, 134, 137
Watts, Jane (daughter), 137
Watts, Robert, 8, 33, 49, 134, 137, 138, 407
Watts, Sarah (Sally), 33, 137, 138, 139
Watts, Sarah, 8, 530, 533, 534, 535

975.7   MAR   '92

Burn, Billie
An island named Daufuskie.